Ubuntu®
The Complete Reference

Richard Petersen

New York   Chicago   San Francisco
Lisbon   London   Madrid   Mexico City
Milan   New Delhi   San Juan
Seoul   Singapore   Sydney   Toronto

The McGraw·Hill Companies

Library of Congress Cataloging-in-Publication Data

Petersen, Richard, 1949-
  Ubuntu : the complete reference / Richard Petersen.
     p. cm.
  ISBN 978-0-07-159846-0 (alk. paper)
  1. Ubuntu (Electronic resource) 2. Operating systems (Computers) I.
Title.
  QA76.76.O63P52383 2008
  005.4'32—dc22

                                    2008028810

McGraw-Hill books are available at special quantity discounts to use as premiums and sales promotions, or for use in corporate training programs. To contact a special sales representative, please visit the Contact Us page at www.mhprofessional.com.

Ubuntu® : The Complete Reference

1234567890   FGR FGR   0198

ISBN   978-0-07-159846-0
MHID   0-07-159846-4

Sponsoring Editor
  Jane K. Brownlow

Editorial Supervisor
  Janet Walden

Project Manager
  Arushi Chawla,
  International Typesetting
  and Composition

Acquisitions Coordinator
  Jennifer Housh

Technical Editor
  Ibrahim Haddad

Copy Editor
  Lisa Theobald

Proofreaders
  Bhavna Gupta and
  Manish Tiwari,
  International Typesetting
  and Composition

Indexer
  Claire Splan

Production Supervisor
  George Anderson

Composition
  International Typesetting
  and Composition

Illustration
  International Typesetting
  and Composition

Art Director, Cover
  Jeff Weeks

Cover Designer
  Pattie Lee

To my cousins, Ken and Carolyn

About the Author

Richard Petersen, MLIS, teaches UNIX and C/C++ courses at the University of California at Berkeley. He is the author of *Linux: The Complete Reference* (all six editions), *Red Hat Enterprise and Fedora Linux: The Complete Reference*, *Red Hat Linux*, *Linux Programming*, *Red Hat Linux Administrator's Reference*, *Linux Programmer's Reference*, *Introductory C with C++*, *Introductory Command Line Unix for Users*, and many other books. He is a contributor to **linux.sys-con.com** (*Linux World Magazine*) with articles on IPv6, Fedora operating system, Yum, Fedora repositories, the Global File System (GFS), udev device management, and the Hardware Abstraction Layer (HAL).

About the Technical Editor

Ibrahim Haddad is director of technology at Motorola, Inc., where he is responsible for defining and developing the requirements for Motorola's open source initiatives. Prior to his work at Motorola, he managed the Carrier Grade Linux and Mobile Linux Initiatives at the Open Source Development Lab (OSDL), which included promoting the development and adoption of Linux and open source software in the communications industry. Prior to joining OSDL, he was a senior researcher at the Research & Innovation Department of Ericsson's Corporate Unit of Research. He is contributing editor of the *Linux Journal* and the *Enterprise Open Source Magazine*. Haddad received his B.Sc. and M.Sc. degrees in Computer Science from the Lebanese American University, and earned his Ph.D. in Computer Science from Concordia University in Montreal, Canada. In 2000, he was awarded by Concordia University both the J. W. McConnell Memorial Graduate Fellowship and the Concordia University 25th Anniversary Fellowship in recognition for academic excellence. In 2007, he was the winner of the Big Idea Innovation Award in Recognition of Leadership and Vision at Motorola Inc.

Contents at a Glance

Contents

Part IV   Using the Shell

Acknowledgments

I would like to thank all those at McGraw-Hill who made this book a reality, particularly Jane Brownlow, acquisitions editor, for her continued encouragement and analysis as well as management of such a complex project; Ibrahim Haddad, the technical editor, whose analysis and suggestions proved very insightful and helpful; Jennifer Housh, editorial assistant, who provided needed resources and helpful advice; Lisa Theobald, copy editor, for her excellent job editing as well as insightful comments; project manager Arushi Chawla incorporated the large number of features found in this book and coordinated the intricate task of generating the final version.

Special thanks to Linus Torvalds, the creator of Linux, and to those who continue to develop Linux as an open, professional, and effective operating system accessible to anyone. Thanks also to the academic community whose special dedication has developed Unix as a flexible and versatile operating system. I would also like to thank professors and students at the University of California, Berkeley, for the experience and support in developing new and different ways of understanding operating system technologies.

I would also like to thank my parents, George and Cecelia, and my brothers, George, Robert, and Mark, for their support and encouragement with such a difficult project. Also Marylou and Valerie and my nieces and nephews, Aleina, Larisa, Justin, Christopher, and Dylan, for their support and deadline reminders.

Introduction

Ubuntu has become one of the major Linux distributions, designed to make Linux an operating system for end users. This book is designed not only to be a complete reference on Ubuntu, but also to provide clear and detailed explanations of its features. No prior knowledge of Unix is assumed; Linux is an operating system anyone can use.

The Ubuntu distribution is designed to be an operating system for people. In the past, most Linux distributions were designed for enterprise-critical server operations, where Linux dominates. Often, difficult administration procedures where required for the simplest tasks. By contrast, Ubuntu supports primarily end users. Ubuntu is Linux for people, ordinary users who just want a powerful and easy-to-use operating system at their fingertips. Linux in general has dramatically increased its ability to handle most tasks automatically. Printers, cameras, USB sticks, and Windows disks are all detected and managed for you. Your graphics card is also detected and configured for you, making full use of the recent greatly improved support for Linux by ATI and Nvidia. Ubuntu pulls all these developments together for the end user, making Linux a user experience that is a simple, effective, reliable, and powerful connection to the information society.

Ubuntu Long-term and Short-term Releases

Ubuntu has split its Linux development into two lines: the long-term and short-term releases. The long-term release aims to provide a stable release for end users, whereas short-term releases take advantage of the latest software and device support. Users who are comfortable with modifying and tweaking their systems often install the short-term releases, whereas those who want only a reliable and stable system install the long-term releases.

Ubuntu Editions

The entire collection of Ubuntu software is available on the Ubuntu repository. Some users, however, might prefer to start with preselected setup applications on an install CD/DVD. These are known as *editions*, but each edition has full access to all Ubuntu software. The Ubuntu Web site lists several editions, including Kubuntu (KDE desktop), Edubuntu (educational packages), and Xubuntu (Xfce4 desktop). Other commonly used editions are Ubuntu Studio (audio, video, and graphic applications) and Mythbuntu (multimedia and MythTV).

Important Features with Ubuntu 8.04, Hardy Heron

With Ubuntu 8.04, several key features are incorporated as standardized and stable components of the Linux operations system. These include changes to distribution methods, device detection, security support, and desktop use. Some of these are listed here, with a complete listing in Chapter 1.

- Ubuntu features automatic detection and configuration of removable devices such as USB printers, digital cameras, and card readers, treating CD/DVD discs as removable devices, as well as fully detecting IDE CD/DVD devices.

- Ubuntu software, both supported and third-party, is easily downloaded and updated from the Ubuntu software repositories.

- Ubuntu is available in several editions, designed for users with particular preferences.

- Audio is managed by the PulseAudio sound interface.

- PolicyKit provides controlled access to system administration tools and shared resources. You can set different levels of control and create your own policies.

- Extensive and simple virtualization support provided using Xen, KVM, and the Virtual Machine Manager.

- GNOME 2.2 with new desktop applications such as the Brasero DVD/CD burner and the World Clock applet.

Linux Features

Ubuntu includes features that have become a standard part of any Linux distribution, such as the desktops, Unix compatibility, network servers, and numerous software applications such as office, multimedia, and Internet applications. GNOME and the K Desktop Environment (KDE) have become standard desktop graphical user interfaces (GUIs) for Linux, noted for their power, flexibility, and ease of use. KDE and GNOME have become the standard GUIs for Linux systems. You can install both, run applications from one on the other, and easily switch from one to the other. Both have become integrated components of Linux, with applications and tools for every kind of task and operation. Instead of treating GNOME and KDE as separate entities, GNOME and KDE tools and applications are presented equally throughout the book.

A wide array of applications operates on Ubuntu. Numerous applications are continually released on the Ubuntu repositories. The GNU general public licensed software provides professional-level applications such as programming development tools, editors, and word processors, as well as numerous specialized applications such as those for graphics and sound.

How to Use This Book

The first two sections of the book are designed to cover tasks you would need to perform to get your system up and running. After an introduction to the working environment, including both GNOME and KDE desktops, you learn some basic configuration tasks, such as setting preferences for your desktop and enabling network connections. Most administrative tasks are now handled for you automatically, detecting devices such as printers and USB drives, as well as providing access. Some tasks, such as adding new users, you will have to perform yourself. The software management is nearly automatic, letting you install software on your system with just a couple of mouse clicks. All these topics are covered in detail in the book, should you ever need to perform a particular task manually.

Since this book is really several books in one—a user interface book, a security book, a server book, and an administration book—how you choose to use it depends upon how you want to use your Ubuntu system. Almost all Linux operations can be carried out using either the GNOME or KDE interface. You can focus on the GNOME and KDE chapters and their corresponding tools and applications in the different chapters throughout the book. On the other hand, if you want to delve deeper into the Unix aspects of Linux, you can check out the shell chapters and the corresponding shell-based commands in other chapters. Single users may concentrate more on the desktops and the Internet features, whereas administrators may make more use of the security and networking features.

Section Topics

The first part of this book is designed to help you start using Ubuntu quickly. It provides an introduction to Ubuntu and its current features. Streamlined installation procedures that take about 30 minutes or less are covered in detail. The installation program provides excellent commentary, describing each step in detail. You then learn the essentials of using the desktop and setting your preferences such as font sizes and backgrounds.

Part II deals with system configuration, network connections, and software management. Commonly performed system configuration tasks such as adding printers and setting up virus protection are presented with the easiest methods, without much of the complex detail described in the administration chapters that is unnecessary for basic operations. Basic network connection tasks are discussed, such as setting up a LAN and wireless connections. You learn how to update and install new software easily using Ubuntu repositories. You can install the latest versions directly from a repository with a few clicks. The software updater automatically detects updates and lets you perform all updates with a single click.

Part III of this book deals with the Ubuntu desktops. Here you are introduced to the two GUIs commonly used on Linux: KDE and GNOME. Different features such as applets, the Control Panel, and configuration tools are described in detail. At any time, you can open up a terminal window in which you can enter standard Linux commands on a command line.

Part IV covers shell commands and configuration as well as files and directory management from the shell. You can choose to use just the standard Unix command line interface to run any of the standard Unix commands. The BASH shell and its various file and directory commands are examined, along with shell configuration files.

Part V of this book discusses in detail the many office, multimedia, and Internet applications you can use on your Linux system, beginning with office suites such as OpenOffice and KOffice. A variety of different text editors are available, including several GNOME and KDE editors, as well as the Vim (enhanced VI). Linux automatically installs mail, news, FTP, and Web browser applications. Both KDE and GNOME come with a full set of mail, news, FTP clients, and Web browsers.

Part VI demonstrates how to implement security precautions using encryption, authentication, and firewalls. Coverage of the GNU Privacy Guard (GPG) tells you how to implement public and private key based encryption, as well as how to configure PolicyKit to control access to administrative tools. AppArmor and SELinux provide comprehensive and refined control of all your network and system resources. Network security topics cover firewalls and encryption using netfilter (iptables) to protect your system, the Secure Shell (SSH) to provide secure remote transmissions, and Kerberos to provide secure authentication.

Part VII discusses system and network administration topics including user, file system, system, device, and kernel administration. Detailed descriptions cover the configuration files used in administration tasks and how to make entries in them. Presentations include both the GUI tools you can use for these tasks and the underlying configurations files and commands. First, basic system administration tasks are covered such as managing runlevels, monitoring your system, and scheduling shutdowns. Then aspects of setting up and controlling users and groups are discussed. Different methods of virtualization are covered, such as full (KVM) and para-virtualizaton (Xen). With the Virtual Machine Manager, both can easily be used to install and run guest operation systems. Different file system tasks are covered such as mounting file systems, managing file systems with HAL and udev, and configuring RAID devices and LVM volumes. Devices are automatically detected with udev and HAL. Backup managements tools are discussed, including BackupPC and Amanda. IPv6 support for Internet addressing is discussed in detail, showing the new IPv6 formats replacing the older IPv4 versions. You also learn how IPv4 Dynamic Host Configuration Protocol (DHCP) server assigns hosts IP addresses dynamically and how IPv6 automatic addressing and renumbering operate.

Part VIII covers local network services such as the CUPS print server network file systems, and Samba Windows servers. The network file system, NFS for Unix, is presented. The chapter on Samba shows how to access Windows file systems and printers.

The appendix provides information, sites, and details for obtaining Ubuntu disc images and creating your own Ubuntu Live and install CD/DVD discs.

PART

Getting Started

Introduction to Ubuntu

Ubuntu is currently one of the most popular end-user Linux distributions (**www .ubuntu.com**). It is managed by the Ubuntu Foundation, which is sponsored by Canonical, Ltd. (**www.canonical.com**), a commercial organization that supports and promotes open source projects. The Ubuntu Project was initiated by Mark Shuttleworth, a Debian Linux developer in South Africa. Ubuntu is based on Debian Linux, one of the oldest Linux distributions, which is dedicated to incorporating cutting-edge developments and features (**www.debian.org**). Debian Linux is an open source operating system that relies on the collaboration of volunteers from around the world.

Ubuntu provides a Debian-based Linux distribution that is stable, reliable, and easy to use. It is designed as a Linux operating system that can be used easily by everyone. The name *Ubuntu* means "humanity to others." As the Ubuntu Project describes it, "Ubuntu is an African word meaning 'Humanity to others,' or 'I am what I am because of who we all are.' The Ubuntu distribution brings the spirit of Ubuntu to the software world."

The official Ubuntu philosophy lists the following principles:

- Every computer user should have the freedom to download, run, copy, distribute, study, share, change, and improve his or her software for any purpose, without paying licensing fees.

- Every computer user should be able to use software in the language of his or her choice.

- Every computer user should be given every opportunity to use software, including users who are affected by any type of disability.

The emphasis on language reflects Ubuntu's international scope. It is meant to be a global distribution that does not focus on any single market. Language support has been integrated into Linux in general by its internationalization projects, denoted by the term *i18n*. You can find information about i18n at sites such as **www.li18nux.net** (The Linux Foundation) and **www.openi18n.org**s.

Making software available to all users involves both full accessibility support for users with disabilities as well as seamless integration of software access using online repositories, making massive amounts of software available to all users at the touch of a button. Ubuntu also makes full use of recent developments in automatic device detection, greatly simplifying installation as well as access to removable devices and attached storage.

Ubuntu aims to provide a fully supported and reliable, open source and free, easy to use and modify, Linux operating system. Ubuntu makes the following promises about its distribution:

- Ubuntu will always be free of charge, including enterprise releases and security updates.

- Ubuntu comes with full commercial support from Canonical and hundreds of companies around the world.

- Ubuntu includes the very best translations and accessibility infrastructure that the free software community has to offer.

- Ubuntu CDs contain only free software applications; you are encouraged to use free and open source software, improve it, and pass it on.

Ubuntu Releases

Ubuntu provides both long-term and short-term releases. Long-term support (LTS) releases, such as Ubuntu 8.04, are released every two years. Short-term releases are provided every six months between the LTS version. They are designed to make available the latest application and support for the newest hardware. Each has its own nickname, such as *Hardy Heron* for the 8.04 LTS release. The long-term releases are supported for three years for desktops and five years for servers, whereas short-term releases are supported for 18 months. Canonical also provides limited commercial support for companies that purchase it.

Installing Ubuntu has been significantly simplified. A core set of applications are installed, and you can add to them as you wish. Following installation, additional software can be downloaded from online repositories. Install screens have been reduced in number and allow users to move quickly through default partitioning, user setup, and time settings. The hardware such as graphics cards and network connections are now configured and detected automatically.

The Ubuntu distribution of Linux is available online at numerous sites. Ubuntu maintains its own site at **www.ubuntu.com/getubuntu**, where you can download the current release of Ubuntu.

Linux

Linux is an fast, stable, and open source operating system for PCs and workstations that features professional-level Internet services, extensive development tools, fully functional graphical user interfaces (GUIs), and a massive number of applications ranging from office suites to multimedia applications. Linux was developed in the early 1990s by Linus Torvalds, along with other programmers around the world (see the history section later in the chapter). As an operating system, Linux performs many of the same functions as Unix, Macintosh, Windows, and Windows NT. However, Linux is distinguished by its power and flexibility, along with being freely available.

Most PC operating systems, such as Windows, began their development within the confines of small, restricted personal computers, which have only recently become more versatile machines. Such operating systems are constantly being upgraded to keep up with the ever-changing capabilities of PC hardware. Linux, on the other hand, was developed in a different context. <u>Linux is a PC version of the Unix operating system</u> that has been used for decades on mainframes and minicomputers and is currently the system of choice for network servers and workstations. Linux brings the speed, efficiency, scalability, and flexibility of Unix to your PC, taking advantage of all the capabilities that PCs can now provide.

Technically, Linux consists of the operating system program, referred to as the *kernel*, which is the part originally developed by Torvalds. But it has always been distributed with a large number of software applications, ranging from network servers and security programs to office applications and development tools. Linux has evolved as part of the open source software movement, in which independent programmers joined forces to provide free and quality software to any user. Linux has become the premier platform for open source software, much of it developed by the Free Software Foundation's GNU project. Many of these applications are bundled as part of standard Linux distributions, and most of them are also incorporated into the Ubuntu repository, using packages that are Debian compliant.

Along with Linux's operating system capabilities come powerful networking features, including support for Internet, intranets, and Windows networking. As a norm, Linux distributions include fast, efficient, and stable Internet servers, such as the Web, FTP, and DNS servers, along with proxy, news, and mail servers. In other words, Linux has everything you need to set up, support, and maintain a fully functional network.

With the both GNOME and K Desktop Environment (KDE), Linux also provides GUIs with the same level of flexibility and power. Linux enables you to choose the interface you want and then customize it, adding panels, applets, virtual desktops, and menus, all with full drag-and-drop capabilities and Internet-aware tools.

Linux does all this at the right price: It is free, including the network servers and GUI desktops. Unlike the official Unix operating system, Linux is distributed freely under a GNU General Public License (GPL) as specified by the Free Software Foundation, making it available to anyone who wants to use it. GNU (which stands for *GNU's Not Unix*) is a project initiated and managed by the Free Software Foundation to provide free software to users, programmers, and developers. Linux is copyrighted, not public domain; however, a GNU public license has much the same effect as the software's being in the public domain. The GNU GPL is designed to ensure that Linux remains free and, at the same time, standardized. Linux is technically the operating system kernel—the core operations—and only one official Linux kernel exists. <u>People sometimes have the mistaken impression that Linux is somehow less than a professional operating system because it is free. Linux is, in fact, a PC, workstation, and server version of Unix. Many actually consider it far more stable and much more powerful than Microsoft Windows. This power and stability have made Linux an operating system of choice as a network server.</u>

Open Source Software

Linux is developed as a cooperative open source effort over the Internet, so no company or institution controls Linux. Software developed for Linux reflects this background. Development often takes place when Linux users decide to work together on a project. The software is posted at an Internet site, and any Linux user can then access the site and download the software. Linux software development has always operated in an Internet environment and is global in scope, enlisting programmers from around the world. The only thing you need to start a Linux-based software project is a Web site.

Most Linux software is developed as open source software, and the source code for an application is freely distributed along with the application. Programmers over the Internet can make their own contributions to a software package's development, modifying and correcting the source code, which is included in all its distributions and is freely available on the Internet. Many major software development efforts are also open source projects, as are the KDE and GNOME desktops along with most of their applications. The OpenOffice office suite supported by Sun is an open source project based on the StarOffice office suite (Sun's commercial version of OpenOffice). You can find more information about the Open Source Initiative at **www.opensource.org**.

Open source software is protected by public licenses that prevent commercial companies from taking control of the software by adding modifications of their own, copyrighting those changes, and selling the software as their own product. The most popular public license is the GNU GPL, under which Linux is distributed, which is provided by the Free Software Foundation. The GNU GPL retains the copyright, freely licensing the software with the requirement that the software and any modifications made to it are always freely available. Other public licenses have been created to support the demands of different kinds of open source projects. The GNU Lesser General Public License (LGPL) lets commercial applications use GNU-licensed software libraries. The Qt Public License (QPL) lets open source developers use the Qt libraries essential to the KDE desktop. You can find a complete listing at **www.opensource.org**.

Linux is currently copyrighted under a GNU public license provided by the Free Software Foundation, and it is often referred to as GNU software (see **www.gnu.org**). GNU software is distributed free, provided it is freely distributed to others. GNU software has proved both reliable and effective. Many of the popular Linux utilities, such as C compilers, shells, and editors, are GNU software applications. Installed with your Linux distribution are the GNU C++ and Lisp compilers, Vi and Emacs editors, BASH and TCSH shells, as well as TeX and Ghostscript document formatters. In addition, many open source software projects are licensed under the GNU GPL. Most of these applications are available on the Ubuntu software repositories. Chapters 6 and 7 describe in detail the process of downloading software applications from Internet sites and installing them on your system.

Under the terms of the GNU GPL, the original author retains the copyright, although anyone can modify the software and redistribute it, provided the source code is included, made public, and provided free. Also, no restriction exists on selling the software or giving it away free. One distributor could charge for the software, while another could provide it free of charge. Major software companies are also providing Linux versions of their most popular applications. Oracle provides a Linux version of its Oracle database. (At present, no plans seem in the works for Microsoft applications, though you can use the Wine, the Windows compatibility layer, to run many Microsoft applications on Linux, directly.)

Ubuntu Editions

Ubuntu is released in several editions, each designed for a distinct group of users or functions (see Table 1-1). Editions install different collections of software such as the KDE, the XFce desktop, servers, educational software, and multimedia applications. ISO images can be downloaded directly or using a BitTorrent application.

Ubuntu Edition	Description
Desktop install	LiveCD using GNOME desktop, **www.ubuntu.com/getubuntu**.
Server install	Install server software (no desktop), **www.ubuntu.com/getubuntu**.
Alternate install	Install enhanced features, **www.releases.ubuntu.com**.
Kubuntu	LiveCD using KDE instead of GNOME, **www.kubuntu.org**.
Xubuntu	Uses the Xfce desktop instead of GNOME, **www.xubuntu.org**. Useful for laptops.
Edubuntu	Installs educational software: Desktop, Server, and Server add-on CDs, **www.edubuntu.org**.
Goubuntu	Uses only open source software; no access to restricted software of any kind, **www.ubuntu.com**.
Ubuntu Studio	Ubuntu Desktop with multimedia and graphics production applications, **www.ubuntustudio.org**.
Mythbuntu	Ubuntu Desktop with MythTV multimedia and digital video recorder (DVR) applications, **www.mythbuntu.org**.

TABLE 1-1   Ubuntu Editions

The Ubuntu Desktop Edition provides standard functionality for end users. The standard Ubuntu release provides a LiveCD using the GNOME desktop. Most users would install this edition. This is the CD image that you download from the Get Ubuntu Download page at **www.ubuntu.com/getubuntu/download**.

Those who want to run Ubuntu as a server to provide an Internet service such as a Web site would use the Ubuntu Server Edition. The Server Edition provides only a simple command line interface; it does not install the desktop. It is primarily designed to run servers. Keep in mind that you could install the desktop first and later download server software from the Ubuntu repositories, running them from a system that also has a desktop. You do not have to install the Server Edition to install and run servers. The Server Edition can be downloaded from the Get Ubuntu Download page.

Users who want more enhanced operating system features such as RAID arrays or file system encryption would use the alternate edition. The alternate edition, along with the Desktop and Server editions, can be downloaded directly from **http://releases.ubuntu.com/hardy** or **http://releases.ubuntu.com/8.04**.

Other editions use either a different desktop or a specialized collection of software for certain groups of users. Links to the editions are listed on the **www.ubuntu.com** Web page. From there you can download their live/install CDs. The Kubuntu edition used KDE instead of GNOME. Xubuntu uses the XFce desktop instead of GNOME. This is a stripped down and highly efficient desktop, ideal for low power use on laptops and smaller computer. The Edubuntu edition provides educational software and can also be used with a specialized Edubuntu server to provide educational software on a school network. The Goubuntu edition is a modified version of the standard edition that includes only open source software, with no access to commercial software of any kind, including restricted vendor graphics drivers such as those from Nvidia or ATI. Only X.org open source display drivers are used. The Ubuntu Studio edition is a new edition that provides a collection of multimedia and image production software. The Mythbuntu edition is designed to install and run the MythTV software, letting you use Ubuntu to operate as a multimedia DVR and video playback system.

The Kubuntu and Edubuntu editions can be downloaded directly from **http://releases .ubuntu.com.**

The Gobuntu, Mythbuntu, Xubuntu, and Ubuntu Studio are all available, along with all the other editions and Ubuntu releases, on the cdimage server at **www.cdimage.ubuntu.com.**

Keep in mind that all these editions are released as LiveCDs or DVD install discs, for which there are two versions: a 32-bit x86 version and a 64-bit x86_64 version. Older computers may support only a 32-bit version, whereas most current computers will support the 64-bit versions. Check your computer hardware specifications to be sure. The 64-bit version should run faster, and most computer software is now available in stable 64-bit packages. Table 1-2 lists Web sites where you can download ISO images for the various editions.

The **http://releases.ubuntu.com** and **www.cdimage.ubuntu.com** also hold BitTorrent and Jigdo download files for the editions they provide.

NOTE *Ubuntu also provides releases for different kinds of installations on hard drives. These include a Server disc for installing only servers, and an alternate disc for supporting specific kinds of file systems and features during an installation, such as RAID and LVM file systems.*

URL	Internet Site
www.ubuntu.com/getubuntu/download	Primary download site for desktop and servers.
http://releases.ubuntu.com/8.04 **www.cdimage.ubuntu.com/releases**	Download sites for alternate, server, and desktop CDs and the Install DVD, as well as BitTorrent files.
http://release.ubuntu.com	Download site for Ubuntu editions, including Kubuntu and Edubuntu. Also check their respective Web sites.
www.cdimage.ubuntu.com	Download site for all Ubuntu editions, including Xubuntu, Mythbuntu, Goubuntu, and Ubuntu Studio. Also check their respective Web sites. Includes Kubuntu, Ubuntu, and Edubuntu.
https://launchpad.net	Ubuntu mirrors.
http://torrent.ubuntu.com	Ubuntu BitTorrent site for BitTorrent downloads of Ubuntu distribution ISO images.

TABLE 1-2   Ubuntu CD ISO Image Locations

Ubuntu 8.04 LTR

Ubuntu 8.04 includes the following features:

- PolicyKit authorization for users, allowing limited controlled administrative access to administration tools and storage and media devices.

- Brasero GNOME CD/DVD burner.

- Kernel-based Virtualization Machine (KVM) support is included with the kernel. KVM uses hardware virtualization enabled processors such as Intel Virtualization Technology (VT) and AMD Secure Virtual Machine (SVM) processors to support hardware-level guest operating systems. Most standard Intel and AMD processors already provide this support.

- Use Virtual Machine Manger to manage and install both KVM and Xen virtual machines.

- The java-gcj-compat collection provides Java runtime environment compatibility. It consists of GNU Java runtime (libgcj), the Eclipse Java compiler (ecj), and a set of wrappers and links (java-gcj-compat).

- New applications such as Transmission BitTorrent client, Vinagre Virtual Network Client, and the World Clock applet with weather around the world.

- Features automatic detection of removable devices such as USB printers, digital cameras, and card readers. CD/DVD discs are treated as removable devices, automatically displayed and accessed when inserted.

- GNOME supports GUI access to all removable devices and shared directories on networked hosts, including Windows folders, using the GNOME Virtual File System, **gvfs**, which replaces **gnomevfs**.

- Any NTFS Windows file systems on your computer are automatically detected and mounted using **ntfs-3g**. Mounted file systems are located in the **media** directory.

- Full IPv6 network protocol support, including automatic addressing and renumbering.

- Network Monitor will automatically detect wireless network connections.

- Information about hotplugged devices is provided to applications with the Hardware Abstraction Layer (HAL) from **www.freedesktop.org**. This allows desktops such as GNOME to display and manage removable devices easily.

- All devices are treated logically as removable and automatically configured by udev. Fixed devices cannot be removed. This feature is meant to let Linux accommodate a wide variety of devices, such as digital cameras, PDAs, and cell phones. PCMCIA and network devices are managed by udev and HAL directly.

- The Update Manager automatically updates your Ubuntu system and all its installed applications, from the Ubuntu online repositories.

- Software management (Synaptic Package Manager) accesses and installs software directly from all your configured online Ubuntu repositories.

- The current version of OpenOffice.org provides effective and MS Office–competitive applications, featuring support for document storage standards.

- Complete range of system and network administration tools featuring easy-to-use GUI interfaces (see Chapters 4 and 5).
- Wine Windows Compatibility Layer lets you run most popular Windows applications directly on your Ubuntu desktop.

Ubuntu LiveCD

The standard Ubuntu Desktop CD and the Install DVD can both operate as LiveCDs (server and alternate editions do not), so you can run Ubuntu from any CD-ROM drive. In effect, you can carry your operating system with you on a CD. New users can also use the LiveCD to try out Ubuntu to see if they like it. The Ubuntu Desktop CD will run as a LiveCD automatically, and with the Install DVD it is a start-up option. Both run GNOME as the desktop. If you want to use the KDE instead, you would use the Kubuntu CD.

Keep in mind that all the LiveCDs also function as install discs for Ubuntu, providing its limited collection of software on a system, but installing a full-fledged Ubuntu operating system that can be expanded and updated from Ubuntu online repositories (see Chapter 2). From the LiveCD desktop, double-click the Install icon on the desktop to start the installation.

The LiveCD provided by Ubuntu includes a limited set of software packages. On the Ubuntu Desktop CD, you use GNOME for desktop support. Other than these limitations, you'll have a fully operational Ubuntu desktop. You have the full set of administrative tools, with which you can add users, change configuration settings, and even add software, while the LiveCD is running. When you shut down, the configuration information is lost, including any software you have added. Files and data can be written to removable devices such as USB drives and CD/DVD write discs, letting you save your data during a LiveCD session.

When you start up the Ubuntu Desktop CD, the GNOME desktop is automatically displayed (see Figure 1-1) and you are logged in as the live session user. The top panel displays menus and application icons for a Web browser (Firefox) and mail. To the right is a network connection icon for NetworkManager, which you can configure (with a right-click) for wireless access. See Chapter 3 for information on basic desktop usage. At the right side of the top panel is a Quit button you can click to shut down your system. It is important to use the Quit button to unmount any removable devices safely.

An icon is displayed for an Examples directory. Click it to access example files for OpenOffice.org (Productivity), Ogg video and SPX/Ogg sound files (Multimedia), and Gimp XCF and image PNG files (Graphics). OpenOffice.org files begin with the prefix **oo-** and include word processing (**odt**), spreadsheets (**xls**), presentation (**odp**), and drawing (**odg**) files. Check the **oo-welcome.odt** file for information about Ubuntu and the **oo-about-these-files.odt** file for information about the example files. Also included are PNG image files of the official Ubuntu logos for Ubuntu, Kubuntu, and Edubuntu.

The Computer window, accessible from the Places menu, displays icons for all partitions on your current computer. These will be automatically mounted as read-only, including Windows file systems. The File System icon will let you peruse the configuration files, but these are located on a Read-Only File System (ROFS) that you can access but not change. These folders and files will show a lock emblem on their icons.

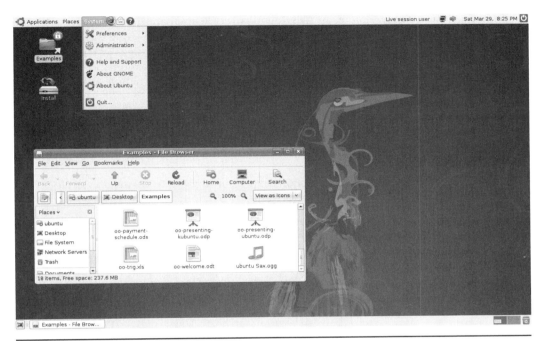

FIGURE 1-1   Ubuntu LiveCD desktop

You can save files to your home directory, but they are only temporary and will disappear at the end of the session. Copy them to a DVD, USB drive, or other removable device to save them. An Install icon lets you install Ubuntu on your computer, performing a standard installation to your hard drive.

Ubuntu Software

You can update to the latest software from the Ubuntu repository using the Update Manager (see Chapter 6). The Ubuntu distribution provides a initial selection of desktop software. Additional applications can be downloaded and installed from online repositories, ranging from office and multimedia applications to Internet servers and administration services. Many popular applications are included in separate sections of the repository. During installation, your system is configured to access Ubuntu repositories.

All Linux software for Ubuntu is currently available from online repositories. You can download applications for desktops, Internet servers, office suites, and programming packages, among others. Software packages are primarily distributed in through Debian-enabled repositories, the largest of which is the official Ubuntu repository. Downloads and updates are handled automatically by your desktop software manager and updater. A complete listing of software packages for the Ubuntu distribution, along with a search capability, is located at **http://packages.ubuntu.com**.

From third-party sources, you can also download software that is in the form of compressed archives or in DEB packages. DEB packages are archived using the Debian Package Manager. Compressed archives have an extension such as **.tar.gz**, whereas Debian packages have a **.deb** extension. You can also download the source version and compile it directly on your system. This has become a simple process, almost as simple as installing the compiled DEB versions.

Due to licensing restrictions, multimedia support for popular operations such as MP3, DVD, and DivX are included with Ubuntu in a separate section of the repository called *multiverse*. Ubuntu also includes on its restricted repository Nvidia and ATI vendor graphics drivers and provides as part of its standard installation the generic X.org that will enable your graphics cards to work.

All software packages in different sections and Ubuntu repositories are accessible directly with the Install and Remove Software and the Synaptic Package Manager.

Ubuntu Help and Documentation

A great deal of help and documentation is available online for Ubuntu, ranging from detailed install procedures to beginners questions (see Table 1-3). The two major sites for documentation are **https://help.ubuntu.com** and the Ubuntu forums at **www.ubuntuformus.org**. In addition, you can consult many blog and news sites as well as the standard Linux documentation. Also helpful is the Ubuntu Guide Wiki at **http://ubuntuguide.org**. Links to Ubuntu documentation, support, blogs, and news are listed at **www.ubuntu.com/community**. Here you will also find links for the Ubuntu community structure, including the code of conduct. A "Contribute" section links to sites where you can make contributions in development, artwork, documentation, and support. For mailing lists, check **http://lists.ubuntu.com**. You'll find lists for categories such as Ubuntu announcements, community support for specific editions, and development for areas such as the desktop, servers, or mobile implementation.

URL	Description
https://help.ubuntu.com	Help pages
http://packages.ubuntu.com	Ubuntu software package list and search
www.ubuntuforums.org	Ubuntu forums
http://ubuntuguide.org	Guide to Ubuntu
http://fridge.ubuntu.com	News and developments
http://planet.ubuntu.com	Member and developer blogs
http://blog.canonical.com	Latest Canonical news
www.tldp.org	Linux Documentation Project Web site
http://ubuntuguide.org	All purpose guide to Ubuntu topics
www.ubuntugeek.com	Specialized Ubuntu modifications
www.ubuntu.com/community	Links to documentation, support, news, and blogs
http://lists.ubuntu.com	Ubuntu mailing lists

TABLE 1-3   Ubuntu Help and Documentation

help.ubuntu.com

Ubuntu-specific documentation is available at **help.ubuntu.com**. Here on tabbed pages you can find specific documentation for different releases. Always check the release help page first for documentation, though it may be sparse and covers mainly changed areas. The Ubuntu LTS release usually includes desktop, installation, and server guides. The guides are complete and cover most topics. For 8.04, use of Desktop Documentation section will cover key desktop topics like software management, music and video applications, Internet application including mail and instant messaging, security topics, and a guide for new users.

The short-term support releases tend to have just a few detailed documentation topics such as software management, desktop customization, security, multimedia and Internet applications, and printing. These will vary depending on what new features are included in the release.

One of the most helpful pages is the Community Contributed Documentation page. Here you will find detailed documentation on installation of all Ubuntu releases, using the desktop, installing software, and configuring devices. Always check the page for your Ubuntu release first. The page includes these main sections:

- **Getting Help**   Links to documentation and FAQs. The official documentation link displays the tabbed page for that release on **help.ubuntu.com**.

- **Getting Ubuntu**   Link to Install page with sections on desktop, server, and alternate installations. Also information on how to move from using other operating systems such as Windows or Mac.

- **Using and Customizing Your System**   Sections on managing and installing software, Internet access, configuring multimedia applications, setting up accessibility, the desktop appearance (eye candy), server configuration, and development tools (programming).

- **Maintain Your Computer**   Links to System Administration, Security, and Troubleshooting Guides pages. System Administration covers topics such as adding users, configuring the GRUB boot loader, setting the time and date, and installing software. The Security page covers lower level issues such as iptables for firewalls and how GPG security works. Of particular interest is the Linux Unified Key Setup (LUKS)–encrypted file system how-tos.

- **Connecting and Configuring Hardware**   Links to pages on drives and partitions, input devices, wireless configuration, printers, sound, video, and laptops.

ubuntuforums.org

Ubuntu Forums provides detailed online support and discussion for users. An Absolute Beginner section provides an area where new users can obtain answers to questions. Sticky threads includes both quick and complete guides to installation for the current Ubuntu release. You can use the search feature to find discussions on your topic of interest.

The main support categories section covers specific support areas such as networking, multimedia, laptops, security, and 64-bit support. Other community discussions cover ongoing work such as virtualization, art and design, gaming, education and science, Wine, assistive technology, and even testimonials. Here you will also find community announcements and news. Of particular interest are third-party projects that include projects such as Mythbuntu (MythTV on Ubuntu), Ubuntu Podcast forum, Ubuntu Women, and Ubuntu Gamers.

The forum community discussion is where you talk about anything else. The **ubuntuforums.org** site also provides a gallery page for posted screenshots as well as RSS feeds for specific forums.

ubuntuguide.org

The Ubuntu Guide is a kind of all-purpose how-to for frequently asked questions. It is independent of the official Ubuntu site and can deal with topics such as how to get DVD-video to work. Areas cover such topics as popular add-on applications such as Flash, Adobe Reader, and MPlayer. The Hardware section deals with specific hardware such as Nvidia drivers and Logitech mice. Emulators such as Wine and VMWare are also discussed.

Ubuntu News and Blog Sites

Several news and blog sites are accessible from the News pop-up menu on the **www.ubuntu.com** site.

- **fridge.ubuntu.com**   The Fridge site lists the latest news and developments for Ubuntu. It features the Weekly Newsletter, latest announcements, and upcoming events.
- **planet.ubuntu.com**   Ubuntu blog for members and developers.
- **blog.canonical.com**   Canonical news.

Linux Documentation

Linux documentation has also been developed over the Internet. Much of the documentation currently available for Linux can be downloaded from Internet FTP sites. A special Linux project called the Linux Documentation Project (LDP), headed by Matt Welsh, has developed a complete set of Linux manuals. The documentation is available at the LDP home site at **www.tldp.org**. The Linux documentation for your installed software will be available at your **/usr/share/doc** directory.

History of Linux and Unix

As a version of Unix, Linux history naturally begins with Unix. The story begins in the late 1960s, when a concerted effort to develop new operating system techniques occurred. In 1968, a consortium of researchers from General Electric, Bell Laboratories, and the Massachusetts Institute of Technology (MIT) carried out a special operating system research project called Multiplexed Information and Computing Service (MULTICS), which incorporated many new concepts in multitasking, file management, and user interaction.

Unix

In 1969, Ken Thompson, Dennis Ritchie, and the researchers at Bell Labs developed the Unix operating system, incorporating many of the features of the MULTICS research project. They tailored the system for the needs of a research environment, designing it to run on minicomputers. From its inception, Unix was an affordable and efficient multiuser and multitasking operating system.

The Unix system became popular at Bell Labs as more and more researchers started using the system. In 1973, Ritchie collaborated with Thompson to rewrite the programming code for the Unix system in the C programming language. Unix gradually grew from one person's tailored design to a standard software product distributed by many different vendors, such as Novell and IBM.

Initially, Unix was treated as a research product. The first versions of Unix were distributed free to the computer science departments of many noted universities. Throughout the 1970s, Bell Labs began issuing official versions of Unix and licensing the systems to different users. One of these users was the Computer Science department of the University of California, Berkeley. Berkeley added many new features to the system that later became standard. In 1975, Berkeley released its own version of Unix, known by its distribution arm, Berkeley Software Distribution (BSD). This BSD version of Unix became a major contender to the Bell Labs version. AT&T developed several research versions of Unix, and in 1983, it released the first commercial version, called System 3. This was later followed by System V, which became a supported commercial software product.

At the same time, the BSD version of Unix was developing through several releases. In the late 1970s, BSD Unix became the basis of a research project by the Department of Defense's Advanced Research Projects Agency (DARPA). As a result, in 1983, Berkeley released a powerful version of Unix called BSD release 4.2. This release included sophisticated file management as well as networking features based on Internet network protocols—the same protocols now used for the Internet. BSD release 4.2 was widely distributed and adopted by many vendors, such as Sun Microsystems.

In the mid-1980s, two competing standards emerged, one based on the AT&T version of Unix and the other based on the BSD version. AT&T's Unix System Laboratories developed System V release 4. Several other companies, such as IBM and Hewlett-Packard, established the Open Software Foundation (OSF) to create their own standard version of Unix. Two commercial standard versions of Unix existed then—the OSF version and System V release 4.

Linux

Originally designed specifically for Intel-based personal computers, Linux started out as a personal project of computer science student Linus Torvalds at the University of Helsinki. At that time, students were making use of a program called *Minix*, which highlighted different Unix features. Minix was created by Professor Andrew Tanenbaum and widely distributed over the Internet to students around the world. Torvalds's intention was to create an effective PC version of Unix for Minix users. It was named Linux, and in 1991, Torvalds released version 0.11. Linux was widely distributed over the Internet, and in the following years, other programmers refined and added to it, incorporating most of the applications and features now found in standard Unix systems. All the major window managers have been ported to Linux. Linux has all the networking tools, such as FTP file transfer support, Web browsers, and the whole range of network services such as e-mail, the Domain Name Service, and Dynamic Host Configuration, along with FTP, Web, and print servers. It also has a full set of program development utilities, such as C++ compilers and debuggers. Given all its features, the Linux operating system remains small, stable, and fast. In its simplest format, Linux can run effectively on only 2MB of memory.

Although Linux has developed in the free and open environment of the Internet, it adheres to official Unix standards. Because of the proliferation of Unix versions in the previous decades, the Institute of Electrical and Electronics Engineers (IEEE) developed an independent Unix standard for the American National Standards Institute (ANSI). This new ANSI-standard Unix is called the Portable Operating System Interface for Computer Environments (POSIX). The standard defines how a Unix-like system needs to operate, specifying details such as system calls and interfaces. POSIX defines a universal standard to which all Unix versions must adhere. Most popular versions of Unix are now POSIX-compliant. Linux was developed from the beginning according to the POSIX standard. Linux also adheres to the Linux File System Hierarchy Standard (FHS), which specifies the location of files and directories in the Linux file structure. See **www.pathname.com/fhs** for more details.

Linux development is now overseen by The Linux Foundation (**www.linux-foundation .org**), which is a merger of The Free Standards Group and Open Source Development Labs (OSDL). This is the group with which Torvalds works to develop new Linux versions. Actual Linux kernels are released at **www.kernel.org**.

Installing Ubuntu

Installing Ubuntu is a very simple procedure with just a few screens with default entries for easy installation. A preselected collection of software is installed. Most of your devices, such as your monitory and network connection, are detected automatically. The most difficult part would be a manual partitioning of the hard drive, but you can use guided partitioning for installs that use an entire hard disk, as is usually the case. As an alternative, you can now install Ubuntu on a virtual hard disk on your Windows system, avoiding partition issues entirely.

Install CD and DVDs

In most cases, installation is performed using an Ubuntu LiveCD that will install the GNOME desktop along with a preselected set of software packages for multimedia players, office applications, and games. The Ubuntu LiveCD is designed to run from a CD drive, while providing the option to install Ubuntu on your hard drive. This is the disc image you will download from the Ubuntu download site at **www.ubuntu.com/getubuntu/download**. The CD has both 32- and 64-bit versions. If you want to use the 64-bit version, be sure you have CPU that is 64-bit compatible (as are all current CPUs). You can also download CD and DVD images directly from **http://releases.ubuntu.com**.

Installation Choices

The LiveCD is not the only Ubuntu installation available. Ubuntu tailors its installs by providing different CD/DVD install discs for different releases and versions (see Table 2-1). Ubuntu provides CDs designed for servers and specialized features such as Logical Volume Manager (LVM) and RAID. The alternate install also supports small installations with less than 320MB of RAM, automated installations, customized OEM systems, and the upgrading of older releases that have no network access. The Wubi installation option will install a fully functional Ubuntu system on a virtual hard disk on a Windows system. This is the easiest installation of Ubuntu and requires no hard disk partitioning.

- **Desktop CD**   Install GNOME desktop with a standard set of applications.
- **Server Install CD**   Install Ubuntu with a standard set of servers.

Ubuntu Release	Description
Ubuntu Desktop CD	Primary Ubuntu release, GNOME desktop
Ubuntu Desktop CD/Wubi	Insert Ubuntu desktop CD in Windows system and you can perform a Wubi installation
Ubuntu Alternate CD	Support for specialized features such as LVM, RAID, encrypted file systems, OEM distributions, and small memory
Ubuntu Server CD	Server only installation, no desktop, command line interface
Ubuntu Install DVD	Installation DVD, primarily for installs, large software collection on disc, can operate as a Live DVD
Ubuntu Editions	
Kubuntu	Installs the KDE desktop and software instead of GNOME, **http://kubuntu.org**
Edubuntu	Installs Educational software: Desktop, Server, and Server add-on CDs, **http://edubuntu.org**
Xubuntu	Installs XFce desktop, **http://xubuntu.org**
Ubuntu Studio	Install Ubuntu multimedia and graphics applications, **http://ubuntustudio.org**

TABLE 2-1   Ubuntu Releases and Versions

- **Alternate CD**   Install specialized features such as LVM, RAID, encrypted file systems, small systems, and OEM configurations.
- **Wubi**   Install to virtual hard disk in Windows.

An Install DVD is meant to install Ubuntu primarily and provides a large selection of software. The DVD can also serve as a LiveDVD and has the advantage of providing a large collection of installable software without needing network access to a repository.

All releases offer 32- and 64-bit versions. You can download these releases from **http://releases.ubuntu.com/8.04** or **http://cdimage.ubuntu.com/releases/hardy**.

Other Ubuntu editions include Kubuntu, Edubuntu, and Goubuntu. The Kubuntu LiveCD installs the K Desktop Environment (KDE) as the desktop instead of GNOME, along with KDE software. You could also install Kubuntu later on a GNOME install by selecting the Kubuntu metapackage for software installation. Kubuntu can then become an option in your login window sessions menu.

The Kubuntu and Edubuntu editions can be downloaded directly from **http://releases.ubuntu.com**.

The Gobuntu, Mythbuntu, Xubuntu, and Ubuntu Studio are all available, along with all the other editions and Ubuntu releases, on the cdimage server at **www.cdimage.ubuntu.com**.

Installing Dual-Boot Systems

The GRUB boot loader already supports dual-booting. Should you have both Linux and Windows systems installed on your hard disk, GRUB will let you choose to boot either the Linux system or a Windows system. During installation, GRUB will automatically detect any other operating systems installed on your computer and configure your boot loader menu to let you access them. You do not have to perform any configuration yourself.

If you want a Windows system installed on your computer, you should install it first if it is not already installed. Windows would overwrite the boot loader installed by a previous Linux system, cutting off access to the Linux system.

To install Windows after Ubuntu, you need to boot from your Ubuntu disk and select the Boot From Hard Disk option. Then run the `grub-install` command with the device name of your hard disk to reinstall the boot loader for GRUB.

Hardware, Software, and Information Requirements

Most hardware today meets the requirements for running Linux. Linux can be installed on a wide variety of systems, ranging from the very weak to the very powerful. The install procedure will detect most of your hardware automatically. You will need to specify only your keyboard, though a default is automatically detected for you.

Hardware Requirements

Following are the minimum hardware requirements for installing a standard installation of the Linux system on an Intel-based PC:

- A 32- or 64-bit Intel- or AMD-based personal computer. At least an Intel or compatible (AMD) microprocessor is required. A 400-MHz Pentium II or better is recommended for a graphical interface and 200 MHz for text.

- For 64-bit systems, be sure to use the 64-bit version of Ubuntu, which includes a supporting kernel.

- A CD-ROM or DVD-ROM drive. Should you need to create a bootable DVD/CD-ROM, you will need a DVD/CD-RW drive.

- Normally, at least 64MB of RAM for text and 192MB for a graphical interface, with 256MB recommended. For 64-bit systems, 128MB for text and 256MB for graphical are required, with 512MB recommended. (Linux can run on as little as 12MB RAM.) For desktop installation, 3GB or more is recommended, and 700MB is necessary for a command line interface–only installation. You will also need 64MB to 2GB for swap space, depending on the amount of available RAM memory.

Hard Drive Configuration

These days, Linux is usually run on its own hard drive, though it can also be run on a hard drive that contains a separate partition for another operating system such as Windows. If you have already installed Windows on your hard drive and configured it to take up the entire hard drive, you need to resize its partition to free up unused space that can be used for a Linux partition. You can use a partition management software package, such as GNU Parted or PartitionMagic, to free up the space.

TIP *You can also use the Ubuntu LiveCD to start up Linux and perform the necessary hard disk partitioning using GParted or QTParted.*

Hardware and Device Information

If you are not installing Linux on your entire hard drive, decide how much of your hard drive (in megabytes) you want to dedicate to your Linux system. If you want to share disk space with Windows, decide how much you want for Windows and how much for Linux. Install Windows first.

Most of the configuration settings are done automatically. Mice are automatically detected (Ubuntu no longer supports serial mice). If you should later need to reconfigure your mouse, you can use the GNOME or KDE mouse configuration tool. Monitor and graphics cards are detected automatically by the X.org service. Should you later need to tweak or modify your configuration, you can use either the vendor configuration tools (ATI or Nvidia) supplied by restricted drivers or the GNOME **displayconfig-gtk** tool (in Ubuntu, choose System | Administration | Screens And Graphics).

Network connections are automatically detected and configured using NetworkManager. Most network connection use DHCP or IPv6, which will automatically set up your network connection. For dial-up and wireless, you may have to configure access later (see Chapter 5).

Installing Ubuntu

Installing Linux involves several processes, beginning with creating Linux partitions, and then loading the Linux software, selecting a time zone, and creating new user accounts. The installation program used for Ubuntu is a screen-based program that takes you through all these processes, step-by-step, as one continuous procedure. You can use either your mouse or the keyboard to make selections. When you finish with a screen, click the Forward button at the bottom to move to the next screen. If you need to move back to the previous screen, click Back. You can also press TAB, the arrow keys, SPACEBAR, and ENTER to make selections. You have little to do other than make selections and choose options.

TIP   *To boot from a CD-ROM or DVD-ROM, you may first have to change the boot sequence setting in your computer's BIOS so that the computer will try to boot first from the CD-ROM. This requires some technical ability and knowledge of how to set your motherboard's BIOS configuration.*

Installation Overview

Installation is a straightforward process. A graphical installation is easy to use and explains each step with detailed instructions on a help pane.

Most systems today already meet hardware requirements and have automatic connections to the Internet (via Dynamic Host Control Protocol, DHCP). They also support booting a DVD-ROM or CD-ROM, though this support may have to be explicitly configured in the system BIOS. In addition, if you know how you want Linux installed on your hard disk partitions, or if you are performing a simple update that uses the same partitions, installing Ubuntu is a fairly simple process. Ubuntu features an automatic partitioning function that will perform the partitioning for you.

A preconfigured set of packages are installed, so you will not even have to select packages. For a quick installation you can simply start up the installation process, placing the DVD or CD in the drive, and start up your system. Graphical installation is a simple matter of following the instructions in each window as you progress. Installation follows seven easy steps:

1. **Welcome and language selection**   A default language is chosen for you, such as English, so you can probably click Forward.

2. **Where are you? and time zone**   Use the map to choose your time zone or select your city from the drop-down menu.

3. **Keyboard Layout**   A default is chosen for you; you can probably click Forward.

4. **Prepare Disk Space and Prepare Partitions**   For automatic partitioning you have the option of using a Guided partition, which will set up your partitions for you, or Manual partitioning, in which you set up partitions yourself.

5. **Who Are You?**   Set up a username and hostname for your computer, as well as a password for that user.

6. **Ready to Install**   At this point, nothing has been changed in your system. You can opt out of the installation if you want. If you click Forward, the install process will take place, making the actual changes. The system will first be formatted, and then packages are installed, with installation progress shown.

7. **Installation Complete**   After the installation, you will be asked to remove the DVD/CD-ROM and click the Exit button. This will reboot your system (do not reboot yourself).

Starting the Installation Program

If your computer can boot from the DVD/CD-ROM, you can start the installation directly from the CD or the DVD. Just place the CD in the CD-ROM drive or the DVD in the DVD drive before you start your computer. After you turn on or restart your computer, the installation program will start up.

LiveCD

The Ubuntu LiveCD (Desktop) is designed for running Ubuntu from the CD and installing Ubuntu. Most users will also use this LiveCD to install or upgrade Ubuntu. First start up Ubuntu and then you can initiate an installation.

The installation program will present a menu listing the following options (see Figure 2-1):

```
Try Ubuntu without any changes to your computer
Install Ubuntu
Install Ubuntu in text mode
Check CD for defects
Test Memory
Boot from first hard disk
```

- **Try Ubuntu without any changes to your computer**   Starts Ubuntu as a LiveCD. However, even if you just opt to try Ubuntu without changes (the first option), you can still perform an installation, just as you would with a LiveCD.

- **Install Ubuntu**   Starts up the installation Welcome screen immediately, beginning the install process (see the next section).

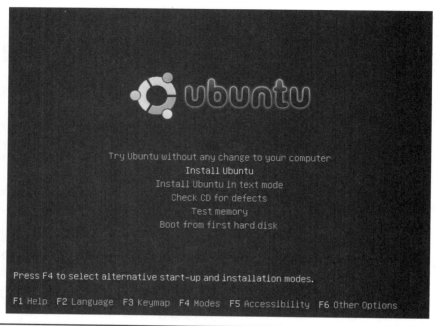

Try Ubuntu without any change to your computer
Install Ubuntu
Install Ubuntu in text mode
Check CD for defects
Test memory
Boot from first hard disk

Press F4 to select alternative start-up and installation modes.

F1 Help   F2 Language   F3 Keymap   F4 Modes   F5 Accessibility   F6 Other Options

FIGURE 2-1   Install disk start menu for Desktop LiveCD

- **Check CD for defects**   Checks whether your CD burn was faulty.
- **Test Memory**   Checks memory.
- **Boot from first hard disk**   Lets your LiveCD work as boot loader, starting up an operating system on the first hard disk, if one is installed. Use it to boot a system that the boot loader is not accessing for some reason.

Along the bottom of the screen are options you can set for the installation process. These are accessible with the function keys F1 through F6:

- F1 **Help**   Boot parameters and install prerequisites.
- F2 **Languages**   List of languages, pop-up menu.
- F3 **Keymap**   Languages for keyboard, pop-up menu.
- F4 **Modes**   List of possible install modes: OEM, Safe Graphics Mode, and Use Of A Driver CD. The Safe Graphics mode uses a low resolution for better compatibility. OEM install is a special kind of install that allows an administrator to configure the install before turning over access. Install With Driver Update CD is used for a CD with more current driver updates, particularly for newer hardware.
- F5 **Accessibility**   Contrast setting, magnifier, on-screen keyboard, and Braille support.

- **F6 Other Options**   Opens an editable text line listing the options of the currently selected menu choice. You can add other options or modify or remove existing ones. As you move down the list of choices you will see the listed options change, showing the boot options for that choice. Press ESC to return or ENTER to start.

Use the arrow keys to move from one menu entry to the next, and press ENTER to select the entry. Should you need to add options, say to the Install or Upgrade entry, press the TAB key. A command line is displayed where you can enter the options. Current options will already be listed. Use the BACKSPACE key to delete and arrow keys to move through the line. Press the ESC key to return to the menu.

TIP *Pressing ESC from the graphics menu places you at the boot prompt,* boot :, *for text mode install.*

The OEM install mode (Modes) is used for organizations that will be installing Ubuntu on several machines but want to add their own applications and configurations to the install later. The OEM install will set up an OEM default user with a password provided by the installer. When the installer is ready to turn over control to a regular user, the installer can run the **oem-prepare** command that will set up a normal user and password, removing the OEM user.

The DVD is designed for users who intend to perform an installation. It is a full DVD with more than 4GB of software on the disc. As with the CD, you have the option of trying Ubuntu or going directly to the installation process.

Starting Up Ubuntu

Your system detects your hardware, providing any configuration specifications that may be required. For example, if you have an IDE CD-RW or DVD-RW drive, it will be configured automatically.

If you cannot start the install process and you are using an LCD display, press F6 on the Install menu and enter **nofb** (no frame buffer) in the options command line.

As each screen appears in the installation, default entries will be already selected, usually by the autoprobing capability of the installation program. Selected entries will appear highlighted. If these entries are correct, you can click Forward to accept them and go on to the next screen.

Installation

If you are installing from the a LiveCD or LiveDVD, the Ubuntu operating system will start up in full LiveCD mode. To install, click the Install icon on the desktop (Figure 2-2). If you are using the DVD, installation will begin immediately.

NOTE *Once you're finished with a step, click the Forward button at the lower right to move on. In some screens, you can click a Back button to return to a previous screen. On most screens, clicking a link at the lower left will display the Release Notes.*

On the Welcome screen, select the language you want from the list on the left. A default language—usually English—will already be selected (Figure 2-3).

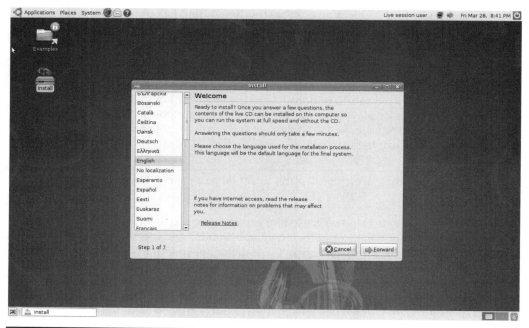

FIGURE 2-2   LiveCD (Desktop) with Install icon

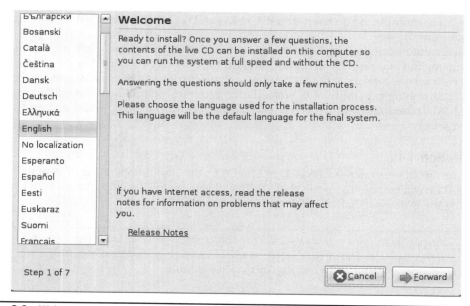

FIGURE 2-3   Welcome and language selection

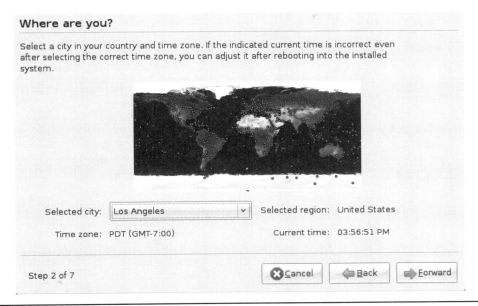

Where are you?

Select a city in your country and time zone. If the indicated current time is incorrect even after selecting the correct time zone, you can adjust it after rebooting into the installed system.

Selected city: [Los Angeles ▾]   Selected region: United States

Time zone: PDT (GMT-7:00)   Current time: 03:56:51 PM

Step 2 of 7   ⊗ Cancel   ⇐ Back   ⇒ Forward

FIGURE 2-4   Where Are You?, setting time zone

On the Where Are You? screen, you can set the time zone by using a map to specify your location or by using Universal Coordinated Time (UTC) entries (Figure 2-4). The Time Zone tool uses a map feature that expands first to your region to let you easily select your city and zone. You can also select your time zone directly from the pop-up menu.

You are then asked to select a keyboard layout—a default is already selected, such as USA (Figure 2-5).

You are asked to designate the Linux partitions and hard disk configurations you want to use on your hard drives. Ubuntu provides automatic partitioning options if you want to use available drives and free space for your Linux system. To let you configure your hard disks manually, Ubuntu offers a simple partitioning interface you can use to set up standard partitions. Unless you are using the alternate install, LVM, RAID, and encrypted file systems are not supported during the install process.

No partitions will be changed or formatted until you select your packages later in the install process. You can opt out of the installation at any time until that point and your original partitions will remain untouched. A default layout sets up a swap partition, a root partition of type *ext3* (Linux native) for the kernel and applications.

A dialog informs you that the partitioner is being started. If you have a single blank hard disk drive connected to your system, the partition screen will give you two options: Guided, using the entire disk, or Manual (Figure 2-6). The options will change according to the number of hard disks on your system. If you have several hard disks, they will be listed. You can also select the disk on which to install Ubuntu.

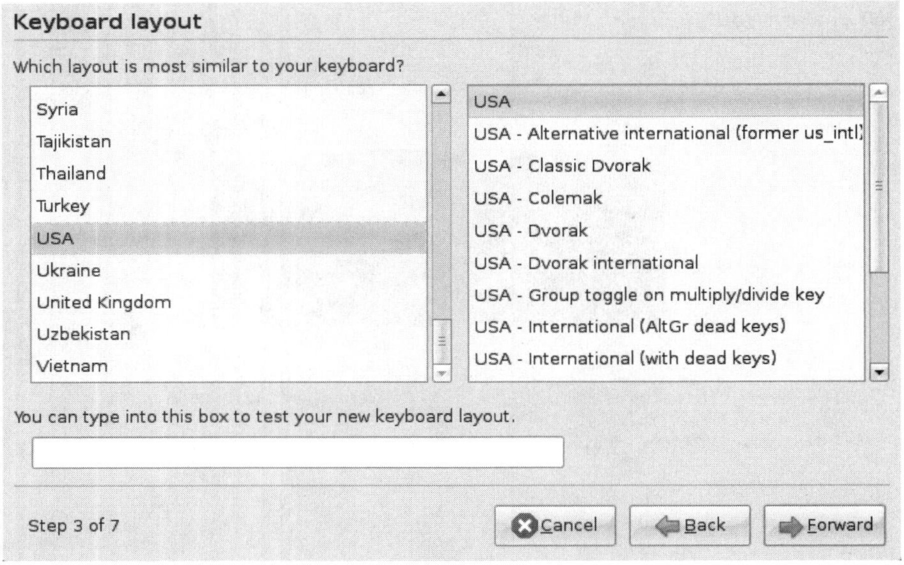

Keyboard layout

Which layout is most similar to your keyboard?

Syria	USA
Tajikistan	USA - Alternative international (former us_intl)
Thailand	USA - Classic Dvorak
Turkey	USA - Colemak
USA	USA - Dvorak
Ukraine	USA - Dvorak international
United Kingdom	USA - Group toggle on multiply/divide key
Uzbekistan	USA - International (AltGr dead keys)
Vietnam	USA - International (with dead keys)

You can type into this box to test your new keyboard layout.

Step 3 of 7   ⊗ Cancel   ⇐ Back   ⇒ Forward

FIGURE 2-5   Keyboard layout selection

Prepare disk space

How do you want to partition the disk?

⦿ Guided - use entire disk

   ⦿ SCSI1 (0,0,0) (sda) - 4.2 GB ATA QEMU HARDDISK

○ Manual

Step 4 of 7   ⊗ Cancel   ⇐ Back   ⇒ Forward

FIGURE 2-6   Prepare disk space

Windows and Linux **/home** partitions will not be overwritten in a guided partition. If you choose the Guided option, free space is required on your hard disk on which to install your system.

If you already have partitions set up on your hard disk, and you want to overwrite existing Linux partitions, you should choose the Manual option so you can edit those partitions, designating them for formatting and installation.

Choose Manual, and the partitioner interface starts up with the Prepare Partitions screen, listing any existing partitions. Each hard disk is listed by its device name, such as **sda** for the first Serial ATA device. Underneath each hard disk are its partitions and/or free space available (Figure 2-7). At the bottom of the screen are actions you can perform on partitions and free space: New Label, Edit, Delete, and Undo Changes To Partitions. When you select the free space entry, the New button will become available. When you select an existing partition, the New Label, Edit, and Delete buttons become available, but not the New button. The Undo Changes To Partitions button is always available.

To create a new partition, select the free space entry for the hard disk and click the New button. A Create A New Partition dialog opens with entries for the partition type (Primary or Logical), the size in megabytes, the location (Beginning or End), the file system type (Use As), and the Mount Point. For the root partition where you will install your system, the file system type would usually be **ext3**, and the root mount point is referenced with the slash (/) symbol (Figure 2-8).

For a swap partition, you would select the swap as the file system type (Use As). Swap partitions have no mount point.

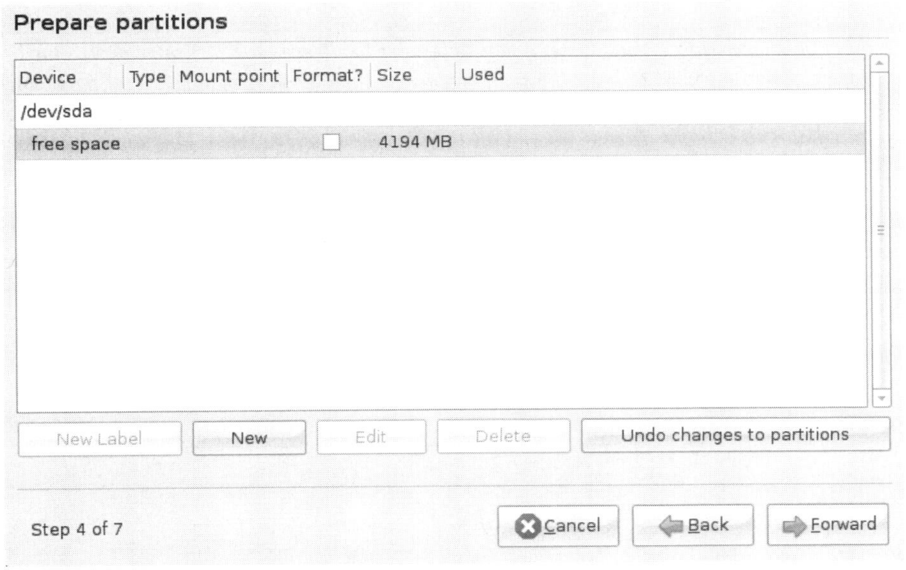

Prepare partitions

Device	Type	Mount point	Format?	Size	Used
/dev/sda					
free space			☐	4194 MB	

New Label | New | Edit | Delete | Undo changes to partitions

Step 4 of 7

❌ Cancel   ⬅ Back   ➡ Forward

FIGURE 2-7   Prepare Partitions

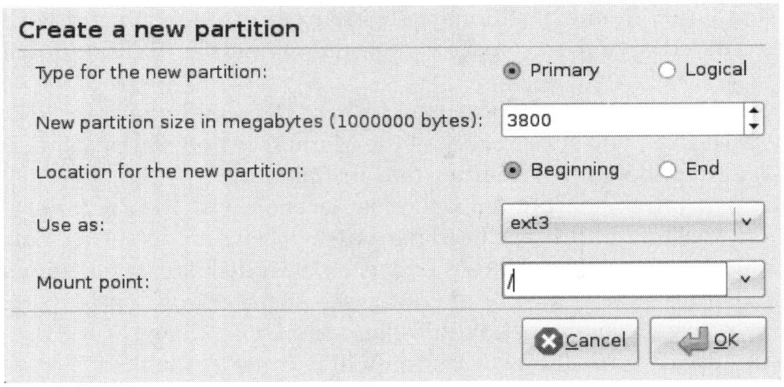

Create a new partition

Type for the new partition: ◉ Primary   ◯ Logical

New partition size in megabytes (1000000 bytes):   [3800   ]

Location for the new partition: ◉ Beginning   ◯ End

Use as: [ext3   ▾]

Mount point: [/   ▾]

                                                [✕ Cancel] [◂ OK]

FIGURE 2-8   Create A New Partition dialog

To edit an existing partition, click its entry in the Prepare Partitions screen and click the Edit button. An Edit A Partition dialog opens with entries for the partition type (Use As) and the Mount Point (Figure 2-9). The backslash (/) refers to the root mount point and is used to install your system.

Once you have created or edited a partition, it will appear in the Prepare Partitions screen. For new partitions, the Format check box will be checked; for edited partitions, be sure to check this box if the partition is for a new root partition. You can click the Undo Changes To Partitions button to undo any changes at this point (Figure 2-10).

TIP *If you have an existing Linux system, you will most likely see several Linux partitions listed. Some of these may be used for just the system software, such as the boot and root partitions. These should be formatted. Others may have extensive user files, such as a /home partition that normally holds user home directories and all the files they have created. You should not format such partitions.*

On the Who Are You? screen, enter your name, your user login name, user password, and the name you want to use for your computer (Figure 2-11). This is the hostname. The user you are creating will have administrative access and will be able to change your system configuration, add new users and printers, and install new software.

Edit a partition

Use as: [ext3   ▾]

Mount point: [/   ▾]

                                    [✕ Cancel] [◂ OK]

FIGURE 2-9   Edit A Partition dialog

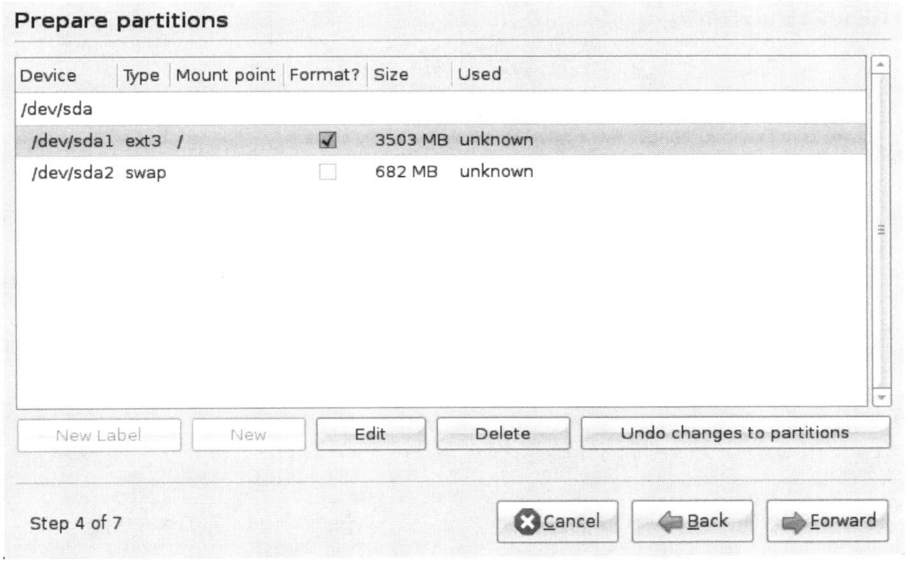

Prepare partitions

Device	Type	Mount point	Format?	Size	Used
/dev/sda					
/dev/sda1	ext3	/	☑	3503 MB	unknown
/dev/sda2	swap		☐	682 MB	unknown

New Label   New   Edit   Delete   Undo changes to partitions

Step 4 of 7   ❌ Cancel   ⬅ Back   ➡ Forward

FIGURE 2-10   Partitions with changes

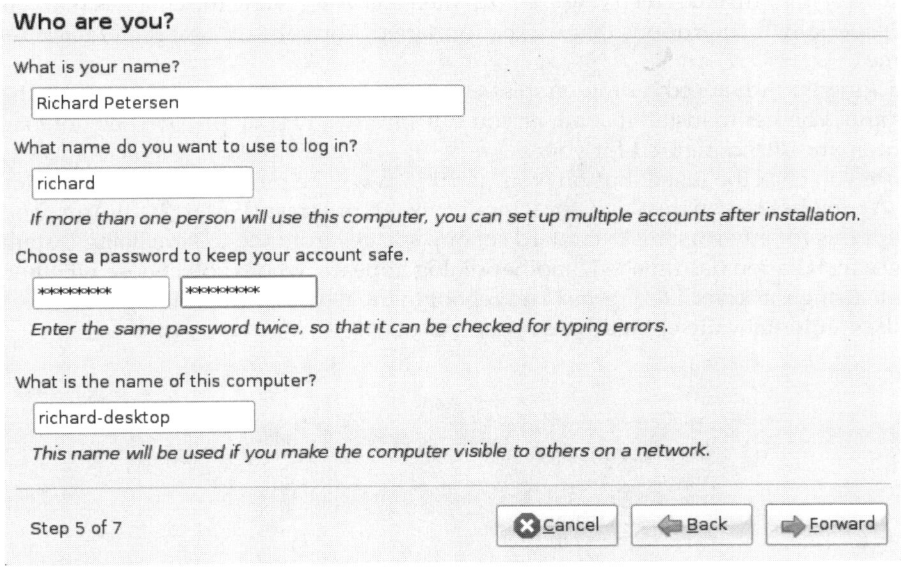

Who are you?

What is your name?

Richard Petersen

What name do you want to use to log in?

richard

If more than one person will use this computer, you can set up multiple accounts after installation.

Choose a password to keep your account safe.

✳✳✳✳✳✳✳   ✳✳✳✳✳✳✳

Enter the same password twice, so that it can be checked for typing errors.

What is the name of this computer?

richard-desktop

This name will be used if you make the computer visible to others on a network.

Step 5 of 7   ❌ Cancel   ⬅ Back   ➡ Forward

FIGURE 2-11   Who Are You?

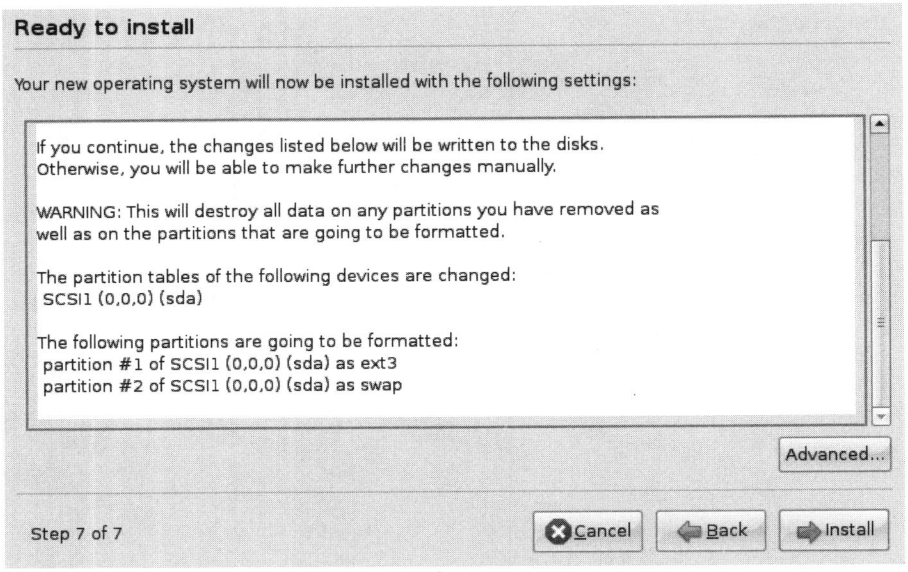

Ready to install

Your new operating system will now be installed with the following settings:

If you continue, the changes listed below will be written to the disks.
Otherwise, you will be able to make further changes manually.

WARNING: This will destroy all data on any partitions you have removed as
well as on the partitions that are going to be formatted.

The partition tables of the following devices are changed:
SCSI1 (0,0,0) (sda)

The following partitions are going to be formatted:
partition #1 of SCSI1 (0,0,0) (sda) as ext3
partition #2 of SCSI1 (0,0,0) (sda) as swap

Advanced...

Step 7 of 7   ❌ Cancel   ⬅ Back   ➡ Install

FIGURE 2-12 Ready To Install

The Ready To Install screen (Figure 2-12) then lets you review the changes that will be made, especially the partitions that will be formatted. You can still cancel and back out at this time.

Clicking the Advanced button on this screen will let you decide where to place the boot loader and whether to install it at all, or you can specify an HTTP proxy. The boot loader was automatically configured for you.

Once you click the Install button, your partitions will be formatted and installation will begin. A progress screen displays, showing the install progress (Figure 2-13). You should not interrupt this for any reason. A standard set of packages from the CD are being installed.

Once installation has finished, another dialog appears, where you choose whether to continue using the LiveCD or restart and reboot to the new installation (Figure 2-14). Your CD will be automatically ejected when your reboot.

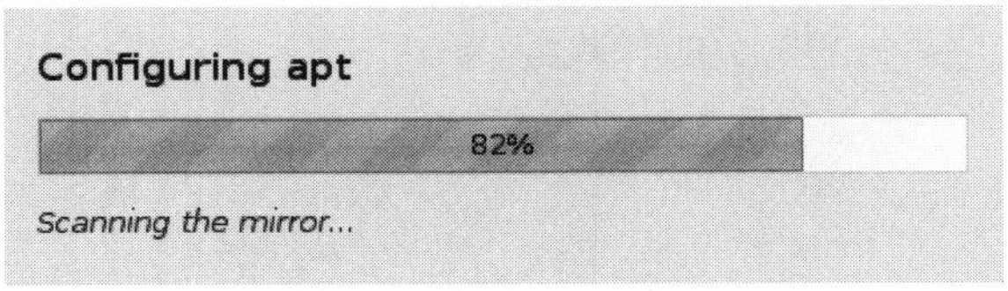

Configuring apt

82%

Scanning the mirror...

FIGURE 2-13 Install progress

Installation is complete. You need to restart the computer in order to use the new installation. You can continue to use this live CD, although any changes you make or documents you save will not be preserved.

Continue using the live CD   Restart now

FIGURE 2-14   Installation completed

Startup Issues

When your system restarts, the GRUB boot loader will quickly select your default operating system and start up its login screen. If you have just installed Ubuntu, the default operating system will be Ubuntu.

Selecting and Editing GRUB

If you have installed more than one operating system, you can select Ubuntu using the GRUB menu. You first need to display the GRUB menu at startup—you will have about a 3 second chance to do this. A quick message will tell you that GRUB is starting up your operating system. At this point, press the ESC key. The GRUB menu will then be displayed, as shown in Figure 2-15.

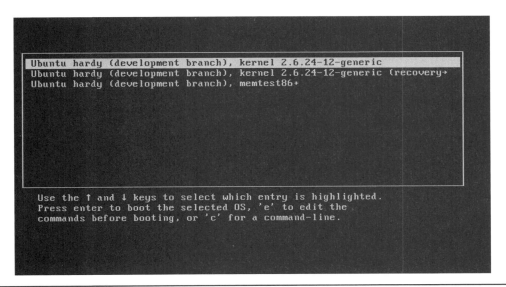

FIGURE 2-15   Ubuntu GRUB menu

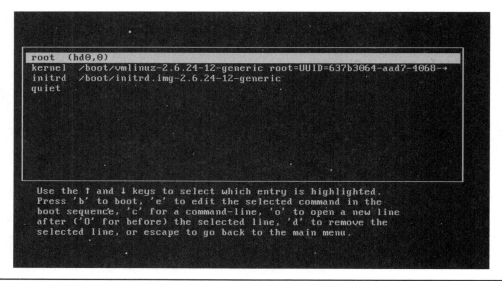

FIGURE 2-16   Editing a GRUB menu item

The GRUB menu will list Ubuntu and other operating systems you specified, such as Windows. Use the arrow keys to move to the entry you want, if it is not already highlighted, and press ENTER.

For graphical installations, some displays may have difficulty running the graphical startup display. If you have this problem, you can edit your Linux GRUB entry and remove the **splash** term at the end of the Grub startup line. Press the E key to edit a Grub entry (see Figure 2-16).

To change a particular line, select it and press the E key. The end of the line is then displayed (see Figure 2-17). You can use the arrow keys to move along the line, the BACKSPACE key to delete characters, and type as you normally do to insert characters. All changes are temporary. Permanent changes can be made only by directly editing the **/boot/grub/menu.lst** file.

```
         [ Minimal BASH-like line editing is supported.   For
           the    first    word,   TAB   lists   possible   command
           completions.   Anywhere else TAB lists the possible
           completions of a device/filename.  ESC at any time
           exits. ]

       4-aad7-4068-8103-ae58dce7f615 ro quiet splash_
```

FIGURE 2-17   Editing a GRUB line

Login and Logout

When your Ubuntu operating system starts up, the login screen appears (Figure 2-18). You can log in to your Linux system using a login name and password for any of the users you set up. An Username entry box displays in the middle of the screen, where you type in your username and press ENTER. The box label will then change to Password and the box will clear. Enter your password and press ENTER.

On the login screen, the Options pop-up menu in the lower-left corner lets you Shut Down or Restart Linux, or Suspend or Hibernate the system. The Select Sessions entry in this menu lets you choose which desktop graphical interface to use, such as KDE or GNOME. The Select Language entry lets you select a language to use.

When you finish, you can shut down your system. From GNOME, you can elect to shut down the entire system. If you log out from either GNOME or KDE and return to the login screen, you can click the Shut Down button to shut down.

If the system should freeze up for any reason, you can hold down the CTRL and ALT keys and press DEL (CTRL-ALT-DEL) to safely restart it. *Never just turn it off.* You can also use CTRL-ALT-F3 to shift to a command line prompt and log in to check out your system, shutting down with the **halt** command (the CTRL-ALT-F7 keys would return you to the graphical interface).

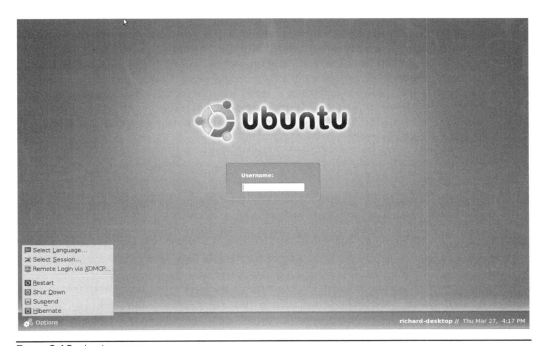

FIGURE 2-18   Login screen

Initial Configuration Tasks

You many want to take care of a few configuration tasks right away, such as the following:

- **Date And Time**   This is configured using either the world clock applet or the Date and Time configuration tool, **date-admin**: System | Administration | Date & Time. The world clock applet is on the right side of the top panel of the Date and Time screen. Right-click the applet and choose Preferences to configure.

- **Create Users**   This is handled by users-admin: System | Administration | Users and Groups.

- **Sound Configuration**   This is handled by PulseAudio: System | Preferences | Sound.

- **Firewall and Virus Projection**   Use Firestarter for your firewall: System | Administration | Firewall. You can install Clam AntiVirus for virus protection and ClamTk virus scanner for the interface: Applications | System Tools | Virus Scanner.

- **Display Configuration**   If you are using a quality graphics card from Nvidia or ATI (AMD), you may want to install their vendor graphics hardware drivers for Linux. These drivers provide better support for Nvidia and ATI graphics cards. To install these drivers, use the Hardware Drivers utility from System | Administration. If you want to configure these drivers yourself, you will also need their configuration interfaces. These you must download using the Synaptic Package Manager. For Nvidia, you install the **nvidia-settings** package, and for ATI the **fglrx-control** package. Alternatively, if you want to use the standard X.org drivers, but you're still having problems, such as in correctly detecting your monitor, you can download an install the GNOME Screen and Graphics Preferences utility (displayconfig-gtk). You may have to start this from a terminal window with the command **gksu displayconfig-gtk**.

Recovery

If for some reason you are not able to boot or access your system, it may be due to conflicting configurations, libraries, or applications. You can boot your Linux system in a recovery mode and then edit configuration files with a text editor such as Vi, remove the suspect libraries, or reinstall damaged software with the Debian Package Manager (DEB). To enter recovery mode, press the ESC key on startup to display the GRUB boot menu. Then select the recovery entry.

Reinstalling the Boot Loader

If you have a dual-boot system that runs both Windows and Linux on the same machine, you may need to reinstall your GRUB boot loader. This problem occurs if your Windows system completely crashes beyond repair and you have to install a new version of Windows, or you are adding Windows to your machine after having installed Linux. Windows will automatically overwrite your boot loader (alternatively, you could install your boot loader on your Linux partition instead of the master boot record, MBR). You will no longer be able to access your Linux system.

To reinstall your boot loader, first boot from your Linux DVD/CD-ROM installation disk, and at the menu select Rescue Installed System. This boots your system in rescue mode. Then use **grub-install** and the device name of your first partition to install the boot loader. Windows normally wants to be on the first partition with the MBR. You would specify this partition. At the prompt, enter **grub-install/dev/sda1** to reinstall your current GRUB boot loader, assuming that Windows is included in the GRUB configuration. You can then reboot, and the GRUB boot loader will start up. If you are adding Windows for the first time, you will have to add an entry for it in the **/boot/grub/menu.lst** file to make it accessible from the boot loader.

Alternate Install

Ubuntu also provides an alternate Install CD to support specialized features such as LVM, RAID, and encrypted file systems. The alternate CD uses a text-based installation interface. You use the TAB key to move between entries and the arrow keys to select items in a menu. Installation tasks are similar to those of the LiveCD and Install DVD. The alternate CD provides several options for setting up LVM partitions (see Figure 2-19).

A default LVM partition will create a separate boot partition and then an LVM Group partition with volumes for the swap and root partitions (see Figure 2-20).

You are informed of the changes in partitions that will be formatted. After you create a new user, the software is installed.

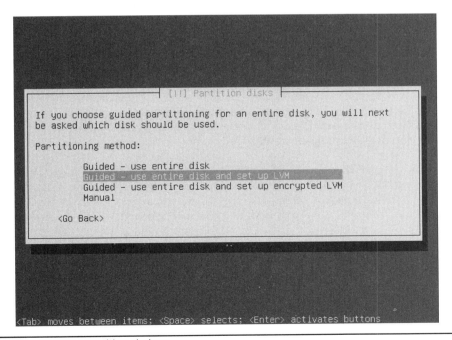

FIGURE 2-19   Alternate partition choices

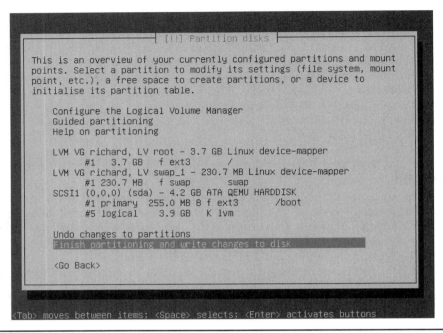

This is an overview of your currently configured partitions and mount
points. Select a partition to modify its settings (file system, mount
point, etc.), a free space to create partitions, or a device to
initialise its partition table.

```
        Configure the Logical Volume Manager
        Guided partitioning
        Help on partitioning

        LVM VG richard, LV root - 3.7 GB Linux device-mapper
            #1   3.7 GB   f ext3        /
        LVM VG richard, LV swap_1 - 230.7 MB Linux device-mapper
            #1 230.7 MB   f swap        swap
        SCSI1 (0,0,0) (sda) - 4.2 GB ATA QEMU HARDDISK
            #1 primary  255.0 MB B f ext3        /boot
            #5 logical    3.9 GB   K lvm

        Undo changes to partitions
        Finish partitioning and write changes to disk

        <Go Back>
```

FIGURE 2-20   Default LVM

Server Install

The Server Install CD includes all the servers available for use on Linux, including the Samba
Windows network server, mail servers, and database servers. These are also included with
the Install DVD. The Server CD is designed for stripped down servers that are used simply
to run servers and do not provide any desktop support. In fact, the GNOME and KDE
desktops are not included or installed with the Server CD. This is a very specialized server
installation.

The Server CD uses the same text-based installation interface used with the alternate
install—with TAB, SPACEBAR, and arrow keys used to make selections. Before the software is
installed, the Software Selection screen displays, where you select the servers you want
to install (Figure 2-21). Use the arrow keys to move to a selection and the SPACEBAR to make
a selection.

When you start up a server installation, you will use the command line interface.
The desktop is not installed. Desktops are considered unnecessary overhead for a server.
The user enters a username at the Ubuntu login: prompt, followed by the password at the
Password: prompt.

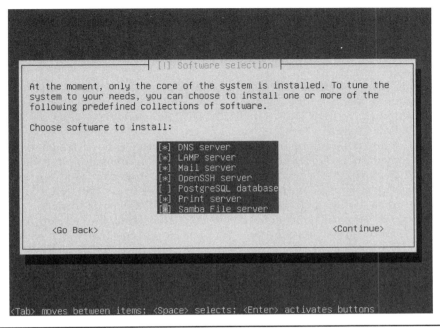

FIGURE 2-21   Software Selection screen, Server CD

Automating Installation with Kickstart

Kickstart is a method for providing a predetermined installation configuration for installing Ubuntu. Instead of having a user enter responses on the install screens, the responses can be listed in a kickstart file from which the install process can read. You will need to create a kickstart configuration file on a working Ubuntu system. (Kickstart configuration files have the extension **.cfg**.) A kickstart file is created for every Ubuntu system that holds the install responses used for that installation. It is located in the **root** directory at **/root/anaconda-ks.cfg**.

If you plan to perform the same kind of installation on computers that would be configured in the same way—such as on a local network with hosts that have the same hardware—you could use this kickstart file as a model for performing installations. It is a text file that you can edit, with entries for each install response, such as the following for keyboard and time zone:

```
keyboard us
timezone America/LosAngeles
```

More complex responses may take options such as **network**, which uses **--device** for the device interface and **bootproto** for the boot client:

```
network --device eth0 --bootproto dhcp
```

Display configuration is more complex, specifying a video card and monitor type, which could vary. You can have the system skip this by using **xskip**.

The first entry is the install source. This will be **cdrom** for a CD/DVD-ROM install. If you want to use an NFS or Web install instead, you could add that information here, specifying the server name or Web site.

You can also use the **system-config-kickstart** tool to create your kickstart file. This provides a graphical interface for each install screen. First install the tool. Then, to start it, choose Applications | System Tools | Kickstart. The help manual provides a detailed description on how to use this tool.

The name of the configuration file should be **ks.cfg**. Once you have created the kickstart file, you can copy it to CD/DVD or even to a floppy disk. You could also place the file on a local hard disk partition (such as a Windows or Linux partition) if you have one. For a network, you could place the file on an NFS server, provided your network is running a DHCP server to enable automatic network configuration on the install computer.

When you start the installation, at the boot prompt you specify the kickstart file and its location. In the following example, the kickstart file is located on a floppy disk as **/dev/fd0**:

```
linux ks=floppy
```

You can use **hd:*device*** to specify a particular device such as a hard drive or second CD-ROM drive. For an NFS site, you would use **nfs:**.

Wubi: Windows-Based Installer

Wubi is an Ubuntu installer that lets you install and run Ubuntu from Windows. It is a simple, safe, and painless way to install Linux for users who want to preserve their Windows system without having to perform any potentially hazardous hard disk partition operations to free up space and create new hardware partitions for Ubuntu.

Wubi is already integrated into the Ubuntu 8.04 Desktop CD. Using Wubi, you do not have to create a separate partition for Ubuntu. A file created on your Window system functions as a *virtual disk*, and Ubuntu is installed on this virtual disk, which operates like a hard disk with a Linux file system installed on it. The Windows boot loader is modified to list a choice for Ubuntu, so when Windows starts up, you can choose to start Ubuntu instead of Windows.

The Wubi installation of Ubuntu is fully functional in every way. Though it uses a virtual hard disk, it is not a virtual system. When you start Ubuntu, you are running only Ubuntu. It differs from a standard install in that the system is installed on a file, rather than an actual hard disk partition, and the original Windows boot loader is used instead of the GRUB boot loader. As far as usage is concerned, operations are the same, though with slightly slower disk access. You can find out more about Wubi at **http://wubi-installer.org**. Check the Ubuntu WubiGuide (**https://wiki.ubuntu.com/WubiGuide**) for detailed information about installation and management issues such as boot problems, virtual disk creation, and details of the Wubi installation for Ubuntu.

To install Ubuntu with Wubi, insert the Ubuntu Desktop CD into your CD/DVD drive. The Ubuntu CD Menu automatically starts up (Figure 2-22), giving you the option of performing the standard install (restart and possibly partition your drive) or installing inside Windows (use a Wubi virtual hard disk file on Windows). The Learn More option opens the Ubuntu Web site.

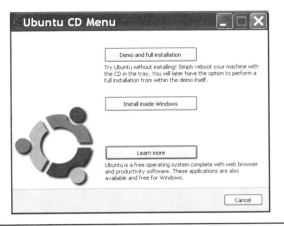

FIGURE 2-22   Ubuntu CD menu on Windows

The Setup screen (Figure 2-23) will prompt you for the drive on which to install the virtual disk file; the installation size, which is the size for the virtual disk file; the desktop environment (Ubuntu); the language to use; and a username and password. You then click the Install button to download and install Ubuntu. Clicking the Accessibility button opens a dialog where you can specify accessibility install options such as Contrast, Magnifier, Braille, and On-screen Keyboard.

Wubi then installs the standard Ubuntu desktop. Your language, keyboard, partitions, and user login have already been determined from the Setup window. Wubi will first copy over files from the Desktop install disk and then prompt you to reboot. When you reboot, your Windows boot menu is displayed with an entry for Ubuntu. Use the arrow keys to select the Ubuntu entry and press ENTER. Ubuntu will then start up. The first time it will complete the installation showing just a progress bar on the desktop, formatting, installing software, detecting hardware, and configuring your system. You do not have to do anything. Once installation tasks are finished, you reboot and select Ubuntu again to start it up.

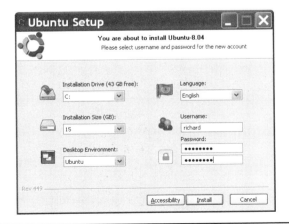

FIGURE 2-23   Ubuntu Setup window for Wubi

Ubuntu is fully functional. You can configure your system, install hardware drivers, and set preferences just as you do for any Ubuntu system.

Wubi sets up an **ubuntu** directory on the hard drive partition on which you installed Ubuntu, usually the **c:** drive. Here you will find **boot** and **disks** subdirectories. In the **disks** subdirectory is your virtual hard disk where Ubuntu is installed. You will also find another virtual hard disk file for your swap disk. Your Ubuntu virtual disk will be named **root.disk**, as in **c:\ubuntu\disks\root.disk**. Keep in mind that Ubuntu is installed as a file on your Windows system. Be careful not to delete the **ubuntu** directory. Should you reformat your Windows partition for any reason, you, of course, would lose you Ubuntu system also.

You can uninstall a Wubi installed Ubuntu system using Window's Add or Remove Software applet.

Interface Basics: Login, Desktop, and Help

Using Linux has become an almost intuitive process, with easy-to-use interfaces, including graphical logins and graphical user interfaces (GUIs) such as GNOME and KDE. Even the standard Linux command line interface has become more user-friendly with editable commands, history lists, and cursor-based tools. To start using Linux, you have to know how to access your Linux system and, once you are on the system, how to execute commands and run applications. Access is supported through a simple window interface with menus for selecting login options and a text box for entering your username and password. Once you access your system, you can interact with it using windows, menus, and icons.

Linux is noted for providing easy access to extensive help documentation. It's easy to obtain information quickly about any Linux command and utility while logged in to the system. You can access an online manual that describes each command or obtain help that provides more detailed explanations of different Linux features. A complete set of manuals provided by the Linux Documentation Project is included on your system and available to browse through or print. Both the GNOME and K Desktop Environment (KDE) desktops provide help systems with easy access to desktop, system, and application help files.

Accessing Your Linux System

If you have installed the GRUB boot loader, when you turn on or reset your computer, the boot loader first decides what operating system to load and run. The boot loader then loads the default operating system, which will be Ubuntu. Ubuntu will use a graphical interface by default, presenting you with a login window in which you enter your username and password.

If other operating systems, such as Windows, are already installed on your computer, you can press the SPACEBAR at startup to display a boot loader menu showing those systems as boot options. If a Windows system is listed, you can choose to start that instead of Ubuntu. (See Chapter 21 for more information on GRUB.)

The GNOME Display Manager: GDM

In Ubuntu, the GNOME Display Manager (GDM) manages the login interface along with authenticating the username and password, and then Ubuntu starts up a selected desktop.

NOTE *If you encounter problems in using the GUI, you can force an exit by pressing CTRL-ALT-BACKSPACE to return to the login screen. In addition, from the GDM, you can switch to the command line interface by pressing CTRL-ALT-F1, and then switch back to the GUI by pressing CTRL-ALT-F7. You can also force your system to reboot at the login prompt by holding down the CTRL and ALT keys and then pressing the DEL key (CTRL-ALT-DEL). Your system will go through the standard shutdown procedure and then your computer will reboot.*

On startup, the GDM displays a login window with a Username text box (Figure 3-1). Various GDM themes are available, which you can select using the GDM configuration tool (see Chapter 4). The default theme currently used is the Ubuntu Human theme. An Options pop-up menu at the lower-left corner of the screen shows entries for Restart, Shut Down, Suspend, and Hibernate your system. In addition, Select Language and Select Session entries display dialogs for selecting the language or user interface you want to use, such as GNOME or KDE.

Enter your username and press ENTER. Then enter your password and press ENTER. By default, the GNOME desktop starts up.

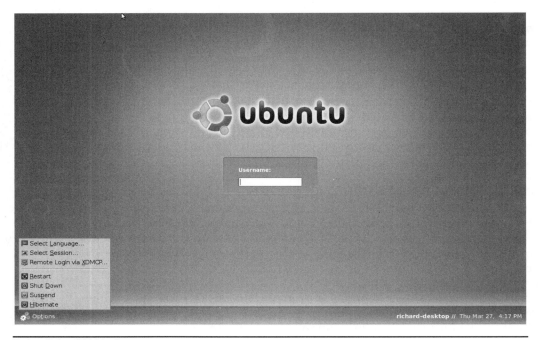

FIGURE 3-1   GDM login screen

When you log out from the desktop, you return to the GDM login screen (Figure 3-1). To shut down your Linux system, choose Options | Shut Down. To restart, choose Options | Restart. You can also shut down the system from GNOME: Choose System | Quit, or click the Quit button on the top panel at the right. GNOME will display a dialog box with two rows of buttons: Suspend, Hibernate, Restart, or Shut Down options appear in the bottom row. Click Restart to shut down and restart your system.

Choose Options | Select Sessions to select the desktop or window manager you want to start up. In the dialog box that shows all installed user interfaces, you can choose KDE to start up the K Desktop, for example, instead of GNOME. The KDE option will not be shown unless you have already installed KDE.

Failsafe entries for both GNOME and the terminal provide a stripped down interface you can use for troubleshooting. For example, the Run Xclient script lets you run just your X Window System configuration script. This script will normally start up GNOME or KDE, but it could be specially configured for other desktops or window managers. Normally, the last session entry would be selected, which starts up the interface you used previously.

Once you have selected your interface, click the Change Session button (or you can opt out of any change by clicking the Cancel button) to return to the login screen.

Selecting Language from the Options menu opens a dialog with a drop-down menu that lists a variety of languages supported by Linux. Choose one and click the Change Language button to change the language used by your interface.

The User Switcher

The user switcher at the upper-right of the top panel of the GNOME desktop lets you switch to another user without having to log out or end your current user session. The user switcher is installed automatically as part of your basic GNOME desktop configuration. Click the username to see a list of all other users, as shown next. Check boxes appear next to the names to indicate which users are logged in and running. To switch to a different user, simply select

the user from this list. If the user is not already logged in, the login screen (GDM) will appear, where you can enter the user's password. If the user is already logged in, the login screen for the lock screen will appear (you can disable the lock screen). Enter the user's password here. The user's original session will continue, and any open windows and applications running when the user switched off will still be open and running. You can easily switch back and forth between logged in users, with each user retaining his session where he left off. When you switch to a new user, the former user's running programs will continue in the background.

Right-clicking the switcher will list several user management options, such as configuring the login screen, managing users, or changing the user's password and personal information. The Preferences item lets you configure how the user switcher is displayed on your screen. For example, instead of the username, you could use the term *Users* or a user icon. You can also choose whether to use a lock screen when the user is switched. Disabling the lock screen option will let you switch seamlessly between logged in users.

Accessing Linux from the Command Line Interface

For the command line interface, you are initially provided a login prompt. On Ubuntu, you can access the command line interface by pressing CTRL-ALT-F1 at any time (ALT-F7 returns to the graphical interface). The login prompt is preceded by the hostname you gave to your system. When you finish using Linux, you first log out. Linux then displays exactly the same login prompt, waiting for you or another user to log in again. This is the equivalent of the login window provided by the GDM. You can then log in to another account.

Once you log in to an account, you can enter and execute commands. Logging in to your Linux account involves two steps: entering your username and then entering your password. Type in the username for your user account. In the next example, the hostname is **turtle**, and the user enters the username **richlp** and is then prompted to enter a password:

```
Ubuntu release 8.04
Kernel 2.6 on an i686

turtle login: richlp
Password:
```

When you type in your password, it does not appear on the screen to protect your password from being seen by others. If you enter either the username or the password incorrectly, the system will respond with the error message "Login incorrect" and will ask for your username again, starting over the login process. You can then re-enter your username and password.

Once you enter your username and password correctly, you are logged in to the system. The command line prompt is displayed, waiting for you to enter a command. Notice the command line prompt is a dollar sign (**$**), not a number sign (**#**). The **$** is the prompt for regular users, whereas the **#** is the prompt solely for the root user. In this version of Ubuntu, your prompt is preceded by the hostname and the directory in which you are working. Both are bounded by a set of brackets:

```
[turtle /home/richlp]$
```

To end your session, issue the **logout** or **exit** command. This returns you to the login prompt, and Linux waits for another user to log in.

```
[turtle /home/richlp]$ logout
```

To log out and shut down your system from the command line, enter the **halt** command:

```
$ halt
```

The Ubuntu Desktop

Ubuntu supports both the GNOME and KDE desktops. The default Ubuntu LiveCD installs GNOME, and the Kubuntu LiveCD installs KDE. The Ubuntu DVD lets you install both, and you can later install one or the other using a Synaptic metapackage. GNOME uses the Ubuntu Human theme for its interface with the Ubuntu screen background and menu icons as its default (Figure 3-2).

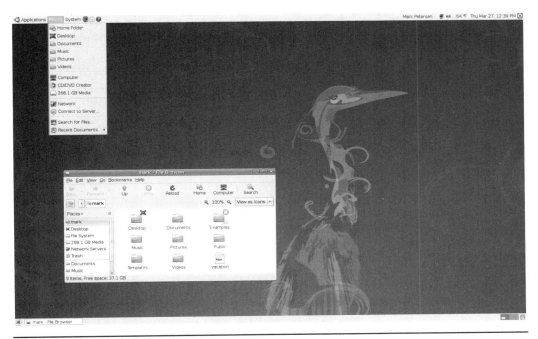

FIGURE 3-2   Ubuntu GNOME desktop

NOTE   *Although the GNOME and KDE interfaces appear similar, they are very different desktop interfaces with separate tools for selecting preferences. The Preferences menus on GNOME and KDE display different selections of desktop configuration tools.*

GNOME Desktop

The Ubuntu GNOME desktop screen initially displays panels at the top and bottom of the screen, as well as any file manager folder icons for your home directory and for the system.

The top panel displays menus, application icons, and notification tasks. Three menus appear in the top panel:

- **Applications**   Submenus such as Office and Internet list the applications installed on your system. Use the Applications menu to start applications. The Install/ Remove Software entry will start the Install and Remove Applications tool for basic package install operations.

- **Places**   This menu lets you easily access commonly used locations such as your home directory; the desktop folder for any files on your desktop; the Computer window, through which you can access devices and removable disks; and Network for accessing shared file systems. It also has entries for searching for files (Search For Files), accessing recently used documents, and logging in to remote servers, such as NFS and FTP servers. This menu has a CD/DVD Creator entry for using Nautilus to burn data CD/DVD-ROMs. A Recent Documents submenu lists all recently accessed files.

- **System** This menu includes Preferences and Administration submenus. The Preferences submenu is used for configuring your GNOME settings, such as the theme you want to use and the behavior of your mouse. The Administration submenu holds all the Ubuntu system configuration tools used to perform administrative tasks such as adding users, setting up printers, configuring network connections, and managing network services such as a web server or Samba Windows access. The System menu also holds entries for locking the screen (Lock) and logging out of the system (Logout).

Next to the menus are application icons for commonly used applications, including Firefox, the mail utility, and help. Click one to start that application. Of course, you can also start these applications from the Applications menu.

You can access your home directory from its entry in the Places menu. A file manager window opens, showing your home directory with default directories created for commonly used files, including **Pictures**, **Documents**, **Music**, and **Videos**. Your office applications will automatically save files to the **Documents** directory by default. Image and photo applications will place image files in the **Pictures** directory. The **Desktop** folder will hold all files and directories saved to your desktop.

The file manager window displays several components, including a browser toolbar, a location bar, and a side pane listing places, which resembles similar areas commonly found on most traditional file managers. When you open a new directory, the same window is used to display it, and you can use the forward and back arrows to move through previously opened directories. In the location bar in text-based mode, a box is displayed where you can enter the pathname for a directory to move directly to it. Figure 3-3 shows the file manager window.

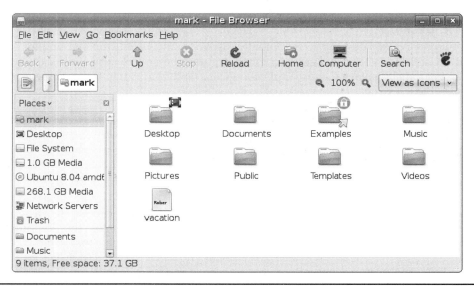

FIGURE 3-3 File manager for home folder

NOTE *For both GNOME and KDE, the file manager is Internet-aware. You can use it to access remote FTP directories and to display or download their files, though in KDE the file manager is also a fully functional Web browser.*

To quit the GNOME desktop, either click the Quit button on the right side of the top panel or choose System | Quit. This displays a dialog with buttons for Log Out, Switch User, Restart, and Shut Down. Click the Shut Down button to shut down the system. Click Log Out to return to the login screen, where you can log in as a different user. Switch User will keep you logged in while you log in as another user. Your active programs will continue to run in the background. Clicking the Restart button will shut down and the restart the system.

NOTE *Ubuntu provides several tools for configuring your GNOME desktop, which you can access by choosing System | Preferences. These tools are discussed in detail in Chapter 8. Click the Help button on each preference window to display detailed descriptions and examples. Some of the commonly used tools are discussed in the "Desktop Operations" section later in this chapter.*

On the far right side of the GNOME desktop's top panel are the user switcher icon, the sound volume control icon, the date and time, and the Quit button.

The bottom panel, shown next, is used for interactive tasks such as selecting workspaces and docking applications. If your desktop becomes too cluttered with open windows and you want to clear it by minimizing all the windows, you can click the Show Desktop button at the left side of the bottom panel. The workspace switcher for virtual desktops appears as two squares on the right side of the panel. Clicking a square moves you to that area of the workspace. On the right of the workspace switcher is the trash icon that you can click to see what items are in your trash.

Moving and Copying Windows and Files

To move a window, click and drag its title bar. Each window sports maximize, minimize, and close buttons, or you can double-click the title bar to maximize the window. Each window has a corresponding minimize and restore button on the bottom panel. The desktop supports full drag-and-drop capabilities and combinations of keypresses and mouse clicks, as shown in the following table. You can drag folders, icons, and applications to the desktop or other file manager windows open to other folders. The move operation is the default drag operation (you can also press the SHIFT key while dragging). To copy files, press the CTRL key and then click and drag before releasing the mouse button. To create a link, hold down both the CTRL and SHIFT keys while dragging the icon to where you want the link to appear, such as the desktop.

SHIFT-click	Move a file or directory, default
CTRL-click	Copy a file or directory
CTRL-SHIFT-click	Create a link for a file or directory

FIGURE 3-4
GNOME Add To
Panel dialog

GNOME Applets

GNOME applets are small programs that you can access from icons on the top panel. It is easy to add applets to the panel: Simply right-click a vacant space on the panel and choose Add To Panel to see all available applets in a dialog (Figure 3-4). You may find some applets to be particularly helpful, such as Dictionary Lookup; the current weather; the system monitor, which shows your CPU usage; the CPU Frequency Scaling Monitor for Cool'n'Quiet processors; and Search For Files. You will need to perform basic configuration for most applets before they can be run. To do this, right-click the applet and choose Preferences to open the Preferences window for that applet, where you can change settings.

The following illustration shows some common applet icons that appear to the right of the Web browser, Email, and Help icons: from left to right, Dictionary Lookup, System Monitor, Tomboy note taker, eyes that follow your mouse around, a fish, DeskBar desktop search, User Switcher, Network Connection Monitor, volume control, weather, date and time (International Clock), and the Quit button.

NOTE *The KDE desktop displays a panel at the bottom of the screen that looks similar to the panel displayed on the top of the GNOME desktop. The file manager for KDE appears slightly different but operates much the same way as the GNOME file manager. See Chapter 9 for details on KDE.*

Desktop Operations

There are several desktop operations that you may want to take advantage of when first setting up your desktop. These include setting up your personal information, burning CD/DVD disks, searching your desktop for files, and using removable media like USB drives, along with access to remote host.

TIP With very large monitors and their high resolutions becoming more common, one feature users find helpful is the ability to increase the desktop font sizes. To increase the font size, open the Font panel on the Appearance preferences located in System | Preferences | Appearance menu. There you can change the font sizes used on your desktop. See Chapter 8 for more information on fonts.

International Clock: Time, Date, and Weather

The International Clock applet displays the current time and date for your region, but you can modify it to display the local weather, as well as the time, date, and weather of any location in the world.

To add a location, right-click the time and choose Preferences. The Clock Preferences dialog displays three tabs: General, Locations, and Weather. To add a new location, click the Add button on the Locations tab. This opens another dialog where you can enter the name, time zone, and coordinates of the location. Click the Find button and open a expandable tree of locations, starting with continent, then region, country, and city (Figure 3-5).

On the Weather tab, you can specify the temperature and wind measures to use. On the General tab, you can set the clock's display options for particular locations and decide whether to show weather, temperature, date, and seconds.

Once you set your location, a weather icon will appear next to the time on the top panel, showing current weather information:

61 ℉ Thu Mar 27, 8:45 AM

To see the locations you have selected, click the time displayed on the top panel. This opens a calendar, with a Locations area with an expandable arrow at the bottom. Click this arrow to display all your locales, their times, and weather, as shown next. A house icon appears next to your home location. A world map shows your world locations as red dots,

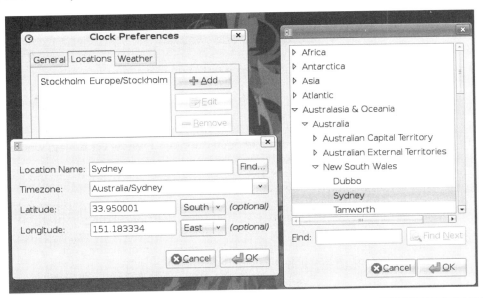

FIGURE 3-5 Selecting a location from the Clock Preferences dialog

with a blue house icon showing your current home location. When you click a location entry, its corresponding dot will blink for a few seconds. Each location also shows a small globe weather icon that indicates the general weather, such as sun or clouds. To see weather details, move your mouse over the weather icon, and a pop-up dialog will display the current weather, temperature, wind speed, and times for sunrise and sunset. The clock icons for each location appear dark, gray, or bright depending on the time of day at that location.

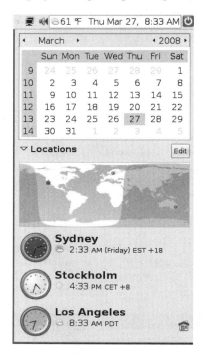

Each location has a Set button that is hidden until you move your mouse over it, on the right side of the clock display.

You can easily change your home location by clicking the Set button to the right the location you want to make your home. The home icon will shift to the new location on the world map. This can be helpful when you're traveling.

To make changes, click the Edit button to open the Clock Preferences dialog, where you can configure the display or add and remove locations.

The calendar shows the current date, but you can move to different months and years using the month and year scroll arrows at the top.

To set the time manually, right-click the time and choose Adjust Date & Time (or, from the General panel of the Clock Preferences window, click the Time Settings button). This opens a Time Settings dialog, where you can enter the time and set the date, as shown next. Use the month and year arrows on the calendar to change the month and year. To set the time for the entire system, click the Set System Time button.

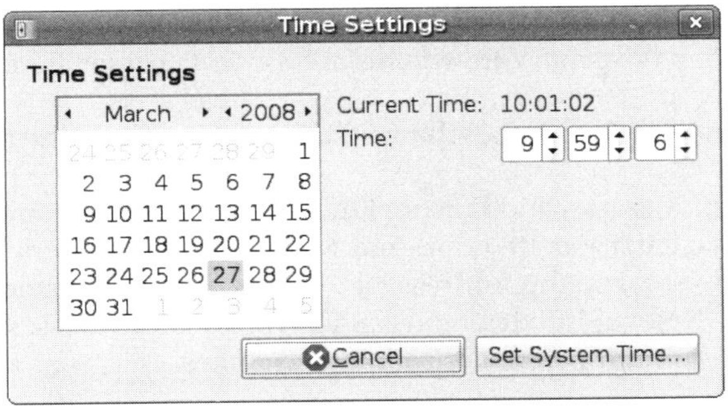

Configuring Personal Information

To set up personal information, including the icon to be used for your graphical login, you use the About Me preferences tool. On the Ubuntu GNOME desktop, choose System | Preferences | About Me. The About Me dialog (Figure 3-6) lets you set up personal information to be used with your desktop applications, as well as change your password. Each user can set up his or her own personal information, including the icon or image to use to represent themselves.

Clicking the image icon in the top-left corner opens a browser window, where you can select a personal image. The Faces directory is selected by default and displays several images. The selected image displays at the right on the browser window. You can even use

FIGURE 3-6   About Me information: System | Preferences | About Me

a personal photograph: select the folder on your home directory where you store images and choose a photograph or image you want to use for your personal image in the login screen when showing your user entry.

To change your password, click the Change Password button at the top right on the About Me dialog.

Three tabs, Contact, Address, and Personal Info, let you change more preferences. On the Contact tab, you can enter e-mail (home and work) addresses, telephone numbers, and instant messaging addresses; on the Address tab, you can enter your home and work addresses; and on the Personal Info tab, you can list your Web addresses and work information. Click Close when you're done making changes.

Desktop Background

You use the Background tab on the Appearance Preferences tool to select or customize your desktop background image (Figure 3-7). You can access this tool in two ways: right-click anywhere on the desktop background and choose Change Desktop Background from the context menu, or choose System | Preferences | Appearance and then select the Background tab. Installed backgrounds are listed here, with the current background selected. To add your own image, either drag-and-drop the image file to the Background window or click the Add button to locate and select the image file. To remove an image, select it and click the Remove button.

From the Style drop-down menu, you can choose display options such as Zoom, Centered, Scaled, Tiled, or Fill Screen. A centered or scaled image will preserve the image proportions. Fill Screen may distort it. Any space not filled, such as with a centered or scaled images, will be filled in with the desktop color. You can change the color if you want, as well as make it a

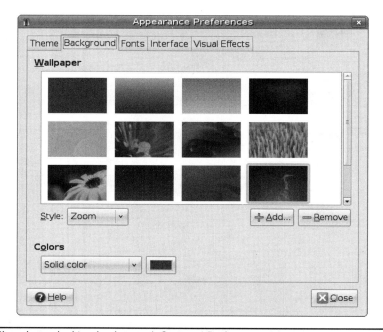

FIGURE 3-7 Choosing a desktop background: System | Preferences | Appearance

horizontal or vertical gradient via the Colors drop-down menu. You select colors from a color wheel that provides an extensive selection.

Initially, only the Ubuntu backgrounds are listed, but you can install the **gnome-background** package to add a collection of GNOME backgrounds. You can download more GNOME backgrounds from **http://art.gnome.org** and **http://gnome-look.org**.

TIP *You can set your screen resolution as well as screen orientation using the Monitor Resolution Settings utility accessible from System | Preferences | Screen Resolution. The utility supports RandR screen management features such as screen rotation, resolution, and refresh rate.*

Using Removable Devices and Media

Removable media such as CDs and DVDs, USB storage disks, digital cameras, and floppy disks will be displayed as icons on your desktop. These icons will not appear until you place the media into their appropriate devices. To open a disk, double-click its icon to display a file manager window and the files on it.

Ubuntu now supports removable devices and media such as digital cameras, PDAs, card readers, and even USB printers. These devices are handled automatically with an appropriate device interface set up on the fly when needed. Such hotplugged devices are identified, and where appropriate, their icons will appear in the file manager window. For example, when you connect a USB drive to your system, it will be detected and displayed as a storage device with its own file system.

CAUTION *If you copy files to a disk, CD, or DVD, be sure to unmount it first before removing it from the drive (right-click the icon and choose Unmount Volume).*

Accessing File Systems, Devices, and Remote Hosts

The GNOME desktop also displays a **Computer** folder. Open this folder to see a list of removable devices along with icons for file system and network connections (Figure 3-8). Click the Filesystem icon to access the entire file system on your computer, starting from the root directory. Regular users will have only read access to many of these directories, whereas the root user will have full read and write access.

Opening the **Network** folder shows a list of hosts on your system with shared directories, such as Windows systems accessible with Samba. GNOME uses Domain Name Service (DNS)–based service discovery to detect these hosts automatically. Clicking a host's icon will list the shared directories available on that system. When opening a shared directory, you will be asked for a user and password, like the user and password required for a directory owned by a Windows user. The first time you access a shared directory, you will also be asked to save this user and password in a *keyring*, which itself can be password-protected. This allows repeated access without your having to enter the password every time.

Burning DVDs and CDs

With GNOME, burning data to a DVD or CD is a simple matter of dragging files to an open blank CD or DVD window and clicking the Write To Disk button. When you insert a blank disc, a CD/DVD Creator window will open. To burn files to the disc, just drag them into that window. All read/write discs, even if they are not blank, are also recognized as writable discs and are opened in a CD/DVD Creator window. Click Write To Disk when

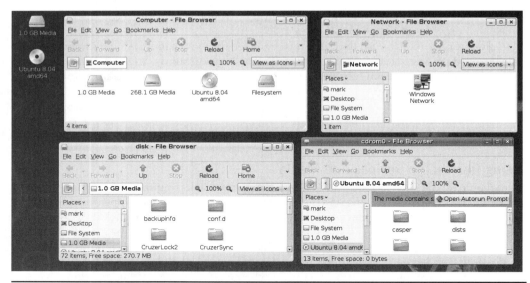

FIGURE 3-8 Removable devices, Computer folder, and shared network folders

you're ready to burn to disc. A dialog will open, as shown in Figure 3-9. You can specify Write Speed, the DVD/CD writer to use (if you have more than one), and the disc label.

GNOME also support burning ISO images. Double-click the ISO image file or right-click the file and choose Open With CD/DVD Creator. This opens the CD/DVD Creator dialog, which prompts you to burn the image. Be sure you insert a blank CD or DVD into your CD/DVD drive first. You can also burn DVD-Video discs.

For more complex DVD/CD burning, you can use the Brasero DVD/CD burner (Figure 3-10) that is included with Ubuntu and is a GNOME project (Ubuntu main repository). Brasero supports drag-and-drop operations for creating audio CDs. In particular, it can handle CD/DVD read/write discs and can erase discs. It also supports multisession burns, adding data to a DVD/CD disc. Initially, Brasero displays a dialog with buttons for the types of project you want to create. You can create a data or audio project, copy a DVD/CD, or burn a DVD/CD image file.

FIGURE 3-9
Writing to a DVD/
CD with GNOME
Nautilus File
Manager

Write to Disc

Information

Write disc to: DVD DD DW1640

Disc name: Personal Data, Mar 27, 2008

Data size: 701.7 KiB

Write Options

Write speed: Maximum possible

❓ Help   ⊗ Cancel   Write

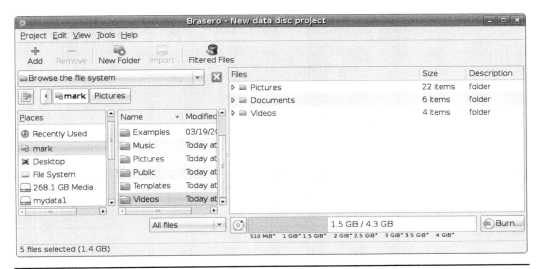

FIGURE 3-10   Burning a DVD/CD with Brasero

Search Tools

Two primary search tools are available for your Ubuntu desktop: Search For Files and Tracker. Search For Files is installed by default and is accessible by choosing Places | Search For Files. The Tracker search and desktop indexer is accessible from Applications | Accessories | Tracker search tool. When you start using Tracker, a Tracker icon will appear in the top panel. Tracker will actually index your files, making access more efficient. The GNOME file manager also provides its own search tool for quickly finding files. As an alternative, you can use the DeskBar search applet, which also makes use of Tracker indexing.

Tracker: Indexed Search

Tracker is a GNOME desktop indexing search tool (**www.gnome.org/projects/tracker/**) that's technically named Meta-Tracker. Tracker is turned off by default as its indexing function can be resource intensive. You can enable Tracker by choosing System | Preferences | Search And Indexing and checking both the Enable Indexing and Enable Watching check boxes on the General tab. If you find that indexing is consuming too many resources, you can turn it off by unchecking the Enable Indexing check box. You can still use Tracker to perform searches if you have Enable Watching checked.

Once enabled, the Tracker applet appears on the right side of the top panel. You can right-click the icon to display a menu for selecting preferences as well as to start Tracker or pausing indexing. Tracker indexes not just by name or location, but also by metadata and content of files and directories. Indexing is performed by the **trackerd** daemon.

To use Tracker, click its icon to open a search window, where you can enter your search and display the results (see Figure 3-11). You can also open this window directly by right-clicking the Tracker icon and choosing Search. Search results are organized into Categories in the side pane. The results for a selected category are shown in the top-right pane. Information about a selected result appears in the lower-right pane.

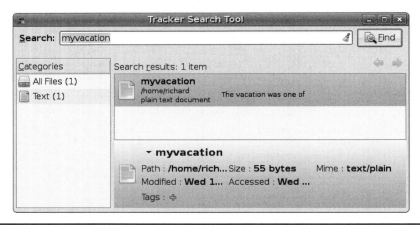

FIGURE 3-11   Search results with Tracker

Tracker also has an indexer that can be configured using the Tracker Preferences window (Figure 3-12). Right-click the Tracker icon and choose Preferences, or choose System | Preferences | Search And Indexing. You'll see tabs for General, Files, Ignored Files, Email, and Performance. On the General tab, you can enable or disable indexing. On the Files tab, you can specify what directories to index. Your home directory is already specified. You can

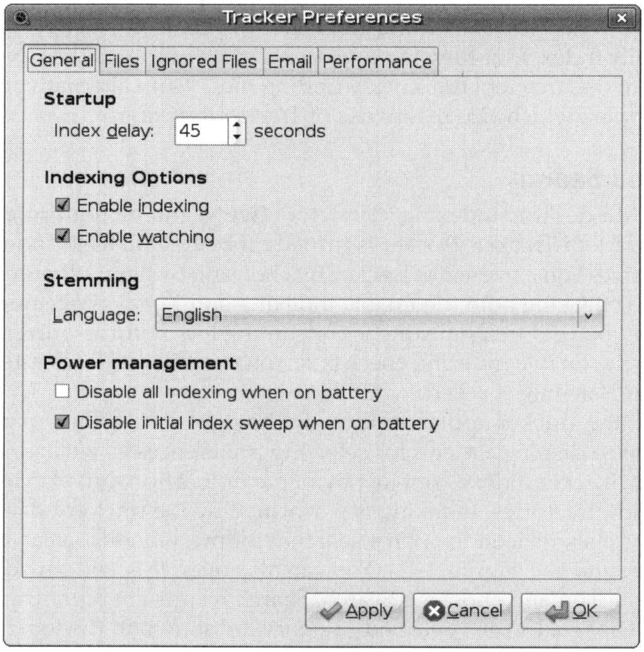

FIGURE 3-12   Tracker configuration

also choose to index the contents of files. The Ignored Files tab lets you exclude directories from indexing, as well as files with certain patterns in their names. On the Email tab, you can index e-mail clients such as Evolution or Thunderbirds, as well as specify particular mbox files. The Performance tab lets you control the amount of resources indexing will use.

Search for Files

The Search For Files tool performs basic file searching (see Figure 3-13). It uses a GNOME front end for the Linux **grep**, **find**, and **locate** tools (see Chapter 10). Choose Places | Search For Files and enter the pattern for which you want to search. File-matching characters (wildcards) will help, such as an ampersand (*) for filename completion or brackets ([]) to specify a range of possible characters or numbers.

Enter the pattern of the search in the Name Contains text box, and then select the folder or file system in which to search from the Look In Folder drop-down menu. The user's home folder is selected by default. You can then elect to specify advanced options such as the Contains The Text text box for searching the contents of text files (**grep**), or additional file characteristics such as the file date, size, or owner type (**find**). You can also use a regular expression to search filenames.

GNOME File Manager Search

The GNOME file manager uses another search tool with similar features. You enter a pattern on which to search, but you can also specify file types. The search begins from the folder opened, but you can specify another folder to search (Location option). Click the plus (+) button to add location and file type search parameters. In the browser mode, you can click the Search button on the toolbar to make the URL box a Search box. Pop-up menus for Location and File Type will appear in the folder window, with + and – buttons for adding or removing location and file type search parameters.

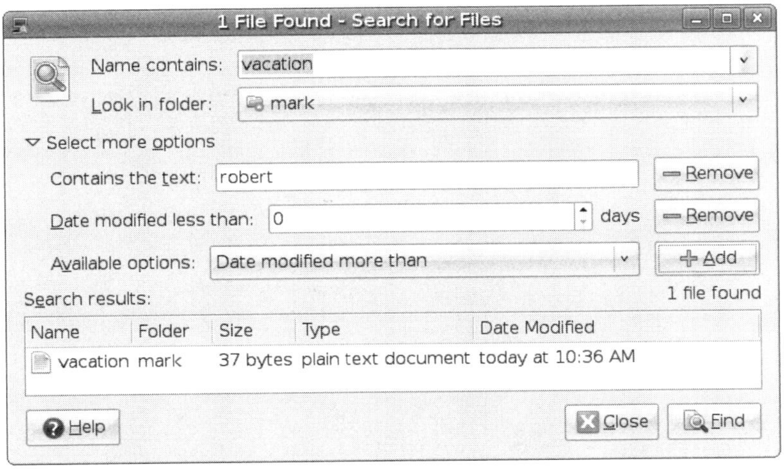

Figure 3-13   Search For Files tool

GNOME Power Management

Ubuntu uses the GNOME Power Manager, **gnome-power-manager**, which makes use of Advanced Configuration and Power Interface (ACPI) support provided by a computer to manage power use. The GNOME Power Manager is configured with the Power Management Preferences window (**gnome-power-preferences**), accessible by choosing System | Preferences | Power Management. Power Manager can be used to configure both a desktop and a laptop.

On a laptop, the battery icon displayed on the top panel will show how much power is available on the battery, as well as when the battery level becomes critical. It will also indicate an AC connection as well as when the battery has been recharged.

TIP *Using the GNOME Screensaver Preferences, you can control when the computer is considered idle and what screen saver to use, if any. You can also control whether to lock the screen when idle. Access the Screensaver Preferences from System | Preferences | Screensaver. To turn off the Screensaver, uncheck the Activate Screensaver When Computer Is Idle check box.*

For a desktop, two tabs appear in the Power Management Preferences window: On AC Power and General. The On AC Power tab offers two sleep options—one for the computer and one for the display screen. You can put each to sleep after a specified interval of inactivity. On the General tab, you set desktop features such as actions to take when you press the power button or whether to display the power icon (see Figure 3-14). The AC Power icon in the top panel will show a plug image for desktops and a battery for laptops.

To see how your laptop or desktop is performing with power, you can use Power Statistics. Right-click the Power Manager icon and choose Power History. This runs the **gnome-power-statistics** tool. You may first have to choose to display the Power Manager icon in its General preferences.

To keep a measure of how much time you have left, you can use the Battery Charge Monitor applet. An icon will appear on the top panel showing you how much time remains

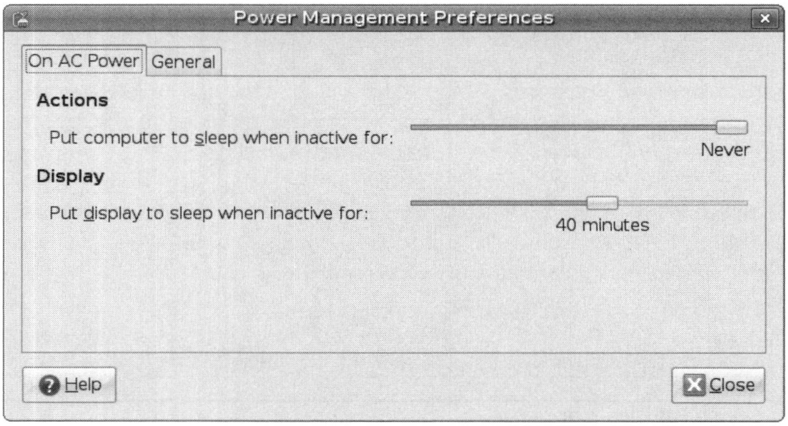

FIGURE 3-14   Power Management Preferences

FIGURE **3-15**
Battery Charge
Monitor

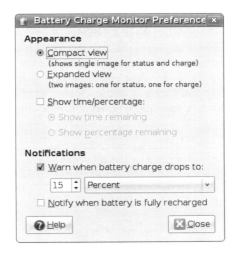

on the battery. The preferences let you specify features such as show time or percentage and when to notify of a low charge (see Figure 3-15).

Using the Command Line Interface

The command line interface provides a simple command prompt at which you type in a command. Even when you're using a GUI, you sometimes need to execute commands on a command line. You can do so in a terminal window, which is accessed by choosing Applications | Accessories | Terminal. You can add the terminal window icon to the desktop by right-clicking the Terminal menu entry and selecting Add Launcher To The Desktop.

Linux commands make extensive use of options and arguments. Be careful to place your arguments and options in their correct order on the command line. The syntax for a Linux command is the command name, followed by options, and then arguments, as shown here:

```
$ command-name options arguments
```

An *option* is a one-letter code preceded by one or two hyphens, which modifies the type of action the command takes. Options and arguments may or may not be optional, depending on the command. For example, the **ls** command can take a **-s** option. The **ls** command displays a listing of files in your directory, and the **-s** option adds the size of each file in blocks. You enter the command and its option on the command line as follows:

```
$ ls -s
```

An *argument* is data the command might need to execute its task. In many cases, this is a filename. An argument is entered as a word on the command line that appears after any options. For example, to display the contents of a file, you can use the **more** command with the filename as its argument. The **less** or **more** command used with the filename **mydata** would be entered on the command line as follows:

```
$ less mydata
```

The command line is actually a buffer of text you can edit. Before you press ENTER to execute the command, you can edit the command on the command line. The editing capabilities provide a way to correct mistakes you may make when typing a command and its options. The BACKSPACE key lets you erase the character you just typed in (the one to the left of the cursor) and the DEL key lets you erase one character to the right of the cursor. With this character-erasing capability, you can BACKSPACE over the entire line if you want, erasing what you entered. CTRL-U erases the whole command line and lets you start over again at the prompt.

TIP *You can use the* UP ARROW *key to redisplay your last-executed command. You can then re-execute that command, or you can edit it and execute the modified command. This is helpful when you have to repeat certain operations over and over, such as editing the same file. This is also helpful when you've already executed a command you entered incorrectly.*

Help Resources

A great deal of support documentation is already installed on your system and is also accessible from online sources. Both the GNOME and KDE desktops feature help systems that use a browser-like interface to display help files. To start the GNOME or KDE Help browser, select the Help entry in the main menu or click the Help icon on the top panel. The Help browsers now support the Ubuntu Help Center, which provides Ubuntu-specific help, as well as the GNOME desktop and system man page support.

If you need to ask a question, you can choose Help | Get Online Help to access the Ubuntu help support at **https://answers.launchpad.net**. Here you can submit your question and check answered questions about Ubuntu.

Ubuntu Help Center

Click the Help icon on the top panel (the ? icon) to start the GNOME help browser (Yelp), which presents the Ubuntu Help Center (see Figure 3-16). The GNOME help browser supports bookmarks for pages you want to access directly. Clicking the Help Topics button on the Ubuntu Help Center will return you to the start page. For detailed documentation and a tutorial on the GNOME help browser, choose Help | Contents, or press F1.

The Ubuntu Help Center displays topics about Ubuntu. Links range from adding software, to managing files and folders, to printing and scanning. A help page will display detailed information on the left and a sidebar of links for more information on the right. These will include any associated links as well. Figure 3-17 shows the Add/Remove Applications help page.

As you progress through a document collection, its bookmarks appear at the top of the page. Figure 3-18 shows the Import Photos From A Digital Camera help page, with bookmarks for Music, Video And Photos, and Photos And Cameras. The sidebar links expand as you progress through the document collection.

The GNOME help browser contents will also show a sidebar listing direct links to all the major help topics (Help | Contents), rather than the Ubuntu-specific links on the Ubuntu Help Center page. These topics include Introduction To The Desktop, Basic Skills, Desktop Overview, Using The Panels, Tools And Utilities, and Configuring Your Desktop. The Introduction To The Desktop topic provides a comprehensive set of links to desktop pages

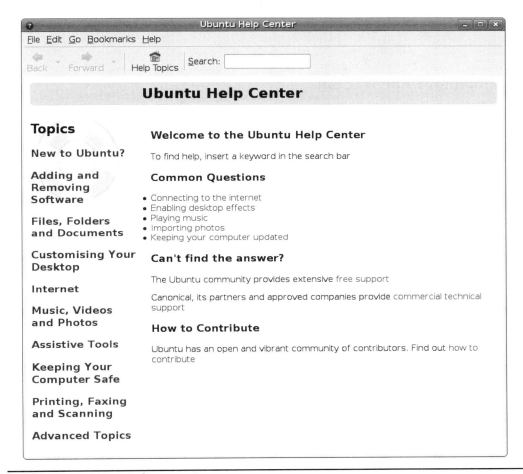

FIGURE 3-16 Ubuntu Help Center

(see Figure 3-19). Many of these topics will also appear as links in pages you access through the Ubuntu Help Center.

You can easily view documentation and user manuals for an application by performing a search on the application name. So, for example, a search on *archive* will show a link to the Archive Manager manual, and a search on *system monitor* will show a link to the System Monitor manual.

Click the Advanced Topics link on the Ubuntu Help Center main page to display links for accessing man pages and info pages.

Context-Sensitive Help

Both GNOME and KDE, along with applications, provide context-sensitive help. Each KDE and GNOME application features detailed manuals that are displayed using their respective help browsers. In addition, system administrative tools feature detailed explanations for each task.

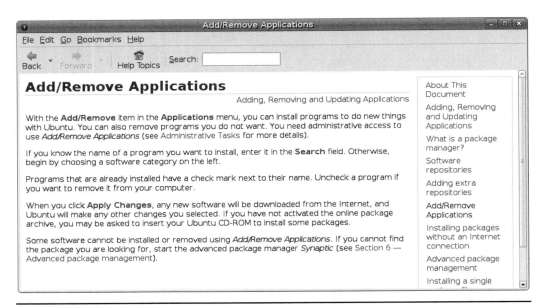

FIGURE 3-17 Help Center page

FIGURE 3-18 Help Center bookmarks and sidebar

FIGURE 3-19   Introduction to the Desktop

Application Documentation

On your system, the **/usr/share/doc** directory contains documentation files installed by each application. Within each directory, you can usually find **HOW-TO**, **README**, and **INSTALL** documents for that application.

Man Pages

You can also access the man pages, which are manuals for Linux commands available from the command line interface, using the **man** command. Enter **man** along with the command on which you want information. The following example asks for information on the ls command:

```
$ man ls
```

Pressing the SPACEBAR advances you to the next page. Pressing the B key moves you back a page. When you finish, press the Q key to quit the man utility and return to the command line. You activate a search by pressing either the slash (/) key or question mark (?) key. The / key searches forward, and the ? key searches backward. When you press the / key, a line opens at the bottom of your screen, where you can enter a word to search for. Press ENTER to activate the search. You can repeat the same search by pressing the N key. You needn't re-enter the pattern.

Info Pages

Online documentation for GNU applications, such as the gcc compiler and the Emacs editor, also exist as *info pages* accessible from the GNOME and KDE help centers. You can also access this documentation by entering the command **info**. This brings up a special screen listing different GNU applications. The **info** interface has its own set of commands. You can learn more about it by entering **info info** at the command prompt. Typing **m** opens a line at the bottom of the screen where you can enter the first few letters of the application. Pressing ENTER brings up the info file on that application.

TIP *You can use either the GNOME or KDE help system to display man pages and info pages.*

Running Windows Software on Linux: Wine

Wine is a Windows compatibility layer that allows you to run many Windows applications natively on Linux. Though you could run the Windows OS on Wine, the actual Windows OS is not required. Windows applications will run as if they were Linux applications, able to access the entire Linux file system and use Linux-connected devices. Applications that are heavily driver-dependent, such as graphics-intensive games, may not run. Others that do not rely on any specialized drivers may run very well, including Photoshop, Microsoft Office, and newsreaders such as NewsBin. For some applications, you may also need to copy over specific Windows dynamic link libraries (DLLs) from a working Windows system to your Wine Windows **system32** or **system** directory.

To install Wine on your system, search for *wine* on the Synaptic Package Manager (see Chapter 6). You will see a wine package listed, described as the *Windows Compatibility Layer*. Once installed, a Wine submenu will appear on the Applications menu. The Wine submenu holds subentries for Wine configuration, the Wine software uninstaller, and Wine file browser, as well as a regedit registry editor, notepad, and a Wine help tool.

To set up Wine, start the Wine Configuration tool. This opens a window with tabs for Applications, Libraries (DLL selection), Audio (sound drivers), Drives, Desktop Integration, and Graphics. On the Applications tab, you can select for which version of Windows an application is designed. The Drives tab lists your detected partitions, as well as your Windows-emulated drives, such as drive C:. (The C: drive is actually just a directory, **.wine/drive_c**, not a partition of a fixed size. Your actual Linux file system will be listed as the Z: drive.)

Once configured, Wine will set up a **.wine** directory on the user's home directory. (The directory is hidden, but you can choose View | Show Hidden Files in the file manager to display it.) Within that directory will be the **drive_c** directory, which functions as the C: drive that holds your Windows system files and program files in the **Windows** and **Program File** subdirectories. The **System** and **System32** directories are located in the **Windows** directory. This is where you would place any needed DLL files. The **Program Files** directory holds your installed Windows programs, just as they would be installed in a Windows **Program Files** directory.

To install a Windows application with Wine, you can open a terminal window and run the **wine** command with the Windows application as an argument. The following example installs the popular NewsBin program:

```
$ wine newsbin.exe
```

Or, instead of using the terminal window, you can right-click the application icon on the desktop and choose Open With | Wine.

Icons for installed Windows software will appear on your desktop. Double-click an icon to start up the application. It will run normally within a Linux window as would any Linux application.

Installing Windows fonts on Wine is a simple matter of copying fonts from a Windows font directory to your Wine **.wine/drive_c/Windows/fonts** directory. You can copy any Windows **.ttf** file to this directory to install a font.

TIP *You can use the commercial Windows emulation framework called CrossOver Office on your Linux system to run certain applications, such as Microsoft Office. Check **www.codeweavers .com** for more details. CrossOver Office is based on Wine, which CodeWeavers supports directly.*

To install applications that have **.msi** extension, you use the msiexec command with **/a** option. The following installs the Mobipocket Ebook Reader:

```
msiexec /a mobireadersetup.msi
```

To add books to the Mobipocket reader library, just drag the book to the open Mobipocket window.

PART

Configuration

4

CHAPTER

Administration Tasks

This chapter reviews a few administrative task and tools you may normally use. Most administrative configurations tasks are performed for you automatically in Ubuntu: For example, devices such as printers, hard drive partitions, and graphics cards are detected and set up automatically by the OS. In some cases, you may need to perform tasks manually—such as adding new users or troubleshooting your display. Administrative operations can be performed with user-friendly system tools.

This chapter discusses a few system administration operations and describes how to perform common tasks such as adding new users and configuring remote printers. Software management is handled in detail in Chapter 6.

TIP *If you have difficulties with your system configuration, check the* **http://ubuntuforums.org** *site for solutions. The site offers helpful forums ranging from desktop and installation problems to games, browsers, and multimedia solutions, Also check the support link at* **www.ubuntu.com** *for documentation, live chat, and mailing lists.*

Ubuntu Administrative Tools

On Ubuntu, administration is handled by a set of separate specialized administrative tools, such as those for user management and printer configuration (see Table 4-1). To access the GUI-based administrative tools, you log in as a user who has administrative access—this is the user you created when you first installed Ubuntu.

On the GNOME desktop, system administrative tools are accessed by choosing System | Administration. Here you will find tools to set the time and date, manage users, configure printers, and install software. Users and Groups lets you create and modify users and groups. Printing lets you install and reconfigure printers. All tools provide easy-to-use and intuitive graphical user interfaces (GUIs). In the Administration menu, tools are identified by simple descriptive terms, whereas their actual names normally begin with terms such as *admin* or *system-config*. For example, the printer configuration tool is listed as *Printing*, but its actual name is **system-config-printer**, whereas Users and Groups is **admin-users**. You can separately invoke any tool by entering its name in a terminal window.

Ubuntu Administration Tools	Description
Synaptic Package Manager	Apt software management using online repositories
Install and Remove Applications	Apt software management using online repositories, add/remove applications
Update Manager	Update tool using apt repositories
system-config-kickstart	Configures automatic install scripts (Fedora/Red Hat)
network-admin	Configures your network interfaces (GNOME)
services-admin	Services tool, manages system and network services such as starting and stopping servers (GNOME)
shares-admin	Configures general open shared directories or files for Linux systems
time-admin	Changes system time and date (GNOME)
users-admin	User and group configuration tool
system-config-cluster	Global File System (GFS) management (Fedora/Red Hat)
system-config-printer	Printer configuration tool (Fedora/Red Hat)
system-config-samba	Configures the Samba server (Fedora/Red Hat), user-level authentication support
gnome-language-selector	Selects a language to use
displayconfig-gtk	Ubuntu display configuration tool, video card and monitor (GNOME)
Firestarter	Configures your network firewall
polkit-gnome-authorization	Sets authentication settings for devices and administration tasks, PolicyKit
system-config-lvm	Configures Logical Volume Manager (LVM) file system volumes (Fedora/Red Hat, unsupported)
ClamAV	Virus protection application

TABLE 4-1   Ubuntu System Administration Tools and Related Applications

Ubuntu uses the GNOME administrative tools with KDE counterparts, administrative tools adapted from the Fedora distribution supported by Red Hat Linux, and independent tools such as Firestarter for your firewall; PolicyKit for device authorizations; and the Synaptic Package Manager for software installation. The GNOME administrative tools are suffixed with *admin*, and the Fedora tools have the prefix *system-config*. With Ubuntu 7.10, the Printing administrative tool is Fedora's **system-config-printer**, replacing the GNOME **printer-admin** tool used in previous Ubuntu releases. A Samba GUI tool is now available for Ubuntu, which is the Fedora **system-config-samba** tool.

Some tools will work on Ubuntu but are not yet supported. The Fedora **system-config-lvm** tool provides a simple and effective way to manage LVM file systems, but it is not yet supported directly by Ubuntu. You can, however, download, convert, and install the software package on Ubuntu, and it will work fine. In addition, virus protection is handled by an entirely separate application such as ClamAV.

NOTE *Many configuration tasks can also be handled on the command line, invoking programs directly. Choose Applications | Accessories | Terminal to open a terminal window with a command line prompt. Commands such as* sudo *and* make *require a terminal window.*

Controlled Administrative Access: PolicyKit, sudo, and gksu

To access administrative tools, you must log in as a user who has administrative permissions (the user you the created during installation). When you select an administrative tool to use, such as a tool available by choosing System | Administration, access is granted either with PolicyKit authorization or **sudo**/**gksu** operation. Many administrative applications, such as the GNOME administration **users-admin** tool, are configured to use PolicyKit. Others, such as the Synaptic Package Manager, still use **sudo**/**gksu**. You can grant any application administrative access by starting it with the **sudo** or **gksu** command, using **gksu** with **gedit**, for example, to edit configuration files. You can find more about **sudo** at **www.sudo.ws**.

You can use the Users and Groups tool to grant or deny particular users administrative access. Both PolicyKit and **gksu**/**sudo** prompt you in a window to enter the user password.

PolicyKit

For PolicyKit-enabled administrative tools, the application will start up with read-only permissions. To use the application to perform administrative tasks, you must first unlock it. Click the Unlock button at the bottom of the window to open a dialog in which you enter your user password. Then the administrative tool's window displays again with full access granted. You can now perform tasks such as adding a new user. With only read access in a locked application, you can scroll through the list of users in the **users-admin** application, for example, but you cannot make any changes or add new users (see Figure 4-1).

Click the Unlock button to open a PolicyKit prompt, where you can enter your user password (see Figure 4-2).

FIGURE 4-1   Users Settings window, locked

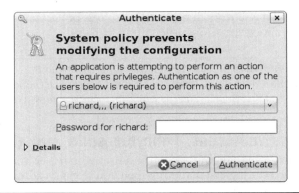

FIGURE 4-2 PolicyKit authorization prompt

After you unlock the **users-admin** window, the Unlock button is grayed out, and you can now make changes (see Figure 4-3).

gksu

Many applications, such as the Synaptic Package Manager, still use **gksu** to grant access. Before the package manager even starts up, you are prompted to enter your password (see Figure 4-4). Only then will the Synaptic Package Manager start, allowing you full access.

For administrative access to desktop applications, use the `gksu` command. Enter the `gksu` command in a terminal window along with the application name. For example, to use the GNOME text editor, **gedit**, to edit system configuration files, you would start **gedit** using the `gksu` command in a terminal window, with `gedit` and the filename as its arguments. This starts up **gedit** with administrator access. You cannot simply start **gedit** directly from the desktop by choosing Applications | Accessories | Text Editor. The following example shows how you can edit the **/boot/grub/menu.lst** file to add or edit operating system entries for the boot manager. You will first be prompted for your user password.

```
gksu gedit /boot/grub/menu.lst
```

FIGURE 4-3 Users Settings window, unlocked

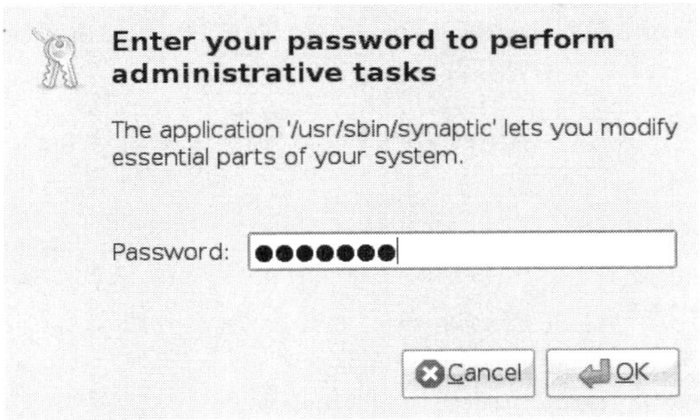

FIGURE 4-4   Administrative Access with gksu

> **NOTE** *To access the command line, you can open a terminal window using the Terminal tool: choose Applications | Accessories | Terminal. For easy access to the terminal window, right-click the menu entry for the Terminal tool and choose Add This Launcher To The Desktop to place a terminal icon on your desktop.*

sudo

The **sudo** and **gksu** commands allow ordinary users limited root user–level administrative access for certain tasks so they can perform specific superuser operations without having full administrative level control.

The **sudo** command is commonly used to run command line commands with administrative access. To access the command line, you can open a terminal window using the Terminal tool accessible from the Applications | Accessories window. To use **sudo** to run an administrative command, the user precedes the command with the **sudo** command. The user is issued a time-sensitive ticket to allow access. Here's an example:

```
sudo date
```

> **NOTE** *Configuration tools are accessible only to the administrative user, so you need to log in to an account that has administrative access. Whenever you access an administrative tool, you will be prompted to re-enter the user password—the password of the user you created during installation. This user has administrative access.*

Login Window Configuration

To change the login window, use the Login Screen Setup window accessible by choosing System | Administration | Login Window. This configures the GNOME Display Manager (GDM), which runs your login process. Here you can set the background image, icons to be displayed, the theme to use, users to list, and even the welcome message (see Figure 4-5).

You can also set up an automatic login for a particular user, skipping the GDM login screen on startup. Login screens can be configured for local or remote users. You can choose

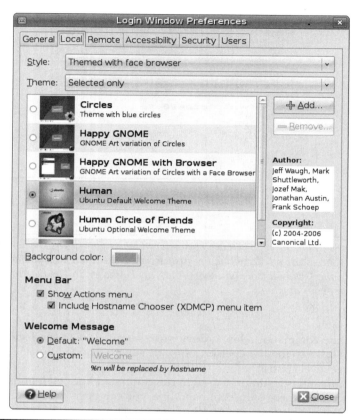

FIGURE 4-5   GDM configuration themes in the Local tab

between a plain screen, a plain screen with face browser, or a themed screen. The Local tab lets you select what screen to use for local logins, and you can browse among available themes. From the Remote tab, you can select Plain, select Plain With Browser, or use the same configuration used for your local logins.

On the Users tab, you can select which users you want displayed when using a face browser. On the Local tab, you can choose from a number of themes. The Ubuntu theme is selected by default. You can also opt to have the theme randomly selected.

On the Security tab, you can set up an automatic login, skipping the login screen on startup (see Figure 4-6). You can even set a timed login, automatically logging in a specific user after displaying the login screen for a given amount of time. In the Security area of the tab, you can set security options such as whether to allow root logins or allow TCP (Internet) access, as well as setting the number of allowable logins. Click the Configure X Server button to open a window for configuring X server access. Check the GNOME Display Manager Reference Manual, accessible with the Help button, for details.

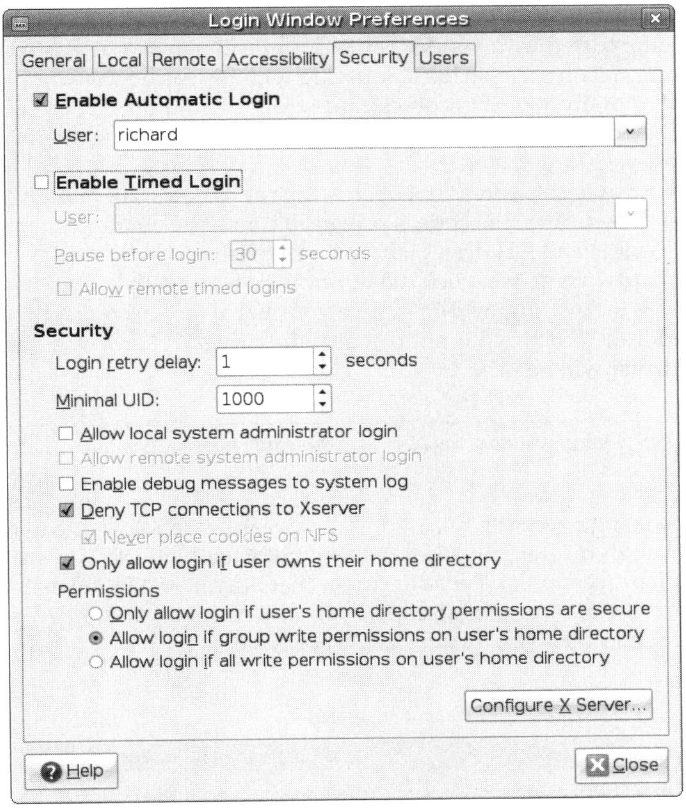

PART II

FIGURE 4-6   Enabling automatic login

TIP *You can configure automatic login for a particular user on the Login Window Preferences configuration's Security tab. This feature is useful for single-user systems in which the same user logs in.*

Display Drivers

The GUI for your desktop display is implemented by the X Window System. The version used on Ubuntu is X.org You can use either vendor-supplied drivers or X.org generic drivers for your graphics card. Ubuntu packages the vendor drivers as restricted graphics software packages, which are designed for compatible installation on Ubuntu and are available on the Ubuntu restricted repository. You can find out more about X.org at **www.x.org**.

When you first install your system, the X.org generic drives are used. Should your graphics card be supported by a vendor (or proprietary) driver, such as ATI or Nvidia drivers, a notification icon for restricted software will appear on the Ubuntu's top panel with a message. For many recent graphics cards from Nvidia or ATI, the vendor driver is recommended. The vendor driver will often support 3-D effects much better that the corresponding generic X.org drivers.

Because vendor driver software is not open source and consists of hidden proprietary code, it is considered restricted. Since the code is private, it cannot be guaranteed to work—though, in most cases, the Nvidia and ATI drives have proven reliable.

To install the hardware driver, click the notification icon on the panel to open the Hardware Drivers window (Figure 4-7), where your hardware drivers will be listed. Click the check box under the Enable column to enable the driver. When you restart your system, the new vendor driver will be used.

NOTE *The Hardware Drivers window is also accessible by choosing System | Administration | Hardware Drivers.*

Should you be using a recently released graphics card, you may have to rely on restricted driver support, though the generic X.org drivers will usually work. You should always use the Ubuntu-compliant version of a vendor driver that is available in the restricted repository. Though possible, it is not recommended that you download a vendor driver for Linux directly from a graphics card vendor such as ATI or Nvidia.

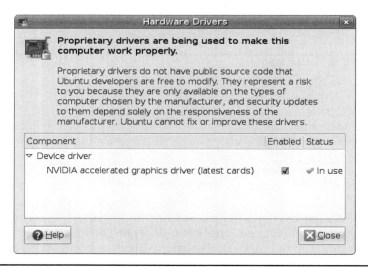

FIGURE 4-7   Restricted Hardware drivers

Manual Display Configuration

Your display will be detected automatically, and Ubuntu will configure both your graphics card and monitor. Normally you should not need to perform any configuration manually. However, with some hardware, your display or graphics card may not be correctly detected. Also, you may want to configure an additional screen(s) for multi-display output.

All configuration tools and drivers will generate an X Window System configuration file called **/etc/X11/xorg.conf**. This is the file the X Window System uses to start up. Whenever you change your settings, your current configuration is saved to **/etc/X11/xorg.backup.conf**. Should you need to restore your old settings manually, you can just replace your current **xorg.conf** file with the backup file. You are advised to make your own backup of an **xorg.conf** file that works. Should your display configuration become unrecoverable, you can always resort to the reliable backup. The following code creates a backup file called **xorg-mybackup.conf**:

```
sudo cp /etc/X11/xorg.conf /etc/X11/xorg-mybackup.conf
```

If you are using a vendor's graphics driver (restricted hardware) such as the Nvidia or ATI graphics driver, the respective vendor configuration tools will be installed for you. You can access these by choosing Applications | System Tools. The Nvidia configuration tool will be named something like *Nvidia X Server Settings*. You should use the vendor's configuration tool for configuring a vendor's drivers.

The Nvidia configuration tool is in the **nvidia-settings** package (see the following line of code). It is not installed with the Nvidia driver. You must use Synaptic Package Manager to install it yourself. You'll then see the Nvidia X Server Settings entry when you choose System | Administration | Nvidia X Server Settings. This interface provides Nvidia vendor access to many of the features of Nvidia graphics cards, such as color correction, video brightness and contrast, thermal monitoring, screen resolution, and color depth (see Figure 4-8).

```
nvidia-settings
```

ATI/AMD provides a Linux version of its Catalyst configuration tool for use on Linux. Much of the ATI video drivers have now become open source, making the ATI video driver much more Linux-compatible. The ATI/AME Catalyst configuration tool for Linux is in the **fglrx-control** package, which you will have to install with the Synaptic Package Manager, like so:

```
fglrx-control
```

Alternatively, if you are not using a vendor driver, and you have to perform specific configurations such as selecting the correct monitor type, you can manually configure your graphics driver using the Screen and Graphics tool (**displayconfig-gtk**). Choose System | Administration | Screen And Graphics. The monitor and resolution should be selected automatically (see Figure 4-9).

If your monitor is not correctly set, you may have to make sure your monitor is selected. Click the small monitor icon next to the Model text box to open a Choose Screen window

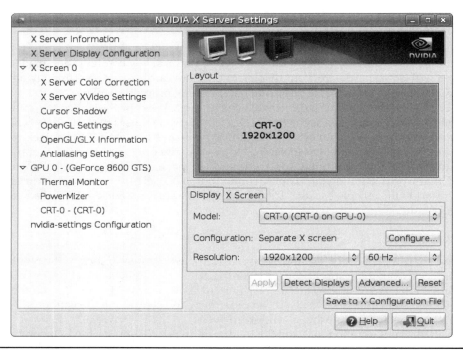

FIGURE 4-8 Nvidia X Server Settings

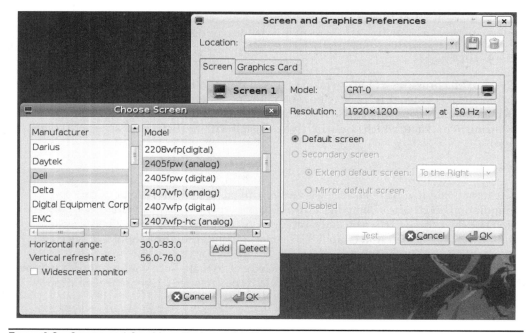

FIGURE 4-9 Screen and Graphics: displayconfig-gtk

with manufacturer and model listings. First select the manufacturer. All supported monitors for that manufacturer will then be listed in the model listings. Then select the correct model. You will see the horizontal and vertical frequencies for that selected monitor displayed. Check with your monitor documentation to make sure they are correct. You can try to use the Detect button to automatically detect the monitor settings, but this may not always be accurate.

You also have the option of creating different location profiles. This is useful if you are using different monitors at certain locations or for different purposes. So, for example, your laptop could have one location for its own screen and another for an attached larger screen. Others could use one location for a standard PC monitor and another for a home theater display such as an LCD TV.

You can also select which driver to use. The appropriate driver will already be selected, but if you are having problems with a vendor's driver, you may want to switch to the X.org driver. Click the Driver button to open a Choose Graphics Card Driver window, where you can then select the drivers from a list or by graphics card model.

Configuring Users

Currently, the easiest and most effective way to add new users on Ubuntu is to use **users-admin**, also known as the User Administration tool. You can access it from the GNOME desktop by choosing System | Administration | Users And Groups. You will be prompted to enter you administrative password. See Chapter 22 for detailed information on how to use the **users-admin** tool to add and manager users.

Printer Management and Configuration

Whenever you first attach a local printer, such as a USB printer, you will be asked to make basic configuration settings such as confirming the make and model. Removable local printers are detected automatically: A message will appear informing you that a new printer was connected, as shown next. Click the Find Driver button on the message to configure the driver and model type. Normally these are chosen for you, and all you need to do on each screen is click the Next button. After a few clicks, your printer is configured and ready to use.

Should you need to perform more complex printer configuration, you can use the Ubuntu printer configuration tool. Ubuntu 804 uses the Fedora Red Hat **system-config-printer** tool for configuring and installing printers. This tool replaces the GNOME **admin-printer** tool used in previous Ubuntu releases. It is accessible by choosing System | Administration | Printing. See Chapter 29 for a detailed description on how to use **system-config-printer**.

To manage print jobs, you use the **system-config-printer-applet** (choose Applications | Accessories | Manage Print Jobs). This opens a Document Print Status window listing current jobs (see Figure 4-10). You can open other windows to show printer status and completed jobs (via the View menu), and you can right-click a job entry to stop, restart, or delete the print job.

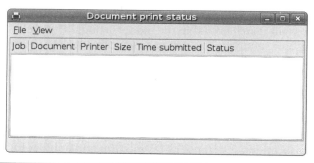

FIGURE **4-10**   Document Print Status window

Sound Configuration

Sound devices are automatically detected by the hardware abstraction layer (HAL) and the **udev** device manager. The sound interface used by default on Ubuntu is PulseAudio. Each user can configure access to sound devices by choosing System | Preferences | Sound, and then configure volume control with and the GNOME or KDE volume panel applets. See Chapter 14 for detailed information about sound devices, volume control, and PulseAudio.

Multimedia Support: MP3, DVD-Video, DivX, and HDTV

Linux, including Ubuntu, does not directly include support for licensed codecs such as MP3 or DVD-Video. A free, open source version of the H.264 HDTV codec, called x264, is available. For DivX, you can use the open source version, **xvid-core**. The **gstreamer-bad** package contains numerous additional codecs for GNOME multimedia applications. On Ubuntu, most of the licensed codecs are available from third parties and are included in packages in the multiverse repository. You can install them directly using the Synaptic Package Manager.

If you try to run a multimedia file and do not have the proper codec, Ubuntu will run a codec wizard that lists the codecs you need to download an install. Often, several choices are available. For MP3, you can use the LAME codec, the licensed Fluendo codec, or both. Alternatively, you could download and install these codecs manually. Most are available on the universe and multiverse repositories, though you would need to know what packages to look for. The codec wizard (see Figure 4-11) does this for you, simplifying the process of installing the various multimedia codecs available for Linux. Appropriate and available codecs are listed for the type of media you are trying to play. Select their check boxes and click the Install button. See Chapter 14 for more information about multimedia codecs, including packages for many third-party multimedia codecs.

If you choose to install a codec that has licensing issues, you will notified and given the option to cancel.

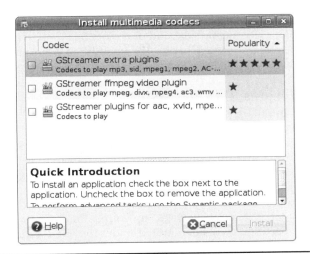

FIGURE 4-11   Ubuntu codec wizard

File System Access

Various file systems can be accessed easily on Ubuntu. Any additional internal hard drive partitions on your system—both Linux and Windows NTFS—will be automatically detected and can be automatically mounted, providing immediate and direct access from your desktop. In addition, you can access remote Windows shared folders and make your own shared folders accessible.

Access Linux File Systems on Internal Drives

Other Linux file systems on internal hard drives will be detect by Ubuntu automatically. Icons for these systems will be displayed on the Computer window (choose Places | Computer). Initially, they will not be mounted. You will first have to validate your authorization before you can mount a disk. To mount a file system for the first time, double-click its icon. A PolicyKit authorization window will appear, similar to that shown in Figure 4-2. You then enter your user password. The option to Remember Authorization is checked, keeping the authorization indefinitely. Whenever you start up your system again, the file system will be mounted for you automatically.

Once your file system is mounted, it displays its icon both in the Computer window and on the desktop. The file system will be mounted under the **/media** directory in a folder named with the name of the file system label, or, if unlabeled, with the device name such as *sda3* for the third partition on the first SATA drive.

Once granted, authentication access will remain in place for a limited time, allowing you to mount other file systems without having to re-enter your password. These file systems will then be automatically mounted as well, provided the Remember Authorization remains checked in the Authenticate window.

Any user with administrative access on the primary console is authorized to mount file systems. You can use PolicyKit agent to expand or restrict this level of authorization, as well as enable access for specific users (see Chapter 17). In addition, your partitions will automatically be displayed on the desktop and in the Computer window as disk icons.

Access for Local Windows NTFS File Systems

If you have installed Ubuntu on a dual-boot system with Windows XP, NT, or 2000, or you otherwise need access to NTFS partitions, Linux NTFS support is installed automatically. Your NTFS partitions are mounted using Filesystem in Userspace (FUSE). The same authentication control used for Linux file systems applies to NTFS file systems. Icons for the NTFS partitions will be displayed in the Computer window.

The first time you access the file system, you may be asked to provide authorization, as shown back in Figure 4-2. The NTFS is then mounted with icons displayed in the Computer widow and on the desktop. Whenever you start up your system, they will be automatically mounted for you. The partitions will be mounted under the **/media** directory with their labels used as folder names. If they have no labels, then they are given the name **disk**, and then numbered as **disk0**, **disk1**, and so on for additional partitions (unlabeled removable devices may also share these names). The NTFS partitions are mounted using ntfs-3g drivers. Chapter 23 provides more detailed information about these drivers.

Access to Local Network Windows NTFS File Systems

Shared Windows folders and printers on any of the computers connected to your local network are automatically accessible from your Ubuntu desktop. The DNS discovery service (Ahavi) automatically detects hosts on your home or local network, and will let you access directly any of the their shared folders.

To access the shared folders, select Network from the Places menu to open the Network Places window. Your connected computers will be listed. If you know the name of the Windows computer you want to access, just click on its icon, otherwise, click on the Windows network icon to see just the Windows machines.

However, local systems cannot access your shared folders until you install a sharing server, Samba for Windows systems, and NFS for Linux/Unix systems. Should you attempt to share a directory, an error notice will be displayed asking you to install Samba or NFS.

Shared Folders for Your Network and Windows: NFS and Samba

To share a folder on your local network, right-click on it and select Sharing options. This opens a window where you can allow sharing, and whether to permit modifying, adding, or deleting files in the folder (see Figure 4-12). You can also allow access to anyone who does not have an account on your system (guest).

To allow others to access your folders be sure the sharing servers are installed, Samba for Windows systems and NFS for Linux/Unix systems. The serves will be automatically configured for you and run. You will not be able to share folders until these servers are installed.

This sharing feature is enabled using **nautilus-share**, and is meant to be used instead of the older GNOME **admin-shares**. You can still use **admin-shares** by entering **admin-shares** in a terminal window, and then clicking the Unlock button to gain administrative access (see Chapter 30).

FIGURE 4-12   Folder Sharing Options

To share folders (directories) with other Linux systems on your network, you use the NFS service (nfs-kernelserver). For Windows systems you use the Samba service (samba).

Bluetooth

Ubuntu provides Bluetooth support for both serial connections and BlueZ protocol–supported devices. Bluetooth is a wireless connection method for locally connected devices such as keyboards, mice, printers, and even PDAs and Bluetooth-capable cell phones. You can think of it as a small local network dedicated to your peripheral devices, eliminating the need for wires. Bluetooth devices can be directly connected through your computer's serial ports or through specialized Bluetooth cards connected to USB ports or inserted in a PCI slot.

BlueZ is the official Linux Bluetooth protocol and has been integrated into the Linux kernel since version 2.4.6. The BlueZ protocol was developed originally by Qualcomm and is now an open source project located at **http://bluez.sourceforge.net**. It is included with Ubuntu in the **bluez-utils** and **bluez-libs** packages, among others. Check the BlueZ site for a complete list of supported hardware, including adapters, PCMCIA cards, and serial connectors.

To configure Bluetooth on Ubuntu, choose System | Preferences | Bluetooth Preferences to open the Bluetooth Preferences window with two tabs, Services and General (see Figure 4-13). The Services pane has entries for Input Service, Audio Service, Network Service, and Serial Service. Use the check boxes to start or stop a service. Input Service and Audio Service are selected and running by default. Add Network Service if you are using a personal area network (PAN). On the General tab, you can select such features as Authorization Requests, Automatic Hardware Detection, and Device Notification.

To enable the Bluetooth service, be sure that the Bluetooth service is checked in **services-admin** by choosing System | Administration | Services.

FIGURE 4-13 Bluetooth Preferences

Bluetooth Configuration

BlueZ includes several modules and drivers, including the core Bluetooth protocols for Host Controller Interface (HCI) devices (HCI USB, UART, PCMCIA) and virtual HCI drivers, along with modules to support protocols for Logical Link Control and Adaptation Protocol (L2CAP), serial port emulation (RFCOMM), Ethernet emulation (BNEP), Synchronous Connection-Oriented (SCO) links for real-time voice, and the Service Discovery Protocol (SDP), which automatically detects services available for an application. In addition, extended services are supported such as PAN and LAN access over Point-to-Point Protocol (PPP).

Configuration information is located in the **/etc/bluetooth** directory, along with the **/etc/ pcmcia** directory for notebooks. The HCI information is saved in **/etc/bluetooth/hcid.conf**, and RFCOMM configuration information is in **/etc/bluetooth/rfcomm.conf**. The Bluetooth service script, **/etc/rc.d/init.d/bluetooth**, is used to start and stop Bluetooth services. This script will start up the Bluetooth daemon for HCI devices, **hcid**, and run any detection and configuration tools, including **sdpd** for the Service Discovery Protocol, and **rfcomm**. It will also activate any serial Bluetooth devices, using **hciattach** to detect them.

From the command line, you can use the `hciconfig` command to configure Bluetooth devices and `hcitool` to configure Bluetooth connections. Use `hciattach` to attach serial devices to a serial port such as **/dev/ttyS1**, and use `rfcomm` to configure and attach RFCOMM devices. Use `l2ping` to detect a Bluetooth device.

PAN allows you to use Bluetooth to implement a PAN supporting IP protocols, much like a wireless LAN for a small number of computers and devices. Bluetooth supports a much smaller bandwidth (1 to 2 megabits) than that used for a standard LAN, but it is sufficient for connecting and transferring data from handheld devices. Several devices and computers can be configured as PAN users, connecting through a central Group Network (GN) computer.

Alternatively, PAN users could connect to a gateway system operating as a network access point connecting the Bluetooth personal network to a large LAN network. The PAN nodes run their own service daemon, **pand**. Dial-up networking uses the **dund** daemon.

System Monitoring

Ubuntu provides the GNOME System Monitor for displaying system information and monitoring system processes: choose System | Administration | System Monitor (see Figure 4-14). Four tabs appear on the System Monitor window: System, Processes, Resources, and File Systems. The System tab shows the amount of memory, available disk space, and the type of CPU on your system. The Resources tab displays graphs for CPU, memory and swap memory, and network usage.

The File Systems tab lists file systems, where they are mounted, and their type, as well as the amount of disk space used and how much is free. This is a fast and easy way to check how much space is left on your system.

The GNOME hardware monitor display detected temperatures for your CPU and, if available, for your graphics card. First download and install the **lm-sensors** package (Ubuntu main repository). In a terminal window enter **sudo sensors-detect** to first activate sensors. These services will detect hardware sensors on your computer. They run as Hardware Sensor services in System | Administration | Services. You can then download and install the **sensors-applet** package, the GNOME applet for sensor information

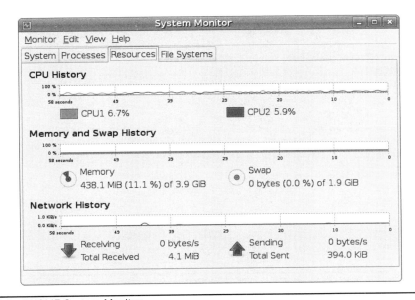

FIGURE 4-14   GNOME System Monitor

(see the next illustration). Once the applet is installed, right-click the applet icon and open its preferences window, where you can set the temperature scale and display information.

Another useful applet is the CPU Frequency Scaling Monitor, which will display CPU use (as shown in the previous illustration). This applet used the **powernowd** service to detect how much of the CPU is being used. Most current CPUs support frequency scaling, which will lower the CPU frequency when it has few tasks to perform. Intel CPUs will scale down to 60 percent and AMD by 50 percent.

Virus Protection

For virus protection, you can use the Linux version of ClamAV from **www.clamav.org**. This virus scanner is included on the Ubuntu universe repository. You will have to download and install it using Synaptic: Choose **clamav**, **clamav-base**, **clamav-freshclam**, and **clamav-data**. In addition you may want either ClamTk (**clamtk** package in GNOME) or KlamAV (KDE) front ends. You can access ClamTk by choosing Applications | System Tools | Virus Scanner. With ClamTk, you can scan specific files and directories, as well as your home directory (see Figure 4-15). Searches can be recursive, including subdirectories. You also have the option to check dot configuration files. Infected files are quarantined.

To update your virus definitions, you need to run **clamtk** with administrative access. Open a terminal window and enter the following:

```
gksu clamtk
```

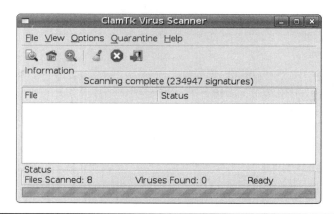

FIGURE 4-15   The ClamTk tool for ClamAV virus protection

You will be prompted for your user password. You can then go to the Help menu and select Update Signatures to update your definitions.

Accessing Devices Remotely

To access devices such as sound cards, digital cameras, or DVD video receivers as a remote user, you will need to modify the PolicyKit permissions. Choose System | Administration | Authorizations to open the PolicyKit client with a sidebar showing an expandable tree. Near the end of the tree is a section for devices that will have the heading *hal*. You'll also see subsections for *storage devices* and *device-access*. Under device-access, you will find entries for many media devices such as video capture, DVB, digital cameras, sound, and DVD drive (optical disk). The right pane will list Implicit Authorizations and Explicit Authorizations segments for allowing access (see Figure 4-16).

The Implicit Authorizations segment will normally deny access to anyone not on the active console. *Anyone* and *Console* are set to No. You can click the Edit button to open a dialog, where

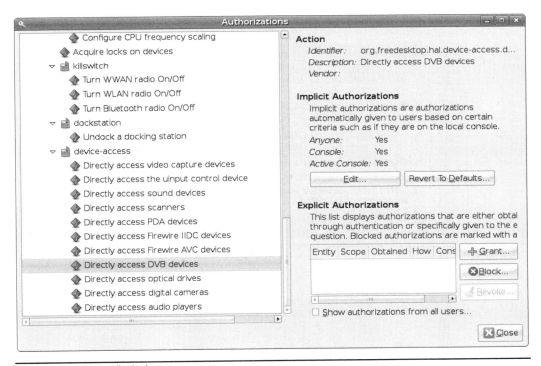

FIGURE 4-16   PolicyKit device access

you can change the Anyone entry from No to Yes. In the Explicit Authorizations segment, you can also set up access for particular users, allowing them full access. See Chapter 17 for more information on PolicyKit.

Managing Services

Many administrative functions operate as services that need to be turned on. They are daemons, constantly running and checking for requests for their services. When you install a service, its daemon is normally turned on automatically. You can check to see if this is so, using the **services-admin** tool by choosing System | Administration | Services. This opens the Services Settings window (see Figure 4-17). Services are listed descriptively with the actual names of their daemons in parentheses. The Hardware Monitor service is run by the **lm-sensors** daemon. Each service will have its own check box. When checked, the service is run when the system starts up. If unchecked, the service is not run. Figure 4-17 shows several commonly use services such as Windows file sharing (**samba**), CPU power management (**powernowd**), and the Graphical Login Manager (**gdm**). See Chapter 30 for more information on **services-admin**.

FIGURE 4-17   services-admin: choose System | Administration | Services

Testing Hardware: Launchpad

Ubuntu provides a hardware testing utility to check your hardware and report any problems. You are encouraged to set up an account at **https://launchpad.net**, where you can send your results. Choose Applications | System Tools | Hardware Testing. You are first asked how you are using your system: Desktop, Laptop, or Server. Then each major hardware device is tested and you can enter your confirmation or add comments (see Figure 4-18). Devices tested include sound, display, video, mouse, keyboard, network card, and network connection.

FIGURE 4-18   Launchpad Hardware Testing window

## 5

CHAPTER

Network Connections

U buntu will automatically detect and configure your network connections with NetworkManager. Should the automatic configuration either fail or be incomplete for some reason, you can use **network-admin** to perform a manual configuration (System | Administration | Network). On GNOME, NetworkManager is managed using a GNOME applet, and on KDE you use KNetworkManager.

Your network will also need a firewall: Firestarter is recommended. (See Chapter 20 for details.) You may also connect to a network with a Windows computer using the Samba server. (See Chapter 30 for information on how to set up access.) To access shared directories and printers on other Linux and Unix computers on your network, you can use the Network File System (NFS) service configured with **shares-admin** (see Chapter 30). For dial-up service, you can use NetworkManager or **network-admin**. If you are working from a command line interface, you can use WvDial. Table 5-1 lists several different network configuration and network-related tools.

NetworkManager

Ubuntu uses NetworkManager to detect both wired and wireless network connections. NetworkManager uses the automatic device detection capabilities of **udev** and the Hardware Abstraction Layer (HAL) to configure your connections. NetworkManager is turned on by default. With multiple wireless access points for Internet connections, a system could have several different network connections from which to choose, instead of a single-line connection such as DSL or cable. This is particularly true for notebook computers that could access different wireless connections at different locations. Instead of manually configuring a new connection each time one is encountered, the NetworkManager tool can automatically configure and select a connection to use.

By default, an Ethernet connection is preferred if available, because direct lines that support Ethernet connections are normally considered faster than wireless connections. For wireless connections, you will need to choose the one you want.

NetworkManager is designed to work in the background, providing status information for your connection and switching from one configured connection to another as needed. For initial configuration, it detects as much information as possible about the new connection. It operates as a GNOME desktop panel applet, monitoring your connection, and it can work on any Linux distribution.

Network Configuration Tool	Description
NetworkManager	Automates wireless and standard network connection selection and notification
network-admin	Ubuntu network configuration tool for all types of connections
KNetworkManager	KDE tool to automate wireless and standard network connection selection and notification
Firestarter	Sets up a network firewall (Chapter 20)
WvDial	PPP modem connection entered on a command line
pand	Implements the Bluetooth personal area network (Chapter 4)
system-config-samba	Configures Samba shares (Chapter 30)
shares-admin	Configures NFS shares (Chapter 30)

TABLE 5-1   Ubuntu Network Configuration and Connection Tools

NetworkManager operates as a daemon. If no Ethernet connection is available, NetworkManager will scan for wireless connections, checking for extended service set identifiers (ESSIDs). If an ESSID identifies a previously used connection, it is automatically selected. If several are found, the most recently used connection is chosen. If only a new connection is available, NetworkManager waits for the user to choose one. A connection is selected only if the user is logged in. If an Ethernet connection is made later, NetworkManager will switch to it from wireless.

NetworkManager is user-specific. When a user logs in, it selects the network preferred by that user. The first time a user runs NetworkManager, the notification applet will display a list of current connections from which the user can choose.

Network interface connection (NIC) hardware is detected using HAL. Information provided by NetworkManager is made available to other applications over D-Bus, the message bus system. Features currently under development include virtual private network (VPN) and application notification. NetworkManager uses the dhcpcd client to gather network information. For user interaction and notification, it uses NetworkManagerInfo.

NetworkManager on GNOME

NetworkManager displays a network icon on the right side of the GNOME desktop's top panel. Click the icon to see a list of all available network connections, including available wireless connections available:

A lock icon appears next to password-protected access points. You can configure hidden access points yourself. Choose Other Wireless Networks from the list to open a dialog where you can enter the ESSID of the network, the key type, and the password. Included is

the option to perform a manual configuration, which will invoke **network-admin**, described in the next section.

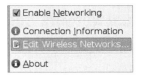

Right-click to access the option for shutting off your connection (Work Offline) or to see information about the connection:

NetworkManager for KDE: KNetworkManager

The KDE interface version of NetworkManager, KNetworkManager, also displays network connections. Click its icon on the panel to display available connections:

To see information about the current connection, right-click the icon. A window displays with tabs for Device, Addresses, Statistics, and Network. KNetworkManager also performs manual configurations such as PPP dial-up configuration and manages wireless connections. To start **kdenetworkmanager** for manual configuration, right-click on its icon in the panel and select Manual Configuration.

Wireless Manual Configuration and Editing

You use the Network Manager Editor to edit and configure your wireless connections manually (see Figure 5-1). Right-click the NetworkManager applet and choose Edit Wireless Connections to open the Wireless Networks window, where you'll see all your wireless connections. You can then select those you want to edit and change a name, bssids, and encryption (Security). You can access this tool directly by choosing Applications | Internet | Network Manager Editor.

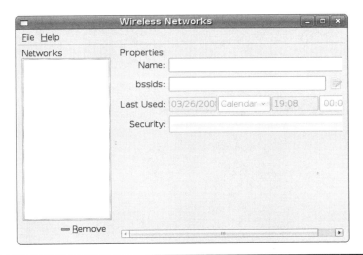

FIGURE 5-1   Network Manager Editor for Wireless Networks

Manual Network Configuration with network-admin

Though rare, if NetworkManager should fail to recognize your network connection, you can use **network-admin** to configure your network card manually. You can access **network-admin** by choosing System I Administration I Network. You will be prompted to enter your administration password, providing root user access for the tool. This tool opens a Network Settings window with four tabs: Connections, General, DNS, and Hosts (see Figure 5-2). These tabs are used for configuring the network settings for your entire system. The Connections tab lists all the detected network connections, and the General tab lists your hostname and domain settings. The DNS tab lists your DNS server and domain searches. The Hosts tab lists static host IP addresses and their domain names, including those for your own system.

You can set up different location profiles where different connections are active or deactivated, as well as use different configuration settings for the connections. To save a location profile, click the button with the disk icon at the right of the Location drop-down menu. You will be prompted to enter a location name. For a laptop, you could have a home and work location profile, using different connections, depending on where you are logging on at the time. Should you want to delete a location profile, first select it and then click the trash button to the right of the disk button.

For most home networks, a router is used to hold all your Internet service provider (ISP) connection information, such as your ISP address, gateway, Domain Name Service (DNS) addresses, and netmask. The router usually functions as a Dynamic Host Control Protocol (DHCP) server, automatically providing your network address to your computer. In this situation, the only information you may want to set with the **network-admin** tool is the hostname—the name of your computer. Wireless connections may need additional encryption information.

Connections

The Connections tab lists current hardware connections. Default entries, such as a wired connection, will already be configured. You will have to enter wireless information manually.

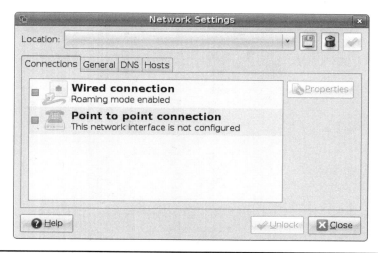

FIGURE 5-2   The Network Settings window Connections tab, network-admin

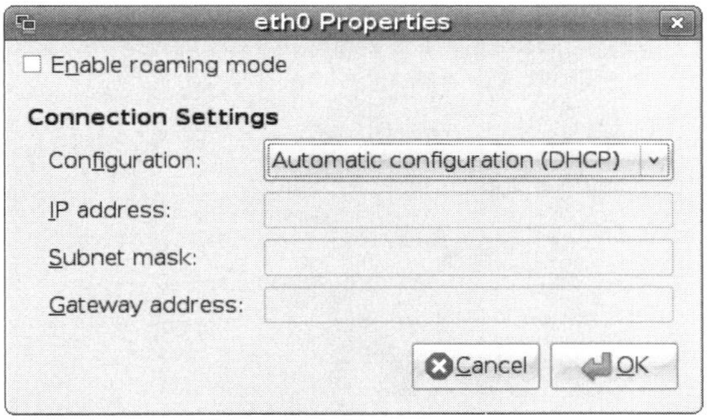

FIGURE 5-3
Connection
Properties window

To configure a connection, select it and click the Properties button to open the Properties window (Figure 5-3), which displays different options according to the type of connection. A wired connection will show Ethernet configuration options. You can choose Automatic Configuration with DHCP, a Static IP Address, or a Zero Configuration Networking (Zeroconf) configuration from the Configuration drop-down menu. Most private and local networks use DHCP. Addresses are automatically assigned by your router. If you have been assigned a static IP address by your network manager, or you are connecting directly to the Internet with a static IP address from your ISP, you should choose the Static IP Address configuration. You will need to enter the IP address, the subnet network mask, and the gateway address.

For a dial-up connection, you will have to enter your ISP's phone number, your username, and password information, as well as set any modem parameters and options.

For wireless connections, you can choose DCHP or manual configuration. With manual configuration you can set the IP address, network mask, and gateway address. You can also set the network name (ESSID).

NOTE *Most local networks use DHCP to provide host and domain addresses automatically.*

General

The General tab of the Network Settings window lists your Host and Domain names (Figure 5-4). Here you can provide a name for your computer. If you are on a private local network, you could simply enter a hostname. For larger networks, you may need to provide a domain name as well.

DNS

The DNS tab includes boxes for entering the IP addresses for your system's DNS servers, needed for static configurations. You can then list your search domain. Local networks should already have a DNS server entry listed. If you are connecting directly to the Internet, you may need to add your ISP's DNS server IP addresses. Both the search domain and the name server addresses are saved in the **/etc/resolv.conf** file.

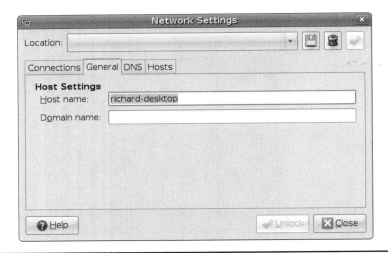

FIGURE 5-4 General tab

Hosts

You use the Hosts tab to associate static IP addresses with certain hosts. The tab has Add, Properties, and Delete buttons and lists entries that associate hostnames with static IP addresses. You can also add aliases (nicknames). The Hosts tab also displays the contents of the **/etc/hosts** file and saves any entries you make to that file.

To add an entry, click Add. A window opens with boxes for the IP address and an alias. When you finish, the entry is added to the Hosts list. To add an alias for an already existing address, select the address and click Add. The selected address will be displayed, and you can add the alias you want for it. To edit a selected entry, click Properties and a similar window opens, enabling you to change any of the fields. To delete an entry, select it and click Delete.

Command Line PPP Access: WvDial

For a dial-up PPP connection, you can use the WvDial dialer, an intelligent dialer that not only dials up an ISP service but also performs login operations, supplying your username and password (Ubuntu main repository). WvDial will automatically detect and configure your modem. It will ask you to enter your phone number, username, and password. It will then set up a configuration for your modem, letting you automatically connect to your dial-up network.

Configuration is saved in the **wvdial.conf** file. Should you need to reconfigure this file, you can use the **wvdialconf** utility to create a default **wvdial.conf** file for you automatically; **wvdialconf** will detect your modem and set default values for basic features. You can also edit the **wvdial.conf** file and modify the Phone, Username, and Password entries with your ISP dial-up information.

The WvDial program first loads its configuration from the **/etc/wvdial.conf** file. You can modify this file directly if necessary. Here, you will find modem and account information, including the modem speed and serial device, as well as the ISP phone number, your username, and password. The **wvdial.conf** file is organized into sections, beginning with a section label enclosed in brackets. A section holds variables for different parameters that are assigned values, such as **username = chris**. The default section holds default values inherited by other sections, so you needn't repeat them. You can also create a named dialer, which is helpful if you log in to several different ISPs.

To start WvDial, enter the command **wvdial**, as shown next, which reads the connection configuration information from the **/etc/wvdial.conf** file. WvDial then dials the ISP and initiates the PPP connection, providing your username and password when requested.

```
$ wvdial
```

You can set up connection configurations for any number of connections in the **/etc/wvdial.conf** file. To select one, enter its label as an argument to the **wvdial** command, as shown here:

```
$ wvdial myisp
```

Manual Wireless Configuration with iwconfig

NetworkManager will automatically detect and configure your wireless connections, as will KNetworkManager. However, you can manually configure your connections with wireless tools such as Network Manager Editor and **iwconfig**. Wireless configuration makes use of the same set of wireless extensions in the Ubuntu main repository, **wireless-tools** package. The **wireless-tools** package is a set of network configuration and reporting tools for wireless devices installed on a Linux system. They are currently supported and developed as part of the Linux Wireless Extension and Wireless Tools project, an open source project maintained by Hewlett-Packard.

As mentioned, you can configure wireless connections manually using the Network Manager Editor (Applications | Internet | Network Manager Editor). This provides a simple interface for standard configurations.

Wireless Tools offer the following command line configuration and reporting tools that you can enter in a command line interface such as terminal window:

Tool	Description
iwconfig	Sets the wireless configuration options basic to most wireless devices
iwlist	Displays current status information of a device
iwspy	Sets the list of IP addresses in a wireless network and checks the quality of their connections
iwpriv	Accesses configuration options specific to a particular device

The **iwconfig** command works similar to **ifconfig**, configuring a network connection. It is the tool used by **network-admin** to configure a wireless card. Alternatively, you can run **iwconfig** directly on a command line, specifying certain parameters. Added parameters let you set wireless-specific features such as the network name (**nwid**), the frequency or channel the card uses (**freq** or **channel**), and the bit rate for transmissions (**rate**). See the **iwconfig** man page for a complete listing of accepted parameters. Some of the commonly used parameters are shown in Table 5-2.

For example, to set the channel used for the wireless device installed as the first Ethernet device, you would use the following, setting the channel to 2:

```
iwconfig eth0 channel 2
```

You can also use **iwconfig** to display statistics for your wireless devices, just as **ifconfig** does. Enter the **iwconfig** command with no arguments or with the name of the device. Information such as the name, frequency, sensitivity, and bit rate is listed.

The **iwpriv** command works in conjunction with **iwconfig**, allowing you set options specific to a particular kind of wireless device. With **iwpriv**, you can also turn on roaming or select the port to use. You use the **private-command** parameter to enter the device-specific options. The following example turns roaming on:

```
iwpriv eth0 roam on
```

To display the quality, signal, and noise levels for your connections, use the **iwspy** command with just the device name:

```
iwspy eth0
```

To obtain more detailed information about your wireless device, such as all the frequencies or channels available, use the **iwlist** tool. Using the device name with a particular parameter,

Parameter	Description
essid	A network name
freq	The frequency of the connection
channel	The channel used
nwid or domain	The network ID or domain
mode	The operating mode used for the device, such as Ad Hoc, Managed, or Auto: Ad Hoc = one cell with no access point; Managed = network with several access points and supports roaming; Master = the node is an access point; Repeater = node forwards packets to other nodes; Secondary = backup master or repeater; Monitor = only receives packets
sens	The sensitivity: the lowest signal level at which data can be received
key or enc	The encryption key used
frag	Cuts packets into smaller fragments to increase better transmission
bit or rate	Speed at which bits are transmitted; the **auto** option automatically falls back to lower rates for noisy channels
ap	Specifies a specific access point
power	Power management for wakeup and sleep operations

TABLE 5-2   Commonly Used Parameters

you can obtain specific information about a device, including the frequency, access points, rate, power features, retry limits, and encryption keys used.

NOTE *The linux-wlan project has developed a separate set of wireless drivers designed for Prism-based wireless cards supporting the new 802.11 wireless standard. The linux-wlan drivers are not currently included with Ubuntu; you will have to download them. The original source code package is available from the linux-wlan Web site at **www.linux-wlan.org**. The current package is **linux-wlan-ng** (Ubuntu main repository).*

Accessing Remote Desktops

Ubuntu also provides tools for accessing remote systems and taking control of their desktops. The X Window System already has built-in support for remotely accessing other user's desktops. On Linux systems, desktop access is performed through the Virtual Network Computing (VNC) protocol. For Windows desktops, you use the Remote Desktop Protocol (RDP).

NOTE *The X Window System allows users to access applications on a remote desktop. Although you can do this directly, you should invoke it through an SSH secure connection:* `ssh -X user@domain`.

Virtual Network Computing

VNC allows a computer to access and control a graphical desktop located on a computer connected to a different network. Anyone with the appropriate permissions can display and control a VNC server on a remote system. To access such a system, a remote computer uses a VNC viewer that connects directly to the remote desktop running a VNC server. Access can be password-protected.

VNC servers export the desktop on ports numbered from 5900. The port used is 5900 plus the number of the port that the desktop uses—usually 1, so this would make the port 5901. Be sure that access is allowed by your firewall. You will also need to open access on port 5800 and 6000. For Firestarter, set up access on the Port dialog. For the Ubuntu Firewall (**ufw**), you'd enter the following in a terminal window:

```
ufw 5900 allow
```

GNOME VNC Client: Vinagre

Vinagre is the GNOME remote desktop viewer used remotely to control a system running a VNC server (Ubuntu main repository). Vinagre is a VNC client that lets you browse your network for VNC servers. You can then connect to a server and remotely control that machine. Vinagre lets you connect to several VNC servers at once, as well as bookmark your favorite ones for easy access later. Vinagre will also keep track of the VNC servers to which you recently connected, letting you easily reconnect. Bookmarks can hold passwords stored in the GNOME keyring, so you do not have to re-enter them each time you connect.

To start Vinagre, choose Applications | Internet | Remote Desktop Viewer, or enter **vinagre** at the command line in a terminal window. This opens the Remote Desktop Viewer window (Figure 5-5) with a side panel that displays bookmarked connections. The toolbar offers Connect, Close, Fullscreen, and Take Screenshot buttons. The menu bar shows menus for Machine, View, Bookmarks, and Help. The Machine menu includes the same options offered on the toolbar, with additional entries for Open and Recent Connections. Vinagre will keep track of all your recent connections here. The View menu configures display options for Vinagre such as displaying the toolbar, status bar, and bookmarks, as well as a full screen display. You use the Bookmarks menu to add, edit, and remove bookmarks for remote connections.

When you click the Connect button, a window opens where you enter the hostname of the remote VNC server and the port to use. You can also click the Find button to have Vinagre search for VNC servers on your network. This opens a Choose VNC Server window that lists all available VNC servers. A Domain button lets you specify a network to search.

NOTE   *Vinagre is supported directly by Ubuntu and installed by default. Other VNC clients include tsclient and krdc (KDE).*

GNOME VNC Server: Vino

Vino is the GNOME VNC server designed to work with Vinagre. You enable and configure Vino on your desktop using **vino-preferences**, accessible by choosing System | Preferences | Remote Desktop. This opens a Remote Desktop Preferences window with General and

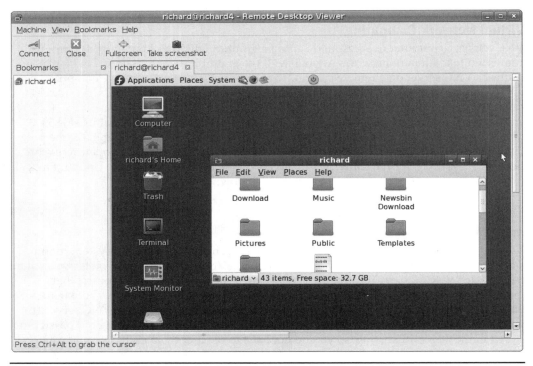

FIGURE 5-5   Vinagre VNC client

Advanced tabs (see Figure 5-6). On the General tab, you can allow sharing and specify security. To enable sharing, select the Allow Other Users To View Your Desktop check box. You'll then see an additional box for allowing other users to control your desktop. For security, you can have a user first ask you for access and then specify a password for entry.

On the Advanced tab, you configure network access, security features, and notification options. For network access, you can restrict access to users on your local network as well as on a specific port. Security can require encryption and screen locking. For notification, a remote desktop connection icon can be displayed on the GNOME desktop panel.

Vino server allows access only to users that are currently logged in to their GNOME desktop. Once enabled by a user, the VNC server is automatically started when the user logs in.

X Window System VNC Servers

Vino is designed to work with GNOME and requires that a user be logged in to the remote desktop. More traditional VNC servers allow remote users to log in to a remote desktop. Such servers can be configured to export desktops and window managers other than GNOME. They use their own X Window System configuration files to determine and set up the display to provide (**.vnc/xstartup**). Here you could specify a window manager or desktop to use: for Ubuntu, they are the **vnc4** and **tightvnc** servers and viewers. These are designed to work with any X Window System window manager, not just GNOME. The **tightvnc** server and view specialize in low-bandwidth access. **Tightvnc** also has a corresponding VNC server for Windows that will allow Linux users to access Windows desktops.

Windows Terminal Servers

Windows has is own method for allowing remote desktop access. Windows servers and some desktops can be configured to run as terminal servers, allowing users to access and use software on those servers. Windows servers as well as Windows XP Professional and

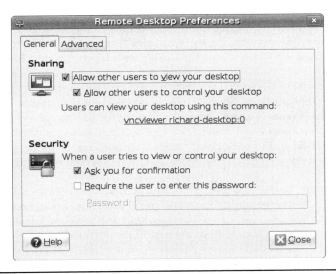

FIGURE 5-6   Remote Desktop Preferences

Windows Vista Business/Enterprise/Ultimate desktops have this feature built-in. On Windows XP Professional and Vista, the Terminal Services feature is referred to as the *Remote Desktop*. Windows Vista also provides Desktop Sharing, which allows more refined multiple access to a particular window or application. Remote Desktops, Terminal Services, and Desktop Sharing are implemented using the RDP.

You can access the Windows RPD–enabled remote system using a Remote Desktop Connection client. On Windows XP Professional and Windows Vista, choose Accessories | Communications | Remote Desktop Connection. A Remote Desktop Connection client can also be downloaded for other versions of Windows such as ME, 98, and XP Home. Linux systems can access a Windows terminal server or Remote Desktop using the **rdesktop** client, which is integrated into other popular clients such as **tsclient**.

NOTE *Instead of using the RDP, you could just install a Windows version of the VNC server, such as the Windows* **tightvnc***, and then use a Linux VNC client to access your Windows system.*

On Windows XP Professional, RDP remote access is configured as Remote Desktop on the Remote tab of the System Properties window (from Control Panel, choose the System icon). Check Allow Users To Connect Remotely To This Computer. On Vista, select the Remote Settings line and then check Allow Connections From Computers Running A Version Of Remote Desktop.

As Windows servers, the terminal server allows remote users to run a virtual Windows system. Access is licensed by Microsoft. Remote systems accessing the server can then run software installed on it, letting many remote users work on the same server as if they were sitting in front of their own Windows systems. On the XP and Vista desktops, the Remote Desktop operates for single users, allowing one client at a time to connect to a particular RDP-enabled desktop. Users can work on files and use storage and printing devices on their own systems for applications running on the terminal server or the Remote Desktop.

Server Linux remote access clients, such as **tsclient** and **rdesktop**, support the RDP, allowing you to access a Windows system (server or desktop) running the Windows Terminal Services feature. The major limitation of clients using the RDP is that they can access only Windows systems running the Windows Terminal Services. You cannot use Windows Remote Desktop Connection client to access a Linux desktop from Windows.

The **tsclient** client lets you connect to Windows desktops running Windows Terminal Services. Though the RDP is selected by default, **tsclient** also supports VNC servers, so you can use it for Linux VNC servers. Start **tsclient** by choosing Applications | Internet | Terminal Server Client. This opens a window with tabs for setting up a connection and configurations for that connection. You click a Connect button to connect to a server. You can save the connection and its configuration for later use. A pop-up menu will list saved connections from which you can choose. Configuration is saved in the user's **.tsclient** directory.

On the General tab, you enter connection information. The Windows RDP will be selected by default. On the remaining tabs, you configure your connections, set display features (Display), select local resources such as sound and keyboard devices to use (Local Resources), or select performance options such as hiding window manager decorations (Performance). The Programs tab allows you choose a application to run automatically when the connection is made.

The **rdesktop** client also sets up Windows Terminal Services access. Start **rdesktop** in a terminal window with the `rdesktop` command, with the hostname of the system to which you want to connect. A Windows Server dialog is then displayed, where you can enter the username and password for the user whose desktop you want to access. You can also use the `-u` and `-p` options to provide the username and password when you invoked `rdesktop`. The `-r` option will let you map local resources such as printers and disks to the Windows system. For example, you could print files on the Windows system from a printer on your Linux system. Disks and storage devices on your Linux system, such as CD/DVD drives, can be accessed by applications on the connected Windows system.

NOTE *As an alternative to **rdesktop**, you can use **gnome-rdp** or **krdc**.*

Software Installation

U buntu software has grown so large that it no longer makes sense to use discs as the primary means of distribution. Instead, distribution is effected using the online Ubuntu software repositories, which contains an extensive collection of Ubuntu-compliant software. This approach heralds a move from thinking of most Linux software included on a few discs, to viewing the disc as just a core from which you can expand your installed software as you like from online repositories. With the integration of repository access into your Linux system, you can now think of that software as an easily installed extension of your current collection.

For Ubuntu, you can add software to your system by accessing software repositories that support Debian packages (DEB) and the Advanced Package Tool (APT). Software is packaged into DEB software package files. These files are, in turn, installed and managed by APT. The Ubuntu software repository is organized into sections, depending on how the software is supported. Software supported directly is located in the *main* Ubuntu repository section. Other Linux software that is most likely compatible is placed in the *universe* repository section.

Many software applications, particularly multimedia applications, have potential licensing conflicts and are placed in the *multiverse* repository section, which is not maintained directly by Ubuntu. Many of the popular multimedia drives and applications such as video and digital music support can be obtained from the Ubuntu multiverse repository using the same simple APT commands you use for Ubuntu-sponsored software.

In addition, some drivers are entirely proprietary and supplied directly by vendors. This is the case with the Nvidia and ATI vendor-provided drivers. These drivers are placed in a *restricted* section—with no open source support, though this situation is being changed by ATI and, to some extent, Nvidia, who are making part of their drivers open source.

You can also download Linux software from many online sources directly, but you are advised to use the Ubuntu-prepared package versions if they're available. Most software for GNOME and KDE have corresponding Ubuntu-compliant packages in the Ubuntu universe and multiverse repositories.

Installing Software Packages

Installing software is an administrative function performed by a user with administrative privileges. Unless you chose to install all your packages during Ubuntu installation, only some of the many applications and utilities available for Linux users were installed on your system. On Ubuntu, you can easily install or remove software from your system with the Add/Remove Applications tool, the Synaptic Package Manager, or the `apt` command. Alternatively, you can install software by downloading and compiling its source code.

APT is integrated as the primary tool used for installing packages. When you install a package with Add/Remove Applications or with the Synaptic Package Manager, APT will be invoked and will automatically select and download the package from the appropriate online repository. (This is a major change of which users may not be aware at first glance.) After having installed your system, when you then want to install additional packages, the install packages tool will use APT to install from an online repository, though it will check a CD or DVD first if you tell it to do so. This will include the entire Ubuntu online repository, including the main repository and universe and multiverse repositories.

A DEB software package installs all the files required for a software application. A Linux software application often consists of several files that must be installed in different directories. The program itself is usually placed in a directory called **/usr/bin**, online manual files go in another directory, and library files go in yet another directory.

NOTE *Be careful not to mix distributions. The distribution segments of all your* **sources.list** *entries should be the same:* hardy *if you are using Ubuntu 8.04,* gutsy *for 7.10,* edgy *for 7.05,* dapper *for 6.06, and so on.*

Ubuntu Package Management Software

Although all Ubuntu software packages have the same DEB format, they can be managed and installed using different package management software tools, such as those listed next. The primary software management tool is APT.

- **APT (Advanced Package Tool)**   Synaptic, Package Manager, **update-manager**, **dpkg**, and **apt-get** are front ends for APT.

- **Synaptic Package Manager**   Graphical front end for managing packages; repository information at **/var/cache/apt**, same as APT.

- **Update Manager**   Ubuntu graphical front end for updating installed software; uses APT.

- **Add/Remove Applications tool, gnome-app-install**   GNOME graphical front end for managing packages; repository info at **/var/cache/apt**, same as APT.

- **dpkg**   Older command line tool used to install, update, remove, and query software packages; uses its own database, **/var/lib/dpkg**; repository info at **/var/cache/apt**, same as APT.

- **apt-get**   Primary command line tool to install, update, and remove software; uses its own database, **/var/lib/apt/**; repository info at **/var/cache/apt**.

- **aptitude**   Front end for tools such as **dpkg** or **apt-get**; cursor based; uses its own database, **/var/lib/aptitude**.

Updating Ubuntu with Update Manager

New versions of Ubuntu are released every few months. In the meantime, new updates are continually being prepared for particular software packages. These are posted as updates you can download from software repositories and install on your system. These include new versions of applications, servers, and even the kernel. Such updates may range from single software packages to whole components.

Updating your Ubuntu system and packages has become a very simple procedure with Update Manager, a graphical update interface for APT. You can update your system by accessing software repositories supporting APT update methods.

The Update Manager applet on your GNOME desktop panel will automatically check for updates whenever you log in. If updates are detected, the Update Manager icon on the panel will flash and display a message telling you the number of updates that are available. Click the Update Manager icon to start Update Manager, or choose System | Administration | Update Manager and click the Check button to check current repository package listings for updates.

All required updates are selected automatically when Update Manager starts up (see Figure 6-1). The check boxes for each entry let you deselect any particular packages you do not want to update. Packages are organized according to importance, beginning with important security updates and followed by recommended updates. You should always install the security updates.

FIGURE 6-1
Update Manager
with selected
packages

Click the Install Updates button to start updating. The packages will be downloaded from their appropriate repository. Once downloaded, the packages are updated. All the APT-compatible repositories that are configured on your system will be checked.

To see a detailed description of an update, select the update and then click the Description Of Update arrow at the bottom of the screen. Two tabs are displayed: Changes and Description (Figure 6-2). Changes lists detailed update information, and Description provides information about the software.

Click the Install Updates button to begin downloading and installing updates. A dialog appears showing the download progress (see Figure 6-3).

You can choose to show the progress for individual files. Click that option to open a window that lists each file and its progress.

Once downloaded, the updates are installed. Click Details button to see install messages for particular software packages.

Managing Packages with Add/Remove Applications

To perform simple installation and removal of software, you can use the Add/Remove Applications tool accessible from the Applications menu. The **gnome-app-install** application is designed for simple package installation and removal. For more detailed and extensive installation such as libraries and kernel packages, you would use the Synaptic Package Manager.

To use the Add/Remove Applications tool, choose Applications | Add/Remove Applications. The Add/Remove Applications tool will start by gathering information on all your packages (see Figure 6-4).

You can display applications in different ways. A pop-up menu lists applications organized by their type of source, such as Ubuntu-supported applications, All open source applications, All available applications, Third party applications, or Installed applications.

The panel on the left lets you list software for different categories, such as Office, Graphics, or Programming, further refining your search. Choose the All option to display or search all available applications.

APT is integrated as the primary install packages tool. When you install a package with Add/Remove Applications, APT will be invoked and will automatically select and download the package from the appropriate online repository.

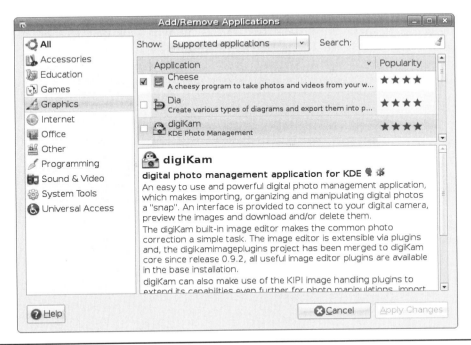

FIGURE 6-4   Add/Remove Applications tool

Synaptic Package Manager

The Synaptic Package Manager gives you more control over all your packages. Packages are listed by name and include supporting packages such as libraries and system-critical packages. You can start up Synaptic by choosing System | Administration | Synaptic Package Manager.

Buttons at the lower left of the Synaptic Package Manager window provide options for organizing and refining the list of packages shown (see Figure 6-5): Sections, Status, Origin, Custom Filters, and Search Results. The dialog pane above the buttons changes depending on which option you choose. Clicking the Sections button will list section categories for your software such as Base System, Communications, and Development. Clicking the Status button will list options for installed and not installed software. Clicking the Origin button shows entries for different repositories, as well as those locally installed (manual or disc-based installations). Clicking Custom Filters lets you choose a filter to use for listing packages. You can create your own filter and use it to display selected packages. Clicking Search Results will list your current and previous searches, letting you move from one to the other.

The Sections option is selected by default (see Figure 6-6). You can choose to list all packages or refine your listing using categories provided in the dialog pane. The All entry in this pane will list all available packages. Packages are organized into categories such as Base System, Cross Platform, and Communications. Each category is in turn subdivided by multiverse, universe, and restricted software.

Status entries further refine installed software as autoremovable or as local or obsolete (see Figure 6-7). Local software are packages you download and install manually.

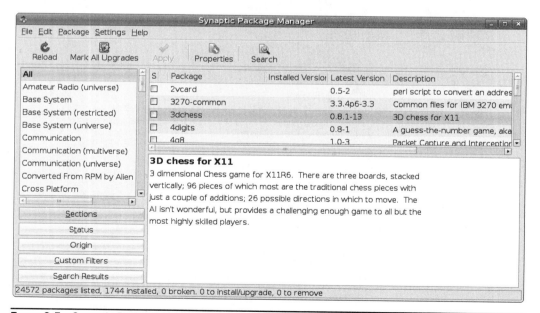

FIGURE 6-5   Synaptic Package Manager

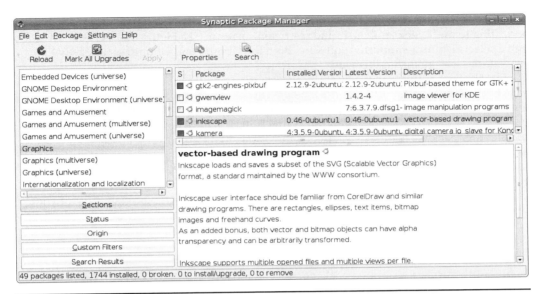

FIGURE 6-6 Synaptic Package Manager: Sections

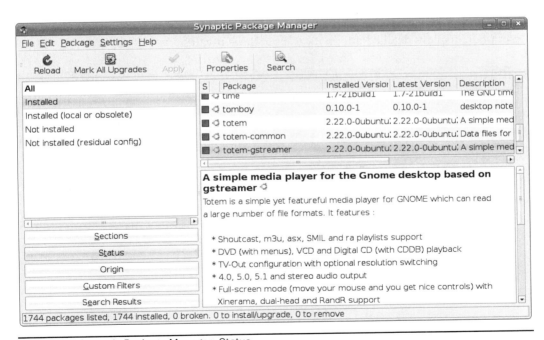

FIGURE 6-7 Synaptic Package Manager: Status

With the Origins options, Ubuntu-compliant repositories may further refine access according to multiverse, universe, and restricted software (see Figure 6-8). A Local/Main entry selects Ubuntu-supported software. Both the Ubuntu and Ubuntu security repositories are organized this way.

Use the Search function for locating software that you'll use most often. To perform a search, click the Search button on the toolbar. This opens a Search dialog with a text box where you can enter search terms. A pop-up menu lets you specify what features of a package to search. The Description And Name feature is most commonly used. You can search other package features such as just the Name, Maintainer, Version, Dependencies, and Provided Packages.

You can also search by keyword; both the package name and the package description will be searched. To perform a search, click the Search button and enter the search term or terms. The results will be displayed with the repository list now replaced by a list of your searches. You can move back and forth between search results by clicking the search entries in this listing (see Figure 6-9).

Properties

To find out information about a package, select the package and click the Properties button. This opens a window with Common, Dependencies, Installed Files, Versions, and Description tabs. The Common tab provides section, versions, and developer information. The Dependencies tab shows all dependent software packages (usually libraries) required by this software. The Install Files tab shows you exactly what files are installed, which is useful for finding the exact location and names for configuration files as well as commands. Description displays detailed information about the software.

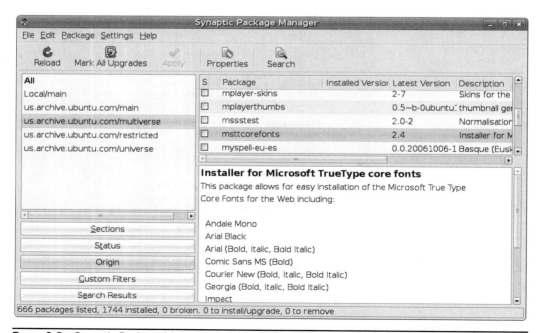

Figure 6-8   Synaptic Package Manager: Origin

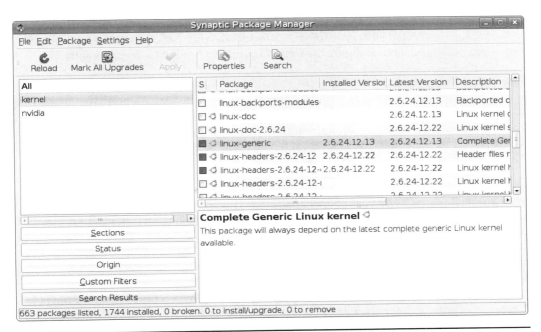

FIGURE 6-9   Synaptic Package Manager: Search

Installing Packages

Before installing, you should click the Reload button to reload the most recent package lists from the active repositories. To install a package, right-click its name and choose Mark For Installation. Should any dependent packages exist, a dialog opens showing those packages. Click the Mark button in the dialog to mark those packages for installation as well. The package entry's check box will then be marked in the Package Manager window.

Once you have selected the packages you want to install, click the Apply button on the toolbar to begin the installation process. A Summary dialog opens, showing all the packages to be installed. You have the option of downloading only the package files. The number of packages to be installed is shown, along with the size of the download and the amount of disk space used. Click the Apply button on the Summary dialog to download and install the packages. A download window will then appear, showing the progress of your package installations. You can choose to show the progress of individual packages, which opens a terminal window listing each package as it is downloaded and installed.

Once downloaded, the dialog name changes to Installing Software. You can choose to have the dialog close automatically when the process is finished.

Sometimes installation requires user input to configure the software. You will be prompted to enter the information if necessary.

When you right-click a package name, you also see options for Mark Suggested For Installation or Mark Recommended For Installation. These will mark applications that can enhance your selected software, though they are not essential.

Certain software, such as desktops or office suites that require a significant number of packages, can be selected all at once using *metapackages*. A metapackage has configuration files that select, download, and configure the range of packages needed for complex software.

Removing Packages

To remove a package, right-click it and select Mark Package For Removal. This will leave configuration files untouched Alternatively, you can mark a package for complete removal, which will also remove any configuration files. Dependent packages will not be removed.

Once you have marked packages for removal, click the Apply button. A summary dialog displays the packages that will be removed. Click Apply to remove them.

Synaptic may not remove dependent packages, especially shared libraries that might or might not be used by other applications. This means that your system could eventually have installed packages that are never being used. Their continued presence will not harm anything, but if you want to conserve disk space, you can clean them out using the **deborphan** tool, which outputs a listing of packages no longer needed by other packages or no longer used. You can then use this list to remove the packages.

Search Filters

You can further refine your search for packages by creating search filters. Select Settings | Filters menu entry to open the Filters window. The Filters window shows two areas, a filter list on the left, and three tabs on the right: Status, Section, and Properties. To create a new filter, click the New button located just below the filter listings.

Click the New Filter 1 entry in the filter list on the left. On the Status tab, you can refine your search criteria according to a package's status (see Figure 6-10). You can search only uninstalled packages or include installed packages. Include or exclude packages marked for removal. Or search for those that are new in the repository. Initially, all criteria are selected. Uncheck those you do not want included in your search.

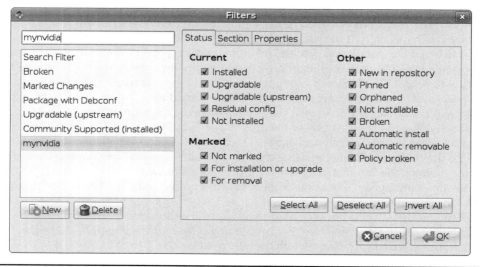

FIGURE 6-10   Synaptic Package Manager: Search Filter Status tab

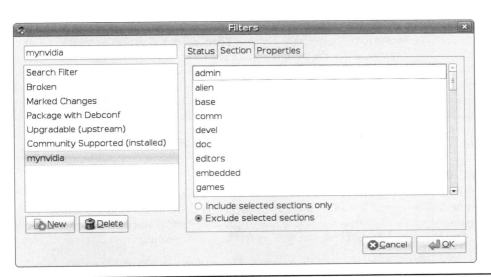

FIGURE 6-11 Synaptic Package Manager: Search Filter Section

The Section tab lets you include or exclude different repository sections such as games, documentation, or administration (see Figure 6-11). If you are looking for a game, you could choose to include just the game section, excluding everything else.

On the Properties tab, you can specify patterns to search on package information such as package names, using Boolean operators to refine your search criteria. Package search criteria are entered using the two pop-up menus and the text box at the bottom of the tab, along with AND or OR Boolean operators (see Figure 6-12).

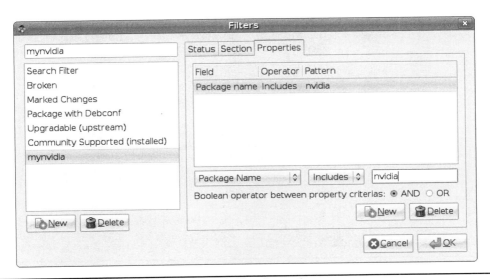

FIGURE 6-12 Synaptic Package Manager: Search Filter Properties

To create a search criteria, select the package feature to search from the pop-up menu, such as Package Name (as shown in the figure). Then select the action to take, such as Includes. In the text box, enter the patterns to be searched. If you have more than one, you can choose either an AND Boolean operation for a small result or an OR operation for an expanded result. Click the New button to add search criteria to the Properties tab. You can create several search criteria, removing old ones by clicking the Delete button.

On the Synaptic Package Manager, when you click the Custom Filters button, you will see the custom filters you created. Click a filter to perform the package selection automatically based on its search criteria (see Figure 6-13).

Synaptic Configuration

To configure the Synaptic Package Manager, choose Settings | Preferences. In the Preferences dialog, you'll see several tabs. Some, such as Columns And Fonts and Colors, configure the tool's appearance. Preferences applicable to how packages are managed are located on the General tab. Here you can set features for marking and applying changes:

- **Consider Recommended Packages as Dependencies**   Installs associated packages that are not necessarily required but would be normally used with package.

- **System Upgrade**   Tries to identify any associated packages to be installed, updated, or removed when installing or updating a package. Not as effective as **apt-get dist-upgrade**.

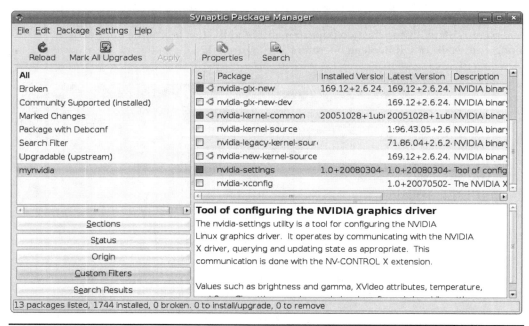

FIGURE 6-13   Synaptic Package Manager: Custom Filters

- **Reload Outdated Package Information**   Automatically keeps its package list up to date.
- **Applying Changes in a Terminal Window**   Useful when interactive installation is required.

NOTE *The aptitude tool provides a simple cursor-based command tool for adding and removing software.*

Ubuntu Software Repositories

Four main components, or sections, make up the Ubuntu repository: main, restricted, universe, and multiverse. These components are described in detail at **http://ubuntu.com/ ubuntu/components**. To see a listing of all packages in the Ubuntu repository, check **http:// packages.ubuntu.com**. To see available repositories and their sections, open the Synaptic Package Manager and choose Settings | Repositories.

Repository Components

The following repository components are included in the main Ubuntu repository:

- **Main**   Officially supported Ubuntu software (canonical), includes GStreamer Good plug-ins.
- **Restricted**   Commonly used and required for many applications, but not open source or freely licensed, such as proprietary graphics card drivers from Nvidia and ATI needed for hardware support. Because they are not open source, they are not guaranteed to work.
- **Universe**   All open source Linux software not directly supported by Ubuntu; includes GStreamer Bad plug-ins.
- **Multiverse**   Linux software that does not meet licensing requirements and is not considered essential. It may not necessarily work. For example, the GStreamer Ugly package is in this repository. Check **http://ubuntu.com/community/ubuntustory/ licensing**.

Repositories

In addition to the main repository, Ubuntu maintains several other repositories used primarily for maintenance and support for existing packages, as shown in the following list:

- **Main repository**   Collection of Ubuntu-compliant software packages for releases.
- **Updates**   Corresponding updates for packages in the main repository, both main and restricted sections. Universe and multiverse sections are not updated.
- **Backports**   Software under development for the next Ubuntu release, but packaged for use in the current one. Not guaranteed or fully tested.
- **Security updates**   Critical security fixes for main software.

In addition, the backports repository provides unfinalized or development versions for new or current software. They are not guaranteed to work but may provide needed features.

Software Sources

With the Software Sources tool, you can enable or disable repository sections as well as add new entries. This tool edits the **/etc/apt/sources.list** file directly. Choose System | Administration | Software Sources. This opens the Software Sources window with five tabs: Ubuntu Software, Third-Party Software, Updates, Authentication, and Statistics (see Figure 6-14). The Ubuntu Software tab lists all your current repository section entries. These include the main repository, universe, restricted, and multiverse, as well as source code. Those that are enabled will be checked. You can enable or disable a repository section by checking or unchecking its entry. You can select the server to use from the Download From drop-down list. To install software from a CD/DVD, just insert it and begin.

On the Third-Party Software tab, you can add repositories for third-party software. The repository for Ubuntu Software Partners will already be listed, but not checked. Check that entry if you want access software from the partners. To add a third-party repository click the Add button. This opens a dialog where you enter the complete APT entry, starting with the DEB format, followed by the URL, distribution, and components or packages. This line will appear in the **/etc/apt/sources.list** file. Once entered, click the Add Channel button.

The Updates tab lets you configure how updates are handled (see Figure 6-15). The tab specifies both your update sources and how automatic updates are handled. You can install Important Security Updates (hardy-security), Recommended Updates (hardy-updates), Pre-released Updates (hardy-proposed), and Unsupported Updates (hardy-backports). The Important Security and Recommended updates will already be selected; these cover updates for the entire Ubuntu repository. Pre-released and Unsupported updates are useful if you have installed any packages from the backports or development repositories.

Your system is already configured to check for updates automatically on a daily basis. You can opt not to check for updates at all by removing the check mark from the Check For

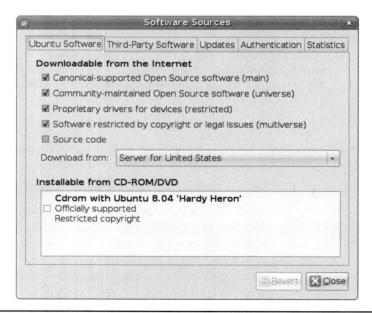

FIGURE 6-14   Software Sources Ubuntu Software repository sections

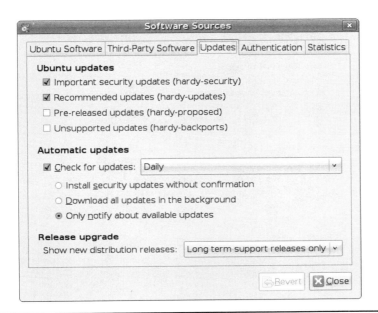

FIGURE 6-15   Software Sources Update configuration

Updates option. You also have options for how updates are handled. You can install any security updates automatically, without confirmation; download updates in the background; or be notified of available updates and then manually choose to install them when you want. The options are exclusive.

The Authentication tab shows the repository software signature keys that are installed on your system (see Figure 6-16). Signature keys will already be installed for Ubuntu repositories, including your CD/DVD-ROM. If you are adding a third-party repository, you will need to add its signature key. Click the Import Key File button to browse for and locate a downloaded signature key file.

Ubuntu requires a signature key for any package that it installs. Signature keys for all the Ubuntu repositories are already installed and are listed on this panel. For third-party repositories, you will have to locate their signature key on their Web site, download it to a file, and then import that file. Most repositories will provide a signature key file for you to download and import. Click the Import Key File to open a file browser, where you can select the downloaded key file. As described in Chapter 7, this procedure is the same as the **apt-key add** operation. Both add keys that APT then uses to verify DEB software packages downloaded from repositories before it installs them.

NOTE   *For added repositories, be sure you have installed the correct signature key as well as a valid URL for the repository.*

The Statistics tab lets you provide Ubuntu with software usage information to let it know what software is being used.

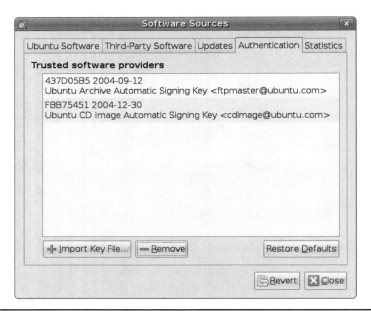

Figure 6-16 Software Sources Authentication, package signature keys

After you have made changes and clicked the Close button, the Software Sources tool will notify you that your software package information is out of date, displaying a Reload button. Click the Reload button to make the new repositories or components available on package managers such as the Synaptic Package Manager. If you do not click Reload, you can run **apt-get update** or perform the check operation on the Synaptic Package Manager to reload the repository configuration.

CAUTION *Though it is possible to add the Debian Linux distribution repository, it is not advisable. Packages are designed for specific distributions. Combining them can lead to unresolvable conflicts.*

Ubuntu Repository Configuration File: sources.list

Repository configuration is managed by APT using configuration files in the **/etc/apt** directory. The **/etc/apt/sources.list** file holds repository entries. The main and restricted sections are enabled by default. An entry consists of a single line with the following format:

```
format URI    distribution    component
```

The *format* is normally **deb**, for Debian package format. The *URI* (universal resource identifier) provides the location of the repository, such as an FTP or Web URL. The *distribution* is the official name of a particular Ubuntu distribution such as dapper or gutsy. Ubuntu 8.04 uses the name hardy. The *component* can be one or more terms that identify a section in that distribution repository, such as *main* for the main repository and *restricted* for the restricted section. You can also list individual packages if you want. Here's an example:

```
deb http://archive.ubuntu.com/ubuntu/   hardy   main restricted
```

Corresponding source code repositories will use a **deb-src** format:

```
deb-src http://us.archive.ubuntu.com/ubuntu/ hardy main restricted
```

Update sections of a repository are referenced by the **-updates** suffix, as in hardy-updates:

```
deb http://archive.ubuntu.com/ubuntu/    hardy-updates    main restricted
```

Security sections for a repository have the suffix **-security**:

```
deb http://archive.ubuntu.com/ubuntu/    hardy-security    main restricted
```

Both universe and multiverse repositories should already be enabled. Each will have an updates repository as well as corresponding source code repositories, such as those shown here for universe:

```
deb http://us.archive.ubuntu.com/ubuntu/ hardy universe
deb-src http://us.archive.ubuntu.com/ubuntu/ hardy universe
deb http://us.archive.ubuntu.com/ubuntu/ hardy-updates universe
deb-src http://us.archive.ubuntu.com/ubuntu/ hardy-updates universe
```

Comments begin with a # mark. You can add comments if you wish. Commenting an entry effectively disables that component of a repository. Placing a # mark before a repository entry will effectively disable it.

Commented entries are included for the backports and Canonical partners repositories. Backports holds applications being developed for future Ubuntu releases and may not work. Partners include companies such as VMWare and Parallels. To activate these repositories, just edit the **/etc/apt/sources.list** file using any text editor, and then remove the # at the beginning of the line. Here's an example comment:

```
# deb http://us.archive.ubuntu.com/ubuntu/ hardy-backports main \
                     restricted universe multiverse
```

You can edit the file directly with the following command:

```
gksu gedit /etc/apt/sources.list
```

Software Management with DEB, APT, and dkpg

Both the Debian distribution and Ubuntu use the Debian package format (DEB) for their software packages. Two basic package managers are available for use with Debian packages: the Advanced Package Tool (APT) and the Debian Package tool (dpkg). APT is designed to work with repositories and is used to install and maintain all your package installations on Ubuntu. Though you can install packages directly as single files with only dpkg, it is always advisable to use APT. Information and package files for Ubuntu-compliant software can be obtained from **http://packages.ubuntu.com**.

You can also download source code versions of applications and then compile and install them on your system. Where this process once was complex, it has been significantly streamlined with the addition of *configure scripts.* Most current source code, including GNU software, is distributed with a configure script that automatically detects your system configuration and generates a *makefile* that is used to compile the application and create a binary file that is compatible with your system. In most cases, you can compile and install complex source code on any system with a few makefile operations.

Software Package Types

Ubuntu uses Debian-compliant software packages whose filenames have a **.deb** extension. Other packages, such as those in the form of source code that you need to compile, may come in a variety of compressed archives. These commonly have the extension **.tar.gz**, **.tgz**, or **.tar.bz2** and are explained in detail later in the chapter. Packages with the **.rpm** extension are Red Hat Package software packages used on Red Hat, Fedora, SuSE, and other Linux distributions that use RPM packages. They are not directly compatible with Ubuntu. You can use the **alien** command to convert most RPM packages to DEB packages that you can then install in Ubuntu.

Table 7-1 lists several common file extensions that you will find in the great variety of Linux software packages available. You can download any Ubuntu-compliant DEB package as well as the original source code package, as single files, directly from **http://packages .ubuntu.com**.

Extension	File
.deb	A Debian Linux package
.gz	A gzip-compressed file (use **gunzip** to decompress)
.bz2	A bzip2-compressed file (use **bunzip2** to decompress; also use the **j** option with **tar**, as in **xvjf**)
.tar	A tar archive file (use **tar** with **xvf** to extract)
.tar.gz	A gzip-compressed tar archive file (use **gunzip** to decompress and **tar** to extract; use the **z** option with **tar**, as in **xvzf**, both to decompress and extract in one step)
.tar.bz2	A bzip2-compressed tar archive file (extract with **tar -xvzj**)
.tz	A tar archive file compressed with the **compress** command
.Z	A file compressed with the **compress** command (use the **decompress** command to decompress)
.bin	A self-extracting software file
.rpm	A software package created with the Red Hat Software Package Manager, used on Fedora, Red Hat, Centos, and SuSE distributions

TABLE 7-1 Linux Software Package File Extensions

DEB Software Packages

A Debian package will automatically resolve dependencies, installing any other needed packages instead of simply reporting their absence. Packages are named with the software name, the version number, and the **.deb** extension. Check **www.us.debian.org/doc** for more information.

Filename format is as follows:

- **Package name**
- **Version number**
- **Distribution label and build number** Packages created specifically for Ubuntu will have the Ubuntu label here. Attached to it will be the build number—the number of times the package was built for Ubuntu.
- **Architecture** The type of system on which the package runs, such as **i386** for Intel 32-bit x86 systems or **amd64** for both Intel and AMD 64-bit systems, x86_64.
- **Package format** This is always **deb**.

For example, the package name for 3dchess is *3dchess*, with a version and build number *0.0.1-13*, and an architecture *amd64* for a 64-bit system. Here's how it looks:

```
3dchess_0.0.1-13_amd64.deb
```

The following package has an Ubuntu label, a package specifically created for Ubuntu. The version number is *1.2* and build number is *4*, with the Ubuntu label *ubuntu2*. The architecture is *i386* for a 32-bit system:

```
spider_1.2-4ubuntu2_i386.deb
```

Managing Software with APT

APT is designed to work with repositories and will handle any dependencies for you. It uses **dpkg** to install and remove individual packages, but it can also determine what dependent packages need to be installed, as well as query and download packages from repositories. Several popular tools for APT help you manage your software easily, such as Synaptic Package Manager, gnome-apt, Aptitude, and deselect.

For APT, you can also use the **apt-get** tool to manage your packages. This tool can download packages as well as compile source code versions for you. By using the `apt-get` command on the command line, you can install, update, and remove packages.

Table 7-2 shows some of these commands. Check the **apt-get** man page for a detailed listing of commands.

The `apt-get` command takes two arguments: the command to perform and the name of the package:

```
apt-get   command   package
```

Other APT package tools follow the same format. The command is a term: use the `install`, `remove`, and `update` commands to install, remove, and update packages. You need to specify only the software name, not the package's full filename; APT will determine that.

Command	Description
update	Download and resynchronize the package listing of available and updated packages for APT-supported repositories. APT repositories updated are those specified in **/etc/apt/sources.list**.
upgrade	Update packages, install new versions of installed packages if available.
dist-upgrade	Update (upgrade) all your installed packages to a new release.
install	Install a specific package, using its package name, not full package filename.
remove	Remove a software package from your system.
source	Download and extract a source code package.
check	Check for broken dependencies.
clean	Remove the downloaded packages held in the repository cache on your system. Used to free up disk space.

TABLE 7-2 apt-get Commands

To install the MPlayer package, for example, you would use the following:

```
sudo apt-get install mplayer
```

To make sure that **apt-get** has a current repository information, use the **apt-get update** command:

```
sudo apt-get update
```

To remove packages, you use the **remove** command:

```
sudo apt-get remove mplayer
```

You can use the **-s** option to check the remove or install first, especially to check whether any dependency problems exist. For remove operations, you can use **-s** to find out what dependent packages will also be removed:

```
sudo apt-get remove -s mplayer
```

A complete log of all install, remove, and update operations are stored in the **/var/log/dpkg.log** file. You can consult this file to find out exactly what files were installed or removed.

As noted in Chapter 6, configuration for APT is held in the **/etc/apt** directory. Here the **sources.list** file lists the distribution repositories from where packages are installed. Source lists for additional third-party repositories (such as that for Wine) are kept in the /**etc/sources.list.d** directory. GPG (GNU Privacy Guard) database files hold validation keys for those repositories. Specific options for **apt-get** can be found in an **/etc/apt.conf** file or in various files located in the **/etc/apt.conf.d** directory.

Upgrading with apt-get

The **apt-get** tool also lets you update and upgrade your entire system at once. In **apt-get**, the terms *update* and *upgrade* not used in the same ways that they are used for other software tools. The **update** command in **apt-get** updates your *package listing*, checking for packages that may need to install newer versions, but *not* installing those versions. Technically, it updates the package list that APT uses to determine what packages need to be installed. The term *upgrade* is used to denote the actual installation of a new version of a software package.

Tip *The terms* update *and* upgrade *can be confusing when used with apt-get. The* update *operation updates the APT package list only, whereas an* upgrade *actually downloads and installs all the packages for a new release.*

Upgrading to a new package is a simple matter of using the **upgrade** command. With no package specified, using **apt-get** with the **upgrade** command will upgrade your entire system, downloading from an FTP site or copying from a CD-ROM and installing packages as needed. Add the **-u** option to list packages as they are upgraded.

First, make sure your repository information (package list) is up to date with the **update** command; then issue the **upgrade** command:

```
sudo apt-get update
sudo apt-get -u upgrade
```

Should you want to upgrade to an entirely new and more recent distribution, you can use the **dist-upgrade** option. A **dist-upgrade** would install a new release—say, 8.04 on a 7.10 system—preserving your original configuration and data. This option will also remove obsolete software packages.

```
sudo apt-get update
sudo apt-get dist-upgrade
```

On the other hand, you may want to keep your current version, particularly if you are using a long-term release (LTR) such as Ubuntu 8.04.

Source Code Files

Although you can install source code files directly, the best way to install them is to use **apt-get**. Use the **source** command with the package name, as shown in the next example. Packages will be downloaded and extracted.

```
sudo apt-get source mplayer
```

The **--download** option lets you just download the source package without extracting it. The **--compile** option will download, extract, compile, and package the source code into a Debian binary package, ready for installation.

No dependent packages will be downloaded. If a software packages requires any dependent packages to run, you will have to download and compile those also. To obtain needed dependent files, you use the **build-dep** option. All your dependent files will be located and downloaded for you automatically. Here's an example:

```
sudo apt-get build-dep mplayer
```

Installing from source code requires that supporting development libraries and source code header files be installed. You can do this separately for each major development platform such as GNOME, KDE, or just the kernel. Alternatively, you can run the APT metapackage **build-essential** for all the Ubuntu development packages, as shown next. You will have to do this only once.

```
sudo apt-get install build-essential
```

Managing Non-repository Packages with dpkg

You can use **dpkg** to install a software package you have already downloaded directly, not with an APT-enabled software tool such as **apt-get** or Synaptic Package Manager. In this case, you are not installing from a repository. Instead, you have manually downloaded the package file from a Web or FTP site to a folder on your system. Such a situation would be rare, reserved for software not available on the Ubuntu- or any APT-enabled repository.

Keep in mind that most software is already on your Ubuntu- or an APT-enabled repository. Check there first before performing a direct download and install with **dpkg**. The **dpkg** configuration files are located in the **/etc/dpkg** directory. Configuration is held in the **dpkg.cfg** file. See the **dpkg** man page for a detailed listing of options.

One situation for which you would use **dpkg** is for packages you have built yourself, such as packages you created when converting a package in another format to a DEB package. This is the case when converting a Red Hat Package Manager (RPM) package to a DEB package format.

Use the **-i** option to install a package:

```
sudo dpkg -i package.deb
```

The major failing for **dpkg** is that it provides no dependency support. It will inform you of needed dependencies, but you will have to install them separately. **dpkg** installs only the specified package. It is ideal for packages that have no dependencies.

Use the **-I** option to obtain package information directly from the DEB package file:

```
sudo dpkg -I package.deb
```

To remove a package, use the **-r** option with the package software name. You do not need version or extension information such as **.386** or **.deb**. With **dpkg**, when removing a package with dependencies, you first have to remove all its dependencies manually. You will not be able to uninstall the package until you do this. Configuration files are not removed.

```
sudo dpkg -r packagename
```

If you install a package that requires dependencies, and then fail to install these dependencies, your install database will be marked as having broken packages. In this case, APT will not allow new packages to be installed until the broken packages are fixed. You can enter the **apt-get** command with the **-f** and **install** options to fix all broken packages at once:

```
sudo apt-get -f install
```

Using Packages with Other Software Formats

You can convert software packages in other software formats into DEB packages that can then be installed on Ubuntu. To do this, you use the **alien** tool, which can convert several different kinds of formats such as RPM and even **.tgz** files. You use the **--to-deb** option to convert to a DEB package format that Ubuntu can then install. The **--scripts** option attempts to convert any pre- or postinstall configuration scripts. Here's an example:

```
alien  --scripts  --to-deb  system-config-lvm-1.1.1-2.fc8.noarch.rpm
```

You can download and install **alien** from the Ubuntu repository using Synaptic Package Manager.

Command Line Search and Information: dpkg-query and atp-cache Tools

The **dpkg-query** command lets you list detailed information about your packages. On the command line (terminal window), use **dpkg-query** with the **-l** option to list all your packages:

```
dpkg-query  -l
```

The **dpkg** command can operate as a front end for **dpkg-query**, detecting its options to perform the appropriate task. The preceding command could also be run like this:

```
dpkg  -l
```

Listing a particular package requires an exact match on the package name, unless you use pattern matching operators. The following command lists the **wine** package (Windows Compatibility Layer):

```
dpkg-query  -l wine
```

A pattern matching operator, such as *, placed after a pattern will display any packages beginning with the specified pattern. The pattern with operators needs to be placed in single quotation marks to prevent an attempt by the shell to use the pattern to match on filenames on your current directory. The following example finds all packages beginning with the pattern *wine*. This would include packages with names such as **wine-doc** and **wine-utils**.

```
dpkg-query  -l   'wine*'
```

You can further refine the results by using **grep** to perform an additional search. The following operation first outputs all packages beginning with *wine*, and from those results, the **grep** operations lists only those with the pattern *utils* in their name, such as **wine-utils**.

```
dpkg  -l   'wine*'  | grep 'utils'
```

Use the **-L** option to list only the files that a package has installed:

```
dpkg-query  -L  wine
```

To see the status information about a package, including its dependencies and configuration files, use the **-s** option. Fields will include Status, Section, Architecture, Version, Depends (dependent packages), Suggests, Conflicts (conflicting packages), and Conffiles (configuration files).

```
dpkg-query -s  wine
```

The status information will also provide suggested dependencies. These are packages not installed, but likely to be used. For the wine package, the **msttcorefonts** Windows fonts package is suggested.

```
dpkg-query  -s  wine | grep Suggests
```

Use the **-S** option to determine to which package a particular file belongs.

```
dpkg-query  -S  filename
```

You can also obtain information with the **apt-cache** tool. Use the **search** command with **apt-cache** to perform a search:

```
apt-cache search wine
```

To find dependencies for a particular package, use the **depends** command:

```
apt-cache depends wine
```

To display just the package description, use the **show** command:

```
apt-cache show wine
```

NOTE   *If you have installed Aptitude to help you manage software, you can use the* **aptitude** *command with the* **search** *and* **show** *options to find and display information about packages.*

Installing Software from Compressed Archives: .tar.gz

Linux software applications in the form of source code are available at different sites on the Internet. You can download any of this software and install it on your system. Recent releases are often available in the form of compressed archive files. Applications will always be downloadable as compressed archives if an RPM version is not available. This is particularly true for the recent versions of GNOME or KDE packages. RPM packages are generated only intermittently.

Decompressing and Extracting Software in One Step

Although you can decompress and extract software in separate operations, you will find that the more common approach is to perform both actions with a single command. The **tar** utility provides decompression options you can use to have **tar** first decompress a file for you, invoking the specified decompression utility. The **z** option automatically invokes **gunzip** to unpack a **.gz** file, and the **j** option unpacks a **.bz2** file. Use the **Z** option for **.Z** files. For example, to combine the decompressing and unpacking operation for a **tar.gz** file into one **tar** command, insert a **z** option to the option list, **xzvf**. (See the later section "Extracting Software" for a discussion of these options.) The next example shows how you can combine decompression and extraction in one step:

```
tar xvzf antigrav_0.0.3.orig.tar.gz
```

For a **.bz2**-compressed archive, you use the **j** option instead of the **z** option:

```
tar xvjf antigrav_0.0.3.orig.tar.bz2
```

Decompressing Software Separately

Many software packages under development or designed for cross-platform implementation may not be in an RPM format. Instead, they may be archived and compressed. The filenames for these files end with the extension **.tar.gz**, **.tar.bz2**, or **.tar.Z**. The different extensions indicate different decompression methods using different commands: **gunzip** for **.gz**, **bunzip2** for **.bz2**, and **decompress** for **.Z**. In fact, most software with an RPM format also has a corresponding **.tar.gz** format. After you download such a package, you must first decompress it and then unpack it with the **tar** command. The compressed archives can hold either source code that you then need to compile or, as is the case with Java packages, binaries that are ready to run.

A *compressed archive* is an archive file created with **tar** and then compressed with a compression tool such as **gzip**. To install such a file, you must first decompress it with a decompression utility such as **gunzip** and then use **tar** to extract the files and directories making up the software package. Instead of the **gunzip** utility, you could also use `gzip-d`. The next example decompresses the **antigrav_0.0.3.orig.tar.gz** file, replacing it with a decompressed version called **antigrav_0.0.3.orig.tar**:

```
ls
 antigrav_0.0.3.orig.gz
gunzip antigrav_0.0.3.orig.tar.gz
ls
antigrav_0.0.3.orig.tar
```

You can download compressed archives from many different sites, including those mentioned previously. Downloads can be accomplished with FTP clients such as NcFTP and gFTP or with any Web browser. Once downloaded, any file that ends with **.Z**, **.bz2**, **.zip**, or **.gz** is a compressed file that must be decompressed.

For files ending with **.bz2**, you use the **bunzip2** command. The following example decompresses a **bz2** version:

```
ls
 antigrav_0.0.3.orig.tar.bz2
bunzip2 antigrav_0.0.3.orig.tar.bz2
ls
antigrav_0.0.3.orig.tar
```

Files ending with **.bin** are self-extracting archives. Run the **.bin** file as if it were a command. You may have to use **chmod** to make it executable.

Selecting an Install Directory

Before you unpack the archive, move it to the directory where you want to store it. Source code packages are often placed in a directory such as **/usr/local/src**, and binary packages go in designated directories. When source code files are unpacked, they generate their own subdirectories from which you can compile and install the software. Once the package is installed, you can delete this directory, keeping the original source code package file (**.tar.gz**).

Packages that hold binary programs ready to run, such as Java packages, are meant to be extracted in certain directories. Usually this is the **/usr/local** directory. Most archives, when they unpack, create a subdirectory named with the application name and its release, placing all those files or directories making up the software package into that subdirectory. For example, the file **antigrav_0.0.3.orig.tar** unpacks to a subdirectory called **antigrav_ 0.0.3.orig**. In certain cases, the software package that contains precompiled binaries is designed to unpack directly into the system subdirectory where it will be used.

Extracting Software

First, use **tar** with the **t** option to check the contents of the archive. If the first entry is a directory, then when you extract the archive, that directory is created and the extracted files are placed in it. If the first entry is not a directory, you should first create one and then copy the archive file to it. Then extract the archive within that directory. If no directory exists as the first entry, files are extracted to the current directory.

You must create a directory yourself to hold these files:

```
# tar tvf antigrav_0.0.3.orig.tar
```

Now you are ready to extract the files from the tar archive. You use **tar** with the **x** option to extract files, the **v** option to display the pathnames of files as they are extracted, and the **f** option, followed by the name of the archive file:

```
# tar xvf antigrav_0.0.3.orig.tar
```

You can also decompress and extract in one step using the **-z** option for **.gz** files and **-j** for **.bz2** files:

```
# tar xvzf antigrav_0.0.3.orig.tar.gz
```

The extraction process creates a subdirectory consisting of the name and release of the software. In the preceding example, the extraction created a subdirectory called **antigrav_ 0.0.3.orig**. You can change to this subdirectory and examine its files, such as the **README** and **INSTALL** files.

```
# cd antigrav_0.0.3.orig
```

Installation of your software may differ for each package. Instructions are usually provided along with an installation program. Be sure to consult the **README** and **INSTALL** files, if included. See the next section for information on how to create and install the application on your system.

Compiling Software

Some software may be in the form of source code that you need to compile before you can install it. This is particularly true of programs designed for cross-platform implementations. Programs designed to run on various Unix systems, such as Sun, as well as on Linux, may be distributed as source code that is downloaded and compiled in those different systems. Compiling such software has been greatly simplified in recent years by the use of configuration scripts that automatically detect a given system's hardware and software configuration and then allow you to compile the program accordingly. For example, the name of the C compiler on a system could be **gcc** or **cc**. Configuration scripts detect which is present and select it for use in the program compilation.

NOTE *Some software will run using scripting languages such as Python instead of programming language code such as C++. These may require only a setup operation (a* **setup** *command), not compiling. Once installed, they will run directly using the scripting language interpreter, such as Python.*

A configure script works by generating a customized makefile that is designed for that particular system. A makefile contains detailed commands to compile a program, including any preprocessing, links to required libraries, and the compilation of program components in their proper order. Many makefiles for complex applications may have to access several software subdirectories, each with separate components to compile. The use of configure and makefile scripts vastly automates the compile process, reducing the procedure to a few simple steps.

First, change to the directory where the software's source code has been extracted:

```
# cd /usr/local/src/antigrav_0.0.3.orig
```

> **NOTE** *Before you compile software, read the **README** or **INSTALL** files included with it. These give you detailed instructions on how to compile and install this particular program.*

Most software can be compiled and installed in three simple steps. The fist step is to issue the **./configure** command, which generates your customized makefile. The second step is to issue the **make** command, which uses a makefile in your working directory (in this case, the makefile you just generated with the **./configure** command) to compile your software. The final step also uses the **make** command, but this time with the **install** option. The makefile generated by the **./configure** command also contains instructions for installing the software on your system. Using the **install** option runs just those installation commands. To perform the installation, you have to be logged in as the root user, giving you the ability to add software files to system directories as needed. If the software uses configuration scripts, compiling and installing usually involves only the following three simple commands:

```
# ./configure
# make
# make install
```

In this example, the **./configure** command performs configuration detection. The **make** command performs the actual compiling, using a makefile script generated by the **./configure** operation. The **make install** command installs the program on your system, placing the executable program in a directory, such as **/usr/local/bin**, and any configuration files in **/etc**. Any shared libraries it created may go into **/usr/local/lib**.

Once you have compiled and installed your application, and you have checked that it is working properly, you can remove the source code directory that was created when you extracted the software. You can keep the archive file (**tar**) in case you need to extract the software again. Use **rm** with the **-rf** options so that all subdirectories will be deleted and you do not have to confirm each deletion.

> **TIP** *Be sure to remember to place the period and slash before the **configure** command. The **./** references a command in the current working directory, rather than another Linux command with the same name.*

Configure Command Options

Certain software may have specific options set up for the **./configure** operation. To find out what these are, use the **./configure** command with the **--help** option:

```
#  ./configure --help
```

A useful common option is the **-prefix** option, which lets you specify the install directory:

```
#  ./configure -prefix=/usr/bin
```

Tip *Some older X Window System applications use* **xmkmf** *directly instead of a configure script to generate the needed makefile. Although* **xmkmf** *has been officially replaced, in this case, enter the command* **xmkmf** *in place of* **./configure**. *Be sure to consult the* **INSTALL** *and* **README** *files for the software.*

Development Libraries

If you are compiling an X Window, GNOME, or KDE-based program, be sure their development libraries have been installed. For X Window applications, be sure the **xmkmf** program is also installed. If you chose a standard install when you installed your distribution system, these most likely were *not* installed. For distributions using RPM packages, these come in the form of a set of development RPM packages, usually with the word *development* or *develop* in their names. You need to install them using **rpm**. GNOME, in particular, has an extensive set of RPM packages for development libraries. Many X Window applications need special shared libraries. For example, some applications may need the **xforms** library or the **qt** library, some of which you must obtain from Web sites.

Shared and StaticLibraries

Libraries can be static, shared, or dynamic. A *static* library's code is incorporated into the program when it is compiled. A *shared* library's code, however, is loaded for access whenever the program is run. When compiled, such a program simply notes the libraries it needs. Then when the program is run, that library is loaded and the program can access its functions. A *dynamic* library is a variation on a shared library. Like a shared library, it can be loaded when the program is run. However, it does not actually load until instructions in the program tell it to do so. It can also be unloaded as the program runs, and another library can be loaded in its place. Shared and dynamic libraries make for much smaller code. Instead of a program including the library as part of its executable file, it needs only a reference to it.

Libraries made available on your system reside in the **/usr/lib** and **/lib** directories. The names of these libraries always begin with the prefix *lib* followed by the library name and a suffix. The suffix differs, depending on whether it is a static or shared library. A shared library has the extension **.so** followed by major and minor version numbers. A static library simply has the **.a** extension. A further distinction is made for shared libraries in the old **a.out** format. These have the extension **.sa**. The syntax for the library name is the following:

```
libname.so.major.minor
libname.a
```

The *name* can be any string, and it uniquely identifies a library. It can be a word, a few characters, or even a single letter. The name of the shared math library is **libm.so.5**, where the math library is uniquely identified by the letter *m* and the major version is *5*, and *libm.a* is the static math library. The name of the X Window library is **libX11.so.6**, where the X Window library is uniquely identified with the letters *X11* and its major version is *6*.

Most shared libraries are found in the **/usr/lib** and **/lib** directories. These directories are always searched first. Some shared libraries are located in special directories of their own. A listing of these is placed in the **/etc/ld.conf** configuration file. These directories will also be searched for a given library. By default, Linux first looks for shared libraries, and then static ones. Whenever a shared library is updated or a new one installed, you need to run the **ldconfig** command to update its entries in the **/etc/ld.conf** file as well as links to it (if you install from an RPM package, this is usually done for you).

Makefile File

If no configure script exists and the program does not use **xmkmf**, you may have to edit the software's makefile directly. Be sure to check the documentation for the software to see whether any changes must be made to the makefile. Only a few changes may be necessary, but more detailed changes require an understanding of C programming and how **make** works with it. If you successfully configure the makefile, you may have to enter only the **make** and **make install** commands. One possible problem is locating the development libraries for C and the X Window System. X libraries are in the **/usr/X11R6/lib** directory. Standard C libraries are located in the **/usr/lib** directory.

NOTE *The Subversion and the Concurrent Versions System (CVS) are software development methods that allow developers from remote locations to work on software stored on a central server. Subversion is an enhanced version of CVS, designed to replace it eventually. Like CVS, Subversion works with CVS repositories, letting you access software in much the same way. Subversion adds features such as better directory and file access as well as support for metadata information.*

Checking Software Package Digital Signatures

One very effective use for digital signatures is to verify that a software package has not been tampered with. A software package could be intercepted in transmission and some of its system-level files changed or substituted. Software packages from your distribution, as well as those by reputable GNU and Linux projects, are digitally signed. The signature provides modification digest information with which to check the integrity of the package. The digital signature may be included with the package file or posted as a separate file. To import a key that APT can use to check a software package, you use the **apt-key** command. APT will automatically check for digital signatures. To check the digital signature of a software package file that is not part of the APT repository system, you use the **gpg** command with the **--verify** option. These would include packages such as those made available as compressed archives, **.tar.gz**, whereas APT can check all DEB packages itself.

Importing Software Public Keys with apt-key

First, however, you will need to make sure that you have the signer's public key. The digital signature was encrypted with the software distributor's private key; that distributor is the signer. Once you have that signer's public key, you can check any data you receive from them. In the case of third-party software repositories, you have to install their public key. Once the key is installed, you do not have to install it again.

Ubuntu includes and installs its public keys with its distribution. For any packages on the Ubuntu repositories, the needed public keys are already installed and checked by APT automatically. For other sites, such as Wine (the Linux Windows emulator), you may need to download the public key from its site and install it (**http://winehq.org**). You may also have to add repository support to access its Ubuntu compatible software. The Wine public key is available from the **winhq.org** site, with the public key for Ubuntu located at **http://wine.budgetdedicated.com/apt/387EE263.gpg**. You could download the public key and then install it on your system with the **apt-key** command. The following downloads the Wine public key:

```
wget -q http://wine.budgetdedicated.com/apt/387EE263.gpg
```

Once the public key is downloaded, you can then use the **apt-key** command to install it for use by APT in software verification. Ubuntu uses the **apt-key** command to maintain public keys for software packages. Use the command with the **add** option to add the key:

```
sudo apt-key add 387EE263.gpg
```

To access the software repository, you would also have to install its APT configuration file in the **/etc/apt/sources.list.d** directory. For Wine, this is named **winehq.ist**. Check the Wine site for download instructions.

Checking Software Compressed Archives

Many software packages in the form of compressed archives, **.tar.gz** or **tar.bz2**, will provide signatures in separate files that end with the **.sig** extension. To check these, use the **gpg** command with the **--verify** option. For example, the most recent Sendmail package is distributed in the form of a compressed archive, **.tar.gz**. Its digital signature is provided in a separate **.sig** file. First you download and install the public key for Sendmail software obtained from the Sendmail Web site (the key may have the year as part of its name). Sendmail has combined all its keys into one armored text file, **PGPKEYS**. You can download and then import the key file with gpg.

```
gpg --import PGPKEYS
```

You can also use the **gpg** command with the **--search-key** and **--keyserver** options to import the key. Keys matching the search term will be displayed in a numbered list. You will be prompted to enter the number of the key you want. The 2007 Sendmail key that results from the following example would be 7. This is the key used for 2007 released software.

```
$ gpg  --keyserver pgp.mit.edu  --search-keys Sendmail
```

Instead of using **gpg** you could use the Encryptions and Password Keys application to find and import the key (choose Applications | Accessories | Encryption and Password Keys).

To check a software archive, **tar.gz** file, you also need to download its digital signature files. For the compressed archive (**.tar.gz**) you can use the **.sig** file ending in **.gz.sig**, and for the uncompressed archive use **.tar.sig**. Then, with the **gpg** command and the **--verify** option, use the digital signature in the **.sig** file to check the authenticity and integrity of the software compressed archive:

```
$ gpg --verify sendmail.8.14.2.tar.gz.sig sendmail.8.14.2.tar.gz
gpg: Signature made Wed 31 Oct 2007 08:23:07 PM PDT using RSA key ID 7093B841
gpg: Good signature from "Sendmail Signing Key/2007 <sendmail@Sendmail.ORG>"$
```

You can also specify just the signature file, and **gpg** will automatically search for and select a file of the same name, but without the **.sig** or **.asc** extension:

```
# gpg --verify sendmail.8.14.2.tar.gz.sig
```

In the future, when you download any software from the Sendmail site that uses this key, you simply have to perform the `--verify` operation. Bear in mind, though, that different software packages from the same site may use different keys. You will have to make sure that you have imported and signed the appropriate key for the software you are checking.

TIP   *You can use the* `--fingerprint` *option to check a key's validity if you wish. If you are confident that the key is valid, you can then sign it with the* `--sign-key` *command.*

PART

III

Desktops

GNOME

The GNU Network Object Model Environment, also known as *GNOME*, is a powerful and easy-to-use environment consisting primarily of a panel, a desktop, and a set of GUI tools with which program interfaces can be constructed. GNOME is designed to provide a flexible platform for the development of powerful applications. Currently, GNOME is supported by several distributions and is the primary interface for Ubuntu. GNOME is free and released under the GNU Public License.

The core components of the GNOME desktop consist of a panel for starting programs and desktop functionality. Other components normally found in a desktop, such as a file manager, Web browser, and window manager, are provided by GNOME-compliant applications. GNOME provides libraries of GNOME GUI tools that developers can use to create GNOME applications. Programs that use buttons, menus, and windows and that adhere to a GNOME standard are said to be *GNOME-compliant*.

Nautilus is the official file manager for the GNOME desktop. The GNOME desktop does not have its own window manager as KDE does. Instead, it uses any GNOME-compliant window manager. The Metacity window manager is bundled with the GNOME distribution.

You can find out more about GNOME at its Web site, **www.gnome.org**. The site provides online documentation, such as the GNOME User's Guide and FAQs, and also maintains extensive mailing lists for GNOME projects to which you can subscribe. The **www.gnomefiles .org** site provides a detailed software listing of current GNOME applications and projects. For detailed documentation check the GNOME documentation site at **http://library.gnome.org**. Documentation is organized by Users, Administrators, and Developers. The "Desktop Users Guide" provides a complete tutorial on desktop use. For administrators, the "GNOME Desktop System Administration Guide" details how administrators can manage user desktops. The "Desktop Administrators' Guide to GNOME Lockdown and Preconfiguration" shows how administrators can control access to tasks such as printing or saving files. Table 8-1 offers a listing of useful GNOME sites.

GNOME 2.22 Features

Check **www.gnome.org** for a detailed description of GNOME features and enhancements, with screen shots and references. GNOME releases new versions on a frequent schedule. Several versions since the 2.0 release have added many new capabilities. GNOME now has efficiencies in load time and memory use, making for a faster response time. Desktop search

Web Sites	Descriptions
gnome.org	Official GNOME Web site
developer.gnome.org	GNOME developer Web site
art.gnome.org	Desktop themes and background art
gnomefiles.org	GNOME software applications, applets, and tools
live.gnome.org/GnomeOffice	GNOME office applications
library.gnome.org	GNOME documentation Web site for Users, Administrators, and Developers

TABLE 8-1   GNOME Resources

is integrated into the file chooser dialog. For laptops, power management has been improved along with battery monitoring. For developers, a new version of the GTK+ toolkit provides better documentation and improved development tools. With GNOME 2.22, the GNOME Virtual File System (GVFS) provides direct file manager support for virtual file systems, letting you access Samba shares and FTP sites directly.

Some GNOME features added since version 2.0 are described in the following sections.

GNOME Desktop Features

Following are new desktop features:

- File Roller can now work on archives on networked systems. You can also copy and paste or drag-and-drop files between archives.
- For right-to-left languages, window, menu, and workspace components are now mirrored, also positioned right-to-left.
- The GNOME documentation site at **http://library.gnome.org** organizes documentation into Users, Administrators, and Developers sections.
- An easy-to-use file permissions dialog allows changing permissions for all files in a folder.
- Basic window compositing is provided using drop shadows, live previews, and transparency effects. Support is included for 3-D effects for windows in the Appearance Visual Effects tab (wobble, shrink, and explode).
- Home directories now have data-specific folders set up including Pictures, Documents, Videos, and Music. GNOME applications may use these as defaults.
- With the GNOME Volume Manager, a computer window is now included, listing your file system devices, including CD-ROMs as well as network file system devices.
- GNOME automatically mounts removable devices at the **/media** directory.

GNOME Applications

The following applications are included:

- The Cheese application manages Web cam photos. For image collections, enhanced browsing is available.

- The GNOME video player, Totem, supports Web access, digital video broadcast (DVB), and DVD. It also provides YouTube and MythTV support.

- Tomboy note taker can now synchronize your notes from different computers. Connecting to a central server, all your notes from different systems can be integrated and synchronized, providing a single set of notes for all your systems.

- The International Clock applet is now used for the time applet on the top panel. It lets you see the time and weather at any location on the planet.

- GNOME sound and video applications can now prompt the user to search for any needed codecs. The mechanism for finding and installing the codec is handled separately by the codec wizard.

- The Disk Usage Analyzer (Accessories | Disk Usage Analyzer) details disk and partition usage, as well as usage by directory, with totals for your entire file systems with space availability.

- GEdit has been reworked to adhere to the Multiple Documentation Interface specs. It now has a new syntax highlighting system for script languages such as PHP, Ruby, and HTML.

- The Vinagre remote desktop viewer lets you access desktops remotely (see Chapter 5).

GNOME Administration Features

Administration features include the following:

- Appearance administrative preferences integrates Theme, Background, Fonts, Interface, and Visual Effects into five tabs in the Appearance Preferences window.

- Seahorse integrates GPG encryption, decryption, and signing of files and text (Applications | Accessories | Passwords And Encryption Keys. For Seahorse configuration, choose System | Preferences | Keyrings And Encryption).

- Integrates PolicyKit controls for GNOME administration tools such as **network-admin** and **users-admin**.

- User Profile Editor (Sabayon) allows administrators to create and manage user profiles on either a current or a remote system. Profiles can contain personal information as well as application preferences, including OpenOffice.

- Integrated power management is controlled with Power Management Preferences.

- The Preferred Applications control panel now has an Accessibility tab with visual and mobility options.

- The GNOME Control Center for basic preferences is integrated into Ubuntu as menus items in the System | Preferences menu. You can also start up the GNOME Control Center directly by entering **gnome-control-center** in a terminal window.

- Mouse accessibility options supporting different kinds of clicks is now integrated with the Mouse Preferences tool.

- The menu editor, Alacarte, lets you customize your menus easily.

- The disk usage analyzer, Baobab, lets you quickly see how much disk space is used.

- For developers, the Anjuta Integrated Development Environment (IDE) provides integrated access to debuggers, Glade UI editor, and Valgrind analysis.

PART III

GNOME File Manager Features

Nautilus is the official file manager for the GNOME desktop. You can find out more about Nautilus from the Nautilus user's manual that is part of the GNOME User's Guide at **www.gnome.org**. The Nautilus file manager, as part of GNOME, also has several new features added:

- Nautilus File manager now includes a disk usage chart when displaying properties for file systems. Images are displayed with their appropriate orientation using Exchangeable Image File (EXIF) camera information.

- Nautilus is now more integrated into other applications such as File Roller for archives, the image viewer for pictures, and the GNOME media player for audio and video. You can now preview sound and video files within a Nautilus window.

- Nautilus uses GNOME Virtual File System (GVFS) for remote file systems, which replaces GnomeVFS. GVFS uses the GO object-based abstraction layer for I/O (GIO). With GVFS, Nautilus can support FUSE user-based file system access. Applications no longer have to be written for GVFS access. Any application can access a GVFS-mounted file system.

- With GVFS, Nautilus now manages automounts for remote file systems. Access is stateful, requiring the user input a password only once, before granting continual access.

- Nautilus can burn files and ISO images to DVD/CD writers.

- Context-sensitive menus let you perform appropriate actions, such as extracting archive files. An Open With option lets you choose from a selection of appropriate applications. Multiple applications can now be registered for use with a file.

- The file manager can display network shares on local networks, using DNS-based service discovery. The file manager also supports access to password-protected FTP sites.

- The file manager can display audio tracks on music CDs with the **cdda://** protocol and access connected digital cameras with the **gphoto2://** protocol.

GTK+

GTK+ is the widget set used for developing GNOME applications. Its look and feel was originally derived from Motif, the widget set was designed from the ground up for power and flexibility. For example, buttons can have labels, images, or any combination thereof. Objects can be dynamically queried and modified at runtime. GTK+ also includes a theme engine that enables users to change the look and feel of applications using these widgets. At the same time, the GTK+ widget set remains small and efficient.

The GTK+ widget set is entirely free under the Lesser General Public License (LGPL). The LGPL enables developers to use the widget set with proprietary software, as well as free software (the GPL would restrict it to just free software). The widget set also features an extensive set of programming language bindings. Internalization is fully supported, permitting GTK+-based applications to be used with other character sets, such as those in Asian languages. The drag-and-drop functionality supports drag-and-drop operations with other widget sets that support these protocols, such as Qt.

The GNOME Interface

The Ubuntu GNOME interface consists of two panels and a desktop, as shown in Figure 8-1. The top panel holds menus, programs, applet icons (an *applet* is a small program that can be launched from the panel), and notification icons such as the user name, date and time, and the clock. You'll also see several menus, which you can click to see entries for commands and applications you can run on your desktop. You can display panels horizontally or vertically or hide them to show you a full screen. The Applications menu is reserved for applications. Other tasks, such as opening a home directory window or logging out, are located in the Places menu. The System menu holds the Preferences submenu for configuring your GNOME interface, as well as the Administration submenu for accessing the distribution administrative tools. The bottom panel offers interactive features for workspaces and docking applications.

The remainder of the interface is the desktop, where you can place directories, files, and programs. You can create them on the desktop directly or drag them from a file manager window. You can use the drag-and-drop operation to move a file from one window to another or to the desktop. A drag-and-drop with the CTRL key held down will copy a file. A drag-and-drop operation with the middle mouse button (two buttons at once on a two-button mouse) enables you to create links on the desktop to installed programs. Initially, the desktop holds only an icon for your home directory. Clicking it opens a file manager window to that directory. A right-click anywhere on the desktop displays a desktop menu with which you can open new windows and create new folders.

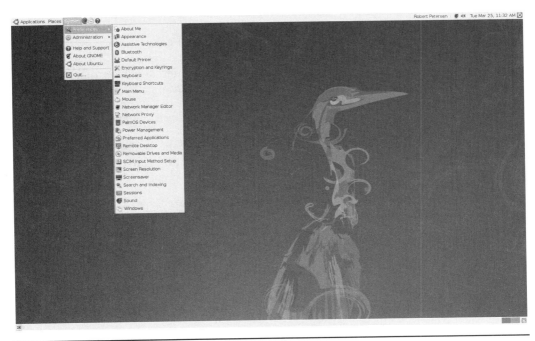

Figure 8-1   GNOME interface showing Preferences submenu

Tip *You can display your GNOME desktop using different themes that change the appearance of desktop objects such as windows, buttons, and scroll bars. GNOME functionality is not affected in any way. You can choose from a variety of themes. Many are posted on the Internet at **http://art.gnome.org**. Technically referred to as GTK themes, these allow the GTK widget set to change its look and feel. To select a theme, choose System | Preferences | Appearance and open the Theme tab.*

GNOME Components

From a user's point of view, the GNOME interface has four components: the desktop, the panels, the main menus, and the file manager. You can display two panels—one used for menus, application icons, and running applets at the top of the screen, and another at the bottom of the screen used primarily for managing your windows and desktop spaces. In its standard default configuration for Ubuntu, the GNOME desktop will display nothing. If you have any removable media, such as CD/DVD discs or attached partitions, icons for those will be displayed.

In addition to menus and items already mentioned, the top panel has icons for the Mozilla Firefox Web browser (globe with fox) and the Evolution mail tool (envelope). At the far right are the time and date icons. An update button will appear if updates are available. You can use the update button to update your system automatically.

The bottom panel holds icons for minimized windows as well as running applets and the trash can. These include a Workspace Switcher (the colored squares) at the right. An icon on the left lets you minimize all your open windows. When you open a window, a corresponding button for it will be displayed in the lower panel, which you can use to minimize and restore the window size. Click the trash can icon on the far right side of the bottom panel to empty deleted files stored there.

Your home directory, as well as any partitions, removable media, and remote file systems, can be accessed from entries on the Places menu on the top panel. If you want an icon for an item displayed on your desktop, right-click the item in the Places menu and choose Add To Desktop. To add the computer icon to the desktop, you would open the Places menu, right-click Computer, and select Add This Launcher To The Desktop. You can do the same for Network, which will show just your remote directories and devices. The home directory icon cannot be added to the desktop.

To start a program, you can select its entry from the Applications menu. You can also click its application icon in the panel (if one appears) or drag-and-drop a data file to its icon. To add an icon for an application to the desktop, right-click its name in the Applications menu and choose Add This Launcher To The Desktop.

Quitting GNOME

To quit GNOME, choose System | Quit. This displays a dialog with two rows of buttons: on top, Logout, Lock Screen, and Switch User buttons, and on the bottom are Suspend, Hibernate, Restart, and Shut Down buttons. The Logout button quits GNOME, returning you to the login window. The Shut Down button shuts down the system. The Restart button shuts down and reboots your system. A Cancel button lets you return to the desktop.

GNOME Help

The GNOME Help browser (Yelp) provides a browser-like interface for displaying the GNOME user's manual, man pages, and info documents (see Chapter 3). To access help, choose System | Help And Support. You'll see a toolbar that enables you to move through the list of previously viewed documents. You can even bookmark specific items. A browser interface lets you to use links to connect to different documents. On the main page, expandable links for several GNOME desktop topics are displayed on left side, with entries for the GNOME User Manual and Administration Guide on the right. At the bottom of the left side listing are links you can click to access the man and info pages. Use the Search box to locate help documents. Special URL-like protocols are supported for the different types of documents: **ghelp** for GNOME help; **man** for man pages; and **info** for the info documents: so, for example, **man:fstab** would display the man page for the **fstab** file.

The GNOME Help browser provides a detailed manual on every aspect of your GNOME interface. The left-hand links display GNOME categories for different application categories such as the System tools and GNOME applets. The GNOME Applets entry provides detailed descriptions of all available GNOME applets. Applications categories such as Internet, Programming, System Tools, and Sound and Video will provide help documents for applications developed as part of the GNOME project, such as the Evolution mail client, the Totem movie player, the Disk Usage Analyzer, and the GNOME System Monitor. Click the Desktop entry at the top of the left-hand list to display links for GNOME User and Administration manuals.

The GNOME Desktop

The GNOME desktop (Figure 8-1) provides all the capabilities of GUI-based operating systems. You can drag-and-drop files, applications, and directories to the desktop, and then drag-and-drop them back to GNOME-compliant applications. If the desktop stops functioning, you can restart it by starting the GNOME file manager (Nautilus). The desktop is actually a back-end process in the GNOME file manager, but you needn't have the file manager open to use the desktop.

NOTE   *As an alternative to using the desktop, you can drag-and-drop any program, file, or directory to the top panel and use the icons from the panel instead.*

Drag-and-Drop Files to the Desktop

Any icon for an item that you drag-and-drop from a file manager window to the desktop also appears on the desktop. However, the default drag-and-drop operation is a **move** operation. If you select a file in your file manager window and drag it to the desktop, you are actually moving the file from its current directory to the GNOME desktop directory, which is located in your home directory and holds all items on the desktop. For GNOME, the desktop directory is **DESKTOP**. In the case of dragging directory folders to the desktop, the entire directory and its subdirectories will be moved to the GNOME desktop directory. To remove an icon from the desktop, you drag-and-drop it in the trash.

You can also copy a file to your desktop by pressing the CTRL key and then clicking and dragging it from a file manager window to your desktop. You will see a small arrow in the upper-right corner of the copied icon change to a + symbol, indicating that you are creating a copy instead of moving the original.

CAUTION *Be careful when removing icons from the desktop. If you have moved the file to the desktop, its original file resides in the **DESKTOP** folder, and if you remove it you are erasing the original. If you have copied or linked the original, you can simply delete the link or the copy; the original will still exist in its original folder. When you drag applications from the menu or panel to the desktop, you are creating a copy of the application launcher button in the **DESKTOP** directory. These you can safely remove.*

You can also create a link on the desktop to any file. This is useful if you want to keep a single version in a specified directory and be able to access it from the desktop. You can also use links for customized programs that you may not want to appear on a menu or panel. You can create a link in two ways: While holding down the CTRL and SHIFT keys (CTRL-SHIFT), drag the file to where you want the link created. A copy of the icon appears with a small arrow in the right corner indicating it is a link. You can click this link to start the program, open the file, or open the directory, depending on the type of file to which you linked. Alternatively, first click and drag the file out of the window, and after moving the file but before releasing the mouse button, press the ALT key. This will display a pop-up menu with selections for Cut, Copy, and Link. Select the Link option to create a link.

GNOME's drag-and-drop file operation works on virtual desktops provided by the GNOME Workspace Switcher. The GNOME Workspace Switcher on the bottom panel creates icons for each virtual desktop in the panel, along with task buttons for any applications open on them.

NOTE *Although the GNOME desktop supports drag-and-drop operations, these normally work only for applications that are GNOME-compliant. You can drag any items from a GNOME-compliant application to your desktop, and vice versa.*

Applications on the Desktop

In some cases, you'll want to create another way on the desktop to access a file without moving it from its original directory. You can do this either by using a GNOME application launcher button or by creating a link to the original program. Application launcher buttons are the GNOME components used in menus and panels to display and access applications.To place an application icon on your desktop, you can simply drag-and-drop the application button from the panel or a menu to the desktop. For example, to place an icon for the Firefox Web browser on your desktop, just drag the Firefox icon from the top panel to anywhere on your desktop space.

For applications that are not on the panel or in a menu, you can create either an application launcher button or a direct link for it. To create an application launcher, right-click the desktop background to display the desktop menu (as discussed next), and then choose Create Launcher.

GNOME Desktop Menu

You can right-click anywhere on the empty desktop to display the GNOME desktop menu that includes entries for common tasks, such as creating an application launcher, creating a new folder, or organizing the icon display. Keep in mind that the New Folder entry creates a new directory on your desktop, specifically in your GNOME desktop directory (**DESKTOP**), not your home directory. The entries for this menu are listed in Table 8-2.

Menu Item	Description
Create Launcher	Creates a new desktop icon for an application
Create Folder	Creates a new directory on your desktop within your **DESKTOP** directory
Create Document	Creates files using installed templates
Clean Up By Name	Arranges your desktop icons
Keep Aligned	Aligns your desktop icons
Cut, Copy, Paste	Cuts, copies, or pastes files, letting you move or copy files between folders
Change Desktop Background	Opens a Background Preferences dialog to let you select a new background for your desktop

TABLE 8-2   GNOME Desktop Menu Items

Window Manager

GNOME works with any window manager. However, desktop functionality, such as drag-and-drop capabilities and the GNOME Workspace Switcher (discussed later in the chapter), works only with window managers that are GNOME-compliant. The current release of GNOME uses the Metacity window manager. It is completely GNOME-compliant and is designed to integrate with the GNOME desktop without any duplication of functionality.

For 3-D support you can use compositing window manager support provided by Compiz Fusion (Ubuntu main repository). Windows are displayed using window decorators, allowing windows to wobble, bend, and move in unusual ways. They employ features similar to current Mac and Windows Vista desktops. A compositing window manager support relies on a graphics card OpenGL 3-D acceleration support. Be sure your graphics card is supported. Compiz Fusion is a merger of Compiz and Beryl compositing window managers. Beryl was developed from Compiz and features its own window decorators. See **http://compiz.org** and **http://beryl-project.org** for more information.

To enable Compiz-fusion effects, you use the Appearance preferences tool, and select the Visual Effects panel (System | Appearance, Visual Effects). On this panel, select the Extra entry.

Metacity employs much the same window operations used on other window managers. You can resize a window by clicking any of its sides or corners and dragging. You can move the window by clicking-and-dragging its title bar. You can also right-click and drag any border to move the window, as well as ALT-click anywhere on the window. The upper-right corner of the GNOME window shows the Maximize, Minimize, and Close buttons. Clicking Minimize creates a button for the window in the panel that you can click to restore it. You can right-click the title bar of a window to display a window menu with entries for window operations. These include workspace entries to move the window to another workspace (virtual desktop) or to all workspaces, which displays the window no matter to what workspace you move.

GNOME Desktop Preferences

You can configure different parts of your GNOME interface using tools listed in System |
Preferences, where Ubuntu also provides several tools for configuring your GNOME
desktop. The GNOME preferences are shown in Table 8-3. Several are discussed in different
sections in this and other chapters. The Help button on each preference window will display
detailed descriptions and examples. Some of the more important tools are discussed here.

The keyboard shortcuts configuration (Keyboard Shortcuts) lets you map keys to certain
tasks, such as mapping multimedia keys on a keyboard to media tasks such as play and
pause. Just select the task and then press the key. You'll find tasks for the desktop,
multimedia, and window management. With window management, you can also map keys
to perform workspace switching. Keys that are already assigned will be shown.

The Windows configuration (Windows) is where you can enable features such as
window roll-up, window movement key, and mouse window selection.

The Mouse and Keyboard preferences are the primary tools for configuring your mouse
and keyboard (Mouse). The Mouse preferences let you choose a mouse image, and configure
its motion and hand orientation. The Keyboard preferences window shows several panels for
selecting your keyboard model (Layout), configuring keys (Layout Options), repeat delay
(Keyboard), and even enforcing breaks from power typing as a health precaution.

To select a sound driver to use for different tasks, as well as specify the sounds to use for
desktop events, you use the Sound Preferences tool (Sound). On the Devices tab, you can
select the sound driver to use, if more than one, for the Sound Events, Music and Videos,
and conferencing. Defaults will already be chosen. On the Sounds tab you can enable
software sound mixing, choosing the sound you want for different desktop events. The
System Beep tab lets you turn off the system beep sound and use visual beep instead, such
as a flashing window title bar.

Appearance

Several appearance-related configuration tasks have been combined into the Appearance
tool. These include Themes, Background, Fonts, Interfaces, and Visual Effects. To change
your theme or background image, or configure your fonts, use the Appearance tool (System |
Preferences | Appearance). The Appearance window shows five tabs: Theme, Background,
Fonts, Interface, and Visual Effects (see Figure 8-2). The Background tab was discussed in
Chapter 3. The Theme and Fonts tabs are covered in the following sections. The Interface tab
lets you modify the appearance of toolbar and menu items, whether to display icons and
where to display text. A preview section shows how menus and toolbar items will appears
depending on your choices. The Visual Effects tab lets you choose the level of desktop effects
ranging from just a simple display to full for 3-D effects for windows (wobble, shrink, and
explode).

Desktop Themes

Themes control your desktop appearance. Use the Themes tab on the Appearance
Preferences dialog to select or customize a theme from a list of icons for currently installed
themes (see Figure 8-3). The icons show key aspects or each theme such as window, folder,
and button images, in effect previewing the theme for you. The Ubuntu theme is initially
selected. You can move through the icons to select a different theme if you wish. If you have

Preferences	Description
About Me	Set and edit personal information such as image, addresses, and password
Appearance	Set desktop appearance configuration: themes, fonts, backgrounds, and interface
Assistive Technologies	Enable features such as accessible login and keyboard screen
Bluetooth	Set Bluetooth notification icon display
Default Printer	Choose a default printer if more than one
Encryption and Keyrings	Configure Seahorse encryption management
Keyboard	Configure your keyboard: selecting options, models, and typing breaks, as well as accessibility features such as repeating, slow, and sticking, and mouse keys setup
Keyboard Shortcuts	Configure keys for special tasks such as multimedia operations
Main Menu	Add or remove categories and menu items for the Applications and System menus
Mouse	Configure mouse: select hand orientation, mouse image, and motion
Network Manager Editor	Manage wireless connections
Network Proxy	Configure proxy if needed: manual or automatic
Power Management	Set power management options for battery use and sleep options
Preferred Applications	Set default Web browser, mail application, and terminal window
Remote Desktop	Allow remote users to view or control your desktop; can control access with password
Removable Drives And Media	Set removable drives and media preferences
SCIM Input Method Setup	Specify custom input methods for keyboard
Screen Resolution	Change screen resolution, refresh rate, and screen orientation
Screensaver	Select and manage screen saver
Seahorse Preferences	Manage encryption key
Search And Indexing	Set search and indexing preferences for desktop searches
Sessions	Manage your session with startup programs and save options (see "Sessions" later in this chapter)
Sound	Select sound driver for events, video and music, and conferencing; select sounds to use for desktop events
Windows	Enable certain window capabilities such as roll-up on title bar, movement key, window selection

TABLE 8-3   GNOME Desktop Preferences

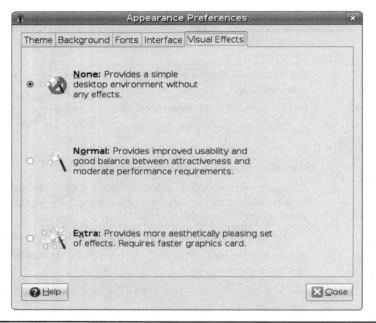

Figure 8-2   Appearance Visual Effects tab

downloaded additional themes from sites such as **http://art.gnome.org**, you can click the Install button to locate and install them. Once installed, the additional themes will also be displayed in the Theme tab. If you download and install a theme or icon set from the Ubuntu repository, it will be automatically installed for you.

TIP   *If you are downloading from **http://art.gnome.org**, you can drag-and-drop the download icon from the Web page directly to the Theme tab, or download first and drop the theme package directly to the Theme tab to install.*

The true power of themes is shown in its ability to let users customize any theme. Themes are organized into three components: controls, window border, and icons. Controls covers the appearance of window and dialog controls such as buttons and slider bars. Window border specifies how title bars, borders, window buttons are displayed. Icons specify how all icons used on the desktop are displayed, whether on the file manager, desktop, or the panel. You can actually mix and match components from any installed theme to create your own theme. You can even download and install separate components such as specific icon sets, which you can then use in a customized theme.

Clicking the Customize button opens a Themes Details window with tabs for different theme components. The components used for the current theme are selected by default. An additional Color tab lets you set the background and text colors for windows, input boxes, and selected items. In the Control, Window Border, and Icon tabs you will see listings

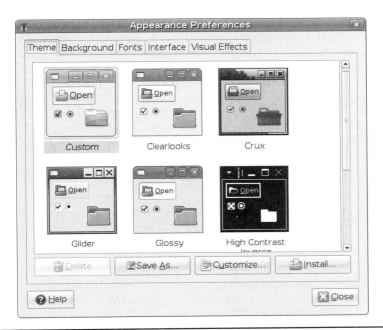

FIGURE 8-3   Selecting GNOME themes

of different themes. You can then mix and match different components from those themes, creating your own customized theme. Upon selecting a component, your desktop will automatically change to display your choices. If you have added a component, such as a new icon set, it will also be shown.

One you have created a new customized theme, a Custom Theme icon will appear in the list on the Theme tab. To save the customized theme, click the Save As button. This opens a dialog where you can enter the theme name, any notes, and specify whether you also want to keep the theme background.

Themes and icons installed directly by a user are placed in the **.themes** and **.icons** directories in the user's home directory. Should you want these themes made available for all users, you can move them from the **.themes** and **.icons** directories to the **/usr/share/icons** and **/usr/share/themes** directories. Be sure to log in as the root user. You then need to change ownership of the moved themes and icons to the root user:

```
chown -R root:root  /usr/share/themes/newtheme
```

Fonts
Ubuntu uses the **fontconfig** method for managing fonts (**http://fontconfig.org/wiki**). You can easily change font sizes, add new fonts, and configure features such as anti-aliasing. Both GNOME and KDE provide tools for selecting, resizing, and adding fonts.

Resizing Desktop Fonts With very large monitors and their high resolutions becoming more common, one feature users find helpful is the ability to increase the desktop font sizes. On a large widescreen monitor, resolutions less than the native one tend not to scale well. A monitor always looks best in its native resolution. However, with a large native resolution such as 1900×1200, text sizes become so small they are hard to read. You can overcome this issue by increasing the font size. The default size is 10; increasing it to 12 makes text in all desktop features such as windows and menus much more readable.

To increase the font size, choose System | Preferences | Appearance and select the Fonts tab (Figure 8-4). You can change the existing font itself as well. You can further refine your fonts display by clicking the Details button to open a window where you can set features such as the dots-per-inch, hinting, and smoothing. To examine a font in more detail, click the Go To Fonts Folder button and click the font.

Adding Fonts To add fonts you open the font viewer by entering the **fonts:/** URL in any file manager window. Click the Location bar toggle to switch to a text-based location bar. In the Location bar text box you can then enter the **fonts://** URL. Once the font viewer is open, you can add a font by simply dragging it to the font viewer window. When you restart, your font will be available for use. Fonts that are Zip archived should first be opened with the Archive manager and can then be dragged from the archive manager to the font viewer. To remove a font, right-click it in the font viewer and select Move To Trash or Delete.

User fonts will be installed to a user's **.fonts** directory. Fonts to be available to all users must be installed in the **/usr/share/fonts** directory, which makes them *system* fonts. Numerous

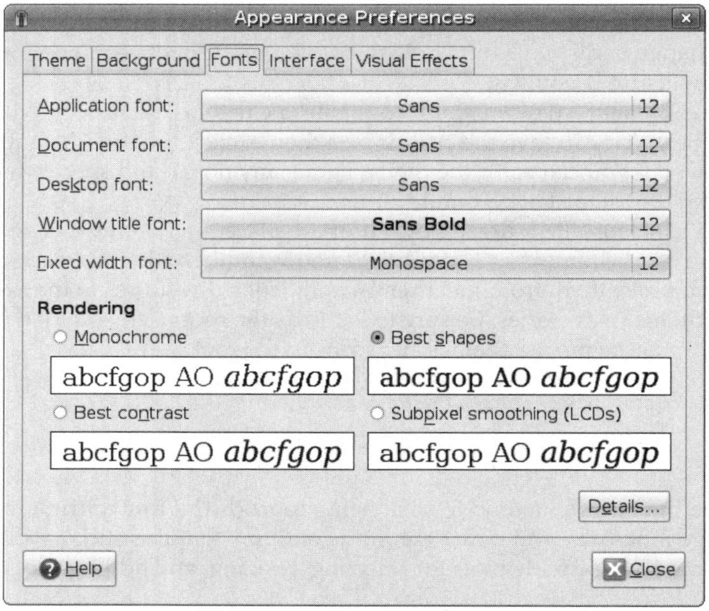

FIGURE 8-4 Manage Fonts, Appearance tool

font packages are available on the Ubuntu repositories. When you install the font packages, the fonts are automatically installed on your system and ready for use. Microsoft TrueType fonts are available from the **msttcorefonts** package (multiverse repository). Many TrueType font packages begin with **ttf-** prefix.

You can also manually install fonts yourself by dragging fonts to the font directory. On GNOME, you must copy fonts manually to the **/usr/share/fonts** directory (with the `sudo` command). If your system has installed both GNOME and KDE, you can install system fonts using KDE (Konqueror file manager) and they will be available on GNOME as well. For dual-boot systems, where Windows is installed as one of the operating systems, you can copy fonts directly from the Windows font directory on the Windows partition (which is mounted automatically in **/media**) to the **fonts:/System** or **fonts:/** window (**/usr/share/fonts** or **.fonts**).

Configuring Fonts   To refine your font display, you can use the *font rendering tool*. Choose System | Preferences | Appearance, and open the Fonts tab. In the Font Rendering section are basic font rendering features such as Monochrome, Best Contrast, Best Shapes, and Subpixel Smoothing. Choose the one that works best. For LCD monitors, choose Subpixel Smoothing. For detailed configuration, click the Details button. Here you can set Smoothing, Hinting (anti-aliasing), and Subpixel color order features. The sub-pixel color order is hardware dependent.

On GNOME, clicking a font entry in the Fonts Preferences tool will open a Pick A Font dialog that lists all available fonts. You can also generate a list by using the `fc-list` command. The list will be unsorted, so you should pipe it first to the `sort` command:

```
fc-list | sort
```

You can use `fc-list` with any font name or name pattern to search for fonts, with options to search by language, family, or styles. See the **/etc/share/fontconfig** documentation for more details.

Sessions

You can configure your desktop to restore your previously opened windows and applications as well as specify startup programs. When you log out, you may want the windows you have open and the applications you have running to be automatically started when you log back in. In effect, you are saving your current session so that it can be restored when you log in again. For example, if you are working on a spreadsheet, you can save your work, but not close the file, and then log out. When you log back in, your spreadsheet will open automatically where you left off.

Saving sessions is not turned on by default. To save sessions, choose System | Preferences | Sessions to open the Session Preferences dialog (Figure 8-5) and then open the Session Options tab. You can save your current session manually or have all your sessions saved automatically when you log out, restoring them whenever you log in.

You can also use the Sessions Preferences dialog to select programs that you want started up automatically. Some are already selected, such as the Software Updater and NetworkManager. On the Startup Programs tab, you can select programs you want started and deselect those you don't want.

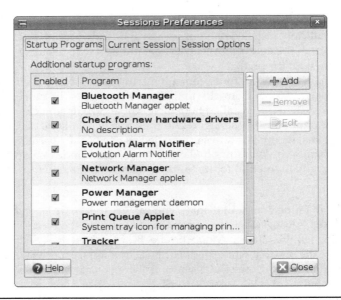

FIGURE 8-5   GNOME Sessions Preferences

The GNOME File Manager: Nautilus

Nautilus is the GNOME file manager that supports the standard features for copying, removing, and deleting items as well as setting permissions and displaying items. It also provides enhancements such as zooming capabilities, user levels, and theme support. You can enlarge or reduce the size of your file icons; select from Novice, Intermediate, or Expert levels of use; and customize the look and feel of Nautilus with different themes. Nautilus also lets you set up customized views of file listings, enabling you to display images for directory icons and run component applications within the file manager window. Nautilus implements a spatial approach to file browsing: a new window is opened for each new folder.

For GNOME 2.22, Nautilus is based on the GVFS, which allows any application to access a virtually mounted file system. File systems mounted with FUSE, the user base file systems access, will be displayed and accessed by Nautilus.

Home Folder Subdirectories

Ubuntu uses the Common User Directory Structure (**xdg-user-dirs** at **http://freedesktop.org**) to set up subdirectories such as **Music** and **Video** in the user home directory. Folders will include **Documents**, **Music**, **Pictures**, and **Videos**. These localized user directories are used as defaults by many desktop applications. Users can change their directory names or place them within other directories using the GNOME file browser. For example, **Music** can be moved into **Documents**: **Documents/Music**. Local configuration is held in the **.config/user-dirs.dirs** file. System-wide defaults are set up in the **/etc/xdg/user-dirs.defaults** file.

Nautilus Window

Nautilus was designed as a desktop shell in which different components can be employed to add functionality. For example, within Nautilus, a Web browser can be executed to provide Web browser capabilities in a Nautilus file manager window. An image viewer can display images. The GNOME media player can run sound and video files. The GNOME File Roller tool can archive files as well as extract them from archives. With the implementation of GStreamer, multimedia tools such as the GNOME audio recorder are now more easily integrated into Nautilus.

When you click the folder for your home directory on your desktop, a file manager window opens showing your home directory. Two methods are used for displaying a folder: *browser* and *spatial*. Ubuntu uses the browser method by default. The Browser window displays several components, including a browser toolbar, a Location bar, and a side pane, commonly found on most traditional file managers (see Figure 8-6). The rest of the window is divided into two panes. The side pane is used to display information about the current working directory. The main window displays the list of files and subdirectories in the current working directory. A status bar at the bottom of the window displays information about a selected file or directory. You can turn any of these elements on or off by selecting their entries in the View menu.

When you open a new directory from a Browser view window, the same window is used to display it, and you can use the Back and Forward arrows to move through previously opened directories. In the Location bar, you can enter the pathname for a directory to move directly to it. To the right of the Location bar (box or button) are magnifying glass icons for zooming out and in the view of the files. Click the minus (–) magnifying glass icon to zoom out and the plus (+) icon to zoom in. Next to the zoom elements is a drop-down menu for selecting the different views for your files, such as icons, small icons, or details.

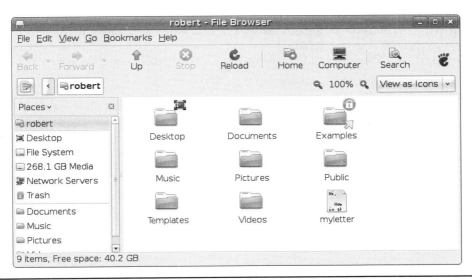

FIGURE 8-6   File Browser view, Nautilus file manager window

Though the Browser view mode is the default for Ubuntu, you can also enable the Spatial view. The Spatial view provides a streamlined display with no toolbars or sidebar. Much of its functionality has been moved to menus and pop-up windows, leaving more space to display files and folders. If you want to use the spatial method for viewing folders, you need to change the file manager behavior preferences. Open any folder and choose Edit | Preferences to open the File Manger Preferences dialog. In the Behavior tab, deselect the entry Always Open In Browser Window. The file manager will then open a new window for each subdirectory you choose. A directory window will show only the menus for managing files and the icons (see Figure 8-7). An information bar at the bottom displays information about the directory or selected files. The menu entries provide the full range of tasks involved in managing your files. On the lower-left is a pop-up menu to access parent directories. The name of the currently displayed directory is shown here.

TIP *To use the Browser view for a particular folder while using the Spatial view, right-click the folder's icon and choose Browser Folder. This will open that folder with the enhanced format. Also, you can select a folder and then choose File | Browser View.*

Nautilus Side Pane: Tree, History, and Notes

The Nautilus sidebar offers several different views you can select from a drop-down menu to display additional information about files and directories: Places, Information, Tree, History, and Notes. The Places view shows file system locations that you would normally access, starting with your home directory. Selecting the File System location places you at top of the file system, letting you move to any accessible part of it. The Information view displays detailed information about the current directory or selected file.

The Tree view displays a tree-based hierarchical view of the directories and files on your system, highlighting the one you have currently selected. You can use this tree to move to other directories and files. The tree maps all the directories on your system, starting from the root directory. You can expand or shrink any directory by clicking the plus or minus symbol to the left of its name. Select a directory by clicking the directory name. The contents of that directory are then displayed. The History view shows previous files or directories you have accessed; this is handy for moving back and forth between directories or files.

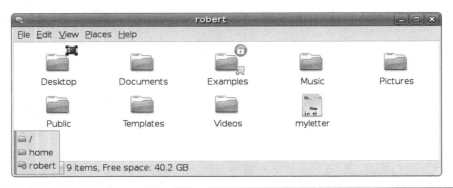

FIGURE 8-7   Spatial view, Nautilus window

The Notes view displays notes you have entered about an item or directory. The Notes view opens an editable text window within the side pane. To add a note for a particular item, such as an image or sound file, just double-click the item to display or run it, and then select the Note view and type your note. You can also right-click the item and choose Preferences, from which you can click a Notes tab. After you have added a note, you will see a note image added to the item's icon in the Nautilus window.

Displaying Files and Folders

You can view a directory's contents as icons or as a detailed list. You use the pop-up menu located on the right side of the Location bar. The View As List view provides the name, permissions, size, date, owner, and group. Buttons are displayed for each field across the top of the main panel. You can use these buttons to sort the lists according to that field. For example, to sort the files by date, click the Date button; to sort by size, click Size. You can also select the different options from the View menu.

In the Icon view, you can sort icons and preview their contents without opening them. To sort items in the Icon view, choose View | Arrange Items and then select a layout option. Certain types of file icons will display previews of their contents: For example, the icons for image files will display a small version of the image; a text file will display in its icon the first few words of its text. The Zoom In entry enlarges your view of the window, making icons bigger, and Zoom Out reduces your view, making them smaller. Normal Size restores them to the standard size. You can also use the plus and minus buttons on the Location bar to change sizes.

You can also change the size of individual icons. Select the icon and then choose Edit | Stretch. Handles appear on the icon image. Click-and-drag the handles to change its size. To restore the icon, choose Edit | Restore Icon's Original Size.

You can also add small emblems to icons, as a kind of visual label. To add an emblem to any file or directory icon, choose Edit | Background & Emblems to open the Background and Emblems window. Here you will see three icons to display panels for color and pattern backgrounds, as well as file and directory emblems. Click Emblems to display the selection of emblems. To add an emblem to a file or directory icon, click and drag the emblem from the Emblem panel to the file or directory icon. The emblem will appear on that icon. If you want to add your own emblem, click the Add Emblem button to search for an emblem image file by name, or browse your file system for the image you want to use (click the Image icon).

Nautilus Pop-up Menu

You can right-click anywhere on the empty space in a file manager window to display a pop-up menu with entries for managing and arranging your file manager icons (see Table 8-4). The menu is the same for both Spatial and Browser views. To create a new folder, choose Create Folder. Choose Arrange Items to display a submenu with entries for sorting your icons by name, size, type, date, or even emblem. Choose Manually to move icons wherever you want. You can also cut, copy, and paste files to move or copy them between folders.

TIP *To change the background used on the file manager window, choose Edit | Background & Emblems. Then drag the background you want to the file manager window. Choose from either Colors or Patterns.*

Menu Item	Description
Create Folder	Creates a new subdirectory within the directory
Create Document	Creates a new document using installed templates
Arrange Items	Displays a submenu to arrange files by name, size, type, date, or emblem
Cut, Copy, Paste	Cuts, copies, or pastes files, letting you move or copy files between folders
Zoom In	Provides a close-up view of icons, making them appear larger
Zoom Out	Provides a distant view of icons, making them appear smaller
Normal Size	Restores view of icons to standard size
Properties	Opens the Properties dialog for the directory opened in the window
Clean Up By Name	Arranges icons by name

TABLE 8-4 Nautilus File Manager Pop-up Menu Options

Navigating Directories

The Spatial and Browser views use different tools for navigating directories. The Spatial view relies more on direct window operations, whereas the Browser view works more like a browser. Recall that to open a directory with the Browser view, you need to right-click the directory icon and choose Browse Folder.

Navigating in the Browser View

The Browser view of the Nautilus file manager operates similarly to a Web browser, using the same window to display opened directories. It maintains a list of previously viewed directories, and you can move back and forth through that list using the toolbar buttons. The Left Arrow button moves you to the previously displayed directory, and the Right Arrow button moves you to the next displayed directory. The Up Arrow button moves you to the parent directory, and the Home button moves you to your home directory. To use a pathname to go directly to a given directory, you can type the pathname in the Location box and press ENTER. Use the toggle icon at the left of the Location bar to toggle between box and button location views.

To open a subdirectory, you can double-click its icon or select the icon and choose File | Open. If you want to open a separate Nautilus Browser view window for that directory, right-click the directory's icon and select Open In A New Window.

Navigating in the Spatial View

In the Spatial view, Nautilus will open a new window for each directory you select. To open a directory, either double-click it or select it and choose File | Open. The parent directory pop-up menu at the bottom left lets you open a window for any parent directories—in effect, moving to a previous directory. To jump to a specific directory, choose File | Open Location. This will open a new window for that directory. Choose File | Open Parent to open a new window for your parent. You will quickly find that moving to different directories entails opening many new windows.

Managing Files

As a GNOME-compliant file manager, Nautilus supports GUI drag-and-drop operations for copying and moving files. To move a file or directory, drag-and-drop it from one directory to another as you would on Windows or Mac interfaces. The move operation is the default drag-and-drop operation in GNOME. To copy a file to a new location, press the CTRL key as you drag-and-drop.

NOTE *If you move a file to a directory on another partition (file system), it will be copied instead of moved.*

Using a File's Pop-up Menu

You can also perform remove, rename, and link creation operations on a file by right-clicking its icon and selecting the action you want from the pop-up menu that appears (see Table 8-5). For example, to remove an item right-click it and select the Move To Trash entry from the pop-up menu. This places it in the **Trash** directory, where you can later delete it by choosing File | Empty Trash. To create a link, right-click the file and select Make Link from the pop-up menu. This creates a new link file that begins with the term *link*.

Renaming Files

To rename a file, right-click the file's icon and choose Rename (or select the icon and press the R key). The name of the icon will be highlighted in a black background, encased in a small text box. Click the name and type a new one over it to replace it. You can also rename a file by entering a new name in its Properties dialog box. Right-click and choose Properties from the pop-up menu to display the Properties dialog box. On the Basic tab, change the name of the file.

Menu Item	Description
Open	Opens the file with its associated application; directories are opened in the file manager; associated applications will be listed
Open In A New Window	Opens a file or directory in a separate window: Browser view only
Open With Other Application	Selects an application with which to open this file; a submenu of possible applications is displayed
Cut, Copy, Paste	Entries to cut, copy, or paste files
Make Link	Creates a link to that file in the same directory
Rename	Renames the file
Move To Trash	Moves a file to the **Trash** directory, where you can later delete it
Create Archive	Archives file using File Roller
Send To	E-mails the file
Properties	Displays the Properties dialog box for this file

TABLE 8-5   Nautilus File Menu Options

Grouping Files

File operations can be performed on a selected group of files and directories. You can select a group of items in several ways: Click the first item and then hold down the SHIFT key while clicking the last item. Click and drag the mouse across items you want to select. To select separated items, hold the CTRL key down as you click the individual icons. If you want to select all the items in the directory, choose Edit | Select All. You can then copy, move, or even delete several files at once.

Opening Applications and Files

You can start any application in the file manager by double-clicking either the application itself or a data file used for that application. If you want to open the file with a specific application, right-click the file and select Open With. A submenu displays a list of possible applications. If your application is not listed, select Other Application to open a Select An Application dialog, where you can choose the application with which you want to open this file. You can also use a text viewer to display the bare contents of a file within the file manager window. Drag-and-drop operations are also supported for applications. You can drag a data file to its associated application icon (say, on the desktop); the application then starts up using that data file.

To change or set the default application to use for a certain type of file, open a file's Properties dialog and open the Open With tab. Here you can choose the default application to use for that kind of file. Once you select your application, it will appear in the Open With list for this file. If you don't want a particular application to appear on the Open With tab, select it and click the Remove button.

If the application you want is not listed on the Open With tab, click the Add button to display a list of commonly used applications and choose the one you want. If the application is not listed, click the Use A Custom Command item at the bottom of the tab to see an entry box and a Browse button. If you already know the full pathname of the application, you can enter its pathname directly. Otherwise, you can click Browse to display a Select An Application dialog that lists applications. Initially, applications in the **/usr/bin** directory are listed, though you can browse to other directories.

For example, to associate BitTorrent files with the original BitTorrent application, right-click any BitTorrent file (one with a **.torrent** extension), choose Properties, and then open the Open With tab. A list of installed applications will be displayed, such as Ktorrent, Azureus, and BitTorrent. Click BitTorrent to use the original BitTorrent application, and then click Close. BitTorrent will then be the default application for all **.torrent** files.

TIP *The Preferred Applications tool will let you set default applications for Internet and system applications—namely the Web browser, mail client, and terminal window console. Available applications are listed in pop-up menus. You can even select from a list of installed applications for select a custom program. You access the Preferred Applications tool by choosing System | Preferences.*

Application Launcher

Certain files, such as shell scripts, are meant to be executed as applications. To run a file using an icon as you would other installed applications, you can create an application launcher for it using the Create Launcher tool. To access this tool, right-click the desktop and choose Create Launcher; or, from the top panel, right-click the panel and choose Add To Panel. This displays the Add To Panel dialog, where you select the Custom Application Launcher entry. When created from the desktop, the new launcher is placed on the desktop; when created from the panel, it will be placed directly on the panel.

The Create Launcher tool will prompt you for the application name, the command that invokes it, and the launch type. The launch type can be an application, file, or file within a terminal. For shell scripts, you use an Application In Terminal option, running the script within a shell.

Use the file type for a data file for which an associated application will be automatically started when opening the file—for example, a Web page will open in a Web browser. Instead of a command, you will be prompted to enter the location of the file.

For Applications and Applications In Terminal, you will be prompted to select the command to use. To do this (the actual application or script file), you can either enter its pathname, if you know it, or use the Browse button to open a file browser window to select it.

To select an icon for your launcher, click the Icon button, initially labeled No Icon. This opens the Icon Browser dialog that lists icons from which you can choose.

Preferred Applications for Web, Mail, Accessibility, and Terminal Windows

Certain types of files will have default applications already associated with them. For example, double-clicking a Web page file will open the file in the Firefox Web browser. If you prefer to set a different default application, you can use the Preferred Applications tool (see Figure 8-8). This tool will let you set default applications for Web pages, mail readers, accessibility tools, and the terminal window. Available applications are listed in drop-down menus. In Figure 8-8 the default mail reader is Evolution. You can even select from a list of installed applications to select a custom program.

To access the Preferred Applications tool from the Ubuntu desktop, choose System | Preferences | Preferred Application. The Preferred Applications tool has tabs for Internet,

FIGURE 8-8 Preferred Applications window

Multimedia, System, and Accessibility. On the Multimedia tab you can select default multimedia applications to run (see Chapter 14). The Accessibility tab has options for selecting a magnifier.

Default Applications for Media

Nautilus directly handles preferences for media operations. The Media tab of the File Management Preferences window (Edit | Preferences) lists entries for CD Audio, DVD Video, Music Player, Photos, and Software. You can select the application to use for the different media (Figure 8-9) from drop-down menus. These menus also include options for Ask What To Do, Do Nothing, and Open Folder. The Open Folder options will open a window displaying the files on the disc. A segment labeled Other Media lets you set up an association for less used media such as Blu-Ray discs. Defaults are already setup for GNOME applications, such as Rhythmbox Music Player for CD Audio discs and Movie Player (Totem) for DVD Video. Photos are opened with the F-Spot photo manager. Software discs will run the **autorun** prompt.

When you insert removable media, such as a CD audio disc, its associated application is automatically started, unless you change that preference. If you want to turn off this feature for a particular kind of media, you can access and select the Do Nothing entry from its application drop-down menu. If you want to be prompted for options, set the Ask What To Do entry in the Media tab pop-up menu . Then, when you insert a disc, a dialog with a drop-down menu for possible actions is displayed (see Figure 8-10). The default application is already selected. From this menu, you can select another application or select the Do Nothing or Open Folder options.

FIGURE 8-9
Nautilus Media
preferences

Figure 8-10
Dialog asking what
application you
want to use

Figure 8-10
Dialog asking what
application you
want to use

You can turn the automatic startup off for all media by checking the box for Never Prompt Or Start Programs On Media Insertion at the bottom of the File Management Preferences dialog box. You can also enable the option Browse Media When Inserted to show all files stored on the disc or other media.

File and Directory Properties

In a file's Properties dialog box, you can view detailed information on a file and set options and permissions (see Figure 8-11). A Properties dialog has five tabs: Basic, Emblems, Permissions, Open With, and Notes. The Basic tab shows detailed information such as Type, Size, Location, and date modified. The MIME Type indicates the type of application associated with it. The file's icon is displayed at the top, and you can edit the filename in the Name text box next to the icon. If you want to change the icon image used for the file or folder, click the icon image to open the Select Custom Icon dialog that shows available icons; select the one you want. The **pixmaps** directory holds the set of current default images, though you can select your own images. Click the image entry to see its icon displayed in the right pane. Double-click to change the icon image.

Figure 8-11
File Properties on
Nautilus

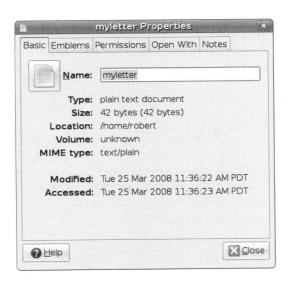

The Emblems tab lets you set the emblem you want displayed for this file. The tab displays all the available emblems. An emblem will appear in the upper-right corner of the icon, providing an indication of the file's contents or importance.

The Permissions tab for files shows the read, write, and execute permissions for Owner, Group, and Others, as set for the file. You can change any of the permissions here, provided the file belongs to you. You configure access for the owner, the group, and others, using drop-down menus. You can set owner permissions as Read Only or Read And Write. For the group and others, you can also set the None option, denying access. The group name expands to a pop-up menu listing different groups; select one to change the file's group. If you want to execute this as an application (say, a shell script) check the Allow Executing File As Program entry. This has the effect of setting the execute permission.

The Permissions tab for directories operates much the same way, but it includes two access entries: Folder Access and File Access. The Folder Access entry controls access to the folder with options for List Files Only, Access Files, and Create And Delete Files. These correspond to the read, read and execute, and read/write/execute permissions given to directories. The File Access entry lets you set permissions for all those files in the directory. They are the same as for files: for the owner, Read or Read and Write; for the group and others, the entry adds a None option to deny access. To set the permissions for all the files in the directory accordingly (not just the folder), click the Apply Permissions To Enclosed Files button.

The Open With tab lists all the applications associated with this kind of file. You can select the one you want to use as the default. This can be particularly useful for media files, where you may prefer a specific player for a certain file or a particular image viewer for pictures. The Notes tab shows any notes you added to the file or directory. It is an editable text window, so you can change or add to your notes directly.

Certain kind of files will have additional tabs, providing information about the file. For example, an audio file will have an Audio tab listing the type of audio file and any other information, such as a song title or compressions method used. An image file will have an Image tab listing the resolution and type of image. A video file will contain a Video tab showing the type of video file along with compression and resolution information.

Nautilus Preferences

You can set preferences for your Nautilus file manager in the Preferences dialog box, which you access by choosing Edit | Preferences. The Preferences dialog box shows a main screen with a side pane with several configuration entries, including Views, Behavior, Display, List Columns, Preview, and Media. You use these tabs to set the default display properties for your Nautilus file manager.

- The Views tab allows you to select how files are displayed by default, such as the list or icon view.

- Behavior lets you choose how to select files, manage the trash, and handle scripts, as well as whether to use the Browser view as the default.

- Display lets you choose what added information you want displayed in a icon caption, such as the size or date.

- The List Columns tab lets you choose both the features to display in the detailed list and the order in which to display them. In addition to the already-selected Name, Size, Date, and Type, you can add Permissions, Group, MIME Type, and Owner.

- The Preview tab lets you choose whether you want small preview content displayed in the icons, such as beginning text for text files.

- The Media tab lets you select default applications for certain media, such as music CDs or blank DVD discs (see the section "Default Applications for Media" earlier in the chapter).

Nautilus as an FTP Browser

Nautilus works as an operational FTP browser. You can use the text-based location bar or choose File | Open Location to access any FTP site. Just enter the URL for the FTP site in the Location box and press ENTER (you do not need to specify **ftp://**). Folders on the FTP site will be displayed, and you can drag files to a local directory to download them. The first time you connect to a site, an Authentication dialog will open letting you select either Anonymous access or access as a User. If you select User, you can then enter your username and password for that site. You can then choose to remember the password for just this session or permanently store it in a keyring.

Once you have accessed the site, you can navigate through the folders as you would with any Nautilus folder, opening directories or returning to parent directories. To download a file, just drag it from the FTP window to a local directory window. A small dialog will appear showing download progress. To upload a file, just drag it from your local folder to the window for the open FTP directory. Your file will be uploaded to that FTP site (if you have permission to do so). You can also delete files on the site's directories.

NOTE   *Unlike KDE's Konqueror file manager, Nautilus is not a functional Web browser. Use Web browsers to access the Internet.*

Removable Drives and Network Folders

From the file manager you can not only access removable media, but can also access all your mounted file systems, remote and local, including any Windows shared directories accessible from Samba. You can browse all your file systems directly from GNOME, which implements this capability with the GNOME virtual file system (GVFS) mapping to your drives, storage devices, and removable media. The Hardware Abstraction Layer (HAL) and **udev** access removable media directly.

You can access your file systems and removable media by choosing Places | Computer (you can also place an icon for this on your desktop). This opens a top-level window showing icons for all removable media (mounted CD-ROMs, floppy disks, and so on), your local file system, and your network shared resources (see Figure 8-12). Double-click any icon to open a file manager window displaying its contents. The file system icon will open a window showing the root-level directory, the top directory for your file system. Access will be restricted for system directories, unless you log in as the root user.

Removable media will also appear automatically as icons directly on your desktop. A DVD/CD-ROM is automatically mounted when you insert it into your DVD/CD-ROM drive,

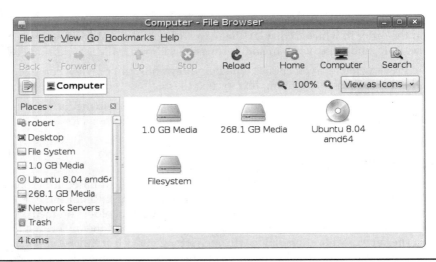

FIGURE 8-12   GNOME Computer window

displaying an icon for it with its label. The same kind of access is also provided for card readers, digital cameras, and USB drives.

NOTE *Be sure that you unmount USB drives before removing them so that data will be written to the device. Otherwise, you may lose data.*

You can then access a disc in the DVD/CD-ROM drive either by double-clicking its icon or by right-clicking it and choosing Open. A file manager window opens to display the contents of the CD-ROM. To eject a disc, right-click its icon and choose Eject. The same procedure works for floppy disks, using the Floppy Disk icon. As with USB drives, be sure you don't remove a mounted floppy disk until you have first unmounted it by right-clicking and selecting Eject.

TIP *Default actions for removable media and drives are now handled by different tools. Nautilus handles removable media such as music CDs and DVD video directly, whereas the Removable Device and Media preferences tool handles devices such as cameras, PDAs, and scanners.*

To see network resources, open the Network window by choosing Places | Network (you can place this icon on your desktop). The Network window lists your connected network hosts. Opening these will display the shares, such as shared directories, to which you have access. Drag-and-drop operations are supported for all shared directories, letting you copy files and folders between a shared directory on another host with a directory on your system. To browse Windows systems on GNOME using Samba, you first have to configure your firewall to accept Samba connections. Use Firestarter (choose System | Administration | Firewall) to allow Samba access, if you have not already done so.

TIP *Nautilus can also burn ISO DVD and CD images, as well as DVD Video. Just insert a blank DVD or CD and then drag the ISO disc image file to a blank CD/DVD icon on your desktop (see Chapter 14).*

GNOME will display icons for any removable devices and perform certain default actions on them. For example, cameras will be started up with F-Spot photo manager. To set preferences for how removable devices are treated, choose System | Preferences | Removable Drives and Media. Certain options are set by default.

Nautilus features built-in DVD/CD-burning support with the **nautilus-cd-burner** package for both files, ISO images, and DVD Video. Burning a data DVD/CD is a simple matter of placing a blank DVD/CD in the appropriate drive. Nautilus automatically recognizes it as a blank disc and allows you to write to it. All read/write discs, even if they are not blank, are also recognized as writable discs and opened in a DVD/CD writer window. To burn a disc, drag the files you want to copy to the blank disc window and then click Write To Disc. A dialog will open with buttons to set options such as the write speed and disc label. After writing the disc, a dialog shows buttons to Eject, Burn Again, or Close. Keep in mind that the newly written disc is not mounted. You can eject it at any time.

NOTE *GNOME now manages all removable media directly with HAL, instead of using **fstab** entries.*

The GNOME Panel

The panel is an important tool on the GNOME interface. Through it you can start your applications, run applets, and access desktop areas. You can think of the GNOME panel as a type of tool accessible from the desktop. You can have several GNOME panels displayed on your desktop, each with applets and menus you have placed in them. In this respect, GNOME is flexible, enabling you to configure your panels any way you want. You can customize a panel to fit your own needs, holding applets and menus of your own selection. You may add new panels, add applications to the panel, and add various applets.

The default GNOME desktop features two panels: a menu panel at the top for your applications and actions, shown next, and a panel at the bottom used for minimized windows and the Workspace Switcher.

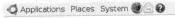

Panel configuration tasks such as adding applications, selecting applets, setting up menus, and creating new panels are handled from a pop-up menu you can access by right-clicking anywhere on the panel. This menu contains entries for Properties, New Panel, Add To Panel, and Delete This Panel, along with Help and About:

- **Properties** Displays a dialog for configuring the features for that panel, such as the position of the panel and its hiding capabilities.
- **New Panel** Lets you add new panels.
- **Add To Panel** Lets you add items to the panel such as application launchers, applets for simple tasks such as the Workspace Switcher, and menus such as the main Applications menu.

To add a new panel, right-click and choose New Panel. A new expanded panel is automatically created and displayed on the side of your screen. You can then use the panel's properties dialog to set different display and background features, as described in the following sections.

Panel Properties

To configure individual panels, you use the Panel Properties dialog box. To display this dialog box, right-click the panel and choose Properties. For individual panels, you can set general configuration features and the background. The Panel Properties dialog box includes General and Background tabs. GNOME uses just one kind of panel with different possible features that give it the same capabilities as the old panel types.

Displaying Panels

On the General tab of a Properties dialog box, you determine how you want the panel to be displayed. You have options for orientation, size, and whether to expand, auto-hide, or display hide buttons. The Orientation entry lets you select on which side of the screen you want the panel to appear. You can then choose whether you want a panel expanded or not. An expanded panel will fill the edges of the screen, whereas a nonexpanded panel is sized to the number of items in the panel and shows handles at each end. Expanded panels will remain fixed to the edge of screen, whereas unexpanded panels can be moved, provided the Show Hide Buttons feature is not selected.

Moving and Hiding Expanded Panels

Expanded panels can be positioned at any edge of your screen. You can move expanded panels from one edge of a screen to another by dragging the panel to another edge. If a panel is already at that location on the screen, the new panel will stack on top of it. You cannot move unexpanded panels in this way. Bear in mind that if you place an expanded panel on the side edge, any menus will be displayed across at the top corner to allow menu items to display properly. The panel on the side edge will expand in size to accommodate its menus. If you have several menus or a menu with a lengthy names, you could end up with a very large panel.

You can hide expanded panels either automatically or manually. These features are specified in the panel Properties General box as Auto Hide and Show Hide Buttons. To automatically hide panels, select the Auto Hide feature. To redisplay the panel, move your mouse to the edge where the panel is located. You can enable or disable the Hide buttons in the panel's Properties dialog box.

If you want to be able to hide a panel manually, select the Show Hide Buttons feature on its Properties dialog. Two handles will be displayed at either end of the panel. You can choose whether these handles will display arrows or not. You can then hide the panel at any time by clicking either of the hide buttons located on each end of the panel. These are thin buttons that display a small arrow that indicates the direction in which the panel will hide.

Unexpanded Panels: Movable and Fixed

Whereas an expanded panel is always located at the edge of the screen, an unexpanded panel is movable. It can be located at the edge of a screen, working like a shrunken version of an expanded panel, or you can move it to any place on your desktop, just as you would an icon.

An unexpanded panel will shrink to the number of its components, showing handles at either end. You can then move the panel by dragging its handles. To access the panel menu with its properties entry, right-click either of its handles.

To fix an unexpanded panel at its current position, select the Show Hide Buttons feature on its Properties dialog. This will replace the handles with Hide buttons and make the panel fixed. Clicking a Hide button will hide the panel to the edge of the screen, just as with expanded panels. If an expanded panel is already located on that edge, the button for a hidden unexpanded panel will be on top of it, just as with a hidden expanded panel. The Auto Hide feature will work for unexpanded panels placed at the edge of a screen.

If you want to fix an unexpanded panel to the edge of a screen, make sure it is placed at the edge you want, and then set its Show Hide Buttons feature.

Panel Background

On the Panel's properties background tab, you can change the panel's background color or image. For a color background, click a color button to display a color selection dialog, where you can choose a color from a color circle and its intensity from an inner color triangle. You can enter its color number if you know it. Once your color is selected, you can use the Style slider to make it more transparent or opaque. To use an image instead of a color, select the image entry and click the Browse button to locate the image file you want. You can also drag-and-drop an image file from the file manager to the panel; that image then becomes the background image for the panel.

Panel Objects

The panel can contain several different types of objects. These include menus, launchers, applets, drawers, and special objects:

- **Menus**   The Applications menu is an example of a panel menu.
- **Launchers**   Launchers are buttons used to start an application or execute a command. The Web browser icon is an example of a launcher button. You can select any application entry in the Applications menu and create a launcher for it on the panel (or the desktop).
- **Applets**   An applet is a small application designed to run within the panel. The Workspace Switcher showing the different desktops is an example of a GNOME applet.
- **Drawers**   A drawer is an extension of the panel that can be open or closed. You can think of a drawer as a shrinkable part of the panel. You can add anything to it that you can to a regular panel, including applets, menus, and even other drawers.
- **Special objects**   Special objects are used for special tasks not supported by other panel objects. For example, the Logout and Lock buttons are special objects.

Moving, Removing, and Locking Objects

To move any object within the panel, right-click it and choose Move Entry. You can either move it to a different place on the same panel or to a different panel. For launchers, you can drag the object directly where you want it to appear. To remove an object from the panel, right-click it and choose Remove From Panel. To prevent an object from being moved or removed, you set its lock feature (right-click the object and choose Lock). Later, to allow it to be moved, you first have to unlock the object (right-click it and choose Unlock).

TIP *On the panel Add To list, common objects such as the clock and the CD player are intermixed with object types such as menus and applications. When adding a particular type of object, such as an application, you will have to search through the list to find the entry for that type; in the case of applications, it is the Application Launcher entry.*

Adding Objects

To add an object to a panel, right-click the panel and select Add To Panel. Then you can select the object from the panel's Add To Panel dialog (Figure 8-13), which displays icon listings of common applets as well as object types. For example, it will display the Main Menu as well as an entry for creating custom menus (Menu Bar). You can choose to add an application that is already in the GNOME Applications menu or to create an application launcher for one that is not. Launchers can be added to a panel by dragging them directly. Launchers include applications, windows, and files.

Application Launchers

If an application already has an application launcher, it's easy to add it to a panel. You simply drag the application launcher to the panel. This will automatically create a copy of the launcher for use on that panel. Launchers can be menu items or desktop icons. All the entries in the Applications menu are application launchers. To add an application from the menu, just select it and drag it to the panel. You can also drag any desktop application icon to a panel to add a copy of it to that panel.

FIGURE 8-13   Add To Panel dialog listing panel objects

Right-click any menu item and select Add This Launcher To Panel to add an application launcher for that application to the panel. Suppose, for example, you use **gedit** frequently and want to add its icon to the panel, instead of having to go through the Applications menu all the time. Open the Applications menu, and then right-click Text Editor and select the Add This Launcher To Panel option. The **gedit** icon now appears in your panel.

You can also select the Add To Panel entry from the panel right-click menu and then choose the Application Launcher entry. This will display a box with a listing of all the Applications menu entries along with System | Preferences and Administration menus, expandable to their items. Just find the application you want added and select it. This may be an easier approach if you are working with many different panels.

NOTE   *For any launcher that you previously created on the desktop, you can drag it to the panel to have a copy of the launcher placed on the panel.*

Folder and File Launchers

To add a folder to a panel, just drag it directly from the file manager window or from the desktop. To add a file, you can also drag it to directly to the panel, but you will then have to create a launcher for it. The Create Launcher window will be displayed, and you can give the file launcher a name and select an icon for it.

Adding Drawers

You can also group applications under a drawer icon. Clicking the drawer icon displays a list of the different application icons you can then select. To add a drawer to your panel, right-click the panel and choose Add To Panel to display the Add To list. From that list select the Drawer entry. This will create a drawer on your panel. You can then drag any items from desktop, menus, or windows to the drawer icon on the panel to have them listed in the drawer.

If you want to add, as a drawer, a whole menu of applications on the main menu to your panel, right-click any item in that menu, choose Entire Menu, and then choose Add This As Drawer To Panel. The entire menu appears as a drawer on your panel, holding icons instead of menu entries. For example, suppose you want to place the Internet Applications menu on your panel. Right-click any entry item in the Internet menu, choose Entire Menu, and choose Add This As Drawer To Panel. A drawer appears on your panel labeled Internet, and clicking it displays a list of icons for all the Internet applications.

Adding Menus

A menu differs from a drawer in that a drawer holds application icons instead of menu entries. You can add menus to your panel much as you add drawers. To add a submenu from the Applications menu to your panel, right-click any item and choose Entire Menu, and then choose Add This As Menu To Panel. The menu title appears in the panel; you can click it to display the menu entries. You can also add a menu from the panel's Add To list by selecting Custom menu.

Adding Folders

You can also add directory folders to a panel. Click and drag the Folder icon from the file manager window to your panel. Whenever you click this new Folder button on the panel, a file manager window opens, displaying that directory. A Folder button for your home directory already appears on the panel. You can add directory folders to any drawer on your panel.

GNOME Applets

Applets are small programs that perform tasks within the panel. To add an applet, right-click the panel and choose Add To Panel. This displays the Add To box, listing common applets along with other types of objects, such as launchers. Select the applet you want. For example, to add a clock to your panel, select Clock from the panel's Add To box. Once added, the Clock applet will appear in the panel. If you want to remove an applet, right-click it and choose Remove From Panel.

GNOME features a number of helpful applets. Some applets monitor your system, such as the Battery Charge Monitor, which checks the battery in laptops, and System Monitor, which shows a graph indicating your current CPU and memory use. The Volume Control applet displays a small scroll bar for adjusting sound levels. The Deskbar tool searches for files on your desktop. Network Monitor lets you monitor a network connection.

Several helpful utility applets provide added functionality to your desktop. The Clock applet can display time in a 12- or 24-hour format. Right-click the Clock applet and choose Preferences to change its setup. The CPU Frequency Scaling Monitor displays CPU usage for CPUs such as AMD and the Intel processors that run at lower speeds when idle.

Workspace Switcher

The Workspace Switcher appears at the lower-right side of the lower panel and shows a view of your virtual desktops, as shown next. Virtual desktops are defined in the window manager. The Workspace Switcher lets you easily move from one desktop to another with the click of a mouse. This panel applet works only in the panel. You can add the Workspace Switcher to any panel by selecting it from that panel's Add To box.

The Workspace Switcher shows your entire virtual desktop as separate rectangles shown next to each other. Open windows show up as small colored rectangles in these squares. You can move any window from one virtual desktop to another by clicking and dragging its image in the Workspace Switcher. To configure the Workspace Switcher, right-click it and select Preferences to display the Preferences dialog box. Here, you can select the number of workspaces. The default is four.

GNOME Window List

The *Window List* icon appears on the bottom panel. This list shows currently opened windows, arranging opened windows in a series of buttons, one for each window. A window can include applications such as a Web browser, or it can be a file manager window displaying a directory. You can move from one window to another by clicking its button. When you minimize a window, you can later restore it by clicking its entry in the Window List. Minimized windows will be grayed out.

Right-clicking a window's Window List button opens a menu that lets you Minimize or Unminimize, Roll Up, Move, Resize, Maximize or Unmaximize, or Close the window. The Minimize operation reduces the window to its Window List entry. Right-clicking the entry displays the menu with an Unminimize option instead of Minimize, which you can then use to redisplay the window. The Roll Up entry reduces the window to its title bar. The Close entry closes the window, ending its application.

If the Window List applet doesn't have enough space to display a separate button for each window, common windows will be grouped under a button that will expand like a menu, listing each window in that group. For example, all open terminal windows will be grouped under a single button, which when clicked will pop up a list of buttons.

The Window List applet is represented by a small serrated bar at the beginning of the window button list. To configure the Window List, right-click this bar and choose Properties. Here, you can set features such as the size in pixels, whether to group windows, whether to show all open windows or those from just the current workspace, or to which workspace to restore windows.

GNOME Directories and Files

GNOME binaries are usually installed in the **/usr/bin** directory on your system. GNOME libraries are located in the **/usr/lib** directory. GNOME also has its own **include** directories with header files for use in compiling and developing GNOME applications, **/usr/include/libgnome-2.0/libgnome** and **/usr/include/libgnomeui** (see Table 8-6). These are installed by the GNOME development packages. The directories located in **/usr/share/gnome** contain files used to configure your GNOME environment.

System GNOME Directories	Contents
/usr/bin	GNOME programs
/usr/lib	GNOME libraries
/usr/include/libgnome-2.0/libgnome	Header files for use in compiling and developing GNOME applications
/usr/include/libgnomeui	Header files for use in compiling and developing GNOME user interface components
/usr/share/gnome	Files used by GNOME applications
/usr/share/doc/gnome*	Documentation for various GNOME packages, including libraries
/etc/gconf	GConf configuration files
User GNOME Directories	**Contents**
.gnome2	Configuration files for the user's GNOME desktop and GNOME applications; includes configuration files for the panel, background, MIME types, and sessions
Desktop	Directory where files, directories, and links you place on the desktop will reside
.gnome2_private	The user's private GNOME directory
.gconf	GConf configuration database
.gconfd	GConf **gconfd** daemon management files
.gstreamer	GNOME GStreamer multimedia configuration files
.gfvs	GVFS virtual file system configuration files
.nautilus	Configuration files for the Nautilus file manager

TABLE 8-6   GNOME Configuration Directories

GNOME User Directories

GNOME sets up several configuration files and directories in your home directory. The **.gnome2** and **.gconf** directories hold configuration files for different desktop components, such as **nautilus** for the file manager and **panel** for the panels. The **Desktop** directory holds all the items you placed on your desktop.

The GConf Configuration Editor

GConf provides underlying configuration support (not installed by default). GConf corresponds to the Registry used on Windows systems. It consists of a series of libraries used to implement a configuration database for a GNOME desktop. This standardized configuration database allows for consistent interactions between GNOME applications. GNOME applications such as Nautilus that are built from a variety of other programs can use GConf to configure all those programs according to a single standard, maintaining configurations in a single database. Currently the GConf database is implemented as XML files in the user's **.gconf** directory. Database interaction and access is carried out by the GConf daemon **gconfd**.

You can use the GConf editor to configure different GNOME applications and desktop functions. To start the GConf editor, enter `gconf-editor` in a terminal window. Configuration elements are specified keys that are organized by application and program. You can edit the keys, changing their values. The GConf editor has four tabs:

- **Tree** Used for navigating keys, with expandable trees for each application, and located on the left. Application entries expand to subentries, grouping keys into different parts or functions for the application.

- **Modification** Used to display the keys for a selected entry and located at the top-right. The Name field will include an icon indicating its type, and the Value field is an editable field showing the current value. You can directly change this value.

- **Documentation** Used to display information about the selected key, showing the key name, the application that owns it, and a short and detailed description. Located at the bottom-right.

- **Results** Appears at the bottom, only when you do a search for a key.

A key has a specific type, such as *numeric* or *string*, and you will be able to make changes only when using the appropriate type. Each key entry has an icon specifying its type, such as a check mark for the Boolean values, a number 1 for numeric values, and a letter *a* for string values. Some keys have pop-up menus with limited choices, represented by an icon with a row of lines. To edit the value of a key, click its value field. Right-click a value field to display the pop-up menu.

Many keys are distributed over several applications and groups. To locate one, you can use the search function. Choose Edit | Find and enter a pattern. The results are displayed in a Results tab, which you can use to scroll through matching keys, selecting the one you want.

Changes can be made either by users or by administrators. Administrators can set default or mandatory values for keys. Mandatory values will prevent users from making changes. For user changes, you can open a Settings window by choosing File | Settings. This opens an identical GConf Editor window. For administrative changes, you first log in as the root user. For default changes, choose File | Default, and for mandatory changes, choose File | Mandatory.

KDE, KDE 4, and Xfce

The *K Desktop Environment (KDE)* is a network-transparent desktop that includes the standard desktop features, such as a window manager and a file manager, as well as an extensive set of applications that covers most Linux tasks. KDE is an Internet-aware system that includes a full set of integrated network/Internet applications, including a mailer, a newsreader, and a Web browser. The file manager doubles as a Web and FTP client, enabling you to access Internet sites directly from your desktop. KDE aims to provide a level of desktop functionality and ease of use found in Macintosh and Windows systems, combined with the power and flexibility of the Unix operating system.

Several editions of Ubuntu, such as Xubuntu, use the Xfce desktop instead of either GNOME or KDE. Xfce is designed as a stripped down desktop with very little resource overhead; it's ideal for laptops or systems dedicated to single tasks.

Ubuntu Hardy, Ubuntu 8.04 LTR, will officially support and include KDE 3.5, not KDE 4.0. This is because the long-term release (LTR) of Ubuntu is designed for stability. KDE 4.0 is too new a release to guarantee that stability. Only KDE 3.5 will be provided the full 18-month support provided for the LTR release (this does include the new Dolphin file manager). However, a KDE 4.0 version for Ubuntu 8.04 will be provided in the Universe repository. This version will offer six-month community-based support until the next Ubuntu short-term release, Ubuntu 8.10. A kubuntu4 disc is available for those who want to install KDE 4 directly.

The situation is complicated by the fact that the Kubuntu edition of Ubuntu for 8.04 has integrated some KDE 4 features, namely the Dolphin file manager and the System Settings configuration tool. Kubuntu still provides the KDE 3.5 Konqueror file manager for use on Kubuntu 8.04. The older 3.5 version used for alternate desktop installation on the original desktop still uses the Konqueror file manager and Control Center configuration tool.

The Kubuntu edition of Ubuntu installs KDE as the primary desktop from the Kubuntu install disc. You can download this disc from the Kubuntu site at **www.kubuntu.org/**. Here you will also find download links for the kubuntu4 disc. You can also download the discs directly from **http://cdimage.unbuntu.com** or **http://releases.ubuntu.com**.

KDE

The KDE desktop is developed and distributed by the KDE Project, a large group of hundreds of programmers from around the world. KDE is open source software provided under a GNU Public License and is available free of charge along with its source code. KDE development is managed by the KDE Core Team. Anyone can apply for team membership, though membership is based on merit.

Numerous applications written specifically for KDE are easily accessible from the desktop. These include editors, photo and paint image applications, spreadsheets, and office applications. Such applications usually have the letter *K* as part of their name—for example, *KWord* or *KMail*. A variety of tools are provided with the KDE desktop. These include calculators, console windows, notepads, and even software package managers.

On a system administration level, KDE provides several tools for configuring your system. With KUser, you can manage user accounts, adding new ones or removing old ones. Practically all your Linux tasks can be performed from the KDE desktop. KDE applications also feature a built-in Help application. Choosing the Contents entry from the Help menu starts the KDE Help viewer, which provides a Web page–like interface with links for navigating through the Help documents. KDE version 3 includes support for the office application suite KOffice, based on KDE's KParts technology. KOffice includes a presentation application, a spreadsheet, an illustrator, and a word processor, among other components. In addition, an integrated development environment (IDE), called KDevelop, is available to help programmers create KDE-based software.

KDE, which was initiated by Matthias Ettrich in October 1996, was designed to run on any Unix implementation, including Linux, Solaris, HP-UX, and FreeBSD. The official KDE Web site is **http://kde.org**, where you'll find news updates, download links, and documentation. KDE software packages can be downloaded from the KDE FTP site at **ftp://ftp.kde.org** and its mirror sites. Several KDE mailing lists are available for users and developers, including announcements, administration, and other topics (see the KDE Web site to subscribe). A great many software applications are currently available for KDE at **http://kde-apps.org**. Development support and documentation can be obtained at **http://developer.kde.org**. Various KDE Web sites are listed in Table 9-1.

Website	Description
http://kde.org	KDE Web site
www.kubuntu.org	Kubuntu site
ftp://ftp.kde.org	KDE FTP site
http://kde-apps.org	KDE software repository
http://developer.kde.org	KDE developer site
http://trolltech.com	Trolltech site for Qt libraries
http://koffice.org	KOffice Project
http://kde-look.org	KDE desktop themes, select KDE entry
http://lists.kde.org	KDE mailing lists

TABLE 9-1 KDE Web Sites

NOTE *New versions of KDE are released frequently, sometimes every few months. KDE releases are designed to enable users to upgrade their older versions easily. The distribution updater should automatically update KDE from distribution repositories, as updates become available. Alternatively, you can download new KDE packages from your distribution's FTP site and install them manually. Packages tailored for various distributions can be also downloaded through the KDE Web site at* **http://kde.org** *or directly from the KDE FTP site at* **ftp://ftp.kde.org** *and its mirror sites in the* **stable** *directory.*

KDE uses as its library of GUI tools the Qt library, developed and supported by Trolltech. Qt is considered one of the best GUI libraries available for Unix/Linux systems. Using Qt has the advantage of relying on a commercially developed and supported GUI library. Also, using the Qt libraries drastically reduces the development time for KDE. Trolltech provides the Qt libraries as open source software that is freely distributable. Certain restrictions exist, however: Qt-based (KDE) applications must be free and open-source, with no modifications made to the Qt libraries. If you develop an application with the Qt libraries and want to sell it, you must first buy a license from Trolltech. In other words, the Qt library is free for free and open source applications but not for commercial applications.

The KDE Desktop

One of KDE's aims is to provide users with a consistent integrated desktop, where all applications use a GUI (see Figure 9-1). To this end, KDE provides its own window manager (KWM), file manager (Konqueror), program manager, and desktop panel (kicker). You can

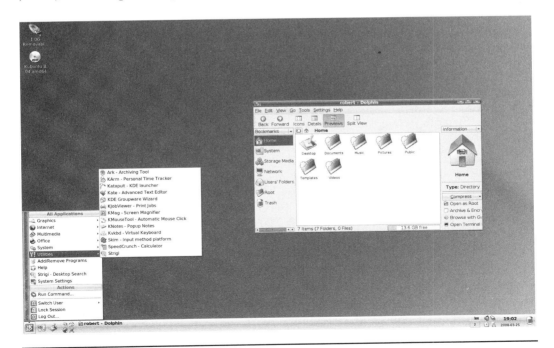

FIGURE 9-1 The KDE desktop

run any other X Window System–compliant application, such as Firefox, in KDE, as well as any GNOME application. In turn, you can also run any KDE application, including the Konqueror file manager, in GNOME.

When you run KDE 3 for the first time for a particular user, you will be prompted to personalize your desktop by the KDE Personalizer. You can select your location and language, desktop behavior, graphic effects level, and theme.

On the desktop, the KDE panel (kicker) is displayed across the bottom of the screen. Kicker is the application launcher panel that includes icons for menus and programs as well as buttons for different desktop screens. The *k* button is the KDE main menu icon. Click this button to access the KDE main menu, which is referred to as the K menu of applications you can run (you can also open the K menu by pressing ALT-F1). From the K menu, you can access numerous submenus for different kinds of applications. The K menu also includes certain key items such as Log Out, Lock Session to lock your desktop, System Settings (called Settings in KDE 3.5) to configure your KDE desktop, Switch User to log in as a different user without logging out first, Run Command to run programs from a command line, Home Directory to browse your home directory quickly, and Help to start the KDE help tool.

TIP *From the KDE menu, choose Settings | Desktop Settings Wizard to change your desktop settings.*

The K menu includes many of the same entries found on the top panel of the GNOME desktop. You can find entries for categories such as Internet, System, Graphics, and Office. If you have installed both GNOME and KDE, these menus list both GNOME and KDE applications you can use. However, some of the K menu entries are for a few more KDE applications, such as KMail on the Internet submenu. Some entries will invoke the KDE version of a tool, such as the Terminal entry in the System Tools menu, which will invoke the KDE terminal window, KConsole. There is no Preferences menu here.

To configure KDE, you use the KDE System Settings tools (choose System Settings in the KDE menu (or choose Control Center from the Settings menu). The System menu will list KDE system tools such as KCron, though it also includes the Ubuntu Administration tools such as the Synaptic Package Manager and Package Manager, Printing configuration, System Monitor, and the Time & Date tool.

TIP *If your CD or DVD-ROM device icons are not displayed when you insert a CD/DVD, you will need to enable the device icon display on your desktop. Right-click the desktop and choose Configure Desktop from the pop-up menu. Select Behavior, and then on the Device Icons pane, select the Show Device Icons check box. A long list of connectable devices is displayed, with default devices already selected. You select and deselect those you want shown or hidden. For most devices, you have both mounted and unmounted options. For example, an unmounted entry for the DVD-ROM will display an DVD-ROM icon even if the DVD-ROM device is empty.*

To quit KDE, you can either select the Log Out entry from the K menu or right-click anywhere on the desktop and select Log Out from the pop-up menu. This displays a screen with icons for Log Out, Suspend, Hibernate, Restart, and Quit. If you leave any applications or windows open when you quit, they are automatically restored when you start up again.

If you want to lock your desktop, you can select the Lock Sessions entry on the KDE menu and your screen saver will appear. To access a locked desktop, click the screen and a box appears prompting you for your login password. When you enter the password, your desktop reappears.

NOTE *You can use the Create New menus to create new folders or files on the desktop, as well as links for applications and devices.*

Next to the K menu is the System Places menu for accessing your file system folders. The term *system* used for this area can be confusing. It refers to places on your system that are commonly accessed, not system configuration tools. It includes entries for your home folder, **Storage Media**, **Remote Places**, **Documents** folder, and **Users** folders. The **Storage Media** folder will display all your mounted file systems, including removable ones. **Remote Places** will let you access connected network shared resources such as Samba-accessible file systems on Windows computers or Unix network-accessible file systems. The **Documents** folder opens your **Document** folder in your home directory, where many applications will save documents by default. The **Users** folders lists icons for the home directories for all users.

Next to the System Places menu, you will find the system tray. The system tray holds buttons for commonly used applications. On Ubuntu these include icons for the Konqueror Web Browser, Amarok media player, Kopete Instant Messenger, and KContact contact address book.

KDE Desktop Operations

The DVD/CD-ROM icons will appear as discs are inserted and mounted, disappearing when ejected. Your home directory is accessed initially from the Home Folder entry the System Places menu.

The Kicker panel displayed across the bottom of the screen initially shows icons for the Kmenu, System Places menu, system tray, minimized windows (in the taskbar), virtual desktops, a clock, and the trash, among others. The desktop supports drag-and-drop operations. For example, to print a document, you can drag it to Kicker's Printer icon. You can place any directories on the desktop by simply dragging them from a file manager window to the desktop. A small menu will appear with options to Copy or Link the folder. To add an icon on the desktop for an active folder, select the Link entry.

Text you copy from one application is held in a desktop clipboard so that you can paste to another application. You can even copy and paste from a KConsole window. For example, you can copy a Web address from a Web page and then paste it into an email message or a word processing document. This feature is supported by the Klipper utility located on the Kicker panel.

You can create new directories on the desktop by right-clicking anywhere on the desktop and choosing Create New | Directory from the pop-up menu. All items that appear on the desktop are located in the **Desktop** directory in your home directory. There you can find the **Trash** directory, along with any others you place on the desktop. You can also create simple text files and HTML files using the same menu.

When you click on the Konqueror Web icon on the panel, Konqueror file manager opens as a Web browser and displays a page with links to commonly used folders on your desktop (see Figure 9-2): Home Folder, Network Folders, Applications, Storage Media, Trash, and

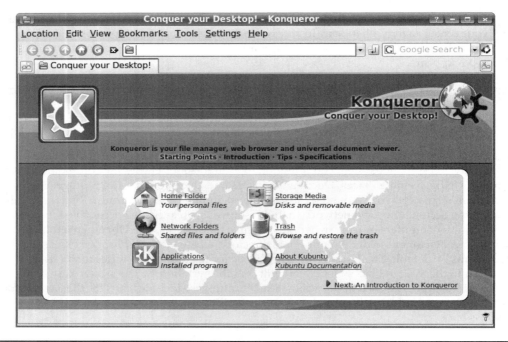

FIGURE 9-2   Konqueror Web Browser

About Kubuntu. You can use the browser to access any of these resources easily. Click Applications to see icons for the main categories, which you can click to display icons for applications.

Applications, Network, Trash, and Storage Media have their own URLs, as shown here:

remote:/	Network folders
applications:/	Applications
media:/	Storage media
trash:/	Trash

Configuration and Administration Access with KDE

KDE uses a set of menus and access points that differ from those in GNOME to access system administration tools. You also access KDE configuration tasks and system administration tools not available through GNOME. Following are the menus available for system configuration and administration:

- **System Settings**   Accessible from the K menu, System Settings, or from any file manager **system:/** URI. This comprehensive KDE configuration window lists all the KDE configuration icons for managing your desktop, file manager, and system, as well as KDE's own administration tools that can be used instead of the GNOME tools. Click an icon to open the window showing the panels for that configuration.

- **System**   This collection of system tools is accessible from the K menu, System. Here you will also find KDE administration tools, such as KUser for managing users.

- **Settings**   Accessible from the K menu, Settings, this configuration menu is used in the original KDE 3.5 (not the Kubuntu edition).

- **Utilities**   Accessible from the K menu, Utilities. Here you will find tools for specific tasks such as KPilot for handheld devices (under Peripherals) and Beagle searching.

Configuring Your Desktop

To configure your desktop, right-click the desktop and choose Configure Desktop. This displays a window with tabs for Behavior, Multiple Desktops, Background, and Screensaver. All these features can also be configured using the System Settings or Control Center Appearance panels:

- Behavior lets you enable the display of certain features, such as displaying a desktop menu across the top of the screen or showing icons on the desktop. You can also select the operations for a mouse click on the desktop. The right-click currently displays the desktop menu. You can also specify which devices to display on the desktop.

- The Multiple Desktops tab lets you select the number of virtual desktops to display.

- Background lets you choose a background color or image for each virtual desktop.

- Screensaver lets you select a screen saver along with its timing. Numerous screen savers are already configured.

TIP   *Additional themes for the KDE desktop can be downloaded from **www.kde-look.org**.*

Special files called *link* files are used to access a variety of elements, including Web sites, applications, and even devices. You can create a link file by right-clicking the desktop and choosing Create New. Then choose the type of link file you want to create.

The Link To Application entry is for launching applications. The Link To Location (URL) entry holds a URL address that you can use to access a Web or FTP site. The Link To Device submenu lets you create links to different kinds of devices, including CD-ROMs, hard disks, and cameras. Bear in mind that these are *links* only. You rarely need to use them. Device icons that display on your desktop are now automatically generated directly by **udev** and the Hardware Abstraction Layer (HAL) as needed.

KDE Windows

A KDE window has the same functionality you find in other window managers and desktops. You can resize the window by clicking and dragging any of its corners or sides. A click-and-drag operation on a side extends the window in that dimension, whereas a corner extends both height and width at the same time. Notice that the corners are slightly enhanced.

The top of the window has a title bar showing the name of the window, the program name in the case of applications, and the current directory name for the file manager windows. The active window has the title bar highlighted. To move the window, click the title bar and drag it where you want. Right-clicking the window title bar displays a pop-up menu with entries for window operations, such as closing or resizing the window. Within the window, menus, icons, and toolbars for the particular application are displayed.

You can configure the appearance and operation of a window by right-clicking the title bar and choosing Window | Configure Window Behavior. Here you can set appearance (Window Decorations), button and key operations (Actions), the focus policy such as a mouse click on the window or just passing the mouse over it (Focus), how the window is displayed when moving it (Moving), and advanced features such as moving a window directly to another virtual desktop (Active Desktop Borders).

Opened windows are also shown as buttons on the KDE taskbar located on the kicker. The taskbar shows icons for the different programs you are running or windows you have open. This is essentially a docking mechanism that lets you change to a window or application just by clicking its icon. When you minimize (iconify) a window, it is reduced to its taskbar icon. You can then restore the window by clicking its taskbar icon.

To the right of the title bar are three small buttons for minimizing, maximizing, or closing the window. You can switch to a window at any time by clicking its taskbar icon. From the keyboard, you can use the ALT-TAB key combination to display a list of current applications. Holding down the ALT key and sequentially pressing TAB moves you through the list.

Application windows may display a Help Notes button, which displays a question mark. Clicking this button changes your cursor to a question mark. You can then move the cursor to an item and click it to display a small help note explaining what the item does. For example, moving the mouse to the Forward button in the file manager taskbar will show a note explaining that this button performs a browser forward operation.

TIP   *The taskbar and pager have three styles: Elegant, Classic, and Transparent.*

Virtual Desktops: The KDE Desktop Pager

KDE, like most Linux window managers, supports virtual desktops. In effect, this extends the desktop area on which you can work. You could have Mozilla running on one desktop and use a text editor in another. KDE can support up to 16 virtual desktops, though the default is 4. Your virtual desktops can be displayed and accessed using the KDE Desktop Pager located on the panel. The KDE Desktop Pager represents your virtual desktops as miniature screens showing small squares for each desktop. It is made to look similar to the GNOME Workspace Switcher. The default four squares are numbered 1, 2, 3, and 4. To move from one desktop to another, click the square for the destination desktop. Clicking 3 displays the third desktop, clicking 1 moves you back to the first desktop, and so on. If you want to move a window to a different desktop, right-click the window's title bar and choose To Desktop, which lists the available desktops. Choose the one you want.

To change the number of virtual desktops, use the System Settings Desktop icon. Either right-click anywhere on the desktop and choose Configure Desktop | Multiple Desktops, or select System Settings from the K menu and open the Desktop heading to select the Multiple Desktops entry. The Visible bar controls the number of desktops. Slide this to the right to add more and to the left to reduce the number. You can change any of the desktop names by clicking a name and entering a new one. Choose the Appearance & Theme's Background entry to change the appearance for particular desktops such as color background and wallpaper (deselect Common Background first).

TIP   *Press CTRL-TAB to move to the next desktop and CTRL-SHIFT-TAB to go the previous desktop. Press CTRL in combination with a function key to switch to a specific desktop: for example, CTRL-F1 switches to the first desktop and CTRL-F3 switches to the third desktop.*

FIGURE 9-3   KDE Kicker

KDE Panel: Kicker

The KDE panel (Kicker) provides access to most KDE functions (see Figure 9-3). The Kicker includes icons for menus, directory windows, specific programs, and virtual desktops.

To add an application to the Kicker, right-click anywhere on the Kicker and choose Add. The Add menu displays the kind of objects you can add, including applets, applications, panels extensions, and special buttons. For KDE applications, choose Applications to list all installed KDE applications on your K menu, and then click the application to add an application button to the Kicker. You can also drag applications from a file manager window or from the K menu to the panel directly and have them automatically placed there. The Kicker displays only desktop files. When you drag-and-drop a file to the Kicker, a desktop file for it is automatically generated.

Kicker also supports numerous applets and several panel extensions

- Applets are designed to run as icons in the panel. These include a clock, a pager, and a system monitor.

- Panel extensions add components to your desktop (right-click on the panel and choose Add New Panel). For example, the Kasbar extension sets up its own panel and list icons for each window you open. You can easily move from one window to another by clicking each corresponding icon in the Kasbar extension panel.

To configure the panel position and behavior, right-click the panel and choose Configure Panel. This displays a customized control module window that collects the panel configuration entries from System Settings or Control Center. The first four of the five configuration windows let you determine how the panel is displayed, and the last window, Taskbar, configures how windows are shown on the taskbar.

The first four windows are Arrangement, Hiding, Menus, and Appearance. The Arrangement window lets you specify the edges of the screen where you want your panel and taskbar displayed. You can also enlarge or reduce it in size. The Hiding window lets you set the hiding mode, whether to enable auto-hiding or to manually hide and display the taskbar. The Menus window lets you control the size of your menus as well as whether to display recently opened documents as menu items. You can also select certain default entries such as Preferences and Bookmarks, as well as edit the KDE menu directly, adding or removing items. The Appearance window lets you set button colors for buttons and background image for the taskbar. With the Taskbar window, you can control windows and tasks displayed on the taskbar, as well as set the button actions.

The KDE Help Center

The KDE Help Center provides a browser-like interface for accessing and displaying both KDE Help files and Linux man and info files. You can start the Help Center by selecting its entry (the life preserver icon) in the K menu, or by right-clicking the desktop and choosing Help. The Help window is divided into two panes. The left pane holds three tabs for

Contents, a Glossary, and for searching the Help resources. The right panes displays currently selected documents. A help tree on the Contents tab lets you choose the kind of Help documents you want to access. Here you can choose manuals, man pages, info documents, or even application manuals. The Help Center includes a detailed user manual, a FAQ, and KDE Web site access.

A navigation toolbar enables you to move through previously viewed documents. KDE Help documents use an HTML format with links you can click to access other documents. The Back and Forward commands move you through the list of previously viewed documents. The KDE Help system provides an effective search tool for searching for patterns in Help documents, including man and info pages. Choose Edit | Find to display a page where you can enter your pattern.

Applications

You can launch an application in KDE in several ways. If an entry for the application is in the K menu, choose that entry to start the application. Some applications also add buttons to the Kicker panel that you can click. Depending on the distribution, the panel will initially hold such applications as the Firefox Web browser and several OpenOffice applications. You can also use the file manager to locate a file that uses the application. Clicking the file's icon starts the application and opens the file. Another way to start an application is to open a shell window, enter the name of the application at the shell prompt, and press ENTER. You can also choose Run Command from the K menu (or press ALT-F2) to open a small window consisting of a box to enter a single command. Previous commands can be accessed from a pop-up menu. An Options button will list options for running the program, such as priority or within a terminal window.

NOTE *You can create a file on your desktop for any application that appears on the KDE menu by clicking and dragging its menu entry to the desktop. Choose Copy, and a desktop file for that application is created on your desktop, showing its icon.*

To create a new desktop file for an application, right-click anywhere on the empty desktop, and choose Create New | Link To Application. Enter the name for the program, and a desktop file for it appears on the desktop with that name. A Properties dialog box then opens with four tabs: General, Permissions, Application, and Preview. The General tab displays the name of the link. To select an icon image for the desktop file, click the icon. The Select Icon window is displayed, listing icons from which you can choose.

On the Permissions tab, be sure to set execute permissions so that the program can be run. You can set permissions for yourself, your group, or any user on the system. The Meta Info tab will list the type of file system used.

To specify the application the desktop file runs, go to the Application tab and either enter the application's program name in the Command box or click Browse to select it. On this tab, you also specify the description and comment. For the description, enter the application name. This is the name used for the link, if you use the file manager to display it. The comment is the Help note that appears when you pass your mouse over the icon.

In the Application tab, you can also specify the type of documents to be associated with this application. At the bottom of the tab are Add and Remove buttons. To specify a MIME type, click Add. This displays a list of file types and their descriptions. Select the one you want associated with this program. Desktop files needn't reside on the desktop. You can place them in any directory and access them through the file manager. You can later make changes to a desktop file by right-clicking its icon and selecting Properties from the pop-up menu. This displays the Properties dialog for this file. You can change its icon and even the application it runs.

The Advanced Options button contains execute options for the application, such as running it in a shell window or as a certain user. To run a shell-based program such as Vi, select the Run In Terminal check box and specify any terminal options. Startup Options let you list the program in the system tray.

TIP   *You can have KDE automatically display selected directories or launch certain applications whenever it starts up. To do so, place links for these directories and applications in the AutoStart directory located in your .kde directory.*

Mounting Devices from the Desktop

To access a CD-ROM, place the disc in your CD-ROM drive and double-click the CD-ROM icon on the desktop. The file manager window then opens, displaying the contents of the disc's top-level directory. To eject the CD, right-click the icon and choose Eject (you can also elect to unmount the CD).

To access a USB drive, connect the USB drive to any USB port. The drive will be automatically detected and a file manager window will open showing the contents of the drive. You can read, copy, move, and delete files on the USB drive. A USB drive icon will appear on the desktop. Moving the cursor over the icon displays detailed information about the drive, such as where it is mounted and how much memory is used. Right-clicking and choosing Properties will display tabs for General, Permissions, Meta Info (space used), and Mounting information. The USB drive menu also has an entry for transferring an image file to the digiKam tool (Download Photos With digiKam). To remove a USB drive, right-click the USB icon and choose Safely Remove. The USB drive icon will disappear from the desktop, and you can then remove the drive.

To access a floppy disk, place the disk in the disk drive and double-click the disk icon. This displays a file manager window with the contents of the disk. Be careful not to remove the disk unless you first unmount it. To unmount the disk, right-click its icon and choose Unmount. You can perform one additional operation with disks: after you insert a blank disk, you can format it. You can choose from several file system formats, including MS-DOS. To format a standard Linux file system, select the ext3 entry.

CAUTION   *Never remove a USB drive directly, as you do with Windows. If you do so, any changes you made, such as adding files, will not be saved. Instead, right-click the USB drive icon and choose Safely Remove. The USB drive icon will disappear from the desktop and you can then remove the USB drive.*

KDE File Managers: Konqueror and Dolphin

The KDE file manager, Konqueror, is a multifunctional utility with which you can manage files, start programs, browse the Web, and download files from remote sites. Traditionally, the term *file manager* is used to refer to managing files on a local hard disk. The KDE file manager extends its functionality well beyond this traditional function because it is Internet capable, seamlessly displaying remote file systems as if they were your own, as well as viewing Web pages with browser capabilities. It is capable of displaying a multitude of different kinds of files, including image, PostScript, and text files. KOffice applications can be run within the Konqueror window. You can even open a separate pane within a file manager window to run a terminal window, where you can enter shell commands (via the Window menu).

Kubuntu supports both the new Dolphin file manager and the older Konqueror file manager. Kubuntu open directories with Dolphin by default. On Kubuntu, you can open any directory with Konqueror by right-clicking the directory icon and choosing Open With Konqueror.

Basic File Manager Operations

You can open a file either by clicking it or by selecting it and then choosing File | Open. If the file is a program, that program starts up. If it is a data file, such as a text file, the associated application is run using that data file. For example, if you double-click a text file, the Kate text editor application starts, displaying that file. If the file manager cannot determine the application to use, it opens a dialog box prompting you to enter the application name. You can click the Browse button on this box to use a directory tree to locate the application program you want.

NOTE *If you want to select the file or directory and not open it, hold down the* CTRL *key while you click it or single-click, because a double-click opens the file.*

The file manager can also extract tar archive files. An *archive* is a file whose name ends in **.tar.gz**, **.tar**, or **.tgz**. Clicking the archive lists the files in it. You can extract a particular file by dragging it out of the window. Clicking a text file in the archive displays it with Kate, while clicking an image file displays it with the Gwenview KDE image viewer. For distributions supporting software packages such as RPM and DEB, selecting the package opens it with the distribution's software install utility, which you can then use to install the package.

Searching Directories

To search for files, choose Tools | Find. This opens a pane within the file manager window in which you can search for filenames using wildcard matching symbols, such as *. Click Find to run the search and Stop to stop it. The search results are displayed in a pane in the lower half of the file manager window. You can click a file and have it open with its appropriate application. Text files are displayed by the Kate text editor. Images are displayed by Gwenview, and PostScript files by KGhostView. Applications are run. The search program also enables you to save your search results for later reference. You can even select files from the search and add them to an archive.

Navigating Directories

Within a file manager window, double-clicking a directory icon moves to that directory and displays its file and subdirectory icons. To move back up to the parent directory, click the up arrow button located on the left end of the navigation toolbar. Double-clicking a directory icon moves you down the directory tree, one directory at a time. By clicking the up arrow button, you move up the tree. To move directly to a specific directory, you can enter its pathname in the Location bar located just above the pane that displays the file and directory icons. Like a Web browser, the file manager remembers the previous directories it has displayed. You can use the back and forward arrow buttons to move through this list of prior directories. You can also use several keyboard shortcuts to perform such operations, as listed in Table 9-2.

Copy, Move, Delete, Rename, and Link Operations

To perform an operation on a file or directory, you first have to select it by clicking the file's icon or listing. To select more than one file, hold down the CTRL key while you click the files you want. You can also use the keyboard arrow keys to move from one file icon to another and then use the ENTER key to select the file you want.

You can use the standard drag-and-drop method to copy and move files. To copy a file, first locate it by using the file manager. Open another file manager window to the directory to which you want the file copied (or in Dolphin use Split View). Then drag-and-drop the file's icon to the new window. A pop-up menu appears with selections for Move, Copy, or Link. Choose Copy. To move a file to another directory, follow the same procedure, but choose Move from the pop-up menu. To copy or move a directory, use the same procedure as for files. All the directory's files and subdirectories are also copied or moved.

Keys	Description
ALT-LEFT ARROW, ALT-RIGHT ARROW	Backward and forward in History
ALT-UP ARROW	One directory up
ENTER	Open a file/directory
ESC	Open a pop-up menu for the current file
LEFT/RIGHT/UP/DOWN ARROWS	Move among the icons
SPACEBAR	Select/unselect file
PAGE UP, PAGE DOWN	Scroll up fast
CTRL-C	Copy selected file to clipboard
CTRL-V	Paste files from clipboard to current directory
CTRL-S	Select files by pattern
CTRL-L	Open new location
CTRL-F	Find files
CTRL-W	Close window

TABLE 9-2   KDE File Manager Keyboard Shortcuts

To rename a file, click its icon and press F2, or right-click the icon and choose Rename from the pop-up menu. The name below the icon will become boxed, editable text that you can then change.

You delete a file either by removing it immediately or placing it in a **Trash** folder to delete later. To delete a file, select it and then choose Edit | Delete. You can also right-click the icon and choose Delete. To place a file in the **Trash** folder, drag-and-drop it to the Trash icon on your desktop or select the file and choose Edit | Move To Trash. You can later open the **Trash** folder and delete the files. To delete all the files in the **Trash** folder, right-click the Trash icon and choose Empty Trash Bin. To restore any files in the Trash bin, open the Trash bin and drag them out of the **Trash** folder.

Each file or directory has properties associated with it that include permissions, the filename, and its directory. To display the Properties dialog for a given file, right-click the file's icon and choose Properties. On the General tab, you see the name of the file displayed. To change the filename, replace the name there with a new one. Permissions are set on the Permissions tab. Here, you can set read, write, and execute permissions for user, group, or other access to the file. The Group entry enables you to change the group for a file. The Meta Info tab lists information specific to that kind of file, such as the number of lines and characters in a text file. An image file will list features such as resolution, bit depth, and color. The Preview tab will display the image used for preview.

Dolphin File Manager: Kubuntu 3 and 4

Dolphin is KDE's dedicated file manager used in Kubuntu and KDE 4. Dolphin is fully supported by Ubuntu 8.04 LTR. A navigation bar shows the current directory either in browse or edit mode. In the browse mode, it show icons for the path of your current directory, and in the edit mode it shows the path name in a text-editable box. You can use either to move to different directories and their subdirectories (see Figure 9-4). Using split

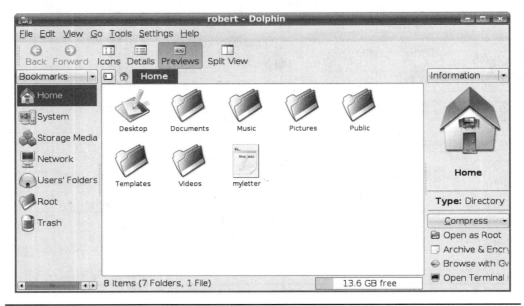

FIGURE 9-4   Kubuntu Dolphin file manager on KDE 3.5

view, you can open directories in the same window, letting you copy and move items between them. Kubuntu displays two sidebars: one for Bookmarks and the other for Information. Passing the mouse over a item displays its information. Dolphin file manager also features integrated desktop search and metadata extraction.

The files listed in a directory can be viewed in several ways, such as icons, detailed listings, and previews (choose View | View Mode). Previews displays contents of the file, such as a thumbnail image of an image file or the first words in a text file. Dolphin also supports *split views*, so you can open two different folders in the same window. Click the Split View button on the toolbar to see a split view.

Konqueror File Manager

The Konqueror file manager window consists of a menu bar, a navigation toolbar, , a status bar, and a sidebar that provides different views of user resources such as a tree view of file and directory icons for your home directory (see Figure 9-5). When you display the file manager window, you'll see the file and subdirectory icons for your home directory. Files and directories are automatically refreshed, so if you add or remove directories, you do not have to refresh the file manager window manually. It automatically updates for your listing, showing added files or eliminating deleted ones.

The files listed in a directory can be viewed in several different ways, such as icons, multicolumn (small icons), expandable trees, file information, or in a detailed listing. To access the different views, choose View | View Mode. The commonly used views are listed as icons at the end of the icon bar. The Tree mode lists your subdirectories as expandable trees whose contents you can display by clicking their plus signs. The Info mode lists file information such as the number of lines and characters in the file. The detailed listing provides permissions, owner, group, and size information. Permissions are the permissions controlling access to this file. The Text view does the same but does not display an icon next to the filename.

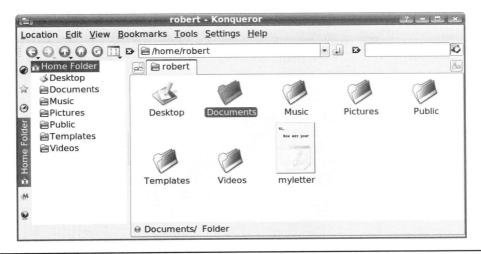

FIGURE 9-5 The Konqueror file manager

Konqueror also supports tabbed displays. Instead of opening a folder in the same file manager window or a new one, you can open a new tab for it using the same file manager window. One tab can display the initial folder opened, and other tabs can be used for folders to be opened later. You can then move from viewing one folder to another simply by clicking a folder's tab. This lets you view multiple folders in one file manager window. To open a folder as a tab, right-click its icon and choose Open in New Tab. To close the folder, right-click its tab label and choose Close Tab. You can also detach a tab, opening it up in its own file manger window.

If you know you want to access particular directories again, you can bookmark them, much as you do a Web page. Just open the directory and choose Bookmarks | Add Bookmarks. An entry for that directory is then placed in the file manager's Bookmark menu. To move to the directory again, select its entry in the Bookmark menu. To navigate from one directory to another, you can use the Location bar or the directory tree. In the Location bar, you can enter the pathname of a directory, if you know it, and press ENTER. The directory tree provides a tree listing all directories on your system and in your home directory. To display the directory tree, choose View | View Mode | Tree View, or click the Tree View icon in the icon bar. To see the tree view for your home or root directory directly, you can use the Navigation panel's Home or Root Folder resources.

> **TIP** *Configuration files, known as hidden files, are not usually displayed. To have the file manager display these files, choose View | Show Hidden Files. Konqueror also supports split views, letting you view different directories in the same window (the View menu). You can split vertically or horizontally.*

Navigation Sidebar
The navigation sidebar lists different resources that a user can access with Konqueror. You can turn the navigation sidebar on or off by selecting its entry in the View menu.

> **TIP** *Konqueror also provides a sidebar media player for running selected media files within your file manager window.*

The sidebar is configured with the Navigation Panel Configuration tool, accessible by right-clicking on the navigation the navigation button bar which also displays items such as your bookmarks, devices, home directory, services, and network resources in an expandable tree. Dragging the mouse over the resource icon displays its full name. When you click an item, its icon will expand to the name of that resource. Double-click it to access it with Konqueror. For example, to move to a subdirectory, expand your home directory entry and then double-click the subdirectory you want. Konqueror will display that subdirectory. To go to a previously bookmarked directory or Web page, find its entry among the bookmarks and select it. The network button lists network resources to which you have access, such as FTP and Web sites. The root folder button displays your system's root directory and its subdirectories.

To configure the Navigation sidebar, right-click the sidebar and choose Multiple Views to allow the display of several resource listings at once, each in its separate sub-sidebar. You can also add a new resource listing, choosing from a bookmark, history, or directory type. A button will appear for the new listing. Right-click the button to select a new icon for it or select a URL, either a directory pathname or a network address. To remove a button and its listing, right-click it and choose Remove.

Konqueror Web and FTP Access

Konqueror also doubles as a full-featured Web browser and an FTP client. It includes a box for entering either a pathname for a local file or a URL for a Web page on the Internet or your intranet. A navigation toolbar can be used to display previous Web pages or previous directories. The Home button will always return you to your home directory. When accessing a Web page, the page is displayed as on any Web browser. With the navigation toolbar, you can move back and forth through the list of previously displayed pages in that session.

Konqueror also operates as an FTP client. When you access an FTP site, you navigate the remote directories as you would your own directories. The operations to download a file are the same as copying a file on your local system. Just select the file's icon or entry in the file manager window and drag it to a window showing the local directory to which you want it downloaded. Then, choose Copy from the pop-up menu that appears. Konqueror also includes KSSL, which provides full Secure Sockets Layer (SSL) support for secure connections, featuring a secure connection status display.

TIP *KDE features the KGet tool for Konqueror, which manages FTP downloads, letting you select, queue, suspend, and schedule downloads, while displaying status information on current downloads.*

Configuring Konqueror

As a file browser, a Web and FTP browser, and an integral part of the KDE desktop, Konqueror has numerous configuration options. To configure Konqueror, open the Configure Konqueror window by choosing Settings | Configure Konqueror from a Konqueror window. This window displays category listings in a sidebar. The initial categories deal with basic file management options such as Appearance, Behavior, Previews, and File Associations. In Behavior, you specify such actions as displaying tooltips and opening folders in new windows. Appearance lets you select the font and size. With Previews you can set the size of previewed icons, as well as specify the kind of files for which you want to retrieve metadata information. File Associations lets you set default applications for different kinds of files.

The remaining categories deal with Web browser configurations, including configuring proxies and Web page displays, as well as such basic behavior as highlighting URLs, fonts to use, managing cookies, and selecting encryption methods. The History category lets you specify the number of history items and their expiration date. With the Plugins category you can see a listing of current browser plug-ins as well as scan for new ones.

KDE Configuration: System Settings

With the KDE configuration tools, you can configure your desktop and system, changing the way it displays and the features it supports (see Figure 9-6). The configuration tools are accessed as from the System Settings entry in the K menu. On Konqueror, you can also select Services (flag icon) from the button sidebar and select System Settings.

The System Settings window shows two tabs: General and Advanced. The General tab is divided into icons for Personal, Look & Feel, Computer Administration, and Network & Connectivity. The Advanced tab has icons for System Administration and Advanced User Settings. Use the icons to display a window with sidebar icons listing configuration panels, with the selected panel shown on the right. The selected panel may have tabs. To change

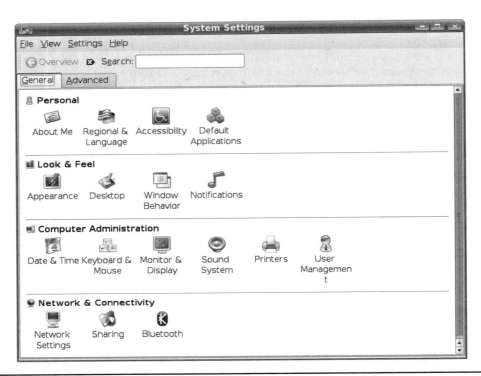

FIGURE 9-6   KDE System Settings

your theme, on the System Settings General tab's Look & Feel section, select the Appearance icon. This opens an Appearance window with a sidebar listing icons for appearance features such as Fonts and Style (see Figure 9-7). To change the theme, select the Style icon. This displays the Style tab of three tabs called Style, Effects, and Toolbar. On the Style tab you can select the widget style. To work with icons, select the Icons icon from the sidebar.

You can also access the System Settings entries from any file manager window by entering the **settings:/** UR in the navigation bar.

NOTE *For the original KDE 3.5 included with the Ubuntu release,* not *the Kubuntu edition, you still use the Control Center, accessible from the Settings menu.*

.kde and Desktop User Directories

The **.kde** directory holds files and directories used to maintain your KDE desktop. As with GNOME, the **Desktop** directory holds KDE desktop files whose icons are displayed on the desktop. Configuration files are located in the **.kde/share/config** directory. Here you can find the general configuration files for different KDE components: **kwinrc** holds configuration commands for the window manager, **kmailrc** for mail, and **kickerrc** for your kicker panel, and **kdeglobals** for keyboard shortcuts along with other global definitions. You can place configuration directives directly in any of these files. **.kde/share/mimelnk**

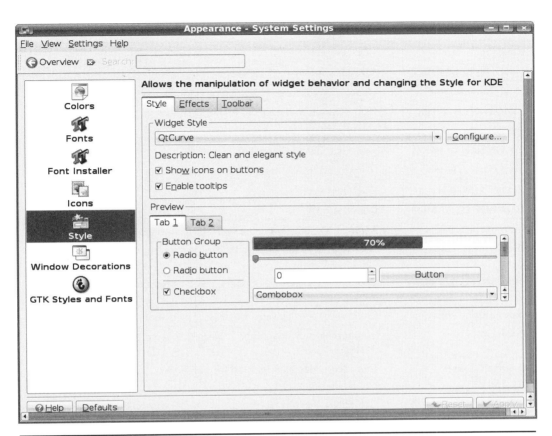

FIGURE 9-7   KDE Appearance Style tab

holds the desktop files for the menu entries added by the user. The **.kde/share/apps**
directory contains files and directories for configuring KDE applications, including **koffice**,
kmail, and even **konqueror**.

KDE Directories and Files
When KDE is installed on your system, its system-wide application, configuration, and
support files may be installed in the same system directories as other GUIs and user
applications. On Ubuntu, KDE is installed in the standard system directories with some
variations, such as **/usr/bin** for KDE program files; **/usr/lib/kde3**, which holds KDE libraries;
and **/usr/include/kde**, which contains KDE header files used in application development.

The directories located in the **share** directory contain files used to configure system
defaults for your KDE environment (the system **share** directory is located at **/usr/share**). The
share/mimelnk directory maps its files to KDE icons and specifies MIME type definitions.
Their contents consist of desktop files having the extension **.desktop**, one for each menu
entry. The **share/apps** directory contains files and directories set up by KDE applications;

System KDE Directories	Description
/usr/bin	KDE programs
/usr/lib/kde3	KDE libraries
/usr/include/kde	Header files for use in compiling and developing KDE applications
/usr/share/config	KDE desktop and application configuration files
/usr/share/mimelnk	Desktop files used to build the KDE menu
/usr/share/apps	Files used by KDE applications
/usr/share/icons	Icons used in KDE desktop and applications
/usr/share/doc	KDE Help system
User KDE Directories	**Description**
.kde/AutoStart	Applications automatically started up with KDE
.kde/share/config	User KDE desktop and application configuration files for user-specified features
.kde/share/mimelnk	Desktop files used to build the user's menu entries on the KDE menu
.kde/share/apps	Directories and files used by KDE applications
Desktop	Desktop files for icons and folders displayed on the user's KDE desktop
Desktop/Trash	Trash folder for files marked for deletion

TABLE 9-3   KDE Installation Directories

share/config contains the configuration files for particular KDE applications. These are the system-wide defaults that can be overridden by users' own configurations in their own **.kde/share/config** directories. The **share/icons** directory holds the default icons used on your KDE desktop and by KDE applications as well as for the Bluecurve interface. As noted previously, in the user's home directory, the **.kde** directory holds a user's own KDE configuration for the desktop and its applications.

Each user has a **Desktop** directory that holds KDE link files for all icons and folders on the user's desktop (see Table 9-3). These include the **Trash** folders and the CD-ROM and home directory links.

KDE 4

The KDE 4 release is a major reworking of the KDE desktop. Though not officially supported in the 8.04 LTR release, a version of 8.04 with KDE 4 is available, called Kubuntu4. You can download it from **www.kubuntu.com** or from **http://cdimage.ubuntu.com**. Check the KDE site for detailed information on KDE 4, including the visual guide: **www.kde.org/announcements/4.0/**.

Every aspect of KDE has been reworked with KDE 4, including a new files manager, desktop, theme, panel, and configuration interface. The KDE window manager supports advanced compositing effects, and Oxygen artwork for user interface theme, icons, and windows.

Device interfaces are managed by Phonon for multimedia devices, and Solid for power, network, and Bluetooth devices. Phonon multimedia framework provides can support different back ends for media playback. Currently it uses the xine back end. With Phonon you can direct media files to specific devices. Solid hardware integration framework integrates fixed and removable devices, as well as network and Bluetooth connections. Solid also connects to your hardware's power management features. ThreadWeaver makes efficient use of multicore processors.

New applications include the Okular document viewer for numerous document formats with various display features such as zoom, page thumbnails, search, and bookmarks. It allows you to add notes to documents. Gwenview is the KDE image viewer with browsing, display, and slideshow features for your images. Terminal window supports tabbed panels, split views for large output, background transparency, and search dialogs for commands. Large output can be scrolled.

KDE 4 Desktop and File Manager

When you log in to KDE 4, the desktop displays the KickOff application launcher in the bottom panel along with the taskbar manager, desktop pager, and the clock (see Figure 9-8). The icon that appears in the upper-right corner is a mouse-activated area that displays a

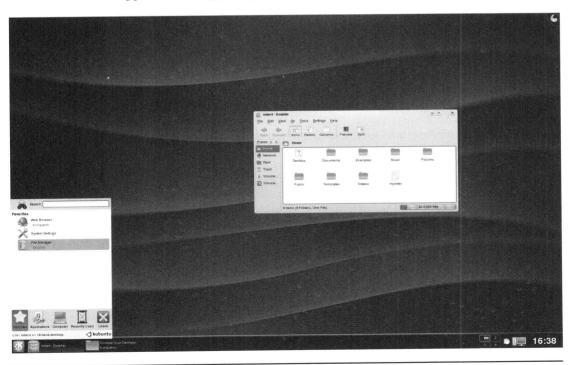

FIGURE 9-8   KDE 4 desktop

menu for adding widgets to the panel as well as zooming in and out the desktop area, in effect minimizing it.

The KickOff application launcher replaces the K menu. It organizes menu entries' tabbed panels that are accessed by icons at the bottom of the KickOff menu: Favorites, Applications, Computer, Recently Used, and Leave. You can add and remove applications on the Favorites panel by right-clicking and selecting Add or Remove To Favorites. The Applications panel shows application categories. Click the Computer icon to open a window with all your fixed and removable storage. The Recently Used panel shows both documents and applications. Click Leave to log out or shut down. KickOff also provides a Search box where you can search for a particular application, instead of working through menus.

The KDE 4 desktop features the Plasma desktop shell with new panel, menu, and widgets, and with a new dashboard function. The dashboard replaces the Show Desktop function. Use the CTRL-F12 key to start the desktop shell. It hides all windows and brings all applets to the front, expanding them to widgets on the desktop area. Click the top-right corner menu to hide the dashboard when you are finished.

Krunner is a quick startup window for applications, where you can type in the application name in a pattern and Krunner will provide possible matches (it even works as a calculator). You can also use the ALT-F2 key to one the Krunner window.

KWin window manager desktop effects can be enabled on the Desktop tab (System Settings | Desktop | Desktop Effects). The Advanced Effects tab lists available effects. Desktop Grid shows a grid of all your virtual desktops , letting you see all your virtual desktops at once. Use the CTRL-F8 key to toggle the display for your virtual desktops on or off. You can then move windows and open applications between desktops. You can also drag the virtual desktop applet to the desktop to view an enlarged version of it. The Taskbar Thumbnails effect will display a live thumbnail of window on the taskbar as your mouse passes over it, showing information on the widget in an expanded window. Some applications and windows can support transparency, letting you see the open windows behind it. The terminal window supports transparency, allowing you to see the terminal text while showing open windows it overlays. You can enable many other effects as well.

Dolphin is KDE 4's dedicated file manager (Konqueror is used as a Web browser). It is also used in Kubuntu, as discussed previously. On Kubuntu4, Dolphin will display two sidebars, a places sidebar for accessing directories and file systems, and an information sidebar. You can close one or both (see Figure 9-9). With the split view you can open directories in the same window, letting you copy and move items between them. The Places sidebar shows icons for often used folders such as **Home**, **Network**, and **Trash**, as well as removable devices. To add a folder to the sidebar, just drag it there. The information pane displays detailed information about a selected file or folder, and the Folders pane displays a directory tree for the file system. You can display panels by choosing View | Panels. The panels are detachable from the file manager window. Dolphin file manager also features integrated desktop search and metadata extraction.

With the KDE configuration panels, you can configure your desktop and system, changing the way it is displayed and the features it supports. The configuration are accessed from the System Settings entry in the Favorites panel of the KDE menu, and appear similar to those used for KDE 3, the Kubuntu edition.

Kubuntu4 uses the same System Settings configuration window as Kubuntu. The System Settings window shows two tabs for General and Advanced. The General tab has sections for Personal, Look & Feel, Computer Administration, and Network & Connectivity.

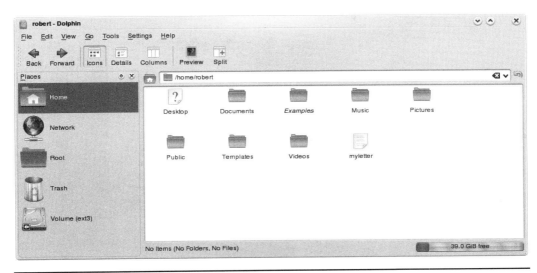

FIGURE 9-9   KDE 4 Dolphin file manager

The Advanced panel has tools for System Administration and Advanced User Settings. Click the icons to display a window with sidebar icons listing configuration panels, with the selected panel shown on the right. The selected panel may have tabs.

Xfce4 Desktop

The Xfce4 desktop is a lightweight desktop designed to run fast without the kind of overhead required for full-featured desktops like KDE and GNOME. You can think of it as a window manager with desktop functionality. It includes its own file manger and panel, but the emphasis is on modularity and simplicity. Like GNOME, Xfce4 is based on GTK+ GUI tools. The desktop consists of a collection of modules such as the Thunar file manager, Xfce4 panel, and the xfwm4 window manager. Keeping with its focus on simplicity, the Xfce4 panel features only a few common applets. Its small scale makes it appropriate for laptops or dedicated systems that have no need for the complex overhead found in other desktops.

Xfce is used primarily on Xubuntu and Mythbuntu, though you can install it on any Ubuntu desktop system. It is useful for desktops designed for just a few tasks, such as multimedia desktops. You can configure your Xfce4 desktop by right-clicking anywhere on the desktop background and choosing Settings | Settings Manager. The Settings Manager window shows icons for your desktop, display, panel, and user interface, among others. Use the user interface tool to resize fonts and select a theme. The Panel tool lets you add new panels and control features such as fixed for freely movable and horizontally or vertically positioned.

Initially, in a new install of Xfce4, only one panel appears with an application launcher icon in it. You can add more items by clicking the panel and choosing Add New Item. This opens a window with several applets such as the clock and Workspace Switcher, as well as menu and application launcher applets (see Figure 9-10). The launcher applet will let you

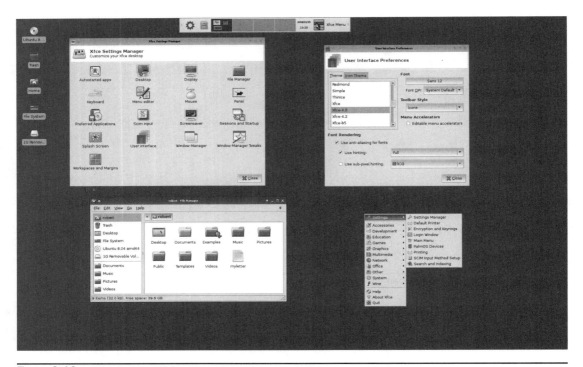

specify a application to start and choose an icon image for it. Using the handles on either side of the panel, you can move it wherever you want on the screen.

Opening the file manager lists entries not just for the home directory, but also for your file system, desktop, and trash contents. The File menu lets you perform file operations such as renaming files or creating new directories.

From the desktop pop-up menu, you can access all the installed applications on your system. A System submenu lets you access all the administrative tools. To quit or log out, right-click the desktop and choose Quit. You have the option of saving your session.

IV
PART

Using the Shell

The Shell

The *shell* is a command interpreter that provides a line-oriented interactive and noninteractive interface between the user and the operating system. You enter commands on a command line; they are interpreted by the shell and then sent as instructions to the operating system.

Several different types of shells have been developed for Linux: the Bourne Again shell (BASH), the Korn shell, the TCSH shell, and the Z shell. TCSH is an enhanced version of the C shell used on many Unix systems, especially Berkeley Software Distribution (BSD) versions. You need only one type of shell to do your work. Linux includes all the major shells, although it installs and uses the BASH shell as the default. If you use the command line shell, you will be using the BASH shell unless you specify another. This chapter primarily discusses the BASH shell, which shares many of the same features as other shells. A brief discussion of the C shell, TCSH, and the Z shell follows at the end of the chapter, noting differences.

You can find out more about shells at their respective Web sites, as listed in Table 10-1. Also, a detailed online manual is available for each installed shell. Use the **man** command and the shell's keyword to access them, **bash** for the BASH shell, **ksh** for the Korn shell, **zsh** for the Z shell, and **tsch** for the TSCH shell. For the C shell you can use **csh**, which links to **tcsh**. For example, the command **man bash** will access the BASH shell online manual.

NOTE   *You can find out more about the BASH shell at **http://gnu.org/software/bash**. A detailed online manual is available on your Linux system using the **man** command with the **bash** keyword.*

Accessing Shells

You can access shells in several ways. From the desktop you can use a terminal window, accessible with either GNOME or KDE. You can run shell scripts that will execute shell commands. You can also boot directly to a command line interface, starting up in a shell command line.

The command line interface for a shell is accessible from GNOME and KDE through a Terminal window – Applications | Accessories | Terminal. It's the most commonly used method for accessing shells. Once a terminal window is open you can enter shell commands.

Shell	Web Site
http://gnu.org/software/bash	BASH Web site with online manual, FAQ, and current releases
http://gnu.org/software/bash/ manual/bash.html	BASH online manual
www.zsh.org	Z shell Web site with referrals to FAQs and current downloads
www.tcsh.org	TCSH Web site with detailed support including manual, tips, FAQ, and recent releases
www.kornshell.com	KornShell site with manual, FAQ, and references

TABLE 10-1   Linux Shells

The terminal window also supports cut, copy, and paste operations from other desktop applications to and from a terminal window (Terminal | Edit menu). You can open as many terminal windows as you want, each working in its own shell. This lets you run several command line operations at once, each in its own terminal window using its own shell. Instead of opening a separate window for each new shell you may want, you can open several shells in the same window, using tabbed panels (SHIFT-CTRL-T opens a new shell). Each panel runs a separate shell, letting you enter different commands in each.

You can also place commands in a script file to be consecutively executed, much like a program. This interpretive capability of the shell provides for many sophisticated features. For example, the shell has a set of file matching characters that can generate filenames. The shell can redirect input and output, as well as run operations in the background, freeing you to perform other tasks.

You can also boot directly into a command line interface, bypassing your graphical login. When you log in, you are placed in the login shell. This is a command line interface using the BASH shell. The runlevel for a command line interface is level 3. You can boot into this level by editing your Grub Linux boot entry and adding a 3 to end that line (see Chapter 2).

The Command Line

The Linux command line interface consists of a single line into which you enter commands with any of their options and arguments. A shell *prompt*, such as the one shown here, marks the beginning of the command line:

```
$
```

By default, the BASH shell uses a dollar sign (**$**) prompt, but Linux has several other types of shells, each with its own prompt (**%** for the C shell, for example). The root user will have a different prompt, the **#**.

You can enter a command along with options and arguments at the prompt. For example, with an **-l** option, the **ls** command will display a line of information about each file, listing such data as its size and the date and time it was last modified. In the next example, the user enters the `ls` command followed by a `-l` option. The dash before the `-l` option is required, as Linux uses it to distinguish an option from an argument.

```
$ ls -l
```

If you want only the information displayed for a particular file, you can add that file's name as the argument, following the `-l` option:

```
$ ls -l mydata
-rw-r--r-- 1 chris weather 207 Feb 20 11:55 mydata
```

TIP *Some commands can be complex and take some time to execute. When you mistakenly execute the wrong command, you can interrupt and stop such commands with the interrupt key—CTRL-C.*

You can enter a command on several lines by typing a backslash just before you press ENTER. The backslash "escapes" the ENTER key, effectively continuing the same command line to the next line. In the next example, the `cp` command is entered on three lines. The first two lines end in a backslash, effectively making all three lines one command line.

```
$ cp -i \
mydata \
/home/george/myproject/newdata
```

You can also enter several commands on the same line by separating them with a semicolon (`;`). In effect the semicolon operates as an execute operation. Commands will be executed in the sequence in which they are entered. The following command executes an `ls` command followed by a `date` command:

```
$ ls ; date
```

You can also conditionally run several commands on the same line with the `&&` operator (see Chapter 11). A command is executed only if the previous command is true. This feature is useful for running several dependent scripts on the same line. In the next example, the `ls` command runs only if the `date` command is successfully executed:

```
$ date && ls
```

TIP *Commands can also be run as arguments on a command line, using their results for other commands. To run a command within a command line, you encase the command in back quotes; see "Values from Linux Commands" later in the chapter.*

Command Line Editing

The BASH shell, which is the default shell, has special command line editing capabilities that you may find helpful as you learn Linux (see Table 10-2).

You can easily modify commands you have entered before executing them, moving anywhere on the command line and inserting or deleting characters. This is particularly helpful for complex commands. You can press CTRL-F or the RIGHT ARROW key to move forward a character or the CTRL-B or LEFT ARROW key to move back a character. CTRL-D or DEL

Movement Commands	Operation
CTRL-F, RIGHT ARROW	Move forward a character
CTRL-B, LEFT ARROW	Move backward a character
CTRL-A or HOME	Move to beginning of line
CTRL-E or END	Move to end of line
ALT-F	Move forward a word
ALT-B	Move backward a word
CTRL-L	Clear screen and place line at top
Editing Commands	**Operation**
CTRL-D or DEL	Delete character cursor is on
CTRL-H or BACKSPACE	Delete character to left of cursor
CTRL-K	Cut remainder of line from cursor position
CTRL-U	Cut from cursor position to beginning of line
CTRL-W	Cut previous word
CTRL-C	Cut entire line
ALT-D	Cut remainder of word
ALT-DEL	Cut from cursor to the beginning of word
CTRL-Y	Paste previous cut text
ALT-Y	Paste from set of previously cut text
CTRL-Y	Paste previous cut text
CTRL-V	Insert quoted text, used for inserting control or meta (ALT) keys as text, such as CTRL-B for backspace or CTRL-T for tabs
ALT-T	Transpose current and previous word
ALT-L	Lowercase current word
ALT-U	Uppercase current word
ALT-C	Capitalize current word
CTRL-SHIFT-_ (underscore)	Undo previous change

TABLE 10-2   Command Line Editing Operations

deletes the character the cursor is on, and CTRL-H or BACKSPACE deletes the character preceding the cursor. To add text, you use the arrow keys to move the cursor to where you want to insert text and type the new characters. You can even cut words with the CTRL-W or ALT-D key combination and then press CTRL-Y to paste them back in at a different position, effectively moving the words.

As a rule, the CTRL version of the command operates on characters, and the ALT version works on words, such as CTRL-T to transpose characters and ALT-T to transpose words. At any time, you can press ENTER to execute the command. For example, if you make a spelling mistake when entering a command, rather than reentering the entire command, you can use the editing operations to correct the mistake. The actual associations of keys and their tasks, along with global settings, are specified in the **/etc/inputrc** file.

TIP *The editing capabilities of the BASH shell command line are provided by Readline, which supports numerous editing operations. You can even bind a key to a selected editing operation. Readline uses the /etc/inputrc file to configure key bindings. This file is read automatically by your /etc/profile shell configuration file when you log in (see Chapter 11). You can customize your editing commands by creating an .inputrc file in your home directory (this is a dot file). It may be best first to copy the /etc/inputrc file as your .inputrc file and then edit it. /etc/profile will first check for a local .inputrc file before accessing the /etc/inputrc file. You can find out more about Readline in the BASH shell reference manual at www.gnu.org/software/bash/manual/.*

Command and Filename Completion

The BASH command line has a built-in feature that performs command line and filename completion. Automatic completions can be effected by pressing the TAB key. If you enter an incomplete pattern as a command or filename argument, you can press the TAB key to activate the command and filename completion feature, which completes the pattern. A directory will have a forward slash (/) attached to its name. If more than one command or file has the same prefix, the shell simply beeps and waits for you to press the TAB key again. It then displays a list of possible command completions and waits for you to add enough characters to select a unique command or filename. In situations for which multiple possibilities are likely, you can press the ESC key instead of two TABs.

In the next example, the user issues a **cat** command with an incomplete filename. When the user presses the TAB key, the system searches for a match and, when it finds one, fills in the filename. The user can then press ENTER to execute the command.

```
$ cat pre <tab>
$ cat preface
```

NOTE *The configuration and directives for completing commands are held in the /etc/bash_completion file, which also invokes more specialized configurations in the /etc/bash_completion.d directory. The bash_completion file includes directives that check whether the user has administrative permission to run or access certain commands or files. If the user does not have permission, a reminder to use sudo is issued. Administrators can modify the completion directives as they wish.*

The automatic completions also works with the names of variables, users, and hosts. In this case, the partial text needs to be preceded by a special character indicating the type of name. Variables begin with a **$**, so any text beginning with a **$** is treated as a variable to be completed. Variables are selected from previously defined variables, such as system shell variables (see Chapter 11). Usernames begin with a tilde (~). Host names begin with an @ sign, with possible names taken from the **/etc/hosts** file. A listing of possible automatic completions follows:

- Filenames begin with any text or /.
- Shell variable text begins with a $ sign.
- Username text begins with a ~ sign.
- Host name text begins with an @.
- Commands, aliases, and text in files begin with normal text.

For example, to complete the variable **HOME** given just **$HOM**, simply press the TAB key:

```
$ echo $HOM <tab>
$ echo $HOME
```

If you enter just an **H**, then you can press TAB twice to see all possible variables beginning with *H*. The command line will be redisplayed, letting you complete the name:

```
$ echo $H <tab> <tab>
$HISTCMD $HISTFILE $HOME $HOSTTYPE HISTFILE   $HISTSIZE $HISTNAME
$ echo $H
```

You can also specifically select the kind of text to complete, using corresponding command keys. In this case, it does not matter what kind of sign a name begins with. For example, pressing ALT-~ will treat the current text as a username. Pressing ALT-@ will treat it as a host name and pressing ALT-$, as a variable. Pressing ALT-! will treat it as a command. To display a list of possible completions, press CTRL-X with the appropriate completion key, as in CTRL-X-$, to list possible variable completions. See Table 10-3 for a complete listing.

Command (CTRL-R for Listing Possible Completions)	Description
TAB	Automatic completion
TAB TAB or ESC	List possible completions
ALT-/, CTRL-R-/	Filename completion, normal text for automatic
ALT-$, CTRL-R-$	Shell variable completion, $ for automatic
ALT-~, CTRL-R-~	Username completion, ~ for automatic
ALT-@, CTRL-R-@	Host name completion, @ for automatic
ALT-!, CTRL-R-!	Command name completion, normal text for automatic

TABLE 10-3   Command Line Text Completion Commands

History

The BASH shell keeps a *history list* of all the commands you enter. You can display each command, in turn, on your command line by pressing the UP ARROW key. Press the DOWN ARROW key to move down the list. You can modify and execute any of these commands when you display them on the command line.

TIP *The ability to redisplay a command is helpful when you've already executed a command you entered incorrectly. In this case, you are presented with an error message and a new, empty command line. By pressing the UP ARROW key, you can redisplay the incorrect command, make corrections to it, and then execute it again. This way, you do not have to enter the whole command again.*

History Events

In the BASH shell, the *history utility* keeps a record of the most recent commands you have executed. The commands are numbered starting at 1, and a limit exists to the number of commands remembered—the default is 500. The history utility is a kind of short-term memory, keeping track of the most recent commands you have executed. To see the set of your most recent commands, type **history** on the command line and press ENTER. A list of your most recent commands is displayed, preceded by a number:

```
$ history
1 cp mydata today
2 vi mydata
10 mv mydata reports
4 cd reports
5 ls
```

Each of these commands is technically referred to as an *event*. An event describes an action that has been taken—a command that has been executed. The events are numbered according to their sequence of execution. The most recent event has the highest number. Each of these events can be identified by its number or beginning characters in the command.

The history utility lets you reference a former event, placing it on your command line so you can execute it. The easiest way to do this is to use the UP ARROW and DOWN ARROW keys to place history events on the command line, one at a time. You needn't display the list first with **history**. Pressing the UP ARROW key once places the last history event on the command line. Pressing it again places the next history event on the command line. Pressing the DOWN ARROW key places the previous event on the command line.

You can use certain control and meta keys to perform other history operations such as searching the history list. A meta key is the ALT key or the ESC key on keyboards that have no ALT key. The ALT key is used here. Pressing ALT-< will move you to the beginning of the history list; ALT-N will search it. CTRL-S and CTRL-R will perform incremental searches, display matching commands as you type in a search string. Table 10-4 lists the different commands for referencing the history list.

TIP *If more than one history event matches what you have entered, you will hear a beep, and you can then enter more characters to help uniquely identify the event.*

History Commands	Description
CTRL-N or DOWN ARROW	Move down to the next event in the history list
CTRL-P or UP ARROW	Move up to the previous event in the history list
ALT-<	Move to the beginning of the history event list
ALT->	Move to the end of the history event list
ALT-N	Forward search, next matching item
ALT-P	Backward search, previous matching item
CTRL-S	Forward search history, forward incremental search
CTRL-R	Reverse search history, reverse incremental search
fc *event-reference*	Edits an event with the standard editor and then executes it **Options** **-l** List recent history events; same as **history** command **-e** *editor event-reference*; invokes a specified editor to edit a specific event
History Event References	
! *event num*	References an event with an event number
! !	References the previous command
! *characters*	References an event with beginning characters
! ? *pattern* **?**	References an event with a pattern in the event
! - *event num*	References an event with an offset from the first event
! *num* **-** *num*	References a range of events

TABLE 10-4 History Commands and History Event References

You can also reference and execute history events using the **!** history command. The **!** is followed by a reference that identifies the command. The reference can be either the number of the event or a beginning set of characters in the event. In the next example, the third command in the history list is referenced first by number and then by the beginning characters:

```
$ !3
mv mydata reports
$ !mv my
mv mydata reports
```

You can also reference an event using an offset from the end of the list. A negative number will offset from the end of the list to that event, thereby referencing it. In the next example, the fourth command, **cd mydata**, is referenced using a negative offset, and then executed. Remember that you are offsetting from the end of the list—in this case, event 5—up toward the beginning of the list, event 1. An offset of 4 beginning from event 5 places you at event 2.

```
$ !-4
vi mydata
```

To reference the last event, you use a following !, as in ! !. In the next example, the command ! ! executes the last command the user executed—in this case, **ls**:

```
$ !!
ls
mydata today reports
```

History Event Editing

You can also edit any event in the history list before you execute it. In the BASH shell, you can do this two ways: You can use the command line editor capability to reference and edit any event in the history list. You can also use a history **fc** command option to reference an event and edit it with the full Vi editor. Each approach involves two different editing capabilities. The first is limited to the commands in the command line editor, which edits only a single line with a subset of Emacs commands. At the same time, however, it enables you to reference events easily in the history list. The second approach invokes the standard Vi editor with all its features, but only for a specified history event.

With the command line editor, not only can you edit the current command, you can also move to a previous event in the history list to edit and execute it. The CTRL-P command then moves you up to the prior event in the list. The CTRL-N command moves you down the list. The ALT-< command moves you to the top of the list, and the ALT-> command moves you to the bottom. You can even use a pattern to search for a given event. The slash followed by a pattern searches backward in the list, and the question mark followed by a pattern searches forward in the list. The **n** command repeats the search.

Once you locate the event you want to edit, you use the Emacs command line editing commands to edit the line. CTRL-D deletes a character. CTRL-F or the RIGHT ARROW moves you forward a character, and CTRL-B or the LEFT ARROW moves you back a character. To add text, position your cursor and type in the characters you want.

If you want to edit an event using a standard editor instead, you need to reference the event using the **fc** command and a specific event reference, such as an event number. The editor used is the specified by the shell in the **FCEDIT** or **EDITOR** variable. This serves as the default editor for the **fc** command. You can assign to the **FCEDIT** or **EDITOR** variable a different editor if you want, such as Emacs instead of Vi. The next example edits the fourth event, **cd reports**, with the standard editor and then executes the edited event:

```
$ fc 4
```

You can select more than one command at a time to be edited and executed by referencing a range of commands. You select a range of commands by indicating an identifier for the first command followed by an identifier for the last command in the range. An identifier can be the command number or the beginning characters in the command. In the next example, the range of commands 2–4 is edited and executed, first using event numbers and then using beginning characters in those events:

```
$ fc 2 4
$ fc vi c
```

The **fc** command uses the default editor specified in the **FCEDIT** special variable. If **FCEDIT** is not defined, it checks for the **EDITOR** variable. If neither is defined it uses Vi, which is usually used. If you want to use the Emacs editor instead, you use the **-e** option and the term **emacs** when you invoke **fc**. The next example edits the fourth event, **cd reports**, with the Emacs editor and then executes the edited event:

```
$ fc -e emacs 4
```

Configuring History: HISTFILE and HISTSIZE

The number of events saved by your system is kept in a special system variable called **HISTSIZE**. By default, this is usually set to 500. You can change this to another value by simply assigning a new value to **HISTSIZE**. In the next example, the user changes the number of history events saved to *10* by resetting the **HISTSIZE** variable:

```
$ HISTSIZE=10
```

The actual history events are saved in a file whose name is held in a special variable called **HISTFILE**. By default, this file is the **.bash_history** file. You can change the file in which history events are saved, however, by assigning a new filename to the **HISTFILE** variable. In the next example, the value of **HISTFILE** is displayed. Then a new filename is assigned to it, **newhist**. History events are then saved in the **newhist** file.

```
$ echo $HISTFILE
.bash_history
$ HISTFILE="newhist"
$ echo $HISTFILE
newhist
```

Filename Expansion: *, ?, [ ]

Filenames are the most common arguments used in a command. Often you will know only part of the filename, or you will want to reference several filenames that have the same extension or begin with the same characters. The shell provides a set of special characters that search out, match, and generate a list of filenames. These are the asterisk, the question mark, and brackets (*, ?, []). Given a partial filename, the shell uses these matching operators to search for files and expand to a list of filenames found. The shell replaces the partial filename argument with the expanded list of matched filenames. These filenames can then become the arguments for commands such as **ls**, which can operate on many files. Table 10-5 lists the shell's file expansion characters.

Matching Multiple Characters

The asterisk (*) references files beginning or ending with a specific set of characters. You place the asterisk before or after a set of characters that form a pattern to be searched for in filenames. If the asterisk is placed before the pattern, filenames that end in that pattern are searched for. If the asterisk is placed after the pattern, filenames that begin with that pattern are searched for. Any matching filename is copied into a list of filenames generated by this operation. In the next example, all filenames beginning with the pattern *doc* are searched for and a list is generated.

Common Shell Symbols	Execution
ENTER	Execute a command line.
;	Separate commands on the same command line.
`command`	Execute a command.
$ (command)	Execute a command.
[]	Match on a class of possible characters in filenames.
\	Quote the following character. Used to quote special characters.
|	Pipe the standard output of one command as input for another command.
&	Execute a command in the background.
!	Reference history command.
File Expansion Symbols	**Execution**
*	Match on any set of characters in filenames.
?	Match on any single character in filenames.
[]	Match on a class of characters in filenames.
Redirection Symbols	**Execution**
>	Redirect the standard output to a file or device, creating the file if it does not exist and overwriting the file if it does exist.
>!	Force the overwriting of a file if it already exists. This overrides the **noclobber** option.
<	Redirect the standard input from a file or device to a program.
>>	Redirect the standard output to a file or device, appending the output to the end of the file.
Standard Error Redirection Symbols	**Execution**
2>	Redirect the standard error to a file or device.
2>>	Redirect and append the standard error to a file or device.
2>&1	Redirect the standard error to the standard output.
>&	Redirect the standard error to a file or device.
|&	Pipe the standard error as input to another command.

TABLE 10-5   Shell Symbols

Then all filenames ending with the pattern *day* are searched for and a list is generated. The last example shows how the * can be used in any combination of characters.

```
$ ls
doc1 doc2 document docs mydoc monday tuesday
```

```
$ ls doc*
doc1 doc2 document docs
$ ls *day
monday tuesday
$ ls m*d*
monday
$
```

Filenames often include an extension specified with a period and followed by a string denoting the file type, such as **.c** for C files, **.cpp** for C++ files, or even **.jpg** for JPEG image files. The extension has no special status and is only part of the characters making up the filename. Using the asterisk makes it easy to select files with a given extension. In the next example, the asterisk is used to list only those files with a **.c** extension. The asterisk placed before the **.c** constitutes the argument for **ls**.

```
$ ls *.c
calc.c main.c
```

You can use * with the **rm** command to erase several files at once. The asterisk first selects a list of files with a given extension or beginning or ending with a given set of characters and then it presents this list of files to the **rm** command to be erased. In the next example, the **rm** command erases all files beginning with the pattern *doc*:

```
$ rm doc*
```

Caution   *Use the * file expansion character carefully and sparingly with the **rm** command. The combination can be dangerous. A misplaced * in an **rm** command without the **-i** option could easily erase all the files in your current directory. The **-i** option will first prompt you to confirm whether the file should be deleted.*

Matching Single Characters

The question mark (**?**) matches only a single incomplete character in filenames. Suppose you want to match the files **doc1** and **docA**, but not the file **document**. Whereas the asterisk will match filenames of any length, the question mark limits the match to one extra character. The next example matches files that begin with the word *doc* followed by a single differing letter:

```
$ ls
doc1 docA document
$ ls doc?
doc1 docA
```

Matching a Range of Characters

Whereas the * and ? file expansion characters specify incomplete portions of a filename, the brackets ([]) enable you to specify a set of valid characters to search for. Any character placed within the brackets will be matched in the filename. Suppose you want to list files beginning with *doc* but ending only in *1* or *A*. You are not interested in filenames ending in *2* or *B*, or any other character. Here is how it's done:

```
$ ls
doc1 doc2 doc3 docA docB docD document
$ ls doc[1A]
doc1 docA
```

You can also specify a set of characters as a range, rather than listing them one by one. A dash placed between the upper and lower bounds of a range of characters selects all characters within that range. The range is usually determined by the character set in use. In an ASCII character set, for example, the range **a-g** will select all lowercase alphabetic characters from *a* through *g*, inclusive. In the next example, files beginning with the pattern *doc* and ending in characters *1* through *3* are selected. Then, those ending in characters *B* through *E* are matched.

```
$ ls doc[1-3]
doc1 doc2 doc3
$ ls doc[B-E]
docB docD
```

You can combine the brackets with other file expansion characters to form flexible matching operators. Suppose you want to list only filenames ending in either a **.c** or **.o** extension, but no other extension. You can use a combination of the asterisk and brackets: ***[co]**. The asterisk matches all filenames, and the brackets match only filenames with extension **.c** or **.o**.

```
$ ls *.[co]
main.c   main.o   calc.c
```

Matching Shell Symbols

At times, a file expansion character is actually part of a filename. In these cases, you need to quote the character by preceding it with a backslash (\) to reference the file. In the next example, the user needs to reference a file that ends with the *?* character, called **answers?**. The *?* is, however, a file expansion character and would match any filename beginning with *answers* that has one or more characters. In this case, the user quotes the *?* with a preceding backslash to reference the filename:

```
$ ls answers\?
answers?
```

Placing the filename in double quotes will also quote the character:

```
$ ls "answers?"
answers?
```

This is also true for filenames or directories that have white space characters such as the space character. In this case, you can either use the backslash to quote the space character in the file or directory name or place the entire name in double quotes:

```
$ ls My\ Documents
My Documents
$ ls "My Documents"
My Documents
```

Generating Patterns

Though not a file expansion operation, {} is often useful for generating names that you can use to create or modify files and directories. The braces operation only generates a list of names. It does not match on existing filenames. Patterns are placed within the braces and separated with commas. Any pattern placed within the braces will generate a version of the pattern, using either the preceding or following pattern, or both. Suppose, for example, you want to generate a list of names beginning with *doc*, but ending only in the patterns *ument*, *final*, and *draft*. Here is how it's done:

```
$ echo doc{ument,final,draft}
document docfinal docdraft
```

Since the names generated do not have to exist, you could use the {} operation in a command to create directories, as shown here:

```
$ mkdir {fall,winter,spring}report
$ ls
fallreport springreport winterreport
```

Standard Input/Output and Redirection

The data in input and output operations is organized like a file. Data input at the keyboard is placed in a data stream arranged as a continuous set of bytes. Data output from a command or program is also placed in a data stream and arranged as a continuous set of bytes. This input data stream is referred to in Linux as the *standard input,* while the output data stream is called the *standard output.* A separate output data stream reserved solely for error messages is called the *standard error.* (See the section "Redirecting and Piping the Standard Error: >&, 2>" later in this chapter.)

Because the standard input and standard output have the same organization as that of a file, they can easily interact with files. Linux has a redirection capability that lets you easily move data in and out of files. You can redirect the standard output so that, instead of displaying the output on a screen, you can save it in a file. You can also redirect the standard input away from the keyboard to a file so that input is read from a file instead of from your keyboard.

When a Linux command is executed and produces output, this output is placed in the standard output data stream. The default destination for the standard output data stream is a device—in this case, the screen. *Devices,* such as the keyboard and screen, are treated as files. They receive and send out streams of bytes with the same organization as that of a byte-stream file. The screen is a device that displays a continuous stream of bytes. By default, the standard output will send its data to the screen device, which will then display the data.

For example, the `ls` command generates a list of all filenames and outputs this list to the standard output. Next, this stream of bytes in the standard output is directed to the screen device. The list of filenames is then printed on the screen. The `cat` command also sends output to the standard output. The contents of a file are copied to the standard output, whose default destination is the screen. The contents of the file are then displayed on the screen.

Redirecting the Standard Output: > and >>

Suppose that instead of displaying a list of files on the screen, you would like to save this list in a file. In other words, you would like to direct the standard output to a file rather than the screen. To do this, you place the output redirection operator, the greater-than sign (>), followed by the name of a file on the command line after the Linux command. Table 10-6

Command	Execution
ENTER	Execute a command line.
;	Separate commands on the same command line.
command\ opts args	Enter backslash before pressing ENTER to continue entering a command on the next line.
`command`	Execute a command.
$ (command)	Execute a command.
Special Characters for Filename Expansion	**Execution**
*	Match on any set of characters.
?	Match on any single characters.
[]	Match on a class of possible characters.
\	Quote the following character. Used to quote special characters.
Redirection	**Execution**
command > filename	Redirect the standard output to a file or device, creating the file if it does not exist and overwriting the file if it does exist.
command < filename	Redirect the standard input from a file or device to a program.
command >> filename	Redirect the standard output to a file or device, appending the output to the end of the file.
command >! filename	In the C shell and the Korn shell, the exclamation point forces the overwriting of a file if it already exists. This overrides the `noclobber` option.
command 2> filename	Redirect the standard error to a file or device in the Bourne shell.
command 2>> filename	Redirect and append the standard error to a file or device in the Bourne shell.
command 2>&1	Redirect the standard error to the standard output in the Bourne shell.
command >& filename	Redirect the standard error to a file or device in the C shell.
Pipes	**Execution**
command | command	Pipe the standard output of one command as input for another command.
command |& command	Pipe the standard error as input to another command in the C shell.

TABLE 10-6   The Shell Operations

PART IV

lists the different ways you can use the redirection operators. In the next example, the output of the **ls** command is redirected from the screen device to a file:

```
$ ls -l *.c > programlist
```

The redirection operation creates the new destination file. If the file already exists, it will be overwritten with the data in the standard output. You can set the **noclobber** feature to prevent overwriting an existing file with the redirection operation. In this case, the redirection operation on an existing file will fail. You can overcome the **noclobber** feature by placing an exclamation point after the redirection operator. You can place the **noclobber** command in a shell configuration file to make it an automatic default operation (see Chapter 11). The next example sets the **noclobber** feature for the BASH shell and then forces the overwriting of the **oldletter** file if it already exists:

```
$ set -o noclobber
$ cat myletter >! oldletter
```

Although the redirection operator and the filename are placed after the command, the redirection operation is not executed after the command. In fact, it is executed before the command. The redirection operation creates the file and sets up the redirection before it receives any data from the standard output. If the file already exists, it will be destroyed and replaced by a file of the same name. In effect, the command generating the output is executed only after the redirected file has been created.

In the next example, the output of the **ls** command is redirected from the screen device to a file. First the **ls** command lists files, and in the next command, **ls** redirects its file list to the **listf** file. Then the **cat** command displays the list of files saved in **listf**. Notice the list of files in **listf** includes the **listf** filename. The list of filenames generated by the **ls** command includes the name of the file created by the redirection operation—in this case, **listf**. The **listf** file is first created by the redirection operation, and then the **ls** command lists it along with other files. This file list output by **ls** is then redirected to the **listf** file, instead of being printed on the screen.

```
$ ls
mydata intro preface
$ ls > listf
$ cat listf
mydata intro listf preface
```

TIP *Errors occur when you try to use the same filename for both an input file for the command and the redirected destination file. In this case, because the redirection operation is executed first, the input file, because it exists, is destroyed and replaced by a file of the same name. When the command is executed, it finds an input file that is empty.*

You can also append the standard output to an existing file using the **>>** redirection operator. Instead of overwriting the file, the data in the standard output is added at the end of the file. In the next example, the **myletter** and **oldletter** files are appended to the **alletters** file. The **alletters** file will then contain the contents of both **myletter** and **oldletter**.

```
$ cat myletter >> alletters
$ cat oldletter >> alletters
```

The Standard Input

Many Linux commands can receive data from the standard input. The standard input itself receives data from a device or a file. The default device for the standard input is the keyboard. Characters typed on the keyboard are placed in the standard input, which is then directed to the Linux command. Just as with the standard output, you can also redirect the standard input, receiving input from a file rather than the keyboard. The operator for redirecting the standard input is the less-than sign (<). In the next example, the standard input is redirected to receive input from the **myletter** file, rather than the keyboard device (use CTRL-D to end the typed input). The contents of **myletter** are read into the standard input by the redirection operation. Then the **cat** command reads the standard input and displays the contents of **myletter**.

```
$ cat < myletter
hello Christopher
How are you today
$
```

You can combine the redirection operations for both standard input and standard output. In the next example, the **cat** command has no filename arguments. Without filename arguments, the **cat** command receives input from the standard input and sends output to the standard output. However, the standard input has been redirected to receive its data from a file, while the standard output has been redirected to place its data in a file.

```
$ cat < myletter > newletter
```

Pipes |

You may encounter situations in which you need to send data from one command to another. In other words, you may want to send the standard output of a command to another command, rather than to a destination file. Suppose, for example, you want to send a list of filenames to the printer to be printed. You need two commands to do this: the **ls** command to generate a list of filenames and the **lpr** command to send the list to the printer. In effect, you need to take the output of the **ls** command and use it as input for the **lpr** command. You can think of the data as flowing from one command to another. To form such a connection in Linux, you use what is called a *pipe*. The *pipe operator* (|, the vertical bar character) placed between two commands forms a connection between them. The standard output of one command becomes the standard input for the other. The pipe operation receives output from the command placed before the pipe and sends this data as input to the command placed after the pipe. As shown in the next example, you can connect the **ls** command and the **lpr** command with a pipe. The list of filenames output by the **ls** command is piped into the **lpr** command.

```
$ ls | lpr
```

You can combine the pipe operation with other shell features, such as file expansion characters, to perform specialized operations. The next example prints only files with a .c extension. The **ls** command is used with the asterisk and .c to generate a list of filenames with the .c extension. Then this list is piped to the **lpr** command.

```
$ ls *.c | lpr
```

In the preceding example, a list of filenames was used as input, but what is important to note is that pipes operate on the standard output of a command, whatever that might be. The contents of whole files or even several files can be piped from one command to another. In the next example, the **cat** command reads and outputs the contents of the **mydata** file, which are then piped to the **lpr** command:

```
$ cat mydata | lpr
```

Many Linux commands generate modified output. For example, the **sort** command takes the contents of a file and generates a version with each line sorted in alphabetic order. The **sort** command works best with files that are lists of items. Commands such as **sort** that output a modified version of its input are referred to as *filters*. Filters are often used with pipes. In the next example, a sorted version of **mylist** is generated and piped into the **more** command for display on the screen. Note that the original file, **mylist**, has not been changed and is not itself sorted. Only the output of **sort** in the standard output is sorted.

```
$ sort mylist | more
```

The standard input piped into a command can be more carefully controlled with the standard input argument (-). When you use the dash as an argument for a command, it represents the standard input.

Redirecting and Piping the Standard Error: >&, 2>

When you execute commands, an error could possibly occur. You may enter the wrong number of arguments, or some kind of system error could take place. When an error occurs, the system issues an error message. Usually such error messages are displayed on the screen, along with the standard output. Linux distinguishes between standard output and error messages, however. Error messages are placed in yet another standard byte stream, called the *standard error*. In the next example, the **cat** command is assigned as its argument the name of a file that does not exist, **myintro**. In this case, the **cat** command simply issues an error:

```
$ cat myintro
cat : myintro not found
$
```

Because error messages are in a separate data stream from the standard output, error messages still appear on the screen for you to see even if you have redirected the standard output to a file. In the next example, the standard output of the **cat** command is redirected to the file **mydata**. However, the standard error, containing the error messages, is still directed to the screen.

```
$ cat myintro > mydata
cat : myintro not found
$
```

You can redirect the standard error, as you can the standard output. This means you can save your error messages in a file for future reference. This is helpful if you need a record of the error messages. Like the standard output, the standard error has the screen device for its default destination. However, you can redirect the standard error to any file or device you choose using special redirection operators. In this case, the error messages will not be displayed on the screen.

Redirection of the standard error relies on a special feature of shell redirection. You can reference all the standard byte streams in redirection operations with numbers. The numbers *0*, *1*, and *2* reference the standard input, standard output, and standard error, respectively. By default, an output redirection, **>**, operates on the standard output, *1*. You can modify the output redirection to operate on the standard error, however, by preceding the output redirection operator with the number 2. In the next example, the **cat** command again will generate an error. The error message is redirected to the standard byte stream represented by the number *2*, the standard error.

```
$ cat nodata 2> myerrors
$ cat myerrors
cat : nodata not found
$
```

You can also append the standard error to a file by using the number 2 and the redirection append operator (**>>**). In the next example, the user appends the standard error to the **myerrors** file, which then functions as a log of errors:

```
$ cat nodata 2>> myerrors
```

Jobs: Background, Kills, and Interruptions

In Linux, you not only have control over a command's input and output, but also over its execution. You can run a job in the background while you execute other commands. You can also cancel commands before they have finished executing. You can even interrupt a command, starting it again later from where you left off. Background operations are particularly useful for long jobs. Instead of waiting at the terminal until a command has finished execution, you can place it in the background. You can then continue executing other Linux commands. You can, for example, edit a file while other files are printing. The background commands, as well as commands to cancel and interrupt jobs, are listed in Table 10-7.

Running Jobs in the Background

You execute a command in the background by placing an ampersand (**&**) on the command line at the end of the command. When you place a job in the background, a user job number and a system process number are displayed. The user job number, placed in brackets, is the number by which the user references the job. The system process number is the number by which the system identifies the job. In the next example, the command to print the file **mydata** is placed in the background:

```
$ lpr mydata &
[1]   534
$
```

You can place more than one command in the background. Each is classified as a job and given a name and a job number. The command **jobs** lists the jobs being run in the background.

Background Jobs	Execution
%*jobnum*	References job by job number, use the `jobs` command to display job numbers.
%	References recent job.
%*string*	References job by an exact matching string.
%?*string*?	References job that contains unique string.
%--	References job before recent job.
&	Execute a command in the background.
`fg` %*jobnum*	Bring a command in the background to the foreground or resume an interrupted program.
`bg`	Place a command in the foreground into the background.
CTRL-Z	Interrupt and stop the currently running program. The program remains stopped and waiting in the background for you to resume it.
`notify` %*jobnum*	Notify you when a job ends.
`kill` %*jobnum* `kill` *processnum*	Cancel and end a job running in the background.
`jobs`	List all background jobs.
`ps -a`	List all currently running processes, including background jobs.
`at` *time date*	Execute commands at a specified time and date. The time can be entered with hours and minutes and qualified as A.M. or P.M.

TABLE 10-7 Job Management Operations

Each entry in the list consists of the job number in brackets, whether it is stopped or running, and the name of the job. The + sign indicates the job currently being processed, and the - sign indicates the next job to be executed. In the next example, two commands have been placed in the background. The `jobs` command then lists those jobs, showing which one is currently being executed.

```
$ lpr intro &
[1]   547
$ cat *.c > myprogs &
[2]   548
$ jobs
[1]  +  Running  lpr intro
[2]  -  Running  cat *.c > myprogs
$
```

Referencing Jobs

Normally, jobs are referenced using the job number, preceded by a % symbol. You can obtain this number with the `jobs` command, which will list all background jobs, as shown in the preceding example. In addition you can also reference a job using an identifying string (see Table 10-7). The string must be either an exact match or a partial unique match. If there is no exact or unique match, you will receive an error message. Also, the **%** symbol itself without any job number references the recent background job. Followed by a - - it references the second previous background job. The following example brings job 1 in the previous example to the foreground:

```
fg %lpr
```

Job Notification

After you execute any command in Linux, the system tells you what background jobs, if you have any running, have been completed so far. The system does not interrupt any operation, such as editing, to notify you about a completed job. If you want to be notified immediately when a certain job ends, no matter what you are doing on the system, you can use the **notify** command to instruct the system to tell you. The **notify** command takes a job number as its argument. When that job is finished, the system interrupts what you are doing to notify you the job has ended. The next example tells the system to notify the user when job 2 has finished:

```
$ notify %2
```

Bringing Jobs to the Foreground

You can bring a job out of the background with the foreground command, **fg**. If only one job is in the background, the **fg** command alone will bring it to the foreground. If more than one job is in the background, you must use the job's number with the command. You place the job number after the **fg** command, preceded with a percent sign. A **bg** command also places a job in the background. This command is usually used for interrupted jobs. In the next example, the second job is brought back into the foreground. You may not immediately receive a prompt again because the second command is now in the foreground and executing. When the command is finished executing, the prompt appears and you can execute another command.

```
$ fg %2
cat *.c > myprogs
$
```

Canceling Jobs

If you want to cancel a job running in the background, you can force it to end with the **kill** command. The **kill** command takes as its argument either the user job number or the system process number. The user job number must be preceded by a percent sign (**%**). You can find out the job number from the **jobs** command. In the next example, the **jobs** command lists the background jobs; then job 2 is canceled:

```
$ jobs
[1]   +   Running   lpr intro
[2]   -   Running   cat *.c > myprogs
$ kill %2
```

Suspending and Stopping Jobs

You can suspend a job and stop it by pressing CTRL-Z. This places the job to the side until it is restarted. The job is not ended; it merely remains suspended until you want to continue. When you're ready, you can continue with the job either in the foreground or the background using the **fg** or **bg** command. The **fg** command restarts a suspended job in the foreground. The **bg** command places the suspended job in the background.

At times, you may need to place a job currently running in the foreground into the background. However, you cannot move a currently running job directly into the background. You first need to suspend it with CTRL-Z and then place it in the background with the **bg** command. In the next example, the current command to list and redirect **.c** files is first suspended with CTRL-Z. Then that job is placed in the background:

```
$ cat *.c > myprogs
^Z
$ bg
```

> **NOTE** *You can also use CTRL-Z to stop currently running jobs such as Vi, suspending them in the background until you are ready to resume them. The Vi session remains as a stopped job in the background until resumed with the **bg** command.*

Ending Processes: ps and kill

You can also cancel a job using the system process number, which you can obtain with the **ps** command. The **ps** command will display your processes, and you can use a process number to end any running process. The **ps** command displays a great deal more information than the **jobs** command. The next example lists the processes a user is running. The PID is the system process number, also known as the process ID. TTY is the terminal identifier. TIME is how long the process has taken so far. COMMAND is the name of the process.

```
$ ps
PID        TTY         TIME        COMMAND
523        tty24       0:05        sh
567        tty24       0:01        lpr
570        tty24       0:00        ps
```

You can then reference the system process number in a **kill** command. Use the process number without any preceding percent sign. The next example kills process 567:

```
$ kill 567
```

Check the **ps** man page for more detailed information about detecting and displaying process information. To just display a process ID number use the output options **-o pid=**. Combining the **ps** command with the **-C** option lets you display just the process ID for a particular command. If more than one process exists for that command, such as multiple bash shells, then all the PIDs will be displayed.

```
$ ps -C lpr -o pid=
567
```

For unique commands, those you know have only one process running, you can safely combine the previous command with the **kill** command to end the process on one line. This avoids interactively having to display and enter the PID to kill the process. The technique can be useful for noninteractive operations such as **cron** and helpful for ending open-ended operations such as video recording. In the following example, a command using just one process, **getatsc**, is ended in a single **kill** operation. The **getatsc** is an HDTV recording command. Backquotes are used first to execute the **ps** command to obtain the PID. (See "Values from Linux Commands" later in the chapter.)

```
kill `ps -C getatsc -o pid=`
```

Shell Variables

A *shell*, by definition, is an interpretive environment within which you execute commands. The BASH, TCSH, and Z shells described previously are types of shells. You can have many instances of a particular kind of shell. You can have many environments running at the same time, of either the same or different types of shells: for example, several shells of the BASH shell type can be running at the same time.

Within each shell, you can enter and execute commands. You can further enhance the capabilities of a shell using shell variables. A shell variable lets you hold data that you can reference over and over again as you execute different commands within a shell. For example, you can define a shell variable to hold the name of complex filename. Then, instead of retyping the filename in different commands, you can reference it with the shell variable.

You define variables within a shell, and such variables are known as *shell variables.* Some utilities, such as the Mail utility, have their own shells with their own shell variables. You can also create your own shell using *shell scripts.* You have a user shell that becomes active as soon as you log in. This is often referred to as the *login shell.* Special system-level parameter variables are defined within this login shell. Shell variables can also be used to define a shell's environment.

NOTE *Shell variables exist as long as your shell is active—that is, until you exit the shell. For example, logging out will exit the login shell. When you log in again, any variables you may need in your login shell must be defined again.*

Definition and Evaluation of Variables: =, $, set, unset

You define a variable in a shell when you first use the variable's name. A variable's name may be any set of alphabetic characters, including the underscore. The name may also include a number, but the number cannot be the first character in the name. A name may not have any other type of character, such as an exclamation point, an ampersand, or even a space. Such symbols are reserved by the shell for its own use. Also, a variable name may not include more than one word. The shell uses spaces on the command line to distinguish different components of a command such as options, arguments, and the command name.

You assign a value to a variable with the assignment operator (=). You type the variable name, the assignment operator, and then the value assigned. Do not place any spaces around the assignment operator. The assignment operation **poet = Virgil**, for example, will fail. (The C shell has a slightly different type of assignment operation.) You can assign any set of characters to a variable. In the next example, the variable **poet** is assigned the string **Virgil**:

```
$ poet=Virgil
```

Once you have assigned a value to a variable, you can then use the variable name to reference the value. Often you use the values of variables as arguments for a command. You can reference the value of a variable using the variable name preceded by the **$** operator. The dollar sign is a special operator that uses the variable name to reference a variable's value, in effect evaluating the variable. Evaluation retrieves a variable's value, usually a set of characters. This set of characters then replaces the variable name on the command line. Wherever a **$** is placed before the variable name, the variable name is replaced with the value of the variable. In the next example, the shell variable **poet** is evaluated and its contents, **Virgil**, are used as the argument for an **echo** command. The **echo** command simply echoes or prints a set of characters to the screen.

```
$ echo $poet
Virgil
```

You must be careful to distinguish between the evaluation of a variable and its name alone. If you leave out the **$** operator before the variable name, all you have is the variable name itself. In the next example, the **$** operator is absent from the variable name. In this case, the **echo** command has as its argument the word *poet*, and so prints out *poet*:

```
$ echo poet
poet
```

The contents of a variable are often used as command arguments. A common command argument is a directory pathname. It can be tedious to retype a directory path that is being used over and over again. If you assign the directory pathname to a variable, you can simply use the evaluated variable in its place. The directory path you assign to the variable is retrieved when the variable is evaluated with the **$** operator. The next example assigns a directory pathname to a variable and then uses the evaluated variable in a copy command. The evaluation of **ldir** (which is **$ldir**) results in the pathname **/home/chris/letters**. The copy command evaluates to **cp myletter /home/chris/letters**.

```
$ ldir=/home/chris/letters
$ cp myletter $ldir
```

You can obtain a list of all the defined variables with the **set** command. If you decide you do not want a certain variable, you can remove it with the **unset** command. The **unset** command undefines a variable.

Values from Linux Commands: Back Quotes

Although you can create variable values by typing in characters or character strings, you can also obtain values from other Linux commands. To assign the result of Linux command to a variable, you first need to execute the command. If you place a Linux command within back quotes (˜) on the command line, that command is first executed and its result becomes an argument on the command line. In the case of assignments, the result of a command can be assigned to a variable by placing the command within back quotes first to execute it. The back quotes can be thought of as an expression consisting of a command to be executed whose result is then assigned to the variable. The characters making up the command itself are not assigned. In the next example, the command `ls *.c` is executed and its result is then assigned to the variable `listc`. `ls *.c`, which generates a list of all files with a .c extension. This list of files is then assigned to the `listc` variable.

```
$ listc=`ls `*.c`
$ echo $listc
main.c prog.c lib.c
```

Keep in mind the difference between single quotes and back quotes. Single quotes treat a Linux command as a set of characters. Back quotes force execution of the Linux command. There may be times when you accidentally enter single quotes when you mean to use back quotes. In the following first example, the assignment for the `lscc` variable has single quotes, not back quotes, placed around the `ls *.c` command. In this case, `ls *.c` are just characters to be assigned to the variable `lscc`. In the second example, back quotes are placed around the `ls *.c` command, forcing evaluation of the command. A list of filenames ending in **.c** is generated and assigned as the value of `lscc`.

```
$ lscc='ls *.c'
$ echo $lscc
ls *.c

$ lscc=`ls *.c`
$ echo $lscc
main.c   prog.c
```

Shell Scripts: User-Defined Commands

You can place shell commands within a file and then have the shell read and execute the commands in the file. In this sense, the file functions as a shell program, executing shell commands as if they were statements in a program. A file that contains shell commands is called a *shell script*.

You enter shell commands into a script file using a standard text editor such as the Vi editor. The `sh` or `.` command used with the script's filename will read the script file and execute the commands. In the next example, the text file called `lsc` contains an `ls` command that displays only files with the extension **.c**:

```
lsc
ls *.c
```

A run of the `lsc` script is shown here:

```
$ sh lsc
main.c calc.c
$ . lsc
main.c calc.c
```

Executing Scripts

You can dispense with the **sh** and **.** commands by setting the executable permission of a script file. When the script file is first created by your text editor, it is given only read and write permission. The **chmod** command with the **+x** option will give the script file executable permission. Once it is executable, entering the name of the script file at the shell prompt and pressing ENTER will execute the script file and the shell commands in it. In effect, the script's filename becomes a new shell command. In this way, you can use shell scripts to design and create your own Linux commands. You need to set the permission only once.

In the next example, the **lsc** file's executable permission for the owner is set to on. Then the **lsc** shell script is directly executed like any Linux command.

```
$ chmod u+x lsc
$ lsc
main.c calc.c
```

You may have to specify that the script you are using is in your current working directory. You do this by prefixing the script name with a period and slash combination, as in **./lsc**. The period is a special character representing the name of your current working directory. The slash is a directory pathname separator. The following example shows how to execute the **lsc** script:

```
$ ./lsc
main.c calc.c
```

Script Arguments

Just as any Linux command can take arguments, so also can a shell script. Arguments on the command line are referenced sequentially starting with 1. An argument is referenced using the **$** operator and the number of its position. The first argument is referenced with **$1**, the second, with **$2**, and so on. In the next example, the **lsext** script prints out files with a specified extension. The first argument is the extension. The script is then executed with the argument **c** (of course, the executable permission must have been set).

lsext
```
ls *.$1
```

A run of the **lsext** script with an argument is shown here:

```
$ lsext c
main.c calc.c
```

In the next example, the commands to print out a file with line numbers have been placed in an executable file called **lpnum**, which takes a filename as its argument. The **cat** command with the **-n** option first outputs the contents of the file with line numbers. Then this output is piped into the **lpr** command, which prints it. The command to print out the line numbers is executed in the background.

lpnum
```
cat -n $1 | lpr &
```

A run of the **lpnum** script with an argument is shown here:

```
$ lpnum mydata
```

You may need to reference more than one argument at a time. The number of arguments used may vary. In **lpnum**, you may want to print out three files at one time and five files at some other time. The **$** operator with the asterisk, **$***, references all the arguments on the command line. Using **$*** enables you to create scripts that take a varying number of arguments. In the next example, **lpnum** is rewritten using **$*** so that it can take a different number of arguments each time you use it:

```
lpnum
cat -n $*  |  lpr &
```

A run of the **lpnum** script with multiple arguments is shown here:

```
$ lpnum mydata preface
```

Control Structures

You can control the execution of Linux commands in a shell script with control structures. Control structures allow you to repeat commands and to select certain commands over others. A control structure consists of two major components: a test and commands. If the test is successful, then the commands are executed. In this way, you can use control structures to make decisions as to whether commands should be executed.

Two different kinds of control structures are used: *loops*, which repeat commands, and *conditions*, which execute commands when certain conditions are met. The BASH shell has three loop control structures—**while**, **for**, and **for-in**—and two condition structures—**if** and **case**. The control structures have as their test the execution of a Linux command. All Linux commands return an exit status after they have finished executing. If a command is successful, its exit status will be 0. If the command fails for any reason, its exit status will be a positive value referencing the type of failure that occurred. The control structures check to see whether the exit status of a Linux command is 0 or some other value. In the case of the **if** and **while** structures, if the exit status is a 0 value, the command was successful and the structure continues.

Test Operations

With the **test** command, you can compare integers and strings, and even perform logical operations. The command consists of the keyword **test** followed by the values being compared, separated by an option that specifies what kind of comparison is taking place. The option can be thought of as the operator, but it is written, like other options, with a minus sign and letter codes. For example, **-eq** is the option that represents the equality comparison. Two string operations, however, actually use an operator instead of an option. When you compare two strings for equality, you use the equal sign (=). For inequality you use **!=**. Table 10-8 lists some of the commonly used options and operators used by **test**. The syntax for the **test** command is shown here:

```
test value -option value
test string = string
```

Integer Comparisons	Function
-gt	Greater-than
-lt	Less-than
-ge	Greater-than-or-equal-to
-le	Less-than-or-equal-to
-eq	Equal
-ne	Not-equal
String Comparisons	
-z	Tests for empty string
=	Equal strings
!=	Not-equal strings
Logical Operations	
-a	Logical AND
-o	Logical OR
!	Logical NOT
File Tests	
-f	File exists and is a regular file
-s	File is not empty
-r	File is readable
-w	File can be written to, modified
-x	File is executable
-d	Filename is a directory name

TABLE 10-8 BASH Shell Test Operators

The next example compares two integer values to determine whether they are equal. In this case, the equality option, **-eq**, should be used. The exit status of the **test** command is examined to determine the result of the test operation. The shell special variable **$?** holds the exit status of the most recently executed Linux command.

```
$ num=5
$ test $num -eq 10
$ echo $?
1
```

Instead of using the keyword **test** for the **test** command, you can use enclosing brackets. The command **test $greeting = "hi"** can be written as

```
$ [ $greeting = "hi" ]
```

Similarly, the command **test $num -eq 10** can be written as

```
$ [ $num -eq 10 ]
```

The brackets themselves must be surrounded by white space: a space, TAB, or ENTER. Without the spaces, the code is invalid.

Conditional Control Structures

The BASH shell has a set of conditional control structures that allow you to choose what Linux commands to execute. Many of these are similar to conditional control structures found in programming languages, but there are some differences. The **if** condition tests the success of a Linux command, not an expression. Furthermore, the end of an **if-then** command must be indicated with the keyword **fi**, and the end of a **case** command is indicated with the keyword **esac**. The condition control structures are listed in Table 10-9.

Condition Control Structures: if, else, elif, case	Function
if *command* **then** *command* **fi**	**if** executes an action if its test command is true

if *command* **then**
  command
 else
  command
 fi
	if-else executes an action if the exit status of its test command is true; if false, the **else** action is executed

if *command* **then**
  command
 elif *command* **then**
  command
 else
  command
 fi
	elif allows you to nest **if** structures, enabling selection among several alternatives; at the first true **if** structure, its commands are executed and control leaves the entire **elif** structure

case *string* **in** *pattern*) *command*;; **esac**	**case** matches the string value to any of several patterns; if a pattern is matched, its associated commands are executed
command **&&** *command*	The logical AND condition returns a true 0 value if both commands return a true 0 value; if one returns a nonzero value, then the AND condition is false and also returns a nonzero value
command **||** *command*	The logical OR condition returns a true 0 value if one or the other command returns a true 0 value; if both commands return a nonzero value, then the OR condition is false and also returns a nonzero value
! *command*	The logical NOT condition inverts the return value of the command

TABLE 10-9   BASH Shell Control Structures

Loop Control Structures: `while, until, for, for-in, select`	

`while` *command*
`do`
 command
`done`
	`while` executes an action as long as its test command is true

`until` *command*
`do`
 command
`done`
	`until` executes an action as long as its test command is false

`for` *variable* `in` *list-values*
`do`
 command
`done`
	`for-in` is designed for use with lists of values; the variable operand is consecutively assigned the values in the list

`for` *variable*
`do`
 command
`done`
	`for` is designed for reference script arguments; the variable operand is consecutively assigned each argument value

`select` *string* `in` *item-list*
`do`
 command
`done`
	`select` creates a menu based on the items in the *item-list*; then it executes the command; the command is usually a `case`

TABLE 10-9 BASH Shell Control Structures (*Continued*)

The `if` structure places a condition on commands. That condition is the exit status of a specific Linux command. If a command is successful, returning an exit status of 0, then the commands within the `if` structure are executed. If the exit status is anything other than 0, the command has failed and the commands within the `if` structure are not executed. The `if` command begins with the keyword `if` and is followed by a Linux command whose exit condition will be evaluated. The keyword `fi` ends the command.

The `elsels` script in the next example executes the `ls` command to list files with two different possible options, either by size or with all file information. If the user enters an `s`, files are listed by size; otherwise, all file information is listed.

```
elsels
echo Enter s to list file sizes,
echo        otherwise all file information is listed.
echo -n "Please enter option: "
read choice
if [   "$choice" = s   ]
     then
          ls -s
     else
            ls -l
fi
echo Good-bye
```

A run of the program follows:

```
$ elsels
Enter s to list file sizes,
otherwise all file information is listed.
Please enter option: s
total 2
     1 monday      2 today
$
```

Loop Control Structures

The **while** loop repeats commands. A **while** loop begins with the keyword **while** and is followed by a Linux command. The keyword **do** follows on the next line. The end of the loop is specified by the keyword **done**. The Linux command used in **while** structures is often a test command indicated by enclosing brackets.

The **for-in** structure is designed to reference a list of values sequentially. It takes two operands: a variable and a list of values. The values in the list are assigned one by one to the variable in the **for-in** structure. Like the **while** command, the **for-in** structure is a loop. Each time through the loop, the next value in the list is assigned to the variable. When the end of the list is reached, the loop stops. Like the **while** loop, the body of a **for-in** loop begins with the keyword **do** and ends with the keyword **done**. The **cbackup** script makes a backup of each file and places it in a directory called **sourcebak**. Notice the use of the ***** special character to generate a list of all filenames with a **.c** extension.

cbackup

```
for backfile in *.c
do
    cp $backfile sourcebak/$backfile
 echo $backfile
done
```

A run of the program follows:

```
$ cbackup
io.c
lib.c
main.c
$
```

The **for** structure without a specified list of values takes as its list of values the command line arguments. The arguments specified on the command line when the shell file is invoked become a list of values referenced by the **for** command. The variable used in the **for** command is set automatically to each argument value in sequence. The first time through the loop, the variable is set to the value of the first argument. The second time, it is set to the value of the second argument.

Filters and Regular Expressions

Filters are commands that read data, perform operations on that data, and then send the results to the standard output. Filters generate different kinds of output, depending on their task. Some filters generate information only about the input, other filters output selected parts of the input, and still other filters output an entire version of the input, but in a modified way. Some filters are limited to one of these, while others have options that specify one or the other. You can think of a filter as operating on a stream of data—receiving data and generating modified output. As data is passed through the filter, it is analyzed, screened, or modified.

The data stream input to a filter consists of a sequence of bytes that can be received from files, devices, or the output of other commands or filters. The filter operates on the data stream, but it does not modify the source of the data. If a filter receives input from a file, the file itself is not modified. Only its data is read and fed into the filter.

The output of a filter is usually sent to the standard output. It can then be redirected to another file or device, or piped as input to another utility or filter. All the features of redirection and pipes apply to filters. Often data is read by one filter and its modified output piped into another filter.

NOTE *Data could easily undergo several modifications as it is passed from one filter to another. However, it is always important to realize the original source of the data is never changed.*

Many utilities and filters use patterns to locate and select specific text in your file. Sometimes, you may need to use patterns in a more flexible and powerful way, searching for several different variations on a given pattern. You can include a set of special characters in your pattern to enable a flexible search. A pattern that contains such special characters is called a *regular expression*. Regular expressions can be used in most filters and utilities that employ pattern searches such as **sed**, **awk**, **grep**, and **egrep**.

TIP *Although many of the special characters used for regular expressions are similar to the shell file expansion characters, they are used in a different way. Shell file expansion characters operate on filenames. Regular expressions search text.*

You can save the output of a filter in a file or send it to a printer. To do so, you need to use redirection or pipes. To save the output of a filter to a file, you redirect it to a file using the redirection operation (>). To send output to the printer, you pipe the output to the **lpr** utility, which then prints it. In the next command, the **cat** command pipes its output to the **lpr** command, which then prints it.

```
$ cat complist | lpr
```

All filters accept input from the standard input. In fact, the output of one filter can be piped as the input for another filter. Many filters also accept input directly from files, however. Such filters can take filenames as their arguments and read data directly from those files.

Searching Files: grep

The **grep** and **fgrep** filters search the contents of files for a pattern. They then tell you in what file the pattern was found and print the lines in which it occurred in each file. Preceding each line is the name of the file in which the line is located. The **grep** command can search for only one pattern, whereas **fgrep** can search for more than one pattern at a time.

The **grep** filter takes two types of arguments. The first argument is the pattern to be searched for; the second argument is a list of filenames, which are the files to be searched. You enter the filenames on the command line after the pattern. You can also use special characters, such as the asterisk, to generate a file list.

```
$ grep pattern filenames-list
```

If you want to include more than one word in the pattern search, you enclose the words within single quotation marks. This is to quote the spaces between the words in the pattern. Otherwise, the shell would interpret the space as a delimiter or argument on the command line, and **grep** would try to interpret words in the pattern as part of the file list. In the next example, **grep** searches for the pattern *text file*:

```
$ grep 'text file' preface
A text file in Linux
text files, changing or
```

If you use more than one file in the file list, **grep** will output the name of the file before the matching line. In the next example, two files, **preface** and **intro**, are searched for the pattern *data*. Before each occurrence, the filename is output.

```
$ grep data preface intro
 preface: data in the file.
 intro: new data
```

As mentioned earlier, you can also use shell file expansion characters to generate a list of files to be searched. In the next example, the asterisk file expansion character is used to generate a list of all files in your directory. This is a simple way of searching all of a directory's files for a pattern.

```
$ grep data *
```

The special characters are often useful for searching a selected set of files. For example, if you want to search all your C program source code files for a particular pattern, you can specify the set of source code files with `*.c`. Suppose you have an unintended infinite loop in your program and you need to locate all instances of iterations. The next example searches only those files with a **.c** extension for the pattern *while* and displays the lines of code that perform iterations:

```
$ grep while *.c
```

Regular Expressions

Regular expressions enable you to match possible variations on a pattern, as well as patterns located at different points in the text. You can search for patterns in your text that have different ending or beginning letters, or you can match text at the beginning or end of a line. The regular expression special characters are the circumflex, dollar sign, asterisk, period, and brackets: `^`, `$`, `*`, `.`, `[]`. The circumflex and dollar sign match on the beginning and end of a line. The asterisk matches repeated characters, the period matches single characters, and the brackets match on classes of characters. See Table 10-10 for a listing of the regular expression special characters.

Character	Match	Operation
^	Start of a line	References the beginning of a line
$	End of a line	References the end of a line
.	Any character	Matches on any one possible character in a pattern
*	Repeated characters	Matches on repeated characters in a pattern
[]	Classes	Matches on classes of characters (a set of characters) in the pattern

TABLE 10-10   Regular Expression Special Characters

NOTE *Regular expressions are used extensively in many Linux filters and applications to perform searches and matching operations. The Vi and Emacs editors and the* **sed**, **diff**, **grep**, *and* **gawk** *filters all use regular expressions.*

Suppose you want to use the long-form output of **ls** to display just your directories. One way to do this is to generate a list of all directories in the long form and pipe this list to **grep**, which can then pick out the directory entries. You can do this by using the ^ special character to specify the beginning of a line. Remember, in the long-form output of **ls**, the first character indicates the file type. A **d** represents a directory, an **l** represents a symbolic link, and an **a** represents a regular file. Using the pattern '^d', **grep** will match only on those lines beginning with a *d*.

```
$ ls -l | grep '^d'
drwxr-x---  2  chris 512 Feb 10 04:30   reports
drwxr-x---  2  chris 512 Jan 6  01:20   letters
```

Shell Configuration

Four different major shells are commonly used on Linux systems: the Bourne Again shell (BASH), the AT&T Korn shell, the TCSH shell, and the Z shell. The BASH shell is an advanced version of the Bourne shell that includes most of the advanced features developed for the Korn shell and the C shell. TCSH is an enhanced version of the C shell, originally developed for BSD versions of Unix. The AT&T Unix Korn shell is open source. The Z shell is an enhanced version of the Korn shell.

Although their Unix counterparts differ greatly, the Linux shells share many of the same features. In Unix, the Bourne shell lacks many capabilities found in the other Unix shells. In Linux, however, the BASH shell incorporates all the advanced features of the Korn shell and C shell, as well as those of the TCSH shell. All four shells are available for your use, though the BASH shell is the default.

For most Linux distributions, when you log in to a command line interface, you are placed in the default BASH shell automatically and shown a shell prompt where you can enter commands. The shell prompt for the BASH shell is a dollar sign ($). In a GUI application, such as GNOME or KDE, you can open a terminal window that will display a command line interface with the prompt for the default BASH shell. Though you log in to your default shell or display it automatically in a terminal window, you can change to another shell by entering its name. Entering **tcsh** invokes the TCSH shell, **bash** the BASH shell, **ksh** the Korn shell, and **zsh** the Z shell. You can exit a shell by pressing CTRL-D or using the **exit** command. You need only one type of shell to do your work. Table 11-1 shows the different commands you can use to invoke different shells. Some shells have additional links you can use the invoke the same shell, such as **sh** and **bsh**, which link to and invoke the **bash** command for the BASH shell.

This chapter describes common features of the BASH shell, such as aliases, as well as how to configure the shell to suit your own needs using shell variables and initialization files. The other shells share many of the same features and use similar variables and initialization files.

NOTE *Though the basic shell features and configurations are shown in this chapter, you should consult the respective online manuals and FAQs for each shell for more detailed examples and explanations. See Table 10-1 in Chapter 10 for the Web sites for each shell.*

Command	Description
bash	BASH shell, **/bin/bash**
bsh	BASH shell, **/bin/bsh** (link to **/bin/bash**)
sh	BASH shell, **/bin/sh** (link to **/bin/bash**)
tcsh	TCSH shell, **/usr/tcsh**
csh	TCSH shell, **/bin/csh** (link to **/bin/tcsh**)
ksh	Korn shell, **/bin/ksh** (also added link **/usr/bin/ksh**)
zsh	Z shell, **/bin/zsh**

TABLE 11-1   Shell Invocation Command Names

Shell Initialization and Configuration Files

Each type of shell has its own set of initialization and configuration files. The TCSH shell uses **.login**, **.tcshrc**, and **.logout** files in place of **.profile**, **.bashrc**, and **.bash_logout**. The Z shell has several initialization files: **.zshenv**, **.zlogin**, **.zprofile**, **.zschrc**, and **.zlogout**. See Table 11-2 for a listing of these files. Check the man pages for each shell to see how they are usually configured. When you install a shell, default versions of these files are automatically placed in the users' home directories. Except for the TCSH shell, all shells use much the same syntax for variable definitions and assigning values (TCSH uses a slightly different syntax, as described in its man pages).

Filename	Function
BASH Shell	
.profile	Login initialization file
.bashrc	BASH shell configuration file
.bash_logout	Logout name
.bash_history	History file
.bash_aliases	Aliases definition file
/etc/profile	System login initialization file
/etc/bash.bashrc	System BASH shell configuration file

TABLE 11-2   Shell Configuration Files

Configuration Directories and Files

Applications often install configuration files in a user's home directory that contain specific configuration information, which tailors the application to the needs of that particular user. This may take the form of a single configuration file that begins with a period, or a directory that contains several configuration files. The directory name will also begin with a period. For example, Mozilla installs a directory called **.mozilla** in the user's home directory that contains configuration files. On the other hand, many mail applications use a single file called **.mailrc** to hold alias and feature settings set up by the user, though others such as Evolution also have their own file, **.evolution**. Most single configuration files end in the letters *rc*. FTP uses a file called **.netrc**. Most newsreaders use a file called **.newsrc**. Entries in configuration files are usually set by the application, though you can usually make entries directly by editing the file. Applications have their own set of special variables to which you can define and assign values. You can list the configuration files in your home directory using the **ls -a** command.

Aliases

You use the **alias** command to create another name for a command. The **alias** command operates like a macro that expands to the command it represents. The alias does not literally replace the name of the command; it simply gives another name to that command. An **alias** command begins with the keyword **alias** and the new name for the command, followed by an equal sign and the command the **alias** will reference.

NOTE *No spaces should be placed around the equal sign used in the **alias** command.*

In the next example, **list** becomes an alias for the **ls** command:

```
$ alias list=ls
$ ls
mydata today
$ list
mydata today
$
```

If you want an alias to be automatically defined, you have to enter the alias operation in a shell configuration file. On Ubuntu, aliases are defined in either the user's **.bashrc** file or a **.bash_aliases** file. To use a **.bash_aliases** file, you must first uncomment the commands in the **.bashrc** file that will read the **.bash_aliases** file. Just edit the **.bashrc** file and remove the preceding **#** so it appears like the following:

```
if [ -f ~/.bash_aliases ]; then
    . ~/.bash_aliases
fi
```

You can also place aliases in the **.bashrc** file directly. Some are already defined, though commented out. You can edit the **.bashrc** file and remove the **#** comment symbols from those lines to activate the aliases:

```
# some more ls aliases
alias ll='ls -l'
alias la='ls -A'
alias l='ls -CF'
```

Aliasing Commands and Options

You can use an alias to substitute for a command and its option, but you need to enclose both the command and the option within single quotes. Any command you alias that contains spaces must be enclosed in single quotes as well. In the next example, the alias **lss** references the **ls** command with its **-s** option, and the alias **lsa** references the **ls** command with the **-F** option. The **ls** command with the **-s** option lists files and their sizes in blocks, and **ls** with the **-F** option places a slash after directory names. Notice how single quotes enclose the command and its option.

```
$ alias lss='ls -s'
$ lss
mydata 14    today  6    reports  1
$ alias lsa='ls -F'
$ lsa
mydata today reports/
$
```

Aliases are helpful for simplifying complex operations. In the next example, **listlong** becomes another name for the **ls** command with the **-l** option (the long format that lists all file information), as well as the **-h** option for using a human-readable format for file sizes. Be sure to encase the command and its arguments within single quotes so that they are taken as one argument and not parsed by the shell.

```
$ alias listlong='ls -lh'
$ listlong
-rw-r--r--    1 root    root    51K  Sep  18  2003 mydata
-rw-r--r--    1 root    root    16K  Sep  27  2003 today
```

Aliasing Commands and Arguments

You may often use an alias to include a command name with an argument. If you execute a command that has an argument with a complex combination of special characters on a regular basis, you may want to alias it. For example, suppose you often list just your source code and object code files—those files ending in either a **.c** or **.o**. You would need to use as an argument for **ls** a combination of special characters such as ***.[co]**. Instead, you can alias **ls** with the **.[co]** argument, giving it a simple name. In the next example, the user creates an alias called **lsc** for the command **ls.[co]**:

```
$ alias lsc='ls *.[co]'
$ lsc
main.c main.o lib.c lib.o
```

Aliasing Commands

You can use the name of a command as an alias. This can be helpful when you should use a command only with a specific option. In the case of the **rm**, **cp**, and **mv** commands, for example, the **-i** option should always be used to ensure an existing file is not overwritten. Instead of always being careful to use the **-i** option each time you use one of these commands, you can alias the command name to include the option. In the next example, the **rm**, **cp**, and **mv** commands have been aliased to include the **-i** option:

```
$ alias rm='rm -i'
$ alias mv='mv -i'
$ alias cp='cp -i'
```

The **alias** command by itself provides a list of all aliases that have been defined, showing the commands they represent. You can remove an alias by using the **unalias** command. In the next example, the user lists the current aliases and then removes the **lsa** alias:

```
$ alias
lsa=ls -F
list=ls
rm=rm -i
$ unalias lsa
```

Controlling Shell Operations

The BASH shell has several features that enable you to control the way different shell operations work. For example, setting the **noclobber** feature prevents redirection from overwriting files. You can turn these features on and off like a toggle, using the **set** command. The **set** command takes two arguments: an option specifying on or off and the name of the feature. To set a feature on, you use the **-o** option, and to set it off, you use the **+o** option. Here is the basic form:

```
$ set -o feature        turn the feature on
$ set +o feature        turn the feature off
```

Three of the most common features are **ignoreeof**, **noclobber**, and **noglob**. Table 11-3 lists these different features, as well as the **set** command. Setting **ignoreeof** enables a feature that prevents you from logging out of the user shell with CTRL-D. CTRL-D is not only used to log out of the user shell, but also to end user input entered directly into the standard input. CTRL-D is used often for the Mail program or for utilities such as **cat**. You can easily enter an extra CTRL-D in such circumstances and accidentally log yourself out. The **ignoreeof** feature prevents such accidental logouts. In the next example, the **ignoreeof** feature is turned on using the **set** command with the **-o** option. The user can then log out only by entering the **logout** command.

```
$ set -o ignoreeof
$ CTRL-D
Use exit to logout
$
```

PART IV

Features	Description
`$ set -+o` *feature*	BASH shell features are turned on and off with the `set` command; `-o` sets a feature on and `+o` turns it off: `$ set -o noclobber` *set noclobber on* `$ set +o noclobber` *set noclobber off*
`ignoreeof`	Disables CTRL-D logout
`noclobber`	Does not overwrite files through redirection
`noglob`	Disables special characters used for filename expansion: *****, **?**, **~**, and **[]**

TABLE 11-3 BASH Shell Special Features

Environment Variables and Subshells: export

When you log in to your account, Linux generates your user shell. Within this shell, you can issue commands and declare variables. You can also create and execute shell scripts. When you execute a shell script, however, the system generates a subshell. You then have two shells, the one you logged in to and the one generated for the script. Within the script shell, you can execute another shell script, which then has its own shell. When a script has finished execution, its shell terminates and you return to the shell from which it was executed. In this sense, you can have many shells, each nested within the other. Variables you define within a shell are local to it. If you define a variable in a shell script, then when the script is run, the variable is defined with that script's shell and is local to it. No other shell can reference that variable. In a sense, the variable is hidden within its shell.

You can define environment variables in all types of shells, including the BASH shell, the Z shell, and the TCSH shell. The strategy used to implement environment variables in the BASH shell, however, is different from that of the TCSH shell. In the BASH shell, environment variables are exported—that is, a copy of an environment variable is made in each subshell. For example, if the **EDITOR** variable is exported, a copy is automatically defined in each subshell for you. In the TCSH shell, on the other hand, an environment variable is defined only once and can be directly referenced by any subshell.

In the BASH shell, an environment variable can be thought of as a regular variable with added capabilities. To make an environment variable, you apply the **export** command to a variable you have already defined. The **export** command instructs the system to define a copy of that variable for each new shell generated. Each new shell will have its own copy of the environment variable. This process is called *exporting variables*. To think of exported environment variables as global variables is a mistake. A new shell can never reference a variable outside of itself. Instead, a copy of the variable with its value is generated for the new shell.

Configuring Your Shell with Shell Parameters

When you log in, Linux will set certain parameters for your login shell. These parameters can take the form of variables or features. (See the earlier section "Controlling Shell Operations" for a description of how to set features.) Linux reserves a predefined set of variables for shell and system use. These are assigned system values, in effect, setting parameters. Linux sets up parameter shell variables you can use to configure your user shell. Many of these parameter shell variables are defined by the system when you log in. Some parameter shell variables are set by the shell automatically, and others are set by initialization scripts, described later. Certain shell variables are set directly by the shell, and others are simply used by it. Many of these other variables are application-specific, used for such tasks as mail, history, or editing. Functionally, it may be better to think of these as system-level variables, as they are used to configure your entire system, setting values such as the location of executable commands on your system or the number of history commands allowable. Table 11-4 shows a list of those shell variables set by the shell for shell-specific tasks; Table 11-5 lists those used by the shell for supporting other applications.

A reserved set of keywords is used for the names of these system variables. You should not use these keywords as the names of any of your own variable names. The system shell variables are all specified in uppercase letters, making them easy to identify. Shell feature variables are in lowercase letters. For example, the keyword **HOME** is used by the system to define the **HOME** variable. **HOME** is a special environment variable that holds the pathname of the user's home directory. On the other hand, the keyword **noclobber** is used to set the **noclobber** feature on or off.

Shell Parameter Variables

Many of the shell parameter variables automatically defined and assigned initial values by the system when you log in can be changed, if you wish. Some parameter variables exist

Shell Variables	Description
BASH	Full pathname of BASH command
BASH_VERSION	The current BASH version number
GROUPS	Groups to which the user belongs
HISTCMD	Number of the current command in the history list
HOME	Pathname for user's home directory
HOSTNAME	Hostname
HOSTTYPE	Type of machine on which the host runs
OLDPWD	Previous working directory
OSTYPE	Operating system in use
PATH	Pathnames for directories searched for executable commands
PPID	Processes ID for shell's parent shell
PWD	User's working directory
RANDOM	Generated random number when referenced
SHLVL	Current shell level, number of shells invoked
UID	User ID of the current user

TABLE 11-4 Shell Variables Set by the Shell

Shell Variables	Description
BASH_VERSION	The current BASH version number
CDPATH	Search path for the **cd** command
EXINIT	Initialization commands for Ex/Vi editor
FCEDIT	Editor used by the history **fc** command
GROUPS	Groups to which the user belongs
HISTFILE	The pathname of the history file
HISTSIZE	Number of commands allowed for history
HISTFILESIZE	Size of the history file in lines
HISTCMD	Number of the current command in the history list
HOME	Pathname for user's home directory
HOSTFILE	Sets the name of the hosts file, if other than **/etc/hosts**
IFS	Interfield delimiter symbol
IGNOREEOF	If not set, EOF character will close the shell; can be set to the number of EOF characters to ignore before accepting one to close the shell (default is 10)
INPUTRC	The **inputrc** configuration file for Readline (command line); default is current directory, **.inputrc**; most Linux distributions set this to **/etc/inputrc**
KDEDIR	The pathname location for the KDE desktop
LOGNAME	Login name
MAIL	Name of specific mail file checked by Mail utility for received messages, if **MAILPATH** is not set
MAILCHECK	Interval for checking for received mail
MAILPATH	List of mail files to be checked by Mail for received messages
HOSTTYPE	Linux platforms, such as i686, x86_64, or PPC
PROMPT_COMMAND	Command to be executed before each prompt, integrating the result as part of the prompt
HISTFILE	The pathname of the history file
PS1	Primary shell prompt
PS2	Secondary shell prompt
QTDIR	Location of the Qt library (used for KDE)
SHELL	Pathname of program for type of shell you are using
TERM	Terminal type
TMOUT	Time that the shell remains active awaiting input
USER	Username
UID	Real user ID (numeric)
EUID	Effective user ID (numeric); usually the same as the UID but can be different when the user changes IDs, as with the **su** command, which allows a user to become an effective root user

TABLE 11-5   System Environment Variables Used by the Shell

whose values should not be changed, however. For example, the **HOME** variable holds the pathname for your home directory. Commands such as **cd** reference the pathname in the **HOME** shell variable to locate your home directory. Some of the more common of these parameter variables are described in this section.

Other parameter variables are defined by the system and given an initial value that you are free to change. To do this, you redefine them and assign a new value. For example, the **PATH** variable is defined by the system and assigned an initial value; it contains the pathnames of directories where commands are located. Whenever you execute a command, the shell searches for it in these directories. You can add a new directory to be searched by redefining the **PATH** variable yourself, so that it will include the new directory's pathname.

Still other parameter variables exist that the system does not define. These are usually optional features, such as the **EXINIT** variable that enables you to set options for the Vi editor. Each time you log in, you must define and assign a value to such variables. Some of the more common parameter variables are **SHELL**, **PATH**, **PS1**, **PS2**, and **MAIL**. The **SHELL** variable holds the pathname of the program for the type of shell you log in to. The **PATH** variable lists the different directories to be searched for a Linux command. The **PS1** and **PS2** variables hold the prompt symbols. The **MAIL** variable holds the pathname of your mailbox file. You can modify the values for any of these to customize your shell.

NOTE *You can obtain a listing of the currently defined shell variables using the* **env** *command. The* **env** *command operates like the* **set** *command, but it lists only parameter variables.*

Using Initialization Files

You can automatically define parameter variables using special shell scripts called *initialization files*. An initialization file is a specially named shell script that is executed whenever you enter a certain shell. You can edit the initialization file and place in it definitions and assignments for parameter variables. When you enter the shell, the initialization file will execute these definitions and assignments, effectively initializing parameter variables with your own values. For example, the BASH shell's **.profile** file is an initialization file executed every time you log in. It contains definitions and assignments of parameter variables. However, the **.profile** file is basically a shell script that you can edit with any text editor, such as the Vi editor, to change, for example, the values assigned to parameter variables.

In the BASH shell, all the parameter variables are designed to be environment variables. When you define or redefine a parameter variable, you also need to export it to make it an environment variable. This means any change you make to a parameter variable must be accompanied by an **export** command. You will see that at the end of the login initialization file, **.profile**, an **export** command is usually included for all the parameter variables defined in it.

Your Home Directory: HOME

The **HOME** variable contains the pathname of your home directory. Your home directory is determined by the parameter administrator when your account is created. The pathname for your home directory is automatically read into your **HOME** variable when you log in.

In the next example, the **echo** command displays the contents of the **HOME** variable:

```
$ echo $HOME
/home/chris
```

The **HOME** variable is often used when you need to specify the absolute pathname of your home directory. In the next example, the absolute pathname of **reports** is specified using **HOME** for the home directory's path:

```
$ ls $HOME/reports
```

Command Locations: PATH

The **PATH** variable contains a series of directory paths separated by colons. Each time a command is executed, the paths listed in the **PATH** variable are searched one by one for that command. For example, the **cp** command resides on the system in the directory **/bin**. This directory path is one of the directories listed in the **PATH** variable. Each time you execute the **cp** command, this path is searched and the **cp** command located. The system defines and assigns **PATH** an initial set of pathnames. In Linux, the initial pathnames are **/bin** and **/usr/bin**.

The shell can execute any executable file, including programs and scripts you have created. For this reason, the **PATH** variable can also reference your working directory; so if you want to execute one of your own scripts or programs in your working directory, the shell can locate it. No spaces are allowed between the pathnames in the string. A colon with no pathname specified references your working directory. Usually, a single colon is placed at the end of the pathnames as an empty entry specifying your working directory. For example, the pathname **//bin:/usr/bin:** references three directories: **/bin**, **/usr/bin**, and your current working directory.

```
$ echo $PATH
/bin:/usr/sbin:
```

You can add any new directory path you want to the **PATH** variable. This can be useful if you have created several of your own Linux commands using shell scripts. You can place these new shell script commands in a directory you create and then add that directory to the **PATH** list. Then, no matter what directory you are in, you can execute one of your shell scripts. The **PATH** variable will contain the directory for that script, so that directory will be searched each time you issue a command.

You add a directory to the **PATH** variable with a variable assignment. You can execute this assignment directly in your shell. In the next example, the user **chris** adds a new directory, called **bin**, to the **PATH**. Although you could carefully type in the complete pathnames listed in **PATH** for the assignment, you can also use an evaluation of **PATH**— **${PATH}**—in its place. In this example, an evaluation of the tilde, ~, is also used to designate the user's **home** directory in the new directory's pathname. Notice the last colon, which specifies the working directory:

```
$ PATH=~/bin:"${PATH}:"
$ export PATH
$ echo $PATH
/bin:/usr/bin::/home/chris/mybin
```

If you add a directory to **PATH** yourself while you are logged in, the directory will be added only for the duration of your login session. When you next log back in, the login initialization file, **.profile**, will again initialize your **PATH** with its original set of directories. The **.profile** file is described in detail a bit later in this chapter (see "Configuring Your Login Shell: .profile"). To add a new directory to your **PATH** permanently, you need to edit your

.profile file and find the assignment for the **PATH** variable. Then, you simply insert the directory, preceded by a colon, into the set of pathnames assigned to **PATH**.

Specifying the BASH Environment: BASH_ENV
The **BASH_ENV** variable holds the name of the BASH shell initialization file to be executed whenever a BASH shell is generated. For example, when a BASH shell script is executed, the **BASH_ENV** variable is checked and the name of the script that it holds is executed before the shell script. The **BASH_ENV** variable usually holds **$HOME/.bashrc**. This is the **.bashrc** file in the user's home directory. (The **.bashrc** file is discussed later in this chapter.) You can specify a different file if you wish, using that instead of the **.bashrc** file for BASH shell scripts.

Configuring the Shell Prompt
The **PS1** and **PS2** variables contain the primary and secondary prompt symbols, respectively. The primary prompt symbol for the BASH shell is a dollar sign (**$**). You can change the prompt symbol by assigning a new set of characters to the **PS1** variable. In the next example, the shell prompt is changed to the **->** symbol:

```
$ PS1= '->'
-> export PS1
->
```

You can change the prompt to be any set of characters, including a string, as shown in the next example:

```
$ PS1="Please enter a command: "
Please enter a command: export PS1
Please enter a command: ls
mydata /reports
Please enter a command:
```

The **PS2** variable holds the secondary prompt symbol, which is used for commands that take several lines to complete. The default secondary prompt is **>**. The added command lines begin with the secondary prompt instead of the primary prompt. You can change the secondary prompt just as easily as the primary prompt, as shown here:

```
$ PS2="@"
```

Like the TCSH shell, the BASH shell provides a predefined set of codes you can use to configure your prompt. With them you can make the time, your username, or your directory pathname a part of your prompt. You can even have your prompt display the history event number of the current command you are about to enter. Each code is preceded by a \ symbol: **\w** represents the current working directory, **\t** the time, and **\u** your username; **\!** will display the next history event number. In the next example, the user adds the current working directory to the prompt:

```
$ PS1="\w $"
/home/dylan $
```

The codes must be included within a quoted string. If no quotes exist, the code characters are not evaluated and are themselves used as the prompt. So, for example, **PS1=\w** sets the prompt to the characters \w, not the working directory. The next example incorporates both the time and the history event number with a new prompt:

```
$ PS1="\t \! ->"
```

The following table lists the codes for configuring your prompt:

Prompt Codes	Description
\!	Current history number
\$	Use $ as prompt for all users except the root user, which has the # as its prompt
\d	Current date
\#	History command number for just the current shell
\h	Hostname
\s	Shell type currently active
\t	Time of day in hours, minutes, and seconds
\u	Username
\v	Shell version
\w	Full pathname of the current working directory
\W	Name of the current working directory
\\	Backslash character
\n	Newline character
\[\]	Allows entry of terminal specific display characters for features such as color or bold font
\nnn	Character specified in octal format

The default BASH prompt is \s-\v\$ to display the type of shell, the shell version, and the $ symbol as the prompt. Some distributions, including Ubuntu, have changed this to a more complex command consisting of the username, the hostname, and the name of the current working directory. A sample configuration is shown next. A simple equivalent is shown here with an @ sign in the hostname and a $ for the final prompt symbol. The home directory is represented with a tilde (~).

```
$ PS1="\u@\h:\w$"
richard@turtle.com:~$
```

Ubuntu also includes some complex prompt definitions in the **.bashrc** file to support color prompts and detect any remote user logins.

Specifying Your News Server

Several shell parameter variables are used to set values used by network applications, such as Web browsers or newsreaders. **NNTPSERVER** is used to set the value of a remote news server accessible on your network. If you are using an ISP, the ISP usually provides a Usenet news server you can access with your newsreader applications. However, you first have to provide your newsreaders with the Internet address of the news server. This is the role of the **NNTPSERVER** variable. News servers on the Internet usually use the NNTP protocol. **NNTPSERVER** should hold the address of such a news server. For many ISPs, the news server address is a domain name that begins with **nntp**. The following example assigns the news server address **nntp.myservice.com** to the **NNTPSERVER** shell variable. Newsreader applications automatically obtain the news server address from **NNTPSERVER**. Usually, this assignment is placed in the shell initialization file, **.profile**, so that it is automatically set each time a user logs in.

```
NNTPSERVER=news.myservice.com
export NNTPSERVER
```

Configuring Your Login Shell: .profile

The **.profile** file is the BASH shell's login initialization file (named **.bash_profile** in SUSE and Fedora Linux). It is a script file that is automatically executed whenever a user logs in. The file contains shell commands that define system environment variables used to manage your shell. They may be either redefinitions of system-defined variables or definitions of user-defined variables. For example, when you log in, your user shell needs to know what directories hold Linux commands. It will reference the **PATH** variable to find the pathnames for these directories. However, first, the **PATH** variable must be assigned those pathnames. In the **.profile** file, an assignment operation does just this. Because it is in the **.profile** file, the assignment is executed automatically when the user logs in.

Exporting Variables

Any new parameter variables you may add to the **.profile** file will also need to be exported, using the **export** command. This makes them accessible to any subshells you may enter. You can export several variables in one **export** command by listing them as arguments. The **.profile** file contains no variable definitions, though you can add some of your own. In this case, the **.profile** file would have an **export** command with a list of all the variables defined in the file. If a variable is missing from this list, you may be unable to access it. The **.bashrc** file contains a definition of the **HISTCONTROL** variable, which is then exported. You can also combine the assignment and **export** command into one operation as shown here for **NNTPSERVER**:

```
export NNTPSERVER=news.myservice.com
```

Variable Assignments

A copy of the standard **.profile** file that's provided for you when your account is created is listed in the next example. Notice how **PATH** is assigned. **PATH** is a parameter variable the system has already defined. **PATH** holds the pathnames of directories searched for any command you enter. The assignment **PATH=HOME/bin${PATH}"** has the effect of redefining **PATH** to include your **bin** directory within your home directory so that your **bin** directory will also be searched for any commands, including those you created yourself, such as scripts or programs.

.profile

```
# ~/.profile: executed by the command interpreter for login shells.
# This file is not read by bash(1), if ~/.bash_profile or ~/.bash_login
# exists.
# see /usr/share/doc/bash/examples/startup-files for examples.
# the files are located in the bash-doc package.

# the default umask is set in /etc/profile
#umask 022

# if running bash
if [ -n "$BASH_VERSION" ]; then
    # include .bashrc if it exists
    if [ -f "$HOME/.bashrc"]; then
        . "$HOME/.bashrc"
    fi
fi
# set PATH so it includes user's private bin if it exists
if [ -d "$HOME/bin"] ; then
    PATH="$HOME/bin:$PATH"
fi
```

Should you want to have your current working directory searched as well, you can use any text editor to modify this line in your **.profile** file: **PATH="$HOME/bin:$PATH"**. You would insert a colon (**:**) after **"$PATH"**. In fact, you can change this entry to add as many directories as you want to search. Making commands automatically executable in your current working directory could be a security risk, allowing files in any directory to be executed, instead of in certain specified directories. An example of how to modify your **.profile** file is shown in the following section.

PATH="$HOME/bin:$PATH:"

Editing Your BASH Profile Script

Your **.profile** initialization file is a text file that can be edited by a text editor, like any other text file. You can easily add new directories to your **PATH** by editing **.profile** and using editing commands to insert a new directory pathname in the list of directory pathnames assigned to the **PATH** variable. You can even add new variable definitions. If you do so, however, be sure to include the new variable's name in the **export** command's argument list. For example, if your **.profile** file does not have any definition of the **EXINIT** variable, you can edit the file and add a new line that assigns a value to **EXINIT**. The definition **EXINIT='set nu ai'** will configure the Vi editor with line numbering and indentation. You then need to add **EXINIT** to the **export** command's argument list. When the **.profile** file executes again, the **EXINIT** variable will be set to the command **set nu ai**. When the Vi editor is invoked, the command in the **EXINIT** variable will be executed, setting the line number and auto-indent options automatically.

In the following example, the user's **.profile** file has been modified to include definitions of **EXINIT** and redefinitions of **PATH**, **PS1**, and **HISTSIZE**. The **PATH** variable has the ending colon added to it that specifies the current working directory, enabling you to execute commands that may be located in either the home directory or the working directory. The redefinition of **HISTSIZE** reduces the number of history events saved, from 1000 defined in the system's **.profile** file, to 30. The redefinition of the **PS1** parameter variable changes the prompt to show just the pathname of the current working directory. Any changes you make to parameter variables within your **.profile** file override those made earlier by the system's **.profile** file. All these parameter variables are then exported with the **export** command.

.profile

```
# ~/.profile: executed by the command interpreter for login shells.
# This file is not read by bash(1), if ~/.bash_profile or ~/.bash_login
# exists.
# see /usr/share/doc/bash/examples/startup-files for examples.
# the files are located in the bash-doc package.

# the default umask is set in /etc/profile
#umask 022

# if running bash
if [ -n "$BASH_VERSION" ]; then
    # include .bashrc if it exists
    if [ -f "$HOME/.bashrc" ]; then
        . "$HOME/.bashrc"
    fi
fi
# set PATH so it includes user's private bin if it exists
if [ -d ~/bin ] ; then
    PATH="$HOME/bin:$PATH:"
fi
HISTSIZE=30
NNTPSERVER=news.myserver.com
EXINIT='set nu ai'
PS1="\w \$"
export PATH HISTSIZE EXINIT PS1 NNTPSERVER
```

Manually Re-executing the .profile Script

Although the **.profile** script is executed each time you log in, it is not automatically re-executed after you make changes to it. The **.profile** file is an initialization file that is executed *only* when you log in. If you want to take advantage of any changes you make to it without having to log out and log in again, you can re-execute the **.profile** shell script with the dot (**.**) command (as you can with any shell script).

```
$ . .profile
```

Alternatively, you can use the **source** command to execute the **.profile** initialization file or any initialization file such as **.login** used in the TCSH shell or **.bashrc**:

```
$ source .profile
```

System Shell Profile Script

Your Linux system also has its own profile file that it executes whenever any user logs in. This system initialization file is simply called **profile** and is found in the **/etc** directory: **/etc/profile**. This file contains parameter variable definitions the system needs to provide for each user. A copy of the system's **profile** file follows. On Ubuntu, the **/etc/profile** script sets the command line shell prompt, checking for the root user (**#**) or a normal user (**$**). It then runs the **/etc/bash.baschrc** script, which performs most of the configuration tasks. The **/etc/profile.d** directory is checked for any specialized scripts to run, assigning system variable values or performing other set up operations. For the standard Ubuntu installation, this directory is currently empty.

```
/etc/profile
# /etc/profile: system-wide .profile file for the Bourne shell (sh(1))
# and Bourne compatible shells (bash(1), ksh(1), ash(1), ...).

if [ -d /etc/profile.d ]; then
  for i in /etc/profile.d/*.sh; do
    if [ -r $i ]; then
      . $i
    fi
  done
  unset i
fi

if [ "$PS1" ]; then
  if [ "$BASH" ]; then
    PS1='\u@\h:\w\$ '
    if [ -f /etc/bash.bashrc ]; then
        . /etc/bash.bashrc
    fi
  else
    if [ "`id -u`" -eq 0 ]; then
      PS1='# '
    else
      PS1='$ '
    fi
  fi
fi
```

Configuring the BASH Shell: .bashrc

The **.bashrc** file is a configuration file executed each time you enter the BASH shell or generate any subshells. If the BASH shell is your login shell, **.bashrc** is executed along with your **.bash_login** file when you log in. If you enter the BASH shell from another shell, the **.bashrc** file is automatically executed and the variable and alias definitions it contains will be defined. If you enter a different type of shell, the configuration file for that shell will be executed instead. For example, if you were to enter the TCSH shell with the **tcsh** command, the **.tcshrc** configuration file would be executed instead of **.bashrc**.

The User .bashrc BASH Script

The **.bashrc** shell configuration file is actually executed each time you generate a BASH shell, such as when you run a shell script. In other words, each time a subshell is created, the **.bashrc** file is executed. This has the effect of exporting any local variables or aliases you have defined in the **.bashrc** shell initialization file. The **.bashrc** file usually contains the definition of aliases and any feature variables used to turn on shell features. Aliases and feature variables are locally defined within the shell. But the **.bashrc** file defines them in every shell. For this reason, the **.bashrc** file usually holds aliases and options you want defined for each shell. As an example of how you can add your own aliases and options, aliases for the **rm**, **cp**, and **mv** commands and the shell **noclobber** and **ignoreeof** options have been added. For the root user **.bashrc**, the **rm**, **cp**, and **mv** aliases have already been included in the root's **.bashrc** file.

The **.bashrc** file will check for aliases in a **.bash_aliases** file and run **/etc/bash_completion** for command completion directives.

The **.bashrc** file will set several features including history, prompt, alias, and command completion settings. The **HISTCONTROL** directive is defined to ignore duplicate commands.

```
# don't put duplicate lines in the history. See bash(1)
# for more options export HISTCONTROL=ignoredups
# ... and ignore same successive entries.
export HISTCONTROL=ignoreboth
```

Several commands then define the shell prompt, beginning with **PS1=**. The code for reading the user's **.bash_aliases** file is included. Possible aliases are also provided. Both are commented. You can remove the comment symbols, **#**, to activate them.

```
# Alias definitions.
# You may want to put all your additions into a separate file like
# ~/.bash_aliases, instead of adding them here directly.
# See /usr/share/doc/bash-doc/examples in the bash-doc package.

#if [ -f ~/.bash_aliases ]; then
#    . ~/.bash_aliases
#fi

# some more ls aliases
#alias ll='ls -l'
#alias la='ls -A'
#alias l='ls -CF'
```

The **.bash_completion** file is then read to set up command completion options:

```
# enable programmable completion features (you don't need to enable
# this, if it's already enabled in /etc/bash.bashrc and /etc/profile
# sources /etc/bash.bashrc).
if [ -f /etc/bash_completion ]; then
    . /etc/bash_completion
fi
```

You can add any commands or definitions of your own to your **.bashrc** file. If you have made changes to **.bashrc** and you want them to take effect during your current login session, you need to re-execute the file with either the **.** or the **source** command:

```
$ . .bashrc
```

The System /etc/bash.bashrc BASH Script

Ubuntu also has a system **bashrc** file executed for all users, called **bash.bashrc**. Currently the **/etc/bash.bashrc** file sets the default shell prompt, as well as instructions for checking whether a user is authorized to use a command. The bash.bashrc file is shown next.

```
# sudo hint
if [ ! -e $HOME/.sudo_as_admin_successful ]; then
    case " $(groups) " in *\ admin\ *)
    if [ -x /usr/bin/sudo ]; then
      cat <<-EOF
      To run a command as administrator (user "root"), use "sudo <com-
mand>".
      See "man sudo_root" for details.

      EOF
    fi
    esac
fi


# if the command-not-found package is installed, use it
if [ -x /usr/lib/command-not-found ]; then
    function command_not_found_handle {
              if [ -x /usr/lib/command-not-found ]; then

              /usr/bin/python /usr/lib/command-not-found -- $1
              return $?
    else
              return 127
    }
fi
```

The BASH Shell Logout File: .bash_logout

The .bash_logout file is also a configuration file, but it is executed when the user logs out. It is designed to perform any operations you want to occur whenever you log out. Instead of variable definitions, the .bash_logout file usually contains shell commands that form a kind of shutdown procedure—actions you always want taken before you log out. One common **logout** command is to clear the screen and then issue a farewell message.

As with .profile, you can add your own shell commands to .bash_logout. In fact, the .bash_logout file is not automatically set up for you when your account is first created. You need to create it yourself, using the Vi or Emacs editor. You could then add a farewell message or other operations. The default .bash_logout file includes instructions to invoke the **clear_console** command to clear the screen. In the next example, the user has added an **echo** command in the .bash_logout file. When the user logs out, the screen is cleared, and then the **echo** command displays the message "Good-bye for now."

.bash_logout
```
# ~/.bash_logout: executed by bash(1) when login shell exits.
# when leaving the console clear the screen to increase privacy
if [ "$SHLVL" = 1 ]; then
    [ -x /usr/bin/clear_console ] && /usr/bin/clear_console -q
fi
```

12

CHAPTER

Files, Directories, and Archives

In Linux, all files are organized into directories that are hierarchically connected in one overall file structure. A file is referenced not only according to its name, but also according to its place in this file structure. You can create as many new directories as you want, adding more directories to the structure. The Linux file commands can perform sophisticated operations, such as moving or copying whole directories along with their subdirectories. You can use file operations such as **find**, **cp**, **mv**, and **ln** to locate files and copy, move, or link them, respectively, from one directory to another. Desktop file managers, such as Konqueror and Nautilus used on the KDE and GNOME desktops, provide a graphical user interface for performing the same operations using icons, windows, and menus (see Chapters 8 and 9). This chapter focuses on the commands you use in the shell command line to manage files, such as **cp** and **mv**. However, whether you use the command line or a GUI file manager, the underlying file structure is the same.

The organization of the Linux file structure into its various system and network administration directories is discussed in detail in Chapter 24. Though not part of the Linux file structure, special tools are available for accessing Windows partitions and floppy disks. These follow much the same format as Linux file commands.

Archives are used to back up files or to combine them into a package, which can then be transferred as one file over the Internet or posted on an FTP site for easy downloading. The standard archive utility used on Linux and Unix systems is tar, for which several GUI front ends exist. You can choose from among several compression programs, including GNU zip (gzip), Zip, bzip, and compress.

NOTE *Linux also allows you to mount and access file systems used by other operating systems such as Unix or Windows. Linux supports a variety of different file systems such as ext2, ext3, and ReiserFS.*

Linux Files

You can name a file using any letters, underscores, and numbers. You can also include periods and commas; however, except in certain special cases, you should never begin a filename with a period. Other characters, such as slashes, question marks, or asterisks, are reserved for use as special characters by the system and should not be part of a filename.

Filenames can be as long as 256 characters. Filenames can also include spaces; however, when you reference such filenames from the command line, be sure to encase them in quotes. On a desktop such as GNOME or KDE, you do not need to include quotes.

You can include an extension as part of a filename. A period is used to distinguish the filename proper from the extension. Extensions can be useful for categorizing your files. You are probably familiar with certain standard extensions that have been adopted by convention. For example, C source code files always have a **.c** extension. Files that contain compiled object code have an **.o** extension. You can, of course, make up your own file extensions.

The following examples are all valid Linux filenames. Keep in mind that to reference the last of these names (the name with spaces) on the command line, you would have to encase it in quotes as **"New book review"**:

```
preface
chapter2
9700info
New_Revisions
calc.c
intro.bk1
New book review
```

Special initialization files are also used to hold shell configuration commands. These are the hidden, or dot, files, which begin with a period. Dot files used by commands and applications have predetermined names, such as the **.mozilla** directory used to hold your Mozilla data and configuration files. Recall that when you use **ls** to display your filenames, the dot files will not be displayed. To include the dot files, you need to use **ls** with the **-a** option. Dot files are discussed in more detail in Chapter 11.

The **ls -l** command displays detailed information about a file. First the permissions are displayed, followed by the number of links, the owner of the file, the name of the group to which the user belongs, the file size in bytes, the date and time the file was last modified, and the name of the file. Permissions indicate who can access the file: the user, members of a group, or all other users. Permissions are discussed in detail later in this chapter. The group name indicates the group permitted to access the file object. The file type for **mydata** is that of an ordinary file. Only one link exists, indicating the file has no other names and no other links. The owner's name is **chris**, the same as the login name, and the group name is **weather**. Other users probably also belong to the **weather** group. The size of the file is 207 bytes, and it was last modified on February 20 at 11:55 A.M. The name of the file is **mydata**. If you want to display this detailed information for all the files in a directory, simply use the **ls -l** command without an argument:

```
$ ls -l
-rw-r--r-- 1 chris weather 207 Feb 20 11:55 mydata
-rw-rw-r-- 1 chris weather 568 Feb 14 10:30 today
-rw-rw-r-- 1 chris weather 308 Feb 17 12:40 monday
```

All files in Linux have one physical format, a *byte stream*, which is simply a sequence of bytes. This allows Linux to apply the file concept to every data component in the system. Directories are classified as files, as are devices. Treating everything as a file allows Linux to organize and exchange data more easily. The data in a file can be sent directly to a device such as a screen because a device interfaces with the system using the same byte-stream file format used by regular files.

This same file format is used to implement other operating system components. The interface to a device, such as the screen or keyboard, is designated as a file. Other components, such as directories, are themselves byte-stream files, but they have a special internal organization. A directory file contains information about a directory, organized in a special directory format. Because these different components are treated as files, they can be said to constitute different *file types.* A character device is one file type. A directory is another file type. The number of these file types may vary according to your specific implementation of Linux. Five common types of files exist, however: ordinary files; directory files; first in, first out (FIFO) pipes; character device files; and block device files. Although you may rarely reference a file's type, it can be useful when searching for directories or devices. Later in the chapter, you'll see how to use the file type in a search criterion with the **find** command to search specifically for directory or device names.

Although all ordinary files have a byte-stream format, they may be used in different ways. The most significant difference is between binary and text files. Compiled programs are examples of binary files. However, even text files can be classified according to their different uses. You can have files that contain C programming source code or shell commands, or even a file that is empty. The file could be an executable program or a directory file. The Linux **file** command helps you determine a file's use. It examines the first few lines of a file and tries to determine a classification for it. The **file** command looks for special keywords or numbers in those first few lines, but it is not always accurate. In the next example, the **file** command examines the contents of two files and determines a classification for them:

```
$ file monday reports
monday: text
reports: directory
```

If you need to examine the entire file, byte by byte, you can do so with the **od** (octal dump) command, which performs a dump of a file. By default, it prints every byte in its octal representation. However, you can also specify a character, decimal, or hexadecimal representation. The **od** command is helpful when you need to detect any special characters in your file or if you want to display a binary file.

The File Structure

Linux organizes files into a hierarchically connected set of directories. Each directory may contain either files or other directories. In this respect, directories perform two important functions: A directory holds files, much like files held in a file drawer, and a directory connects to other directories, much as a branch in a tree is connected to other branches. Because of the similarities to a tree, such a structure is often referred to as a *tree structure.*

The Linux file structure branches into several directories beginning with a root directory, */*. Within the root directory, several system directories contain files and programs that are features of the Linux system. The root directory also contains a directory called **/home** that contains the home directories of all the users in the system. Each user's home directory, in turn, contains the directories the user has made for his or her own use. Each of these can also contain directories. Such nested directories branch out from the user's home directory.

NOTE *The user's home directory can be any directory, though it is usually the directory that bears the user's login name. This directory is located in the directory named /home on your Linux system. For example, a user named dylan will have a home directory called dylan located in the system's /home directory. The user's home directory is a subdirectory of the directory called /home on your system.*

Home Directories

When you log in to the system, you are placed within your home directory. The name given to this directory by the system is the same as your login name. Any files you create when you first log in are organized within your home directory. You can also create more directories within your home directory and make changes to these directories and store files in them. The same is true for other users on the system. Each user has his or her own home directory, identified by the appropriate login name. Users, in turn, can create their own directories.

You can access a directory either through its name or by making it your working directory. When it is created, each directory is given a name, and you can use this name in file operations to access files within that directory. You can also make the directory your working directory. If you do not use any directory names in a file operation, the working directory (the one from which you are currently working) will be accessed. When you log in, the working directory is your home directory, which usually has the same name as your login name. You can use the **cd** command to designate another directory as the working directory.

Pathnames

The name you give to a directory or file when you create it is not its full name. Instead, the full name of a directory is its *pathname.* The hierarchically nested relationship among directories forms paths, and these paths can be used to identify and reference any directory or file uniquely or absolutely. Each directory in the file structure can be said to have its own unique path. The actual name by which the system identifies a directory always begins with the root directory and consists of all directories nested below that directory.

In Linux, you write a pathname by listing each directory in the path separated from the last by a forward slash. A slash preceding the first directory in the path represents the root. So, for example, the pathname for the **chris** directory is **/home/chris**, and the pathname for the **reports** directory could be **/home/chris/reports**. Pathnames also apply to files. When you create a file within a directory, you give the file a name. The actual name by which the system identifies the file, however, is the filename combined with the path of directories from the root to the file's directory. As an example, the pathname for **monday** is **/home/chris/reports/ monday** (the root directory is represented by the first slash). The path for the **monday** file consists of the root, **home**, **chris**, and **reports** directories and the filename **monday**.

Pathnames may be *absolute* or *relative.* An absolute pathname is the complete pathname of a file or directory beginning with the root directory. A relative pathname begins from your working directory; it is the path of a file relative to your working directory. Using the previous example, if **chris** is your working directory, the relative pathname for the file **monday** is **reports/monday**. The absolute pathname for **monday** is **/home/chris/reports/ monday**.

The absolute pathname from the root to your home directory can be especially complex and, at times, even subject to change by the system administrator. To make it easier to reference, you can use the tilde (~) character, which represents the absolute pathname of your home directory. In the next example, from the **thankyou** directory, the user references the **monday** file in the home directory by placing a tilde and slash before **monday**:

```
$ pwd
/home/chris/letters/thankyou
$ cat ~/monday
raining and warm
$
```

You must specify the rest of the path from your home directory. In the next example, the user references the **monday** file in the **reports** directory. The tilde represents the path to the user's home directory, **/home/chris**, and then the rest of the path to the **monday** file is specified.

```
$ cat ~/reports/monday
```

System Directories

The root directory that begins the Linux file structure contains several system directories that contain files and programs used to run and maintain the system. Many also contain other subdirectories with programs for executing specific features of Linux. For example, the directory **/usr/bin** contains the various Linux commands that users execute, such as **lpl**. The directory **/bin** holds system level commands. Table 12-1 lists the basic system directories.

Directory	Function
/	Begins the file system structure, called the *root*
/home	Contains users' home directories
/bin	Holds all the standard commands and utility programs
/usr	Holds those files and commands used by the system; this directory breaks down into several subdirectories
/usr/bin	Holds user-oriented commands and utility programs
/usr/sbin	Holds system administration commands
/usr/lib	Holds libraries for programming languages
/usr/share/doc	Holds Linux documentation
/usr/share/man	Holds the online man files
/var/spool	Holds spooled files, such as those generated for printing jobs and network transfers
/sbin	Holds system administration commands for booting the system
/var	Holds files that vary, such as mailbox files
/dev	Holds file interfaces for devices such as the terminals and printers (dynamically generated by udev, do not edit)
/etc	Holds system configuration files and any other system files

TABLE 12-1 Standard System Directories in Linux

Listing, Displaying, and Printing Files: ls, cat, more, less, and lpr

One of the primary functions of an operating system is the management of files. You may need to perform certain basic output operations on your files, such as displaying them on your screen or printing them. The Linux system provides a set of commands that perform basic file-management operations, such as listing, displaying, and printing files, as well as copying, renaming, and erasing files. These commands are usually made up of abbreviated versions of words. For example, the `ls` command is a shortened form of *list* and lists the files in your directory. The `lpr` command is an abbreviated form of *line print* and will print a file. The `cat`, `less`, and `more` commands display the contents of a file on the screen. Table 12-2 lists these commands with their different options. When you log in to your Linux system, you may want a list of the files in your home directory. The `ls` command, which outputs a list of your file and directory names, is useful for this. The `ls` command has many possible options for displaying filenames according to specific features.

Displaying Files: cat, less, and more

You may also need to look at the contents of a file. The `cat` and `more` commands display the contents of a file on the screen. The name `cat` stands for *concatenate*.

```
$ cat mydata
computers
```

The `cat` command outputs the entire text of a file to the screen at once. This presents a problem when the file is large, because its text quickly speeds past on the screen. The `more` and `less` commands are designed to overcome this limitation by displaying one screen of text at a time. You can then move forward or backward in the text at your leisure.

Command or Option	Execution
`ls`	Lists file and directory names.
`cat` *filenames*	Displays a file. Can take filenames for its arguments. Outputs the contents of those files directly to the standard output, which, by default, is directed to the screen.
`more` *filenames*	Displays a file screen by screen. Press SPACEBAR to continue to the next screen and Q to quit.
`less` *filenames*	Displays a file screen by screen. Press SPACEBAR to continue to the next screen and Q to quit.
`lpr` *filenames*	Sends a file to the line printer to be printed; a list of files may be used as arguments. Use the `-P` option to specify a printer.
`lpq`	Lists the print queue for printing jobs.
`lprm`	Removes a printing job from the print queue.

TABLE 12-2   Listing, Displaying, and Printing Files

You invoke the **more** or **less** command by entering the command name followed by the name of the file you want to view (**less** is a more powerful and configurable display utility):

```
$ less mydata
```

When **more** or **less** invokes a file, the first screen of text is displayed. To continue to the next screen, you press the F key or the SPACEBAR. To move back in the text, you press the B key. You can quit at any time by pressing the Q key.

Printing Files: lpr, lpq, and lprm

With the printer commands such as **lpr** and **lprm**, you can perform printing operations such as printing files or canceling print jobs (see Table 12-2). When you need to print files, use the **lpr** command to send files to the printer connected to your system. In the next example, the user prints the **mydata** file:

```
$ lpr mydata
```

If you want to print several files at once, you can specify more than one file on the command line after the **lpr** command. In the next example, the user prints out both the **mydata** and **preface** files:

```
$ lpr mydata preface
```

Printing jobs are placed in a queue and printed one at a time in the background—you can continue with other work as your files print. You can see the position of a particular printing job at any given time with the **lpq** command, which gives the owner of the printing job (the login name of the user who sent the job), the print job ID, the size in bytes, and the temporary file in which it is currently held.

If you need to cancel an unwanted printing job, you can do so with the **lprm** command, which takes as its argument either the ID number of the printing job or the owner's name. It then removes the print job from the print queue. For this task, **lpq** is helpful, for it provides you with the ID number and owner of the printing job you need to use with **lprm**.

Managing Directories: mkdir, rmdir, ls, cd, and pwd

You can create and remove your own directories, as well as change your working directory, with the **mkdir**, **rmdir**, and **cd** commands. Each of these commands can take as its argument the pathname for a directory. The **pwd** command displays the absolute pathname of your working directory. In addition to these commands, the special characters represented by a single dot, a double dot, and a tilde can be used to reference the working directory, the parent of the working directory, and the home directory, respectively. Taken together, these commands enable you to manage your directories. You can create nested directories, move from one directory to another, and use pathnames to reference any of your directories. Those commands commonly used to manage directories are listed in Table 12-3.

Command	Execution
`mkdir` *directory*	Creates a directory.
`rmdir` *directory*	Erases a directory.
`ls -F`	Lists directory name with a preceding slash.
`ls -R`	Lists working directory as well as all subdirectories.
`cd` *directory name*	Changes to the specified directory, making it the working directory. `cd` without a directory name changes back to the home directory: `$ cd reports`
`pwd`	Displays the pathname of the working directory.
directory name/*filename*	A slash is used in pathnames to separate each directory name. In the case of pathnames for files, a slash separates the preceding directory names from the filename.

`..`	References the parent directory. You can use it as an argument or as part of a pathname:
	`$ cd ..`
	`$ mv ../thisletter oldletters`

`.`	References the working directory. You can use it as an argument or as part of a pathname: `$ ls .`
`~/`*pathname*	The tilde is a special character that represents the pathname for the home directory. It is useful when you need to use an absolute pathname for a file or directory: `$ cp monday ~/today`

TABLE 12-3   Directory Commands

Creating and Deleting Directories

You create and remove directories with the **mkdir** and **rmdir** commands. In either case, you can also use pathnames for the directories. In the next example, the user creates the directory **reports**. Then the user creates the directory **letters** using a pathname:

```
$ mkdir reports
$ mkdir /home/chris/letters
```

You can remove a directory with the **rmdir** command followed by the directory name. In the next example, the user removes the directory **reports** with the **rmdir** command:

```
$ rmdir reports
```

To remove a directory and all its subdirectories, you use the **rm** command with the **-r** option. This is a very powerful command and can easily be used to erase all your files. If your **rm** command is aliased as **rm -i** (interactive mode), you will be prompted for each file.

To remove all files and subdirectories without prompts, add the `-f` option. The following example deletes the **reports** directory and all its subdirectories:

```
rm -rf reports
```

Displaying Directory Contents

You have seen how to use the `ls` command to list the files and directories within your working directory. To distinguish between file and directory names, however, you need to use the `ls` command with the `-F` option. A slash is then placed after each directory name in the list.

```
$ ls
weather reports letters
$ ls -F
weather reports/ letters/
```

The `ls` command also takes as an argument any directory name or directory pathname. This enables you to list the files in any directory without first having to change to that directory. In the next example, the `ls` command takes as its argument the name of a directory, **reports**. Then the `ls` command is executed again, only this time the absolute pathname of **reports** is used.

```
$ ls reports
monday tuesday
$ ls /home/chris/reports
monday tuesday
$
```

Moving Through Directories

The `cd` command takes as its argument the name of the directory that you want to change. The name of the directory can be the name of a subdirectory in your working directory or the full pathname of any directory on the system. If you want to change back to your home directory, you need to enter only the `cd` command by itself, without a filename argument.

```
$ cd props
$ pwd
/home/dylan/props
```

Referencing the Parent Directory

A directory always has a parent (except, of course, for the root). For example, in the preceding listing, the parent for **props** is the **dylan** directory. When a directory is created, two entries are made: one represented with a dot (`.`), and the other with double dots (`..`). The dot represents the pathname of the directory, and the double dots represent the pathname of its parent directory. Double dots, used as an argument in a command, reference a parent directory. The single dot references the directory itself.

You can use the single dot to reference your working directory, instead of using its pathname. For example, to copy a file to the working directory retaining the same name, the dot can be used in place of the working directory's pathname. In this sense, the dot is another name for the working directory. In the next example, the user copies the **weather** file from the **chris** directory to the **reports** directory. The **reports** directory is the working directory and can be represented with the single dot.

```
$ cd reports
$ cp /home/chris/weather .
```

The **..** symbol is often used to reference files in the parent directory. In the next example, the **cat** command displays the **weather** file in the parent directory. The pathname for the file is the **..** symbol (for the parent directory) followed by a slash and the filename.

```
$ cat ../weather
raining and warm
```

TIP   *You can use the* **cd** *command with the* **..** *symbol to step back through successive parent directories of the directory tree from a lower directory.*

File and Directory Operations: find, cp, mv, rm, and ln

As you create more and more files, you may want to back them up, change their names, erase some of them, or even give them added names. Linux provides several file commands you can use to search for files, copy files, rename files, or remove files (see Table 12-5 later in this chapter). If you have a large number of files, you can also search them to locate a specific one. The commands are again shortened forms of full words, consisting of only two characters. The **cp** command stands for *copy* and copies a file, **mv** stands for *move* and renames or moves a file, **rm** stands for *remove* and erases a file, and **ln** stands for *link* and adds another name for a file, often used as a shortcut to the original. One exception to the two-character rule is the **find** command, which performs searches of your filenames to find a file. All these operations can be handled by the GUI desktops such as GNOME and KDE (see Chapters 8 and 9).

Searching Directories: find

Once a large number of files have been stored in many different directories, you may need to search them to locate a specific file, or files, of a certain type. The **find** command enables you to perform such a search from the command line. The **find** command takes as its arguments directory names followed by several possible options that specify the type of search and the criteria for the search; it then searches within the directories listed and their subdirectories for files that meet these criteria. The **find** command can search for a file by name, type, owner, and even the time of the last update.

```
$ find directory-list -option criteria
```

TIP   *From the GNOME desktop you can use the Search tool in the Places menu to search for files. From the KDE Desktop you can use the find tool in the file manager.*

The **-name** option has as its criteria a pattern and instructs **find** to search for the filename that matches that pattern. To search for a file by name, you use the **find** command with the directory name followed by the **-name** option and the name of the file:

```
$ find directory-list -name filename
```

The **find** command also has options that merely perform actions, such as outputting the results of a search. If you want **find** to display the filenames it has located, you simply include the **-print** option on the command line along with any other options. The **-print** option is an action that instructs **find** to write to the standard output the names of all the files it locates (you can also use the **-ls** option instead to list files in the long format). In the next example, the user searches for all the files in the **reports** directory with the name **monday**. Once located, the file, with its relative pathname, is printed.

```
$ find reports -name monday -print
reports/monday
```

The **find** command prints out the filenames using the directory name specified in the directory list. If you specify an absolute pathname, the absolute path of the found directories will be output. If you specify a relative pathname, only the relative pathname will be output. In the preceding example, the user specified a relative pathname, **reports**, in the directory list. Located filenames were output beginning with this relative pathname. In the next example, the user specifies an absolute pathname in the directory list. Located filenames are then output using this absolute pathname.

```
$ find /home/chris -name monday -print
/home/chris/reports/monday
```

TIP *Should you need to find the location of a specific program or configuration file, you can use* **find** *to search for the file from the root directory. Log in as the root user and use* **/** *as the directory. This command searches for the location of the* **more** *command and files on the entire file system:* **find / -name more -print**.

Searching the Working Directory

If you want to search your working directory, you can use the dot in the directory pathname to represent your working directory. The next example searches all files and subdirectories in the working directory, using the dot to represent the working directory. If your working directory is your home directory, this is a convenient way to search through all your own directories. Notice that the located filenames that are output begin with a dot.

```
$ find . -name weather -print
./weather
```

You can use shell wildcard characters as part of the pattern criteria for searching files. The special characters must be quoted, however, to avoid evaluation by the shell. In the next example, all files (indicated by the asterisk) with the **.c** extension in the **programs** directory are searched for and then displayed in the long format using the **-ls** action:

```
$ find programs -name '*.c' -ls
```

Locating Directories

You can also use the **find** command to locate other directories. In Linux, a directory is officially classified as a special type of file. Although all files have a byte-stream format, some files, such as directories, are used in special ways. In this sense, a file can be said to have a file type. The **find** command has an option called **-type** that searches for a file of a given type. The **-type** option takes a one-character modifier that represents the file type. The modifier that represents a directory is a **d**. In the next example, both the directory name and the directory file type are used to search for the directory called **thankyou**:

```
$ find /home/chris -name thankyou -type d -print
/home/chris/letters/thankyou
$
```

File types are not so much different types of files as they are the file format applied to other components of the operating system, such as devices. In this sense, a device is treated as a type of file, and you can use **find** to search for devices and directories, as well as ordinary files. Table 12-4 lists the different types available for the **find** command's **-type** option.

Command or Option	Execution
find	Searches directories for files according to search criteria. This command has several options, which follow, that specify the type of criteria and actions to be taken.
-context *scontext*	Searches for files according to security context (SE Linux).
-exec *command*	Executes command when files found.
-gid *name*	Searches for files belonging to a group according to group ID.
-group *name*	Searches for files belonging to the group *name*.
-lname *pattern*	Searches for symbolic link files.
-ls	Provides a detailed listing of each file, with owner, permission, size, and date information.
-mtime *num*	Searches for files last modified *num* days ago.
-name *pattern*	Searches for files with *pattern* in the name.
-newer *pattern*	Searches for files modified after the one matched by *pattern*.
-perm *permission*	Searches for files with certain permissions set. Use octal or symbolic format for permissions.
-print	Outputs the result of the search to the standard output. The result is usually a list of filenames, including their full pathnames.
-size *numc*	Searches for files with the size *num* in blocks. If **c** is added after *num*, the size in bytes (characters) is searched for.
-type *filetype*	Searches for files with the specified file type. File type can be **b** for block device, **c** for character device, **d** for directory, **f** for file, or **l** for symbolic link.
-uid *name*	Searches for files belonging to a user according to user ID.
-user *name*	Searches for files belonging to a user.

TABLE **12-4**   The find Command Types

You can also use the find operation to search for files by ownership or security criteria, such as files belonging to a specific user or those with a certain security context. The **-user** option lets you locate all files belonging to a certain user. The following example lists all files that the user **chris** has created or owns on the entire system:

```
$ find / -user chris -print
```

To list files stored only in the users' home directories, you use **/home** for the starting search directory. This finds all files in the home directory as well as any owned by that user in other user directories.

Copying Files

To make a copy of a file, you simply give **cp** two filenames as its arguments (see Table 12-5). The first filename is the name of the file to be copied—the one that already exists. This is often referred to as the *source file*. The second filename is the name you want for the copy. This will be a new file containing a copy of all the data in the source file. This second argument is often referred to as the *destination file*. The syntax for the **cp** command follows:

```
$ cp source-file destination-file
```

Command	Execution
cp *filename filename*	Copies a file. **cp** takes two arguments: the original file and the name of the new copy. You can use pathnames for the files to copy across directories: `$ cp today reports/monday`
cp -r *dirname dirname*	Copies a subdirectory from one directory to another. The copied directory includes all its own subdirectories: `$ cp -r letters/thankyou oldletters`
ln *filename filename*	Creates added names for files referred to as links. A link can be created in one directory that references a file in another directory: `$ ln today reports/monday`
mv *filename filename*	Moves (renames) a file. The **mv** command takes two arguments: the first is the file to be moved. The second argument can be the new filename or the pathname of a directory. If it is the name of a directory, then the file is literally moved to that directory, changing the file's pathname: `$ mv today /home/chris/reports`
mv *dirname dirname*	Moves directories. In this case, the first and last arguments are directories: `$ mv letters/thankyou oldletters`
rm *filenames*	Removes (erases) a file. Can take any number of filenames as its arguments. Removes links to a file. If a file has more than one link, you need to remove all of them to erase a file: `$rm today weather weekend`

TABLE 12-5   File Operations

In the next example, the user copies a file called **proposal** to a new file called **oldprop**:

```
$ cp proposal oldprop
```

You can unintentionally destroy another file with the **cp** command. The **cp** command generates a copy by first creating a file and then copying data into it. If another file has the same name as the destination file, that file will be destroyed and a new file with that name created. By default, Red Hat configures your system to check for an existing copy by the same name (**cp** is aliased with the -**i** option; see Chapter 11). To copy a file from your working directory to another directory, you need to use that directory name as the second argument in the **cp** command. In the next example, the **proposal** file is overwritten by the **newprop** file. The **proposal** file already exists.

```
$ cp newprop proposal
```

You can use any of the wildcard characters to generate a list of filenames to use with **cp** or **mv**. For example, suppose you need to copy all your C source code files to a given directory. Instead of listing each one individually on the command line, you can use an ***** character with the **.c** extension to match on and generate a list of C source code files (all files with a **.c** extension). In the next example, the user copies all source code files in the current directory to the **sourcebks** directory:

```
$ cp *.c sourcebks
```

If you want to copy all the files in a given directory to another directory, you can use ***** to match on and generate a list of all those files in a **cp** command. In the next example, the user copies all the files in the **props** directory to the **oldprop** directory. Notice the use of a **props** pathname preceding the ***** special characters. In this context, **props** is a pathname that will be appended before each file in the list that ***** generates.

```
$ cp props/* oldprop
```

You can, of course, use any of the other special characters, such as **.**, **?**, or **[]**. In the next example, the user copies both source code and object code files (**.o** and **.c**) to the **projbk** directory:

```
$ cp *.[oc] projbk
```

When you copy a file, you can give the copy a name that's different from the original. To do so, place the new filename after the directory name, separated by a slash:

```
$ cp filename directory-name/new-filename
```

Moving Files

You can use the **mv** command either to rename a file or move a file from one directory to another. When using **mv** to rename a file, you simply use the new filename as the second argument. The first argument is the current name of the file you are renaming. If you want to rename a file when you move it, you can specify the new name of the file after the directory name. In the next example, the **proposal** file is renamed with the name **version1**:

```
$ mv proposal version1
```

As with **cp**, the **mv** command can erase a file. When renaming a file, you might accidentally choose a filename already used by another file. In this case, that other file will be erased. The **mv** command also has an **-i** option that checks first to see whether a file by that name already exists.

You can also use any of the special characters described in Chapter 10 to generate a list of filenames to use with **mv**. In the next example, the user moves all source code files in the current directory to the **newproj** directory:

```
$ mv *.c newproj
```

If you want to move all the files in a given directory to another directory, you can use ***** to match on and generate a list of all those files. In the next example, the user moves all the files in the **reports** directory to the **repbks** directory:

```
$ mv reports/* repbks
```

NOTE *On GNOME or KDE, the easiest way to copy files to a CD-R/RW or DVD-R/RW disc is to use the built-in desktop burning capability. Just insert a blank disk, open it as a folder, and drag-and-drop files onto it. You will be prompted automatically to burn the files. You can also use any number or CD/DVD burning tools, such as K3B.*

Copying and Moving Directories

You can also copy or move whole directories at once. Both **cp** and **mv** can take as their first argument a directory name, enabling you to copy or move subdirectories from one directory into another (see Table 12-5). The first argument is the name of the directory to be moved or copied, and the second argument is the name of the directory within which it is to be placed. The same pathname structure used for files applies to moving or copying directories.

You can just as easily copy subdirectories from one directory to another. To copy a directory, the **cp** command requires that you use the **-r** option, which stands for *recursive*. It directs the **cp** command to copy a directory as well as any subdirectories it may contain. In other words, the entire directory subtree, from that directory on, will be copied. In the next example, the **thankyou** directory is copied to the **oldletters** directory. Now two **thankyou** subdirectories exist—one in **letters** and one in **oldletters**.

```
$ cp -r letters/thankyou oldletters
$ ls -F letters
/thankyou
$ ls -F oldletters
/thankyou
```

Erasing Files and Directories: The rm Command

As you use Linux, you will find the number of files you use increases rapidly. Generating files in Linux is easy. Applications such as editors, and commands such as **cp**, can easily be used to create files. Eventually, many of these files may become outdated and useless. You can then remove them with the **rm** command. The **rm** command can take any number of arguments, enabling you to list several filenames and erase them all at the same time. In the next example, the file **oldprop** is erased:

```
$ rm oldprop
```

Be careful when using the **rm** command, because *it is irrevocable*. Once a file is removed, it cannot be restored (there is no undo). With the **-i** option, you are prompted separately for each file and asked whether you really want to remove it. If you enter **y**, the file will be removed. If you enter anything else, the file is not removed. In the next example, the **rm** command is instructed to erase the files **proposal** and **oldprop**. The **rm** command then asks for confirmation for each file. The user decides to remove **oldprop**, but not **proposal**.

```
$ rm -i proposal oldprop
Remove proposal? n
Remove oldprop? y
$
```

Links: The ln Command

You can give a file more than one name using the **ln** command. You might do this because you want to reference a file using different filenames to access it from different directories. The added names are often referred to as *links*. Linux supports two different types of links: *hard links* are literally another name for the same file, whereas *symbolic links* function like shortcuts referencing another file. Symbolic links are much more flexible and can work over many different file systems, while hard links are limited to your local file system. Furthermore, hard links introduce security concerns, as they allow direct access from a link that may have public access to an original file that you may want protected. Because of this, links are usually implemented as symbolic links.

Symbolic Links

To set up a symbolic link, you use the **ln** command with the **-s** option and two arguments: the name of the original file and the new, added filename. The **ls** operation lists both filenames, but only one physical file will exist.

```
$ ln -s original-filename added-filename
```

In the next example, the **today** file is given the additional name **weather**. In this case, **weather** is another name for the **today** file.

```
$ ls
today
$ ln -s today weather
$ ls
today weather
```

You can give the same file several names by using the **ln** command on the same file many times. In the next example, the file **today** is assigned the names **weather** and **weekend**:

```
$ ln -s today weather
$ ln -s today weekend
$ ls
today weather weekend
```

If you list the full information about a symbolic link and its file, you will find the information displayed is different. In the next example, the user lists the full information for both **lunch** and **/home/george/veglist** using the `ls` command with the `-l` option. The first character in the line specifies the file type. Symbolic links have their own file type, represented by an l. The file type for **lunch** is l, indicating it is a symbolic link, not an ordinary file. The number after the term `group` is the size of the file. Notice the sizes differ. The size of the **lunch** file is only 4 bytes. This is because **lunch** is only a symbolic link—a file that holds the pathname of another file—and a pathname takes up only a few bytes. It is not a direct hard link to the **veglist** file.

```
$ ls -l lunch /home/george/veglist
-rw-rw-r-- 1 george group 793 Feb 14 10:30 veglist
lrw-rw-r-- 1 chris group 4 Feb 14 10:30 lunch
```

To erase a file, you need to remove only its original name (and any hard links to it). If any symbolic links are left over, they will be unable to access the file. In this case, a symbolic link will hold the pathname of a file that no longer exists.

Hard Links

You can give the same file several names by using the `ln` command on the same file many times. To set up a hard link, you use the `ln` command with no `-s` option and two arguments: the name of the original file and the new, added filename. The `ls` operation lists both filenames, but only one physical file will exist.

```
$ ln original-filename added-filename
```

In the next example, the **monday** file is given the additional name **storm**. In this case, **storm** is just another name for the **monday** file.

```
$ ls
today
$ ln monday storm
$ ls
monday storm
```

To erase a file that has hard links, you need to remove all its hard links. The name of a file is actually considered a link to that file—hence the command **rm** removes the link to the file. If you have several links to the file and remove only one of them, the others stay in place and you can reference the file through them. The same is true even if you remove the original link—the original name of the file. Any added links will work just as well. In the next example, the **today** file is removed with the **rm** command. However, a link to that same file exists, called **weather**. The file can then be referenced under the name **weather**.

```
$ ln today weather
$ rm today
$ cat weather
The storm broke today
and the sun came out.
$
```

NOTE *Each file and directory in Linux contains a set of permissions that determine who can access them and how. You set these permissions to limit access in one of three ways: you can restrict access to yourself alone, you can allow users in a group to have access, or you can permit anyone on your system to have access. You can also control how a given file or directory is accessed. A file and directory may have read, write, and execute permissions. When a file is created, it is automatically given read and write permissions for the owner, enabling you to display and modify the file. You may change these permissions to any combination you want (see Chapter 23 for more details).*

Archiving and Compressing Files

Archives are used to back up files or to combine them into a package, which can then be transferred as one file over the Internet or posted on an FTP site for easy downloading. The standard archive utility used on Linux and Unix systems is tar, for which several GUI front ends exist. You can choose from among several compression programs, including GNU zip (gzip), Zip, bzip, and compress. Table 12-6 lists the commonly used archive and compression applications.

TIP *You can use the unrar tool to read and extract the popular rar archives but not to create them. unrar is available from* **http://rpm.livna.org** *and can be downloaded and installed with yum. File Roller is able to extract RAR files once the unrar tool is installed. Other graphical front ends such as Xarchiver and Linrar are available from* **http://freshmeat.net**. *To create rar archives, you have to purchase the archiver from Rarlab at* **http://rarlab.com**.

Archiving and Compressing Files with File Roller

GNOME provides the File Roller tool (choose Accessories | Archive Manager) that operates as a GUI front end to archive and compress files, letting you perform Zip, gzip, tar, and bzip2 operation using a graphical interface. You can examine the contents of archives, extract the files you want, and create new compressed archives. When you create an archive, you determine its compression method by specifying its filename extension, such as **.gz** for gzip or **.bz2** for bzip2. You can select the different extensions from the File Type

Applications	Description
tar	Archive creation and extraction **www.gnu.org/software/tar/manual/tar.html**
File Roller (Archive Manager)	GNOME front end for tar and gzip/bzip2
gzip	File, directory, and archive compression **www.gnu.org/software/gzip/manual/**
bzip2	File, directory, and archive compression **www.gnu.org/software/gzip/manual/**
zip	File, directory, and archive compression

TABLE 12-6   Archive and Compression Applications

menu or enter the extension yourself. To archive and compress files, you can choose a combined extension such as **.tar.bz2**, which both archives with tar and compresses with bzip2. Click Add to add files to your archive. To extract files from an archive, open the archive to display the list of archive files. You can then click Extract to extract particular files or the entire archive.

TIP *File Roller can also be used to examine the contents of an archive file easily. From the file manager, right-click the archive and choose Open With Archive Manager. The list of files and directories in that archive will be displayed. For subdirectories, double-click their entries. This method also works for RPM software files, letting you browse all the files that make up a software package.*

Archive Files and Devices: tar

The tar utility creates archives for files and directories. With tar, you can archive specific files, update them in the archive, and add new files as you want to that archive. You can even archive entire directories with all their files and subdirectories, all of which can be restored from the archive. The tar utility was originally designed to create archives on tapes. (The term *tar* stands for tape archive.) However, you can create archives on any device, such as a floppy disk, or you can create an archive file to hold the archive. The tar utility is ideal for making backups of your files or combining several files into a single file for transmission across a network (File Roller is a GUI interface for tar). For more information on tar, check the man page or the online man page at **www.gnu.org/software/tar/manual/tar.html**.

NOTE *As an alternative to tar, you can use pax, which is designed to work with different kinds of Unix archive formats such as cpio, bcpio, and tar. You can extract, list, and create archives. The pax utility is helpful if you are handling archives created on Unix systems that are using different archive formats.*

Displaying Archive Contents

Both file managers in GNOME and KDE have the ability to display the contents of a tar archive file automatically. The contents are displayed as though they were files in a directory. You can list the files as icons or with details, sorting them by name, type, or other fields. You can even display the contents of files. Clicking a text file opens it with a text editor, and an image is displayed with an image viewer. If the file manager cannot determine what program to use to display the file, it prompts you to select an application. Both file managers can perform the same kinds of operations on archives residing on remote file systems, such as tar archives on FTP sites. You can obtain a listing of their contents and even read their readme files. The Nautilus file manager (GNOME) can also extract an archive: right-click the Archive icon and choose Extract.

Creating Archives

On Linux, tar is often used to create archives on devices or files. You can direct tar to archive files to a specific device or a file by using the **f** option with the name of the device or file. The syntax for the **tar** command using the **f** option is shown in the next example. The device or filename is often referred to as the *archive name*. When creating a file for a tar archive, the filename is usually given the extension **.tar**. This is only a convention and is not required.

You can list as many filenames as you want. If a directory name is specified, all its subdirectories are included in the archive.

```
$ tar optionsf archive-name.tar directory-and-filenames
```

To create an archive, use the **c** option. Combined with the **f** option, **c** creates an archive on a file or device. You enter the **c** option before and next to the **f** option. No dash precedes a tar option. Table 12-7 lists the different options you can use with tar. In the next example,

Commands	Execution
tar *options files*	Backs up files to tape, device, or archive file.
tar *optionsf archive_name filelist*	Backs up files to a specific file or device specified as *archive_name*. *filelist* can be filename or directory.
Options	
c	Creates a new archive.
--delete	Removes a file from the archive.
f *archive-name*	Saves the tape archive to the file archive name, instead of to the default tape device. When given an archive name, the **f** option saves the tar archive in a file of that name.
f *device-name*	Saves a tar archive to a device such as a floppy disk or tape. **/dev/fd0** is the device name for your floppy disk; the default device is held in **/etc/default/tar-file**.
j	Compresses or decompresses archived files using **bzip2**.
m	When extracting a file from an archive, no new timestamp is assigned.
M	Creates a multiple-volume archive that may be stored on several floppy disks.
r	Appends files to an archive.
t	Lists the names of files in an archive.
U	Updates an archive with new and changed files; adds only those files modified since they were archived or files not already present in the archive.
w	Waits for a confirmation from the user before archiving each file; enables you to update an archive selectively.
x	Extracts files from an archive.
v	Displays each filename as it is archived.
z	Compresses or decompresses archived files using **gzip**.

TABLE 12-7 File Archives: `tar`

the directory **mydir** and all its subdirectories are saved in the file **myarch.tar**. In this example, the **mydir** directory holds two files, **mymeeting** and **party**, as well as a directory called **reports** that has three files: **weather**, **monday**, and **friday**.

```
$ tar cvf myarch.tar mydir
mydir/
mydir/reports/
mydir/reports/weather
mydir/reports/monday
mydir/reports/friday
mydir/mymeeting
mydir/party
```

Extracting Archives

The user can later extract the directories from the tape using the **x** option. The **xf** option extracts files from an archive file or device. The tar extraction operation generates all subdirectories. In the next example, the **xf** option directs **tar** to extract all the files and subdirectories from the tar file **myarch.tar**:

```
$ tar xvf myarch.tar
mydir/
mydir/reports/
mydir/reports/weather
mydir/reports/monday
mydir/reports/friday
mydir/mymeeting
mydir/party
```

You use the **r** option to add files to an already created archive. The **r** option appends the files to the archive. In the next example, the user appends the files in the **mydocs** directory to the **myarch.tar** archive. Here, the directory **mydocs** and its files are added to the **myarch.tar** archive:

```
$ tar rvf myarch.tar mydocs
mydocs/
mydocs/doc1
```

Updating Archives

If you change any of the files in directories you previously archived, you can use the **u** option to instruct tar to update the archive with any modified files. The **tar** command compares the time of the last update for each archived file with those in the user's directory and copies into the archive any files that have been changed since they were last archived. Any newly created files in these directories are also added to the archive. In the next example, the user updates the **myarch.tar** file with any recently modified or newly created files in the **mydir** directory. In this case, the **gifts** file was added to the **mydir** directory:

```
tar uvf myarch.tar mydir
mydir/
mydir/gifts
```

If you need to see what files are stored in an archive, you can use the **tar** command with the **t** option. The next example lists all the files stored in the **myarch.tar** archive:

```
tar tvf myarch.tar
drwxr-xr-x root/root 0 2000-10-24 21:38:18 mydir/
drwxr-xr-x root/root 0 2000-10-24 21:38:51 mydir/reports/
-rw-r--r-- root/root 22 2000-10-24 21:38:40 mydir/reports/weather
-rw-r--r-- root/root 22 2000-10-24 21:38:45 mydir/reports/monday
-rw-r--r-- root/root 22 2000-10-24 21:38:51 mydir/reports/friday
-rw-r--r-- root/root 22 2000-10-24 21:38:18 mydir/mymeeting
-rw-r--r-- root/root 22 2000-10-24 21:36:42 mydir/party
drwxr-xr-x root/root 0 2000-10-24 21:48:45 mydocs/
-rw-r--r-- root/root 22 2000-10-24 21:48:45 mydocs/doc1
drwxr-xr-x root/root 0 2000-10-24 21:54:03 mydir/
-rw-r--r-- root/root 22 2000-10-24 21:54:03 mydir/gifts
```

NOTE *To back up a files using several CD/DVD-ROMs, you would first use the* **-M** *(multi-volume) option to create a split archive that consists of several files. The tape size for an ISO DVD would be specified with the tape-length option,* **--tape-length=2294900***.*

Compressing Archives

The **tar** operation does not perform compression on archived files. If you want to compress archived files, you can instruct tar to invoke the gzip utility to compress them. With the lowercase **z** option, tar first uses gzip to compress files before archiving them. The same **z** option invokes gzip to decompress them when extracting files.

```
$ tar czf myarch.tar.gz mydir
```

To use bzip instead of gzip to compress files before archiving them, you use the **j** option. The same **j** option invokes bzip to decompress them when extracting files.

```
$ tar cjf myarch.tar.bz2 mydir
```

Remember that a difference exists between compressing individual files in an archive and compressing the entire archive as a whole. Often, an archive is created for transferring several files at once as one tar file. To shorten transmission time, the archive should be as small as possible. You can use the compression utility gzip on the archive tar file to compress it, reducing its size, and then send the compressed version. The person receiving it can decompress it, restoring the tar file. Using gzip on a tar file often results in a file with the extension **.tar.gz**. The extension **.gz** is added to a compressed gzip file. The next example creates a compressed version of **myarch.tar** using the same name with the extension **.gz**:

```
$ gzip myarch.tar
$ ls
$ myarch.tar.gz
```

Instead of retyping the **tar** command for different files, you can place the command in a script and pass the files to it. Be sure to make the script executable. In the following example, a simple **myarchprog** script is created that will archive filenames listed as its arguments.

```
myarchprog
tar   cvf    myarch.tar     $*
```

A run of the **myarchprog** script with multiple arguments is shown here:

```
$ myarchprog mydata preface
mydata
preface
```

Archiving to Tape

If you have specified a default device, such as a tape, and you want to create an archive on it, you can simply use **tar** without the **f** option and a device or filename. This can be helpful for making backups of your files. The name of the default device is held in a file called **/etc/default/tar**. The syntax for the **tar** command using the default tape device is shown in the following example. If a directory name is specified, all its subdirectories are included in the archive.

```
$ tar option directory-and-filenames
```

In the next example, the directory **mydir** and all its subdirectories are saved on a tape in the default tape device:

```
$ tar c mydir
```

In this example, the **mydir** directory and all its files and subdirectories are extracted from the default tape device and placed in the user's working directory:

```
$ tar x mydir
```

NOTE *You can use other archive programs such as cpio, pax, and shar. However, tar is the most commonly used program for archiving application software.*

File Compression: gzip, bzip2, and zip

You may want to reduce the size of a file for several reasons: the two most common are to save space and, if you are transferring the file across a network, to save transmission time. You can effectively reduce a file size by creating a compressed copy of it. Any time you need the file again, you can decompress it. Compression is used in combination with archiving to enable you to compress entire directories and their files at once. Decompression generates a copy of the archive file, which can then be extracted, generating a copy of those files and directories. File Roller provides a GUI for these tasks. For more information on gzip, check the man page or the online man page at **www.gnu.org/software/gzip/manual/**. For bzip2, also check its man page or the online documentation at **www.bzip.org/docs.html**.

Compression with gzip

Several compression utilities are available for use on Linux and Unix systems. Most software for Linux systems uses the GNU gzip and gunzip utilities. The gzip utility compresses files, and gunzip decompresses them. To compress a file, enter the command **gzip** and the filename. This replaces the file with a compressed version of it with the extension **.gz**.

```
$ gzip mydata
$ ls
mydata.gz
```

To decompress a gzip file, use either **gzip** with the **-d** option or the command **gunzip**. These commands decompress a compressed file with the **.gz** extension and replace it with a decompressed version with the same root name but without the **.gz** extension. When you use gunzip, you needn't even type in the **.gz** extension; **gunzip** and **gzip** **-d** assume it. Table 12-8 lists the different gzip options.

```
$ gunzip mydata.gz
$ ls
mydata
```

TIP *On your desktop, you can extract the contents of an archive by locating it with the file manager and double-clicking it. You can also right-click and choose Open With Archive Manager. This will start the File Roller application, which will open the archive, listing its contents. You can then choose to extract the archive. File Roller will use the appropriate tools to decompress the archive (bzip2, zip, or gzip) if compressed, and then extract the archive (tar).*

Option	Execution
-c	Sends compressed version of file to standard output; each file listed is separately compressed: `gzip -c mydata preface > myfiles.gz`

-d	Decompresses a compressed file; or you can use gunzip:
	`gzip -d myfiles.gz`
	`gunzip myfiles.gz`

-h	Displays help listing.
-l *file-list*	Displays compressed and uncompressed size of each file listed: `gzip -l myfiles.gz.`
-r *directory-name*	Recursively searches for specified directories and compresses all the files in them; the search begins from the current working directory. When used with **gunzip**, compressed files of a specified directory are uncompressed.
-v *file-list*	For each compressed or decompressed file, displays its name and the percentage of its reduction in size.
-*num*	Determines the speed and size of the compression; the range is from –1 to –9. A lower number gives greater speed but less compression, resulting in a larger file that compresses and decompresses quickly. Thus, –1 gives the quickest compression but with the largest size; –9 results in a very small file that takes longer to compress and decompress. The default is –6.

TABLE 12-8 The gzip Options

You can also compress archived tar files. This results in files with the extensions **.tar.gz**. Compressed archived files are often used for transmitting extremely large files across networks.

```
$ gzip myarch.tar
$ ls
myarch.tar.gz
```

You can compress tar file members individually using the **tar z** option that invokes gzip. With the **z** option, tar invokes gzip to compress a file before placing it in an archive. Archives with members compressed with the **z** option, however, cannot be updated, and it is not possible to add to them. All members must be compressed, and all must be added at the same time.

The compress and uncompress Commands

You can also use the **compress** and **uncompress** commands to create compressed files. They generate a file that has a **.Z** extension and use a compression format different from gzip. The **compress** and **uncompress** commands are not that widely used, but you may run across **.Z** files occasionally. You can use the **uncompress** command to decompress a **.Z** file. The gzip utility is the standard GNU compression utility and should be used instead of **compress**.

Compressing with bzip2

Another popular compression utility is bzip2. It compresses files using the Burrows-Wheeler block-sorting text compression algorithm and Huffman coding. The command line options are similar to gzip by design, but they are not exactly the same. (See the bzip2 man page for a complete listing.) You compress files using the **bzip2** command and decompress with **bunzip2**. The **bzip2** command creates files with the extension **.bz2**. You can use **bzcat** to output compressed data to the standard output. The **bzip2** command compresses files in blocks and enables you to specify their size (larger blocks give you greater compression). As when using gzip, you can use bzip2 to compress tar files. The following example compresses the **mydata** file into a bzip compressed file with the extension **.bz2**:

```
$ bzip2 mydata
$ ls
mydata.bz2
```

To decompress, use the **bunzip2** command on a bzip file:

```
$ bunzip2 mydata.bz2
```

Using Zip

Zip is a compression and archive utility modeled on PKZIP, which was used originally on DOS systems. Zip is a cross-platform utility used on Windows, Mac, MS-DOS, OS/2, Unix, and Linux systems. Zip commands can work with archives created by PKZIP and can use Zip archives. You compress a file using the **zip** command. This creates a Zip file with the **.zip** extension. If no files are listed, **zip** outputs the compressed data to the standard output. You can also use the - argument to have **zip** read from the standard input.

To compress a directory, you include the **-r** option. This example archives and compresses a file:

```
$ zip mydata
$ ls
mydata.zip
```

This example archives and compresses the **reports** directory:

```
$ zip -r reports
```

A full set of archive operations is supported. With the **-f** option, you can update a particular file in the Zip archive with a newer version. The **-u** option replaces or adds files, and the **-d** option deletes files from the Zip archive. Options also exist for encrypting files, making DOS-to-Unix end-of-line translations and including hidden files.

To decompress and extract the Zip file, you use the **unzip** command:

```
$ unzip mydata.zip
```

Applications

13

Office and Database Applications

A variety of office suites are now available for Linux (see Table 13-1). These include professional-level word processors, presentation managers, drawing tools, and spreadsheets. The freely available versions are described in this chapter. Sun has initiated development of an open source office suite using StarOffice code. The applications, known as OpenOffice.org, provide Office applications integrated with GNOME and are currently the primary office applications supported by most Linux distributions. KOffice is an entirely free office suite designed for use with KDE. The GNOME Office suite integrates GNOME applications into a productivity suite that is freely available. CodeWeavers CrossOver Office provides reliable support for running Microsoft Office Windows applications directly on Linux, integrating them with KDE and GNOME. You can also purchase commercial office suites such as StarOffice from Sun. For desktop publishing, especially PDF generation, you can use Scribus.

A variety of database management systems are available for Linux. These include high-powered, commercial-level database management systems, such as Oracle, IBM's DB2, and Sybase. Open source Linux databases are also available, such as MySQL and PostgreSQL. These are among the most widely used on Linux systems. Most of the database management systems available for Linux are designed to support large relational databases. For small personal databases, you can use the desktop database management systems being developed for KDE and GNOME. In addition, some software is available for databases accessed with the XBase database programming language. These are smaller databases using formats originally developed for dBase on the PC. (Various database management systems available to run under Linux are listed in Table 13-8 later in this chapter.)

Linux also provides several text editors that range from simple text editors for simple notes to editors with more complex features such as spell-checkers, buffers, or pattern matching. All generate character text files and can be used to edit any Linux text files. Text editors are often used in system administration tasks to change or add entries in Linux configuration files found in the **/etc** directory or a user's initialization or application dot files located in a user's home directory. You can use any text editor to work on source code files for any of the programming languages or shell program scripts.

Web Site	Description
www.openoffice.org	OpenOffice.org open source office suite based on StarOffice
http://koffice.org	KOffice Suite, for KD
http://live.gnome.org/GnomeOffice	GNOME Office, for GNOME
www.sun.com/staroffice	StarOffice Suite
www.codeweavers.com	CrossOver Office (MS Office support)
www.scribus.net	Scribus desktop publishing tool

TABLE 13-1   Linux Office Suites

Running Microsoft Office on Linux: CrossOver and Wine

One of the primary concerns for new Linux users is what kind of access they will have to their Microsoft Office files, particularly Word files. The Linux operating system and many applications for it are designed to provide seamless access to MS Office files. The major Linux office suites, including KOffice, OpenOffice.org, and StarOffice, all read and manage any MS Office files. In addition, these office suites are fast approaching the same level of features and support for office tasks as found in MS Office.

If you want to use any Windows application on Linux, three important alternatives are the Wine virtual Windows API support, VMware virtual platform technology, and CrossOver Office by CodeWeavers. VMware and CrossOver are commercial packages.

Wine allows you to run many Windows applications directly, using a supporting virtual Windows API. See the Wine Web site (**www.winehq.com**) for a list of supported applications. Well-written applications may run directly from Wine, such as the NewsBin newsreader. Often you will have to have a working Windows system from which you need to copy system DLLs needed by particular applications. You can also import Windows fonts by directly copying them to the Wine font directory. Each user can install his or her own version of Wine with its own simulated **c:** partition on which Windows applications are installed. The simulated drive is installed as **drive_c** in your **.wine** directory. The **.wine** directory is a hidden directory. It is not normally displayed with the **ls** command or the GNOME file manager. You can also use any of your Linux directories for your Windows application data files instead of your simulated **c:** drive. These are referenced by Windows applications as the **z:** drive.

In a terminal window, using the **wine** command with an install program will automatically install that Windows application on the simulated **c:** drive. The following example installs MS Office:

```
$ wine /media/OFFICE/setup.exe
```

Though you may encounter difficulties in working with latest MS Office versions, earlier versions such as Office 2003 should not pose problems. When you insert the Office CD, it will be mounted to the **/media** directory using the disc label as its folder name. Check the **/media** folder (click File system in the Computer window) to see the actual name. You then run the **setup.exe** program for Office with Wine. Depending on the Office version, you may encounter more subfolders for the Office **setup.exe** program. The preceding example assumes that the label for Office is *OFFICE* and that the **setup.exe** program for Office is on the top level directory of that CD.

The install program will start up and you will be prompted to enter your product key. Be sure to use only uppercase as you type. Choose Applications | Wine | Programs | Microsoft Office and then choose the application name to start up the application normally. If you right-click a menu entry, such as Microsoft Word, you can choose Add Launcher To Desktop to add an icon for the application on your desktop. The application is referenced by Wine on the users simulated **c:** drive, such as the following for Word:

```
wine  "C:\Program Files\Microsoft Office\OFFICE11\WINWORD.EXE"
```

The Windows **My Documents** folder is set up by Wine to be the user's home directory.

Wine is constantly being updated to accommodate the latest versions of Windows applications. However, for some applications, you may need to copy DLL files from a working Windows system to the Wine folder **.wine/drive_c/windows**, usually to the **system** or **system32** directories.

Though effective, Wine support is as stable as that of CrossOver Office. CrossOver Office is a commercial product that lets you install and run most MS Office applications. CrossOver Office was developed by CodeWeavers, which also supports Windows Web browser plug-ins as well as several popular Windows applications such as Adobe Photoshop. CrossOver features both standard and professional versions, providing reliable application support. You can find out more about CrossOver Office at **www.codeweavers.com**.

CrossOver can be installed either for private multiuser mode or managed multiuser mode. In private multiuser mode, each user installs his or her own Windows software, such as full versions of Office. In managed multiuser mode, the Windows software is installed once and all users share it.

When you install new software, you first open the CrossOver startup tool, and then on the Add/Remove panel you will see a list of supported software. This will include Office applications as well as some Adobe applications, including earlier versions of Photoshop. From an Install Software panel, you can select whether to install from a CD-ROM or an **.exe** file. For Office on a CD-ROM, select CD-ROM, place the Windows CD-ROM in your CD drive, and then click Next. The Windows Office installer will start up in a Linux window and will proceed as if you were using a Windows system. When the install requires a restart of the system, CrossOver will simulate it for you. Once the software is installed, you will see a Windows Applications menu on the main menu, from which you can start your installed Windows software. The applications will run within a Linux window, but they'll appear just as if they were running in Windows. You can also try CrossOver for unsupported applications, which may or may not run.

With VMware, you can run Windows under Linux; you can run Windows applications, including Office, on your Linux system. For more information, check the VMware Web site at **http://vmware.com**.

PART V

NOTE *Though Linux allows users to directly mount and access any of the old DOS or FAT32 partitions used for Windows 95, 98, and Me, it can mount NTFS partitions (Windows Vista, XP, 2000, and NT) with the NTFS, **ntfs-3g**, and the original NTFS project drivers. The **ntfs-3g** drivers support writing NTFS partitions and are installed on Ubuntu by default.*

OpenOffice.org

OpenOffice.org is a fully integrated suite of office applications developed as an open source project and freely distributed to all. It is included as the primary office suite for most Linux distributions, accessible from an Office menu. It includes word processing, spreadsheet, presentation, and drawing applications (see Table 13-2). Versions of OpenOffice.org exist for Linux, Windows, and Mac OS. You can obtain information such as online manuals and FAQs as well as current versions from **www.openoffice.org**.

NOTE *Development for OpenOffice.org is being carried out as an open source project called openoffice.org. The core code is based on the original StarOffice. The code developed in the openoffice.org project will be incorporated into future releases of StarOffice.*

OpenOffice.org is an integrated suite of applications. You can open the writer, spreadsheet, or presentation application directly. In addition, in most OpenOffice.org applications, you can choose File | New and choose a different application if you wish. The Writer word processor supports standard word processing features, such as cut and paste, spell-checker, and text formatting, as well as paragraph styles. Context menus let you format text easily. Wizards (Letter, Web Page, Fax, and Agenda) let you quickly generate different kinds of documents. You can embed objects within documents, such as using Draw to create figures that you can then drag-and-drop to the Writer document. You can find out more about each component at their respective product pages from the OpenOffice Web site.

Calc is a professional-level spreadsheet. With Math, you can create formulas that you can embed in a text document. With the Impress presentation manager, you can create images for presentations—such as circles, rectangles, and connecting elements such as arrows—as well as vector-based illustrations. Impress supports advanced features such as morphing objects, grouping objects, and defining gradients. Draw is a sophisticated drawing tool that includes 3-D modeling tools. You can create simple or complex images, including animation text aligned on curves. OpenOffice.org also includes a printer setup tool with which you can select printers, fonts, paper sizes, and page formats.

NOTE *StarOffice is a fully integrated and Microsoft Office–compatible suite of office applications developed and supported by Sun Microsystems, **www.sun.com/staroffice**. Sun provides StarOffice as a commercial product, though educational use is free.*

Application	Description
Base	Basic database with support for MySQL, PostgreSQL, and MaxDB
Calc	OpenOffice.org spreadsheet
Draw	OpenOffice.org drawing application
Impress	OpenOffice.org presentation manager
Math	OpenOffice.org mathematical formula composer
Writer	OpenOffice.org word processor

TABLE 13-2 OpenOffice.org Applications

OpenOffice.org features an underlying component model that can be programmed to develop customized applications. Check the OpenOffice.org API project for more details (**http://api.openoffice.org**). The OpenOffice.org Software Development Kit (SDK) provides support for using OpenOffice.org components in applications written in C++ or Java. The Unified Network Objects (UNO) model is the component model for OpenOffice.org, providing interaction between programming languages, other object models, and network connections.

NOTE *Also for use on GNOME is the desktop publishing tool Scribus,* ***www.scribus.net****.*

KOffice

KOffice is an integrated office suite for the K Desktop Environment (KDE) consisting of several office applications, including a word processor, a spreadsheet, and graphics applications. You can download it using the Synaptic Package Manager. All applications are written for the KOM component model, which allows components from any one application to be used in another. This means you can embed a spreadsheet from KSpread or diagrams from Karbon14 in a KWord document. You can obtain more information about KOffice from the KOffice Web site at **http://koffice.org**.

TIP *KOffice applications have import and export filters that allow them to import or export files from popular applications such as AbiWord, OpenOffice.org applications, MS Word, and even documents on handheld devices. The reliability of these filters varies, and you should check the KOffice Filters Web page for a listing of the various filters and their stability.*

KOffice Applications

Currently, KOffice includes KSpread, KPresenter, KWord, Karbon14, KFormula, KChart, Kugar, Krita, and Kivio (see Table 13-3). The contact application, Kontact, has been spun off as a separate project. Kontact is an integrated contact application including KMail, KOrganizer, KAddressbook, and KNotes. KSpread is a spreadsheet, KPresenter is a presentation application, Karbon14 is a vector graphics program, KWord is a MS Publisher-like word processor, KFormula is a formula editor, and KChart generates charts and diagrams. Kugar is a report generator, Krita is a bitmap image editor, and Kivio creates flow charts. Kexi provides database integration with KOffice applications, currently supporting PostgreSQL and MySQL.

KSpread, the spreadsheet application, incorporates the basic operations found in most spreadsheets, with formulas similar to those used in MS Excel. You can also embed charts, pictures, or formulas using KChart, Krita, Karbon14, or KFormula.

With KChart, you can create different kinds of charts, such as bar graphs, pie charts, and line graphs, as well as create diagrams. To generate a chart, you can use data in KSpread to enter your data. With KPresenter, you can create presentations consisting of text and graphics modeled using different fonts, orientations, and attributes such as colors. You can add such elements as speech bubbles, arrows, and clip art, as well as embed any KOffice component. Karbon14 is a vector-based graphics program, much like Adobe Illustrator and OpenOffice.org Draw. It supports the standard graphic operations such as rotating, scaling, and aligning objects.

Application	Description
Karbon14	Vector graphics program
KChart	Tool for drawing charts and diagrams
Kexi	Database integration
KFormula	Mathematical formula editor
Kivio	Flow chart generator and editor (similar to Visio)
Kontact (separate project)	Contact application including mail, address book, and organizer
Kontour	Vector drawing program
KPlato	Project management and planning
KPresenter	Presentation program
Krita	Paint and image manipulation program
KSpread	Spreadsheet
Kugar	Report generator
KWord	Word processor (desktop publisher)

TABLE 13-3   KOffice Applications

KWord can best be described as a desktop publisher, with many of the features found in publishing applications such as MS Publisher and FrameMaker. Although it is also a fully functional word processor, KWord is not page-based like Word or WordPerfect. Instead, text is set up in frames that are placed on the page like objects. Frames, like objects in a drawing program, can be moved, resized, and even reoriented. You can organize frames into a frame set, having text flow from one to the other.

KParts

Embedded components support real-time updates. For example, if you use KChart to generate a chart in a KWord document using data in a KSpread spreadsheet and then change the selected data in the spreadsheet, KChart automatically updates the chart in the KWord document. In effect, you are creating a *compound document* made up of several applications. This capability is implemented by the KDE component model known as KParts, which provides communication between distributed objects. In this respect, you can think of an application working also as a server, providing other applications with its specialized services. A word processor, specializing in services such as paragraph formatting or spell-checking, could provide these services to all KOffice applications. In that way, other applications do not need to have their own text formatting functions written into them.

KParts is implemented with the Desktop Communications Protocol (DCOP). This is a very simple, small, and fast interprocess communication/Remote Procedure Call (IPC/RPC) mechanism that is based on the X Window System's Inter-Client Exchange (ICE) protocol. KDE applications now use DCOP libraries to manage their communications with each other. DCOP makes development of KOffice applications much easier and more stable.

GNOME Office

The GNOME Office project supports three office applications: AbiWord, Gnumeric, and GNOME-DB. Former members of GNOME Office still provide certain Office tasks, such as Novell's Evolution e-mail and contact client. Many former members are still GNOME projects, with information listed for them at **www.gnome.org/projects**. You can find out more from the GNOME Office site at **http://live.gnome.org/GnomeOffice**. A current listing for common GNOME Office applications, including those not part of the GNOME Office suite, is shown in Table 13-4. All implement the CORBA model for embedding components, ensuring drag-and-drop capability throughout the GNOME interface.

Gnumeric is a professional-level GNOME spreadsheet program meant to replace commercial spreadsheets. Like GNOME, Gnumeric is freely available under the GNU Public License. Gnumeric is included with the GNOME release, and you will find it installed on any distribution that supports GNOME. You can download current versions from **www.gnome .org/projects/gnumeric**. Gnumeric supports standard GUI spreadsheet features, including autofilling and cell formatting, and it provides an extensive number of formats. It supports drag-and-drop operations to move or copy cells to another location. Gnumeric also supports plug-ins, making it possible to extend and customize its capabilities easily.

AbiWord is an open source word processor that aims to be a complete cross-platform solution, running on Mac, Unix, and Windows, as well as Linux. It is part of a set of desktop productivity applications being developed by the AbiSource project (**http://abisource.com**).

The GNOME-DB project provides a GNOME Data Access (GDA) library supporting several kinds of databases, such as PostgreSQL, MySQL, MS Access, and unixODBC. It provides an API to which databases can plug in. These back-end connections are based on CORBA. Through this API, GNOME applications can access a database. You can find out more about GNOME-DB at **www.gnome-db.org**.

Application	Description
GNOME Office	
AbiWord	Cross-platform word processor
GNOME-DB	Database connectivity
Gnumeric	Spreadsheet
Other GNOME Office Apps	
Balsa	E-mail client (GNOME project)
Dia	Diagram and flow chart editor (GNOME project)
Evolution	Integrated e-mail, calendar, and personal organizer (Novell)
GnuCash	Personal finance manager (GNOME project)
OpenOffice.org	OpenOffice.org office suite
Planner	Project manager (GNOME project)

TABLE 13-4   GNOME Office and Other Office Applications for GNOME

PART V

Dia is a drawing program designed to create diagrams (GNOME project), such as database, circuit object, flow chart, and network diagrams. You can easily create elements along with lines and arcs with different types of endpoints such as arrows or diamonds. Data can be saved in XML format, making it easily transportable to other applications.

GnuCash (**http://gnucash.org**) is a personal finance application for managing accounts, stocks, and expenses (GNOME project). It includes support for home banking with the OpenHBCI interface. OpenHBCI is the open source home banking computer interface (**http://openhbci.sourceforge.net**).

Document Viewers (PostScript, PDF, and DVI)

Though located under Graphic submenu in the Applications menu, PostScript, PDF, and Digital Visual Interface (DVI) viewers are more commonly used with Office applications (see Table 13-5). Evince and Ghostview can display both PostScript (**.ps**) and PDF (**.pdf**) files. Ghostview's X Window System front end is **gv**. KPDF and Xpdf are PDF viewers. KPDF includes many of the standard Adobe Reader features such as zoom, two-page display, and full-screen mode. Alternatively, you can download Acrobat Reader for Linux from Adobe to display PDF files. All these viewers also have the ability to print documents. To generate PDF documents, you can use Scribus desktop publisher (**www.scribus.net**), and to edit PDF documents you can use pdfedit.

Linux also features a professional-level typesetting tool, called *TeX*, commonly used to compose complex mathematical formulas. TeX generates a DVI document that can be displayed by DVI viewers, several of which are available for Linux. DVI files generated by the TeX document application can be viewed by KDVI, which is a plug-in to the KViewShell tool. KViewShell can display and print any kind of document for which it has a plug-in.

Viewer	Description
Acrobat Reader	Adobe PDF and PostScript display application
Evince	Document Viewer for PostScript and PDF files
Gnome-gv	Gnome Ghostscript viewer
KDVI	KDE tool for displaying TeX DVI files (plug-in to KViewShell)
KGhostView	KDE interface for displaying PostScript and PDF files
KPDF	KDE tool for displaying PDF files
pdfedit	Edit PDF documents
Scribus	Desktop publisher for generating PDF documents
xpdf	X Window System tool for displaying PDF files only

TABLE 13-5 PostScript, PDF, and DVI Viewers

PDA Access

For many PDAs you can use the pilot tools to access your handheld device, transferring information between it and your system. The **pilot-link** package holds tools you can use to access your PDA. Check **www.pilot-link.org** for detailed documentation and useful links. The tool name usually begin with *pilot*—for instance, **pilot-addresses** reads addresses from an address book. Other tools whose names begin with *read* allow you to convert PDA device data for access by other applications; **read-expenses**, for instance, outputs expense data as standard text. One of the more useful tools is **pilot-xfer**, used to back up your PDA.

Instead of using command line commands directly, you can use the J-Pilot, KPilot, and GNOMEPilot applications to access your PDA. To use your PDA on GNOME, you can use the gnome-pilot applet from your GNOME panel to configure your connection. In the gnome-pilot applet's Preferences windows (right-click on the gnome-pilot applet), the Conduits tab lets you enable several hotsync operations to perform automatically, including e-mail, memos, and installing files. Click the Help button for a detailed manual.

J-Pilot provides a GUI that lets you perform basic tasks such as synchronizing address books and writing memos. KPilot is included with the **kpim** package installed as part of the KDE desktop. When you start up **kpilot** it will first let you automatically sync with your PDA. You then have the option to use Evolution or Kontact with your PDA, or to perform backups. You can then perform such operations as creating hotsyncs, viewing addresses, and installing files. For text and Palm format conversions, you can use KPalmDoc. This tool will convert text files to Palm files, and Palm files to text files.

TIP *The device name used for your PDA is /dev/pilot, which is managed by **udev**. Should you manually need to specify a port for your handheld, you have to modify **udev** rules, not change the /dev/pilot file directly.*

Editors

Traditionally, most Linux distributions install the cursor-based editors Vim and Emacs. Vim is an enhanced version of the Vi text editor used on the Unix system. These editors use simple, cursor-based operations to give you a full-screen format. You can start these editors from the shell command line without any kind of X Window System support. In this mode, their cursor-based operations do not have the ease of use normally found in window-based editors. There are no menus, scroll bars, or mouse-click features. However, KDE and GNOME do support powerful GUI text editors with all these features. These editors operate much more like those found on Macintosh and Windows systems. They have full mouse support, scroll bars, and menus. You may find them much easier to use than the Vi and Emacs editors. These editors operate from their respective desktops, requiring you first have either KDE or GNOME installed, though the editors can run on either desktop. Vim and Emacs have powerful editing features that have been refined over the years. Emacs, in particular, is extensible to a full-development environment for programming new applications. Newer versions of Emacs, such as GNU Emacs and XEmacs, provide X Window System support with mouse, menu, and window operations. They can run on any window manager or desktop. In addition, the gvim version of the Vim editor also provides basic window operations. You can access it on both GNOME and KDE desktops. Table 13-6 lists several GUI-based editors for Linux.

The K Desktop	Description
Kate	Text and program editor
KEdit	Text editor
KWord	Desktop publisher, part of KOffice
GNOME	
AbiWord	Word processor
Gedit	Text editor
X Window System	
GNU Emacs	Emacs editor with X Window System support
gvim	Vim version with X Window System support (vim-x11)
OpenWriter	OpenOffice.org word processor that can edit text files
XEmacs	X Window System version of Emacs editor

TABLE 13-6 Desktop Editors

GNOME Editor: Gedit

The Gedit editor is a basic text editor for the GNOME desktop. It provides full mouse support, implementing standard GUI operations, such as cut and paste to move text, and click and drag to select and move/copy text. It supports standard text editing operations such as find and replace. You can use Gedit to create and modify your text files, including configuration files. Gedit also provides more advanced features such as print preview and configurable levels of undo/redo operations, and it can read data from pipes. It features a plug-in menu that provides added functionality, and it includes plug-ins for spell-checking, encryption, e-mail, and text-based Web page display.

KDE Editors: Kate and KEdit

All the KDE editors provide full mouse support, implementing standard GUI operations, such as cut and paste to move text and click and drag to select and move/copy text. Kate is an advanced editor, with such features as spell-checking, font selection, and highlighting. Most commands can be selected using menus. A toolbar of icons for common operations is displayed across the top of the Kate window. A sidebar displays panels for a file selector and a file list. With the file selector, you can navigate through the file system selecting files to access. Kate also supports multiple views of a document, letting you display segments in their own windows, vertically or horizontally. You can also open several documents at the same time, moving among them with the file list. Kate is designed to be a program editor for editing software programming/development-related source code files. Although Kate does not have all the features of Emacs or Vi, it can handle most major tasks. Kate can format the syntax for different programming languages, such as C, Perl, Java, and XML. In addition, Kate has the ability to access and edit files on an FTP or Web site.

KEdit is an older, simple text editor meant for editing simple text files such as configuration files. A toolbar of buttons at the top of the KEdit window enables you to execute common editing commands easily using just a mouse click. With KEdit, you can also mail files you are editing over a network. The entry for KEdit in the K menu is listed simply as Text Editor.

The Emacs Editor

Emacs can best be described as a working environment featuring an editor, a mailer, a newsreader, and a Lisp interpreter. The editor is tailored for program development, enabling you to format source code according to the programming language you use. Many versions of Emacs are currently available for use on Unix and Linux systems. The versions usually included with Linux distributions are either GNU Emacs or XEmacs. GNU Emacs is X Window System–capable, enabling GUI features such as menus, scroll bars, and mouse-based editing operations. Check the update FTP sites for your distribution for new versions as they are released as well as the GNU Web site at **www.gnu.org** and the Emacs Web site at **www.gnu.org/software/emacs**. You can also find out more information about XEmacs at its Web site, **http://xemacs.org**.

Emacs derives much of its power and flexibility from its ability to manipulate buffers. Emacs can be described as a *buffer-oriented editor*. Whenever you edit a file in any editor, the file is copied into a work buffer, and editing operations are made on the work buffer. Emacs can manage many work buffers at once, so you can edit several files at the same time. You can edit buffers that hold deleted or copied text. You can even create buffers of your own, fill them with text, and later save them to a file. Emacs extends the concept of buffers to cover any task. When you compose mail, you open a mail buffer, and when you read news, you open a news buffer. Switching from one task to another is simply a matter of switching to another buffer.

The Emacs editor operates much like a standard word processor. The keys on your keyboard represent input characters. Commands are implemented with special keys, such as the CTRL key and ALT key. There is no special input mode, as in Vi. You type in your text, and if you need to execute an editing command, such as moving the cursor or saving text, you use a CTRL key. Such an organization makes the Emacs editor easy to use. However, Emacs is anything but simple—it is a sophisticated and flexible editor with several hundred commands. Emacs also has special features, such as multiple windows. You can display two windows for text at the same time. You can also open and work on more than one file at a time, displaying each on the screen in its own window. You invoke the Emacs editor with the command **emacs**. You can enter the name of the file you want to edit, and if the file does not exist, it is created. In the next example, the user prepares to edit the file **mydata** with Emacs:

```
$ emacs mydata
```

The GNU Emacs editor now supports an X Window System GUI. To enable X support, start Emacs within an X Window System environment, such as a KDE, GNOME, or Xfce desktop. The basic GUI editing operations are supported: selection of text with click-and-drag mouse operations; cut, copy, and paste; and a scroll bar for moving through text. The Mode line and Echo areas are displayed at the bottom of the window, where you can enter keyboard commands. The scroll bar is located on the left side. To move the scroll bar down, click it with the left mouse button. To move the scroll bar up, click it with the right mouse button.

NOTE *XEmacs is the complete Emacs editor with a GUI and Internet applications, including a Web browser, a mail utility, and a newsreader.*

The Vi Editor: Vim and Gvim

The Vim editor included with most Linux distributions is an enhanced version of the Vi editor that includes all the same commands and features. Vi, which stands for *visual*, remains one of the most widely used editors in Linux. Keyboard-based editors such as Vim and Emacs use a keyboard for two different operations: to specify editing commands and to receive character input.

Used for editing commands, certain keys perform deletions, some execute changes, and others perform cursor movement. Used for character input, keys represent characters that can be entered into the file being edited. Usually, these two different functions are divided among different keys on the keyboard. Alphabetic keys are reserved for character input, while function keys and control keys specify editing commands, such as deleting text or moving the cursor. Such editors can rely on the existence of an extended keyboard that includes function and control keys. Editors in Unix, however, were designed to assume a minimal keyboard with alphanumeric characters and some control characters, as well as the ESC and ENTER keys.

Instead of dividing the command and input functions among different keys, the Vi editor has three separate modes of operation for the keyboard: command and input modes, and a line editing mode. In *command* mode, all the keys on the keyboard become editing commands; in *input* mode, the keys on the keyboard become input characters. Some of the editing commands, such as **a** or **i**, enter the input mode. On typing **i**, you leave the command mode and enter the input mode. Each key then represents a character to be input to the text. Pressing ESC automatically returns you to the command mode, and the keys once again become editor commands. As you edit text, you are constantly moving from the command mode to the input mode and back again. With Vim, you can use the CTRL-O command to jump quickly to the command mode and enter a command, and then automatically return to the input mode. Table 13-7 lists a basic set of Vi commands to get you started.

Command	Cursor Movement
h	Moves the cursor left one character.
l	Moves the cursor right one character.
k	Moves the cursor up one line.
j	Moves the cursor down one line.
CTRL-F	Moves forward by a screen of text; the next screen of text is displayed.
CTRL-B	Moves backward by a screen of text; the previous screen of text is displayed.
Input	*All input commands place the user in input; the user leaves input by pressing ESC.*
a	Enters input after the cursor.
i	Enters input before the cursor.
o	Enters input below the line on which the cursor resides; inserts a new empty line below the line on which the cursor resides.

TABLE 13-7 Vi Editor Commands

Command	Cursor Movement
Text Selection (Vim)	**Cursor Movement**
v	Visual mode; move the cursor to expand selected text by character. Once selected, press key to execute action: c change, d delete, y copy, : line editing command, J join lines, U uppercase, u lowercase.
V	Visual mode; move cursor to expand selected text by line.
Delete	**Effect**
x	Deletes the character on which the cursor resides.
dd	Deletes the line on which the cursor resides.
Change	*Except for the replace command, r, all change commands place the user into input after deleting text.*
cw	Deletes the word the cursor is on and places the user into the input mode.
r	Replaces the character the cursor is on. After pressing r, the user enters the replacement character. The change is made without entering input; the user remains in the Vi command mode.
R	First places into input mode, and then overwrites character by character. Appears as an overwrite mode on the screen but actually is in input mode.
Move	*Move text by first deleting it, moving the cursor to desired place of insertion, and then pressing the p command. (When text is deleted, it is automatically held in a special buffer.)*
p	Inserts deleted or copied text after the character or line on which the cursor resides.
P	Inserts deleted or copied text before the character or line on which the cursor resides.
dw p	Deletes a word, and then moves it to the place you indicate with the cursor (press p to insert the word *after* the word on which the cursor resides).
yy or Y p	Copies the line on which the cursor resides.
Search	*The two search commands open up a line at the bottom of the screen and enable the user to enter a pattern to be searched for; press ENTER after typing in the pattern.*
/pattern	Searches forward in the text for a pattern.
?pattern	Searches backward in the text for a pattern.
n	Repeats the previous search, whether it was forward or backward.
Line Editing Commands	**Effect**
w	Saves file.
q	Quits editor; q! quits without saving.

TABLE 13-7   Vi Editor Commands

Although the Vi command mode handles most editing operations, it cannot perform some, such as file saving and global substitutions. For those operations, you need to execute line editing commands. You enter the line editing mode using the Vi colon (:) command. The colon is a special command that enables you to perform a one-line editing operation. When you type the colon, a line opens up at the bottom of the screen with the cursor placed at the beginning of the line, signaling that you are now in the line editing mode. In this mode, you enter an editing command on a line, press ENTER, and the command is executed. Entry into this mode is usually only temporary. Upon pressing ENTER, you are automatically returned to the Vi command mode, and the cursor returns to its previous position on the screen.

Although you can create, save, close, and quit files with the Vi editor, the commands for each are not all that similar. Saving and quitting a file involves the use of special line editing commands, whereas closing a file is a Vi editing command. Creation of a file is usually specified on the same shell command line that invokes the Vi editor. To edit a file, type **vi** or **vim** and the name of a file on the shell command line. If a file by that name does not exist, the system creates it. In effect, entering the name of a file that does not yet exist instructs the Vi editor to create that file. The following command invokes the Vi editor, working on the file **booklist**. If **booklist** does not yet exist, the Vi editor creates it:

```
$ vim booklist
```

After executing the **vim** command, you enter Vi's command mode. Each key becomes a Vi editing command, and the screen becomes a window onto the text file. Text is displayed screen by screen. The first screen of text is displayed, and the cursor is positioned in the upper-left corner. With a newly created file, there is no text to display. This fact is indicated by a column of tildes at the left side of the screen. The tildes represent the part of a screen that is not part of the file.

Remember, when you first enter the Vi editor, you are in the command mode. To enter text, you need to enter the input mode. In the command mode, **a** is the editor command for appending text. Pressing this key places you in the input mode. Now the keyboard operates like a typewriter and you can input text to the file. If you press ENTER, you merely start a new line of text. With Vim, you can use the arrow keys to move from one part of the entered text to another and work on different parts of the text. After entering text, you can leave the input mode and return to the command mode by pressing ESC. Once finished with the editing session, you exit Vi by typing two capital Zs: **ZZ** (hold down the SHIFT key and press **z** twice). This sequence first saves the file and then exits the Vi editor, returning you to the Linux shell. To save a file while editing, you use the line editing command **w**, which writes a file to the disk; **w** is equivalent to the Save command found in other word processors. You first type a colon to access the line editing mode, and then type **w** and press ENTER. (Note that the combination **:wq** is the same as **ZZ**.)

You can use the **:q** command to quit an editing session. Unlike the **ZZ** command, the **:q** command does not perform any save operation before it quits. In this respect, it has one major constraint. If any modifications have been made to your file since the last save operation, the **:q** command will fail and you will not leave the editor. However, you can override this restriction by placing a ! qualifier after the **:q** command. The command **:q!** will quit the Vi editor without saving any modifications made to the file in that session since the last save.

To obtain online help, enter the `:help` command. This is a line editing command. Type a colon, enter the word **help** on the line that opens at the bottom of the screen, and then press ENTER. You can add the name of a specific command after the word **help**. Pressing the F1 key also brings up online help.

As an alternative to using Vim in a command line interface, you can use **gvim**, which provides X Window System–based menus for basic file, editing, and window operations. Gvim is installed as the **vim-gui-common** package, which includes several links to Gvim such as **evim**, **gview**, and **gex** (open Ex editor line). To use Gvim, you can select it from your distribution's main menu, or enter the **gvim** command at an X Window System terminal prompt.

The standard Vi interface is displayed, but with several menu buttons displayed across the top along with a toolbar with buttons for common commands like searches and file saves. All the standard Vi commands work just as described previously. However, you can use your mouse to select items on these menus. You can open and close a file, or open several files using split windows or different windows. The editing menu enables you to cut, copy, and paste text as well as undo or redo operations. In the editing mode, you can select text with your mouse with a click-and-drag operation, or use the Editing menu to cut or copy and then paste the selected text. Text entry, however, is still performed using the **a**, **i**, or **o** command to enter the input mode. Searches and replacements are supported through a dialog window. Some buttons on the toolbar can be used for finding next and previous instances. Gview also features programming support, with color coding for programming syntax, for both shell scripts and C++ programs. It also provides a Make button for running makefiles.

You can also split the view into different windows to display parts of the same file or different files. Use the `:split` command to open a window, and use `:hide` to close the current one. Use CTRL-W with the UP and DOWN ARROW keys to move between them. On Gvim, you use entries in the Windows menu to manage windows. Configuration preferences can be placed in the user's **.vimrc** file.

Database Management Systems

Database software can be generally organized into three categories: SQL, XBase, and desktop databases. *SQL-based databases* are professional-level relational databases whose files are managed by a central database server program. Applications that use the database do not access the files directly. Instead, they send requests to the database server, which then performs the actual access. SQL is the query language used on these industrial-strength databases. Both are open source projects freely available for your use. The easiest way to set up a small personal database is with OpenOffice.org Base. You can quickly create a database that can interface easily with other applications. Table 13-8 lists database management systems (DBMSs) currently available for Linux.

NOTE *The* XBase *language is an enhanced version of the dBase programming language used to access database files whose formats were originally developed for dBase on the PC. XBase is used mainly for smaller personal databases, with database files often located on a user's own system.*

System	Site
OpenOffice.org Base database	**www.openoffice.org**
PostgreSQL database	**www.postgresql.org**
MySQL database	**www.mysql.com**
Oracle database	**www.oracle.com**
Sybase database	**www.sybase.com**
IBM DB2 database	**www-306.ibm.com/software/data/db2/**
Informix database	**www-306.ibm.com/software/data/informix/**
MaxDB, SAP database	**www.sdn.sap.com/irj/sdn/maxdb**
GNU SQL database	**http://ispras.ru/~kml/gss**
FlagShip interface for XBase database files	**http://fship.com/free.html**
XBase tools and libraries	**http://linux.techass.com/projects/xdb**

TABLE 13-8   Database Management Systems for Linux

OpenOffice.org Base

OpenOffice.org's basic database application can access many database files. You can set up and operate a simple database as well as access and manage files from other database applications. When you start up OpenOffice. org Base, you will be prompted either to start a new database or connect to an existing one. File types supported include Open Database Connectivity (ODBC 3), Java Database Connectivity (JDBC), ActiveX Data Objects (ADO), MySQL, dBase, Comma Separated Values (CSV), PostgreSQL, and Microsoft Access (MDB) database files (install the **unixodbc** and **java-libmysql** packages). Check the OpenOffice.org Base page and Project page for detailed information on drivers and supported databases.

SQL Databases (RDMS)

SQL databases are relational database management systems (RDMSs) designed for extensive professional and commercial database management tasks. Many of the major SQL databases now have Linux versions, including Oracle, Informix, Sybase, and IBM (but not, of course, Microsoft). These are commercial and professional database management systems of the highest order. Linux has proved itself capable of supporting complex and demanding database management tasks. In addition, many free SQL databases are available for Linux that offer much the same functionality. Most commercial databases also provide free personal versions, as do Oracle, Adabas D, and MySQL.

PostgreSQL

PostgreSQL is based on the POSTGRES database management system, though it uses SQL as its query language. POSTGRES is a next-generation research prototype developed at the University of California, Berkeley. Linux versions of PostgreSQL are included in most distributions. PostgreSQL is an open source project, developed under the GPL license.

MySQL

MySQL is a true multiuser, multithreaded SQL database server, supported by MySQL AB. MySQL is an open source product available free under the GPL license. The MySQL Web site includes detailed documentation, including manuals and FAQs.

Oracle

Oracle offers a fully functional version of its Oracle9*i* database management system for Linux, as well as the Oracle Application Server. You can download trial versions from the Oracle Web site. Oracle is a professional DBMS for large databases specifically designed for Internet e-business tasks. The Oracle Application Server provides support for real-time and commerce applications on the Web. As Linux is a fully functional version of Unix, Oracle is particularly effective on it. Oracle was originally designed to operate on Unix, and Linux is a far better platform for it than other PC operating systems.

Oracle offers extensive documentation for its Linux version that you can download from its Documentation page, to which you can link from the Support pages on its Web site. The documentation available includes an installation guide, an administrator's reference, and release notes, as well as the generic documentation. You can find specific information on installing and configuring Oracle for Linux in the Oracle Database HOW-TO.

Informix

Informix (now controlled by IBM) offers an integrated platform of Internet-based applications called Informix Internet Foundation.2000 on Linux. These include the Informix Dynamic Server, the company's database server. Informix Dynamic Server features Dynamic Scalable Architecture, making it capable of effectively using any hardware setup. Informix provides only commercial products. No free versions exist, though the company currently provides special promotions for Linux products. Informix strongly supports Linux development of its Informix line.

Sybase

For Linux, Sybase offers the Sybase Adaptive Server Enterprise server. You can currently download the Adaptive Server Enterprise server from the Sybase Web site. The Sybase Enterprise database features data integration that coordinates all information resources on a network. SQL Anywhere is a database system designed for smaller databases, though with the same level of complexity found in larger databases.

DB2

IBM provides a Linux version of its DB2 Universal Database software. You can download it free from the IBM DB2 Web page for Linux. DB2 Universal Database for Linux includes Internet functionality along with support for Java and Perl. With the Web Control Center, administrators can maintain databases from a Web browser. DB2 features scalability to expand the database easily, support for Binary Large Objects, and cost-based optimization for fast access. DB2 is still very much a mainframe database, though IBM is currently working on refining its Unix/Linux version.

MaxDB

MaxDB is a SAP-certified database, originally developed by SAP. It provides capabilities comparable to many of the professional-level databases.

GNU SQL

GNU SQL is the GNU relational database developed by a group at the Institute for System Programming of the Russian Academy of Sciences and supported by the GNU organization. It is a portable multiuser database management system with a client/server structure that supports SQL. The server processes requests and performs basic administrative operations, such as unloading parts of the database used infrequently. The clients can reside on any computer of a local network. GNU SQL uses a dialect of SQL based on the SQL-89 standard and is designed for use on a Unix-like environment. You can download the database software from the GNU FTP site at **ftp.gnu.org**.

XBase Databases

Databases accessed with XBase are smaller in scale, designed for small networks or for personal use. Many are originally PC database programs, such as dBase III, Clipper, FoxPro, and Quicksilver. Currently, only FlagShip provides an interface for accessing XBase database files.

FlagShip is a compiler with which you can create interfaces for querying XBase database files. The interfaces support menus and dialog boxes, and they have function calls that execute certain database queries. FlagShip can compile dBase III+ code and up. It is compatible with dBase and Clipper and can access most XBase file formats, such as **.dbf**, **.dbt**, **.fmt**, and **.frm**. One of FlagShip's key features is that its interfaces can be attached to a Web page, enabling users to update databases. FlagShip is commercial software, though you can download a free personal version its Web site at **www.fship.com**.

Graphics Tools and Multimedia

Linux supports a wide range of graphics and multimedia applications and tools, including simple image viewers such as GwenView, sophisticated image manipulation programs such as GIMP, music and CD players such as Rhythmbox, and video viewers such as Totem. Graphics tools available for use under Linux are listed later in this chapter in Table 14-2. Additionally, strong support is provided for multimedia tasks, from video and DVD to sound and music editing (Table 14-6). Thousands of multimedia and graphics projects, as well as standard projects, are under development or currently available from online sites such as those shown in Table 14-1. Most are available on Ubuntu's multiverse and universe repositories. For information on graphics hardware and drivers, see **www.phoronix.com**.

TIP *K Desktop Environment (KDE) programs, including graphics and multimedia applications, can be run from GNOME, and GNOME programs can be run by KDE. You simply need to have one of the desktops installed and the supporting libraries from the other. So, for example, to run a KDE graphics applications on GNOME, you do not have to install the full KDE desktop, only the required KDE supporting libraries. Ubuntu will automatically install any needed libraries when the application is installed.*

NOTE *Support for many popular multimedia operations, specifically MP3, DVD, and DivX, are not included with many distributions because of licensing and other restrictions. To play MP3, DVD, or DivX files, you will have to download and install support packages manually. For Ubuntu, precompiled packages for many popular media applications and libraries, such as MPlayer and XviD as well as MP3 and DVD video support, are available at Ubuntu multiverse and universe repositories.*

Graphics Tools

GNOME, KDE, and the X Window System support an impressive number of graphics tools, including image viewers, window grabbers, image editors, and paint tools. On the KDE and GNOME desktops, these tools can be found under a Graphics submenu on the Utilities menu.

Sites	Description
http://sourceforge.net	Extensive amount of multimedia software for Linux, much under development
http://kde-apps.org	KDE multimedia applications: KDE supports an extensive set of multimedia software applications
http://gnomefiles.org	GNOME files, GNOME multimedia applications: Many multimedia applications have been developed for GNOME
http://linux-sound.org	Sound & MIDI Software for Linux: Wide range of multimedia and sound software
http://alsa-project.org	Advanced Linux Sound Architecture (ALSA): The ALSA project is under development on Linux under the GNU Public License (GPL)
http://opensound.com	Open Sound System: Wide range of supporting multimedia applications
www.pulseaudio.org	PulseAudio sound interface
www.phoronix.com	Phoronix site for the latest news and reviews of hardware compatibility, including graphics cards

TABLE 14-1   Linux Multimedia Sites

NOTE *Linux has become a platform of choice for many professional-level multimedia tasks such as generating computer-generated images (CGIs) and animation for movie special effects, using such demanding software as Maya and Softimage. Linux graphic libraries include those for OpenGL, MESA, and SGI.*

Photo Management Tools: F-Spot and digiKam

The F-Spot photo manager (**http://f-spot.org**) provides a simple and powerful way to manage, display, and import your photos and images (see Figure 14-1). Photos can be organized by different categories such as events, people, and places. You can perform standard display operations such as rotation or full-screen viewing, along with slide shows. Image editing support is provided. Selected photos can be directly burned to a CD (using Nautilus burning capabilities).

Features include a simple and easy-to-use interface. A timeline feature lets you see photos as they were taken. You can also display photos in full-screen mode or as slide shows. F-Spot includes a photo editor that provides basic adjustments and changes such as rotation, red-eye correction, and standard color settings including temperature and saturation. You can tag photos and place them in groups, making them easier to access. With a tag, you can label a collection of photos, then use the tag to access them instantly. The tag itself can be a user-selected icon including one that the user can create with the Tag icon editor. F-Spot provides several ways to upload photos to a Web site. It provides direct access to a Flickr account (**http://flickr.com**) or to Gallery-supported sites (**http://gallery .menalto.com**). Photos can also be saved to a folder for later uploading to a Web site, either as plain files or as static HTML files.

DigiKam (**www.digiKam.org**) is a KDE photo manager with many of the same features. A side panel allows easy access by album, date, tags, or previous searches. The program

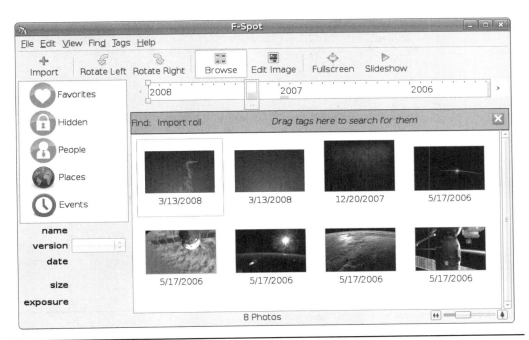

FIGURE 14-1   F-Spot photo management

also provides image-editing capabilities, with numerous effects. The digiKam configuration (Settings menu) provides extensive options, including image editing, digital camera support, and interface configuration.

Cheese (**www.gnome.org/projects/cheese/**) is a Web cam picture-taking and video-recording tool for GNOME (see Figure 14-2). You can snap pictures from your Web cam and apply simple effects, manage photos, and record video. The effects panel shows effects that can be turned on or off for the current image. You can also export a selected photo or video to F-Spot, as well as e-mail it as an attachment.

TIP   *The Windows version of Photoshop is now supported by Wine. You can install Photoshop CS on Ubuntu using Wine and then access it through the Wine Windows support tool. Once started, Photoshop will operate similar to any Linux desktop application.*

GNOME Graphics Tools

GNOME features several powerful and easy-to-use graphics tools. Some are installed with Linux, and you can download others, such as GView and Gtkam, from **http://gnomefiles.org**. In addition, many of the KDE tools work effectively in GNOME and are accessible from the GNOME desktop. Most are available on the Ubuntu main repository.

The GTHUMB application is an image viewer and browser that lets you display images using thumbnails and organize them into catalogs or easy reference. See **http://gthumb .sourceforge.net/** for more information.

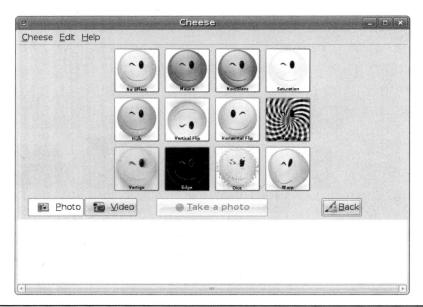

Figure 14-2 Cheese Web cam photo/video manager

The GNU Image Manipulation Program (GIMP) is a sophisticated image editing application much like Adobe Photoshop. You can use GIMP for such tasks as photo retouching, image composition, and image authoring. It supports features such as layers, channels, blends, and gradients. GIMP makes particular use of the GTK+ widget set. You can find out more about GIMP and download the newest versions from its Web site at **http://gimp.org**. GIMP is freely distributed under the GPL.

Inkscape (Figure 14-3) is a GNOME-based vector graphics application for Scalable Vector Graphics (SVG) images (**www.inkscape.org/**). Its features are similar to those of professional-level vector graphics applications such as Adobe Illustrator. The SVG format allows easy generation of images for Web use as well as complex art. Though its native format is SVG, it can also export to Portable Network Graphics (PNG) format. It features layers and easy object creation, including stars and spirals. A color bar lets you quickly change color fills.

The gPhoto project (**http://gphoto.org**) provides software for accessing digital cameras. Several front-end interfaces are provided for a core library, called **libgphoto2**, consisting of drivers and tools that can access numerous digital cameras.

KDE Graphics Tools

The KDE desktop features the same variety of graphics tools found on the GNOME desktop. Many are available from the Ubuntu main repository. Most do not require a full installation of the KDE desktop.

GwenView is a simple image viewer for GIF and JPEG image files. The KSnapshot program is a simple screen grabber for KDE, which currently supports only a few image formats. KuickShow is an easy-to-use, comfortable image browser and viewer supporting

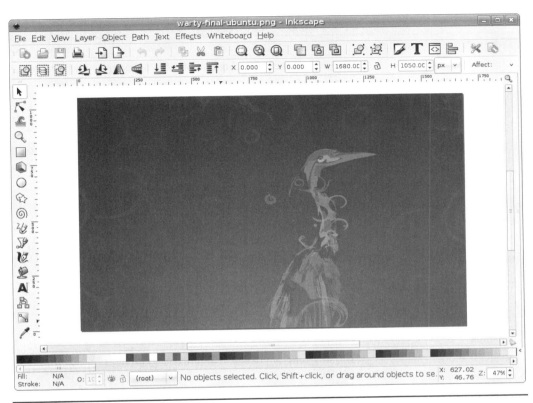

FIGURE 14-3   Inkscape

slide shows and numerous image formats based on **imlib**. KolourPaint is a simple paint program with brushes, shapes, and color effects; it supports numerous image formats. Krita (**www.koffice.org/krita/**, formerly known as Krayon and KImageShop) is the KOffice professional image paint and editing application, with a wide range of features such as the ability to create Web images and modify photographs.

X Window System Graphic Programs

X Window System–based applications run directly on the underlying X Window System, which supports the more complex GNOME and KDE desktops. These applications tend to be simpler, lacking the desktop functionality found in GNOME or KDE applications. Most are available on the Ubuntu universe repository. Xpaint is a paint program much like MacPaint that allows you to load graphics or photographs and then create shapes, add text and colors, and use brush tools with various sizes and colors. Xfig is a drawing program, and Xmorph lets you morph images, changing their shapes. ImageMagick (**www.imagemagick.org/script/ index.php**) lets you convert images from one format to another; you can, for instance, change a TIFF image to a JPEG image. Table 14-2 lists some popular graphics tools for Linux.

Tools	Description
Photo Management	
Cheese	GNOME Web cam applications for taking pictures and videos
digiKam	KDE digital camera application and image library manager
F-Spot	GNOME digital camera application and image library manager
KDE	
KolourPaint	Simple paint program
Krita	Image editor
KSnapshot	Screen grabber
KuickShow	Image browser and viewer
GwenView	Simple image viewer for image files
ShowFoto	Simple image viewer, works with digiKam
GNOME	
GIMP	GNU Image Manipulation Program
gpaint	GNOME paint program
GTHUMB	Image browser, viewer, and cataloger
Inkscape	GNOME vector graphics application
OpenOffice.org Draw	Drawing program (**www.openoffice.org/product/draw.html**)
X Window System	
ImageMagick	Image format conversion and editing tool
Xfig	Drawing program
Xpaint	Paint program
Xmorph	Tool that morphs images

TABLE 14-2   Graphics Tools for Linux

Multimedia Tools

Many applications are available for both video and sound, including sound editors, MP3 players, and video players. Linux sound applications include mixers, digital audio tools, CD audio writers, MP3 players, and network audio support. Literally thousands of projects are currently under development at sourceforge.net. If you are looking for a specific kind of application, odds are you will find it there. Current projects include a full-featured video player, a digital video recorder, and a digital audio mixer. Many applications designed specifically for the GNOME or KDE user interface can be found at their respective software site (**http://gnomefiles.org** or **http://kde-apps.org**). Precompiled binary Red Hat Package Manager (RPM) or Debian (DEB) packages can be easily downloaded and installed from distribution repositories.

Multimedia applications use various codecs to run different kinds of media, such as MP3 for music files. The Codec Buddy tool will detect the codec you need and download it if not installed. You can purchase third-party commercial codecs such as Windows Media or Dolby codecs from Fluendo (**www.fluendo.com**)

NOTE *You can configure the ability to watch video on your browser by using a variety of plug-ins for different embedded media players. For Adobe Flash files, you can use the original Adobe Flash plug-in,* **flashplugin-nonfree,** *or* **gnash,** *the GNOME free flash player. VLC and GXine provide Mozilla plug-ins for Firefox for playing video (**mozilla-plugin** packages).*

Ubuntu Codec Wizard

Ubuntu provides a codec wizard that will automatically detect whenever you need to install a new multimedia codec (see Chapter 4). If you try to run a media file for which you do not have the proper codec, the codec wizard will appear, listing the codecs you need to download and install. For MP3, you can use the lame codec, the licensed Fluendo codec, or both. Alternatively, you could download and install these codecs manually. Most are available on the universe and multiverse repositories, though you would need to know what packages to look for. For the Fluendo codecs, search in the Synaptic Package Manager.

The codec wizard will select and install these packages for you, simplifying the process of installing the various multimedia codecs available for Linux. Table 14-3 lists several popular multimedia codec packages.

GStreamer

Many GNOME-based applications use GStreamer, a streaming media framework based on graphs and filters. Using a plug-in structure, GStreamer applications can accommodate a wide variety of media types. You can download modules and plug-ins from **http:// gstreamer.freedesktop.org**. GNOME on Linux includes several GStreamer applications:

- The Totem video player uses GStreamer to play DVDs, VCDs, DVB broadcasts, DivX, and MPEG media.

- Rhythmbox provides integrated music management. It is similar to the Apple iTunes music player.

- Sound Juicer is an audio CD ripper.

- A CD player, a sound recorder, and a volume control are all provided as part of the GStreamer GNOME Media package.

Multimedia System Selector

GStreamer can be configured to use different input and output sound and video drivers and servers. You can make these selections using the GStreamer properties tool. To open this tool you enter `gstreamer-properties` in a terminal window. This opens a window labeled Multimedia Systems Selector which displays two tabbed panels, one for sound and the other for video. The output drivers and servers are labeled Default Sink, and the input divers are labeled Default Source. Pop-up menus list the available sound or video drivers or servers. For example, the sound server used is ALSA, but you can change that to OSS.

Package	Description
lliba52	HDTV audio (ATSC A/52, AC3)
audacious-plugins-extra	MP3, AAC, and WMA for Audacious
faac	MPEG2/ 4 AAC sound encoding and decoding
faad2	MPEG2/ 4 AAC audio decoding, high quality
libfame	Fast Assembly MPEG video encoding
ffmpeg	Play, record, convert, stream audio and video; includes digital streaming server, conversion tool, and media player; **libavcodec** holds **FFmpeg** originally developed video and audio codec code
gstreamer-bad	Not fully reliable codecs and tools for GStreamer, including some with possible licensing issues
gstreamer-dll	DLL (Windows) media loader for GStreamer
gstreamer-ffmpeg	**FFmpeg** plug-in for GStreamer
gstreamer-fluendo-mp3	Fully licensed MP3 codec from Fluendo for GStreamer
gstreamer-fluendo-mpeg	Fully licensed MPEG2 video codec from Fluendo for GStreamer
gstreamer-ugly	Reliable video and audio codecs for GStreamer that may have licensing issues
lame	MP3 playback capability, not an official MP3 decoder
libdts	DTS Coherent Acoustics playback capability
libdvdread3	DVD video playback capability, includes CSS decoding
libdvdnav	DVD video menu navigation
libdvbpsi	MPEG TS stream (DVB and PSI) decoding and encoding capability, VideoLAN project
libmad	MPEG1 and MPEG2 audio decoding
libmpeg3	MPEG video audio decoding (MPEG1/2 audio and video, AC3, IFO, and VOB)
libquicktime	QuickTime playback
libopendaap	iTunes support
mpeg2dec	MPEG2 and MPEG1 playback
libsmpeg	Smpeg MPEG video and audio decoder for SPLAY
swfdec	FLASH animation decoding
totem-xine	Totem movie player using Xine libraries instead of GStreamer
twolame	MPEG audio layer 2, MP2 encoding
x264	H264/AVC decoding and encoding (high-definition media)
libxine1-plugins	Additional video and audio playback capability
xvidcore	OpenDivX codec (DivX and Xvid playback)

TABLE 14-3   Multimedia Third-Party Codecs

GStreamer Plug-ins: The Good, the Bad, and the Ugly

Many GNOME multimedia applications such as Totem use GStreamer to provide multimedia support. To use such features as DVD video and MP3, you must install GStreamer extra plug-ins.

The supporting packages can be confusing. For version 1 and above, GStreamer establishes four different support packages called the base, the good, the bad, and the ugly:

- **The base**   Reliable commonly used plug-ins
- **The good**   Reliable additional and useful plug-ins
- **The ugly**   Reliable but not fully licensed plug-ins (DVD/MP3 support)
- **The bad**   Possibly unreliable but useful plug-ins (possible crashes)

As an alternative to the ugly package, you can use Fluendo packages for MP3 and MPEG2 support, **gstreamer-fluendo-mp3**, and **gstreamer-fluendo-mpegmux**.

GStreamer MP3 Compatibility and iPod

For your iPod and other MP3 devices to work with GNOME applications such as Rhythmbox, you will need to install MP3 support for GStreamer. MP3 support is not installed by Ubuntu because of licensing issues. You can, however, install the GStreamer **gstreamer-fluendo-mp3** or **gstreamer-plugins-ugly** support packages as noted previously. The Fluendo package provides a fully licensed MP3 codec.

To sync and import data from your iPod, you can use iPod management software such as GUI for iPod (**gtkpod**). Several scripts and tools are currently available for iPod operations; they include SyncPOD, myPod, gtkpod, and iPod for Linux. Search **http://sourceforge.net** for iPod.

Sound Drivers and Interfaces

Sound devices on Linux are supported by hardware sound drivers. With the current kernel, hardware support is implemented by the Advanced Linux Sound Architecture (ALSA) system. ALSA replaces the free version of the Open Sound System used in previous releases as well as the original built-in sound drivers. You can find more about ALSA at **www.alsa-project.org**. Table 14-4 lists sound device and interface tools.

Your sound cards and devices should be automatically detected by ALSA when you start up your system. ALSA is invoked by **udev** when your system starts up. Removable devices, such as USB sound devices, will also be detected. The detected devices configuration is saved at **/etc/asound.state**.

In GNOME, you can select preferences for your sounds by choosing System | Preferences | Sound. This opens the Sound Preferences window with three tabs: Devices, Sounds, and System Beep (see Figure 14-4). On the Devices tab, you can select the sound interface to use for Sound Events, Music and Movies, and Audio Conferencing, as well as for Default Mixer Tracks. Normally the ALSA interface is selected. You can use PulseAudio instead.

The Sounds tab lets you enable system sounds for particular tasks such as check boxes or logouts. The System Beep tab lets you use either sounds or visual sounds such as flashes on the desktop for your system sounds.

Tools	Description
GNOME Volume Control	GNOME sound connection configuration and volume tool
KMix	KDE sound connection configuration and volume tool
alsamixer	ALSA sound connection configuration and volume tool
amixer	ALSA command for sound connection configuration
GNOME Sound Preferences	Used to select interfaces such as ALSA or PulseAudio (choose System | Preferences | Hardware | Sound)
PulseAudio	Sound interface, selected from Sound Preferences
PulseAudio Volume Control	Controls stream input, output, and playback, PulseAudio Volume Control (**pavucontrol**) package (choose Applications | Sound And Video)
PulseAudio Volume Meter	Displays active sound levels (choose Applications | Sound And Video)
PulseAudio Manager	Manages information and PulseAudio, **pman** package (choose Applications | Sound And Video)
PulseAudio Device Chooser	Device selection (choose Applications | Sound And Video)
PulseAudio Preferences	Options for network access and virtual output (choose System | Preferences)

TABLE 14-4   Sound Device and Interface Tools

Connection Configuration: GNOME Volume Control

Various output and input connections are activated and configured during automatic configuration. The standard connections are activated, but others, such as SPDIF digital connections, may not. You can mute and unmute, as well as control the volume of different connection with either GNOME Volume Control or KDE KMix. KMix will provide a complete display of every connection on your system, whereas GNOME Volume Control will show only those selected for display. KMix will show SPDIF connections, but the GNOME tool will not.

As an alternative either to GNOME Volume Control or KMix, you can also use the command-line ALSA control tool, **alsamixer**. This will display all connections and allow you to use keyboard commands to select (ARROW keys), mute (M key), or set sound levels (PG UP and PG DN). Press ESC to exit. The **amixer** command lets you perform the same tasks for different sound connections from the command line. To play and record from the command line, you can use the **play** and **rec** commands.

You can access the GNOME Volume Control tool either from the sound applet on the desktop to panel (right-click and choose Preferences), or by choosing System \| Preferences \| Volume Control. Depending upon the kind of sound devices displayed, the mixer can show as many as four tabs: Playback, Recording, Switches, and Options (Figure 14-5). The Switches tab usually includes just an entry for headphones. The Options tab shows a pop-up menu for streams such as PCM, if they're available.

On the Playback tab, you can set the sound levels for different connections, both right or left, locking them together, or muting the connections altogether. Only a few commonly

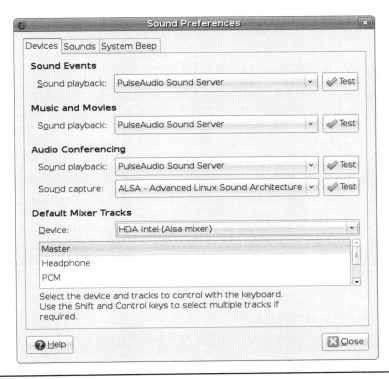

FIGURE 14-4 Sound Preferences

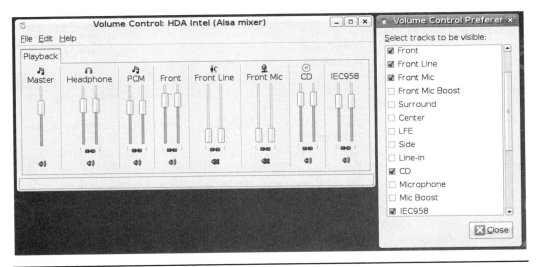

FIGURE 14-5 GNOME Volume Control mixer

used connections are displayed. To display others, you need to configure the Volume Control properties.

To set the default sound device, choose File | Change Device. Available devices will be displayed with radio buttons for each. These are the same devices listed in the Sound Preferences Device pop-up menu. You can easily switch between defaults using just he Volume Control.

Configuring digital output for SPDIF (digital) connectors can be confusing. The digital output may be muted by default. You will first have to configure GNOME Volume Control Preferences to display the SPDIF digital connection. To display the Preferences window, either right-click the sound applet and choose Preferences, or choose Edit | Preferences. The Preferences window lists all possible connections (tracks) on your system, with checks for those that will be displayed. From the list of tracks find the device name of the optical output and click its check box. This will make it show up on the Volume Control window.

The name of the SPDIF output is not always obvious. You may need to run `aplay -L` in a terminal window to determine the name of the digital output device on your system. It will be the entry with *Digital* in it. On an Intel chip system, this could be something like *IEC958* for Intel HDA sound devices found on many computer motherboards. Once your digital output is selected, you can then unmute it by clicking the Volume Control applet and then clicking the digital output sound segment's sound icon. The red *X* should disappear.

PulseAudio and Sound Interfaces

In addition to hardware drivers, sound system also uses sound interfaces to direct encoded sound streams from an application to the hardware drivers and devices. Many sound interfaces are available, but Ubuntu now uses the PulseAudio server, as do many other distributions. PulseAudio aims to combine and consolidate all sound interfaces into a simple, flexible, and powerful server. The ALSA hardware drivers are still used, but the application interface is handled by PulseAudio.

PulseAudio provides packages for interfacing with GStreamer, MPlayer, ALSA, X Multimedia System (XMMS), and xine, replacing those sound interfaces with PulseAudio. The KDE aRts interface is not supported as aRts also performs its own synthesizing.

PulseAudio is a cross-platform sound server that allows you to modify the sound level for different audio streams separately. PulseAudio offers complete control over all your sound streams, letting you combine sound devices and direct the stream anywhere on your network. PulseAudio is not confined to a single system. It is network capable, letting you direct sound from one PC to another.

Each user can choose whether or not to use PulseAudio. Activation is performed from GNOME or KDE desktop preferences. On GNOME, choose System | Preferences | Sound. Then on the Devices tab, you can select PulseAudio from the various pop-up menus. Once you do, you can then use the PulseAudio Volume Control by choosing Applications | Sound And Video | PulseAudio to set the should levels for different sound sources (input streams). You will have to install the **pavucontrol** package. PulseAudio can be difficult to set up and enable.

For full easy configuration, be sure to install all the PulseAudio GUI tools (universe repository). Most begin with the prefix **pa** in the package name. You will have to use synaptic software installer to find and install the others. Search on *pulseaudio*. Menu entries are not set up for these tools. You will have to open a terminal window and enter their commands. They will then run as GUI GNOME applications. PulseAudio command line tools are included in the setup and used for managing PulseAudio and playing sound files. The **paplay** and **pacat** packages will play a sound files, **pactl** will let you control the sound server, and **pacmd** lets you reconfigure it. Other tools include the following:

- PulseAudio Volume Control, **pavucontrol**
- PulseAudio Volume Meter, **pavumeter**
- PulseAudio Manager, **paman**
- PulseAudio Device Chooser, **padevchooser**
- PulseAudio Preferences, **paprefs**

Once PulseAudio is activated, you can use the Volume Control tool to set the sound levels for different playback applications (enter **pavucontrol** in a terminal window). The PulseAudio Volume Control tool window features three tabs: Playback, Output Devices, and Input Devices (see Figure 14-6). The Playback tab shows all the applications currently using PulseAudio. You can adjust the volume for each applications separately. You can use the Output Devices tab to set the volume control at the source. The Input Devices tab is used for capture or microphone input, which can also be adjusted.

You can use the PulseAudio Volume control to direct different applications (streams) to different outputs (devices). For example, you could have two sound sources running, one for video and another for music. The video could be directed through one device to headphones and the music through another device to speakers or even to another PC. To redirect an application to a different device, right-click its name in the Playback tab. A pop-up menu will list the available devices so you can choose the one you want.

The PulseAudio Volume Meter window will show the actual volume of your devices (enter **pavumeter** in a terminal window). The PulseAudio Manager will show information about your PulseAudio configuration (enter **paman** in a terminal window). The Devices tab shows the currently active sinks (outputs or directed receivers) and sources. The Clients tab shows all the applications currently using PulseAudio for sound.

To configure network access, you use the PulseAudio Configuration tool (choose System | Preferences | PulseAudio Configuration). Here you can permit network access and enable

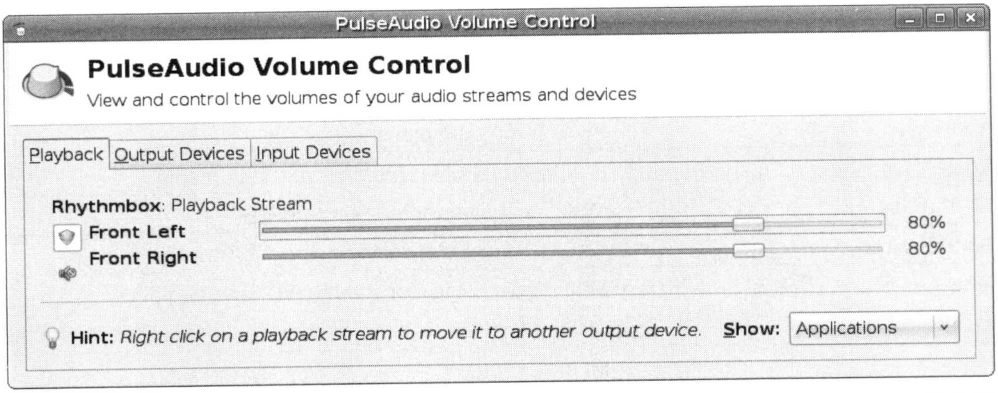

FIGURE 14-6   Pulse AudioVolume Control

multicast and *simultaneous* output. Simultaneous output creates a virtual output device to the same hardware device. This lets you channel two sources onto the same output. With PulseAudio Volume Control, you could then channel playback streams to the same output device, but using a virtual device as the output for one. This lets you change the output volume for each stream independently. You could have music and voice directed to the same hardware device, using a virtual device for music and the standard device for voice. You can then reduce the music stream or raise the voice stream.

Music Applications

Many music applications are currently available for GNOME, including sound editors, MP3 players, and audio players (see Table 14-5). You can use Rhythmbox and Sound Juicer to play music CDs and the GNOME Sound Recorder to record sound sources. Check **http://gnomefiles.org** for current releases.

A variety of applications are also available for KDE, including two media players (Kaiman and Kaboodle), a mixer (KMix), and a CD player (Kscd). Check **http://kde-apps.org** for recent additions. Several X Window System–based multimedia applications are installed with most distributions. These include XMMS and Xplaycd, CD music players, and Xanim, an animation and video player.

GNOME includes sound applications such as the XMMS multimedia player, GNOME CD Player, Sound Juicer (Audio CD Extractor), and Rhythmbox in the Sound And Video menu (see Figure 14-7). KDE applications include KMidi, Kaboodle, and Noatun. Linux systems also

Player	Description
aKtion	KDE video player
Audacious	Multimedia player
GNOME CD Player	Plays music CD
GNOME Sound Recorder	Sound recorder
Grip	CD audio ripper
HelixPlayer	Open source version of RealPlayer (**www.real.com**)
Kaboodle	A media player
Krec	KDE sound recorder
Kscd	Music CD player
Noatun	KDE multimedia player
RealPlayer	RealMedia and RealAudio streaming media
Rhythmbox	Music management (GStreamer)
Sound Juicer	GNOME audio player and ripper (GStreamer)
Xine	Multimedia player for video, DVD, and audio
XMMS	CD player
Xplaycd	Music CD player

TABLE 14-5 Music Players and Rippers

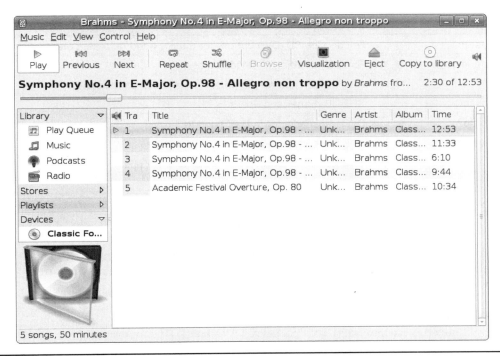

FIGURE 14-7   Rhythmbox Multimedia Player

support HelixPlayer, the open source project used for RealPlayer. HelixPlayer runs only open source media such as Ogg Vorbis files (though you can obtain RealPlayer audio and video codecs for the player). See **https://helixcommunity.org** for more information. You can also download a copy of RealPlayer, the Internet streaming media player, from **www.real.com**. Be sure to choose RealPlayer for Unix.

Due to licensing and patent issues, Ubuntu does not install MP3 support by default. The Ubuntu codec wizard will prompt you to install MP3 support when you first try to play an MP3 file. One option is the free Fluendo MP3 codec. Just install the **gsreamer-fluendo-mp3** package (universe repository). Another option is LAME (which originally stood for Lame Ain't an MP3 Encoder), which has evolved into a full MP3 encoder whose software is available under the LPGL license.

TIP   *As an alternative to MP3, you can use Ogg Vorbis compression for music files (**http://vorbis.com**).*

CD/DVD Burners and Rippers

Several CD ripper and writer programs can be used for CD music and MP3 writing (burners and rippers). These include Sound Juicer, Brasero (see Chapter 3), K3b, Grip, and KAudioCreator. Table 14-6 shows more.

For burning DVD/CD data discs, you can use Brasero and the Nautilus CD/DVD burner, which is integrated into the Nautilus file manager, the default file manager for the GNOME desktop. Qdvdauthor, dvdauthor, Brasero, and K3b can all be used to create DVD-Video discs.

Application	Description
Brasero	Full service CD/DVD burner, for music, video, and data discs
dvdauthor	Tools for creating DVD-Video discs
K3b	KDE CD/DVD burner, for music, video, and data discs
KAudioCreator	KDE CD burner and ripper
ogmrip	DVD transcoding with DivX support
Qdvdauthor	KDE front end for dvdauthor
Sound Juicer	GNOME music player and CD burner and ripper
Serpentine	GNOME music CD burner and ripper

TABLE **14-6**   DVD Burners

All use mkisofs, cdrecord, and cdda2wav DVD/CD writing programs, which are installed as part of your distribution. DVD-Video and CD music rippers may require addition codecs installed, for which the codec wizard will prompt you.

Video Applications

Several Linux projects provide TV, video, DivX, DVD, and DTV support for Linux, as shown in Table 14-7.

Sites	Description
http://linuxtv.org	LinuxTV Project: Links to video, TV, and DVD sites
http://xinehq.de	Xine video player
www.gnome.org/projects/totem/	Totem video and DVD player for GNOME based on xine and using GStreamer
www.videolan.org	VideoLAN Network multimedia streaming, includes x264 high definition support
www.mplayerhq.hu	MPlayer DVD/multimedia player
www.kde-apps.org/	Kdetv KDE TV viewer
http://tvtime.sourceforge.net	Tvtime TV viewer
http://labs.divx.com/ DivXLinuxCodec	DivX for Linux
www.xvid.org	XviD Open Source DivX, may be included with distributions

TABLE **14-7**   Video and DVD Projects and Applications

Video and DVD Players

Most current DVD and media players are provided on the following Ubuntu repositories:

- **The VideoLAN Project** Offers network streaming support for most media formats, including MPEG-4 and MPEG-2. It includes a multimedia player, VLC, that can work on any kind of system (**vlc** package, universe repository).

- **MPlayer** One of the most popular and capable multimedia/DVD players in use. It is a cross-platform open source alternative to RealPlayer and Windows Media Player, and it includes support for DivX. MPlayer uses an extensive set of supporting libraries and applications such as **lirc**, **lame**, **lzo**, and **aalib**, which are also on the site. If you have trouble displaying video, be sure to check the preferences for different video devices and select one that works best (**mplayer** package, multiverse repository).

- **xine** This multipurpose video player for Linux/Unix systems can play video, DVD, and audio discs. Many applications such as Totem, KMPLayer, and Kaffeine use xine support to playback DVD Video (**xine** support packages, Ubuntu main repository).

- **Totem** This GNOME movie player uses GStreamer (see Figure 14-8). To expand Totem capabilities, you need to install added GStreamer plug-ins, such as the DVB plug-in for DVB broadcasts. The codec wizard will prompt you to install any needed media codecs and plug-ins (**totem** package, Ubuntu main repository, installed with GNOME desktop).

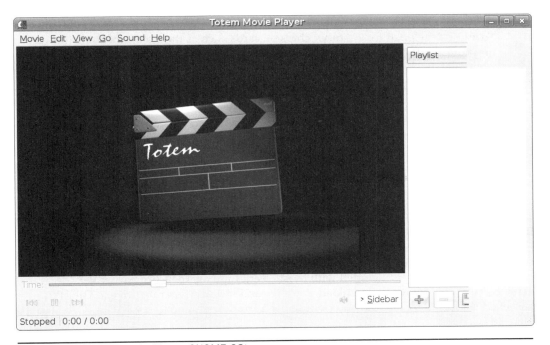

FIGURE 14-8 Totem Movie Player, GNOME GStreamer

- **KMPlayer**   This is a KDE movie player (**kmplayer** package, Ubuntu main repository, installed with KDE desktop).

- **Kaffeine**   This KDE multimedia player is based on xine (**kaffeine** package, Ubuntu main repository).

- **Additional codec support: FFmpeg and x264**   The x264 codec is an open source version of the high definition H.264 codec developed by VideoLAN (**x264** and **FFmpeg** packages, multiverse repository, installed by codec wizard when first required).

None of the DVD-Video applications will initially play commercial DVD-Video discs. That requires Content Scrambling System (CSS) decryption of commercial DVDs. The codec wizard will prompt you to download and install the **libdvdcss** library, which works around CSS decryption by treating the DVD as a block device, allowing you to use any of the DVD players to run commercial DVDs. It is also provides region-free access.

Originally, many of these players did not support DVD menus. With the **libdvdnav** library, these players now feature full DVD menu support. The **libdvdread** library provides basic DVD interface support, such as reading IFO files.

TV Players

The following TV players are provided on several Ubuntu repositories:

- **LinuxTV Project**   The site **http://linuxtv.org** provides detailed links to DVD, digital video broadcasting (DVB), and multicasting. The site also provides downloads of many Linux video applications.

- **Tvtime**   This TV player works with many common video capture cards, relying on drivers developed for TV tuner chips on cards such as the Conexant chips (universe repository). It can only display a TV image and has no recording or file playback capabilities.

- **Kaffeine and Kdetv**   These KDE multimedia players will also play TV(Universe repository).

- **MythTV**   This is a popular video recording and playback application on Linux systems (**mythtv** package, multiverse repository). See **www.mythv.org** for information.

Several video applications are available or currently under development for KDE and GNMOE: Check **www.kde-apps.org**. for KDE players and **http://gnomefiles.org** for GNOME players. Most are available on the Ubuntu repositories.

DVB and HDTV Support

For DVB and HDTV reception you can use most DVB cards as well as many HDTV cars such as the pcHDTV video card (**www.pchdtv.com/**). For example, the latest pcHDTV card uses the cx88-dvb drivers included with most recent Linux kernels (for earlier kernels versions you would have to download, compile, and install a separate driver). The DVB kernel driver install by default. You can use the `lsmod` command to see if your DVB module is loaded.

TIP *Many graphics cards do not provide support for HDTV (H264) hardware acceleration in Linux, though software acceleration with the x264 codec is adequate.*

Many DVB-capable applications such as Kaffeine already have DVB accessibility installed. Totem, for example, has a DVB plug-in for viewing DVB channels. You can also use the **dvb-tools** package to manage access. The DVB tools can also be used to record HDTV and DVB broadcasts to transport stream (TS) files. The TS (**.ts** or **.tp**) file can then be viewed with an HDTV-capable viewer, such as the HDTV versions of xine or VideoLAN VLC media player. You can use MythTV and vdr (video disk recorder) to view and record.

Be sure appropriate decoders are installed, such as MPEG-2, FFmpeg, and A52/AC3. For DVB broadcasts, many DVB-capable players and tools such as Kaffeine and Klear, as well as vdr, will tune and record DVB broadcasts. The **dvb-tools** package holds sample configurations.

MPEG-4 Files: DivX and Xvid on Linux

MPEG-4 compressed files provide DVD-quality video with relatively small file sizes. They have become popular for distributing high-quality video files over the Internet. When you first try to play an MPEG-4 file, the codec wizard will prompt you to install the needed codec packages to play it. Many multimedia applications such as VLC already support MPEG-4 files.

DivX is a commercial video version of MPEG-4 compress video files, free for personal use. You can download the Linux version of DivX for free from **http://labs.divx.com/ DivXLinuxCodec**. You must manually install the package.

As an alternative, you can use the open source version of DivX known as Xvid (**xvidcore** package, multiverse repository). Most DivX files can be run using Xvid. Xvid is an entirely independent open source project, but it's compatible with DivX files. You can download the Xvid source code from **www.xvid.org**.

To convert DVD-Video files to an MPEG-4/DivX format, you can use **transcode** (multiverse repository) or **FFmpeg** (universe repository). Many DVD burners can convert DVD video files to DivX/Xvid files.

Mail and News Clients

Your Linux system supports a wide range of both electronic mail and news clients. Mail clients let you send and receive messages to and from other users on your system or users accessible from your network. News clients let you read articles and messages posted in newsgroups, which are open to access by all users.

Mail Clients

You can send and receive e-mail messages in a variety of ways, depending on the type of mail client you use. Although all e-mail utilities perform the same basic tasks of receiving and sending messages, they tend to use different interfaces. Some mail clients operate on a desktop, such as KDE and GNOME. Others run on any X Window System managers. Several popular mail clients were designed to use a screen-based interface and can be started only from the command line. Other traditional mail clients were developed for the command line interface, which requires you to type your commands on a single command line.

Most mail clients described in this chapter are included in standard Linux distributions and come in a standard package for easy installation. For web-based Internet mail services, such as Hotmail, Google, and Yahoo!, you use a web browser instead of a mail client to access mail accounts provided by those services.

Table 15-1 lists several popular Linux mail clients. Mail is transported to and from destinations using mail transport agents. Sendmail, Exim, and Smail send and receive mail from destinations on the Internet or at other sites on a network. To send mail over the Internet, they use the Simple Mail Transport Protocol (SMTP). Most Linux distributions automatically install and locally configure Sendmail for you. On starting up your system, having configured your network connections, you can send and receive messages over the Internet.

You can sign your e-mail message with the same standard signature information, such as your name, an Internet address or addresses, or a farewell phrase. Having your signature information automatically added to your messages is helpful. To do so, you need to create a signature file in your home directory and enter your signature information in it. A *signature file* is a standard text file you can edit using any text editor. Mail clients such as KMail enable you to specify a file to function as your signature file. Others, such as Mail, expect the signature file to be named **.signature**.

Mail Client	Description
Kontact (KMail, KAddressbook, KOrganizer)	Includes the K Desktop mail client, KMail; integrated mail, address book, and scheduler
Evolution	E-mail client
Balsa	GNOME mail client
Thunderbird	Mozilla group standalone mail client and newsreader
Netscape	Web browser–based mail client
GNU Emacs and XEmacs	Emacs mail clients
Mutt	Screen-based mail client
Sylpheed	Gtk mail and news client
Mail	Original Unix-based command line mail client
SquirrelMail	Web-based mail client
Claws Mail	Extended version of Sylpheed

TABLE 15-1   Linux Mail Clients

MIME

Multipurpose Internet Mail Extensions (MIME) is used to enable mail clients to send and receive multimedia files and files using different character sets such as those for different languages. Multimedia files can be images, sound clips, or even video. Mail clients that support MIME can send binary files automatically as attachments to messages. MIME-capable mail clients maintain a file called **mailcap** that maps different types of MIME messages to applications on your system that can view or display them. For example, an image file will be mapped to an application that can display images. Your mail clients can then run that program to display the image message. A sound file will be mapped to an application that can play sound files on your speakers. Most mail clients have MIME capabilities built in and use their own version of the **mailcap** file. Others use a program called *metamail* that adds MIME support. MIME is used not only in mail clients; both the KDE and GNOME file managers use MIME to map a file to a particular application so that you can launch the application directly from the file.

NOTE *Secure/MIME (S/MIME) and OpenPGP/MIME are authentication protocols for signing and encrypting mail messages. S/MIME was originally developed by RSA Data Security. OpenPGP is an open standard based on the PGP/MIME protocol developed by the PGP (Pretty Good Privacy) group. Clients such as KMail and Evolution can use OpenPGP/MIME to authenticate messages. Check the Internet Mail Consortium for more information: www.imc.org.*

Applications are associated with binary files by means of the **mailcap** and **mime.types** files. The **mime.types** file defines different MIME types, associating a MIME type with a certain application. The **mailcap** file then associates each MIME type with a specified application. Your system maintains its own MIME types file, usually **/etc/mime.types**.

Though you can create your own MIME types, a standard set is already in use. The types text, image, audio, video, application, multipart, and message, along with their subtypes, have already been defined for your system. You will find that commonly used file extensions such as **.tif** and **.jpg** for TIFF and JPEG image files are already associated with a MIME type and an application. Though you can easily change the associated application, it is best to keep the MIME types already installed. The current official MIME types are listed at the IANA Web site (**http://iana.org**) under the name Media Types, provided as part of their Assignment Services. You can access the media types file directly on this site.

Entries in the MIME types file associate a MIME type and possible subtype of an application with a set of possible file extensions used for files that run on a particular kind of application. The MIME type is usually further qualified by a subtype, separated from the major type by a slash. For example, a MIME type image can have several subtypes, such as JPEG, GIF, or TIFF. A sample MIME type entries defining a MIME type for JPEG files and QuickTime video files are shown next. Spaces indicate a logical OR. The MIME type is **image/jpeg**, and the list of possible file extensions is **jpeg jpg jpe**.

```
image/jpeg          jpeg jpg jpe
video/quicktime     qt mov
```

The applications specified will depend on those available on your particular system. The application is specified as part of the application type. In many cases, X Window System–based programs are specified. Comments are indicated with a **#**. The following entries associate **odt** files with the OpenOffice.org writer, **kwd** and **kwt** files with KOffice KWord, and **qtl** files with the QuickTime player.

```
application//vnd.oasis.opendocument.text    odt
application/x-kword                         kwd kwt
application/x-quicktimeplayer               qtl
```

NOTE *On KDE, use the KDE Control Center's File Association entry under KDE Components. This will list MIME types and their associated filename extensions. Select an entry to edit it and change the applications associated with it. KDE saves its MIME type information in a separate file called **mimelnk** in the KDE configuration directory.*

Evolution

Evolution is the primary mail client for the GNOME desktop. It is installed by default on the Ubuntu desktop. Though designed for GNOME, it will work equally well on KDE. Evolution is an integrated mail client, calendar, and address book. The Evolution mailer is a powerful tool with support for numerous protocols (SMTP, POP, and IMAP), multiple mail accounts, and encryption. With Evolution, you can create multiple mail accounts on different servers, including those that use different protocols such as POP or IMAP. You can also decrypt Pretty Good Privacy (PGP)– or GNU Privacy Guard (GPG)–encrypted messages.

The Evolution mailer provides a simple GUI with a toolbar for commonly used commands and a sidebar for e-mail accounts and applications (see Figure 15-1). A menu of Evolution commands allows access to other operations. For automatic mail notification, you use the mail notification plug-in for Evolution. The main panel is divided into two panes, one for listing the mail headers and the other for displaying the currently selected message.

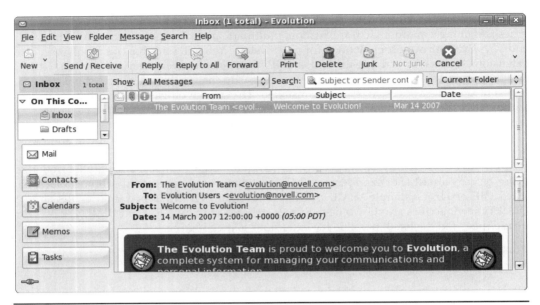

Figure 15-1   Evolution e-mail client

You can click any header title to sort your headers by that category. Evolution also supports the use of search (virtual) folders that can be created by the user to hold mail that meets specified criteria. Incoming mail can be automatically distributed to a particular search folder.

To configure Evolution, choose Edit | Preferences. On the Evolution Preferences window, a sidebar shows icons for main accounts, auto-completion, mail preferences, composition preference, calendar and tasks, and certificates. The main accounts entry displays a list of current accounts. An Add button lets you add new accounts, and the Edit button allows you to change current accounts. When you're editing an account, the Account Editor displays tabs for Identity, Receiving Email (your incoming mail server), Sending Email (outgoing mail server), and Security (encryption and digital signatures). In the Mail Preferences entry, you configure how Evolution displays and manages messages. In the Compose Preferences entry, you set up composition features such as signatures, formatting, and spell-checking. The Automatic Contact tab in Mail Preferences is where you can specify that addresses of mail to which you reply should be automatically added to the Evolution Contacts list. To see and manage your contacts, click the Contacts button on the left sidebar.

With Evolution, you can also create search folders to organize access to your messages. A search folder is not an actual folder; it simply collects links to messages based on certain search criteria. Using search folders, you can quickly display messages on a topic or subject, or from a specific user. In effect, it performs an automatic search on messages as they arrive. To set up a search folder, choose Edit | Search Folders and click Add to open the Add Rule window. Here you can add criteria for searches and the folders to search. You can also right-click a message header that meets a criteria you want searched and choose Create Rule From Message, and then select one of the Search Rule entries.

Numerous plug-ins are available to extend Evolution's capabilities. Most are installed and enabled for you automatically, including the SpamAssassin plug-in for handling junk mail. To manage your plug-ins, choose Edit | Plugin to open the Plugin Manager, with plug-ins listed in a left scroll window and configuration tabs located for a selected plug-in on the right side.

Evolution also supports filters. You can use filters to direct some messages automatically to certain folders, instead of having all incoming messages placed in the **Inbox** folder. To create a filter, choose Edit | Message Filters and click Add to open the Add Rule window. You can also right-click the header of a message whose heading meets your criteria, such as a subject or sender, and select Create Rule From Message | Filter for sender, subject, or recipient. On the Add Rule window, you can add other criteria and also specify the action to take, such as moving the message to a particular folder. You can also add other actions such as assigning a score, changing the color, copying the message, or deleting it.

NOTE *Other GNOME mail clients include Sylpheed and Claws Mail (both are on the Ubuntu universe repository). Sylpheed is a mail and news client with an interface similar to Windows mail clients. Claws Mail is an extended version of Sylpheed with many additional features (www.claws-mail.org).*

Thunderbird

Thunderbird is a full-featured standalone e-mail client provided by the Mozilla project (**www.mozilla.org**), Ubuntu main repository. It is designed to be easy to use, highly customizable, and heavily secure. It features advanced intelligent spam filtering, as well as security features such as encryption, digital signatures, and S/MIME. To protect against viruses, e-mail attachments can be examined without being run. Thunderbird supports both Internet Message Access Protocol (IMAP) and Post Office Protocol (POP), as well as the use of Lightweight Directory Access Protocol (LDAP) address books. It functions as a newsreader and features a built-in RSS reader. In addition, Thunderbird is an extensible application, allowing customized modules to be added to enhance its abilities. You can download extensions such as dictionary search and contact sidebars from the Web site. GPG encryption can be supported with the **enigmail** extension (Ubuntu main repository).

The interface uses a standard three-pane format, with a side pane for listing mail accounts and their boxes. The top pane lists main entries, and the bottom pane shows text. Commands can be run via the toolbar, menus, or keyboard shortcuts. You can even change the appearance using different themes. Thunderbird also supports HTML mail, displaying web components such as URLs in mail messages.

The message list pane shows several fields by which you can sort your messages. Some use symbols such as the Threads, Attachments, and Read icons. Clicking Threads will gather the messages into respective threads with replies grouped together. The last icon in the message list fields is a pop-up menu that lets you choose which fields to display. Thunderbird provides a variety of customizable display filters, such as People I Know, which displays only messages from people included in your address book, and Attachments, which displays messages with attached files. You can even create your own display filters. Search and sorting capabilities also include filters that can match selected patterns in any field, including subject, date, or the message body.

When you first start up Thunderbird, you will be prompted to create an e-mail account. You can add more e-mail accounts or modify current ones by choosing Edit | Account Settings. Then click Add Account to open a dialog with four options, one of which is an e-mail account. Select the Email option, and you are prompted to enter your e-mail address and name. In the next screen you specify either POP or IMAP and enter the name of the incoming e-mail server, such as **smtp.myemailserver.com**. You then specify an incoming username given you by your e-mail service. Then you enter an account name label to identify the account on Thunderbird. A final verification screen lets you confirm your entries. In the Account Settings window you will see an entry for your news server, with tabs for Server Settings, Copies & Folders, Composition & Addressing, Offline & Disk Space, Return Receipt, and Security. The Server Settings tab has entries for your server name, port, username, and connection and task configurations such as automatically downloading new messages. The Security tab opens the Certificate Manager, where you can select security certificates to digitally sign or encrypt messages.

Thunderbird provides an address book where you can enter complete contact information, including e-mail addresses, street addresses, phone numbers, and notes. Choose Tools | Address Book to open the Address Book window. Three tabs appear: one for the address books available; another listing the address entries with field entries such as Name, E-mail, and Organization; and one for displaying address information. You can sort the entries by these fields. Clicking an entry will display the address information, including e-mail address, street addresses, and phone. Only fields with values are displayed. To create a new entry in an address book, click New Card to open a window with tabs for Contact and Address information. To create mailing lists from the address book entries, click the New List button, specify the name of the list, and enter the e-mail addresses.

After you set up the Address Book, you can use its addresses when creating mail messages. On the Compose window, click the Contacts button to open a Contacts pane. Your address book entries will be listed using the contact's name. Just click the name to add it to the address box of your e-mail message. Alternatively, you can open the Address Book and drag-and-drop addresses to an address box on the message window.

A user's e-mail messages, addresses, and configuration information are kept in files located in the **.thunderbird** directory within the user's home directory. Backing up this information is as simple as making a copy of that directory. Messages for the different mail boxes are kept in a **Mail** subdirectory. If you are migrating to a new system, you can copy the directory from the older system. To back up the mail for any mail account, copy the **Mail** subdirectory for that account. Though the default address books, **abook.mab** and **history.mab**, can be interchangeably copied, nondefault address books need to be exported to LDAP Data Interchange Format (LDIF) and then imported to the new Thunderbird application. It is advisable to export your address books regularly to LDIF files as backups.

The K Desktop Mail Client: KMail

The KDE mail client, KMail, provides a full-featured GUI for composing, sending, and receiving e-mail messages (Ubuntu main repository). KMail is now part of the KDE Personal Information Management suite (KDE-PIM), which also includes an address book (KAddressbook), an organizer and scheduler (KOrganizer), and a note writer (KNotes). All these components are also directly integrated on the desktop into Kontact.

To start up KMail, you start the Kontact application. The KMail window displays three panes for folders, headers, and messages. The upper-left pane displays your mail folders:

an inbox folder for received mail, an outbox folder for mail you have composed but have not sent yet, and a sent-mail folder for messages you have previously sent. You can create your own mail folders and save selected messages in them, if you wish. The top-right pane displays mail headers for the currently selected mail folder. To display a message, click its header. The message is then displayed in the large pane below the header list. You can also send and receive attachments, including binary files. Pictures and movies that are received are displayed using the appropriate KDE utility. If you right-click the message, a pop-up menu displays options for actions you may want to perform on it. You can move or copy it to another folder or simply delete it. You can also compose a reply or forward the message. KMail, along with Kontact, KOrganizer, and KAddressbook, are accessible from the KDE Desktop, Office, and Internet menus.

To set up KMail for use with your mail accounts, you must first enter account information. Choose Settings | Configure. Several tabs will appear on the Settings window, which you can display by clicking their icons in the left column. For accounts, you select the Network tab. You may have more than one mail account on mail servers maintained by your ISP or LAN. A Configure window is displayed where you can enter login, password, and host information. For secure access, KMail now supports Secure Sockets Layer (SSL), provided OpenSSL is installed. Messages can now be encrypted and decoded by users. It also supports IMAP in addition to POP and SMTP.

SquirrelMail Webmail Client

You can use the SquirrelMail Webmail tool to access mail on a Linux system using your Web browser (universe repository). It will display a login screen for mail users. It features an inbox list and message reader, support for editing and sending new messages, and a plug-in structure for adding new features. You can find out more about SquirrelMail at **www.squirrelmail.org**. The Apache configuration file is **/etc/httpd/conf.d/squirrelmail.conf**, and SquirrelMail is installed in **/usr/share/squirrelmail**. Be sure that the IMAP mail server is also installed.

To configure SquirrelMail, you use the **config.pl** script in the **/usr/share/squirrelmail/ config** directory. This displays a simple text-based menu where you can configure settings such as the server to use, folder defaults, general options, and organizational preferences:

```
./config.pl
```

To access SquirrelMail, use the Web server address with the **/squirrelmail** extension, as in **localhost/squirrelmail** for users on the local system or **mytrek.com/squirrelmail** for remote users.

Command Line Mail Clients

Several mail clients use a simple command line interface. They can be run without any other kind of support, such as the X Window System, desktops, or cursor support. They are simple and easy to use but include an extensive set of features and options. Two of the more widely used mail clients of this type are Mutt and Mail. Mutt is a cursor-based client that can be run from the command line. Mail is the mailx mail client that was developed for the Unix system. It is considered a kind of default mail client that can be found on all Unix and Linux systems.

NOTE *You can also use the Emacs mail client from the command line, as described in "Mail Client" section in the chapter.*

Mutt

Mutt has an easy-to-use screen-based interface and an extensive set of features, such as MIME support (Ubuntu main repository). You can find more information about Mutt from the Mutt Web site, **www.mutt.org**. Here you can download recent versions of Mutt and access online manuals and help resources. On most distributions, the Mutt manual is located in the **/usr/doc** directory under **Mutt**. The Mutt newsgroup is **comp.mail.mutt**, where you can post queries and discuss recent Mutt developments.

Mail/mailx

What is known now as the Mail utility was originally created for BSD Unix and called simply *mail* (Ubuntu main repository, **mailx** package). Later versions of Unix System V adopted the BSD mail utility and renamed it *mailx*; now it is referred to as Mail. Mail functions as a de facto default mail client on Unix and Linux systems. All systems have the mail client called Mail, whereas they may not have other mail clients. Check the mail man page for detailed information and commands.

To send a message with Mail, type **mail** on the command line along with the address of the person to whom you are sending the message. Press ENTER and you are prompted for a subject. Enter the subject of the message and press ENTER again. At this point, you are placed in input mode. Anything you type is considered the contents of the message. Pressing ENTER adds a new line to the text. When you finish typing your message, press CTRL-D on a line of its own to end the message. You will then be prompted to enter a user to whom to send a carbon copy of the message (Cc). If you do not want to send a carbon copy, just press ENTER. You will then see *EOT (end-of-transmission)* displayed after you press CTRL-D to end your message.

You can send a message to several users at the same time by listing those users' addresses as arguments on the command line following the **mail** command. In the next example, the user sends the same message to both **chris** and **aleina**:

```
$ mail chris aleina
```

To receive mail, you first enter the **mail** command and press ENTER. This invokes a Mail shell with its own prompt and mail commands. A list of message headers is displayed. Header information is arranged into fields beginning with the status of the message and the message number. The status of a message is indicated by a single uppercase letter, usually **N** for *new* or **U** for *unread*. A message number, used for easy reference to your messages, follows the status field. The next field is the address of the sender, followed by the date and time the message was received and then the number of lines and characters in the message. The last field contains the subject the sender gave for the message. After the headers, the Mail shell displays its prompt, an ampersand (**&**). At the Mail prompt, you enter commands that operate on the messages. An example of a Mail header and prompt follows:

```
$ mail
Mail version 8.1 6/6/93. Type ? for help.
"/var/spool/mail/larisa": 3 messages 2 unread
 1 chris@turtle.mytrek. Thu Jun 7 14:17 22/554 "trip"
```

```
>U 2 aleina@turtle.mytrek  Thu Jun 7 14:18 22/525 "party"
 U 3 dylan@turtle.mytrek.  Thu Jun 7 14:18 22/528 "newsletter"
& q
```

Mail references messages either through a message list or through the current message marker, the greater-than sign (>), which is placed before a message considered the current message. The current message is referenced by default when no message number is included with a **mail** command. You can also reference messages using a message list consisting of several message numbers. Given the messages in the preceding example, you can reference all three messages with **1-3**.

You use the **R** and **r** commands to reply to a message you have received. The **R** command entered with a message number generates a header for sending a message and then places you into input mode to type the message. The **q** command quits Mail. When you quit, messages you have already read are placed in a file called **mbox** in your home directory. Instead of saving messages in the **mbox** file, you can use the **s** command to save a message explicitly to a file of your choice. Mail has its own initialization file, called .mailrc, that is executed each time Mail is invoked, either for sending or receiving messages. Within it, you can define Mail options and create aliases. You can set options that add different features to mail, such as changing the prompt or saving copies of messages you send. To define an alias, enter the keyword **alias**, followed by the alias you have chosen and then the list of addresses it represents. In the next example, the alias **myclass** is defined in the .mailrc file.

.mailrc
```
alias myclass chris dylan aleina justin larisa
```

In this example, the contents of the file **homework** are sent to all the users whose addresses are aliased by **myclass**:

```
$ mail myclass < homework
```

Notifications of Received Mail

As your mail messages are received, they are automatically placed in your mailbox file, but you are not automatically notified when you receive a message. You can use a mail client to retrieve any new messages, or you can use a mail monitor tool to tell you when new mail has arrived in your inbox. Applications such as Evolution and Thunderbird will install their own notification plug-ins. Several independent mail notification tools are also available, such as gnubiff and Mail Notification (both in universe repository). Mail Notification will support Gmail as well as Evolution (for Evolution, install the separate plug-in package). When you first log in after Mail Notification has been installed, the Mail Notification configuration window is displayed. Here you can add new mail accounts to check, such as Gmail accounts, as well as set other features such as summary pop-ups. When you receive mail, a Mail icon will appear in the notification applet of your desktop panel. Move your cursor over it to check for any new mail. Clicking it will display the Mail Notification configuration window, though you can configure this to go directly to your e-mail application. The gnubiff tool will notify you of any POP3 or IMAP mail arrivals.

The KDE desktop has a mail monitor utility called *Korn* that works in much the same way (universe repository). Korn shows an empty inbox tray when there is no mail and a tray with slanted letters in it when mail arrives. You can specify the mail client to use and the polling interval for checking for new mail. If you have several mail accounts, you can set up a Korn profile for each one. Different icons can appear for each account, telling you when mail arrives in one of them.

For command line interfaces, you can use the biff utility (universe repository), which notifies you immediately when a message is received. This is helpful when you are expecting a message and want to know as soon as it arrives. Then biff automatically displays the header and beginning lines of messages as they are received. To turn on biff, you enter `biff y` on the command line. To turn it off, you enter `biff n`. To find out if biff is turned on, enter `biff` alone.

You can temporarily block biff by using the `mesg n` command to prevent any message displays on your screen. The `mesg n` command not only stops any Write and Talk messages, it also stops biff and Notify messages. Later, you can unblock biff with a `mesg y` command. A `mesg n` command comes in handy if you don't want to be disturbed while working on some project.

Accessing Mail on Remote POP Mail Servers

Most newer mail clients are equipped to access mail accounts on remote servers. For such mail clients, you can specify a separate mail account with its own mailbox. For example, if you are using an ISP, most likely you will use that ISP's mail server to receive mail. You will have set up a mail account with a username and password for accessing your mail. Your e-mail address is usually your username and the ISP's domain name. For example, a username of *justin* for an ISP domain named **mynet.com** would have the address **justin@mynet.com**. The username would be *justin*. The address of the actual mail server could be something like **mail .mynet.com**. The user **justin** would log in to the **mail.mynet.com** server using the username *justin* and password to access mail sent to the address **justin@mynet.com**. Mail clients, such as Evolution, KMail, Balsa, and Thunderbird, enable you to set up a mailbox for such an account and access your ISP's mail server to check for and download received mail. You must specify what protocol a mail server uses. This is usually either POP or IMAP. This procedure is used for any remote mail server. Using a mail server address, you can access your account with your username and password.

TIP *Many mail clients, such as Mutt and Thunderbird, support IMAP and POP directly.*

Should you have several remote e-mail accounts, instead of creating separate mailboxes for each in a mail client, you can arrange to have mail from those accounts sent directly to the inbox maintained by your Linux system for your Linux account. All your mail, whether from other users on your Linux system or from remote mail accounts, will appear in your local inbox. This feature is helpful if you are using a mail client, such as Mail, that does not have the ability to access mail on your ISP's mail server. You can implement this feature with Fetchmail, which checks for mail on remote mail servers and downloads it to your local inbox, where it appears as newly received mail (Ubuntu main repository).

You must know the remote mail server's Internet address and mail protocol. Most remote mail servers use the POP3 protocol, but others may use the IMAP or POP2 protocols. Enter `fetchmail` on the command line with the mail server address and any needed options. The mail protocol is indicated with the `-p` option and the mail server type, usually POP3.

If your e-mail username is different from your Linux login name, you use the **-u** option and the e-mail name. Once you execute the **fetchmail** command, you are prompted for a password. The syntax for the **fetchmail** command for a POP3 mail server follows:

```
fetchmail -p POP3 -u username mail-server
```

You will see messages telling you whether mail is available and, if so, how many messages are being downloaded. You can then use a mail client to read the messages from your inbox. You can run Fetchmail in daemon mode to have it automatically check for mail. You must include an option specifying the interval in seconds for checking mail, like so:

```
fetchmail -d 1200
```

You can specify options such as the server type, username, and password in a **.fetchmailrc** file in your home directory. You can also include entries for other mail servers and accounts. Once Fetchmail is configured, you can enter **fetchmail** with no arguments; it will read entries from your **.fetchmailrc** file. You can also make entries directly in the **.fetchmailrc** file. An entry in the **.fetchmailrc** file for a particular mail account consists of several fields and their values: poll, protocol, username, and password. *Poll* is used to specify the mail server name, and *protocol* is the type of protocol used. You can also specify your password, instead of having to enter it each time Fetchmail accesses the mail server.

Mailing Lists

As an alternative to newsgroups, you can subscribe to mailing lists. Users on mailing lists automatically receive messages and articles sent to the lists. Mailing lists work much like a mail alias, broadcasting messages to all users on the list.

Mailing lists were designed to serve small, specialized groups of people. Instead of posting articles for anyone to see, only those who subscribe receive them. Numerous mailing lists, as well as other subjects, are available for Linux. For example, at the **www.gnome.org** site, you can subscribe to several mailing lists on GNOME topics, such as **gnome-themes-list@gnome.org**, which deals with GNOME desktop themes. You can do the same at **http://lists.kde.org** for KDE topics. At **liszt.com**, you can search for mailing lists on various topics. By convention, to subscribe to a list, you send a request to the mailing list address with a **–request** term added to its username. For example, to subscribe to **gnome-themes-list@gnome.org**, you send a request to **gnome-themes-list-request@gnome.org**. At **www.linux.org**, on the Documentation page you can access a listing of mailing lists and submit subscriptions. Lists exist for such topics as the Linux kernel, administration, security, and different distributions. For example, **linux-admin** covers administration topics, and **linux-apps** discusses software applications; **vger.kernel.org** provides mailing list services for Linux kernel developers.

NOTE *You can use the Mailman and Majordomo programs to manage your mailing lists automatically. Mailman is the GNU mailing list manager (**http://list.org**). You can find out more about Majordomo at **www.greatcircle.com/majordomo** and about Mailman at **http://sourceforge.net**.*

PART V

Usenet News

Usenet is an open mail system on which users post messages that include news, discussions, and opinions. It operates like a mailbox to which any user on your Linux system can read or send messages. Users' messages are incorporated into Usenet files, which are distributed to any system signed up to receive them. Each system that receives Usenet files is referred to as a *site*. Certain sites perform organizational and distribution operations for Usenet, receiving messages from other sites and organizing them into Usenet files, which are then broadcast to many other sites. Such sites are called *backbone sites,* and they operate like publishers, receiving articles and organizing them into different groups.

To access Usenet news, you need access to a news server. A news server receives the daily Usenet newsfeeds and makes them accessible to other systems. Your network may have a system that operates as a news server. If you are using an ISP, a news server is probably maintained by your ISP for your use. To read Usenet articles, you use a *newsreader*—a client program that connects to a news server and accesses the articles. On the Internet and in TCP/IP networks, news servers communicate with newsreaders using the Network News Transfer Protocol (NNTP) and are often referred to as *NNTP news servers*. You can also create your own news server on your Linux system to run a local Usenet news service or to download and maintain the full set of Usenet articles. Several Linux programs, called *news transport agents,* can be used to create such a server. This chapter focuses on the variety of newsreaders available for the Linux platform.

Usenet files were originally designed to function like journals. Messages contained in the files are referred to as *articles.* A user could write an article, post it in Usenet, and have it immediately distributed to other systems around the world. Someone could then read the article on Usenet, instead of waiting for a journal publication. Usenet files themselves were organized as journal publications. Because journals are designed to address specific groups, Usenet files are organized according to groups called *newsgroups.* When a user posts an article, it is assigned to a specific newsgroup. If another user wants to read that article, he or she looks at the articles in that newsgroup. You can think of each newsgroup as a constantly updated magazine. For example, to read articles on the Linux operating system, you access the Usenet newsgroup on Linux. Usenet files are also used as bulletin boards on which people carry on debates. Again, such files are classified into newsgroups, though their articles read more like conversations than journal articles. You can also create articles of your own, which you can then add to a newsgroup for others to read. Adding an article to a newsgroup is called *posting* the article.

Linux has newsgroups on various topics. Some are for discussion, and others are sources of information about recent developments. On some, you can ask for help for specific problems. A selection of some of the popular Linux newsgroups is provided here:

- **comp.os.linux.announce**   Announcements of Linux developments
- **comp.os.linux.admin**   System administration questions
- **comp.os.linux.misc**   Special questions and issues
- **comp.os.linux.setup**   Installation problems
- **comp.os.linux.help**   Questions and answers for particular problems
- **linux.help**   Help for Linux problems

Newsreaders

You read Usenet articles with a newsreader, such as KNode, Pan, Mozilla, trn, or tin, which enable you to select a specific newsgroup and then read the articles in it. A newsreader operates like a user interface, letting you browse through and select available articles for reading, saving, or printing. Most newsreaders employ a sophisticated retrieval feature called *threads* that pulls together articles on the same discussion or topic.

Newsreaders are designed to operate using certain kinds of interfaces. For example, KNode is a KDE newsreader that uses an interface designed for KDE. Pan uses a GNOME interface. Pine is a cursor-based newsreader, meaning that it provides a full-screen interface that you can work with using a simple screen-based cursor that you can move with arrow keys. It does not support a mouse or any other GUI feature. The tin program uses a simple command line interface with limited cursor support. Most commands you type in and press ENTER to execute.

As of this writing, no good binary-based newsreader exists that can convert text messages to binary equivalents, such as those found in **alt.binaries** newsgroups. One solution is to use the Windows version of the popular NewsBin newsreader running under Wine (Windows compatibility layer for Linux), as shown Figure 15-2. You need to install Wine first (see Chapter 3). The current version of NewsBin runs stable and fast with Wine (you may need to use the video hardware drives for your graphics card). Several popular newsreaders are listed in Table 15-2.

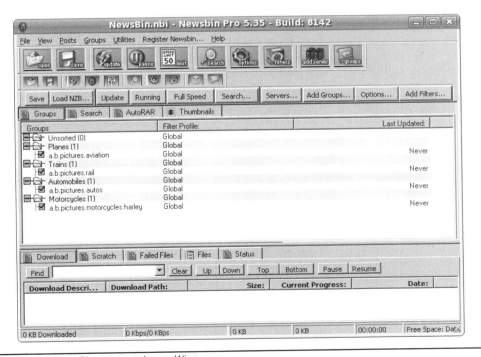

FIGURE 15-2 NewsBin newsreader on Wine

Newsreader	Description
Pan	GNOME Desktop newsreader
KNode	KDE Desktop newsreader
Thunderbird	Mail client with newsreader capabilities (X based)
Sylpheed	GNOME Windows-like newsreader
slrn	Newsreader (cursor based)
Emacs	Emacs editor, mail client, and newsreader (cursor based)
trn	Newsreader (command line interface)
NewsBin	Newsreader (Windows version works under Wine)

TABLE 15-2 Linux Newsreaders

Most newsreaders can read Usenet news provided on remote news servers that use the NNTP. Many such remote news servers are available through the Internet. Desktop newsreaders, such as KNode and Pan, have you specify the Internet address for the remote news server in their own configuration settings. Several shell-based newsreaders, however, such as trn and tin, obtain the news server's Internet address from the **NNTPSERVER** shell variable. Before you can connect to a remote news server with such newsreaders, you first have to assign the Internet address of the news server to the **NNTPSERVER** shell variable, and then export that variable. You can place the assignment and export of **NNTPSERVER** in a login initialization file, such as **.bash_profile**, so that it is performed automatically whenever you log in. Administrators can place this entry in the **/etc/profile** file for a news server available to all users on the system.

```
$ NNTPSERVER=news.domain.com
$ export NNTPSERVER
```

You may also need to open the newsreader port 119 on your firewall. The following would open up the newsreader port on ufw firewall:

```
sudo ufw allow 119/tcp
```

The slrn newsreader is screen-based. Commands are displayed across the top of the screen and can be executed using the listed keys. Different types of screens exist for the newsgroup list, article list, and article content, each with its own set of commands. An initial screen lists your subscribed newsgroups with commands for posting, listing, and subscribing to your newsgroups. When you start slrn for the first time, you will have to create a **.jnewsrc** file in your home directory. Use the following command: **slrn -f .jnewsrc -create**. Also, you will have to set the **NNTPSERVER** variable and make sure it is exported.

The slrn newsreader features a new utility called **slrnpull** that you can use to download articles in specified newsgroups automatically. This allows you to view your selected newsgroups offline. The **slrnpull** utility was designed as a simple single-user version of Leafnode; it will access a news server and download its designated newsgroups, making them available through slrn whenever the user chooses to examine them. Newsgroup articles are downloaded to the **SLRNPULL_ROOT** directory, usually **/var/spool/srlnpull**. The selected newsgroups to be downloaded are entered in the **slrnpull.conf** configuration file placed in the **SLRNPULL_ROOT** directory. In this file, you can specify how many articles to download for each group and when they should expire. To use slrn with **slrnpull**, you will have to configure the **.slrnrc** file to reference the **slrnpull** directories where newsgroup files are kept.

NOTE   *Usenet news is provided over the Internet as a daily newsfeed of articles and postings for thousands of newsgroups. This newsfeed is sent to sites that can then provide access to the news for other systems through newsreaders. These sites operate as news servers; the newsreaders used to access them are their clients. The news server software, called* news transport agents, *provides newsreaders with news, enabling you to read newsgroups and post articles. For Linux, three of the popular news transport agents are INN, Leafnode, and Cnews. Both Cnews and Leafnode are small, simple, and useful for small networks. INN is more powerful and complex, designed with large systems in mind (see* ***www.isc.org*** *for more details).*

Web Browsers, FTP, Java, VoIP, and IM

U buntu provides powerful Web and FTP clients for accessing Internet sites, as well as instant messaging (IM) and Voice over Internet Protocol (VoIP) clients for direct communication between users. Many of these applications are installed automatically and are ready to use when you first start up your Ubuntu system. Ubuntu also includes full Java development support, letting you run and construct Java applets.

Web Protocols

The World Wide Web (WWW, or the Web) is a hypertext database of different types of information, distributed across many different sites on the Internet. A *hypertext database* consists of items linked to other items, which, in turn, may be linked to yet other items, and so on. Upon retrieving an item, you can use that item to retrieve any related items. For example, you can retrieve an article on the Amazon rain forest and then use it to retrieve a map or a picture of the rain forest. In this respect, a hypertext database is like a web of interconnected data you can trace from one data item to another. Information is displayed in *Web pages*, where highlighted keywords or graphics form links to other Web pages or to items, such as pictures, articles, or files.

On your Linux system, you can choose from several Web browsers, including Firefox, Konqueror, Epiphany, and Lynx. Firefox, Konqueror, and Epiphany are X Window System–based browsers that provide full picture, sound, and video display capabilities. Most distributions also include the Lynx browser, a line-mode browser that displays only lines of text. The K Desktop incorporates Web browser capabilities into its file manager, letting a directory window operate as a Web browser. GNOME-based browsers, such as Express and Mnemonic, are also designed to be easily enhanced.

Web browsers and FTP clients are commonly used to conduct secure transactions such as logging in to remote sites, ordering items, or transferring files. Such operations are currently secured by encryption methods provided by the Secure Sockets Layer (SSL). If you use a browser for secure transactions, it should be SSL enabled. Most browsers such as Mozilla and ELinks include SSL support. For FTP operations, you can use the SSH version of ftp, sftp, or the Kerberos 5 version. Linux distributions include SSL as part of a standard installation.

An Internet resource is accessed using a Universal Resource Identifier (URI), also known as a Universal Resource Locator (URL), which is composed of three elements: the transfer protocol, the hostname, and the pathname. The transfer protocol and the hostname are separated by a colon and two slashes, *://*. The *pathname* always begins with a single slash:

```
transfer-protocol://host-name/path-name
```

The *transfer protocol* is usually HTTP (Hypertext Transfer Protocol), indicating a Web page. Other possible values for transfer protocols are **ftp** and **file**. As their names suggest, **ftp** initiates FTP sessions, whereas **file** displays a local file on your own system, such as a text or HTML file. Table 16-1 lists the various transfer protocols.

The *hostname* is the computer on which a particular Web site is located. You can think of this as the address of the Web site. By convention, most hostnames begin with **www**. In the next example, the URL locates a Web page called **guides.html** on the **tldp.org** Web site:

```
http://tldp.org/guides.html
```

If you do not want to access a particular Web page, you can leave the file reference out, and then you automatically access the Web site's home page. To access a Web site directly, use its hostname. If no home page is specified for a Web site, the file **index.html** in the top directory is often used as the home page. In the next example, the user brings up the GNOME home page:

```
http://www.gnome.org/
```

The pathname specifies the directory where the resource can be found on the host system, as well as the name of the resource's file. For example, **/pub/Linux/newdat.html** references an HTML document called **newdat** located in the **/pub/Linux** directory.

The resource file's extension indicates the type of action to be taken on it. A picture has a **.gif** or **.jpeg** extension and is converted for display. A sound file has an **.au** or **.wav** extension and is played. The following URL references a **.gif** file. Instead of displaying a Web page, your browser invokes a graphics viewer to display the picture. Table 16-2 provides a list of the more common file extensions.

```
http://www.train.com/engine/engine1.gif
```

Protocol	Description
http	Uses Hypertext Transfer Protocol for Web site access
ftp	Uses File Transfer Protocol for anonymous FTP connections
fish	Uses File Transfer Protocol using SSH secure connections
telnet	Makes a Telnet connection
news	Reads Usenet news; uses Network News Transfer Protocol (NNTP)

TABLE 16-1 Web Protocols

File Type	Description
.html	Web page document formatted using HTML
Graphics Files	
.gif	Graphics, using GIF compression
.jpeg	Graphics, using JPEG compression
.png	Graphics, using PNG compression (Portable Network Graphics)
Sound Files	
.au	Sun (Unix) sound file
.wav	Microsoft Windows sound file
.aiff	Macintosh sound file
Video Files	
.QT	QuickTime video file, multiplatform
.mpeg	Video file
.avi	Microsoft Windows video file

TABLE 16-2   Web File Types

Web Browsers

Most Web browsers are designed to access several different kinds of information. Web browsers can access a Web page on a remote Web site or a file on your own system. Some browsers can also access a remote news server or an FTP site. The type of information for a site is specified by the keyword *http* for Web sites, *nntp* for news servers, *ftp* for FTP sites, or *file* for files on your own system. As mentioned, several popular browsers are available for Linux. Three distinctive ones described here are Mozilla, Konqueror, and Lynx. Mozilla is an X Window System–based Web browser capable of displaying graphics, video, and sound, as well as operating as a newsreader and mailer. Konqueror is the KDE file manager. KDE has integrated full Web-browsing capability into the Konqueror file manager, letting you seamlessly access the Web and your file system with the same application. Lynx and ELinks are command line–based browsers with no graphics capabilities, but in every other respect they are fully functional Web browsers.

To search for files on FTP sites, you can use search engines provided by Web sites such as Yahoo! or Google. These usually search for both Web pages and FTP files. To find a particular Web page you want on the Internet, you can use any of these search engines or perform searches from any number of web portals. Web searches have become a standard service of most Web sites. Hypertext databases are designed to access any kind of data, whether it is text, graphics, sound, or even video. Whether you can actually access such data depends to a large extent on the type of browser you use.

Firefox: The Mozilla Framework

The Mozilla project is an open source project based on the original Netscape browser code that provides a development framework for web-based applications, primarily the Web browser and e-mail client. Originally, the aim of the Mozilla project was to provide an end user Web browser called *Mozilla*. Its purpose has since changed to providing a development framework that anyone can use to create Web applications, though the project also provides its own. Table 16-3 lists some Mozilla resources.

Currently the framework is used for Mozilla products such as the Firefox Web browser and the Thunderbird mail client, as well for non-Mozilla products such as the Netscape, Epiphany, and Galeon Web browsers. In addition, the framework is easily extensible, supporting numerous add-ons in the form of plug-ins and extensions.

The first-generation product of the Mozilla project was the Mozilla Web browser, which is still available. Like the original Netscape, it included a mail client and newsreader, all in one integrated interface. The second-generation products have split this integrated package into separate standalone applications, the Firefox Web browser and the Thunderbird e-mail/ newsreader client. Also under development is the Camino Web browser for Mac OS X and the Sunbird calendar application.

In 1998, Netscape made its source code freely available under the Netscape Public License (NPL). Mozilla is developed on an open source model much like Linux, KDE, and GNOME. Developers can submit modifications and additions over the Internet to the Mozilla Web site. Mozilla releases are referred to as *Milestones*, and Mozilla products are currently released under both the NPL license for modifications of Mozilla code and the Mozilla Public License (MPL) for new additions.

The Firefox Web Browser

Ubuntu uses Firefox 3.0 as its primary browser. Firefox is a streamlined browser featuring fast Web access. Firefox is based on the Netscape **mozilla** core source code. Firefox is an X Window System application you can operate from any desktop, including GNOME, KDE, and Xfce. Firefox is installed by default with both a menu entry in the main menu's Internet menu and an icon on the different desktop panels. When opened (Figure 16-1), Firefox displays an area at the top of the screen for entering a URI address and a navigation toolbar with series of buttons for various Web page operations. Menus on the top menu bar provide access to such Firefox features as Tools, View, and Bookmarks. A status bar at the bottom shows the state of the current page.

Web Site	Description
www.mozilla.org	The Mozilla project
http://mozdev.org	Mozilla plug-ins and extensions
www.oreillynet.com/mozilla	Mozilla documentation and news
www.mozillazine.org	Mozilla news and articles
http://mozillanews.org	Mozilla news and articles
www.bugzilla.org	Mozilla bug reporting and tracking system

TABLE 16-3 Mozilla Resources

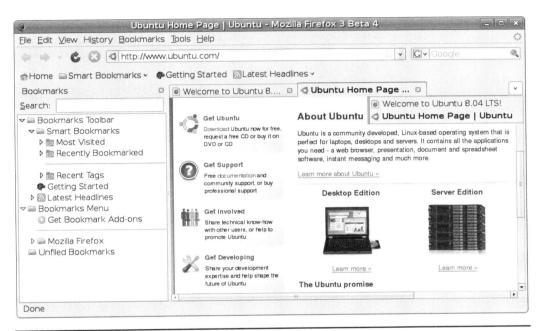

FIGURE 16-1 Firefox Web browser

To the right of the URI box is a search box where you can use different search engines for searching the Web, selected sites, or particular items. A pop-up menu lets you select a search engine. Currently included are Google, Yahoo!, Amazon, and eBay, along with Dictionary.com for looking up word definitions. Firefox also features button links and tabbed pages. You can drag the URI from the URI box to the button link bar to create a button with which to access the site quickly. Use this for frequently accessed sites.

For easy browsing, Firefox features tabbed panels for displaying Web pages. To open an empty tabbed panel, press CTRL-T or choose File | New Tab. To display a page in that panel, drag its URL from the URL box or from the bookmark list to the panel. You can have several panels open at once, moving from one page to the next by clicking their tabs. You can elect to open all your link buttons as tabbed panels by right-clicking the link bar and selecting Open In Tabs.

TIP *Right-clicking on the Web page background displays a pop-up menu with options for most basic operations such as page navigation, saving, and sending pages.*

To search a current page for certain text, press CTRL-F. This opens a search toolbar at the bottom of Firefox where you can enter a search term. You can choose to highlight found entries or match character case. Next and Previous buttons let you move to the next found pattern.

When you download a file using Firefox, the download is managed by the Download Manager. You can download several files at once. Downloads can be displayed in the Download Manager toolbar. You can cancel a download at any time, or pause a download, resuming it later. Right-clicking a download entry will display the site from which it was downloaded as well as the directory in which you saved the entry. To remove an entry, select it and click Remove from toolbar.

Firefox Bookmarks and History

Firefox refers to the URIs of Web pages you want to keep as *bookmarks,* marking pages you want to access directly. You can add favorite Web pages using the Bookmarks menu, or press CTRL-T to add a bookmark. You can then view a list of your bookmarks and select one to view. You can also edit your list, adding or removing bookmarks. When adding a bookmark, an Add Bookmark window opens with pop-up menus for folders and tags. The **Folder** menu is set to **Bookmarks** folder by default. You can also select the Bookmarks Toolbar or unfilled bookmarks.

History is a list of previous URIs you have accessed. The URI box also features a pop-up menu listing your previous history sites. Bookmarks and History can be viewed as sidebars, selectable from the View menu.

Firefox also features Bookmark toolbar you use for frequently accessed sites. The Bookmark toolbar is displayed just above the Web page. You can drag the URI from the URI box to the Bookmark toolbar to create a button for quick access to a site. Buttons can also be folders, containing button links for several pages. Clicking a folder button will display the button links in a pop-up menu. You can also right-click the Bookmark toolbar to display a pop-up menu with entries for adding a bookmark and creating a new folder. Entries include Open All In Tabs, which lets you open a group of commonly used Web pages at once.

To manage your bookmarks, choose Bookmarks | Show All Bookmarks. This opens the Library window with bookmark folders displayed in a sidebar. Bookmarks in a folder are shown in the upper-right panel, and properties for a selected bookmark in that list is displayed in the lower-right panel. The Organize menu has an option to create a new folder. The View menu lets you sort your bookmarks. The Import And Backup menu has options to save backups of your bookmark as well as export your bookmark for use on other systems using Firefox. You can also import exported Firefox bookmarks from other systems.

Bookmarks also maintains a **Smart Bookmarks** folder that keeps a list of Most Visited, Recently Bookmarked, and Recent Tags. This lets you find sites you visit most often or those you consider important.

Firefox supports *live bookmarks*, which are used to connect to a site that provides a live RSS feed—a page that is constantly being updated, such as a news site. Live bookmarks are indicated by a live bookmark icon to the right of its URI. Click this icon or choose Bookmark | Subscribe To This Page to subscribe to the site. A pop-up menu is displayed in the main window with the prompt "Subscribe to this feed using." Live Bookmarks is selected by default, but you can also choose My Yahoo!, Bloglines, or Google. You can also choose to Always Use Live Bookmarks For Feeds. You can then click Subscribe Now to set up the live bookmark. This opens a dialog where you can choose to place the live bookmark, either in the Bookmark menu or on the Bookmark toolbar. In the Bookmark toolbar, the live bookmark becomes a pop-up menu listing the active pages, with an entry at the end for the main site.

When you open the live bookmark in the Bookmark toolbar or from the live bookmark icon in its URI entry, a list of active pages is displayed. An Open All In Tabs entry at the bottom of the listing lets you open all the active pages at once. News pages on a site are often RSS feeds that you can set up as a live bookmarks. At the Ubuntu site (**www.ubuntu.com**), you can subscribe to many news links as live bookmarks, such as the Canonical Blog, the

Fridge, and Planet Ubuntu. When you select a subscribed site on the Bookmark menu, a submenu of active pages is displayed from which you can choose. On Ubuntu, the BBC site is a live bookmark available from the Latest Headlines Bookmark Toolbar button.

Firefox Configuration

Choose Edit | Preferences in Firefox to set several options in the Preferences window (Figure 16-2), with buttons for Main, Tabs, Content, Applications, Privacy, Security, and Advanced. On the Main page, you can set you home page, download options, and access add-ons management. Tabs control tab opening and closing behavior. Content lets you set the font and font size, as well as color and language to use. You can also block pop-ups and enable Java. Applications associate content with applications to run it, such as video or MP3. Privacy controls history, cookies, and private data. Security is where you can remember passwords and set warning messages. The Advanced page has several tabs: General, Network, Update, and Encryption. The General tab provides features such as spell-checking and keyboard navigation. The Network tab has a Setting button for the Connection feature, which is where you set up your network connections such as the direct connection to the internet or proxy settings. Here you can also set up offline storage size. The Encryption tab is where you can manage certificates, setting up validation methods, viewing, and revocation.

If you are on a network that connects to the Internet through a firewall, you must use the Proxies screen to enter the address of your network's firewall gateway computer. A *firewall* is a computer that operates as a controlled gateway to the Internet for your network.

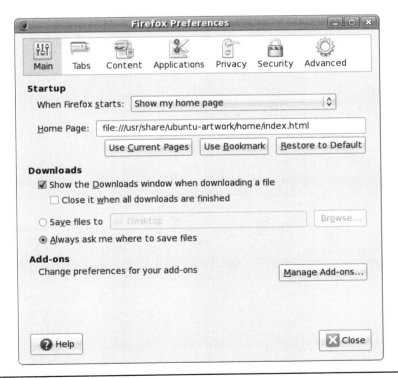

FIGURE 16-2   Firefox Preferences window

Several types of firewalls exist. The most restrictive kinds of firewalls use programs called *proxies*, which receive Internet requests from users and then make those requests on their behalf. There is no direct connection to the Internet.

Firefox also support *profiles*. You can set up different Firefox configurations, each with its own preferences and bookmarks. This is useful for computers such as laptops that connect to different networks or are used for different purposes. You can select and create profiles by starting the Profile Manager. Enter the **firefox** command in a terminal window with the **-P** option:

```
firefox -P
```

A default profile is already set up. You can create a new profile, which runs the Profile Wizard to prompt you for the profile name and directory to use. Select a profile to use and click Start Firefox. The last profile you used will be used the next time you start Firefox. You can have Firefox prompt you for the profile to use at startup, or run the **firefox -P** command again to change your profile.

Firefox Add-ons

The Add-ons Management button, on the Preferences Main screen, opens a window with tabs for Extensions, Themes, and Plugins. From the Add-ons window (Figure 16-3) you can select the Get Add-ons tab to see links to add-ons sites and to load Ubuntu Extensions. The Get Ubuntu Extensions link opens an Install/Remove Extension window that lists available extension packages designed to work well with Ubuntu. Check those you want and click Apply Changes.

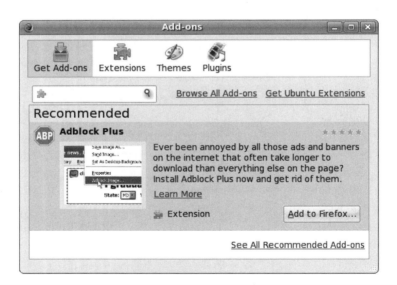

FIGURE 16-3   Firefox Add-ons Management

The K Desktop File Manager: Konqueror

If you are using KDE, you can use a file manager window as a Web browser. The KDE file manager is automatically configured to act as a Web browser. It can display Web pages, including graphics and links. The file manager supports standard Web page operation, such as moving forward and backward through accessed pages. Clicking a link accesses and displays the Web page referenced. In this respect, the Web becomes seamlessly integrated into the KDE desktop.

GNOME Web Browsers: Epiphany, Galeon, and Kazehakase

Several GNOME-based Web browsers, such as Epiphany, Galeon, and Kazehakase, support standard Web operations. Epiphany is designed to be a fast, clean, and simple browser interface. It is also integrated with the KDE desktop, featuring a download applet that will continue even after closing Epiphany. In addition, Epiphany supports tabbed panels for multiple Web site access. You can find out more about Epiphany at **www.gnome.org/ projects/epiphany**.

Galeon is a fast, light browser also based on the Mozilla browser engine (Gecko). Kazehakase emphasizes a customizable interface with download boxes and RSS bookmarks.

You can also download numerous support tools, such as the RSSOwl to display news feeds and the GWGET Download Manager for controlling Web-based downloads. The Downloader for X is useful for both FTP and Web file downloads. It has numerous features, letting you control download speeds as well as download subdirectories.

Lynx and ELinks: Line-Mode Browsers

Lynx is a line-mode browser you can use without the X Window System. A Web page is displayed as text only. A text page can contain links to other Internet resources but does not display graphics, video, or sound. Except for the display limitations, Lynx is a fully functional Web browser. You can use Lynx to download files or to make telnet connections. All information on the Web is still accessible to you. Because it does not require as much overhead as graphics-based browsers, Lynx can operate much faster, quickly displaying Web page text. To start the Lynx browser, you enter **lynx** on the command line and press ENTER.

Another useful text-based browser shipped with most distributions is ELinks, a powerful screen-based browser that includes features such as frame, form, and table support. It also supports SSL secure encryption. To start ELinks, enter the **elinks** command in a terminal window.

Java for Linux

To develop Java applications, use Java tools, and run many Java products, you must install the Java 2 Software Development Kit (SDK) and the Java 2 Runtime Environment (JRE) on your system. Together, they make up the Java 2 Platform, Standard Edition (J2SE). Sun currently supports and distributes Linux versions of these products. They are included as Ubuntu packages on the multiverse repository, which you can install with the Synaptic Package Manager.

Many Linux distributions include numerous free Java applications and support, such as Jakarta. The main JRE and SDK are not included directly. From the Ubuntu main repository,

PART V

a compatible set of GNU packages (Java-like) are provided that allow you to run Java applets. From the Ubuntu multiverse repository you can install the original JRE and SDK from Sun packaged for Ubuntu.

Ubuntu supports a Java-like collection of support packages that enable the use of Java Runtime operations. There is no official name for this collection, though it is usually referred to as **java-gci-compat**, as well as **Java-like**. This collection provides a free and open source environment, consisting of three packages: GNU Java runtime (**libgcj**), the Eclipse Java compiler (**ecj**), and a set of wrappers and links (**java-gcj-compat**). It is available as part of the Ubuntu main repository. Use the **gcj-web-plugin** for supporting Java in Web browsers.

You can also download and install the Sun version of the JRE, now included in the Ubuntu multiverse repository. Use the Synaptic Package Manager and search on *sun-java5*. These Debian versions are packaged for installation on Ubuntu (mulitverse development repository).

Alternatively, you can download and install the JRE and SDK directly from Sun (**www.java.com**). The SDK and JRE are available in the form of self-extracting compressed archives, **.bin**.

> **NOTE** *Numerous additional Java-based products and tools are currently adaptable for Linux. Many of the products such as the Java Web server run directly as provided by Sun. You can download several directly from the Sun Java Web site at* **http://java.sun.com**.

Sun now provides an open source development environment called *Iced Tea*, which is designed for developing completely open source Java applications. OpenJDK provides a Java development platform; detailed descriptions of features can be found in the SDK documentation, **http://java.sun.com/docs**.

FTP Clients

With File Transfer Protocol (FTP) clients, you can connect to a corresponding FTP site and download files from it. FTP clients are commonly used to download software from public FTP sites that operate as software repositories. Most Linux software applications can be downloaded to your Linux system from such sites, which feature anonymous logins that let any user access their files. A distribution site such as **ftp.redhat.com** is an example of one such FTP site, holding an extensive set of packaged Linux applications you can download using an FTP client and then easily install on your system. Basic FTP client capabilities are incorporated into the Konqueror (KDE) and Nautilus (GNOME) file managers. You can use a file manager window to access an FTP site and drag files to local directories to download them. Effective FTP clients are also now incorporated into most Web browsers, making browsers a primary downloading tool. Firefox in particular has strong FTP download capabilities.

Although file managers and Web browsers provide effective access to public (anonymous login) sites, you may need a standalone FTP client such as curl, wget, gFTP, or ftp to access private sites. These clients let you enter usernames and passwords with which you can access a private FTP site. The standalone clients are also useful for large downloads from public FTP sites, especially those with little or no Web display support. Popular Linux FTP clients are listed in Table 16-4.

FTP Clients	Description
Firefox	Mozilla Web and FTP browser
Konqueror	KDE file manager
Nautilus	GNOME file manager
gFTP	GNOME FTP client
ftp	Command line FTP client
lftp	Command line FTP client capable of multiple connections
NcFTP	Screen-based FTP client
curl	Internet transfer client (FTP and HTTP)

TABLE 16-4   Linux FTP Clients

Network File Transfer: FTP

You can transfer extremely large files directly from one site to another using FTP, which can handle both text and binary files. This TCP/IP protocol operates on systems connected to networks that use TCP/IP, such as the Internet. FTP performs a remote login to another account on another system to which you connect through your network. Once logged in to that other system, you can transfer files to and from it. To log in, you need to know the login name and password for the account on the remote system. For example, if you have accounts at two different sites on the Internet, you can use FTP to transfer files from one to the other. Many sites on the Internet allow public access using FTP, however. Such sites serve as depositories for large files that anyone can access and download. These sites are often referred to as *FTP sites,* and in many cases, their Internet addresses usually begin with *ftp,* such as **ftp.gnome.org** or **ftp.ubuntu.com**. These public sites allow anonymous FTP login from any user. For the login name, use the word *anonymous,* and for the password, use your e-mail address. You can then transfer files from that site to your own system.

You can perform FTP operations using an FTP client program; for Linux systems, you can choose from several FTP clients. Many now operate using GUIs such as GNOME. Some, such as Firefox, have limited capabilities, whereas others, such as NcFTP, include an extensive set of enhancements. The original FTP client is just as effective, though not as easy to use. It operates using a simple command line interface and requires no GUI or cursor support as other clients do.

The Internet has a great many sites open to public access that contain files anyone can obtain using FTP. Unless you already know where a file is located, however, finding it can be difficult. To search for files on FTP sites, you can use search engines such as Yahoo! or Google. For Linux software, you can check sites such as **http://freshmeat.net, http://sourceforge.net**, **http://apps.kde.com**, and **www.gnome.org**. These sites usually search for both Web pages and FTP files.

Web Browser–Based FTP: Firefox

You access an FTP site and download files from it with any Web browser. When you access an FTP site, the entire list of files in a directory is listed as a Web page. You can move to a subdirectory by clicking its entry. With Firefox, you can easily browse through an FTP site to download files: just click the download link. This will start the transfer operation, opening a dialog for selecting your local directory and the name for the file. The default name is the same as on the remote system. You can manage your downloads with the download manager, which will let you cancel a download operation in progress or remove other downloads requested. The manager will show the time remaining, the speed, and the amount transferred for the current download. Browsers are useful for locating individual files, though not for downloading a large set of files, as is usually required for a system update.

The KDE File Managers: Konqueror and Dolphin

On KDE, the Konqueror and Dolphin desktop file managers have built-in FTP capability. The FTP operation has been seamlessly integrated into standard desktop file operations. Downloading files from an FTP site is as simple as copying files by dragging them from one directory window to another, but one of the directories happens to be located on a remote FTP site. On the KDE desktop, you can use a file manager window to access a remote FTP site. Files in the remote directory are listed just as your local files are.

To download files from an FTP site, you open a window to access that site, entering the URL for the FTP site in the window's location box. Use the **ftp://** protocol for FTP access. You can also use the **fish://** protocol for FTP access using SSH secure connections. Once connected, open the directory you want, and then open another window for the local directory to which you want the remote files copied. In the window showing the FTP files, select the ones you want to download. Then drag-and-drop those files to the window for the local directory. A pop-up menu appears with choices for Copy, Link, or Move. Select Copy to download the selected files. Another window opens, showing the download progress and displaying the name of each file in turn, along with a bar indicating the percentage downloaded so far.

GNOME Desktop FTP: Nautilus

The easiest way to download files is to use the built-in FTP capabilities of the GNOME file manager, Nautilus. The FTP operation has been seamlessly integrated into standard desktop file operations. Downloading files from an FTP site is as simple as dragging files from one directory window to another, where one of the directories happens to be located on a remote FTP site. Use Nautilus to access a remote FTP site, listing files in the remote directory, just as local files are. Just enter the FTP URL following the prefix **ftp://** and press ENTER. The top directory of the remote FTP site will be displayed. Use Nautilus to progress through the remote FTP site's directory tree until you find the file you want. Then open another window for the local directory to which you want the remote files copied. In the window showing the FTP files, select those you want to download. Then CTRL-click and drag those files to the window for the local directory. CTRL-clicking performs a copy operation, not a move. As files are downloaded, a dialog appears showing the progress.

gFTP

The gFTP program is a simpler GNOME FTP client designed to let you make standard FTP file transfers. The gFTP window consists of several panes: The top-left pane lists files in your local directory, and the top-right pane lists your remote directory. Subdirectories have folder icons preceding their names. The parent directory can be referenced by the double period entry (..) with an up arrow at the top of each list. Double-click a directory entry to access it. The pathnames for all directories are displayed in boxes above each pane. You can enter a new pathname to change to a different directory.

Two buttons between the panes are used for transferring files. The left arrow button downloads selected files in the remote directory, and the right arrow button uploads files from the local directory. To download a file, click it in the right pane and then click the left arrow button. When the file is downloaded, its name appears in the left pane, your local directory. Menus across the top of the window can be used to manage your transfers. A connection manager enables you to enter login information about a specific site. You can specify whether to perform an anonymous login or provide a username and password. Click Connect to connect to that site. A drop-down menu for sites lets you choose the site you want. Interrupted downloads can be restarted easily.

wget

The wget tool lets you access Web and FTP sites for particular directories and files. Directories can be recursively downloaded, letting you copy an entire Web site. The **wget** command takes as its option the URL for the file or directory you want. Helpful options include **-q** for quiet, **-r** for recursive (directories), **-b** to download in the background, and **-c** to continue downloading an interrupted file. One of the drawbacks is that your URL reference can be very complex. You have to know the URL already; you cannot interactively locate an item as you would with an FTP client. The following would download the Ubuntu DVD in the background:

```
wget -b  http://cdimage.ubuntu.com/dvd/currnet/hardy-dvd-amd64.iso
```

TIP *With the GNOME wget tool, you can run wget downloads using a GUI.*

curl

The curl Internet client operates much like wget but with much more flexibility. You can specify multiple URLs on curl's command line, and you can use braces to specify multiple matching URLs, such as different Web sites with the same domain name. You can list the different Web site hostnames within braces followed by their domain name (or vice versa). You can also use brackets to specify a range of multiple items. This can be very useful for downloading archived files that have the same root name with varying extensions, such as different issues of the same magazine. Curl can download using any protocol and will try to intelligently guess the protocol to use if none is provided. Check the curl man page for more information.

ftp

The name *ftp* designates the original FTP client used on Unix and Linux systems. The ftp client uses a command line interface, and it has an extensive set of commands and options you can use to manage your FTP transfers. Alternatively you can use sftp for more secure access. The sftp client has the same commands as ftp, but provided Secure Shell (SSH) encryption. Also, if you installed the Kerberos clients, a Kerberized version of ftp is set up, which provides for secure authentication from Kerberos servers. It has the same name as the ftp client (an ftp link to Kerberos ftp) and also the same commands.

You start the ftp client by entering the command **ftp** at a shell prompt. If you want to connect to a specific site, you can include the name of that site on the command line after the **ftp** keyword. Otherwise, you need to connect to the remote system with the ftp command **open**. You are then prompted for the name of the remote system with the prompt *(to)*. When you enter the remote system name, ftp connects you to the system and then prompts you for a login name. The prompt for the login name consists of the word *Name* and, in parentheses, the system name and your local login name. Sometimes the login name on the remote system is the same as the login name on your own system. If the names are the same, press ENTER at the prompt. If they are different, enter the remote system's login name. After entering the login name, you are prompted for the password.

In the next example, the user connects to the remote system **garnet** and logs in to the **robert** account:

```
$ ftp
ftp> open
(to) garnet
Connected to garnet.berkeley.edu.
220 garnet.berkeley.edu FTP server ready.
Name (garnet.berkeley.edu:root): robert
password required
Password:
user robert logged in
ftp>
```

Once you're logged in, you can execute Linux commands on either the remote system or your local system. You execute a command on your local system in ftp by preceding the command with an exclamation point. Any Linux commands without an exclamation point are executed on the remote system. One exception exists to this rule: Whereas you can change directories on the remote system with the **cd** command, to change directories on your local system, you need to use a special ftp command called **lcd** (local **cd**).

In the next example, the first command lists files in the remote system, while the second command lists files in the local system:

```
ftp> ls
ftp> !ls
```

The ftp program provides a basic set of commands for managing files and directories on your remote site, provided you have the permission to do so (see Table 16-5). You can use **mkdir** to create a remote directory and **rmdir** to remove one. Use the **delete** command to erase a remote file. With the **rename** command, you can change the names of files. You close your connection to a system with the **close** command. You can then open another connection if you want. To end the ftp session, use the **quit** or **bye** command:

```
ftp> close
ftp> bye
Good-bye
$
```

To transfer files to and from the remote system, use the **get** and **put** commands. The **get** command receives files from the remote system to your local system, and the **put** command sends files from your local system to the remote system. In a sense, your local

Command	Effect
`ftp`	Invokes the ftp program.
`open` *site-address*	Opens connection to another system.
`close`	Closes connection to a system.
`quit` or `bye`	Ends ftp session.
`ls`	Lists the contents of a directory.
`dir`	Lists the contents of a directory in long form.
`get` *filename*	Sends file from remote system to local system.
`put` *filename*	Sends file from local system to remote system.
`mget` *regular-expression*	Enables you to download several files at once from a remote system. You can use special characters to specify the files; you are prompted to transfer each file in turn.
`mput` *regular-expression*	Enables you to send several files at once to a remote system. You can use special characters to specify the files; you are prompted for each file to be transferred.
`runique`	Toggles storing of files with unique filenames. If a file already exists with the same filename on the local system, a new filename is generated.
`reget` *filename*	Resumes transfer of an interrupted file from where you left off.
`binary`	Transfers files in binary mode.
`ascii`	Transfers files in ASCII mode.
`cd` *directory*	Changes directories on the remote system.
`lcd` *directory*	Changes directories on the local system.
`help` or `?`	Lists ftp commands.
`mkdir` *directory*	Creates a directory on the remote system.
`rmdir`	Deletes a remote directory.
`delete` *filename*	Deletes a file on the remote system.
`mdelete` *file-list*	Deletes several remote files at once.
`rename`	Renames a file on a remote system.
`hash`	Displays progressive hash signs during download.
`status`	Displays current status of ftp.

TABLE 16-5   The ftp Client Commands

system gets files *from* the remote and puts files *to* the remote. In the next example, the file **weather** is sent from the local system to the remote system using the **put** command:

```
ftp> put weather
PORT command successful.
ASCII data connection
ASCII Transfer complete.
ftp>
```

If a download is interrupted, you can resume the download with **reget**. This is helpful when working with extremely large files; the download resumes from where it left off, so the whole file needn't be downloaded again. Be sure to download binary files in binary mode. For most FTP sites, the binary mode is the default, but some sites might have ASCII (text) as the default. The command **ascii** sets the character mode, and the command **binary** sets the binary mode. Most software packages available at Internet sites are archived and compressed files, which are binary files. In the next example, the transfer mode is set to binary, and the archived software package **mydata.tar.gz** is sent from the remote system to your local system using the **get** command:

```
ftp> binary
ftp> get mydata.tar.gz
PORT command successful.
Binary data connection
Binary Transfer complete.
ftp>
```

You may often want to send several files, specifying their names with wildcard characters. The **put** and **get** commands, however, operate only on a single file and do not work with special characters. To transfer several files at a time, you have to use two other commands, **mput** and **mget**. When you use **mput** or **mget**, you are prompted for a file list. You can then either enter the list of files or a file-list specification using special characters. For example, ***.c** specifies all the files with a .c extension, and ***** specifies all files in the current directory. In the case of **mget**, files are sent one by one from the remote system to your local system. Each time, you are prompted with the name of the file being sent. You can type **y** to send the file or **n** to cancel the transmission. You are then prompted for the next file. The **mput** command works in the same way, but it sends files from your local system to the remote system. In the next example, all files with a .c extension are sent to your local system using **mget**:

```
ftp> mget
(remote-files) *.c
mget calc.c? y
```

Answering the prompt for each file can be a tedious prospect if you plan to download a large number of files, such as those for a system update. In this case, you can turn off the prompt with the **prompt** command, which toggles the interactive mode on and off. The **mget** operation then downloads all files it matches, one after the other.

```
ftp> prompt
Interactive mode off.
```

NOTE *To access a public FTP site, you must perform an anonymous login. Instead of a login name, you enter the keyword* anonymous *(or ftp). Then, for the password, you enter your e-mail address. Once the ftp prompt is displayed, you are ready to transfer files. You may need to change to the appropriate directory first or set the transfer mode to binary.*

Automatic Login and Macros: .netrc

The ftp client has an automatic login ability and support for macros. Both are entered in a user's ftp configuration file called **.netrc**. Each time you connect to a site, the **.netrc** file is checked for connection information, such as a login name and password. In this way, you needn't enter a login name and password each time you connect to a site. This feature is particularly useful for anonymous logins. Instead of having to enter the username *anonymous* and your e-mail address as your password, this information can be automatically read from the **.netrc** file. You can even make anonymous login information your default so that, unless otherwise specified, an anonymous login is attempted for any FTP site to which you try to connect. If you must log in to an FTP site, you can specify it in the **.netrc** file and, when you connect, either automatically log in with your username and password for that site or be prompted for them.

Entries in the **.netrc** file have the following syntax. An entry for a site begins with the term `machine`, followed by the network or Internet address, and then the login and password information:

```
machine system-address login remote-login-name password password
```

lftp

The lftp program is an enhanced FTP client with advanced features such as the ability to download mirror sites and run several FTP operations in the background at the same time (Ubuntu main repository). Lftp uses a command set similar to that for the ftp client: you use **get** and **mget** commands to download files, with the **-o** option to specify local locations for them. Use **lcd** and **cd** to change local and remote directories.

To manage background commands, you use many of the same commands used for the shell. The **&** placed at the end of a command puts it into the background, and pressing CTRL-Z puts an already-running job in the background. Commands can be grouped with parentheses and placed together into the background. Use the **jobs** command to list your background jobs and the **wait** or **fg** command to move jobs from the background to the foreground. When you exit lftp, the program will continue to run any background jobs. In effect, lftp becomes a background job itself.

When you connect to a site, you can queue commands with the **queue** command, setting up a list of FTP operations to perform. This feature allows you to queue several download operations to a site. The queue can be reordered and entries deleted if you wish. You can also connect to several sites and set up a queue for each one. The **mirror** command lets you maintain a local version of a mirror site. You can download an entire site or just update newer files, as well as remove files no longer present on the mirror.

You can tailor lftp with options set in the **.lftprc** file. System-wide settings are placed in the **/etc/lftp.conf** file. Here, you can set features such as the prompt to use and your anonymous password. The **.lftp** directory holds support files for command history, logs, bookmarks, and startup commands. The lftp program also supports the **.netrc** file, checking it for login information.

TIP *The NcFTP program runs as a command line operation similar to ftp with many of the same commands (Ubuntu universe repository). To start up NcFTP, you enter the* **ncftp** *command on the command line. It also provides* **ncftpput** *and* **ncftpget** *for use in shell scripts.*

Network Talk and Messenger Clients: VoIP, IRC, and IM

You may, at times, want to communicate directly with other users on your network. You can do so with VoIP, Talk, ICQ, IM, and IRC utilities, provided the other user is also logged in to a connected system at the same time (see Table 16-6). With VoIP applications, you can speak over Internet connections as if you're on a telephone. With an Internet Relay Chat (IRC) utility, you can connect to a remote server where other users are also connected and talk with them. IM clients operate much the same way, allowing users on the same IM system to communicate anywhere across the Internet. Ubuntu uses Pidgin as its standard interface for IM.

Ekiga

Ekiga (Figure 16-4) is GNOME's VoIP application providing Internet IP telephone and video conferencing support. It is installed by default on the Ubuntu desktop and is accessible by choosing Applications | Internet | Ekiga Softphone.

To use Ekiga, you will need a Session Initiation Protocol (SIP) address. You can obtain a free address from **http://ekiga.net**, but you will first have to subscribe to the service. When you start Ekiga, you will be prompted to configure your connection. Here you provide your name, set up your user ID and password, detect your network connection, and specify a sound driver and video device.

Use the call pad to make a call. The sound and video panels let you adjust sound levels and video image appearance. Use the address book to connect to another Ekiga user. A white pages directory lets you search for people who are also using Ekiga.

Ekiga was formerly called GnomeMeeting, and its Web site is still at **www.gnomemeeting .org**. Ekiga supports both the H.323 and SIP protocols. It is compatible with Microsoft's NetMeeting. H.323 is a comprehensive protocol that includes the digital broadcasting protocols such as digital video broadcast (DVB) and H.261 for video streaming, as well as the supporting protocols such as the H.450 series for managing calls.

Clients	Description
Ekiga	VoIP application
Pidgin	Messenger interface for all IM protocols including MSN, AIM, Yahoo!, MySpaceIM, ICQ, XMPP, and IRC
X-Chat	IRC client
Konversation	KDE IRC client
Gabber	Jabber client (XMPP)
Gaim	GNOME AIM client
psi	Jabber client using QT (KDE)
nalm	Command line cursor–based IRC, ICQ, and AIM client

TABLE 16-6 Talk and Messenger Clients

FIGURE 16-4
Ekiga

NOTE *IRC operates like a chat room. You can enter channels and talk to other users already online. You must first select an IRC server to which you want to connect. Various servers are available for different locales and topics. Several IRC clients are available for use on Ubuntu, including sirc, ksirc, Konversation, and irssi. Most IM applications, such as Pidgin, can also support IRC.*

Instant Messenger: Pidgin

IM clients operate much the same way as ICQ (**www.icq.com**), allowing users on the same IM system to communicate anywhere across the Internet. Currently some of the major IM systems are AIM (AOL), Microsoft Network (MSN), Yahoo!, ICQ, and Jabber. Unlike the others, Jabber is an open source IM service (**www.jabber.org**). It uses an XML protocol it developed called Extensible Messaging and Presence Protocol (XMPP) (**www.xmpp.org**).

TIP *Pidgin will not start up unless you have at least one account configured. The first time you start Pidgin, the Add Account window is displayed with Basic and Advanced tabs for setting up an account. Later you can edit the account by selecting it in the Accounts window (Accounts | Manage) and clicking the Modify button.*

Ubuntu will install Pidgin as its standard interface for IM. Pidgin, formerly known as GAIM, is a multiprotocol IM client that works with most IM protocols including AIM, MSN, Jabber, Google Talk, ICQ, IRC, Yahoo!, MySpaceIM, and more. Pidgin is accessible by choosing Applications | Internet | Pidgin Instant Messenger. To create a new account, choose Accounts | Manage and click the Add button. This opens an Add Account window with Basic and Advanced tabs. Set protocol and account settings on the Basic tab; choose the protocol from a pop-up menu that shows items such as AIM, Bonjour, MySpaceIM, Yahoo!, and IRC. The configuration entries for both Basic and Advanced will change depending on the protocol. AIM shows entries for Screen Name, Password, and Alias. You can also select a buddy icon. Specify the server and network connection settings on the Advanced tab; the AIM server will already be entered.

To configure your setup, choose Tools | Preferences. The Conversations tab lets you set the font, images, and smiley icons for your messages. The Network tab lets you configure your network connection, and the Logging tab lets you turn message logging on or off. The Sounds tab allows you to choose sounds for different events. You can find out more about Pidgin at **http://pidgin.im**. Pidgin is a GNOME front end that used the **libpurple** library for actual IM tasks (formerly **libgaim**). The **libpurple** library is used by many different IM applications such as Finch.

VI PART

Security

Authorization, Encryption, and Permissions

Authorization, encryption, and permissions are all methods for controlling access. Authorizations can control access to administrative tools, making sure only valid and trusted users make changes to your system setup. Encryption can protect messages and files you may send, and digital signatures can confirm the source of a message or file. Users can also place their own access controls on their files using permissions and access control lists (ACLs). You can even encrypt entire file systems, making them accessible only with a valid key.

Certain security packages control access to resources such as devices, messages, directories, and file systems. PolicyKit provides controls for accessing devices and administrative tools by users. It is designed to permit limited administrative access to particular users, instead of allowing full root user access.

You can use encryption, integrity checks, and digital signatures to protect data transmitted over a network. For example, the GNU Privacy Guard (GnuPG) encryption as supported by Seahorse encryption management lets you encrypt your e-mail messages or files you want to send, and it lets you sign them with an encrypted digital signature authenticating that the message was sent by you. The digital signature also includes encrypted modification digest information that provides an integrity check, allowing the recipient to verify that the message received is the original and not one that has been changed or substituted.

Permissions can be set on file and directories to allow access to the owner, members of a group, or to all other users. This is the traditional method of controlling access to files. You can also use ACLs to add further restrictions. ACLs provide more refined access, but they are more difficult to manage. You can also encrypt entire file systems, using the same public key encryption method used for messages and archives.

Controlled Access with PolicyKit: Authorizations

Designed by the Freedesktop.org project, PolicyKit allows ordinary users and applications access to administrative-controlled applications and devices. Currently it works primarily with Hardware Abstraction Layer (HAL)–enabled devices and some GNOME desktop tasks. Though its functions could be accomplished with other operations such as group permissions,

PolicyKit aims to provide a simple and centralized interface for granting users access to administration-controlled devices and tools. PolicyKit is used to grant access to most of the devices on your system, including removable devices. It is also used to control access to several administrative tools such as **users-admin** and **services-admin** (GNOME administration tools). It is not used for access for other administrative tools such as Synaptic Package Manager or the login window. For these uses, you would use sudo and gksu. PolicyKit also controls access to the GNOME desktop clock applet.

For administrative tools, read-only access is granted to everyone, but the application is locked to prevent any changes. To gain full access, you click a Lock button in the lower-right corner of the application. You are then prompted to enter your administrative password, as you would for sudo or gksu. The application will unlock, allowing full access and displaying an Unlock button.

PolicyKit can also allow more refined access. Instead of an all-or-nothing approach, in which a user had to gain full root level control over the entire system just to access a specific administration tool, PolicyKit can allow access to a specific administrative application (currently only the GNOME clock is supported). All other access can be denied. Without PolicyKit, this kind of access could be configured in a limited way for some devices, such as while mounting and unmounting CD/DVD discs but not for applications. A similar kind of refined control is provided on Ubuntu with sudo and gsku, allowing access to specific administrative applications; administrative password access is still required, and root level access, though limited to that application, is still granted. You can find out more about PolicyKit at **http://hal.freedesktop.org/docs/PolicyKit/**.

Using PolicyKit, administrator-controlled devices and applications are set up to communicate with ordinary users, allowing them to request certain actions. If the user is allowed to perform the action, the request is authorized and the action is performed. In the case of devices, which are now controlled and managed by HAL, the request can be sent to HAL, which then can authorize the action. Technically, all devices and administrative tools are considered mechanism to which requests are sent by user PolicyKit agents. Administration mechanisms use a shared library called **policykit** to decide whether to grant access. Users and application requests are validated by a **libpolkit-grant** shared library. The **policykit** library will check the validations provided by **libpolkit-grant** and allow access accordingly.

Authentication can be required for the user (user password) or for an administrator (root user password). On Ubuntu, no root user access is defined, unless you first set up a root user password. You would be given user level access requiring only your user password, as is the case for sudo. Access can further be controlled by time limits: indefinite, for the rest of the current session, or as long as the process is active.

PolicyKit Agent

To gain access, a user makes use of an authentication agent. The PolicyKit GNOME agent is installed with PolicyKit and can be run by any administration-enabled user by choosing System | Administration | Authorization. Both the **policykit** and **gnome-policykit** packages are part of the Ubuntu main repository and installed by default. This runs the **polkit-gnome-authorization** tool with which you can set PolicyKit access.

PolicyKit Sidebar

The PolicyKit agent will display a window with a sidebar showing and expandable tree of supported PolicyKit devices and applications. Collapsing the tree gives you a better view of what is available (Figure 17-1). There are main entries for **gnome** and **freedesktop**.

FIGURE **17-1**
PolicyKit sidebar,
collapsed

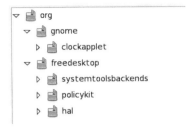

The **freedesktop** entry holds freedesktop-supported tools including **hal** and **policykit**, as well as **systemtoolsbackends** for administrative tool support.

The **hal** entry lets you control access to devices, with subsections for storage devices, device access to other devices, and power management, among others (see Figure 17-2). The **storage** section lets you control mounting for internal and removable drives, as well as encryption configuration.

PolicyKit Implicit and Explicit Authorizations

A selected entry will display its PolicyKit configuration on the right panel. This is divided into three segments: Action, Implicit Authorizations, and Explicit Authorizations (see Figure 17-3).

Implicit Authorizations are applied to the device or tool for all users. These are set for Anyone, Console, and Active Console. For single-user systems such as most laptops, the logged in user will be the active console. Console and Anyone would cover remote users. A Yes entry allows complete automatic access, and a No entry denies all access. You can click the Edit button to change the settings (see Figure 17-4). You can choose to restrict access to administrative users or users that provide their password, as well as limiting authorization to the duration of the session.

To grant access to specific users, click the Grant button on the Explicit Authorizations area. This opens a Grant Authorization dialog where you can select a user and specify the level of access (Figure 17-5).

In the **device access** section under **hal** you can permit access by remote users to certain devices such as video, sound, and DVB devices. In this case, the implicit authorizations could be modified to allow access by anyone. Or you could allow access to specific users.

In the **freedesktop** entry (see Figure 17-1), you can use entries under **policykit** to configure PolicyKit authorization. Here you can specify who can revoke, read, modify, or grant PolicyKit authorizations.

FIGURE **17-2**
Storage devices
in hal

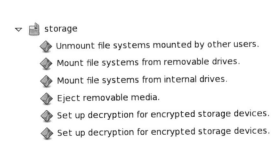

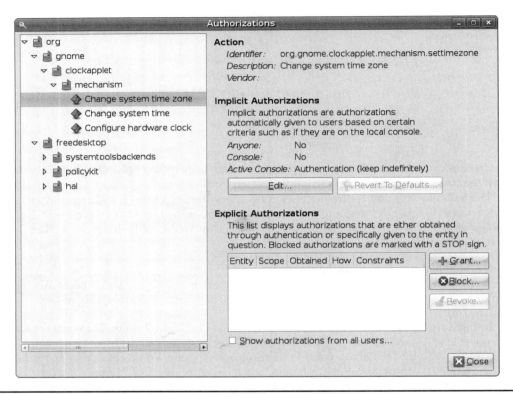

Figure 17-3   PolicyKit Authorizations window

For administrative tools such as user, services, and networking, you use the **freedesktop |
systemtoolsbackends | manage system configuration** entry. Implicit authorizations are set
for the active console only with administrative authentication (see Figure 17-6). There are no
explicit authorizations. You can use the Grant and Block buttons in the Explicit
Authorizations area to grant or block access for particular users.

Figure 17-4
Editing implicit
authorizations

FIGURE 17-5
Grant Authorization
dialog

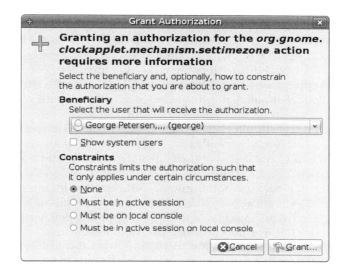

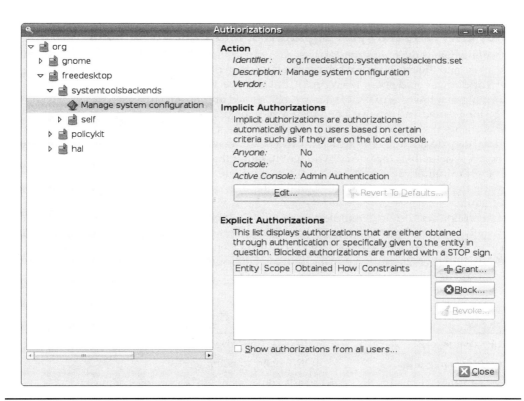

FIGURE 17-6   Managing system configuration for systemtoolsbackends

PolicyKit Configuration Files and Tools

Devices and administrative applications that want to make use of PolicyKit must be modified to access it. Currently, HAL, which controls access to most devices, provides PolicyKit control for devices. On GNOME, the clock applet is configured for PolicyKit control. PolicyKit for devices and applications are configured using XML files with the extension **.policy** in the **/usr/share/PolicyKit/policy** directory. Here you will find **.policy** files for the gnome-clock-applet as well as several for HAL and one for PolicyKit.

The **/etc/PolicyKit/PolicyKit.conf** file is used to permit overriding any PolicyKit authorizations for users. Currently the configuration file is set up always to allow access to the root user and to any users with administrative access (admin group). It can be configured for specific users.

Though you would use **polkit-gnome-authorization** to configure PolicyKit, several command line tools are also available. These include **polkit-auth** to manage authorization, **polkit-action** to list and modify allowed actions, **polkit-policy-file-validate** to validate a PolicyKit policy file, and **polkit-config-file-validate** to validate the PolicyKit configuration file. Should you make changes directly to the **PolicyKit.conf** file, you should run **polkit-config-file-validate** to make sure the file is valid. If you add or modify any of the **.policy** files, you can run **polkit-policy-file-validate** on them to verify that they are correctly configured.

Public Key Encryption, Digital Signatures, and Integrity Checks

Encrypting data is the only sure way to secure data transmitted over a network. Encrypt data with a key, and the receiver or receivers can later decrypt it. To protect data transmitted over a network, you should not only encrypt it, but also check that it has not been modified, confirming that it was actually created by the claimed author. An encrypted message could still be intercepted and modified and then reencrypted. Integrity checks such as modification digests ensure that the data was not altered. Though encryption and integrity checks protect the data, they do not authenticate it. You also need to know that the user who claims to send a message is actually is the person who sent it, rather than an imposter. To authenticate a message, the author can sign it using a digital signature. This signature can also be encrypted, allowing the receiver to validate it. Digital signatures ensure that the message you receive is authentic.

Encryption was originally implemented with Pretty Good Privacy (PGP). Originally a privately controlled methodology, it was handed over to the Internet Engineering Task Force (IETF) to support an open standard for PGP called OpenPGP (see Table 17-1). Any project can use OpenPGP to create encryption applications, such as GnuPG. Commercial products for PGP are still developed by the PGP Corporation, which also uses the OpenPGP standard.

Web Site	Description
http://gnupg.org	GnuPG, Gnu Privacy Guard
http://openpgp.org	IETF open standard for PGP
www.pgp.com	PGP Corporation, PGP commercial products

TABLE 17-1 PGP Sites

Public Key Encryption

Encryption uses a key to encrypt data in such a way that a corresponding key can decrypt it. In the past, older forms of encryption used the same key both to encrypt and decrypt a message. This, however, involved providing the receiver with the key, opening up the possibility that anyone who obtained the key could decrypt the data. Public key encryption uses two keys to encrypt and decrypt a message: a *private key* and a *public key*. The private key is always kept and used to decrypt messages you have received. The public key is made available to people to whom you send messages. They then use your public key to encrypt any message that they want to send to you. The private key decrypts messages, and the public key encrypts them. Each user has a set of private and public keys, securely kept in keyrings.

Reciprocally, if you want to send messages to another user, you first obtain that user's public key and use it to encrypt the message you want to send to the user. The user then decrypts the messages with his or her own private key. In other words, your public key is used by others to encrypt the messages you receive, and you use other users' public keys to encrypt messages you send to them. All the users on your Linux system can have their own public and private keys. They will use the **gpg** program to generate them and keep their private key in their own keyrings.

Digital Signatures

A *digital signature* is used both to authenticate a message and provide an integrity check. Authentication guarantees that the message has not been modified—that it is the original message sent by you—and the integrity check verifies that it has not been changed. Though usually combined with encrypted messages to provide a greater level of security, digital signatures can also be used for messages that can be sent in the clear. For example, you would want to know if a public notice of upgrades of a Ubuntu release was actually sent by Ubuntu and not by someone trying to spread confusion. Such a message still needs to be authenticated and checked to see whether it was actually sent by the sender or, if sent by the original sender, was not somehow changed en route. Verification like this protects against modification or substitution of the message by someone pretending to be the sender.

Integrity Checks

Digitally signing a message involves generating a checksum value from the contents of the message using an encryption hash algorithm such as the SHA2 modification digest algorithm. This is a unique value that accurately represents the size and contents of your message. Any kind of changes to the message will generate a different value. The value provides a way to check the integrity of the data. Commonly known as the MD5 value, it is reflective of the MD5 hash algorithm that was used encrypt the value. The MD5 algorithm has since been replaced by the more secure SHA2 algorithms.

The MD5 value is encrypted with your private key. When the user receives your message, your digital signature is decrypted using your public key. Then an MD5 value of the message received is generated and compared with the MD5 value you sent. If the values are the same, the message is authenticated as the original message sent by you, not a false one sent by a user pretending to be you. The user can use GnuPG to decrypt and check digital signatures.

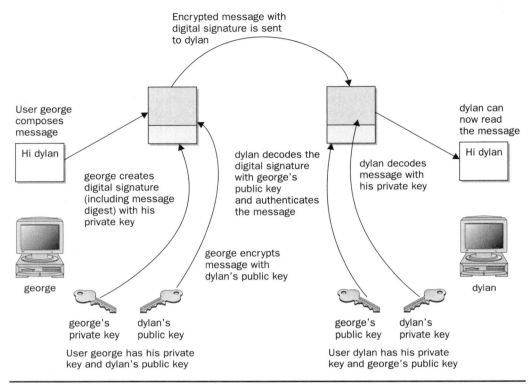

Figure 17-7 Public key encryption and digital signatures

Combining Encryption and Signatures

Normally, digital signatures are combined with encryption to provide a more secure level of transmission. The message is encrypted with the recipient's public key, and the digital signature is encrypted with your private key. The user decrypts both the message (with his private key) and then the signature (with your public key). The user then compares the signature with one that he generates from the message to authenticate it. When GnuPG decodes a message, it will also decode and check a digital signature automatically. Figure 17-7 shows the process for encrypting and digitally signing a message.

Managing Keys with Seahorse

For GPG and SSH encryption, signing, and decryption of files and text, GNOME provides Seahorse. Seahorse lets you manage your encryption keys stored in keyrings as well as SSH keys and passphrases. You can import keys, sign keys, search for remote keys, create your own keyrings, and specify a keyserver to search and publish to. All these operations can also be performed using the **gpg** command.

FIGURE 17-8
Seahorse
Passwords and
Encryption Keys
window: Seahorse

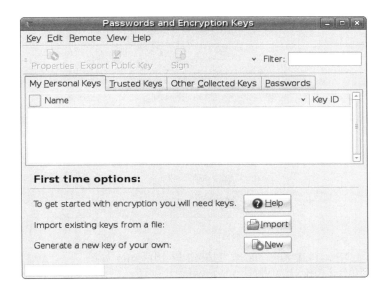

Passwords and Encryption Keys: Seahorse

To import, sign, and locate keys, you use the Seahorse encryption key manager. On the GNOME desktop, Seahorse is referred to as "Passwords and Encryption Keys." Choose Applications | Accessories | Passwords And Encryption Keys. This entry will run the **seahorse** command that will display the "Passwords And Encryption Keys" window. This window shows four tabs: My Personal Keys, Trusted Keys, Other Collected Keys, and Passwords. When you first start up the utility, it will display three buttons on the lower part of the panel: Help, Import, and New (see Figure 17-8).

Creating a New Private Key

Click the New button (or choose Key | Create New Key) to create your own private/public keys (Figure 17-9). Keep in mind that before you can perform any encryption, you must first set up your own GPG (GPG is the GNU version of PGP) key pair, private and public. You choose whether to set up a PGP or SSH key. Choose the PGP Key entry to set up a GPG key, and then click Continue.

FIGURE 17-9
Choose encryption
key type

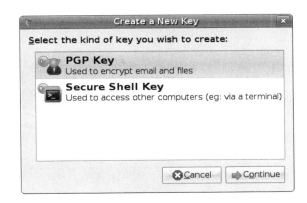

PART VI

Figure 17-10
New PGP Key
dialog

In the New PGP Key dialog (Figure 17-10), enter your name and e-mail address. Click the Advanced Key Options drop-down arrow to set Encryption Type, Key Strength, and Expiration Date. Then click the Create button.

You are then asked to enter a passphrase (Password) for the encryption key (Figure 17-11). This passphrase will allow you to decrypt any data encrypted by your key.

The key is then generated. This can take a some time. During the generation process, a busy notification will let you know the generation is still in process (Figure 17-12).

Once the key is created, it will appear in the My Personal Keys tab of the Passwords And Encryption Keys window (Figure 17-13).

Importing Public Keys

In the Passwords And Encryption Keys window, click the Import button (or choose Key | Import) to import any public keys you may have downloaded. If you know the name of the key file, you can try searching the key servers for it. Choose Remote | Find Remote Keys to open the Find Remote Keys dialog, where you can enter a search string for the key (Figure 17-14). The search term is treated as a prefix, matching on all possible completions.

An expandable tree lists you key servers; choose which ones to search. Results are listed in a new window. Select the one you want, and then either click Import to import the key directly or click Save Key As to save the key as an ASC key file that you can later import. To see information about a key, select it and click the Properties button. Information about the owner and the key is displayed.

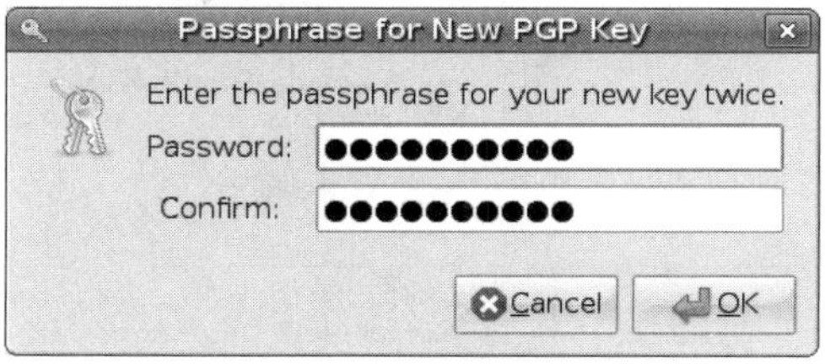

Figure 17-11
Passphrase for
encryption key

Figure 17-12
Generating
encryption key

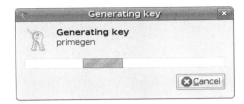

Once you have imported the key, it will appear in the Other Collected Keys tab of the Passwords And Encryption Keys window (Figure 17-15). If you know that you can trust the key, you can sign it, making it a trusted key. Right-click its entry and choose Sign to open a signing dialog, or click the Sign button. You are asked to specify how carefully you have checked this key (Not At All, Casually, and Very Carefully). The key will be moved from the Other Collected Keys tab to the Trusted Keys tab.

When you created your own private key, you also generated a corresponding public key that others can use to decrypt data encrypted with that key. To make your public key available to others, you can export it to a file to send directly to other users, automatically share it with other users on your system, or publish it on a keyserver.

To export your public key to a file, select your key in the My Personal Keys tab and click the Export Public Key button. You can do this for your public keys also. To make keys automatically available to other users, or to publish them on a keyserver, you use the Password And Encryption Settings window which configures Seahorse preferences: choose System | Preferences | Encryption And Keyrings.

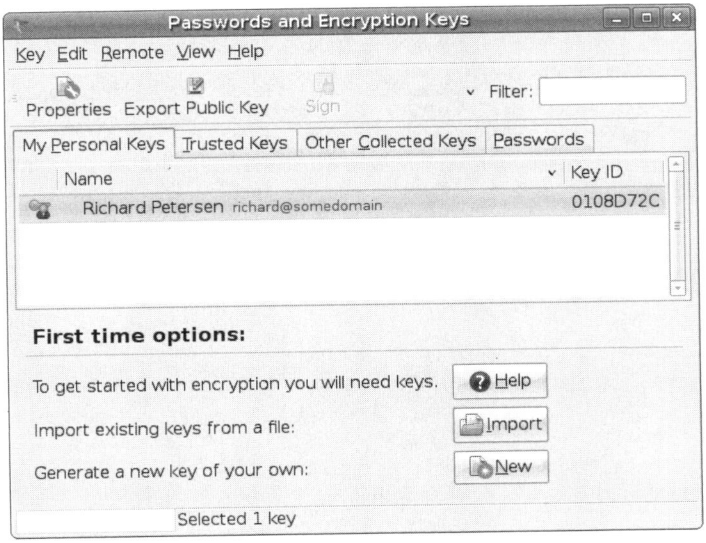

Figure 17-13   My Personal Keys

FIGURE 17-14
Searching for keys

Seahorse integrates support for GPG. Should you import a key with the **gpg** command, it will appear in the Other Collected Keys tab. You can also sign a key using the **gpg** command with the **--sign-key** option, and the key will appear in the Trusted Keys tab.

Seahorse Settings

To manage and configure key support, you use the Password And Encryption Settings window which sets Seahorse preferences. Access it from System | Preferences | Encryption And Keyrings, which runs the **seahorse-preferences** command. The Password And Encryption Settings window opens with five tabs: Password Keyrings, Encryption, PGP Passphrases, Key Servers, and Key Sharing (Figure 17-16).

On the Password Keyrings tab, you can add keyrings and manage their passwords. To create a new keyring, click the Add Keyring button to open a dialog where you can enter the keyring name and password. On the Encryption tab, you can select a default key use. On the PGP Passphrases tab, you can configure passphrase remembering. By default, passphrases are never remembered. You can choose always to remember passphrases or remember them for a particular period of time.

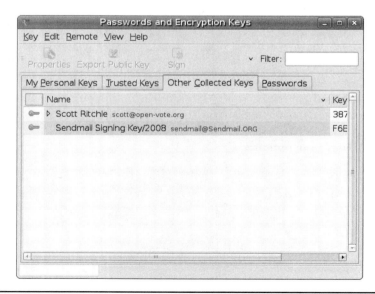

FIGURE 17-15   Other Collected Keys tab

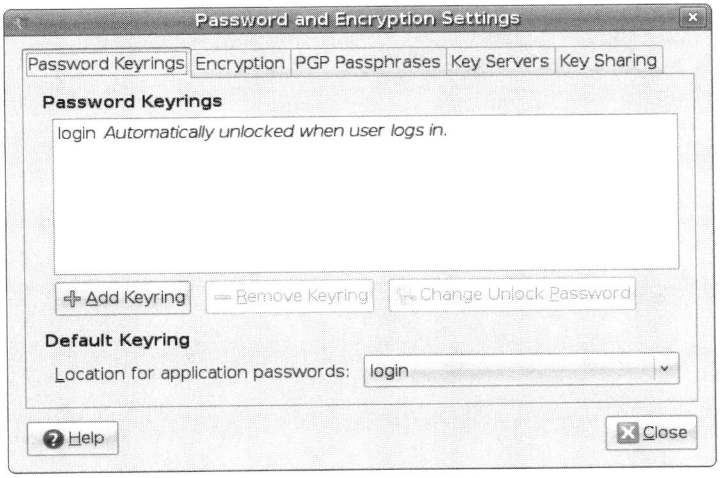

Figure 17-16   Password and Encryption Settings

The Key Servers tab lists keyservers to use. Click the Add key to add a key server, entering its host name (URI). You can choose to publish your public keys on the keyservers (off by default). You can also choose to retrieve keys automatically from the key servers and to synchronize modified keys.

The Key Sharing tab gives you the option to share public keys automatically with other users on your network. Users will have access to all your public keys, which they can use to encrypt messages for files they send to you. You do not have to send them your public keys manually.

Making Your Public Keys Available with Seahorse

To allow other users to decrypt your messages, you must make your public key available to them. They, in turn, have to send you their public keys so that you can decrypt any messages you receive from them. In effect, enabling encrypted communications among users involves all of them exchanging their public keys. The public keys then must be verified and signed by each user who receives them. The public keys can then be trusted to decrypt messages safely.

If you are sending messages to just a few users, you can manually e-mail them your public key. For general public use, you can post your public key on a keyserver, from which anyone can then download and use the key to decrypt any message they receive from you. A keyserver can be accessed using e-mail, Lightweight Directory Access Protocol (LDAP), or the HTTP Horowitz Keyserver Protocol (HKP). (For more information, see the OpenPGP Public Keyserver project at **http://pks.sourceforge.net**.) In Ubuntu, **hkp://pgp.mit.edu:11371** and **ldap://keyserver.pgp.com** will already be selected by Seahorse. On the Password And Encryption Settings window's Key Servers tab, you can choose a keyserver to publish to (Figure 17-17). (To have systems on your local network receive your public keys automatically, click the Share My Keys With Others On My Network check box on the Key Sharing tab.)

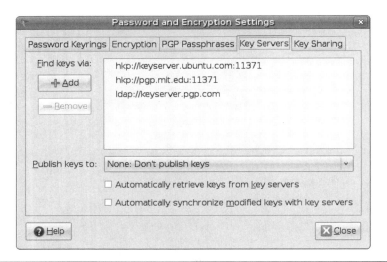

FIGURE 17-17 Key Server management

GNU Privacy Guard: gpg

To protect messages and text files, Ubuntu, like most Linux distributions, provides GnuPG encryption and authentication (**http://gnupg.org**). GnuPG is the GNU open source software that works much like Pretty Good Privacy (PGP) encryption. It is the OpenPGP encryption and signing tool. With GnuPG, you can both encrypt and digitally sign your messages and files—protecting the message or file and authenticating that it is from you.

To protect messages that you send by e-mail, Evolution and KMail both support GnuPG encryption and authentication, along with Thunderbird with added GPG plug-ins. On Evolution, you can select PGP encryption and signatures from the Security menu to use GnuPG (the PGP options use GnuPG). On KMail, you can select the encryption to use on the Security tab in the Options window. For Thunderbird, you can use the **enigmail** extension to support OpenGPG and PGP encryption (**http://enigmail.mozdev.org**).

TIP *You should always send a copy of your encrypted message to yourself. This way, you can decrypt the message and read it as a sent message.*

You can encrypt text files using Gedit as well as the Nautilus file manager. Other applications such as Openoffice.org support digital signatures, authenticating your files.

GnuPG operations are carried out with the **gpg** command, which uses both commands and options to perform tasks. Commonly used commands and options are listed in Table 17-2.

NOTE *Some commands and options have short forms that use only one hyphen, but normally, two hyphens are used.*

GPG Commands	Description
`-s, --sign`	Signs a document, creating a signature; may be combined with `--encrypt`.
`--clearsign`	Creates a clear-text signature.
`-b, --detach-sign`	Creates a detached signature.
`-e, --encrypt`	Encrypts data; may be combined with `--sign`.
`--decrypt` [*file*]	Decrypts file (or **stdin** if no file is specified) and writes it to **stdout** (or the file specified with `--output`). If the decrypted file is signed, the signature is verified.
`--verify` [[*sigfile*] [*signed-files*]]	Verifies a signed file. The signature can be contained with the file or in a separate detached signature file.
`-k, --list-keys` [*names*], `--list-public-keys` [*names*]	Lists all keys from the public keyrings or those specified.
`-K, --list-secret-keys` [*names*]	Lists your private (secret) keys.
`--list-sigs` [*names*]	Lists your keys along with any signatures they have.
`--check-sigs` [*names*]	Lists keys and their signatures and verifies the signatures.
`--fingerprint` [*names*]	Lists fingerprints for specified keys.
`--gen-key`	Generates a new set of private and public keys.
`--edit-key` *name*	Edits your keys. Commands perform most key operations, such as **sign** to sign a key or **passwd** to change your passphrase.
`--sign-key` *name*	Signs a public key with your private key. Same as **sign in --edit-key**.
`--delete-key` *name*	Removes a public key from the public keyring.
`--delete-secret-key` *name*	Removes private and public keys from both the secret and public keyrings.
`--gen-revoke`	Generates a revocation certificate for your own key.
`--export` [*names*]	Exports a specified key from your keyring. With no arguments, exports all keys.
`--send-keys` [*names*]	Exports and sends specified keys to a keyserver. The option `--keyserver` must be used to provide the name of this keyserver.
`--import` [*files*]	Imports keys contained in files into your public keyring.

TABLE **17-2**   GPG Commands and Options

PART VI

GPG Options	Description
`-a, --armor`	Creates ASCII-armored output, ASCII version of encrypted data.
`-o, --output` *file*	Writes output to a specified file.
`--default-key` *name*	Specifies the default private key to use for signatures.
`--keyserver` *site*	Looks up public keys not on your keyring. Can also specify the site to which to send your public key. `host -l pgp.net	grep www.keys` will list the keyservers.
`-r, --recipient` *names*	Encrypts data for the specified user, using that user's public key.
`--default-recipient` *names*	Specifies the default recipient to use for encrypting data.

TABLE 17-2 GPG Commands and Options (*Continued*)

For managing your encryption keys, you can use the GNOME Seahorse Encryption and Keyrings window (Applications | Accessories | Passwords and Encryption Keys), instead of **gpg** commands directly (as discussed in the preceding section). Encryption for text files and the Gedit text editor are provided by the Seahorse plug-in. Other applications, such as Evolution, support encryption directly.

NOTE *If you want to verify the validity of a digital signature, you can use* **gpgv** *instead of* **gpg**. *This is a stripped-down version of* **gpg** *used for signature verification.*

The first time you use **gpg**, a **.gnupg** directory is created in your home directory with a file named **options**. The **.gnupg/gpg.conf** file contains commented default options for GPG operations. You can edit this file and uncomment or change any default options you want implemented for GPG. You can use a different options file by specifying it with the `--options` parameter when invoking **gpg**. Helpful options include keyserver entries. The **.gnupg** directory will also hold encryption files such as **secring.gpg** for your secret keys (secret keyring), **pubring.gpg** for your public keys (public keyring), and **trustdb.gpg**, which is a database for trusted keys.

Generating Your Public Key with gpg

Before you can use GnuPG, you will have to generate your private and public keys. You can do this with the Passwords and Encryption Keys utility described earlier, or use the **gpg** command entered in a terminal window. On the command line (terminal window), enter the **gpg** command with the `--gen-key` command:

```
gpg --gen-key
```

The **gpg** program will then prompt with different options for creating your private and public keys. You can check the **gpg** man page for information on using the **gpg** program.

You are first asked to select the kind of key you want. Normally, you keep the default entry by pressing the ENTER key. Then you choose the key size, usually the default of 1024. You then specify how long the key is to be valid—usually, there is no expiration.

You are then asked to enter a user ID, a comment, and an e-mail address. Press ENTER to see prompts for each in turn. These elements, any of which can be used as the key's name, identify the key. You use the key name when performing certain GPG tasks such as signing a key or creating a revocation certificate. For example, the following elements create a key for the user **richlp** with the comment **author** and the e-mail address **richlp@turtle.mytrek.com**:

```
Richard Petersen (author) <richlp@turtle.mytrek.com>
```

You can use any unique part of a key's identity to reference that key. For example, the string *Richard* would reference the preceding key, provided there are no other keys that have the string *Richard* in them. The string *richlp* would also reference the key, as would *author*. Where a string matches more than one key, all those matched would be referenced.

After you have entered your user ID, comment, and e-mail address, the elements are displayed along with a menu that will allow you to change any element:

```
Change (N)ame, (C)omment, (E)mail or (O)kay/(Q)uit?
```

Enter **o** to approve and accept the key.

The **gpg** program will then ask you to enter a passphrase, used to protect your private key. Be sure to use a real phrase, including spaces—not just a password. **gpg** then generates your public and private keys and places them in the **.gnupg** directory. This may take a few minutes.

The private keys are kept in a file called **secring.gpg** in your **.gnupg** directory. The public key is placed in the **pubring.gpg** file, to which you can add the public keys of other users. You can list these keys with the **--list-keys**, **--list-public-keys**, or **-k** command:

```
gpg --list-keys
```

To list your private keys you would use the **--list-secret-keys** or **-K** command:

```
gpg --list-secret-keys
```

If you need to change your keys later, you can create a revocation certificate to notify others that the public key is no longer valid. For example, if you forget your password or someone else discovers it, you can use the revocation certificate to tell others that your public key should no longer be used. In the next example, the user creates a revocation certificate for the key **richlp** and places it in the file **myrevoke.asc**:

```
gpg --output myrevoke.asc --gen-revoke richlp
```

Importing Public Keys

To decode messages from other users, you will need to have their public keys. Either they can send them to you or you can download them from a keyserver. Save the message or Web page containing the public key to a file. You will then need to import the key, and you should also verify and sign the key. Use the file you received to import the public key to your **pubring** file. As noted previously, you can also use the Seahorse Passwords and Encryption

Keys utility (Applications | Accessories | Passwords And Encryption Keys) to import and sign keys. In the following example, the user imports **george**'s public key, which he has received as the file **georgekey.asc**:

```
gpg --import georgekey.asc
```

You can also use the **gpg --search-key** and **--keyserver** options to import a key. Keys matching the search term will be displayed in a numbered list. You will be prompted to enter the number of the key you want. The 2007 Sendmail key from the results from the following example would be 7. This is the key used for 2007 released software.

```
$ gpg --keyserver pgp.mit.edu  --search-keys Sendmail
gpg: searching for "Sendmail" from hkp server pgp.mit.edu
(1)     Sendmail Signing Key/2008 <sendmail@Sendmail.ORG>
          1024 bit RSA key F6B30729, created: 2008-01-18
. . . . . .
(7)     Sendmail Signing Key/2007 <sendmail@Sendmail.ORG>
          1024 bit RSA key 7093B841, created: 2006-12-16
Enter number(s), N)ext, or Q)uit > 7
gpg: requesting key 7093B841 from hkp server pgp.mit.edu
gpg: key 7093B841: public key "Sendmail Signing Key/2007
<sendmail@Sendmail.ORG>" imported
gpg: 3 marginal(s) needed, 1 complete(s) needed, PGP trust model
gpg: depth: 0  valid:   1  signed:   0  trust: 0-, 0q, 0n, 0m, 0f, 1u
gpg: Total number processed: 1
gpg:                    imported: 1  (RSA: 1)
```

NOTE *You can remove any key, including your own private key, using the* **--delete-key** *and* **--delete-secret-key** *commands.*

Signing Your Public Keys

If you trust the imported key, you can then sign it, making it a trusted key (these will show up in the Trusted Keys tab of the Passwords and Encryption Keys window). To sign a key, you use the **gpg** command with the **--sign-key** command and the key's name:

```
gpg --sign-key george@rabbit
```

Alternatively, you can edit the key with the **--edit-key** command to start an interactive session in which you can enter the command **sign** to sign the key and **save** to save the change. Signing a key involves accessing your private key, so you will be prompted for your passphrase.

In this example, the e-mail address is used for the key name. You are prompted to make sure you want to sign it. Then you have to enter the passphrase for your own GPG key.

```
$ gpg --sign-key sendmail@Sendmail.ORG
pub  1024R/7093B841  created: 2006-12-16  expires: never       usage: SCEA
                     trust: unknown      validity: unknown
[ unknown] (1). Sendmail Signing Key/2007 <sendmail@Sendmail.ORG>
pub  1024R/7093B841  created: 2006-12-16  expires: never       usage: SCEA
                     trust: unknown      validity: unknown
```

```
Primary key fingerprint: D9 FD C5 6B EE 1E 7A A8  CE 27 D9 B9 55 8B 56 B6
     Sendmail Signing Key/2007 <sendmail@Sendmail.ORG>
Are you sure that you want to sign this key with your
key "Richard Petersen <richard@somedomain>" (0108D72C)
Really sign? (y/N) y
You need a passphrase to unlock the secret key for
user: "Richard Petersen <richard@somedomain>"
1024-bit DSA key, ID 0108D72C, created 2008-03-26
```

For public keys in your keyrings, you can set different trust levels. GPG supports several trust levels, including marginal, full trust, and ultimate. You use the **--edit-key** command with the **trust** option to set the trust level:

```
gpg --edit-key george@rabbit trust
```

This will display a menu of several options:

```
1 = I don't know or won't say
2 = I do NOT trust
3 = I trust marginally
4 = I trust full
5 = I trust ultimately
m = back to main menu
```

The **--edit-key** command actually runs a shell in which you can enter a variety of different key modification operations, such as **trust** to set the trust level, **keyserver** to indicate where the key can be found, and **sign** to sign the key. Use the **quit** command to quit the edit-key shell.

You can also check the fingerprint of the key for added verification. To check manually that a public key file was not modified in transit, you can check its fingerprint. This is a hash value generated from the contents of the key, much like a modification digest. Using the **--fingerprint** option, you can generate a hash value from the key you installed, and then contact the sender and ask her what the hash value should really be. If they are not the same, you know the key was tampered with in transit.

TIP *You can use the* **--fingerprint** *option to check a key's validity. If you are confident that the key is valid, you can then sign it with the* **--sign-key** *command.*

You do not have to check the fingerprint to have **gpg** operate. This is just an advisable precaution you can perform on your own. The point is that you need to be confident that the key you received is valid. Normally, you can accept most keys from public servers or known sites as valid, although it is easy to check their posted fingerprints. Once assured of the key's validity, you can then sign it with your private key. Signing a key notifies **gpg** that you officially accept the key.

Publishing Keys

You can use the **gpg** command with the **-keyserver** option and **--send-key** command to send keys directly to a keyserver. The **--send-key** command takes as its argument your e-mail address. You need to send only to one keyserver, as it will share your key with other keyservers automatically. You can also use the Seahorse Password and Encryption Settings window's Key Sharing and Key Servers tabs to publish your keys. The following command publishes a key to the **pgp.mit.edu** keyserver:

```
gpg --keyserver pgp.mit.edu:11371 --send-key chris@turtle.mytrek.com
```

If you want to send your key directly to another user, you should generate an armored text version of the key that you can then e-mail. You do this with the **--armor** and **--export** options, using the **--output** option to specify a file in which to place the key. The **--armor** option will generate an ASCII text version of the encrypted file so that it can be e-mailed directly, instead of as an attached binary. Files that hold an ASCII-encoded version of the encryption normally have the extension **.asc**, by convention. Binary encrypted files normally use the extension **.gpg**. You can then e-mail the file to users to which you want to send encrypted messages.

```
# gpg --armor --export richlp@turtle.mytrek.com --output richlp.asc
# mail -s 'mypubkey' george@rabbit.mytrek.com < richlp.asc
```

Many companies and institutions post their public key files on their Web sites, where they can be downloaded and used to verify encrypted software downloads or official announcements.

NOTE *Some commands and options for GPG have both long and short forms. For example, the* **--armor** *command can be written as* **-a**, **--output** *as* **-o**, **--sign** *as* **-s**, *and* **--encrypt** *as* **-e**. *Most others, such as* **--export**, *have no short form.*

Using GPG

GPG encryption is currently supported by most mail clients, including KMail, Thunderbird, and Evolution. You can use the **gpg** command to encode and decode messages manually, including digital signatures. Seahorse provides several GPG encryption plug-ins for use with Evolution and Gedit.

Encrypting and Decrypting Data with the gpg Command

The **gpg** command provides several options for managing secure messages. The **e** option encrypts messages, the **a** option generates an armored text version, and the **s** option (used by e-mail applications) adds a digital signature. You will need to specify the recipient's public key, which you should already have imported into your **pubring** file. This key is used to encrypt the message. The recipient will then be able to decode the message with her private key. Use the **--recipient** or **-r** option to specify the name of the recipient key. You can use any unique substring in the user's public key name, but the e-mail address usually suffices. You use the **d** option to decode received messages. In the following example, the user encrypts (**e**) and signs (**s**) a file generated in armored text format (**a**). The **-r** option indicates the recipient for the message (whose public key is used to encrypt the message):

```
gpg e -s -a -o myfile.asc -r george@rabbit.mytrek.com myfile
# mail george@rabbit.mytrek.com < myrile.asc
```

You can leave out the ASCII armor option if you want to send or transfer the file as a binary attachment. Without the **--armor** or **-a** option, **gpg** generates an encoded binary file, not an encoded text file. This is the method used for encryption by Nautilus. A binary file can be transmitted through e-mail only as an attachment. As noted previously, ASCII-armored versions usually have an extension of **.asc**, whereas binary version use **.gpg**.

When the other user receives the file, they can save it to a file named something like **myfile.asc** and then decode the file with the **-d** option. The **-o** option will specify a file in which to save the decoded version. GPG will automatically determine whether this is a binary file or an ASCII-armored version.

```
gpg -d -o myfile.txt myfile.asc
```

To check the digital signature of the file, use the **gpg** command with the **--verify** option. This assumes that the sender has signed the file.

```
gpg --verify myfile.asc
```

NOTE *You can use* **gpgsplit** *to split a GPG message into its components to examine them separately.*

As you perform GPG tasks, you will need to reference the keys you have using their key names. Bear in mind that you need only a unique identifying substring to select the key you want. GPG performs a pattern search on the string you specify as the key name in any given command. If the string matches more than one key, all matching keys will be selected.

Seahorse Plug-ins: Choose Recipients

Plug-ins are provided for Gedit to encrypt text files, the Epiphany Web browser for text phrases, and Nautilus to perform encryption from the context menu. A panel applet lets you encrypt, sign, and decrypt clipboard content.

The Seahorse Choose Recipients plug-in opens a window in which you can choose the key to use for encryption (Figure 17-18). A pop-up menu lets you use all keys, only selected recipients, or search results. A search box lets you search for keys, selecting them based on a pattern you enter. Available keys will be listed in the window by name and key ID. You also have the option of signing the message, by selecting signatures from the Sign Message As pop-up menu. Once you make your selection, you will be prompted to enter the passphrase for that encryption key.

Encrypting and Decrypting Files with Nautilus

Nautilus will generate an encrypted copy of a file with the extension **.gpg**. This tool operates like **gpg** with the **-e** option, and no **-a** option. To encrypt a file from Nautilus, select the file and then right-click to open the Nautilus pop-up menu. Choose the Encrypt option. Or select the file and choose Edit | Encrypt. The Choose Recipients window then opens, letting you select the encryption keys and digital signature to use. Select the encryption key, and you will be prompted to enter the key's passphrase. Then an encrypted copy of the file will be generated with the extension **.pgp**. The original is left untouched.

If you only want to sign a file, you can choose Edit | Sign (or right-click the filename and choose Sign). This opens a dialog with a pop-up menu listing digital signatures you can use.

Figure 17-18
Choose Recipients
window

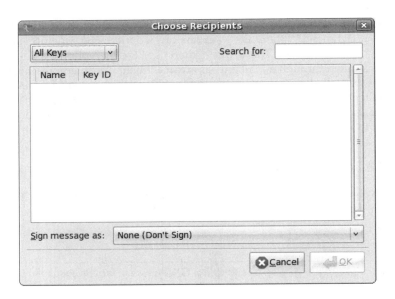

Figure 17-18
Choose Recipients
window

To decrypt the encrypted **.pgp** file, double-click it, or right-click and select "Open With Decrypt File." This opens the file with the decrypt tool, which generates a decrypted copy of the file. A "Choose decrypted file name" dialog will then open, where you can enter the name for the copy and the directory in which save it. You are then prompted for the passphrase.

Encrypting Data with Gedit

Gedit is designed to create armored text–encrypted files, the kind you would send as an e-mail. It will change the original text file, transforming the text into an encoded armor ASCII equivalent, with *BEGIN* and *END* entries for the encoded data. You could then send the text directly as a message. To decode, be sure to select the entire encoded text, including the *BEGIN* and *END* lines. You will be prompted for the passphrase for the key. If signed, the signature will also be checked.

To encrypt files with Gedit, you first have to enable encryption. Open Gedit and choose Edit | Preferences. On the Preferences window, select the Plugins tab. Scroll down the list of active plug-ins and click the check box for Text Encryption. Now, on the Gedit Edit menu, you will see entries for Sign, Decrypt/Verify, and Encrypt.

Choose Edit | Encrypt to encrypt the message or Edit | Sign to sign it. When you choose Encrypt, the Choose Recipients dialog, opens where you can select the encryption keys to use. If you choose Sign, a small dialog appears with a pop-up menu listing digital signatures you can use. To decrypt or verify, first select the text and then select the Decrypt/Verify entry.

Decrypting a Digital Signature

You will need to have the signer's public key to decode and check the digital signature. If you do not have they key, you will receive a message saying that the public key was not found. In this case, you will have to obtain the signer's public key. You can access a keyserver that you think may have the public key or request the public key directly from a Web site or from the signer. Then import the key as described earlier.

Signing Messages

Most applications that handle text and data files provide the ability to sign those files. For the Gedit editor and Nautilus file browser, a window opens with a pop-up menu letting you choose the key to use to sign the file. On Evolution you can select the PGP Signature entry from the Security menu in the Compose Message window.

NOTE   *One very effective use for digital signatures is to verify that a software package has not been altered. A software package could be intercepted in transmission and some of its system-level files changed or substituted. Software packages for Ubuntu, as well as those by reputable GNU and Linux projects, are digitally signed. The signature provides modification digest information with which to check the integrity of the package (see Chapter 7).*

You do not have to encrypt a file to sign it. A digital signature is a separate component. You can either combine the signature with a file or generate a signature file separately. To combine a signature with a file, you generate a new version that incorporates both. Use the **--sign** or **-s** option to generate a version of the document that includes the digital signature. In the following example, the **mydoc** file is digitally signed with **mydoc.gpg** file containing both the original file and the signature:

```
gpg  -o mydoc.gpg  --sign mydoc
```

If, instead, you want to generate a separate signature file, you use the **--detach-sig** command. This has the advantage of not having to generate a complete copy of the original file. That file remains untouched. The signature file usually has an extension such as **.sig**. In the following example, the user creates a signature file called **mydoc2.sig** for the **mydoc2** file:

```
gpg -o mydoc2.sig --detach-sig mydoc2
```

To verify the file using a detached signature, the recipient user specifies both the signature file and the original file:

```
gpg --verify mydoc2.sig  mydoc2
```

To verify a trusted signature, you can use **gpgv**. You can also generate a clear sign signature to be used in text files. A *clear sign* signature is a text version of the signature that can be attached to a text file. The text file can be further edited by any text editor. Use the **--clearsign** option to create a clear sign signature. The following example creates a clear signed version of a text file called **mysignotice.txt**:

```
gpg -o mysignotice.txt --clearsign mynotice.txt
```

Permissions: Discretionary Access Control

Each file and directory in Linux contains a set of permissions that determine who can access it and how. These are known as *discretionary access controls (DACs)*. You set these permissions to limit access in one of three ways: you can restrict access to yourself alone, you can allow users in a predesignated group to have access, or you can permit anyone on your system to have access. You can also control how a given file or directory is accessed.

Read, Write, and Execute

A file or directory may have read, write, and execute permissions. When you create a file, you, as the creator/owner, are automatically given read and write permissions, enabling you to display and modify the file. You may change these permissions to any combination you want. A file can also have read-only permission, which prevents any modifications.

TIP   *From GNOME and KDE desktops, you can change permissions easily by right-clicking a file or directory icon and choosing Properties. On the Properties window's Permissions tab, you will see options for setting Owner, Group, and Other permissions.*

Three different categories of users can have access to a file or directory: the owner, the group, and all others not belonging to that group. The *owner* is the user who created the file. Any file you create, you own. You can also permit a *group* to have access to a file. Users are often collected into groups, especially in network situations in businesses. For example, all the users for a given class or project can be formed into a group by the system administrator. A user can grant access to a file to the members of a designated group. Finally, you can also open up access to a file to all other users on the system. In this case, every user who is not part of the file's group can have access to that file. In this sense, every other user on the system makes up the "others" category. If you want to give the same access to all users on your system, you set the same permissions for both the group and others. That way, you include both members of the group (group permission) and all those users who are not members (others permission).

Each category has its own set of read, write, and execute permissions. The first set controls the user's own access to his or her files—the owner access. The second set controls the access of the group to a user's files. The third set controls the access of all other users to the user's files. The three sets of read, write, and execute permissions for the three categories—owner, group, and other—make a total of nine types of permissions.

The `ls` command with the `-l` option displays detailed information about the file, including the permissions. In the following example's second line, the first few characters show the permissions set for the **mydata** file:

```
$ ls -l mydata
-rw-r--r-- 1 chris weather 207 Feb 20 11:55 mydata
```

An empty permission is represented by a dash (-). The read permission is represented by **r**, write by **w**, and execute by **x**. Notice that 10 permission characters are displayed here. The first character indicates the file type. In a general sense, a directory can be considered a type of file. If the first character is a dash, it means a file is being listed. If the first character is **d**, information about a directory is being displayed. The next 9 characters are arranged according to the different user categories. The first set of 3 characters is the owner's set of permissions for the file. The second set of 3 characters is the group's set of permissions for the file. The last set of 3 characters is the other users' set of permissions for the file.

Permissions on GNOME and KDE

On GNOME, you can set a directory or file permission using the Permissions tab in the Properties window. Right-click the file or directory entry in the file manager window and choose Properties and open the Permissions tab (Figure 17-19). Here you will find pop-up

FIGURE **17-19**
Setting file
permissions on
GNOME

menus for Read, Write, and Execute along with rows for Owner, Group, and Other. You can set owner permissions as Read Only or Read And Write. For the group and others, you can also set the None option, denying access. The group name expands to a pop-up menu listing different groups; select one to change the file's group. If you want to execute this as an application (say, a shell script) check the Allow Executing File As Program entry. This has the effect of setting the execute permission.

The Permissions tab for directories (Figure 17-20) operates much the same way, but it includes two access entries: Folder Access and File Access. The Folder Access entry controls access to the folder with options for List Files Only, Access Files, and Create And Delete Files. These correspond to the read, read and execute, and read/write/execute permissions granted to directories. The File Access entry lets you set permissions for all those files in the directory. They are the same as those for files: for the owner, Read or Read and Vi Write; for the group and others, the entry adds a None option to deny access. To set the permissions for all the files in the directory accordingly (not just the folder), click the Apply Permissions To Enclosed Files button.

On KDE, you can set a directory or file permission using the Permissions tab of the Properties window. Right-click the file or directory entry in the file manager window and choose Properties. On the Permissions tab, you'll find pop-up menus for Owner, Group, and Others. Options include Can Read, Can Read and Write, and Forbidden. For more refined access, click the Advanced Permissions button to display a table for checking read, write, and execute access (**r**, **w**, **x**) for owner, group, and others. You can also set the sticky bit and user and group ID permissions. The Add Entry button lets you set up ACL access, specifying certain users or groups that can or cannot have access to the file.

Directories have slightly different options: Can View Content and Can View and Modify Content, which are the read and write permissions. You have the option to apply changes to all subdirectories and the files in them. Clicking the Advanced Permissions button displays the same read, write, and execute table for owner, group, and others. Click a table entry to toggle a permission on or off. The selected permissions are shown in the Effective column. Use the Add Entry button to add ACL entries to control access by specific users and groups.

PART VI

FIGURE 17-20
Directory
Permissions on
GNOME

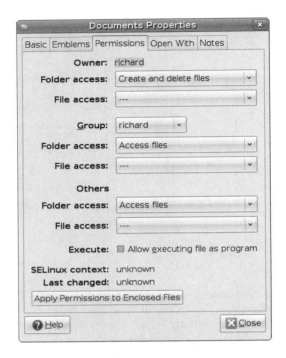

FIGURE 17-20
Directory
Permissions on
GNOME

chmod

You use the **chmod** command to change permission configurations. The **chmod** command takes two lists as its arguments: permission changes and filenames. You can specify the list of permissions in two different ways: One way uses permission symbols and is called the *symbolic method*. The other uses what is known as a *binary mask* and is called either the *absolute* or the *relative* method. Table 17-3 lists options for the **chmod** command.

NOTE   *When a program is owned by the root, setting the user ID permission will give the user the ability to execute the program with root permissions. This can be a serious security risk for any program that can effect changes—such as* **rm***, which removes files.*

Ownership

Files and directories belong both to an owner and a group. A group usually consists of a collection of users that all belong to the same group. In the following example, the **mydata** file is owned by the user **robert** and belongs to the group **weather**:

```
-rw-r--r-- 1 robert weather 207 Feb 20 11:55 mydata
```

A group can also consist of one user, normally the user who creates the file. Each user on the system, including the root user, is assigned her own group of which she is the only

Command or Option	Execution
chmod	Changes the permission of a file or directory.
Options	
+	Adds a permission.
-	Removes a permission.
=	Assigns entire set of permissions.
r	Sets read permission for a file or directory. A file can be displayed or printed; a directory can have the list of its files displayed.
w	Sets write permission for a file or directory. A file can be edited or erased, and a directory can be removed.
x	Sets execute permission for a file or directory. If the file is a shell script, it can be executed as a program. A directory can be changed to and entered.
u	Sets permissions for the user who created and owns the file or directory.
g	Sets permissions for group access to a file or directory.
o	Sets permissions for access to a file or directory by all other users on the system.
a	Sets permissions for access by the owner, group, and all other users.
s	Sets user ID and group ID permission; program owned by owner and group.
t	Sets sticky bit permission; program remains in memory.
Commands	
chgrp *groupname filenames*	Changes the group for a file or files.
chown *user-name filenames*	Changes the owner of a file or files.
ls -l *filename*	Lists a filename with its permissions displayed.
ls -ld *directory*	Lists a directory name with its permissions displayed.
ls -l	Lists all files in a directory with its permissions displayed.

TABLE 17-3   File and Directory Permission Operations

member, ensuring access by that user only. In the next example, the report file is owned by the **robert** user and belongs to that user's single-user group, **robert**:

```
-rw-r--r-- 1 robert robert 305 Mar 17 12:01 report
```

The root user, the system administrator, owns most of the system files that also belong to the root group, of which only the root user is a member. Most administration files, such as configuration files in the **/etc** directory, are owned by the root user and belong to the root group. Only the root user has permission to modify them, whereas normal users can read and, in the case of programs, also execute them. In the next example, the **root** user owns the **fstab** file in the **/etc** directory, which also belongs to the **root** user group:

```
-rw-r--r-- 1 root root 621 Apr 22 11:03 fstab
```

Certain directories and files located in the system directories are owned by a service, rather than the root user, because the services need to change those files directly. This is particularly true for services that interact with remote users, such as Internet servers. Most of these files are located in the **/var** directory. Here you will find files and directories managed by services such as the Squid proxy server and the Domain Name Server (named). In this example, the Squid proxy server directory is owned by the **squid** user and belongs to the **squid** group:

```
drwxr-x--- 2 squid squid 4096 Jan 24 16:29 squid
```

Changing a File's Owner or Group: chown and chgrp

Although other users may be able to access a file, only the owner can change its permissions. If, however, you want to give some other user control over one of your file's permissions, you can change the owner of the file from yourself to the other user. The **chown** command transfers control over a file to another user. This command takes as its first argument the name of the other user. Following the username, you list the files you are transferring. In the next example, the user gives control of the **mydata** file to user **robert**:

```
$ chown robert mydata
$ ls -l mydata
-rw-r--r-- 1 robert weather 207 Feb 20 11:55 mydata
```

You can also, if you wish, change the group for a file, using the **chgrp** command. **chgrp** takes as its first argument the name of the new group for a file or files. Following the new group name, you list the files you want changed to that group. In the next example, the user changes the group name for **today** and **weekend** to the **forecast** group. The **ls -l** command then reflects the group change:

```
$ chgrp forecast today weekend
$ ls -l
-rw-rw-r-- 1 chris forecast 568 Feb 14 10:30 today
-rw-rw-r-- 1 chris forecast 308 Feb 17 12:40 weekend
```

You can combine the **chgrp** operation with the **chown** command by attaching a group to the new owner with a colon:

```
$ chown george:forecast tomorrow
-rw-rw-r-- 1 george forecast 568 Feb 14 10:30 tomorrow
```

Setting Permissions: Permission Symbols

The symbolic method of setting permissions uses the characters **r**, **w**, and **x** for read, write, and execute, respectively. Any of these permissions can be added or removed. The symbol to add a permission is the plus sign, **+**. The symbol to remove a permission is the minus sign, **-**.

In the next example, the **chmod** command adds the execute permission and removes the write permission for the **mydata** file for all categories. The read permission is not changed.

```
$ chmod +x-w mydata
```

Permission symbols also specify each user category. The owner, group, and others categories are represented by the **u**, **g**, and **o** characters, respectively. Notice the owner category is represented by a **u** and can be thought of as the user. The symbol for a category is placed before a plus and minus sign preceding the read, write, and execute permissions. If no category symbol is used, all categories are assumed, and the permissions specified are set for the user, group, and others. In the next example, the first **chmod** command sets the permissions for the group to read and write. The second **chmod** command sets permissions for other users to read. Notice no spaces are between the permission specifications and the category. The permissions list is simply one long phrase, with no spaces.

```
$ chmod g+rw mydata
$ chmod o+r mydata
```

A user may remove permissions as well as add them. In the next example, the read permission is set for other users, but the write and execute permissions are removed:

```
$ chmod o+r-wx mydata
```

Another permission character exists, **a**, which represents all the categories. The **a** character is the default. In the next example, the two commands are equivalent. The read permission is explicitly set with the **a** character denoting all types of users—other, group, and user:

```
$ chmod a+r mydata
$ chmod +r mydata
```

One of the most common permission operations is setting a file's executable permission. This is often done in the case of shell program files. The executable permission indicates a file contains executable instructions and can be directly run by the system. In the next example, the file **lsc** has its executable permission set and then executed:

```
$ chmod u+x lsc
$ lsc
main.c lib.c
$
```

Absolute Permissions: Binary Masks

Instead of using the permission symbols shown in Table 17-3, many users find it convenient to use the absolute method. The *absolute method* changes all the permissions at once, instead of specifying one or the other. It uses a *binary mask* that references all the permissions in each category. The three categories, each with three permissions, conform to an octal binary format. Octal numbers have a Base 8 structure. When translated into a binary number, each octal digit becomes three binary digits. A binary number is a set of *1* and *0* digits. Three octal digits in a number translate into three sets of three binary digits, which is nine altogether—and the exact number of permissions for a file.

You can use the octal digits as a mask to set the different file permissions. Each octal digit applies to one of the user categories. You can think of the digits matching up with the permission categories from left to right, beginning with the owner category. The first octal digit applies to the owner category, the second to the group, and the third to the others category. The actual octal digit you choose determines the read, write, and execute permissions for each category. At this point, you need to know how octal digits translate into their binary equivalents.

Calculating Octal Numbers

A simple way to calculate the octal number makes use of the fact that any number used for permissions will be a combination derived from adding in decimal terms the numbers 4, 2, and 1. Use 4 for read permission, 2 for write, and 1 for execute. The read, write, execute permission is simply the addition of 4 + 2 + 1 to get 7. The read and execute permission adds 4 and 1 to get 5. You can use this method to calculate the octal number for each category. To get 755, you would add 4 + 2 + 1 for the owner read, write, and execute permission; 4 + 1 for the group read and execute permission; and 4 + 1 again for the other read and execute permission.

Binary Masks

When dealing with a binary mask, you need to specify three digits for all three categories, as well as their permissions. This makes a binary mask less versatile than the permission symbols. To set the owner execute permission on and the write permission off for the **mydata** file and retain the read permission, you need to use the octal digit 5 (binary 101). At the same time, you need to specify the digits for group and other users access. If these categories are to retain read access, you need the octal number 4 for each (100). This gives you three octal digits, 544, which translate into the binary digits 101 100 100.

```
$ chmod 544 mydata
```

Execute Permissions

One of the most common uses of the binary mask is to set the execute permission. You can create files that contain Linux commands, called *shell scripts.* To execute the commands in a shell script, you must first indicate that the file is executable—that it contains commands the system can execute. You can do this in several ways, one of which is to set the executable permission on the shell script file. Suppose, for example, that you just completed a shell script file and you need to give it executable permission to run it. You also want to retain read and write permission but deny any access by the group or other users. The octal digit 7 (111) will set all three permissions, including execute (you can also add 4-read, 2-write, and 1-execute to get 7). Using 0 for the group and other users denies them access. This gives you the digits 700, which are equivalent to the binary digits 111 000 000. In this example, the owner permission for the **myprog** file is set to include execute permission:

```
$ chmod 700 myprog
```

If you want others to be able to execute and read the file but not change it, you can set the read and execute permissions and turn off the write permission with the digit 5 (101). In this case, you use the octal digits 755, having the binary equivalent of 111 101 101:

```
$ chmod 755 myprog
```

Directory Permissions

You can also set permissions on directories. The read permission set on a directory allows the list of files in a directory to be displayed. The execute permission enables a user to change to that directory. The write permission enables a user to create and remove his files in that directory. If you allow other users to have write permission on a directory, they can add their own files to it. When you create a directory, you are automatically given read, write, and execute permissions. You may list the files in that directory, change to the directory, and create files in it.

Like files, directories have sets of permissions for the owner, the group, and all other users. Often, you may want to allow other users to change to and list the files in one of your directories but not let them add their own files to the directory. In this case, you set read and execute permissions on the directory but you don't set a write permission. This allows other users to change to the directory and list the files in it but not to create new files or to copy any of their files into it. The next example sets read and execute permissions for the group for the **thankyou** directory but removes the write permission. Members of the group may enter the **thankyou** directory and list the files there, but they may not create new ones.

```
$ chmod g+rx-w letters/thankyou
```

Just as with files, you can also use octal digits to set a directory permission. To set the same permissions as in the preceding example, you use the octal digits *750*, which have the binary equivalents of *111 101 000*.

```
$ chmod 750 letters/thankyou
```

Displaying Directory Permissions

The **ls** command with the **-l** option lists all files in a directory. To list only the information about the directory itself, add a **d** modifier. In the next example, **ls -ld** displays information about the **thankyou** directory. Notice the first character in the permissions list is **d**, indicating it is a directory:

```
$ ls -ld thankyou
drwxr-x--- 2 chris 512 Feb 10 04:30 thankyou
```

Parent Directory Permissions

If you want other users to have access to a file, you not only need to set permissions for that file, but you must make sure the permissions are set for the directory in which the file is located. To access your file, a user must first access the file's directory. The same applies to parents of directories. Although a directory may give permission to others to access it, if its parent directory denies access, the directory cannot be reached. Therefore, you must pay close attention to your directory tree. To provide access to a directory, all other directories above it in the directory tree must also be accessible to other users.

Ownership Permissions

In addition to the read/write/execute permissions, you can also set ownership permissions for executable programs. Normally, the user who runs a program owns it while it is running, even though the program file itself may be owned by another user. The Set User ID permission allows the original owner of the program to own it always, even while another user is running the program. For example, most software on the system is owned by the root user but is run by ordinary users. Some such software may have to modify files owned by the root. In this case, the ordinary user needs to run that program with the root retaining ownership so that the program can have the permissions to change those root-owned files. The Group ID permission works the same way, except it applies to groups. Programs owned by a group retain ownership, even when run by users from another group. The program can then change the owner group's files. A potential security risk is involved in that you are essentially giving a user some limited root-level access.

Using Symbols

To add both the User ID and Group ID permissions to a file, you use the **s** option. The following example adds the User ID permission to the **pppd** program, which is owned by the root user. When an ordinary user runs **pppd**, the root user retains ownership, allowing the **pppd** program to change root-owned files.

```
# chmod +s /usr/sbin/pppd
```

The Set User ID and Set Group ID permissions show up as an **s** in the execute position of the owner and group segments. Set User ID and Group ID are essentially variations of the execute permission, **x**. Read, write, and User ID permissions are **rws** instead of **rwx**.

```
# ls -l /usr/sbin/pppd
-rwsr-sr-x 1 root root 184412 Jan 24 22:48 /usr/sbin/pppd
```

Using the Binary Method

For the ownership permissions, you add another octal number to the beginning of the octal digits. The octal digit for User ID permission is *4* (*100*) and for Group ID, it is *2* (*010*) (use *6* to set both—*110*). The following example sets the User ID permission to the **pppd** program, along with read and execute permissions for the owner, group, and others:

```
# chmod 4555 /usr/sbin/pppd
```

Sticky Bit Permissions

Another special permission provides for greater security on directories. Originally, the *sticky bit* was used to keep a program in memory after it finished execution to increase efficiency. Current Linux systems ignore this feature. Instead, it is used for directories to protect files within them. Files in a directory with the sticky bit set can be deleted or renamed only by the root user or the owner of the directory.

Using Symbols

The sticky bit permission symbol is **t**. The sticky bit shows up as a **t** in the execute position of the other permissions. A program with read and execute permissions with the sticky bit has its permissions displayed as **r-t**. Here's an example:

```
# chmod +t /home/dylan/myreports
# ls -l /home/dylan/myreports
-rwxr-xr-t 1 root root 4096 /home/dylan/myreports
```

Using the Binary Method

As with ownership, for sticky bit permissions, you add another octal number to the beginning of the octal digits. The octal digit for the sticky bit is *1 (001)*. The following example sets the sticky bit for the **myreports** directory:

```
# chmod 1755 /home/dylan/myreports
```

The next example sets both the sticky bit and the User ID permission on the **newprogs** directory. The permission *5755* has the binary equivalent of *101 111 101 101*:

```
# chmod 5755 /usr/bin/newprogs
# ls -l /usr/bin/newprogs
drwsr-xr-t 1 root root 4096  /usr/bin/newprogs
```

Permission Defaults: umask

Whenever you create a file or directory, it is given default permissions. You can display the current defaults or change them with the **umask** command. The permissions are displayed in binary or symbolic format as described in the following sections. The default permissions include any execute permissions that are applied to a directory. Execute permission for a file is turned off by default when you create it because standard data files do not use the executable permissions (to make a file executable like a script, you have to set its execute permission manually). To display the current default permissions, use the **umask** command with no arguments. Use the **-S** option for the symbolic format:

```
$ umask -S
u=rwx,g=rx,o=rx
```

This default **umask** provides **rw-r--r--** permission for standard files and adds execute permission for directories, **rwxr-xr-x**.

You can set a new default by specifying permissions in either symbolic or binary format. To specify the new permissions, use the **-S** option. The following example denies others read permission, while allowing user and group read access, which results in permissions of **rwxr-x---**:

```
$ umask -S  u=rwx,g=rx,o=
```

When you use the binary format, the mask is the inverse of the permissions you want to set. To set both the read and execute permissions on and the write permission off, you use the octal number *2*, (binary *010*). To set all permissions on, you use an octal *0* (binary *000*). The following example shows the mask for the permission defaults **rwx**, **rx**, and **rx** (**rw**, **r**, and **r** for files):

```
$ umask
0022
```

To set the default to deny all permissions only for others, you use *0027*, using the binary mask *0111* for the other permissions:

```
$ umask 0027
```

Access Control Lists: FACL

Users can provide more refined control of their files and directories by using ACLs, which maintain lists of users and groups and the rights they have to access certain files and directories. ACLs allow for much more refined access to directories, instead of just the all-or-nothing approach of owners, groups, and other. With ACLs, only specific users could be granted write access to a file, while some others could be given only read access. Instead of opening up a file to all members of a group or everyone else on the system or network, an ACL could limit access to a few specified users, regardless of their group membership. Like permissions, ACLs are controlled by the user, allowing access to a file to be set by particular individuals or groups.

On Ubuntu, ACL support can be installed with the **acl** package (universe repository). Check the man pages for **acl**, **setfacl**, and **getfacl** for detailed descriptions and examples.

ACL entries have the three fields, separated by colons: a type (user, group, other, mask), a qualifier (specific user or group), and the discretionary access permissions (read, write, execute). The type can be **u**, **g**, **o**, and **m**, referencing user, group, other, and mask, respectively. For the qualifier, you can enter a user or group. Instead of a name, you can use a user or group ID, UID, or GID. Permissions can be read, write, or execute: **r**, **w**, or **x**. The permissions can be managed with binary or symbolic methods. In a standard binary method, the **rwx** permissions are positional, with read being first, write second, and execute third. If a dash (-) appears in any of these positions, it is denying that kind of access. **r-x** would allow read and execute permission, but deny write access. With a symbolic method, you use a + or ^ symbol to specify a permission you want to add or remove: **+r^w+x** would add read and execute permissions and remove write permission.

The entry **u:chris:rw** would allow the user **chris** to have read and write permissions for the specified file. You can list several entries on the same line, separated by commas, or place each entry in a file on its own line.

ACL for File Systems

File systems need to be mounted with the **acl** option. The ACL tools (**acl** package) include **setfacl** and **getfacl** commands to set permissions. See the respective man pages for more information.

Once permissions are set for a file system, you can use the **mount** command with the **acl** option to mount it. With Fedora 8, be sure the file system is labeled. Use **???** to create a label.

```
sudo mount  -o acl  LABEL=myvideos /myvideo1
```

To have the device automatically mounted with the ACL options, add the **acl** option to its entry in the **/etc/fstab** file:

```
LABEL=myvideos     /myvideo1     ext3        defaults,acl    0    0
```

Displaying ACL Controls

Once the file system has been mounted with ACL attributes enabled, you can then use the **getfacl** command to display the ACL attributes for particular files and directories. The **getfacl** command will list the filename, owner, and group. It will then list permissions for user, group, mask, and other. The permission entry will have three fields, the first being the type (user, group, mask, or other). The second is a list of users and groups that are permitted access, and the third is the permission granted to the listed users and groups. You can have several permissions of the same type, listing users and groups that would have different permissions. Default permissions are initially listed with empty user and group lists (empty second field). The following command will show the ACL settings for the **myfirstvid** file:

```
getfacl  myfirstvid
```

To see the ACL for the current working directory, use the period as the argument:

```
getfacl .
```

When you use the **ls** command with the **–l** option on an ACL file or directory, as shown next, a plus sign (**+**) will appear at the end of the permissions field indicating that ACLs are in effect.

```
ls -l myfirstvid
```

To copy an ACL file, use the **–p** permission (the move/rename operation, **mv**, will preserve the ACL permissions):

```
cp -p myfirstvid  myvidback
```

ACL Settings

With the **setfacl** command, you can control access by specific users, setting read, write, and execute permissions. Use the **-m** option to add new permissions and change current ones (**-x** removes a setting). As noted previously, users and permissions are referenced with a colon-separated list with permissions specified using the **r**, **w**, and **x** options, and **u**, **g**, and **o** referencing user, group, and other categories. The argument **u:chris:rw** would allow the user **chris** to have read and write permissions for the specified file:

```
setfacl  -m u:chris:rw  myfirstvid
```

The **getfacl** operation will then display added permission entry:

```
getfacl  myfirstvid
```

Tip *You can install and use the **Eiciel** tool to provide a graphical user interface for setting ACL controls on files and directories.*

To change a particular entry, use the **–m** option:

```
setfacl  -m u:chris:r  myfirstvid
```

To remove an entire entry, use the **–x** option. Specify just the type and the user or group name:

```
setfacl  -x u:chris  myfirstvid
```

Tip *You can also use the **chacl** command to change ACL settings.*

PART VI

For each file ACL, an effective mask is set up whenever you add a new entry. The effective rights mask is calculated by the **setfacl** command as the union of all other permissions already specified for ACL entries, and the current one specified. In effect, when you use the **setfacl** command with the **-m** option to add an ACL entry, a mask entry is calculated by **setfacl** and added to the operation. You can turn off this implied calculation with the **-n** option. You would then have to set the effective rights mask explicitly.

```
setfacl -n -m u:chris:r,m::rw  myfirstvid
```

TIP Instead of repeating the same ACL entries for each file, you can create a file that holds the entries and then read them to your file.

Should you use **chmod** to changes permissions on an ACL file, you are changing the mask entry. The mask entry takes precedence over all other entries. If you change a mask to read-only for all permissions, all other entries are overridden. This is indicated by an effective comment displayed after the entry, showing the actual permission allowed. The original entries remain, they are just not effective. No modification of the original entry has been made. This feature lets you shut off access to all users and groups, without having to change all the particular entries. You can then use **chmod** or change the mask entry directly to turn access back on for all the original entries.

Encrypted File Systems

Linux lets you encrypt nonroot and swap file systems, allowing access only to those users with the appropriate encrypted password. You can apply encryption to both fixed and removable file systems such as USB devices. It is recommended that you use the Luks (Linux Unified Key Setup) encryption tools to encrypt file systems. Ubuntu supports encrypted file systems during installation using the Alternate install disc.

You can use either **luksformat** tool to set up and format a Luks encrypted file system. The **luksformat** tool is a front end for both **cryptsetup** and **mkfs**, which perform the setup and formatting. It is used primarily for removable devices such as USB drives. The **cryptsetup** tool sets up the encrypted file system, and you can use it directly, later formatting it with **mkfs**.

Both **luksformat** and **cryptsetup** are installed as part of the **cryptsetup** package (Ubuntu main repository). You can also install **gdecrypt** to provide a GNOME interface for accessing your encrypted file systems (Ubuntu universe repository). Check **/usr/share/doc/cryptsetup** for HOWTO files and example for managing encrypted partitions. Support for encrypted file systems is provided by the **/etc/init.d/cryptdisks** script. Default options are set in the **/etc/defaults/cryptdisks** file, which enable encrypted disk support.

To set up and format a file system with **luksformat**, enter the device name. The default file system type is **vfat**. Use the **-t** option to specify a file system. You will be prompted to enter a passphrase. The **cryptsetup** tool is invoked with the **luksFormat** option. Be sure the file system is not mounted.

Once your encrypted file system is set up and formatted, restart your system. You can then access the encrypted partition or removable drive. For a USB drive or disk, from the file system window, double-click the USB drive icon. This opens a window in which you are prompted for a password with the option to forget, remember for the session, or always remember. A message tells you the device is encrypted. Once you enter your password, you can then mount and access the device (double-click it again). The volume name will appear with an icon on your desktop. HAL will handle all mounting and access for removable media. Use the same procedure for fixed partitions.

Instead of restarting your system after the initialization and format, you can use **cryptsetup** with the **luksOpen** option to open the encrypted file system. If you want to manage fixed drives manually, you can place entries in the **/etc/crypttab** and **/etc/fstab** files for them.

Instead of using **luksformat**, you can use the **cryptsetup** command directly to set up your encrypted file system manually. You first use the **cryptsetup** command with the **luksFormat** option to initialize and create an encrypted volume. You will be prompted to specify a key (or add the key file as an argument). Add an entry for the volume in the **/etc/ crypttab** file. Then either reboot or use the **cryptsetup** command with the **luksOpen** option to access the volume. You will be prompted for the passphrase (or use **--keyfile** to specify the file with the passphrase). You can then format the file system, specifying its name and type. Place an entry for the new file system in the **/etc/fstab** file.

If you did not use Luks, you will have to specify a encryption method with the **cypher** option. Use the **--cypher** option with **cryptsetup** in the **/etc/crypttab** entry. For an Encrypted Salt-Sector Initialization Vector (ESSIV) cypher, you use **aes-cbc-essiv: sha256**. For a plain cypher, you use **aes-cbc-plain**.

Intrusion Detection: Tripwire and AIDE

When an attacker breaks into a system, he will usually try to gain control by making his own changes to system administration files, such as password files. He can create his own user and password information, allowing him access at any time, or he can simply change the root user password. He can also replace entire programs, such as the login program, with his own version. One method of detecting such actions is to use an integrity checking tool such as Tripwire or Advanced Intrusion Detection Environment (AIDE) to detect any changes to system administration files. AIDEI is a free and enhanced alternative to Tripwire (Ubuntu main repository). It provides easy configuration and detailed reporting.

An integrity checking tool works by first creating a database of unique identifiers for each file or program to be checked. These can include features such as permissions and file size, but more important, they can also include checksum numbers generated by encryption algorithms from the file's contents. Default identifiers are checksum numbers created by algorithms such as the SHA2 modification digest algorithm. An encrypted value that provides such a unique identification of a file is known as a *signature*. In effect, a signature provides an accurate snapshot of the contents of a file. Files and programs are then periodically checked by generating their identifiers again and matching them with those in the database. The intrusion detection application will generate signatures of the current files and programs and match them against the values previously generated for its database. Any differences are noted as changes to the file, and you are notified of the changes.

NOTE *You can also check your log files for any suspicious activity. The /var/log/messages file in particular is helpful for checking for critical events such as user logins, FTP connections, and superuser logins.*

AppArmor and Security-Enhanced Linux

L inux and Unix systems normally use a discretionary access control (DAC) method for restricting access. In this approach, users and the objects they own, such as files, determine permissions. The user has complete discretion over the objects she owns. The weak point in many Linux/Unix systems has typically been user administrative accounts. If an attacker manages to gain access to an administrative account, he will have complete control over the services the account manages. Access to the root user provides control over the entire system, all its users, and any network services it is running. To counter this weakness, you can use the mandatory access control (MAC) structure. Instead of an all-or-nothing set of privileges based on accounts, services and administrative tasks are compartmentalized and separately controlled with policies detailing what can and cannot be done. Access is granted not just because a user is an authenticated user, but when specific security criteria are met. Users, applications, processes, files, and devices can be granted only the access they need to do their jobs, and nothing more.

Ubuntu provides two methods for implementing MACs on your system: AppArmor (Application Armor) and Security-Enhanced Linux (SELinux). The two are incompatible, and you can use only one or the other. AppArmor is installed by default; if you later install SELinux, AppArmor will be removed. It is a more limited tool that is easier to use than SELinux and uses profiles that can be learned automatically from application usage. SELinux is much more complex but provides completed control over all objects in your system, labeling each with security permissions.

AppArmor

Ubuntu installs AppArmor as its default security system. AppArmor is designed as an alternative to SELinux. It is much less complicated but makes use of the same kernel support provided for SELinux. AppArmor is a simple method for implementing MAC for specified Linux applications. AppArmor is used primarily to control network servers such as Web, FTP, Samba, and Common UNIX Printing System (CUPS) servers. In this respect, it is much more limited in scope than SELinux, which tries to cover every object. Instead of labeling each object, as SELinux does, AppArmor identifies an object by its pathname.

The object does not have to be affected by AppArmor. Originally developed by Immunix and later supported for a time by Novell (OpenSUSE), AppArmor is available under the GNU Public License. You can find out more about AppArmor at http://en.opensuse.org/Apparmor. Ubuntu will install the **apparmor** and **apparmor-utils** packages (Ubuntu main repository). Also available are the **apparmor-profiles** and **apparmor-doc** packages (universe repository).

AppArmor works by setting up a profile for supported applications. The profile is a security policy that is similar to SELinux policies. A profile defines what an application can access and use on the system.

AppArmor is started with the **/etc/init.d/apparmor** script, which you can also use to stop and restart AppArmor. As you modify profiles, you may need to stop or restart AppArmor. The following would restart AppArmor

```
sudo /etc/init.d/apparmor restart
```

Most servers have profiles like the Apache Web server or the Samba Windows file sharing server. Initially there are two profiles loaded, both for the CUPS printer server, controlling access to the system printers. The **apparmor-profiles** package will install many preconfigured profiles for use on Ubuntu. There are profiles for most servers such as the vsftp FTP server, the Apache Web server, and Squid proxy server, and the Postfix mail server.

AppArmor can apply either an enforce or a complain mode to a particular profile. In the enforce mode, a profile's restrictions are executed, denying access to processes or user not permitted to access the profiled application. In the complain mode, restrictions are not executed. Warning messages are issued instead.

AppArmor Utilities

The **apparmor-utils** packages installs several AppArmor tools, including **enforce**, which enables AppArmor to enforce restrictions on a profile, and **complain**, which instructs AppArmor to only issues warning messages for a profile. The **unconfined** tool lists applications that have no AppArmor profiles. The **audit** tool turns on AppArmor message logging for an application (uses enforce mode). The **apparmor_status** tool displays current profile information. The **--complaining** option lists only those applications that are in complain mode, and the **--enforced** option lists applications that are in enforcing mode. The following show the current status for apparmor, showing what profiles are loaded and what mode is applied to it.

```
sudo apparmor_status
```

The **logprof** tool analyzes AppArmor logs to determine whether any changes are needed in any of the application profiles. Suggested changes are displayed, and the user can allow (**A**) or deny them (**D**). In complain mode, allow is the default, and in enforce mode, deny is the default. You can also make your own changes with the new (**N**) option. Should you want the change applied to all files and directories in a suggested path, you can select the global option (**G**), essentially replacing the last directory or file in a path with the * global file matching symbol.

The **autodep** tool generates a basic AppArmor profile for a new or unconfined application. If you want a more effective profile, you can use **genprof** to analyze the application's use and generate profile controls accordingly.

The **genprof** tool will update or generate a detailed profile for a specified application. It will first set the profile to complain mode. You then use the application, logging complain mode messages on that usage. **genprof** prompts you either to scan the complain messages to refine the profile (**S**) further, or to finish (**F**). When scanned, violations are detected and you are prompted to allow or deny recommended controls. You can then repeat the scan operation until you think the profile is acceptable. Select finish (**F**) to finalize the profile and quit.

Table 18-1 lists several AppArmor utilities/commands.

AppArmor Configuration

AppArmor configuration is located in the **/etc/apparmor** directory. Configurations for different profiles are located in the **/etc/apparmor.d** directory. Loaded profile configuration files have as their name their pathname, using periods instead of slashes to separate directory names. The profile file for the **smbd** (Samba) application is **usr.sbin.smbd**. For CUPS (**cupsd**) it is **usr.sbin.cupsd**.

Configuration rules for AppArmor profiles consist of a path and permissions allowable on that path. A detailed explanation of AppArmor rules and permissions can be found in the **apparmor.d** man page, including a profile example. A path ending in a * matching symbol will select all the files in that directory. The ** selects all file in the parent directory. All file matching operations are supported: *****, **[]**, **?**. Permissions include **r** (read), **w** (write), **x** (execute), and **l** (link). The **u** permission allows unconstrained access.

The following entry allows all the files in the **/var/log/samba** directory with the prefix **log.** to be written to:

```
/var/log/samba/log.* w,
```

Utility/Command	Description
`apparmor_status`	Provides status information about AppArmor policies
`audit` *applications*	Enables logging for AppArmor messages for specified applications
`autodep` *application*	Generates a basic profile for new applications
`complain`	Set AppArmor to complain mode
`enforce`	Sets AppArmor to enforce mode
`genprof` *application*	Generates a profile for an application
`logprof`	Analyzes AppArmor complain messages for a profile and suggests profile modifications
`unconfined`	Lists applications not controlled by AppArmor (no profiles)

TABLE 18-1   AppArmor Utilities

The **abstractions** subdirectory contains files with profile rules that are common to different profiles. Rules from these files are read into actual profiles using the `include` directive. There are abstractions for applications such as GNOME, Samba, and FTP. Some abstractions will include other more general abstractions, such as those for X Window Server or GNOME. For example, the profile for the Samba **smbd** server, **usr.sbin.smbd**, will have a `include` directive for the `samba` abstraction. This abstraction holds rules common to both the **smbd** and **nmbd** servers, both used by the Samba service. The `<>` used in an `include` directive indicates the **/etc/apparmor.d** directory. A list of abstraction files can be found on the **apparmor.d** man page. The include line for Samba is shown here.

```
#include <abstractions/samba>
```

In some cases, such as with the Web server profile, a profile may need access to particular files in a directory to which it normally should not have access. In such a case, the application may need to use a subprofile to allow access. In effect, the application changes hats, taking on permissions does not have in the original profile.

The app**armor-profiles** package provides profile default files for numerous applications in the **/usr/share/doc/apparmor-profiles/extras** directory. It can also be used to activate several commonly used profiles, setting up profile files for them in the **/etc/apparmor.d** directory, such as those for Samba (**nmbd** and **smbd**), Avahi, and the Network Time Protocol daemon (**ntpd**).

Security Enhanced Linux

Although numerous security tools have existed for protecting specific services, user information, and data, no tool has been available for protecting the entire system at the administrative level—at least not until SELinux, which provides built-in administrative protection for aspects of your Linux system. Instead of relying on users to protect their files or on a specific network program to control access, security measures are built into SELinux's basic file management system and network access methods. All controls can be managed directly by an administrator as part of Linux system administration.

Resource	Location
NSA SELinux	**www.nsa.gov/selinux/**
SELinux FAQ	**www.nsa.gov/selinux/info/faq.cfm**
SELinux for Distributions at sourceforge.net	**http://selinux.sourceforge.net**
Writing SELinux Policy HOWTO	**www.lurking-grue.org/writingselinuxpolicyHOWTO.html**
NSA SELinux Documentation	**www.nsa.gov/selinux/info/docs.cfm**
Configuring SELinux Policy	**www.nsa.gov/selinux/papers/policy2-abs.cfm**
SELinux Reference Policy Project	**http://oss.tresys.com/projects/refpolicy**

TABLE 18-2   SELinux Resources

SELinux was developed and is maintained by the U.S. National Security Agency (NSA), which chose Linux as its platform for implementing a secure operating system. Most Linux distributions have embraced SELinux and incorporated it as a standard feature. Detailed documentation is available from resources listed in Table 18-2, including sites provided by the NSA and SourceForge. In addition, check your Linux distribution's Web site for any manuals, FAQs, or documentation on SELinux.

Though Ubuntu provides shared library support for SELinux, it does not include SELinux as part of the main repository. Instead, SELinux is made available as part of the universe repository. Though not integrated into Ubuntu, SELinux is still a critically important and powerful security service. You can use the Synaptic Package Manager to search for, download, and install SELinux packages. Select the **selinux** metapackage to include the required policy packages. Documentation is located in the **selinux-doc** and **selinux-policy-refpolicy-doc** packages. You should also install the **policycoreutils** package, which contains SELinux management tools.

The SELinux reference policy package (**selinux-policy-refpolicy**) is installed with SELinux. In addition, several supporting packages are provided. The **selinux-policy-refpolicy-dev** package installs the supporting header files for creating your own SELinux modules. The **selinux-policy-refpolicy-cups** package provides a SELinux CUPS policy module for use on Ubuntu. The **selinux-policy-refpolicy-unconfined** package holds the unconfined policy module that in effect changes your policy to a targeted policy. Without this package, the reference policy will enforce a strict policy.

NOTE *MLS adds a more refined security access method, designed for servers. MLS adds a security level value to resources. Only users with access to certain levels can access the corresponding files and applications. Within each level, access can be further controlled with the use of categories. Categories work much like groups, allowing access only to users cleared for that category. Access becomes more refined, instead of an all-or-nothing situation. Multi-Category Security (MCS) extends SELinux for use not only by administrators, but also by users.*

Flask Architecture

The Flux Advanced Security Kernel (Flask) operating system security architecture provides support for security policies. It organizes OS components and data into subjects and objects, for which a security context is defined. *Subjects* are processes: applications, drivers, and system tasks that are currently running. *Objects* are fixed components such as files, directories, sockets, network interfaces, and devices. A *security context* is a set of security attributes that determines how a subject or object can be used. This approach provides very fine-grained control over every element in the OS as well as all data on your computer.

The attributes designated for the security contexts and the degree to which they are enforced are determined by an overall *security policy*, which is enforced by a *security server*. Distributions may provide different preconfigured policies from which to work.

SELinux uses a combination of the Type Enforcement (TE), Role-based Access Control (RBAC), and Multilevel Security (MLS) security models. TE focuses on objects and processes such as directories and applications. For the TE model, the security attributes assigned to an object are known as either *domains* or *types*. Types are used for fixed objects such as files, and domains are used for processes such as running applications.

For user access to processes and objects, SELinux makes use of the RBAC model. When new processes or objects are created, transition rules specify the type or domain to which they belong in their security contexts. With the RBAC model, users are assigned roles for which permissions are defined. The roles restrict what objects and processes a user can access. The security context for processes include a role attribute, controlling what objects it can assess. The new MLS adds a security level that contains both a sensitivity and capability value.

Users are given separate SELinux user identities. Normally these correspond to the user IDs set up under the standard Linux user creation operations. Though the separate user IDs may use the same names, they are not the same identifiers. Standard Linux identities can be easily changed with commands such as **setuid** and **su**. Changes to the Linux user ID will not affect the SELinux ID, however. This means that even if a user changes her ID, SELinux will still be able to track it, maintaining control over that user.

System Administration Access

It is critically important that you make sure you have system administrative access under SELinux before you enforce its policies. This is especially true if you are using a strict or MLS policy, which imposes restrictions on administrative access. You should always use SELinux in permissive mode first and check for any messages denying access. With SELinux enforced, it may no longer matter whether you can access the root user or not. What matters is whether your user, even the root user, has **sysadm_r** role and **sysadm_t** object access and an administrative security level. You may not be able to use the **su** command to access the root user and expect to have root user administrative access. Recall that SELinux keeps its own security identities that are not the same as Linux user IDs. Although you may change your user ID with **su**, you will not have changed your security ID.

The targeted approach to policy implementation will set up rules that allow standard system administrator access using normal Linux procedures. The root user will be able to access the root user account normally. In the strict policy, however, the root user needs to access her account using the appropriate security ID. Both are now part of a single reference policy. If you want administrative access through the **su** command (from another user), you first use the **su** command to log in as the root user. You then have to change your role to the **sysadm_r** role—however, you must already be configured by SELinux policy rules to be allowed to take on the **sysadm_r** role. A user can be allowed to assume several possible roles. To change a role, the user can use the **newrole** command with the **-r** option:

```
newrole -r sysadm_r
```

Terminology

SELinux uses several terms that have different meanings in other contexts. The terminology can be confusing because some of the terms, such as *domain*, have different meanings in other, related, areas. For example, a *domain* in SELinux is a *process* as opposed to an *object*, whereas in networking the term refers to network DNS addresses. A *policy* is a set of rules used to determine the relationships between users, roles, and types or domains. These rules state what types a role can access and what roles a user can have.

Identity

SELinux creates *identities* that are used to control access. Identities are not the same as traditional user IDs. Although each SELinux user normally has an user ID, identities and user IDs are not linked. Therefore, operations that affect a user do not affect the corresponding SELinux identity.

SELinux can set up a separate corresponding identity for each user, though on less secure policies, such as unconfined (targeted) policies, general identities are used. A general user identity is used for all normal users, restricting users to user-level access, whereas administrators are assigned administrative identities. You can further define security identities for particular users.

The identity makes up part of a security context that determines what a user can or cannot do. Should a user change her user ID, that user's security identity will not change. A user will always have the same security identity. In traditional Linux systems, a user can use commands such as **su** to change her user ID, becoming a different user. On SELinux, even though a user can still change her Linux user ID, the user still retains the same original security ID. You always know what a particular person is doing on your system, no matter what user ID that person may assume.

The security identity can have limited access. So even though a user may use the Linux **su** command to become the root user, the user's security identity could prevent her from performing any root user administrative commands. As noted, to gain an administrative access, the role for the user's security identity would have to change as well.

Security identities have roles that control what they can do. Use **id -Z** to see the security context for your security identity, what roles you have, and what kinds of objects you can access. This command lists the user security context that starts with the security ID, followed by a colon, and then the roles the user has and the objects the user can control. A user role is **user_r**, and a system administration role is **system_r**. The general security identity is **user_u**, whereas a particular security identity will normally use the username. The following example shows the security context for a standard user with the general security identity:

```
$ id -Z
 user_u:user_r:user_t
```

In this example, the user has a security identity called **george**:

```
$ id -Z
 george:user_r:user_t
```

You can use the **newrole** command to change a user's role. Changing to a system administrative role, for example, can give the user equivalent root access.

```
$ newrole -r sysadm_r
$ id -Z
 george:sysadm_r:sysadm_t
```

Domains

Domains are used to identify and control processes. Each process is assigned a domain within which it can run. A domain sets restrictions on what a process can do. Traditionally, a process was given a user ID to determine what it could do, and many processes required a root user ID to gain access to the full file system. A process with a root user ID could be used to gain full administrative access over the entire system. A domain, on the other hand, can be tailored to access some areas but not others. Attempts to break into another domain such as the administrative domain would be blocked. For example, the administrative domain is **sysadm_t**, whereas the DNS server uses only **named_t**, and users have a **user_t** domain.

Types

Whereas domains control processes, *types* control objects such as files and directories. Files and directories are grouped into types that can be used to control who can have access to them. The type names use the same format used by the domain names, ending with a **_t** suffix. Unlike domains, types reference objects, including files, devices, and network interfaces.

Roles

Types and domains are assigned to *roles*. Users (security identities) with a given role can access types and domains assigned to that role. For example, most users can access **user_t** type objects but not **sysadm_t** objects. The types and domains a user can access are set by the role entry in configuration files. The following example allows users to access objects with the user password type:

```
role user_r types user_passwd_t
```

Security Context

Each object has a *security context* that sets its security attributes, such as identity, role, domain, or type. A file will have a security context listing the kind of identity that can access it, the role under which it can be accessed, and the security type to which it belongs. Each component adds its own refined level of security. Passive objects are usually assigned a generic role, **object_r**, which has no effect, as such objects cannot initiate actions.

A normal file created by a user in his own directory will have an identity, role, and type, as shown next. The *identity* is a user and the *role* is that of an object. The *type* is the user's home directory. This type is used for all subdirectories and their files created within a user's home directory.

```
user_u:object_r:user_home_t
```

A file or directory created by that same user in a different part of the file system will use a different type. For example, the type for files created in the **/tmp** directory will be **tmp_t**:

```
user_u:object_r:tmp_t
```

Transition: Labeling

A *transition* assigns a security context to a process or file. For a file, the security context is assigned when it is created, while for a process, the security context is determined when the process is run.

Making sure every file has an appropriate security context is called *labeling*. Adding another file system requires that you label (add security contexts) to the directories and files on it. Labeling varies, depending on the policy you use. Each policy may have different security contexts for objects and processes. Relabeling is carried out using the **fixfiles** command in the policy source directory:

```
fixfiles relabel
```

Management Operations for SELinux

Certain basic operations, such as checking the SELinux status, checking a user's or file's security context, or disabling SELinux at boot, can be very useful in managing SELinux.

Turning Off SELinux

To turn off SELinux permanently, set the **SELINUX** variable in the **/etc/selinux/config** file to **disabled**:

```
SELINUX=disabled
```

To turn off (permissive mode) SELinux temporarily without rebooting, use the **setenforce** command with the **0** option; use **1** to turn it back on (enforcing mode). You can also use the terms **permissive** or **enforcing** as the arguments instead of **0** or **1**.

```
setenforce 1
```

You must have the **sysadm_r** role to use these commands, which you can obtain by logging in as the root user.

Checking Status and Statistics

To check the current status of your SELinux system, use **sestatus**. Adding the **-v** option will also display process and file contexts, as listed in **/etc/sestatus.conf**. The contexts will specify the roles and types assigned to a particular process, file, or directory.

```
sestatus -v
```

Use the **seinfo** command to display your current SELinux statistics:

```
seinfo
```

Checking Security Context

The **-Z** option used with the **ls**, **id**, and **ps** commands to check the security context for files, users, and processes, respectively. The security context tells you the roles that users must have to access given processes or objects. In the following, the first line list files with their security context, the second lists a user's security context, and the last will list the security context for processes.

```
ls -lZ
id -Z
ps -eZ
```

SELinux Management Tools

SELinux provides a number of tools that let you manage your SELinux configuration and policy implementation, including **semanage** to configure your policy (**policycoreutils** and **setools**). The **setools** collection provides SELinux configuration and analysis tools including **apol**, the Security Policy Analysis tool, for domain transition analysis; **sediffx** for policy differences; and **seaudit** to examine the audit logs (see Table 18-3). The command line user management tools, **useradd**, **usermod**, and **userdel**, all have SELinux options that can be applied when SELinux is installed. In addition, the **audit2allow** tool will convert SELinux denial messages into policy modules that will allow access.

PART VI

Command	Description
apol	Analyzes SELinux policy
autid2allow	Generates policy to allow rules for modules using audit AVC Denial messages
chcon	Changes context
checkpolicy	Compiles SELinux policy
chsid	Changes a security ID
fixfiles	Checks file systems and sets security contexts
newrole	Assigns a new role
restorecon	Sets security features for particular files
seaudit	Examines SELinux log files
sediffx	Examines SELinux policy differences
seinfo	Displays policy statistics
sesearch	Searches for Type Enforcement rules in policies
sestatus	Checks status of SELinux on your system, including the contexts of processes and files
setfiles	Sets security context for files

TABLE 18-3 SELinux Tools

With the modular version of SELinux, policy management is no longer handled by editing configuration files directly. Instead, you use the SELinux management tools such as **semanage**. These tools make use of interface files to generate changed policies.

Semanage
The **semanage** tool lets you change your SELinux configuration without having to edit SELinux source files directly. It covers several major categories including users, ports, file contexts, and logins. Check the man page for **semanage** for detailed descriptions. Options let you modify specific security features: **-s** for the username, **-R** for the role, **-t** for the type, and **-r** for an MLS security range, for example. The following example adds a user with role **user_r**:

```
semanage user -a -R user_r  justin
```

semanage is configured with the **/etc/selinux/semanage.conf** file, where you can configure **semanage** to write directly on modules (the default) or work on the source.

SELinux AVC Denial messages are saved in the **/var/log/audit/audit.log** file. These entries are particularly important if you are using the permissive mode to test a policy you want to enforce later. You need to find out whether you are being denied access where appropriate and afforded control when needed. To see only the SELinux messages, you can use the **seaudit** tool. Startup messages for the SELinux service are logged in **/var/log/messages**.

Allowing Access: chcon and audit2allow

Whenever SELinux denies access to a file or application, the kernel issues an AVC Denial notice. In many cases, the problem can be fixed simply by renaming the security context of a file to allow access. You use the **chcon** command to change a file's security context. To rename the security context of a file, access needs to be granted to the Samba server for a **log.richard3** file in the **/var/lib/samba** directory, like so:

```
chcon -R -t samba_share_t log.richard3
```

More complicated problems, especially those that are unknown, may require that you create a new policy module using the AVC messages in the audit log. To do this, you can use the **audit2allow** command. This command will audit AVC messages and generate commands to allow SELinux access. The audit log is at **/var/log/autid/audit.log** and is output to **audit2allow**, which then can use its **-M** option to create a policy module:

```
cat /var/log/audit/audit.log | audit2allow -M local
```

You then use the **semodule** command to load the module:

```
semodule -i local.pp
```

If you want to edit the allowable entries first, you can use the following command to create a **.te** file of the local module, **local.te**, which you can then edit:

```
audit2allow -m local -i  /var/log/audit/audit.log   >  local.te
```

Once you have edited the **.te** file, you can use **checkmodule** to compile the module, and then **semodule_package** to create the policy module, **local.pp**. Then you can install it with **semodule**. Here's how to create a **.mod** file with **checkmodule** and then create a **.pp** file with **semodule_package**:

```
checkmodule -M -m -o local.mod local.te
semodule_package -o local.pp  -m local.mod
semodule -i local.pp
```

In this example, the policy module is called **local**. If you later want to create a new module with **audit2allow**, you should use either a different name or append the output to the **.te** file using the **-o** option.

The SELinux Reference Policy

A SELinux operating system is secured using a *policy*. SELinux now uses a single policy, called the *Reference Policy*, instead of the two separate targeted and strict policies used in previous editions (see **http://oss.tresys.com/projects/refpolicy**). Instead of giving users only two alternatives, *strict* and *targeted*, the SELinux Reference Policy project aims to provide a basic policy that can be easily adapted and expanded as needed. The SELinux Reference Policy configures SELinux into modules that can be handled separately. You can still have strict and targeted policies, but there are variations on a basic reference policy. In addition you can create an MLS policy. The strict policy is installed by default. On Ubuntu, you can implement a targeted policy by installing the **selinux-policy-refpolicy-unconfined** package.

This loads an unconfined module that allows access to any object that is not being controlled by a specific module.

The targeted approach is used to control specific services, such as network and Internet servers such as Web, DNS, and FTP servers. It also can control local services with network connections. The policy will not affect only the daemon itself, but all the resources it uses on your system.

The strict policy, the default, provides complete control over your system. It is with this kind of policy that users and even administrators can be inadvertently locked out of the system. A strict policy needs to be carefully tested to make sure access is appropriately denied and granted.

Policies are implemented in policy files, binary files that are compiled from source files. The policy binary files are in policy subdirectories in the **/etc/selinux** configuration directory, **/etc/selinux/refpolicy**. For example, the policy file for the refpolicy policy is **/etc/selinux/refpolicy/policy/policy.22**.

The reference development files that hold the interface header files are installed at **/usr/share/selinux/repolicy/include.** You can use the development files to create your own policy modules that you can then load.

SELinux Configuration

Configuration for general SELinux server settings is carried out in the **/etc/selinux/config** file. Currently, only two settings are available: the *state* and the *policy*. You set the **SELINUX** variable to the state, such as **enforcing** or **permissive**, and set the **SELINUXTYPE** variable to the kind of policy you want. These correspond to the **Securitylevel-config** SELinux settings for **disabled** and **enforcing**, as well as the policy to use, such as **refpolicy**. A sample config file is shown here:

```
# This file controls the state of SELinux on the system.
# SELINUX= can take one of these three values:
#     enforcing - SELinux security policy is enforced.
#     permissive - SELinux prints warnings instead of enforcing.
#     disabled - SELinux is fully disabled.
SELINUX=permissive
# SELINUXTYPE= type of policy in use.
SELINUXTYPE=refpolicy
```

SELinux Policy Rules

Policy rules can be made up of either TE or RBAC statements, along with security levels (MLS). A type statement can be a type or attribute declaration or a transition, change, or assertion rule. The RBAC statements can be role declarations or dominance, or they can allow roles. A security level specifies a number corresponding to the level of access permitted. Policy configuration can be difficult, as it involves extensive and complicated rules. For this reason, many rules are implemented using GNU M4 macros in **fi** files that will in turn generate the appropriate rules. (Sendmail, for example, uses M4 macros in a similar way.) You will find these rules in files in the SELinux Reference Policy source code package that you need to download and install. Some of the basic rules are discussed here.

Type and Role Declarations

A type declaration starts with the keyword **type**, followed by the type name (identifier) and any optional attributes or aliases. The type name will have a _t suffix. Standard type definitions are included for objects such as files. The following is a default type for any file, with attributes **file_type** and **sysadmfile**:

```
type file_t, file_type, sysadmfile;
```

The root will have its own type declaration:

```
type root_t, file_type, sysadmfile;
```

A role declaration determines the roles that can access objects of a certain type. These rules begin with the keyword **role** followed by the role and the objects associated with that role. In this example, the amanda objects (**amanda_t**) can be accessed by a user or process with the system role (**system_r**):

```
role system_r types amanda_t;
```

A more specific type declaration is provided for executables, such as the following for the Amanda server (**amanda_exec_t**). This defines the Amanda executable as a system administration–controlled executable file:

```
type amanda_exec_t, file_type, sysadmfile, exec_type;
```

Types are also set up for the files created in the user home directory:

```
type user_home_t, file_type, sysadmfile, home_type;
type user_home_dir_t, file_type, sysadmfile, home_dir_type;
```

File Contexts

File contexts associate specific files with security contexts. The file or files are listed first, with multiple files represented with regular expressions. Then the role, type, and security level are specified. The following command creates a security context for all files in the **/etc** directory (configuration files). These are accessible from the system user (**system_u**) and are objects of the **etc_t** type with a security level of 0, **s0**.

```
/etc(/.*)?              system_u:object_r:etc_t:s0
```

Certain files can belong to other types; for instance, the **resolve.conf** configuration file belongs to the **net_conf** type:

```
/etc/resolv/.conf.*    --    system_u:object_r:net_conf_t:s0
```

Certain services will have their own security contexts for their configuration files:

```
/etc/amanda(/.*)?             system_u:object_r:amanda_config_t:s0
```

User Roles

User roles define what roles a user can take on. A user role begins with the keyword **user** followed by the username, then the keyword **roles**, and finally the roles it can use. You will find these rules in the SELinux Reference Policy source code files. The following example is a definition of the **system_u** user:

```
user system_u roles system_r;
```

If a user can have several roles, the roles are listed in brackets. The following is the definition of the standard user role, which allows users to take on system administrative roles:

```
user user_u roles { user_r sysadm_r system_r };
```

The strict policy lists only the **user_r** role:

```
user user_u roles { user_r };
```

SELinux Policy Configuration Files and Modules

Configuration files are normally changed using **.te** an **.fc** files. These are missing from the module headers in **/usr/share/selinux**. If you are adding a module, you will need to create the **.te** and **.fc** files for it. Then you can create a module and add it as described in the next section. If you want to create or modify your own policy, you will need to download and install the source code files for the SELinux Reference Policy. The reference policy code holds the complete set of **.te** and **.fc** configuration files.

Instead of compiling the entire source each time you want to make a change, you can simply compile a module for the area you changed. The modules directory holds the different modules. Each module is built from a corresponding **.te** file. The **checkmodule** command is used to create a **.mod** module file from the **.te** file, and then the **semodule_package** command is use to create the loadable **.pp** module file as well as a **.fc** file context file. As noted in the SELinux documentation, if you need to change the configuration for **syslogd**, you first use the following command to create a **syslogd.mod** file using **syslogd.te**. The **-M** option specifies support for MLS security levels.

```
checkmodule -M -m syslogd.te  -o syslogd.mod
```

Then use the **semodule_package** command to create a **syslogd.pp** file from the **syslogd.mod** file. The **-f** option specifies the file context file:

```
semodule_package -m syslogd.mod  -o syslogd.pp -f syslogd.fc
```

To add the module, you use **semodule** and the **-i** option. You can check whether a module is loaded with the **-l** option.

```
semodule -i syslogd.pp
```

Changes to the base policy are made to the **policy.conf** file, which is compiled into the **base.pp** module.

SELinux: Administrative Operations

You can perform several tasks on your SELinux system without having to recompile your entire configuration. Security contexts for certain files and directories can be changed as needed. For example, when you add a new file system, you will need to label it with the appropriate security contexts. Also, when you add users, you may need to have a user be given special attention by the system.

Several tools are available for changing your objects' security contexts. The **fixfiles** command can set the security context for file systems. You use the **relabel** option to set security contexts and the **check** option to see what should be changed. The **fixfiles** tool is a script that uses **setfiles** and **restorecon** to make actual changes.

The **restorecon** command will let you restore the security context for files and directories, but **setfiles** is the basic tool used for setting security contexts. It can be applied to individual files or directories. It is used to label the file when a policy is first installed.

With **chcon**, you can change the permissions of individual files and directories, much as **chmod** does for general permissions.

You can manage users with the **semanage** command with the **user** option. To see what users are currently active, you can list them with the **semanage user** command and the **-l** option:

```
# semanage user -l
system_u: system_r
user_u: user_r sysadm_r system_r
root: user_r sysadm_r system_r
```

The **semanage user** command has **a, d, m,** options for adding, removing, or changing users, respectively. The **a** and **m** options let you specify roles to add to a user, whereas the **d** option will remove the user.

19

Secure Shell and Kerberos

To protect remote connections from hosts outside your network, transmissions can be encrypted. For Linux systems, you can use the Secure Shell (SSH) suite of programs to encrypt and authenticate transmissions, preventing them from being read or modified by anyone else, as well confirming the identity of the sender. SSH programs are meant to replace the remote tools such as rsh and rcp, which perform no encryption and include security risks such as transmitting passwords in clear text. SSH is included in the main Ubuntu repository. It is considered an integral part of the Ubuntu distribution.

User authentication can be controlled for certain services by Kerberos servers. Kerberos authentication provides another level of security whereby individual services can be protected, allowing use of a service only to users who are cleared for access. Kerberos is provided as part of the universe repository.

Table 19-1 lists several SSH and Kerberos resources on the Web.

The Secure Shell: OpenSSH

Although a firewall can protect a network from attempts to break into it from the outside, the problem of securing legitimate communications to the network from outside sources still exists. A particular problem stems from users who want to connect to your network remotely. Such connections could be monitored, and information such as passwords and user IDs used when the user logs in to your network could be copied and used later to break in. One solution is to use SSH for remote logins and other kinds of remote connections such as FTP transfers. SSH encrypts any communications between the remote user and a system on your network.

Two implementations of SSH currently use what are, in effect, two different and incompatible protocols. The first version of SSH, known as SSH1, uses the original SSH protocol. Version 2.0, known as SSH2, uses a completely rewritten version of the SSH protocol. Encryption is performed in different ways, encrypting different parts of a packet. SSH1 uses server and host keys to authenticate systems, whereas SSH2 uses only host keys. Furthermore, certain functions, such as the secure file transfer program (sftp), are supported only by SSH2.

Web Site	Description
http://openssh.org	OpenSSH, open source version of SSH
http://ssh.com	SSH Communications Security, commercial SSH version
http://web.mit.edu/kerberos	Kerberos authentication

TABLE 19-1   SSH and Kerberos Resources

NOTE   *A commercial version of SSH is available from SSH Communications Security at **http://ssh.com**. SSH Communications Security provides an entirely commercial version called SSH Tectia, designed for enterprise and government use. The older noncommercial SSH package is still freely available to download and use.*

The SSH protocol has become an official Internet Engineering Task Force (IETF) standard. A free and open source version is developed and maintained by the OpenSSH project, currently supported by the OpenBSD project. OpenSSH is the version supplied with most Linux distributions, including Ubuntu and Debian. You can find out more about OpenSSH at **http://openssh.org**, where you can download the most recent version, although your distribution will provide current Red Hat Package Manager (RPM) versions.

SSH Encryption and Authentication

SSH secures connections by authenticating users and encrypting their transmissions. The authentication process is handled with public key encryption. Once authenticated, transmissions are encrypted by a cipher agreed upon by the SSH server and client for use in a particular session. SSH supports multiple ciphers. Authentication is applied to hosts and users. SSH first authenticates a particular host, verifying that it is a valid SSH host that can be securely communicated with. Then the user is authenticated, verifying that the user is who he says he is.

SSH uses strong encryption methods, and their export from the United States may be restricted. Currently, SSH can deal with the following kinds of attacks:

- IP spoofing, in which a remote host sends out packets that pretend to come from another, trusted host
- IP source routing, where a host can pretend an IP packet comes from another, trusted host
- DNS spoofing, where an attacker forges name server records
- Interception of clear-text passwords and other data by intermediate hosts
- Manipulation of data by people in control of intermediate hosts
- Attacks based on listening to X Window authentication data and spoofed connections to the X11 server

Encryption

The public key encryption used in SSH authentication makes use of two keys: a public key and a private key. The public key is used to encrypt data, while the private key decrypts it.

Each host or user has its own public and private keys. The public key is distributed to other hosts, who can then use it to encrypt authentication data that only the host's private key can decrypt. For example, when a host sends data to a user on another system, the host encrypts the authentication data with a public key, which it previously received from that user. The data can be decrypted only by the user's corresponding private key. The public key can safely be sent in the open from one host to another, allowing it to be installed safely on different hosts. You can think of the process as taking place between a client and a server. When the client sends data to the server, it first encrypts the data using the server's public key. The server can then decrypt the data using its own private key.

It is recommended that SSH transmissions be authenticated with public-private keys controlled by passphrases. Unlike Pretty Good Privacy (PGP), SSH uses public key encryption for the authentication process only. Once authenticated, participants agree on a common cipher to use to encrypt transmission. Authentication will verify the identity of the participants. Each user who intends to use SSH to access a remote account first needs to create the public and private keys along with a passphrase to use for the authentication process. A user then sends her public key to the remote account she wants to access and installs the public key on that account. When the user attempts to access the remote account, that account can then use the user's public key to authenticate that the user is legitimate. The process assumes that the remote account has set up its own SSH private and public key. For the user to access the remote account, she will have to know the remote account's SSH passphrase. SSH is often used in situations where a user has two or more accounts located on different systems and wants to be able to access them securely from each other. In that case, the user already has access to each account and can install SSH on each, giving each its own private and public keys along with their passphrases.

Authentication
The mechanics of authentication in SSH versions 1 and 2 differ slightly. However, the procedure on the part of users is the same. Essentially, a user creates both public and private keys using the `ssh-keygen` command. The user's public key then is distributed to those users to which the original user wants access. Often this is an account a user holds on another host. A passphrase further protects access. The original user will need to know the other user's passphrase to access the account.

SSH1 uses RSA Authentication. When a remote user tries to log in to an account, that account is checked to see whether it has the remote user's public key. If it does, that public key is used to encrypt a *challenge* (usually a random number) that can be decrypted only by the remote user's private key. When the remote user receives the encrypted challenge, that user decrypts the challenge with its private key. SSH2 can use either RSA or DSA Authentication. The remote user will first encrypt a session identifier using its private key, signing it. The encrypted session identifier is then decrypted by the account using the remote user's public key. The session identifier has been previously set up by SSH for that session.

SSH authentication is first carried out with the host, and then with users. Each host has its own public and private keys used for authentication. Once the host is authenticated, the user is queried. Each user has his own public and private keys. Users on an SSH server who want to receive connections from remote users should keep a list of those remote user's public keys. Similarly, an SSH host will maintain a list of public keys for other SSH hosts.

SSH Packages, Tools, and Server

SSH is implemented on Linux systems with OpenSSH. The full set of OpenSSH packages includes the OpenSSH metapackage (**ssh**), the OpenSSH server (**openssh-server**), and the OpenSSH client (**openssh-clients**). These packages also require OpenSSL (**openssl**), which installs the cryptographic libraries that SSH uses.

The SSH tools are listed in Table 19-2. They include several client programs such as **scp** and **ssh**, as well as the SSH server. The SSH server (**sshd**) provides secure connections to anyone from the outside using the SSH client to connect. Several configuration utilities are also included, such as **ssh-add**, which adds valid hosts to the authentication agent, and **ssh-keygen**, which generates the keys used for encryption.

For SSH2, names of the actual tools have a *2* suffix. SSH1 tools have a *1* as their suffix. During installation, however, links are set for each tool to use only the name with the suffix. For example, if you have installed SSH2, a link called **scp** to the **scp2** application exists. You can then use the link to invoke the tool. Using **scp** starts **scp2**. Table 19-2 specifies only the link names, as these are the same for each version. Remember, though, that some applications, such as **sftp**, are available only with version 2.

You can configure the OpenSSH server (**sshd**) to start up automatically using **services-admin** (System | Administration | Services) and selecting Remote Shell Server (ssh). You can start, stop, and restart the server manually with the **/etd/init.d/ssh** script:

```
sudo /etc/init.d/ssh restart
```

Application	Description
ssh	SSH client
sshd	SSH server (daemon)
sftp	SSH FTP client, Secure File Transfer Program for SSH2 only; use **?** to list SFTP commands
sftp-server	SSH FTP server for SSH2 only (SFTP)
scp	SSH copy command client
ssh-keygen	Utility for generating keys: **-h** for help
ssh-keyscan	Tool to gather public host keys automatically to generate **ssh_known_hosts** files
ssh-add	Adds RSD and DSA identities to the authentication agent
ssh-agent	SSH authentication agent that holds private keys for public key authentication (RSA, DSA)
ssh-askpass	X Window System utility for querying passwords, invoked by `ssh-add` (**openssh-askpass**)
ssh-askpass-gnome	GNOME utility for querying passwords, invoked by `ssh-add`
ssh-signer	Signs host-based authentication packets for SSH2 only; must be SUID root (performed by installation)
slogin	Remote login (SSH1)

TABLE 19-2   SSH Tools

You must configure your firewall to allow access to the **sshd** server. The SSH server is normally accessed on port 22. You can configure a different port to use in the **/etc/ssh/shd_config** file if you want and then open that port on the firewall. If you are using a **ufw** firewall, simply allow access on port 22:

```
sudo ufw allow 22/tcp
```

If you are using Firestarter (System | Administration | Firestarter), on the Policy tab, select the Inbound menu item and then right-click the Services pane to add a rule. On the Add New Inbound Rule window, select SSH from the Name pop-up menu, and the 22 port will be selected for you. The SSH rule will show up in the Allow Service section of the Policy Inbound panel.

If you are managing your iptables firewall directly, you could manage access directly by adding the following iptables rule. This accepts input on port 22 for TCP/IP protocol packages.

```
iptables -A INPUT -p tcp --dport 22 -j ACCEPT
```

SSH Setup

Using SSH involves creating your own public and private keys and then distributing your public key to other users or user accounts of your own on remote systems. Perhaps, for example, you remotely log in from a local client to an account on a remote server from a home computer to a company computer. Your home computer would be your client account, and the account on your company computer would be your server account. On your client account, you need to generate your public and private keys and then place a copy of your public key in the server account. You can do this simply by e-mailing the key file or copying the file to a floppy disk. Once the account on your server has a copy of your client user's public key, you can access the server account from your client account. You will also be prompted for the server account's passphrase, which you'll need to know to access that account. Figure 19-1 illustrates the SSH setup that allows user **george** to access the account **cecelia**.

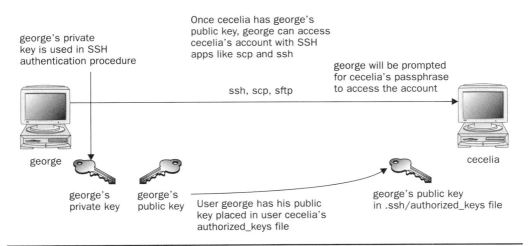

Figure 19-1   SSH setup and access

To use SSH to access other accounts, the follow must occur:

- You must create public and private keys on your account along with a passphrase. You will need to use this passphrase to access your account from another account.
- You must distribute your public key to other accounts you want to access, placing them in the **.ssh/authorized_keys** file.
- Other accounts also have to set up public and private keys along with a passphrase.
- You must know the other account's passphrase to access it.

Creating SSH Keys with ssh-keygen

You create your public and private keys using the **ssh-keygen** command. You then specify the kind of encryption you want to use—either DSA or RSA encryption—using the **-t** option and the encryption name in lowercase (**dsa** or **rsa**). In the following example, the user creates a key with the RSA encryption:

```
ssh-keygen -t rsa
```

The **ssh-keygen** command prompts you for a passphrase, which it will use as a kind of password to protect your private key. The passphrase should consist of several words. You are also prompted to enter a filename for the keys. If you do not enter a filename, SSH will use its defaults. The public key will have the extension **.pub**. The **ssh-keygen** command generates the public key and places it in your **.ssh/id_dsa.pub** or **.ssh/id_dsa.pub** file, depending on the type of key you specified; it places the private key in the corresponding **.ssh/id_dsa.pub** or **.ssh/id_rsa.pub** file.

NOTE   *The .ssh/identity filename is used in SSH1; it may be installed by default on older distribution versions. SSH2 uses a different filename, .ssh/id_dsa or .ssh/id_rsa, depending on whether RSA or DSA authentication is used.*

If you need to change your passphrase, you can do so with the **ssh-keygen** command and the **-p** option. Each user will have her own SSH configuration directory, called **.ssh**, located in her own home directory. The public and private keys, as well as SSH configuration files, are placed here. If you build from the source code, the **make install** operation will automatically run **ssh-keygen**. Table 19-3 lists the SSH configuration files.

Authorized Keys

A public key is used to authenticate a user and the user's host. You use the public key on a remote system to allow that user access. The public key is placed in the remote user account's **.ssh/authorized_keys** file. Recall that the public key is held in the **.ssh/id_dsa.pub** file. If a user wants to log in remotely from a local account to an account on a remote system, he would first place his public key in the **.ssh/authorized_keys** file in the account on the remote system he wants to access. If the user **larisa** on **turtle.mytrek.com** wants to access the **aleina** account on **rabbit.mytrek.com**, larisa's public key from **/home/larisa/.ssh/id_dsa.pub** first must be placed in **aleina**'s **authorized_keys** file, **/home/aleina/.ssh/authorized_keys**. User **larisa** can send the key or have it copied over. A simple **cat** (concatenation) operation can append a key to the authorized key file.

File	Description
$HOME/.ssh/known_hosts	Records host keys for all hosts the user has logged in to (that are not in **/etc/ssh/ssh_known_hosts**).
$HOME/.ssh/random_seed	Seeds the random number generator.
$HOME/.ssh/id_rsa	Contains the RSA authentication identity of the user.
$HOME/.ssh/id_dsa	Contains the DSA authentication identity of the user.
$HOME/.ssh/id_rsa.pub	Contains the RSA public key for authentication. The contents of this file should be added to **$HOME/.ssh/ authorized_keys** on all machines that you want to log in to using RSA authentication.
$HOME/.ssh/id_dsa.pub	Contains the DSA public key for authentication. The contents of this file should be added to **$HOME/.ssh/ authorized_keys** on all machines that you want to log in to using DSA authentication.
$HOME/.ssh/config	Contains the per-user configuration file.
$HOME/.ssh/authorized_keys	Lists the RSA or DSA keys that can be used for logging in as this user.
/etc/ssh/ssh_known_hosts	Contains the systemwide list of known host keys.
/etc/ssh/ssh_config	Contains the systemwide configuration file. This file provides defaults for those values not specified in the user's configuration file.
/etc/ssh/sshd_config	Contains the SSH server configuration file.
/etc/ssh/sshrc	Contains the system default. Commands in this file are executed by **ssh** when the user logs in just before the user's shell (or command) is started.
$HOME/.ssh/rc	Contains commands executed by **ssh** when the user logs in just before the user's shell (or command) is started.

TABLE 19-3   SSH Configuration Files

In the next example, the user adds the public key for **aleina** in the **larisa.pub** file to the authorized key file. The **larisa.pub** file is a copy of the **/home/larisa/.ssh/id_dsa.pub** file that the user received earlier.

```
cat larisa.pub >>  .ssh/authorized_keys
```

Loading Keys

If you regularly make connections to a variety of remote hosts, you can use the **ssh-agent** command to place private keys in memory where they can be accessed quickly to decrypt received transmissions. The **ssh-agent** command is intended for use at the beginning of a login session. For GNOME, you can use the **openssh-askpass-gnome** utility, invoked by **ssh-add**, which allows you to enter a password when you log in to GNOME. GNOME will automatically supply that password whenever you use an SSH client.

Although the `ssh-agent` command enables you to use private keys in memory, you also must specifically load your private keys into memory using the `ssh-add` command. `ssh-add` with no arguments loads your private key from your .ssh/id_dsa or .ssh/id_rsa.pub file. You are prompted for your passphrase for this private key. To remove the key from memory, use `ssh-add` with the `-d` option. If you have several private keys, you can load them all into memory. `ssh-add` with the `-l` option lists currently loaded private keys.

SSH Clients

SSH was originally designed to replace remote access operations, such as rlogin, rcp, and telnet, which perform no encryption and introduce security risks such as transmitting passwords in clear text. You can also use SSH to encode X Window Server sessions as well as FTP transmissions (sftp). The **ssh-clients** package contains corresponding SSH clients to replace these applications. With slogin or ssh, you can log in from a remote host to execute commands and run applications, much as you can with rlogin and rsh. With scp, you can copy files between the remote host and a network host, just as with rcp. With sftp, you can transfer FTP files secured by encryption.

ssh

With ssh, you can remotely log in from a local client to a remote system on your network operating as the SSH server. The term *local client* here refers to a client outside the network, such as your home computer, and the term *remote* refers to a host system on the network to which you are connecting. In effect, you connect from your local system to the remote network host. Ssh is designed to replace rlogin, which performs remote logins, and rsh, which executes remote commands. With ssh, you can log in from a local site to a remote host on your network and then send commands to be executed on that host. The **ssh** command is also capable of supporting X Window System connections. This feature is automatically enabled if you make an ssh connection from an X Window System environment, such as GNOME or KDE. A connection is set up for you between the local X server and the remote X server. The remote host sets up a dummy X server and sends any X Window System data through it to your local system to be processed by your own local X server.

The **ssh** login operation function is much like the **rlogin** command. You enter the **ssh** command with the address of the remote host, followed by a `-l` option and the login name (username) of the remote account you are logging in to. The following example logs in to the **aleina** user account on the **rabbit.mytrek.com** host:

```
ssh rabbit.mytrek.com -l aleina
```

You can also use the username in an address format with **ssh**, as in

```
ssh aleian@rabbit.mytrek.com
```

The following listing shows how the user **george** accesses the **cecelia** account on **turtle.mytrek.com**:

```
[george@turtle george]$ ssh turtle.mytrek.com -l cecelia
cecelia@turtle.mytrek.com's password:
[cecelia@turtle cecelia]$
```

A variety of options is available to enable you to configure your connection. Most options have corresponding configuration options that can be set in the configuration file. For example, with the **-c** option, you can designate which encryption method you want to use, for instance, **idea**, **des**, **blowfish**, or **arcfour**. With the **-i** option, you can select a particular private key to use. The **-C** option enables you to have transmissions compressed at specified levels. (See the **ssh** man page for a complete list of options.)

scp

You use scp to copy files from one host to another on a network. Designed to replace rcp, scp uses ssh to transfer data and employs the same authentication and encryption methods. If authentication requires it, scp requests a password or passphrase. The scp program operates much like rcp. Directories and files on remote hosts are specified using the username and the host address before the filename or directory. The username specifies the remote user account that scp is accessing, and the host is the remote system where that account is located. You separate the user from the host address with an @, and you separate the host address from the file or directory name with a colon. The following example copies the file **party** from a user's current directory to the user **aleina**'s **birthday** directory, located on the **rabbit.mytrek.com** host:

```
scp party aleina@rabbit.mytrek.com:/birthday/party
```

Of particular interest is the **-r** (recursive) option, which enables you to copy whole directories. (See the **scp** man page for a complete list of options.)

In the next example, the user copies the entire **reports** directory to the user **justin**'s **projects** directory:

```
scp -r reports justin@rabbit.mytrek.com:/projects
```

In the next example, the user **george** copies the **mydoc1** file from the user **cecelia**'s home directory:

```
[george@turtle george]$ scp cecelia@turtle.mytrek.com:mydoc1   .
cecelia@turtle.mytrek.com's password:
mydoc1     0% |                          |    0 --:--
ETA
mydoc1   100% |**************************|   17 00:00
[george@turtle george]$
```

From a Windows system, you can also use **scp** clients such as **winscp**, which will interact with Linux scp-enabled systems.

sftp and sftp-server

With sftp, you can transfer FTP files secured by encryption. The sftp program uses the same commands as ftp. This client, which works only with SSH2, operates much like ftp, with many of the same commands. Use **sftp** instead of **ftp** to invoke the sftp client:

```
sftp releases.ubuntu.com
```

To use the sftp client to connect to an FTP server, that server needs to be operating the **sftp-server** application. The SSH server invokes **sftp-server** to provide encrypted FTP transmissions to those using the sftp client. The sftp-server and client use the SSH File Transfer Protocol (SFTP) to perform FTP operations securely.

Port Forwarding (Tunneling)

If, for some reason, you can connect to a secure host only by going through an insecure host, ssh provides a feature called *port forwarding*, which lets you secure the insecure segment of your connection. This involves simply specifying the port at which the insecure host is to connect to the secure one. This sets up a direct connection between the local host and the remote host, through the intermediary insecure host. Encrypted data is passed through directly. This process is referred to as *tunneling*, creating a secure tunnel of encrypted data through connected servers.

You can set up port forwarding to a port on the remote system or to one on your local system. To forward a port on the remote system to a port on your local system, use **ssh** with the **-R** option, followed by an argument holding the local port, the remote host address, and the remote port to be forwarded, each separated from the next by a colon. This works by allocating a socket to listen to the port on the remote side. Whenever a connection is made to this port, the connection is forwarded over the secure channel and a connection is made to a remote port from the local machine. In the following example, port 22 on the local system is connected to port 23 on the **rabbit.mytrek.com** remote system:

```
ssh -R 22:rabbit.mytrek.com:23
```

To forward a port on your local system to a port on a remote system, use the **ssh -L** command, followed by an argument holding the local port, the remote host address, and the remote port to be forwarded, each two arguments separated by a colon. A socket is allocated to listen to the port on the local side. Whenever a connection is made to this port, the connection is forwarded over the secure channel and a connection is made to the remote port on the remote machine. In the following example, port 22 on the local system is connected to port 23 on the **rabbit.mytrek.com** remote system:

```
ssh -L 22:rabbit.mytrek.com:23
```

You can use the **LocalForward** and **RemoteForward** options in your **.ssh/config** file to set up port forwarding for particular hosts or to specify a default for all hosts to which you connect.

SSH Configuration

The SSH configuration file for each user is in the user's **.ssh/config** file. The **/etc/ssh/ssh_config** file is used to set sitewide defaults. In the configuration file, you can set various options, as listed in the **ssh_config** man document. The configuration file is designed to specify options for different remote hosts to which you might connect. It is organized into segments, where each segment begins with the keyword **HOST**, followed by the IP address of the host. The following lines hold the options you have set for that host. A segment ends at the next **HOST** entry. Of particular interest are the **User** and **Cipher** options. Use the **User** option to specify the names of users on the remote system who are allowed access. With the **Cipher** option, you can select which encryption method to use for a particular host. Encryption methods include IDEA, DES (standard), triple-DES (3DES), Blowfish (128 bit), Arcfour (RSA's RC4), and Twofish. The following example allows access from **larisa** at **turtle.mytrek.com** and uses Blowfish encryption for transmissions:

```
Host turtle.mytrek.com
     User larisa
     Compression no
     Cipher blowfish
```

To specify global options that apply to any host to which you connect, create a **HOST** entry with the asterisk as its host: **HOST ***. This entry must be placed at the end of the configuration file because an option is changed only the first time it is set. Any subsequent entries for an option are ignored. Because a host matches on both its own entry and the global one, its specific entry should come before the global entry. The asterisk (*****) and the question mark (**?**) are both wildcard matching operators that enable you to specify a group of hosts with the same suffix or prefix. Here's an example:

```
Host *
   FallBackToRsh yes
   KeepAlive no
   Cipher idea
```

Kerberos

User authentication can further be controlled for certain services by Kerberos servers. Kerberos authentication provides another level of security whereby individual services can be protected, allowing use of a service only to users who are cleared for access.

The name *Kerberos* comes from Greek mythology and is the name of the three-headed watchdog for Hades. Kerberos is a network authentication protocol that provides encrypted authentication to connections between a client and a server. As an authentication protocol, Kerberos requires a client to prove its identity using encryption methods before it can access a server. Once authenticated, the client and server can conduct all communications using encryption.

While firewalls protect only from outside attacks, Kerberos is designed to protect from attacks inside the network as well. Users already within a network could try to break into local servers. To prevent this, Kerberos places protection around the servers themselves, rather than around an entire network or a computer. A free version is available from the Massachusetts Institute of Technology at **http://web.mit.edu/kerberos** under the MIT Public License, which is similar to the GNU Public License. Be sure to check the MIT site for recent upgrades and detailed documentation, including FAQs, manuals, and tutorials.

Ubuntu installs the Kerberos support libraries by default. You can install the Kerberos server and several Kerberos clients using the **krb5** packages. The server is **krb5-server**, which will also select the kdc server. The **krb5-clients** package includes the Kerberos secured replacements for RSH, RCP, telnet, and the FTP client. Selecting **krb5-server** or **krb5-clients** will install needed support packages including **krb5-config**, configuration files for Kerberos on Ubuntu. Tools you need to communicate with the server, such as **kadmin**, are included in the **krb5-user** package. Detailed configuration is available on the **krb5-doc** package. Kerberos secured servers are also available for FTP, telnet, and RSH. All the Kerberos packages, except for the configuration and documentation packages, are on the universe repository.

TIP *The Kerberos V5 package includes its own versions of network tools such as telnet, RCP, FTP, and RSH. These provide secure authenticated access by remote users. The tools operate in the same way as their original counterparts. The package also contains a Kerberos version of the* **su** *administrative login command,* **ksu***.*

Kerberos Servers

The key to Kerberos is a Kerberos server through which all requests for any server services are channeled. The Kerberos server then authenticates a client, identifying the client and validating the client's right to use a particular server. The server maintains a database of authorized users. Kerberos then issues the client an encrypted ticket that the client can use to gain access to the server. For example, if a user needs to check her e-mail, a request for use of the mail server is sent to the Kerberos server, which then authenticates the user and issues a ticket that is used to access the mail server. Without a Kerberos-issued ticket, no one can access any of the servers. Originally, this process required that users undergo a separate authentication procedure for each server to which they wanted access. However, users now need to perform only an initial authentication that is valid for all servers.

This process involves the use of two servers: an authentication server (AS) and a ticket-granting server (TGS). Together they make up what is known as the *key distribution center* (KDC). In effect, they distribute keys used to unlock access to services. The authentication server first validates a user's identity. The AS issues a ticket called the *ticket-granting ticket* (TGT) that allows the user to access the TGS. The TGS then issues the user another ticket to access a service. This way, the user never has any direct access of any kind to a server during the authentication process. The process is somewhat more complex than described. An authenticator using information such as the current time, a checksum, and an optional encryption key is sent along with the ticket and is decrypted with the session key. This authenticator is used by a service to verify a user's identity.

NOTE *You can view your list of current tickets with the* **klist** *command.*

Authentication Process

The AS validates a user with information in its user database. Each user needs to be registered in the AS database. The database will include a user password and other user information. To access the AS, the user provides a username and password. The password is used to generate a user key with which communication between the AS and the user is encrypted. The user will have his own copy of the user key with which to decrypt communications. The authentication process is illustrated in Figure 19-2.

Accessing a service with Kerberos involves the following steps:

1. The user must be validated by the AS and granted access to the TGS with a ticket access key. You do this by issuing the **kinit** command, which will ask you enter your Kerberos username and then send it on to the AS (the Kerberos username is usually the same as your username):

```
kinit
```

2. The AS generates a TGT with which to access the TGS. This ticket will include a session key that will be used to let you access the TGS. The TGT is sent back to you encrypted with your user key (password).

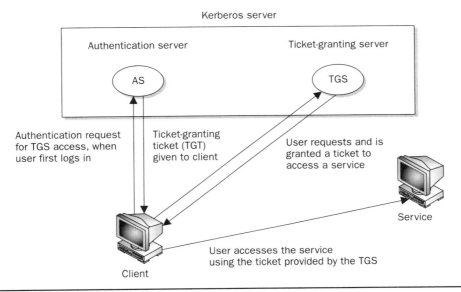

Kerberos server

Authentication server   Ticket-granting server

AS   TGS

Authentication request   Ticket-granting
for TGS access, when   ticket (TGT)   User requests and is
user first logs in   given to client   granted a ticket to
                                                access a service

                                                                    Service

                           User accesses the service
                           using the ticket provided by the TGS

Client

FIGURE 19-2   Kerberos authentication

3. The **kinit** program then prompts you to enter your Kerberos password, which it uses to decrypt the TGT. You can manage your Kerberos password with the **kpasswd** command.

4. Now you can use a client program such as a mail client program to access the mail server, for instance. When you do so, the TGT accesses the TGS, which then generates a ticket for accessing the mail server. The TGS generates a new session key for use with just the mail server. This is provided in the ticket sent to you for accessing the mail server. In effect, a TGT session key is used for accessing the TGS, and a mail session key is used for accessing the mail server. The ticket for the mail server is sent to you encrypted with the TGS session key.

5. The client then uses the mail ticket received from the TGS to access the mail server.

6. If you want to use another service such as FTP, when your FTP client sends a request to the TGS for a ticket, the TGS will automatically obtain authorization from the AS and issue an FTP ticket with an FTP session key. This kind of support remains in effect for a limited period of time, usually several hours, after which you again have to use **kinit** to undergo the authentication process and access the TGS. You can manually destroy any tickets you have with the **kdestroy** command.

NOTE *With Kerberos V5, a Kerberos login utility is provided whereby users are automatically granted TGTs when they log in normally. This avoids the need to use* **kinit** *to obtain a TGT manually.*

PART VI

Kerberized Services

Setting up a particular service to use Kerberos (known as *Kerberizing*) can be a complicated process. A Kerberized service needs to check the user's identity and credentials, check for a ticket for the service, and if one is not present, obtain one. Once Kerberized services are set up, their use is nearly transparent to the user. Tickets are automatically issued and authentication carried out without any extra effort by the user. The **/etc/services** file should contain a listing of specific Kerberized services. These are services such as **kpasswd**, **kshell**, and **klogin** that provide Kerberos password, superuser access, and login services.

Kerberos also provides its own Kerberized network tools for ftp, rsh, rcp, and rlogin. These are located at **/usr/bin** and use the same names as the original network tools with the prefix **krb5-**, as in **krb5-ftp** for the command line FTP client. The **/usr/bin/ftp** entry become a link to the **/etc/alternatives/ftp** item, which in turn is a link to **/usr/bin/krb5-ftp**. The `rsh`, `rcp`, and `rlogin` commands have the same kind of links. The `telnet` command will link to **/usr/bin/telnet.krb5**.

Kerberos Servers and Clients

Installing and configuring a Kerberos server is a complex process. Carefully check the documentation for installing the current versions. Some of the key areas are listed here. In the Kerberos configuration file, **krb5.conf**, you can set such features as the encryption method used and the database name. When installing Kerberos, be sure to follow the instructions carefully for providing administrative access. You can start, stop, and restart the Kerberos server with the **krb5-admin-server** and the **krb5-kdc** scripts in the **/etc/init.d** directory.

You will need to configure the server for your network, along with clients for each host (the **krb5-server** package for servers and **krb5-clients** for clients). To configure your server, you first specify your Kerberos realm and domain. You then create a database with the **kdb5_util** command and the `create` option:

```
kdb5_util create -s
```

You will be prompted to enter a master key. You then need to add a local principal, a local user with full administrative access from the host on which the server runs. Start the **kadmin.local** tool and use the **addprincipal** command to add the local principal. You can then start the **krb5-admin-server** and **krb5-kdc** scripts.

On each client host, use the **kadmin** tool with the **addprincipal** command to add a principal for the host. Also add a host principal for each host on your network with a `host/` qualifier, as in **host/rabbit.mytrek.com**. You can use the `-randkey` option to specify a random key. Then save local copies of the host keys, using the `ktadd` command to save them in the **/etc/krb5.keytab** file. Each host needs to also have the same **/etc/krb5.conf** configuration file on its system, specifying the Kerberos server and the kdc host.

NOTE *When you configure Kerberos with the authentication tool, you will be able to enter the realm, KDC server, and Kerberos server. Default entries will be displayed using the domain* **example.com**. *Be sure to specify the realm in uppercase letters. A new entry for your realm will be made in the realms segment of* **/etc/krb5.conf**, *listing the kdc and server entries you made.*

20

CHAPTER

Firewalls

Most systems currently connected to the Internet are open to attempts by outside users to gain unauthorized access. Outside users can try to gain access directly by setting up an illegal connection, by intercepting valid communications from users remotely connected to the system, or by pretending to be valid users. Firewalls, encryption, and authentication procedures can be used to protect against such attacks. A *firewall* prevents any direct unauthorized attempts at access, *encryption* protects transmissions from authorized remote users, and *authentication* verifies that a user requesting access has the right to do so. The current Linux kernel incorporates support for firewalls using the **netfilter** (iptables) packet filtering package. To implement a firewall, you simply provide a series of rules to govern what kind of access you want to allow on your system. If that system is also a gateway for a private network, the system's firewall capability can effectively help protect the network from outside attacks.

Like all Linux systems, Ubuntu implements its firewall using iptables. However, you can choose from several different popular firewall management tools. Ubuntu now provides its own firewall management tool called the Uncomplicated Firewall (**ufw**). iptables and ufw are on the Ubuntu main repository, and all other firewall tools are in the universe repository. You can also choose to use other popular management tools such as Firestarter or Firewall Builder (**fwbuilder**). Firestarter provides a desktop interface whereas ufw is command line only. Both ufw and Firestarter are covered in this chapter, along with the underlying iptables firewall application. Search Synaptic for *firewall* to see a more complete listing. Firewall tools are listed in Table 20-1.

Uncomplicated Firewall

The Uncomplicated Firewall, ufw, is now the official firewall application for Ubuntu. It provides a simple firewall that can be managed with a few command line operations. Like all firewall applications, ufw uses iptables to define rules and run the firewall. The ufw application is a management interface for iptables. Default iptables rules are kept in before and after files, with added rules in user files. The iptables rule files are held in the **/etc/ufw** directory. Firewall configuration for certain packages will be placed in the **/usr/share/ufw.d** directory. The ufw firewall is started up at boot using the **/etc/init.d/ufw** script.

Firewall	Description
iptables	netfilter, NAT, and mangle: **netfilter.org** (main repository)
ufw	Uncomplicated Firewall: **https://wiki.ubuntu.com/UbuntuFirewall** (Ubuntu Main repository); also see Ubuntu Server Guide at **http://doc.ubuntu.com**
Firestarter	Firestarter firewall configuration tool, **www.fs-security.com** (universe repository)
Firewall Builder	Firewall configuration tool: allow for more complex configuration, **www.fwbuilder.org** (universe repository)
gnome-lokkit	Basic firewall configuration (universe repository)
Shorewall	Shoreline firewall: **www.shorewall.net** (universe repository)
Guarddog	KDE firewall configuration tool: **www.simonzone.com/software/guarddog** (universe repository)

TABLE 20-1 Ubuntu Firewall Configuration Tools

iptables firewall rules are set up using ufw commands entered on a command line in a terminal window. Most users may only need to use ufw commands to allow or deny access by services like the Web server or Samba server. To check the current firewall status, listing those services allowed or blocked, use the **status** command:

```
sudo ufw status
```

If the firewall is not enabled, you will first have to enable it with the **enable** command:

```
sudo ufw enable
```

You can restart the firewall, reloading your rules, using the **/etc/init.d/ufw restart** command:

```
sudo /etc/init.d/ufw restart
```

You can then add rules using the **allow** and **deny** commands and their options, as listed in Table 20-2. To allow a service, use the **allow** command and the service name—the name for the service listed in the **/etc/services** file. The following command allows the ftp service:

```
sudo ufw allow ftp
```

If the service you want is not listed in **/etc/services**, and you know the port and protocol it uses, can specify the port and protocol directly. For example, the Samba service uses port 137 and protocol TCP:

```
sudo ufw allow 137/tcp
```

The **status** operation will then show what services are allowed:

```
sudo ufw status
To                      Action              From
21:tcp                  ALLOW               Anywhere
21:udp                  ALLOW               Anywhere
137:tcp                 ALLOW               Anywhere
```

Commands	Description
`enable, disable`	Turn the firewall on or off
`status`	Display status along with services allowed or denied
`logging on, logging off`	Turn logging on or off
`default allow, default deny`	Set the default policy, **allow** is open, **deny** is restrictive
`allow` *service*	Allow access by a service; services are defined in **/etc/services** which specifies the ports for that service
`allow` *port-number/protocol*	Allow access on a particular port using specified protocol; the protocol is optional
`deny` *service*	Deny access by a service
`delete` *rule*	Delete an installed rule; use **allow** or **deny** and include rule specifics
`proto` *protocol*	Specify *protocol* in **allow** or **deny** rule
`from` *address*	Specify source *address* in **allow** or **deny** rule
`to` *address*	Specify destination *address* in **allow** or **deny** rule
`port` *port*	Specify *port* in **allow** or **deny** rule for **from** and **to** address operations

TABLE 20-2   ufw Firewall Operations

To remove a rule, prefix it with the `delete` command:

```
sudo ufw delete allow 137/tcp
```

More detailed rules can be specified using **address**, **port**, and **protocol** commands. These are similar to the actual iptables commands. Packets to and from particular networks, hosts, and ports can be controlled. The following denies SSH access (port 22) from host 192.168.03:

```
sudo ufw deny proto tcp from 192.168.03 to any port 22
```

The rules you add are placed in the **/var/lib/ufw/user.rules** file as iptables rules. Ufw is just a front end for **iptables-restore**, which will read this file and set up the firewall using iptables commands. ufw will also have **iptables-restore** read the **before.rules** and **after.rules** files in the **/etc/ufw** directory. These files are considered administrative files that include required supporting rules for your iptables firewall. Administrators can add their own iptables rules to these files for system specific features such as IP masquerading.

NOTE *The Ubuntu Server Guide (**http://doc.ubuntu.com**) shows information on how to implement IP masquerading on ufw.*

The **before.rules** file will specify a table with the * symbol, as in *****filter** for the netfilter table. For the NAT table, you would use ***nat**. At the end of each table segment, a **COMMIT** command is needed to instruct ufw to apply the rules. Rules use **-A** for allow and **-D** for deny, assuming the **iptables** command. The following would implement IP forwarding when placed at the end of the **before.rules** file (see Ubuntu firewall server documentation). This particular rule works on the first Ethernet device (eth0) for a local network (192.168.0.0/24):

```
# nat Table rules
*nat
:POSTROUTING ACCEPT [0:0]
# Forward traffic from eth1 through eth0.
-A POSTROUTING -s 192.168.0.0/24 -o eth0 -j MASQUERADE
# don't delete the 'COMMIT' line or these NAT table rules won't be processed
COMMIT
```

Default settings for ufw are placed in **/etc/defaults/ufw**. Here you will find the default INPUT, OUTPUT, and FORWARD policies. A **default deny** command will set the default INPUT to DROP and OUTPUT to ACCEPT, whereas **default allow** will set both INPUT and OUTPUT defaults to ACCEPT. FORWARD will be set to DROP. To allow IP masquerading, FORWARD would have to be set to ACCEPT. Any user rules you have set up would not be affected. You would have to change these manually.

Firestarter

Like all Linux systems, firewalls are implemented using iptables. Setting up the iptables rules can become very complicated, and firewall configuration tools can be used to set up your firewall, with most rules being automatically generated for you. Ubuntu provides the Firestarter firewall configuration tool for this purpose. To access Firestarter, choose System | Administration | Firewall. Much of the configuration is automatic. If you are using a local home or work network, you may have to add rules for services such as Samba Windows network access or the network address of your local network.

The first time you start up Firestarter, the Firewall Wizard will prompt you for your network device and Internet connection sharing information. After the Welcome screen, the Network Device Setup window lets you select your network device, such as an Ethernet device or a modem, as well as whether to use DHCP (Dynamic Host Control Protocol) to detect your address information (Figure 20-1).

The Internet Connection Sharing Setup window is rarely used. You can probably skip it. It is used only for local networks on which your computer is used as a gateway through which other computers can access the Internet. A second Ethernet device is usually connected to the local network as well as a local DHCP server controlling local network addressing. Most Internet gateways are now handled by dedicated routers, rather than computers.

Firestarter starts with a window titled with your computer name, with three tabs: Status, Events, and Policy (Figure 20-2). The toolbar entries will change with each tab you select. The Status tab lets you start and stop your firewall using the Stop/Start Firewall button in the toolbar. Its status is shown as a play or stop icon in the Status area of the Status tab. The Events area of this tab shows inbound and outbound traffic, and the Network area lists your

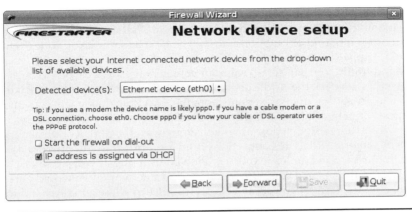

FIGURE 20-1   Firestarter Firewall Wizard, Network Device Setup window

network devices along with device information such as the number of packets received, sent, and average activity. Usually only one device is listed (a computer functioning as a gateway will have several). An expansion list will show Active Connections, revealing what kind of connection is active, such as Samba or Internet connections.

The Events tab lists any rejected connections as blocked connections. The Save, Clear, and Reload buttons on the toolbar let you save the event log, clear it, or reload to see the latest events.

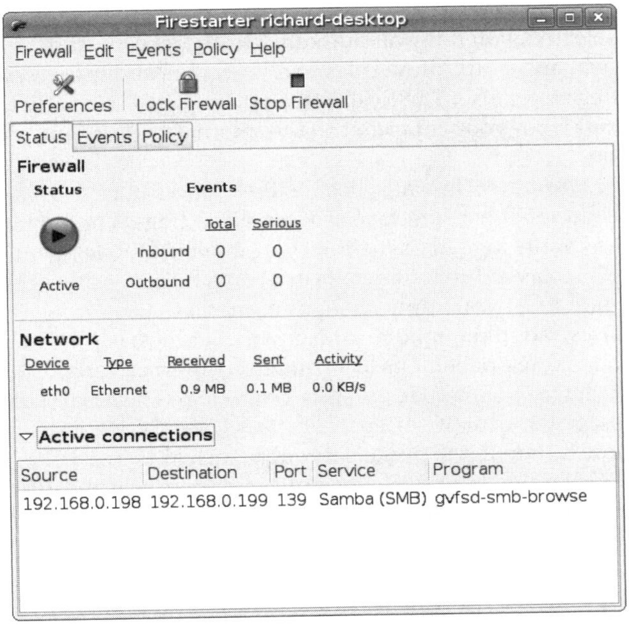

FIGURE 20-2   Firestarter firewall

The Policy tab shows rules for allowing host and service connections. A pop-up menu lets you see inbound traffic or outbound traffic policies. On this tab, you can add your own simplified rules for inbound or outbound hosts. The toolbar shows Add Rule, Remove Rule, Edit Rule, and Apply Rule buttons.

For inbound traffic, you can set up rules for connections, services, or forwarding. Click the segment, and then click the Add Rule button. The dialog that appears depends on the type of rule you are setting up. For a connection, the Add Rule dialog lets you enter the host, IP address, or network from which you can receive connections. For a service, you can select the service to allow from a pop-up menu, along with the port, as well as whether to allow access by anyone or only to connections from a specific host or network. By default, all inbound traffic is denied, unless explicitly allowed by a rule. If you are setting up a firewall for only your personal computer connected to a network, you would enter a rule for the local network address. You could also set up rules to allow access by services such as Samba or BitTorrent.

Setting up outbound traffic is more complex. You can set either a permissive or restrictive policy. The Permissive policy is selected by default. The Permissive entry will reject blacklisted hosts and services, and the Restrictive entry will allow whitelisted hosts and services. Each has both a connection and service segment, just like the inbound connections, with the same options.

If Permissive is selected, you will allow all outbound traffic, except traffic you specifically deny. For this configuration, you can create Deny rules for certain hosts and services. When setting up a Deny rule for a service, you can choose a service from a pop-up menu and specify its port. You can then reject either anyone using this service, or specify a particular host or network. For a connection, you specify the host, IP address, or network that can connect. The connection rules act like your own blacklist, listing hosts or networks to which you or others on your network cannot connect.

If Restrictive is selected, you deny all outbound traffic, except traffic you specifically allow. In this case, you can set up Allow rules to allow connections by certain hosts and services, rejecting everything else. The Restrictive option is not normally used, as it would cut off any connections from your computer to the Internet, unless you added a rule to permit the connection.

To configure your Firestarter firewall, click the Preferences button. This opens a Preference window, where you can set either Interface or Firewall settings. For the Interface settings, you can set either the Events logged or the Policy. The Events tab lets you eliminate logging of unwanted events, such as redundant events or events from specific hosts or ports. The Policy tab has an option to let you apply changes immediately.

For Firewall Settings, tabs offer options for Network Settings, ICMP Filtering, ToS Filtering, and Advanced Options. Network Settings lets you select your network device. Here you could change your network device to Ethernet, wireless, or modem. The ICMP Filtering tab blocks Internet Control Message Protocol (ICMP) packet attacks (see "ICMP Packets" later in the chapter). Options allow certain ICMP packets through, such as Unreachable to notify you of an unknown site. The ToS Filtering tab lets you prioritize your packets by both the kind of service and maximized efficiency. For the kind of service, you can choose either Workstations, Servers, or the X Window System. For maximized efficiency, you can choose Reliability, Throughput, or Interactivity. Workstations and Throughput are selected by default.

The Advanced Options tab lets you select the drop method (Silent or Error Reported), the Broadcast traffic rejection policy for internal and external connections (External broadcasts are blocked by default), and traffic validation block reserved addresses.

iptables, NAT, Mangle, and ip6tables

Firewalls are implemented on Linux systems, including Ubuntu, with the **Netfilter** software package. Netfilter implements packet filtering, network address translations (NAT), and packet mangling for the Linux 2.4 kernel and above. Packet filtering, NAT, and packet mangling are implemented using tables of rules. The Netfilter software is developed by the Netfilter Project, at **http://netfilter.org**, which offers detailed documentation and tutorials.

Packet filtering is the process of deciding whether a packet received by the firewall host should be passed on to the local network. The packet filtering software checks the source and destination addresses of the packet and sends the packet on, if it's allowed. Even if your system is not part of a network but connects directly to the Internet, you can still use the firewall feature to control access to your system. Of course, this also provides much more security.

An additional task performed by firewalls is network address translation (NAT), which performs tasks such as redirecting packets to certain hosts, forwarding packets to other networks, and changing the host source of packets to implement IP masquerading. The *packet mangling* table is used to modify packet information. Rules applied specifically to this table are often designed to control the mundane behavior of packets, such as routing, connection size, and priority.

iptables

The command used to execute packet filtering, NAT tasks, and packet mangling is `iptables`, and the software is commonly referred to as simply iptables. However, netfilter implements packet filtering, NAT tasks, and packet mangling separately using different tables and commands. A table will hold the set of commands for its application. This approach streamlines the packet-filtering task, letting iptables perform packet-filtering checks without the overhead of also having to do address translations or mangling. NAT operations are also freed from being mixed in with packet-filtering checks. You use the `iptables` command for packet filtering, NAT tasks, and packet mangling. Each operation has its own table of rules: *filter* for packet filtering, *nat* for NAT tasks, and *mangle* for packet mangling. For NAT you specify the NAT table with the `-t nat` option. For the mangle table you use the `-t mangle` option. The packet filtering is the default. It can be specified with the `-t filter` option, but it's usually left out, assuming that if a table is not specified it is a filter operation. In addition, netfilter also handles certain exemptions to connection tracking operations in a **raw** table.

On Ubuntu, firewall applications such as fvw and Firestarter will set up their own iptables files containing `iptables` commands. When these are run, they will set up the tables and rules used to filter, translate, and mangle packets. The Firestarter iptables files are located at **/etc/firestarter**, whereas in ufw they are located at **/etc/ufw**.

ip6tables

The ip6tables package provides support for IPv6 addressing. It is identical to iptables except that it allows the use of IPv6 addresses instead of IPv4 addresses. Both filter and mangle tables are supported in ip6tables, but not NAT tables. The filter tables support the same options and commands supported in iptables. The mangle tables will allow specialized packet changes such as those for iptables, using **PREROUTING**, **INPUT**, **OUTPUT**, **FORWARD**, and **POSTROUTING** rules. Some extensions have **ipv6** labels for their names, such as **ipv6-icmp**, which corresponds to the iptables **icmp** extension. The **ipv6headers** extension is used to select IPv6 headers.

Modules

Unlike its predecessor ipchains, netfilter is designed to be modularized and extensible. Capabilities can be added in the form of modules such as the state module, which adds connection tracking. Most modules are loaded as part of the iptables service. Others are optional; you can elect to load them before installing rules. The iptables modules are located at **/usr/lib/*kernel-version*/kernel/net/ipv4/netfilter**, where *kernel-version* is your kernel number. For IPv6 modules, check the **ipv6/netfilter** directory. Modules that load automatically will have an **ipt_** prefix, and optional modules have just an **ip_** prefix. If you are writing you own iptables script, you would have to add **modprobe** commands to load optional modules directly.

Packet Filtering

Netfilter is essentially a framework for packet management that can check packets for particular network protocols and notify parts of the kernel listening for them. Built on the netfilter framework is the packet selection system implemented by iptables. With iptables, different tables of rules can be set up to select packets according to differing criteria. Netfilter currently supports three tables: filter, NAT, and mangle. Packet filtering is implemented using a filter table that holds rules for dropping or accepting packets. Network address translation operations such as IP masquerading are implemented using the NAT table that holds IP masquerading rules. The mangle table is used for specialized packet changes. Changes can be made to packets before they are sent out, when they are received, or as they are being forwarded. This structure is extensible in that new modules can define their own tables with their own rules. This also greatly improves efficiency: Instead of all packets checking one large table, they access only the table of rules they need.

IP table rules are managed using the **iptables** command. For this command, you will need to specify the table you want to manage. The default is the filter table, which doesn't need to be specified. You can list the rules you have added at any time with the **-L** and **-n** options, as shown next. The **-n** option says to use only numeric output for both IP addresses and ports, avoiding a DNS lookup for hostnames. You could, however, just use the **-L** option to see the port labels and hostnames:

```
iptables -L -n
```

NOTE *In iptables commands, chain names must be entered in uppercase, as with the chain names INPUT, OUTPUT, and FORWARD.*

Chains

Rules are combined into different *chains*. The kernel uses chains to manage packets it receives and sends out. A chain is simply a checklist of rules that specify what action to take for packets containing certain headers. The rules operate with an if-then-else structure. If a packet does not match the first rule, the next rule is then checked, and so on. If the packet does not match any rules, the kernel consults chain policy. Usually, at this point the packet is rejected. If the packet does match a rule, it is passed to its target, which determines what to do with the packet. If a packet does not match any of the rules, it is passed to the chain's default target. The standard targets are listed in Table 20-3.

Target	Function
ACCEPT	Allow packet to pass through the firewall
DROP	Deny access by the packet
REJECT	Deny access and notify the sender
QUEUE	Send packet to user space
RETURN	Jump to the end of the chain and let the default target process it

TABLE 20-3   iptables Targets

Targets

A *target* can, in turn, be another chain of rules, even a chain of user-defined rules. A packet could be passed through several chains before it finally reaches a target. In the case of user-defined chains, the default target is always the next rule in the chains from which it was called. This sets up a procedure- or function call–like flow of control found in programming languages. When a rule has a user-defined chain as its target, when activated, that user-defined chain is executed. If no rules are matched, execution returns to the next rule in the originating chain.

TIP   *Specialized targets and options can be added by means of kernel patches provided by the netfilter site. For example, the SAME patch returns the same address for all connections. A patch-o-matic option for the netfilter make file will patch your kernel source code, adding support for the new target and options. You can then rebuild and install your kernel.*

Firewall and NAT Chains

The kernel uses three firewall chains: INPUT, OUTPUT, and FORWARD. When a packet is received through an interface, the INPUT chain is used to determine what to do with it. The kernel then uses its routing information to decide where to send it. If the kernel sends the packet to another host, the FORWARD chain is checked. Before the packet is actually sent, the OUTPUT chain is also checked. In addition, two NAT table chains, POSTROUTING and PREROUTING, are implemented to handle masquerading and packet address modifications. The mangle table has its own versions of POSTROUTING, PREROUTING, INPUT, and FORWARD that can modify packets. The built-in netfilter chains are listed in Table 20-4.

Chain	Description
INPUT	Rules for incoming packets
OUTPUT	Rules for outgoing packets
FORWARD	Rules for forwarded packets
PREROUTING	Rules for redirecting or modifying incoming packets, NAT and mangle tables only
POSTROUTING	Rules for redirecting or modifying outgoing packets, NAT and mangle tables only

TABLE 20-4   Netfilter Built-in Chains

Adding and Changing Rules

You add and modify chain rules using an `iptables` command, which consists of the command `iptables`, followed by an argument denoting the command to execute. For example, `iptables -A` adds a new rule, whereas `iptables -D` deletes a rule. The `iptables` commands are listed in Table 20-5. The following command lists the chains along with their rules currently defined for your system. The output shows the default values created by `iptables` commands.

```
iptables -L -n
Chain input (policy ACCEPT):
Chain forward (policy ACCEPT):
Chain output (policy ACCEPT):
```

To add a new rule to a chain, you use `-A`. Use `-D` to remove it, and `-R` to replace it. Following the command, list the chain to which the rule applies, such as the INPUT, OUTPUT, or FORWARD chain, or a user-defined chain. Next, you list different options that specify the actions you want taken (most are the same as those used for iptables, with a few exceptions). The `-s` option specifies the source address attached to the packet, `-d` specifies the destination address, and the `-j` option specifies the target of the rule. The ACCEPT target will allow a packet to pass. The `-i` option now indicates the input device and can be used only with the INPUT and FORWARD chains. The `-o` option indicates the output device and can be used only for OUTPUT and FORWARD chains. Table 20-6 lists several basic options.

Option	Function
`-A` *chain*	Appends a rule to a chain
`-D` *chain* [*rulenum*]	Deletes matching rules from a chain; deletes rule *rulenum* (1 = first) from *chain*
`-I` *chain* [*rulenum*]	Inserts in *chain* as *rulenum* (default 1 = first)
`-R` *chain rulenum*	Replaces rule *rulenum* (1 = first) in *chain*
`-L` [*chain*]	Lists the rules in *chain* or all chains
`-E` [*chain*]	Renames a chain
`-F` [*chain*]	Deletes (flushes) all rules in *chain* or all chains
`-R` *chain*	Replaces a rule; rules are numbered from 1
`-Z` [*chain*]	Zero counters in *chain* or all chains
`-N` *chain*	Creates a new user-defined chain
`-X` chain	Deletes a user-defined chain
`-P` *chain target*	Changes policy on *chain* to *target*
`-t` *table*	Specify the table in which to add the chain; the **filter** table is the default, **nat** for NAT rules, **mangle** for packet mangling, **raw** for connection tracking exceptions

TABLE 20-5 iptables Commands

Option	Function
`-p` `[!]` *proto*	Specifies a protocol, such as TCP, UDP, ICMP, or ALL.
`-s` `[!]` *address*`[`/*mask*`]` `[!]` `[`*port*`[`:*port*`]]`	Specifies source address to match. With the *port* argument, you can specify the port.
`--sport` `[!]` `[`*port*`[`:*port*`]]`	Specifies source port. You can specify a range of ports using the colon, *port*:*port*.
`-d` `[!]` *address*`[`/*mask*`]` `[!]` `[`*port*`[`:*port*`]]`	Specifies destination address to match. With the *port* argument, you can specify the port.
`--dport` `[!]` `[`*port*`[`:*port*`]]`	Specifies destination port.
`--icmp-type` `[!]` *typename*	Specifies ICMP type.
`-i` `[!]` *name*`[+]`	Specifies an input network interface using its name (for example, `eth0`). The + symbol functions as a wildcard. The + attached to the end of the name matches all interfaces with that prefix (`eth+` matches all Ethernet interfaces). Can be used only with the INPUT chain.
`-j` *target* `[`*port*`]`	Specifies the target for a rule (specify `[port]` for REDIRECT target).
`--to-source` `<` *ipaddr*`>` `[-<` *ipaddr*`>]` `[:` *port*`-` *port*`]`	Used with the SNAT target, rewrites packets with new source IP address.
`--to-destination` `<` *ipaddr*`>` `[-<` *ipaddr*`>]` `[:` *port*`-` *port*`]`	Used with the DNAT target, rewrites packets with new destination IP address.
`-n`	Specifies numeric output of addresses and ports, used with `-L`.
`-o` `[!]` *name*`[+]`	Specifies an output network interface using its name (for example, `eth0`). Can be used only with FORWARD and OUTPUT chains.
`-t` *table*	Specifies a table to use, as in `-t nat` for the NAT table.
`-v`	Verbose mode, shows rule details, used with `-L`.
`-x`	Expands numbers (displays exact values), used with `-L`.
`[!]` `-f`	Matches second through last fragments of a fragmented packet.
`[!]` `-V`	Prints package version.
`!`	Negates an option or address.
`-m`	Specifies a module to use, such as state.
`--state`	Specifies options for the state module such as NEW, INVALID, RELATED, and ESTABLISHED. Used to detect packet's state. NEW references SYN packets (new connections).
`--syn`	SYN packets, new connections.
`--tcp-flags`	TCP flags: SYN, ACK, FIN, RST, URG, PS, and ALL for all flags.
`--limit`	Option for the limit module (`-m limit`). Used to control the rate of matches, matching a given number of times per second.
`--limit-burst`	Option for the limit module (`-m limit`). Specifies maximum burst before the limit kicks in. Used to control denial-of-service attacks.

TABLE 20-6   iptables Options

iptables Options

The **iptables** package is designed to be extensible, and a number of options with selection criteria can be included with iptables. For example, the TCP extension includes the **--syn** option that checks for SYN packets. The ICMP extension provides the **--icmp-type** option for specifying ICMP packets as those used in ping operations. The limit extension includes the **--limit** option, with which you can limit the maximum number of matching packets in a specified time period, such as a second.

In the following example, the user adds a rule to the INPUT chain to accept all packets originating from the address 192.168.0.55. Any packets that are received (**INPUT**) whose source address (**-s**) matches 192.168.0.55 are accepted and passed through (**-j ACCEPT**):

```
iptables -A INPUT -s 192.168.0.55 -j ACCEPT
```

Accepting and Denying Packets: DROP and ACCEPT

Two built-in targets can be used: DROP and ACCEPT. Other targets can be either user-defined chains or extensions added on, such as REJECT. Two special targets are used to manage chains: RETURN and QUEUE. RETURN indicates the end of a chain and returns to the chain from which it started. QUEUE is used to send packets to user space.

```
iptables -A INPUT -s www.myjunk.com -j DROP
```

You can turn a rule into its inverse with an **!** symbol. For example, to accept all incoming packets except those from a specific address, place an **!** symbol before the **-s** option and that address. The following example will accept all packets except those from the IP address 192.168.0.45:

```
iptables -A INPUT -j ACCEPT ! -s 192.168.0.45
```

You can specify an individual address using its domain name or its IP number. For a range of addresses, you can use the IP number of their network and the network IP mask. The IP mask can be an IP number or simply the number of bits making up the mask. For example, all of the addresses in network 192.168.0 can be represented by 192.168.0.0/ 225.255.255.0 or by 192.168.0.0/24. To specify any address, you can use 0.0.0.0/0.0.0.0 or simply 0/0. By default, rules reference any address if no **-s** or **-d** specification exists. The following example accepts messages coming in that are from (source) any host in the 192.168.0.0 network and that are going (destination) anywhere at all (the **-d** option is left out or could be written as **-d 0/0**):

```
iptables -A INPUT -s 192.168.0.0/24  -j ACCEPT
```

The iptables rules are usually applied to a specific network interface such as the Ethernet interface used to connect to the Internet. For a single system connected to the Internet, you will have two interfaces, one that is your Internet connection and a loopback interface (**lo**) for internal connections between users on your system. The network interface for the Internet is referenced using the device name for the interface. For example, an Ethernet card with the device name **/dev/eth0** would be referenced by the name **eth0**. A modem using PPP protocols with the device name **/dev/ppp0** would have the name **ppp0**. In iptables rules, you use the **-i** option to indicate the input device; it can be used only with the INPUT and FORWARD chains. The **-o** option indicates the output device and can be used only for OUTPUT and FORWARD chains. Rules can then be applied to packets arriving and leaving on particular network devices. In the following examples, the first rule references the Ethernet device **eth0**, and the second references the localhost:

```
iptables -A INPUT -j DROP -i eth0 -s 192.168.0.45
iptables -A INPUT -j ACCEPT  -i lo
```

User-Defined Chains

With iptables, the FORWARD and INPUT chains are evaluated separately; one does not feed into the other. This means that if you want to completely block certain addresses from passing through your system, you will need to add both a FORWARD rule and an INPUT rule for them:

```
iptables -A INPUT -j DROP -i eth0 -s 192.168.0.45
iptables -A FORWARD -j DROP -i eth0 -s 192.168.0.45
```

A common method for reducing repeated INPUT and FORWARD rules is to create a user chain into which both the INPUT and FORWARD chains feed. You define a user chain with the **-N** option. The next example shows the basic format for this arrangement. A new chain is created called *incoming* (it can be any name you choose). The rules you define for your FORWARD and INPUT chains are now defined for the incoming chain. The INPUT and FORWARD chains then use the incoming chain as a target, jumping directly to it and using its rules to process any packets they receive.

```
iptables -N incoming

iptables -A incoming -j DROP -i eth0 -s 192.168.0.45
iptables -A incoming -j ACCEPT  -i lo

iptables -A FORWARD -j incoming
iptables -A INPUT -j incoming
```

ICMP Packets

Firewalls often block certain Internet Control Message Protocol (ICMP) messages. ICMP redirect messages, in particular, can take control of your routing tasks. You need to enable some ICMP messages, however, such as those needed for ping, traceroute, and particularly destination-unreachable operations. In most cases, you always need to make sure destination-unreachable packets are allowed; otherwise, domain name queries could hang. Some of the more common ICMP packet types are listed in Table 20-7. You can enable an ICMP type of packet with the **--icmp-type** option, which takes as its argument a number or a name representing the message. The following examples enable the use of **echo-reply**, **echo-request**, and **destination-unreachable** messages, which have the numbers 0, 8, and 3:

```
iptables -A INPUT -j ACCEPT  -p icmp -i eth0 --icmp -type  echo-reply -d 10.0.0.1
iptables -A INPUT -j ACCEPT  -p icmp -i eth0 --icmp-type  echo-request -d 10.0.0.1
iptables -A INPUT -j ACCEPT -p icmp -i eth0 --icmp-type  destination-unreachable -d
10.0.0.1
```

Number	Name	Required By
0	**echo-reply**	ping
3	**destination-unreachable**	Any TCP/UDP traffic
5	**redirect**	Routing if not running routing daemon
8	**echo-request**	ping
11	**time-exceeded**	traceroute

TABLE **20-7**   Common ICMP Packets

Their rule listing will look like this:

```
ACCEPT      icmp --  0.0.0.0/0           10.0.0.1            icmp type 0
ACCEPT      icmp --  0.0.0.0/0           10.0.0.1            icmp type 8
ACCEPT      icmp --  0.0.0.0/0           10.0.0.1            icmp type 3
```

Ping operations need to be further controlled to avoid the ping-of-death security threat. You can do this in several ways. One way is to deny any ping fragments. Ping packets are normally very small. You can block ping-of-death attacks by denying any ICMP packet that is a fragment. Use the **-f** option to indicate fragments:

```
iptables -A INPUT -p icmp -j DROP -f
```

Another way is to limit the number of matches received for ping packets. You use the limit module to control the number of matches on the ICMP ping operation. Use **-m limit** to use the limit module and **--limit** to specify the number of allowed matches. **1/s** will allow one match per second.

```
iptables -A FORWARD -p icmp --icmp-type echo-request -m limit --limit 1/s -j ACCEPT
```

Controlling Port Access

If your system is hosting an Internet service, such as a web or FTP server, you can use iptables to control access to it. You can specify a particular service by using the source port (**--sport**) or destination port (**--dport**) options with the port that the service uses. iptables lets you use names for ports such as **www** for the web server port. The names of services and the ports they use are listed in the **/etc/services** file, which maps ports to particular services. For a domain name server, the port would be **domain**. You can also use the port number if you want, preceding the number with a colon. The following example accepts all messages to the web server located at 192.168.0.43:

```
iptables -A INPUT -d 192.168.0.43 --dport www -j ACCEPT
```

You can also use port references to protect certain services and deny others. This approach is often used if you are designing a firewall that is much more open to the Internet, letting users make freer use of Internet connections. Certain services that you know can be harmful, such as telnet and NTP, can be denied selectively. For example, to deny any kind of telnet operation on your firewall, you can drop all packets coming in on the telnet port, 23. To protect NFS operations, you can deny access to the port used for the portmapper, 111. You can use either the port number or the port name. Here's an example:

```
# deny outside access to portmapper port on firewall.
iptables -A arriving  -j DROP -p tcp -i eth0  --dport 111
# deny outside access to telnet port on firewall.
iptables -A arriving  -j DROP -p tcp -i eth0  --dport telnet
```

The rule listing will look like this:

```
DROP      tcp  --  0.0.0.0/0    0.0.0.0/0    tcp dpt:111
DROP      tcp  --  0.0.0.0/0    0.0.0.0/0    tcp dpt:23
```

One port-related security problem is access to your X server on the XFree86 ports that range from 6000 to 6009. On a relatively open firewall, these ports could be used illegally to access your system through your X server. A range of ports can be specified with a colon, as in *6000:6009*. You can also use *x11* for the first port, *x11:6009*. Sessions on the X server can be secured by using SSH, which normally accesses the X server on port 6010.

```
iptables -A arriving  -j DROP -p tcp -i eth0  --dport 6000:6009
```

Common ports checked and their labels are shown here:

Service	Port Number	Port Label
Auth	113	auth
Finger	79	finger
FTP	21	ftp
NTP	123	ntp
Portmapper	111	sunrpc
Telnet	23	telnet
Web server	80	www
XFree86	6000:6009	x11:6009

Packet States: Connection Tracking

One of the more useful extensions is the state extension, which can easily detect tracking information for a packet. Connection tracking maintains information about a connection such as its source, destination, and port. It provides an effective means for determining which packets belong to an established or related connection. To use connection tracking, you specify the state module first with **-m state**. Then you can use the **--state** option. Here you can specify any of the following states:

State	Description
NEW	A packet that creates a new connection
ESTABLISHED	A packet that belongs to an existing connection
RELATED	A packet that is related to, but not part of, an existing connection, such as an ICMP error or a packet establishing an FTP data connection
INVALID	A packet that could not be identified for some reason
RELATED+REPLY	A packet that is related to an established connection but is not part of one directly

If you are designing a firewall that is meant to protect your local network from any attempts to penetrate it from an outside network, you may want to restrict packets coming in. Simply denying access by all packets is unfeasible, because users connected to outside servers—say, on the Internet—must receive information from them. You can, instead, deny access by a particular kind of packet used to initiate a connection. The idea is that an attacker must initiate a connection from the outside. The headers of these kinds of packets have their SYN bit set on and their FIN and ACK bits empty. The state module's NEW state matches on any such SYN packet. By specifying a DROP target for such packets, you deny access by any packet that is part of an attempt to make a connection with your system. Anyone trying to connect to your system from the outside is unable to do so. Users on your local system who have initiated connections with outside hosts can still communicate with them. The following example will drop any packets trying to create a new connection on the **eth0** interface, though they will be accepted on any other interface:

```
iptables -A INPUT -m state --state NEW -i eth0 -j DROP
```

NOTE *The raw table can be used to disable connection tracking for packets using the NOTRACK target. It supports a PREROUTING and OUTPUT chains.*

You can use the **!** operator on the **eth0** device combined with an ACCEPT target to compose a rule that will accept any new packets except those on the **eth0** device. If the **eth0** device is the only one that connects to the Internet, this still effectively blocks outside access. At the same time, input operation for other devices such as your localhost are free to make new connections. This kind of conditional INPUT rule is used to allow access overall with exceptions. It usually assumes that a later rule such as a chain policy will drop remaining packets. Here's an example:

```
iptables -A INPUT -m state --state NEW ! -i eth0 -j ACCEPT
```

The next example will accept any packets that are part of an established connection or related to such a connection on the **eth0** interface:

```
iptables -A INPUT -m state --state ESTABLISHED,RELATED -j ACCEPT
```

TIP *You can use the iptstate tool to display the current state table.*

Specialized Connection Tracking: ftp, irc, Amanda, tftp

To track certain kinds of packets, iptables uses specialized connection tracking modules. These are optional modules that you have to load manually. To track passive FTP connections, you would have to load the **ip_conntrack_ftp** module. To add NAT table support, you would also load the **ip_nat_ftp** module. For IRC connections, you use **ip_conntrack_irc** and **ip_nat_irc**. Corresponding modules exist for Amanda (the backup server) and TFTP (Trivial FTP).

If you are writing your own iptables script, you would have to add **modprobe** commands to load the modules:

```
modprobe ip_conntrack ip_conntrack_ftp ip_nat_ftp
modprobe ip_conntrack_amanda ip_nat_amanda
```

Network Address Translation

Network address translation (NAT) is the process whereby a system will change the destination or source of packets as they pass through the system. A packet will traverse several linked systems on a network before it reaches its final destination. Normally, they will simply pass the packet on. However, if one of these systems performs a NAT on a packet, it can change the source or destination. A packet sent to a particular destination can have its destination address changed. To make this work, the system also needs to remember such changes so that the source and destination for any reply packets are altered back to the original addresses of the packet being replied to.

NAT is often used to provide access to systems that may be connected to the Internet through only one IP address. Such is the case with networking features such as IP masquerading, support for multiple servers, and transparent proxying. With IP masquerading, NAT operations will change the destination and source of a packet moving through a firewall/gateway linking the Internet to computers on a local network. The gateway has a single IP address that the other local computers can use through NAT operations. If you have multiple servers but only one IP address, you can use NAT operations to send packets to the alternate servers. You can also use NAT operations to have your IP address reference a particular server application such as a web server (transparent proxy). NAT tables are not implemented for ip6tables.

NOTE *Using proxies, you can control access to specific services, such as web or FTP servers. You need a proxy for each service you want to control. The web server has its own web proxy, while an FTP server has an FTP proxy. Proxies can also be used to cache commonly used data, such as web pages, so that users needn't constantly access the originating site. The proxy software commonly used on Linux systems is Squid.*

Adding NAT Rules

Packet selection rules for NAT operations are added to the NAT table managed by the **iptables** command. To add rules to the NAT table, you have to specify the NAT table with the **-t** option. Thus, to add a rule to the NAT table, you would have to specify the NAT table with the **-t nat** option, as shown here:

```
iptables -t nat
```

With the **-L** option, you can list the rules you have added to the NAT table:

```
iptables -t nat -L -n
```

Adding the **-n** option will list IP addresses and ports in numeric form. This will speed up the listing, as iptables will not attempt to do a DNS lookup to determine the hostname for the IP address.

NAT Targets and Chains

Two types of NAT operations can be used: source NAT, specified as SNAT target, and destination NAT, specified as DNAT target. SNAT target is used for rules that alter source addresses, and DNAT target is used for those that alter destination addresses.

Three chains in the NAT table are used by the kernel for NAT operations: PREROUTING, POSTROUTING, and OUTPUT. PREROUTING is used for destination NAT (DNAT) rules, which are packets that are arriving. POSTROUTING is used for source NAT (SNAT) rules, which are for packets leaving. OUTPUT is used for DNAT rules for locally generated packets.

As with packet filtering, you can specify source (**-s**) and destination (**-d**) addresses, as well as the input (**-i**) and output (**-o**) devices. The **-j** option will specify a target such as MASQUERADE. You implement IP masquerading by adding a MASQUERADE rule to the POSTROUTING chain:

```
# iptables -t nat -A POSTROUTING -o eth0 -j MASQUERADE
```

To change the source address of a packet leaving your system, you use the POSTROUTING rule with the SNAT target. For the SNAT target, you use the **--to-source** option to specify the source address:

```
# iptables -t nat -A POSTROUTING -o eth0 -j SNAT --to-source 192.168.0.4
```

To change the destination address of packets arriving on your system, you use the PREROUTING rule with the DNAT target and the **--to-destination** option:

```
# iptables -t nat -A PREROUTING -i eth0 \
          -j DNAT --to-destination 192.168.0.3
```

Specifying a port lets you change destinations for packets arriving on a particular port. In effect, this lets you implement port forwarding. In the next example, every packet arriving on port 80 (the web service port) is redirected to 10.0.0.3, which in this case would be a system running a web server:

```
  # iptables -t nat -A PREROUTING -i eth0 -dport 80 \
          -j DNAT --to-destination 10.0.0.3
```

With the TOS and MARK targets, you can mangle the packet to control its routing or priority. A TOS target sets the type of service for a packet, which can set the priority using criteria such as normal-service, minimize-cost, or maximize-throughput, among others.

The targets valid only for the NAT table are shown here:

SNAT	Modify source address, use **--to-source** option to specify new source address
DNAT	Modify destination address, use **--to-destination** option to specify new destination address
REDIRECT	Redirect a packet
MASQUERADE	IP masquerading
MIRROR	Reverse source and destination and send back to sender
MARK	Modify the Mark field to control message routing

NAT Redirection: Transparent Proxies

NAT tables can be used to implement any kind of packet redirection, a process transparent to the user. Redirection is commonly used to implement a transparent proxy. Redirection of packets is carried out with the REDIRECT target. With transparent proxies, packets received can be automatically redirected to a proxy server. For example, packets arriving on the web service port, 80, can be redirected to the Squid proxy service port, usually 3128. This involves a command to redirect a packet, using the REDIRECT target on the PREROUTING chain:

```
# iptables -t nat -A PREROUTING -i eth1 --dport 80 -j REDIRECT --to-port 3128
```

Packet Mangling: The Mangle Table

The *packet mangling* table is used to modify packet information. Rules applied specifically to this table are often designed to control the mundane behavior of packets, such as routing, connection size, and priority. Rules that modify a packet, rather than simply redirecting or stopping it, can be used only in the mangle table. For example, the TOS target can be used directly in the mangle table to change the Type of Service field to modifying a packet's priority. A TCPMSS target can be set to control the size of a connection. The ECN target lets you work around ECN black holes, and the DSCP target will let you change DSCP bits. Several extensions such as the ROUTE extension will change a packet, in this case, rewriting its destination rather than just redirecting it. The mangle table has its own versions of POSTROUTING, PREROUTING, INPUT, and FORWARD commands that are capable of changing packets.

The mangle table is indicated with the **-t mangle** option. Use the following command to see what chains are listed in your mangle table:

```
iptables -t mangle  -L
```

Several mangle table targets are shown here:

TOS	Modify the Type of Service field to manage the priority of the packet
TCPMSS	Modify the allowed size of packets for a connection, enabling larger transmissions
ECN	Remove ECN black hole information
DSCP	Change DSCP bits
ROUTE	Extension TARGET to modify destination information in the packet

---

TIP *Though you can enter iptables rules from the shell command line, when you shut down your system, these commands will be lost. You will most likely need to place your iptables rules in a script that can then be executed directly. This way you can edit and manage a complex set of rules, adding comments and maintaining their ordering.*

IP Masquerading

On Linux systems, you can set up a network in which one connection to the Internet is used by several systems on your network, so that only one IP address is required to connect to the Internet. This method is called *IP masquerading*, which refers to the way a system masquerades as another system, using that system's IP address. In such a network, one system is connected to the Internet with its own IP address, while the other systems are connected on a local area network (LAN) to this system. When a local system wants to access the network, it masquerades as the Internet-connected system, borrowing its IP address.

IP masquerading is implemented on Linux using the iptables firewall tool. In effect, you set up a firewall, which you then configure to do IP masquerading. You can find out more information on IP masquerading from the Linux Masquerade HOWTO files at the Linux Documentation Project, **http://tldp.org**, where you'll find both an IP-Masquerade-HOWTO and a Masquerading-Simple-HOWTO. They provide detailed, step-by-step guides to setting up IP masquerading on your system. IP masquerading must be supported by the kernel before you can use it.

In netfilter, IP masquerading is a NAT operation and is not integrated with packet filtering. IP masquerading commands are placed on the NAT table and treated separately from the packet-filtering commands. Use iptables to place a masquerade rule on the NAT table. First reference the NAT table with the **-t nat** option. Then add a rule to the POSTROUTING chain with the **-o** option specifying the output device and the **-j** option with the **MASQUERADE** command.

```
iptables -t nat -A POSTROUTING -o eth0 -j MASQUERADE
```

You will have to turn on IP forwarding for your system, by editing the **/etc/sysctl.conf** file and uncommenting the following lines for **net.ipv4.ip_forward** and **net.ipv6.ip_forward** variables:

```
net.ipv4.ip_forward = 1
net.ipv6.ip.forward = 1
```

VII

PART

System Administration

Basic System Administration

L inux is designed to serve many users at the same time, providing an interface between the users and the system with its resources, services, and devices. Users have their own shells through which they interact with the operating system, but you may need to configure the operating system itself in different ways. You may need to add new users, devices such as printers and scanners, and even file systems. Such operations come under the heading of *system administration*. The person who performs such actions requires administrative access. In this sense, two types of interaction can occur with Linux: regular users' interactions and interactions with the superuser who performs system administration tasks.

The chapters in this part of the book focus on operations such as managing users, configuring printers, adding file systems, and compiling the kernel. You perform most of these tasks only rarely, such as adding a new printer or mounting a file system. Other tasks, such as adding or removing users, are performed on a regular basis. Basic system administration covers topics such as gaining system administrative access, scheduling tasks, runlevels, boot configuration, and performance monitoring.

With Linux, you can load different versions of the kernel as well as other operating systems that you have installed on your system. The task of selecting and starting up an operating system or kernel is managed by a boot management utility called the *Grand Unified Bootloader (GRUB)*. This versatile tool lets you load operating systems that share the same disk drive and let you choose from different Linux kernels that may be installed on the same Linux system.

Ubuntu Administrative Tools

Administration is handled by a set of separate specialized administrative tools developed and supported by Ubuntu, such as those for user management and display configuration. To access the GUI-based Ubuntu tools, you log in as a user who has administrative access. (This is the user you created when you first installed Ubuntu.)

On the GNOME desktop, you can access system administrative tools from the System | Administration menu. Here you will find tools to set the time and date, to manage users, configure printers, and install software. Users and Groups lets you create and modify users and groups. Printing lets you install and reconfigure printers. All tools provide intuitive GUIs that are easy to use. In the Administration menu, tools are identified by simple descriptive terms, whereas their actual names normally begin with terms such as *admin* or *system-config*. For example, the printer configuration tool is called Printing on the Administration menu, but its actual name is **system-config-printer**, whereas Users and Groups is **admin-users**. You can separately invoke any tool by entering its name in a terminal window.

The GUI tools are normally either GNOME administrative tools, with KDE counterparts, or administrative tools adapted from the Fedora distribution supported by Red Hat Linux. The GNOME administrative tools are suffixed with the term *admin*, and the Fedora tools use the prefix *system-config*. In Ubuntu, the Printing administrative tool is Fedora's **system-config-printer**, replacing the GNOME **printer-admin** tool used in previous Ubuntu releases. A Samba GUI tool is now available for Ubuntu, which is the Fedora **system-config-samba** tool. Some tools will work with Ubuntu but are not yet supported.

The Fedora **system-config-lvm** tool provides a simple and effective way to manage Logical Volume Manager (LVM) file systems, but it is not yet supported directly by Ubuntu. You can, however, download, convert, and install its software package on Ubuntu and it will work fine.

Table 21-1 shows Ubuntu administration tools.

Ubuntu Administration Tools	Description
Synaptic Package Manager	APT software management using online repositories
Update Manager	Updates using APT repositories
time-admin	Changes system time and date (GNOME)
displayconfig-gtk	Ubuntu display configuration tool, video card and monitor (GNOME)
system-config-kickstart	Automatically installs scripts (Fedora/Red Hat)
network-admin	Configures network interfaces (GNOME)
system-config-cluster	Manages Global File System (GFS) (Fedora/Red Hat)
system-config-printer	Configures printer (Fedora/Red Hat)
system-config-samba	Configures Samba server (Fedora/Red Hat); user level authentication support
shares-admin	Configures general open shared directories or files; no authentication support
Firestarter	Configures network firewall
services-admin	Services tool, manages system and network services such as starting and stopping servers (GNOME)
users-admin	Configures users and groups
gnome-language-selector	Selects language
system-config-lvm	Configures LVM file system volumes (Fedora/Red Hat, unsupported)
sudo and gksu	Provide administrative access to systemwide commands and applications
PolicyKit service	Authorizes access by users to specific administrative tools

TABLE 21-1   Ubuntu Administrative Tools

Administrative Access

To access administrative tools, you must log in as a user who has administrative permissions. The user created during installation is automatically granted administrative permissions, so you can log in as that user. You must also type in the administrator password when prompted.

To perform system administration operations such as adding new users, you must have the appropriate access rights. There are several ways to gain such access, each with more refined access controls. In each case you have to login as a user who has been granted administrative access. The access methods are: logging in as the root user, login as a sudo supported user (gksu is the graphical version of sudo), and unlocking an administrative tool for access by a PolicyKit authorized users. PolicyKit is the newest and preferred access method and is appropriate for accessing most administrative tools. The sudo-granted access method (gksu is the graphical version of sudo) was used in previous Ubuntu releases and is still used for software upgrade and installation tasks (Synaptic and Update Manager). Root user access was and is still discouraged, but it provides complete control over the entire system.

- **PolicyKit**   Provides access only to specific applications and only to users with specific administrative access for that application. Requires that the application be configured for use by PolicyKit. You do not have to log in first as an authorized user.

- **gksu and sudo**   Provides access to any application will full root-level authorization. A time limit helps reduce risk. The `gsku` command is used for graphical administrative tools such as Synaptic Package Manager. You need to use sudo to perform standard Unix commands at the root level, such as editing configuration files. You must use a valid administrative username and password to gain access to any administrative tool and perform any operation on the system.

- **root user access, `su`**   Provides complete direct control over the entire system. This is the traditional method for accessing administrative tools but is disabled by default on Ubuntu, but it can be enabled. Any person, user or not, who knows the root user password can log in as the root user and gain complete control over the system. The `su` command will allow any user to log in as the root user if they know the root user password. Logging in as the root user.

Controlled Administrative Access with PolicyKit

PolicyKit will let any user start an administrative tool, but access is restricted to read-only. The **users-admin** tool for managing users provides a list of users on your system, but you cannot make any changes or add new users. In effect, you are locked out. For PolicyKit-controlled utilities, a Lock/Unlock button appears in the lower-right corner of the tool's window. To gain full access to the tool, you need to unlock it. Click the Unlock button to open a dialog where you can type in the username and password for the authorized user (see Figure 21-1). The list of authorized users is selectable from a pop-up menu. Each authorized user is granted administrative access when he or she sets up an account.

With PolicyKit, you can log in as any user and later gain access to a particular administrative tool by entering the appropriate username and password in the Authenticate window. Without using PolicyKit, you must first log in as an administrative user with full access to use administrative tools.

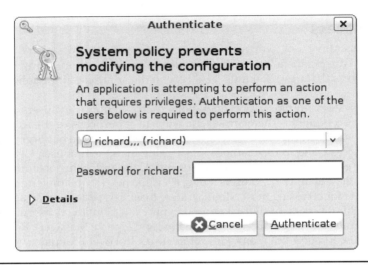

FIGURE 21-1 PolicyKit Authenticate dialog

Controlled Administrative Access with gksu and sudo

The sudo service provides administrative access to specific users. You have to be a user on the system with a valid username and password that has been authorized by the sudo service for administrative access. This allows other users to perform specific superuser operations without having full administrative level control. You use the **sudo** command to run a command with administrative access. The **gksu** tool is the graphical version of sudo used on the Ubuntu GNOME desktop. You can find more about sudo at **www.sudo.ws**.

gksu

The gksu tool is actually a front end to sudo that does not require a terminal window . (another name for gksu is gksudo). You can use the **gksu** command to run graphical applications with administrative access. The gsku tool will prompt you to enter your password (Figure 21-2), assuming you are logged in as a user with sudo-authorized administrative access.

You can enter the **gksu** command in a terminal window with the application as an argument or set up an application launcher using the **gksu** command. The following

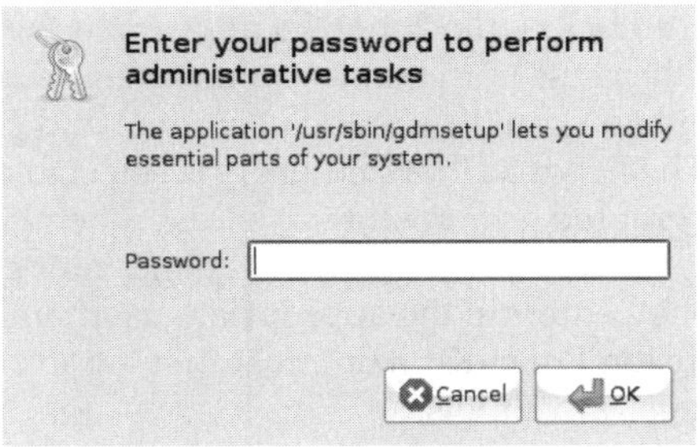

FIGURE 21-2
The gksu prompt
for access to
administrative
tools

Enter your password to perform administrative tasks

The application '/usr/sbin/gdmsetup' lets you modify essential parts of your system.

Password: [   ]

⊗ Cancel   ⏎ OK

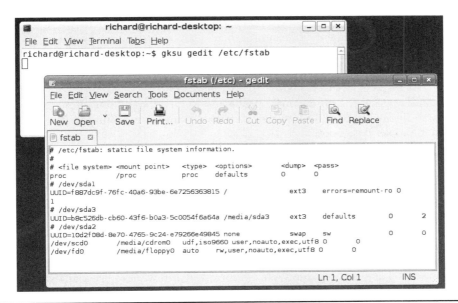

FIGURE 21-3   Invoking Gedit with the `gksu` command

example starts up the Gedit editor with administrative access (Figure 21-3), allowing you to edit system configuration files directly:

```
gksu gedit
```

The administrative tools on your desktop actually invoke their applications using gksu, as in **gksu synaptic**. You will see this command in the Launcher tab in the application's Properties window. If you run **gksu** directly without any application specified, it will prompt you to enter the application name. You can set up a GNOME or KDE application launcher for an application with the **gksu** command prefixing the application command.

sudo

Some administrative operations require access from the command line in the terminal window. For such operations, you would use the **sudo** command from a terminal window. You can open a terminal window using the Terminal tool accessible from the Applications | Accessories window. For easier access, you can drag the menu entry for the Terminal tool to the desktop to create a desktop Terminal icon for creating a terminal window:

```
sudo
```

To use sudo to run an administrative command, the user precedes the command with the **sudo** command, as shown next. The user is prompted to enter a password and, if access is granted, the user is issued a time-restricted ticket to allow access.

```
sudo date 0406145908
password:
```

From the terminal window, you would enter the **sudo** command with the administrative program name as an argument. For example, here's how you'd launch Vi to edit system configuration files:

```
sudo vi /etc/fstab
```

This starts up Vi with administrator privileges. This command line allows you to edit the **/etc/fstab** file to add or edit file system entries for automatic mounting. You will be prompted for a user password.

sudo Configuration   Access is controlled by the **/etc/sudoers** file that lists users and the commands they can run, along with the password for access. If the **NOPASSWD** option is set, users will not need a password. **ALL**, depending on the context, can refer to all hosts on your network, all root-level commands, or all users. (See the man page for **sudoers** for detailed information on all options.)

To make changes or add entries, you must edit the file with the special **visudo** editing command. This invokes the Vi editor to edit the **/etc/sudoers** file. Unlike a standard editor, **visudo** will lock the **/etc/sudoers** file and check the syntax of your entries. You are not allowed to save changes unless the syntax is correct. If you want to use a different editor, you can assign it to the **EDITOR** shell variable.

A sudoers entry has the following syntax:

```
user    host=command
```

The *host* is a host on your network. You can specify all hosts with the **ALL** option. The command line can be a list of commands, some or all qualified by options such as whether a password is required. To specify all commands, you can use the **ALL** option. The following gives the user **george** full root-level access to all commands on all hosts:

```
george  ALL = ALL
```

By default, sudo will deny access to all users, including the root. For this reason, the default **/etc/sudoers** file sets full access for the root user to all commands. The **ALL= (ALL) ALL** entry allows access by the root to all hosts as all users to all commands:

```
root    ALL=(ALL)    ALL
```

To specify a group name, prefix the group with a **%** sign, as in **%mygroup**. This lets you grant the same access to a group of users. By default, sudo grants access to all users in the **admin** group, who are granted administrative access. The **ALL= (ALL) ALL** entry allows access by the **admin** group to all hosts as all users to all commands.

```
%admin  ALL=(ALL)    ALL
```

You can also allow members of a certain group access without requiring a password by using the **NOPASSWD** option. A commented configuration entry allowing permission for all members of the **sudo** group is provided in the **/etc/sudoers** file.

```
%admin  ALL=NOPASSWD    ALL
```

In addition, you can let a user work as another user on a given host. Such alternative users are placed within parentheses in front of the commands. For example, if you want to give **george** access to the **beach** host as the user **mydns**, you'd use the following:

```
george beach = (mydns) ALL
```

To give **robert** access on all hosts to the **date** command, you would use this:

```
robert ALL=/usr/bin/system-config-date
```

If a user wants to see what commands he can run, he would use the **sudo** command with the **-l** option:

```
sudo -l
```

Full Administrative Access with root, su, and superuser

Ubuntu is designed never to let anyone directly access the **root** user. The **root** user has total control over the entire system. Instead, certain users are granted administrative access with which they can separately access administrative tools and perform specific administrative tasks. Even though a **root** user exists, a password for the **root** user is not defined so that access to the user is never allowed.

You can, however, activate the **root** user by using the **passwd** command to create a **root** user password. Enter the **passwd** command with the root user name in a **sudo** operation:

```
sudo passwd root
```

You will be prompted for your administrative password, and then prompted by the **passwd** command to enter a password for the **root** user. You will then be prompted to re-enter the password.

You can then log in as the root user with the username **root**, making you the superuser. Because a superuser has the power to change almost anything on the system, such a password is usually a carefully guarded secret, is changed very frequently, and is given out only to those who manage the system. With the correct password, you can log in to the system as a system administrator and configure the system in various ways. You can add or remove users, add or remove whole file systems, back up and restore files, and even designate the system's name and address.

You can also use the **su** command to log in as the **root** user:

```
su root
```

The **su** command used alone will assume the **root** username. The **su** command can be used to log in as any user, provided you have the user's password.

You can access the root user using the **sudo** command or the **su** command. The **su** command is the superuser command (and the superuser *is* the **root** user). A user granted administrative access by **sudo** could then become the **root** user. The following logs in as the **root** user:

```
sudo su
```

To exit from a **su** login operation when you are finished working in that account, just enter the following:

```
exit
```

Table 21-2 shows some common system administration access commands.

CAUTION *For security reasons, Linux distributions do not allow the use of **su** in a telnet session to access the **root** user. For SSH- or Kerberos-enabled systems, secure login access is provided using **slogin** (SSH) and **rlogin** (Kerberos).*

Editing User Configuration Files Directly

Although the administrative and preferences tools will handle all configuration settings for you, at times you will need to make changes by directly editing configuration files. These are usually systemwide administrative text files in the **/etc** directory or user configuration files (often called *dot files* because they are prefixed with a period) in a user directory, such as **.profile**. As noted, to change system files, you will need administrative access, invoking an editor using the **sudo** command.

CAUTION *Be careful when editing your configuration files. Editing mistakes can corrupt your configurations. It is advisable to make a backup of the original configuration files you are working on before making changes.*

You can use any standard editor such as Vi or Emacs to edit these files, though one of the easiest ways to edit them is to use Gedit on the GNOME desktop. Gedit lets you edit several files at once, opening a tabbed pane for each. You can use Gedit to edit any text file, including files you create yourself. The **.profile** file configures your login shell.

User configuration files such as **.profile** must be chosen from the file manager window. These are hidden files that will not be shown initially. To view these files temporarily, choose View | Show Hidden Files. To have hidden files show permanently, in any file manager window choose Edit | Preferences to open the Preferences window and check the

Command	Description
`su root`	Logs a superuser into the root from a user login. Root user access disabled by default on Ubuntu.
`sudo` *command*	Restricts administrative access to specified users.
`passwd` *login-name*	Sets a new password for the login name.
`gksu` *command*	Runs gksu application with administrative access.

TABLE 21-2 System Administration Access Commands

Show Hidden Files entry. After making the change, click Reset View To Defaults to redisplay your files. This displays the dot files in your file manager window. Double-click a filename to open it in Gedit.

Administrative Access from the File Browser

You may often want to perform file management operations on system directories or files, such as editing system configuration files or creating new folders onto which you can mount new file systems. The file browser on your administrative user account does not have permission to make changes to the system files or directories. To gain this kind of access, you can invoke the file browser with the **gksu** command from a terminal window. Enter the following command to open the Nautilus GNOME browser shown in Figure 21-4:

```
gksu nautilus
```

You will be prompted to enter your administrative user password. Then Nautilus opens at the root user home directory.

***

TIP   *For easy access, you can create an application launcher using the gksu nautilus command in the Launcher panel. Then you can double-click the launcher from the desktop to start up the file browser with root access.*

You can perform any administrative action on files, such as changing permissions to folders and directories, creating new folders and directories, or deleting old folders and directories anywhere in the system. You can also edit any configuration files, which are usually found in the **/etc** directory. These are text files that can be edited by Gedit. Double-click a file to open it in a Gedit text editor window.

FIGURE 21-4   Administrative access with the GNOME File Browser (Nautilus)

System Time and Date

You can set the system time and date using the shell **date** command or the GNOME **time-admin** tool. You probably set the time and date when you first installed your system, so you should not need to do so again. However, if you entered the time incorrectly or are working in a different time zone, you can use this utility to change the time. Or perhaps you want to have your time checked and set automatically using Network Time Protocol (NTP) time servers.

Using the time-admin Date and Time Utility

The preferred way to set the system time and date is to use the GNOME Date and Time utility (**time-admin**) or the world clock applet (see Chapter 3). To start **time-admin**, choose System | Administration | Date & Time. The time and date values will be displayed, but grayed out. The **time-admin** tool is controlled by PolicyKit. Click the Unlock button and enter an administrative user password to gain access.

In the Time and Date Settings dialog (Figure 21-5), the current time is shown in hours, minutes, and seconds. Use the arrow buttons to change these values. On the calendar, you can select the year, month, and day by using the arrow keys to move to the next or previous month or year. Clicking the Time Zone button at the top of the dialog displays the Time Zone dialog, which shows a map with location, along with a pop-up menu for specific cities. Select the city nearest you to set your time zone. Clicking the map zooms to that area.

The Configuration pop-up menu lets you choose to set the time manually or have a time server set it for you automatically. The Manual setting is the default. Alternatively, you can use time servers to set the time automatically. In this case, the Calendar and Time boxes will not be displayed (Figure 21-6). Time servers use the Network Time Protocol (NTP), which allows a remote server to set the date and time, instead of using local settings. NTP allows for the most accurate synchronization of your system's clock. It is often used to manage the time and date for networked systems, freeing the administrator from having to synchronize clocks manually. You can download current documentation and NTP software from **www.ntp.org**.

Figure 21-5
GNOME Time and
Date Settings

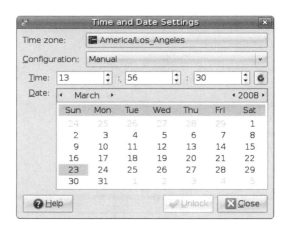

Figure 21-6
NTP time server
access

To use the NTP time servers, in the Configuration pop-up, select Keep Synchronized With Internet Servers. Initially, NTP support may not be installed. Ubuntu will prompt you to install it (just click Install NTP Support). Once installed, the Calendar and Time boxes are replaced by a Select Servers button.

NTP servers tend to be overworked, so you can choose more than one to access. Click the Select Servers button to display a list of NTP servers. The Ubuntu NTP server will already be selected, or you can select others in your area. You can even add NTP servers, as many local networks have their own. You can find out more about NTP servers at the NTP Public Services Project site (Time Servers link) at **http://ntp.isc.org**.

Using the date Command

You can use the **date** command on your root user command line to set the date and time for the system. As an argument to **date**, you list (with no delimiters) the month, day, time, and year. In the next example, the date is set to 2:59 P.M., April 6, 2008 (*04* for April, *06* for the day, *1459* for the time, and *08* for the year 2008):

```
sudo date 0406145908
Sun Apr 6 02:59:22 PST 2008
```

Scheduling Tasks with cron

Scheduling regular system maintenance tasks is managed by the **cron** service on Linux, implemented by a **cron** daemon. A daemon is a continually running server that constantly checks for certain actions to take. These tasks are listed in the **crontab** file. The **cron** daemon constantly checks the user's **crontab** file to see if it is time to take these actions. Any user can set up a **crontab** file of her own. The root user can set up a **crontab** file to take care of system administrative actions, such as backing up files at a certain time each week or month.

The easiest way to schedule tasks is to use the desktop **cron** tool. In KDE, you can use the KCRON tool and for GNOME you can use GNOME Schedule. Both let you choose the month, date, and time for a process, though you will have to enter the command you want run manually, as if on a command line. A listing of **cron** entries lets you modify or delete tasks. If you have an open-ended operation, be sure to schedule a command to shut it down.

The name of the **cron** daemon is **crond**. Normally it is started automatically when your system starts up. You can set this feature using **services-admin** (GNOME). You can also start and stop the **crond** service manually, which you may want to do for emergency maintenance or during upgrades.

crontab Entries

A `crontab` entry has six fields: the first five are used to specify the time for an action, while the last field is the action itself.

- The first field specifies minutes (0–59).
- The second field specifies the hour (0–23).
- The third field specifies the day of the month (1–31).
- The fourth field specifies the month of the year (1–12, or month prefixes like *Jan* and *Sep*).
- The fifth field specifies the day of the week (0–6, or day prefixes like *Wed* and *Fri*), starting with 0 as Sunday.

In each of the time fields, you can specify a range, a set of values, or use the asterisk to indicate all values. For example, **1-5** for the day-of-week field specifies Monday through Friday. In the hour field, **8, 12, 17** would specify 8 A.M., 12 noon, and 5 P.M. An ***** in the month-of-year field indicates every month. The format of a `crontab` field follows:

```
minute  hour  day-month  month  day(s)-week  task
```

The following example backs up the **projects** directory at 2:00 A.M. every weekday:

```
0 2 * * 1-5   tar cf /home/backp /home/projects
```

The same entry is listed here again using prefixes for the month and weekday:

```
0 2 * * Mon-Fri tar cf /home/backp /home/projects
```

To specify particular months, days, weeks, or hours, you can list them individually, separated by commas. For example, to perform the previous task on Sunday, Wednesday, and Friday, you can use **0,3,5** in the day-of-week field, or their prefix equivalents, **Sun,Wed,Fri**:

```
0 2 * * 0,3,5   tar cf /home/backp /home/projects
```

cron also supports comments. A *comment* is any line beginning with a **#** sign, which indicates that the information that follows is not part of a command:

```
# Weekly backup for Chris's projects
0 2 * * Mon-Fri  tar cf /home/backp /home/projects
```

Environment Variables for cron

The **cron** service also lets you define environment variables for use with tasks performed. Linux defines variables for **SHELL**, **PATH**, **MAILTO**, and **HOME**:

- **SHELL**   Designates the shell to use tasks, in this case the BASH shell.
- **PATH**   Lists the directories where programs and scripts can be found. The following example lists the standard directories, **/usr/bin** and **/bin**, as well as the system directories reserved for system applications, **/usr/sbin** and **/sbin**.

- **MAILTO**   Designates to whom the results of a task are to be mailed. By default, these are mailed to the user who schedules it, but you can have the results sent to a specific user, such as the administrator's e-mail address, or an account on another system in a network.
- **HOME**   Is the home directory for a task, in the example's case, the top directory.

```
SHELL=/bin/bash
PATH=/sbin:/bin:/usr/sbin:/usr/bin
MAILTO=root
HOME=/
```

The cron.d Directory

On a heavily used system, the **/etc/crontab** file can easily become crowded. There may also be instances in which certain entries require different variables. For example, you may need to run some task under a different shell. To help you organize your `crontab` tasks, you can place `crontab` entries in files within the **cron.d** directory. The files in the **cron.d** directory all contain `crontab` entries of the same format as **/etc/crontab**. They may be given any name. They are treated as added `crontab` files, with **cron** checking them for tasks to run. For example, Linux installs a **sysstat** file in the **cron.d** that contains `crontab` entries to run tools to gather system statistics.

The crontab Command

You use the `crontab` command to install your entries into a **crontab** file. To do this, first create a text file and type your `crontab` entries. Save this file with any name you want, such as **mycronfile**. Then, to install these entries, enter `crontab` and the name of the text file. The `crontab` command takes the contents of the text file and creates a **crontab** file in the **/var/spool/cron** directory, adding the name of the user who issued the command.

In the following example, the root user installs the contents of **mycronfile** as the root's **crontab** file:

```
sudo crontab mycronfile
```

This creates a file called **/var/spool/cron/root**. If a user named **justin** installs a **crontab** file, it creates a file called **/var/spool/cron/justin**. You can control use of the `crontab` command by regular users with the **/etc/cron.allow** file. Only users whose names appear in this file can create **crontab** files of their own. Conversely, the **/etc/cron.deny** file lists those users denied use of the **cron** tool, preventing them for scheduling tasks. If neither file exists, access is denied to all users. If a user is not in an **/etc/cron.allow** file, access is denied. However, if the **/etc/cron.allow** file does not exist, and the **/etc/cron.deny** file does, then all users not listed in **/etc/cron.deny** are automatically allowed access.

Editing in cron

Never try to edit your **crontab** file directly. Instead, use the `crontab` command with the **-e** option. This opens your **crontab** file in the **/var/spool/cron** directory with a standard text editor, such as Vi (`crontab` uses the default editor as specified by the **EDITOR** shell environment variable). To use a different editor for `crontab`, change the default editor by assigning the editor's program name to the **EDITOR** variable and exporting that variable. Normally, the **EDITOR** variable is set in the **/etc/profile** script. Running `crontab` with the -**l** option displays the contents of your **crontab** file, and the -**r** option deletes the entire file. Invoking `crontab` with another text file of `crontab` entries overwrites your current **crontab** file, replacing it with the contents of the text file.

Organizing Scheduled Tasks

You can organize administrative **cron** tasks into two general groups: common administrative tasks that can be run at regular intervals, and specialized tasks that need to be run at a unique time. Unique tasks can be run as entries in the **/etc/crontab** file, as described in the next section. Common administrative tasks, though they can be run from the **/etc/crontab** file, are better organized into specialized **cron** directories. Within such directories, each task is placed in its own shell script that will invoke the task when run. Suppose that several administrative tasks need to be run each week on the same day—for example, maintenance for a system is scheduled on a Sunday morning. For these kinds of tasks, **cron** provides several specialized directories for automatic daily, weekly, monthly, and yearly tasks. Each contains a **cron** prefix and a suffix for the time interval. The **/etc/cron.daily** directory is used for tasks that need to be performed every day, whereas weekly tasks can be placed in the **/etc/cron.weekly** directory. The **cron** directories are listed in Table 21-3.

cron Command and Tools	Description
`crontab` *options filename*	With *filename* as an argument, installs `crontab` entries in the file to a **crontab** file; these entries are operations executed at specified times: -**e** edits the **crontab** file -**l** lists the contents of the **crontab** file -**r** deletes the **crontab** file
Kcron	KDE GUI interface **cron** management tool
Schedule	GNOME GUI interface **cron** management tool
cron Files and Directories	
`/etc/crontab`	System `crontab` file, accessible only by the root user
`/etc/cron.d`	Directory containing multiple `crontab` files, accessible only by the administrative user
`/etc/cron.d/cron.hourly`	Directory for tasks performed hourly
`/etc/cron.d/cron.daily`	Directory for tasks performed daily
`/etc/cron.d/cron.weekly`	Directory for tasks performed weekly
`/etc/cron.d/cron.monthly`	Directory for tasks performed monthly
`/etc/cron.d/cron.yearly`	Directory for tasks performed yearly
`/etc/cron.d/cron.allow`	Users allowed to submit **cron** tasks
`/etc/cron.d/cron.deny`	Users denied access to **cron**

TABLE 21-3   Cron Command, Tools, Files, and Directories

Running cron Directory Scripts

Each directory contains scripts that are all run at the same time. The scheduling for each group is determined by an entry in the **/etc/crontab** file. The actual execution of the scripts is performed by the **/usr/bin/run-parts** script, which runs all the scripts and programs in a given directory. Scheduling for all the tasks in a given directory is handled by an entry in the **/etc/crontab** file. Linux provides entries with designated times, which you may change for your own needs. The default **crontab** file is shown here, with times for running scripts in the different **cron** directories. Here you can see that most scripts are run at about 4 A.M. either daily (4:02), Sunday (4:22), or first day of each month (4:42). Hourly scripts are run one minute after the hour.

```
SHELL=/bin/bash
PATH=/sbin:/bin:/usr/sbin:/usr/bin
MAILTO=root
HOME=/
# run-parts
01 * * * * root run-parts /etc/cron.hourly
02 4 * * * root run-parts /etc/cron.daily
22 4 * * 0 root run-parts /etc/cron.weekly
42 4 1 * * root run-parts /etc/cron.monthly
```

TIP *Scripts within a **cron** directory are run alphabetically. If you need a certain script to run before any others, you may have to alter its name. One method is to prefix the name with a numeral. For example, in the /cron.weekly directory, the **anacron** script is named **0anacron** so that it will run before any others.*

Keep in mind that these are simply directories that contain executable files. The actual scheduling is performed by the entries in the **/etc/crontab** file. For example, if the weekly field in the **cron.weekly crontab** entry is changed to ***** instead of **0**, and the monthly field to **1** (**22 4 1 * *** instead of **22 4 * * 0**), tasks in the **cron.weekly** file will end up running monthly instead of weekly.

cron Directory Names

The names used for these directories are merely conventions. They have no special meaning to the **cron** daemon. You could, in fact, create your own directory, place scripts within it, and schedule **run-parts** to run those scripts at a given time. In the next example, scripts placed in the **/etc/cron.mydocs** directory will run at 12 noon every Wednesday:

```
* 12 * * 3 root run-parts /etc/cron.mydocs
```

Anacron

For a system that may normally be shut down during times that **cron** is likely to run, you may want to supplement **cron** with **anacron**, which activates only when scheduled tasks need to be executed. For example, if a system is shut down on a weekend when **cron** jobs are scheduled, the jobs will not be performed; **anacron**, however, checks to see what jobs need to be performed when the system is turned on again, and then runs them. It is designed for jobs that run only daily or weekly.

For **anacron** jobs, you place `crontab` entries in the **/etc/anacrontab** file. For each scheduled task, you specify the number of intervening days when it is executed (7 is weekly, *30* is monthly), the time of day it is run (numbered in minutes), a description of the task, and the command to be executed. For backups, the command used is the `tar` operation.

System Directories

Your Linux file system is organized into directories that contain files used for different system functions, as listed in Table 21-4. For basic system administration, you should be familiar with the system program directories where applications are kept, the system configuration directory (**/etc**) where most configuration files are placed, and the system log directory (**/var/log**) that holds the system logs, recording activity on your system. Other system directories are covered in their respective chapters, with many discussed in Chapter 25.

Directory	Description
/bin	System-related programs
/sbin	System programs for specialized tasks
/lib	System and application libraries
/etc	Configuration files for system and network services and applications
/home	User home directories and server data directories, such as web and FTP site files
/media	Where CD-ROM and floppy disk file systems are mounted (Chapter 23)
/var	System directories whose files continually change, such as logs, printer spool files, and lock files (Chapter 25)
/usr	User-related programs and files; includes several key subdirectories, such as **/usr/bin**, **/usr/X11**, and **/usr/doc**
/usr/bin	Programs for users
/dev	Dynamically generated directory for device files (Chapter 25)
/etc/X11	X Window System configuration files
/usr/share	Shared files
/usr/share/doc	Documentation for applications
/tmp	Directory for system temporary files
/var/log	Logging directory
/var/log/	System logs generated by **syslogd**
/var/log/audit	Audit logs generated by **auditd**

TABLE 21-4   System Directories

Program Directories

Directories with *bin* in the name are used to hold programs. The **/bin** directory holds basic user programs, such as login shells (BASH, TCSH, and ZSH) and file commands (`cp`, `mv`, `rm`, `ln`, and so on). The **/sbin** directory holds specialized system programs for such tasks as file system management (`fsck`, `fdisk`, `mkfs`) and system operations such as shutdown and startup (`init`). The **/usr/bin** directory holds program files designed for user tasks. The **/usr/sbin** directory holds user-related system operations, such as `useradd` to add new users. The **/lib** directory holds all the libraries your system uses, including the main Linux library, **libc**, and subdirectories such as **modules**, which holds all the current kernel modules.

Configuration Directories and Files

When you configure different elements of your system, such as users, applications, servers, or network connections, you use configuration files kept in the **/etc** directory. The **/etc** directory holds your system, network, server, and application configuration files. Here you can find the **fstab** file listing your file systems, the **hosts** file with IP addresses for hosts on your system, and **/etc/profile**, the systemwide default BASH shell configuration file. This directory includes various subdirectories, such as **/etc/apache** for the Apache web server configuration files, **/etc/X11** for the X Window System and window manager configuration files, and **/etc/udev** for rules to generate device files in **/dev**. You can configure many applications and services by directly editing their configuration files, though it is best to use a corresponding administration tool. Table 21-5 lists several commonly used configuration files found in the **/etc** directory.

System Logs: /var/log and syslogd

Various system logs for tasks performed on your system are stored in the **/var/log** directory. Here you can find logs for mail, news, and all other system operations, such as web server logs. The **/var/log/messages** file is a log of all system tasks not covered by other logs. This usually includes startup tasks, such as loading drivers and mounting file systems. If a driver for a card failed to load at startup, you will find an error message for it here. Logins are also recorded in this file, showing you who attempted to log in to what account. The **/var/log/maillog** file logs mail message transmissions and news transfers.

NOTE *To view logs, you can use the GNOME System Log Viewer.*

syslogd and syslog.conf

The **syslogd** daemon manages all the logs on your system and coordinates with any of the logging operations of other systems on your network. Configuration information for **syslogd** is held in the **/etc/syslog.conf** file, which contains the names and locations for your system log files. Here you find entries for **/var/log/messages** and **/var/log/maillog**, among others. Whenever you make changes to the **syslog.conf** file, you need to restart the **syslogd** daemon.

File	Description
/etc/bashrc	Default shell configuration file Bash shell
/etc/group	A list of groups with configurations for each
/etc/fstab	File systems that are automatically mounted when you start your system
/boot/grub/menu.lst	The GRUB configuration file for the GRUB bootloader, linked to by **/etc/menu.lst**
/etc/event.d	Upstart startup scripts
/etc/inittab	Dummy **inittab** file used for specifying default runlevel
/etc/profile	Default shell configuration file for users
/etc/modules	Modules on your system to be automatically loaded
/etc/motd	System administrator's message of the day
/etc/mtab	Currently mounted file systems
/etc/passwd	User password and login configurations
/etc/services	Services run on the system and the ports they use
/etc/shadow	User-encrypted passwords
/etc/shells	Shells installed on the system that users can use
/etc/sudoers	sudo configuration to control administrative access
/etc/termcap	A list of terminal type specifications for terminals that could be connected to the system
/etc/xinetd.conf	Xinetd server configuration
Directory	
/etc/cron.d	**cron** scripts
/etc/cups	CUPS printer configuration files
/etc/init.d	Service scripts for distribution that support SysV init scripts
/etc/mail	Sendmail configuration files
/etc/openldap	Configuration for Open LDAP server
/etc/event.d	Configuration scripts for Upstart startup operations, replaces System V init
/etc/rc.N	Startup scripts for different runlevels
/etc/skel	Versions of initialization files, such as **.bash_profile**, which are copied to new users' home directories
/etc/X11	X Window System configuration files
/etc/xinetd.d	Configuration scripts for services managed by Xinetd server
/etc/udev	Rules for generating devices (Chapter 25)
/etc/hal	Rules for generating removable devices (Chapter 25)

TABLE 21-5   Common System Configuration Files and Directories

Entries in syslogd.conf

An entry in **syslog.conf** consists of two fields: a *selector* and an *action*. The selector is the kind of service to be logged, such as mail or news, and the action is the location where messages are to be placed. The action is usually a log file, but it can also be a remote host or a pipe to another program. The kind of service is referred to as a *facility*. The **syslogd** daemon has several terms it uses to specify certain kinds of service (see Table 21-6).

Facilities	Description
`auth_priv`	Security/authorization messages (private)
`cron`	Clock daemon (**cron** and **at**) messages
`daemon`	Other system daemon messages
`kern`	Kernel messages
`lpr`	Line printer subsystem messages
`mail`	Mail subsystem messages
`mark`	Internal use only
`news`	Usenet news subsystem messages
`syslog`	Syslog internal messages
`user`	Generic user-level messages
`uucp`	UUCP subsystem messages
`local0` through `local7`	Reserved for local use
Priorities	**Description**
`debug`	7, debugging messages, lowest priority
`info`	6, informational messages
`notice`	5, notifications, normal, but significant condition
`warning`	4, warnings
`err`	3, error messages
`crit`	2, critical conditions
`alert`	1, alerts, action must be taken immediately
`emerg`	0, emergency messages, system is unusable, highest priority
Operators	**Description**
`*`	Match all facilities or priorities in a sector
`=`	Restrict to a specified priority
`!`	Exclude specified priority and higher ones
`/`	A file to save messages to
`@`	A host to send messages to
`|`	A FIFO pipe to send messages to

TABLE 21-6 Syslogd Facilities, Priorities, and Operators

A facility can be further qualified by a priority. A *priority* specifies the kind of message generated by the facility; **syslogd** uses several designated terms to indicate different priorities. A *sector* is constructed from both the facility and the priority, separated by a period. For example, to save error messages generated by mail systems, you use a sector consisting of the **mail** facility and the **err** priority, as shown here:

```
mail.err
```

To save these messages to the **/var/log/maillog** file, you specify that file as the action, giving you the following entry:

```
mail.err /var/log/maillog
```

The **syslogd** daemon also supports the use of * as a matching character to match either all the facilities or all the priorities in a sector: **cron.*** matches on all **cron** messages no matter what the priority; ***.err** matches on error messages from all the facilities; and ***.*** matches on all messages. The following example saves all mail messages to the **/var/log/maillog** file and all critical messages to the **/var/log/mycritical** file:

```
mail.* /var/log/maillog
*.crit /var/log/mycritical
```

Priorities

When you specify a priority for a facility, all messages with a higher priority are also included. Thus the **err** priority also includes the **crit**, **alert**, and **emerg** priorities. If you just want to select the message for a specific priority, you qualify the priority with the = operator. For example, **mail.=err** will select only error messages, not **crit**, **alert**, or **emerg** messages. You can also restrict priorities with the ! operator. This will eliminate messages with the specified priority and higher. For example, **mail.!crit** will exclude **crit** messages, as well as the higher **alert** and **emerg** messages. To exclude specifically all the messages for an entire facility, you use the **none** priority; for instance, **mail.none** excludes all mail messages. This is usually used when you're defining several sectors in the same entry.

You can list several priorities or facilities in a given sector by separating them with commas. You can also have several sectors in the same entry by separating them with semicolons. The first example saves to the **/var/log/messages** file all messages with **info** priority, excluding all mail and authentication messages (**authpriv**). The second saves all **crit** messages and higher for the **uucp** and **news** facilities to the **/var/log/spooler** file:

```
*.info;mail.none;news.none;authpriv.none /var/log/messages
uucp,news.crit /var/log/spooler
```

Actions and Users

In the action field, you can specify files, remote systems, users, or pipes. An action entry for a file must always begin with a / and specify its full pathname, such as **/var/log/messages**. To log messages to a remote host, you simply specify the hostname preceded by an @ sign. The following example saves all kernel messages on **rabbit.trek.com**:

```
kern.* @rabbit.trek.com
```

To send messages to users, you list their login names. The following example will send critical news messages to the consoles for the users **chris** and **aleina**:

```
news.=crit chris,aleina
```

You can also output messages to a named pipe (FIFO). The pipe entry for the action field begins with a |. The following example pipes kernel debug messages to the named pipe |**/usr/adm/debug**:

```
kern.=debug |/usr/adm/debug
```

NOTE *The Linux Auditing System provides system call auditing. You can download and install it from the Ubuntu universe repository. The auditing is performed by a server called **auditd**, with logs saved to the **/var/log/audit** directory. It is designed to complement SELinux, which saves its messages to the **auditd** log in the **/var/log/audit/audit.log** file. Logs are located at **/var/log/audit**. The audit package includes the **auditd** server and three commands:* `autrace`, `ausearch`, *and* `auditctl`*. You use* `ausearch` *to query the audit logs. You can control the behavior of the **auditd** server with the* `auditctl` *tool.*

Performance Analysis Tools and Processes

Linux treats each task performed on your system as a process, which is assigned a number and a name. You can examine these processes and even stop them. Linux provides several tools for examining processes as well as your system performance. Easy monitoring is provided by the GNOME System Monitor. Other system monitoring tools are also available, such as GKrellM and KSysguard.

A number of utilities on your system provide detailed information on your processes, as well as other system information such as CPU and disk use (see Table 21-7). Although these tools were designed to be used on a shell command line, displaying output in text lines, several now have KDE and GNOME versions that provide a GUI for displaying results and managing processes. Many of the command line tools such as **sar** and **iostat** are included in the **systat** package on the universe repository.

GNOME System Monitor

The GNOME System Monitor displays system information and monitoring system processes on four tabs: System, Processes, Resources, and File Systems (see Figure 21-7). The System tab shows the version of Ubuntu, GNOME, and Linux kernel being used. The CPU and the amount of RAM memory, and the available hard disk space on the primary partition. The Processes tab lists processes, letting you sort or search for processes. You can use field buttons to sort by name, process ID, user, and memory. The View pop-up menu lets you select all processes, just your own, or active processes. You can easily stop any process by selecting it and then clicking the End Process button. Right-clicking an item displays actions you can take on the process such as stopping or hiding it. The Resources tab displays graphs for CPU, Memory and Swap History, and Network History. The File Systems tab lists file

Performance Tool	Description
vmstat	Performance of system components
top	Listing of most CPU-intensive processes
free	Listing of free RAM
sar	System activity information
iostat	Disk usage
GNOME System Monitor	System monitor for processes and usage monitoring
GKrellM	Stackable, flexible, and extensible monitoring tool that displays information on a wide variety of system, network, and storage operations, as well as services; easily configurable with themes
KDE Task Manager and Performance Monitor	KDE system monitor for processes and usage monitoring
System Tap	Tool to analyze performance bottlenecks
GNOME Power Manager	Manages power efficiency features of your system
PowerNowd	Implements CPU speed reduction during idle times (AMD Cool'n'Quiet)

TABLE 21-7 Performance Tools

systems, where they are mounted, and their types, as well as the amount of disk space used and how much is free. To see information on virtual memory, inodes, and flags, choose View | Memory Maps.

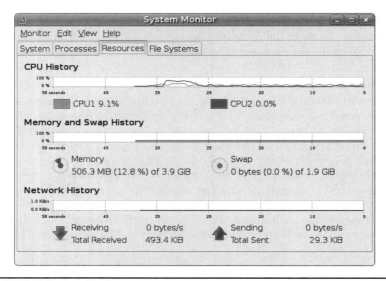

FIGURE 21-7 GNOME System Monitor

The ps Command

From the command line, you can use the **ps** command to list processes. With the **-aux** option, you can list all processes. Piping the output to a **grep** command with a pattern enables you to search for a particular process. A pipe funnels the output of a preceding command as input to a following command. The following command lists all X Window System processes:

```
ps -aux | grep 'X'
```

vmstat, top, free, Xload, iostat, and sar

The **vmstat** command outputs a detailed listing indicating the performance of different system components, including CPU, memory, I/O, and swap operations. A report is issued as a line with fields for the different components. If you provide a time period as an argument, it repeats at the specified interval—usually a few seconds. The **top** command provides a listing of the processes on your system that are the most CPU intensive, showing what processes are using most of your resources. The listing is in real time and updated every few seconds. Commands are provided for changing a process's status, such as its priority.

The **free** command lists the amount of free RAM memory on your system, showing how much is used and how much is free, as well as what is used for buffers and swap memory. **Xload** is an X Window System tool showing the load, CPU, and memory; **iostat** displays your disk usage; and **sar** shows system activity information.

SystemTap

SystemTap (**http://sourceware.org/systemtap/**) is a diagnostic tool for providing information about complex system implementations. It essentially analyzes performance bottlenecks, letting you home in on where a problem could be located. SystemTap relies on Kprobes (Kernel Dynamic Probes), which allows kernel modules to set up simple probes.

GNOME Power Manager

The GNOME Power Manager is designed to take full advantage of the efficiency features available on both laptops and desktops. It supports such tasks as reducing CPU frequency, dimming the display, shutting down unused hard drives, and automatic shutdown or suspension. See **www.gnome.org/projects/gnome-power-manager** for a detailed description. The GNOME Power Manager is integrated with HAL (Hardware Abstraction Layer) and dbus to detect hardware states and issue hardware notifications. Hardware notifications are issued using notification icons for devices, such as the battery icon. The notification icons are located on the desktop panel. A tooltip on the battery icon will show the remaining time available on your battery.

Power management preferences for laptops let you set sleep, brightness, and action settings for battery and direct power (AC). For desktops, you can set the inactivity time for putting the display to sleep or suspending the system. You can access the preferences by choosing System | Preferences | More Preferences | Power Management.

Features like Cool 'n'Quiet for Athlon CPUs and Pentium M frequency controls are handled separately by the CPU Frequency Manager. CPU frequency reporting tools are provided part of the GNOME applets package. The CPU Frequency Manager is the **powernowd** daemon that provides simple direct control of the CPU speed.

GKrellM

GKrellM is a GTK-based set of small stackable monitors for various system, network, and device operations (universe repository). A title bar at the top of the stack will display the hostname of your system. By default, GKrellM displays the hostname, system time, CPU load, process chart, disk access, network devices such as **eth0**, memory use, and a mail check. You can change the chart display of a monitor, its height, for instance, by right-clicking it to show a display options screen.

KDE Task Manager and Performance Monitor (KSysguard)

The KDE Task Manager and Performance Monitor, KSysguard, is accessible from the KDE desktop. This tool allows you to monitor the performance of your own system as well as remote systems. KSysguard can provide simple values or detailed tables for various parameters. A System Load panel provides graphical information about CPU and memory usage, and a Process Table lists current processes using a tree format to show dependencies. You can design your own monitoring panels with worksheets, showing different types of values you want to display and the form you want to display them in, such as a bar graph or a digital meter. The Sensor Browser pane is an expandable tree of sensors for information such as CPU System Load or Memory's Used Memory. A top entry appears for each host to which you are connected, including your own, localhost. To design your own monitor, create a worksheet and drag and drop a sensor onto it.

Grand Unified Bootloader

The Grand Unified Bootloader (GRUB) is a multiboot bootloader used for most Linux distributions. With GRUB, users can select operating systems to run from a menu interface displayed when a system boots up. Use arrow keys to move to an entry and press ENTER. Type **e** to edit a command, change kernel arguments, or specify a different kernel. The **c** command places you in a command line interface. Provided your system BIOS supports very large drives, GRUB can boot from anywhere. Linux and Unix operating systems are known as *multiboot operating systems* and take arguments passed to them at boot time. Check the GRUB man page for GRUB options. GRUB is a GNU project with its home page at **www.gnu.org/software/grub** and wiki at **http://grub.enbug.org**.

Officially, the GRUB configuration settings are held in the **/boot/grub/menu.lst** file. You can make your entries in the configuration file and GRUB will automatically read them when you reboot. You can set several options, such as the timeout period and the background image to use. Check the GRUB info documentation for a detailed description Use the **info grub** command to access the GRUB info documentation.

If you want to edit the **menu.lst** file, you will have to edit it with administrative access. Use **gksu gedit** or **sudo** with an editor such as Vi to edit the file with administrative access. You will be prompted to enter your user password.

```
gksu gedit /boot/grub/menu.lst
```

The **menu.lst** file generated by Ubuntu will initially list several commented GRUB options, as shown in the next example. Some will be uncommented, and thereby made active. You can activate other options by editing the **menu.lst** file and removing the preceding **#**. The actual menu entries are located at the end of the file, beginning with the term title. Three options are already set for you: **default**, **timeout**, and **hiddenmenu**. The **default** option will specify the entry to run and will be set to the main kernel. If you want to make another operating system the default instead (such as a Mac or Windows OS on a dual-boot system), you could change the number to that entry (counting from 0). The **timeout** option is the time allotted before the default system is started up automatically. The **hiddenmenu** option hides the GRUB menu display, letting you display it if you press any key before the timeout.

```
## default num
# Set the default entry to the entry number NUM. Numbering starts from 0, and
# the entry number 0 is the default if the command is not used.
default         0

## timeout sec
# Set a timeout, in SEC seconds, before automatically booting the default entry
# (normally the first entry defined).
timeout         3

## hiddenmenu
# Hides the menu by default (press ESC to see the menu)
hiddenmenu
```

You can specify a system to boot by creating a title entry for it, beginning with the term **title**, as shown next. You then specify where the operating system kernel or program is located, which hard drive to use, and what partition to use on that hard drive. This information is listed in parentheses following the **root** option. Numbering starts from 0, not 1, and hard drives are indicated with an **hd** prefix, whether they are IDE or SCSI hard drives. Thus **root(hd0,2)** references the first hard drive (**hda**) and the third partition on that hard drive (**hda3**). For Linux systems, you will also have to use the **kernel** option to indicate the kernel program to run, using the full pathname and any options the kernel may need. The RAM disk is indicated by the **initrd** option.

```
title    Ubuntu hardy (8.04), kernel 2.6.24-11-generic
root     (hd0,1)
kernel   /boot/vmlinuz-2.6.24-11-generic root=UUID=a179d6e6-b90c-4cc4-982d-
a4cfcedea7df ro quiet splash
initrd   /boot/initrd.img-2.6.24-11-generic
quiet
```

The kernel option specifies the kernel to run. The kernel is located in the **/boot** directory and has the name **vmlinux** with the kernel version number. Several kernels can reside in the **/boot** directory, and you can use GRUB to choose the one to use. After the kernel program you specify any options you want for the kernel. This includes the **ro** option, which initially starts the kernel as read only. The **root** option is used to specify the device on which your system was installed, your root directory. Ubuntu uses a special Universally Unique Identifier (UUID), which was created during installation, for your boot partition.

If you installed the standard workstation configuration, your root directory will be installed on a logical volume. Your **root** option references the boot partition.

For recovery, you can start up in the single user mode. This provides administrative access without any services starting up, since services could be failing. The following example shows a recovery mode GRUB entry. It is exactly the same as the main entry, but with the **single** option as the end of kernel line to indicate the single runlevel. The **splash** and **quiet** options are removed. The Upstart startup script, **/etc/event.d/rc-default**, is programmed to detect the single option, and then startup in runlevel **S**, single user mode using the **telinit** command.

```
title    Ubuntu hardy (8.04), kernel 2.6.24-11-generic (recovery mode)
root     (hd0,1)
kernel   /boot/vmlinuz-2.6.24-11-generic root=UUID=a179d6e6-b90c-4cc4-982d-
a4cfcedea7df ro single
initrd   /boot/initrd.img-2.6.24-11-generic
```

Following the main and recovery entries will be the main and recovery entries for your previously installed kernel. These are kept in case you have problems with the new kernel. You can always use GRUB to boot to the old kernal. Should you have problems with the old kernel, you can boot to the recovery mode (single runlevel) for the old kernel.

In multiboot systems, you can use GRUB to boot to another installed operating system, such as Windows. For another non-Linux operating system such as Windows, you use the **rootnoverify** option to specify where Windows is installed, as shown next. This option instructs GRUB not to try to mount the partition. Use the **chainloader+1** option to allow GRUB to access it. The **chainloader** option tells GRUB to use another boot program for that operating system. The number indicates the sector on the partition where the boot program is located—for example, **+1** indicates the first sector.

```
title Windows XP
      rootnoverify (hd0,0)
      chainloader +1
```

Windows systems will all want to boot from the first partition on the first disk. This becomes a problem if you want to install several versions of Windows on different partitions or you install Windows on a partition other than the first one. For Windows partitions on the same disk, you can work around this issue by hiding other partitions in line, and then unhiding the one you want, making it appear to be the first partition. In the following example, the first partition is hidden and the second is unhidden. This assumes a Windows system is on the second partition on the first hard drive (**hd0,1**). Now that the first partition is hidden, the second one appears as the first partition:

```
hide (hd0,0)
unhide (hd0,1)
rootnoverify (hd0,1)
```

For systems with multiple hard drives, you may have Windows installed on a drive other than the first hard drive. GRUB numbers hard drives from 0, with **hd0** referencing the first hard drive and **hd1** referencing the second hard drive. Windows will always want to boot from the first partition on the first hard drive. For a version of Windows installed on a hard drive other than the first one, you can work around this by renumbering your drives with the **map** command. The first drive can be renumbered as another drive, and that drive can then be remapped as the first drive. In the next example, the first drive is remapped as the second drive, and the second drive is mapped as the first drive. This example assumes that a Windows system is used on the first partition on the second hard drive (**hd1,0**). Once the first drive is remapped as the second one, the second drive can operate as the first drive. However, the **chainloader** operation still detects the actual location of that Windows OS on the second hard drive, **(hd1,0)+1**, in this example on the first partition. GRUB will then boot the Windows partition on the second hard drive as if it where located on a first hard drive.

```
map (hd0) (hd1)
map (hd1) (hd0)
chainloader (hd1,0)+1
```

TIP   *If you have problems booting to Linux, and you can fix the issue by editing the GRUB configuration file (by changing hard drive numbers). You can boot up with your CD/DVD Linux install disk and type* **linux rescue** *at the boot prompt. Follow the prompts to boot up your system with the command line interface. Issue the* **chroot /mnt/sysimage** *command. You can then change to the /boot/grub directory and edit your GRUB configuration file with an editor such as Vi.*

A sample segment from a GRUB configurations file (**menu.lst**) follows with entries for both Linux and Windows. There are entries for both a newer 2.6.24-11 kernel and the previous 2.5.3-8 kernel.

```
title    Ubuntu hardy (8.04), kernel 2.6.24-11-generic
root     (hd0,0)
kernel      /boot/vmlinuz-2.6.24-11-generic root=UUID=1313d608-a6cb-4457-a493-
e973bb89e4dd ro quiet splash
initrd      /boot/initrd.img-2.6.24-11-generic
quiet

title    Ubuntu hardy (8.04), kernel 2.6.24-11-generic (recovery mode)
root     (hd0,0)
kernel      /boot/vmlinuz-2.6.24-11-generic root=UUID=1313d608-a6cb-4457-a493-
e973bb89e4dd ro single
initrd      /boot/initrd.img-2.6.24-11-generic

title    Ubuntu hardy (8.04), kernel 2.6.24-8-generic
root     (hd0,0)
kernel      /boot/vmlinuz-2.6.24-8-generic root=UUID=1313d608-a6cb-4457-a493-
e973bb89e4dd ro quiet splash
initrd      /boot/initrd.img-2.6.24-8-generic
quiet

title    Ubuntu hardy (8.04), kernel 2.6.24-8-generic (recovery mode)
root     (hd0,0)
kernel      /boot/vmlinuz-2.6.24-8-generic root=UUID=1313d608-a6cb-4457-a493-
e973bb89e4dd ro single
initrd      /boot/initrd.img-2.6.24-8-generic
```

```
title      Ubuntu hardy (8.04), memtest86+
root       hd0,0)
kernel       /boot/memtest86+.bin
quiet

title Windows XP
       rootnoverify (hd0,0)
       chainloader +1
```

Virtualization

Several methods of virtualization are now available for use on Linux. These range from the paravirtualization implementation employed by Xen to the hardware acceleration used by the Kernel-based Virtual Machine (KVM) for Intel and AMD processors with hardware virtualization support. You can even use software emulation. All of these can be installed and managed with the Virtual Machine Manager (**virt-manager**), a GNOME-based tool that provides a simple GUI for managing your virtual machines and installing new ones. Linux also provides the GNOME VM applet, **gnome-applet-vm**, a panel applet that can monitor your virtual machines. See Table 21-8 for a listing of virtualization resources. See **http://virt.kernelnewbies.org** for general virtualization links and overview.

All virtualization methods can be installed and managed with the Virtual Machine Manager, which greatly simplifies the process of installing and managing virtual operating systems (guest OSs). With just a few steps you can install Windows or other Linux distributions on your Linux system and run them as guest operating systems whenever you need them. KVM virtual hosts will run directly from the processor, running almost as fast and as stably as if they were installed separately with a dual-boot configuration.

Two major methods are currently used for virtualization: full and paravirtualization. Full virtualization (KVM or QEMU) runs a guest OS independently, whereas paravirtualization (Xen) requires that you first boot up a Xen Linux kernel from which you can launch paravirtualized guest OSs. This means that a fully virtualized OS can be started with the Virtual Machine Manager from a normal Linux kernel, whereas a paravirtualized OS requires booting up with a Xen kernel.

Resource	Description
http://virt.kernelnewbies.org	Virtualization kernel documentation
http://virt-manager.et.redhat.com/	Virtual Machine Manager, **virt-manager**
http://citrixxenserver.com	Xen XenServer site
http://bellard.org/qemu/	QEMU software virtualization
http://kvm.qumranet.com/kvmwiki	KVM hardware virtualization wiki
http://libvirt.org	libvirt toolkit for accessing Linux virtualization capabilities

TABLE 21-8 Virtualization Resources

Virtual Machine Manager: virt-manager

The Virtual Machine Manager is a project developed and supported by Red Hat and is currently available on Ubuntu (**virt-manager** package). You can easily manage and set up virtual machines using **virt-manager**. After **virt-manager** is installed and started, a window lists your virtual machines. Features such as the machine ID, name, status, CPU, and memory usage are displayed. You can use the View menu to determine what features to display. Click the Help entry in the Help menu to show a detailed manual for Virtual Machine Manager.

For detailed information about the host machine, choose Edit | Host Details. The Overview tab shows information such as the hostname, the number of CPUs, and the kind of hypervisor (virtual machine monitor) it can launch. The Virtual Network tab shows your virtual networks, listing IPv4 connection information, the device name, and the network name. A default virtual network will already be set up. Select Guest and click Details for guest information.

To create a virtual machine, choose File | New Machine to start the **virt-install** wizard. You will be prompted for the name, the kind of virtualization, the location of the operating system install disk or files, the storage to use for the guest operating system, and the amount of system memory to allocate for the guest OS.

After entering a name, choose your virtualization method. If you are running a standard kernel, you will have only the option to use a fully virtualized method. On systems with Intel VT and AMD SVM processors, you will also have the option to enable hardware acceleration. This means using KVM support that will provide processor-level hardware virtualization. For processors without hardware virtualization support, a software emulation is used.

If, instead, you are running Virtual Machine Manager from the Xen kernel (as **domain** 0), you can use paravirtualization. For versions of a guest OS specially modified for use by Xen, that guest OS can be run with virtualization employed as required. In addition, for Intel VT and AMD SVM, Xen HVM methods can be used to employ hardware virtualization when virtualization is needed.

TIP *With a system with extensive memory and processor support, you can even run or install guest operating systems simultaneously using KVM from the Virtual Machine Manager.*

You then choose the location of the OS install media. For a fully virtualized OS, this can either be a disk image or a CD/DVD-ROM, such as a Windows install disk. You then choose the type of operating system you are installing, first selecting a category such as Linux or Windows, and then a particular distribution or version such as CentOS Linux or Windows XP. For a paravirtualized OS (Xen), you choose a network location for the install media.

Next, choose the storage method, either an existing partition or a file. If you choose a file, you can either set a fixed size (such as a fixed partition) or have the file expand as needed. Should the file be on a partition with a great deal of free space, size may not be an issue. Initially the file will be 4GB, but you may want to make it larger to allow for regular use.

You then choose a virtual network or a physical device for your network connection. Then choose the amount of system memory to allocate to each virtual machine, as well as the number of virtual CPUs to use. A final screen displays all your configuration information for the new virtual machine before you start installation. You can still cancel at this point. When you start installation, the install window for the guest OS is displayed and you install as you normally would. An installed OS is run in the virtual machine console window that offers buttons to run, pause, and shut down the OS.

TIP *You can also manage your virtual machines from the command line with* `virsh`*.*

KVM Hardware Virtualization

Hardware virtualization is now directly supported in the kernel (pervious versions used a kernel module). Hardware virtualization is implemented by Intel and AMD as a Hardware Virtual Machine (HVM) abstraction layer. Intel processors that have hardware virtualization support are labeled *VT* (Virtualization Technology), and AMD processors are labeled *SVM* (Secure Virtual Machine). An HVM system can provide full virtualization, not requiring a specially modified versions of an OS kernel like Xen's paravirtualization method uses. You can even run Windows XP directly from Linux using HVM. KVM is a open source project developed by Qumranet, **http://kvm.qumranet.com/kvmwiki**, where you can check for KVM information in the virtualization documentation. The KVM applications are included in the Ubuntu **kvm** package.

NOTE *KVM is run with a modified version of QEMU, which has limited virtual device support, such as the graphics driver (Xen has full native device driver access).*

KVM uses the hardware virtualization in a processor to run a virtual machine directly from hardware. No underlying software translation is used; whereas Xen will work through an underlying **domain 0** kernel, KVM operates directly with processor.

The following hardware is required for KVM support:

- An Intel (VT) or AMD (SVM) virtualization enabled processor (such as AMD AM2 socket processors or Intel Core2Duo processors). You may need to enable virtualization support in your motherboard. Some motherboards will work better than others. In some cases you may have to disable ACPI support in the motherboard BIOS to allow Windows XP to run.

- At least 1GB of system memory to allow space for the virtual OS to run. The hardware virtual OS requires its own memory.

KVM is launched as a process directly from the Linux kernel, as if booting to a new OS. It can be managed like any Linux process. KVM adds a quest process mode with its own user and kernel mode. This is in addition to the Linux kernel and user modes. KVM uses its own device driver to interface with the processor's virtualization hardware, **/dev/kvm**. KVM uses the kernel module **kvm-intel** or **kvm-amd** to interface with the processor's virtualization hardware. A modified version of a software emulator QEMU is used to run the OS guest. QEMU was originally designed as an emulator and is also available as such for processors without hardware virtualization. You do not have to install Xen to run KVM; KVM can be run separately, though installing Xen will not interfere with KVM installs.

TIP *You can implement KVM manually using QEMU, a processor emulator for full virtualization. First you create an image file for the new OS with* `qemu-img`*. Then use* `kvm` *to start the guest OS.*

Be sure to boot into the standard kernel, not into the Xen kernel. Start the Virtual Machine Manager on your GNOME desktop. Choose File | New Machine. This starts the **virt-install** wizard. When choosing the type of virtualization to use, select Fully Virtualized and make sure hardware acceleration is selected (Enabled kernel/hardware acceleration). You are then prompted for various features such as the name, the amount of system memory to use, whether to use a given partition or an image file along with the file size, graphics support, and where the install image is located (this can be a CD/DVD-ROM, though a disk image is preferred for Windows).

Once installed, you can use the Virtual Machine Manager to start up your guest OS at any time. Your guest OS is run in a virtual machine console.

NOTE *To access data directly on your virtual disks or files, you can use* `lomount` *or* `kpartx`*.*

Xen Virtualization Kernel

Distributions will normally provide versions of the kernel that incorporate Xen Virtualization. Xen Virtualization technology allows you to run different operating systems on a Linux system as well as run virtual versions of the kernel to test new applications.

Xen is an open source project originally developed by the University of Cambridge Computer Laboratory in coordination with the Open Source Development Labs and several Linux distributors. You can find more about Xen at **www.cl.cam.ac.uk/Research/SRG/netos/xen**. Xen development is currently managed by Citrix, a commercial service that provides both free open source versions of Xen and commercial implementations with support. You can find detailed documentation on the latest Xen releases, **www.citrixxenserver.com**.

NOTE *VMware provides a free version of its virtualization server. You can also purchase the virtualization desktop to install other OSs, as well as VMware's ESX virtualization server that is more stable and efficient.*

On a single Xen server, you can use several virtual machines to run different operating systems at the same time. Commercial virtualization is currently provided by VMware, and it also offers a free version of its virtualization server. Xen is a *paravirtualized* system, meaning that the guest operation system has to be modified to run on Xen. It cannot run without modification as it can on a fully virtualized system like VMware. This approach increases efficiency, giving its virtual machines nearly the same level of efficiency as the native kernel, which makes virtualization practical for enterprise-level systems. Some of the advantages cited for Xen are setting up a separate test system, isolating servers in virtual machines on the same system, and letting virtual machine access the hardware support provided by the native kernel. For an operating system to work on Xen, it must be configured to access the Xen interface. Currently only Unix and Linux operating systems are configured to be Xen compatible, though work is progressing on Windows compatibility.

You must first install the Xen kernel package as well as the Xen server, tools, and documentation. One Xen kernel package incorporates support for running Xen in **domain 0** (**xen0**), as a server, and for unprivileged (**xenU**) user access. Detailed documentation will be in **/usr/share/doc/xen-***version*. Configuration files are placed in **/etc/xen** directory, and corresponding kernels are in the **/boot** and **/lib/modules** directories. In the **/etc/xen** directory you will find the **xend-config** file for configuring the Xen **xend** server, as well as example Xen configuration files.

Once the package is installed, reboot and select the Xen kernel from the GRUB screen. Your standard original kernel will also be listed, which you can select to return to a normal kernel. Selecting Xen will start up the Xen kernel that allows you to create your Xen-based virtual systems. If you have the GNOME VM monitor applet running, it will now detect a 0 domain.

Xen sets up separate virtual machines called *domains*. When the Xen kernel starts up, it creates a primary domain, **domain 0**, which manages your system and sets up virtual machines for other operating systems. Management of the virtual machines is handled by the **xend** server. Your native kernel is installed on **domain 0**, which will handle most of the hardware devices for all the other virtual machines.

You control the domains with the **xend** server. **xend** messages are placed in the **/var/log/ xend.log** file. The **xend** server should automatically be started when you start up with the Xen kernel.

NOTE *Xen also provides support for the Hardware Virtual Machine (HVM), the HVM abstraction layer that Intel is implementing in its processors as Intel VT-x. AMD will implement HVM as SVM. The example configuration file for HVM in the **/etc/xen** directory has the extension **.hvm**. In this file, options are set to detect and use HVM. The **virt-install** script also checks for HVM.*

XenMan

You can use XenMan (**http://xenman.sourceforge.net**) to manage your Xen virtual machines. The XenMan tool provides a desktop interface from which you can manage Xen domains, adding new ones or deleting old ones. Dashboards let you check statistics such as CPU and memory usage. You can manage each virtual machine, starting, stopping, or rebooting. You can even save a snapshot of a machine and restore to that point. To start XenMan, enter the **xenman** command from a terminal window. The XenMan configuration file is **xenman.conf**.

Users have their own configuration file in the **.xenman** directory. Global definitions and Xen configuration files are held in the **/etc/xenman/xenman.conf** file, which defines paths for your virtual block devices and provides the location of snapshots. It also provides environment (current domain), any specific application configurations, and client configuration such as GNOME support. XenMan also supports the use of images, collected into an image store. An image is a predefined virtual machine from which numerous other virtual machines can be generated. You could, for example, set up Ubuntu images, and then generate several Ubuntu virtual machines using those images.

virt-install

Instead of configuring a file directly or using **virt-manager**, you can use the **virt-install** script. It currently can install only from a remote network location using an **http://**, **nfs://**, or

ftp:// prefix. This script will not allow you to use less than 256MB for each virtual machine. If you want to use less memory than that, say for a scaled-down version of Linux, you will have to use the configuration files directly as described in the preceding section.

If your system has a limited amount of available RAM, you may need to limit the amount the **domain 0** virtual machine is using. You can reduce this to the recommended 256MB with the following command:

```
xm mem-set 0 256
```

To start the **virt-install** script, open a terminal window and enter the script name:

```
virt-install
```

You will be prompted to set several parameters, and then a configuration file will be automatically generated. You are asked to name the virtual machine: this is your hostname. Then you are asked how much RAM to allocate. A minimum of 256MB is required. This means that for just one virtual machine you have to have at least 500MB of RAM—256MB for the Xen0 server (**domain 0**) and 256MB for the guest/user machine (**domain 1**). More virtual machines would use correspondingly more RAM.

You are then prompted to enter the disk path for the virtual machine image file. You are then prompted for the size of the image file in gigabytes. Virtual machines use an image file where its entire system is kept. Finally, you are prompted for the location of installation files for the operating system you want to install. Here you can enter an FTP or Website.

Managing Users

A s a system administrator, you must manage the users of your system. You can add or remove users, as well as add and remove groups, and you can modify access rights and permissions for both users and groups. You also have access to system initialization files you can use to configure all user shells, and you have control over the default initialization files copied into a user account when it is first created. You can decide how new user accounts should be configured initially by configuring these files.

GUI User Management Tools: users-admin

Currently, the easiest and most effective way to add new users on Ubuntu is to use GNOME's **users-admin** tool. You can access it from the GNOME desktop by choosing System | Administration | Users And Groups. GNOME's **users-admin** tool provides a simple interface for adding, modifying, and removing users and groups. The Users Settings window (Figure 22-1) lists users' names, login names, and home directories, along with the users' icons they chose with the About Me tool (System | Preferences). To the right are buttons for adding new users, editing a user's properties, deleting users, and managing groups.

Read-only access is provided to all users; before you can use **users-admin**, you have to unlock it. User entries will be grayed out. Users will be able to see the list of users on your system, but they cannot modify their entries, add new ones, or delete current users. Administrative access is required to perform these operations. Administrative access for the **users-admin** tool is controlled by PolicyKit. Click the Unlock button at the bottom of the window to open a Authenticate dialog, where you enter your user password (Figure 22-2). Click the Authenticate button, and user entries will no longer be grayed out in the Users Settings window. With administrative access granted, the bottom Unlock button will be grayed out.

Create a New User

To create a new user, click Add User in the Users Settings window. This opens a New User Account window with three tabs: Account, User Privileges, and Advanced (see Figure 22-3). The Account tab has entries for the Username, Real Name (the user's full name), Profile, Contact Information, and Password information. The Profile entry is a pop-up menu listing Desktop User, Administrator, and Unprivileged. Administrator will allow the user to use the administration tools and the **sudo** command to perform systemwide administration tasks.

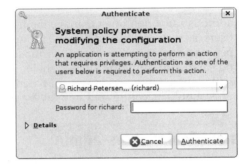

Desktop users do not have administration access. Unprivileged denies access to most resources, though online access is allowed—it operates much like a dumb terminal.

On the User Privileges tab, you can control device access as well as administrative access. You can restrict or allow access to CD-ROMs, scanners, and external storage such as USB drives. You can also determine whether the user can perform administrative tasks. The Administer The System check box is left unchecked by default; if you want to allow the user to perform administration tasks, be sure to check this box.

The Advanced tab lets you select a home directory, the shell to use, a main group, and a user ID. Defaults will already be chosen for you. A home directory in the name of the new user will be specified and the shell used will be the BASH shell. Normally you would not want to change these settings, though you might prefer to use a different shell, such as the C shell. For the group, the user will have a group with its own username. In addition, the user will have access to all system resource groups such as CD-ROM, audio, video, and scanner.

To change settings, select the user in the Users Settings window and click the Properties button. The Account Properties window opens with Account, Privileges, and Advanced tabs. To delete a user, for example, select the username and click the Delete button.

Manage Groups

To manage groups, click the Manage Groups button in the Users Settings window. This opens a Group Settings window that lists all groups. To add or remove users to or from a group, click the group name in the Group Settings window and click Properties. You can then check or uncheck users from the Group Members listing.

To add a new group, click the Add Group button in the Users Settings window to open a New Group dialog (Figure 22-4), where you can specify the Group Name and ID, and select members to include in the group.

User Configuration Files

User management utilities, such as GNOME's **users-admin** or KDE's KUser, contain default files called *configuration files* and directories to set up the new account. A set of pathnames is used to locate these default files or to indicate where to create certain user directories. Table 22-1 shows a list of common configuration file pathnames.

FIGURE 22-4
New Group dialog

Directory and File	Description
/home	User's home directory
/etc/shells	Supported login shells
/etc/passwd	User's password
/etc/group	Group to which the user belongs
/etc/shadow	Encrypted password file
/etc/gshadow	Encrypted password file for groups
/etc/login.defs	Default login definitions for users

TABLE 22-1   Paths for User Configuration Files

NOTE *Every file is owned by a user who can control access to it. System files are owned by the root user and accessible by the root only. Services such as FTP are an exception to this rule. Though accessible by the root, a service's files are owned by their own special user. For example, FTP files are owned by an **ftp** user. This provides users to access a service's files without them also having root user access.*

The Password Files

A user gains access to an account by providing a correct login and password. The system maintains passwords in password files, along with login information such as the username and ID. Tools such as the **passwd** command let users change their passwords by modifying these files; **/etc/passwd** was the file that traditionally held user passwords, though in encrypted form. However, all users are allowed to read the **/etc/passwd** file, which allows users to access the encrypted passwords. For better security, password entries are now kept in the **/etc/shadow** file, which is restricted to the root user.

TIP *You can find out which users are currently logged in by using the **w** or **who** command from a terminal window. The **w** command displays detailed information about each connected user, such as from where they logged in and how long they have been inactive, and the date and time of login. The **who** command provides less detailed data.*

/etc/passwd

When you add a user, an entry for that user is made in the **/etc/passwd** file, commonly known as the *password file*. Each entry takes up one line that has the following fields, separated by colons:

- **Username**   Login name of the user
- **Password**   Encrypted password for the user's account
- **User ID**   Unique number assigned by the system
- **Group ID**   Number used to identify the group to which the user belongs
- **Comment**   Any user information, such as the user's full name

- **Home directory**   The user's home directory
- **Login shell**   Shell to run when the user logs in; this is the default shell, usually **/bin/bash**

CAUTION *Although it is technically possible to edit entries in the **/etc/passwd** file directly, it is not recommended. In particular, deleting an entry does not remove any other information, permissions, and data associated with a user, which opens a possible security breach whereby an intruder could take over the deleted user's ID or disk space.*

Depending on whether or not you are using shadow passwords, the password field (the second field) will be either an **x** or an encrypted form of the user's password. Linux implements shadow passwords by default, so these entries should have an **x** for their passwords. The following is an example of an **/etc/passwd** entry. For such entries, you must use the `passwd` command to create a password. Notice also that user IDs in this particular system start at 500 and increment by 1. The group shown is not the generic User, but a group consisting uniquely of one user. For example, the **dylan** user belongs to a group named **Dylan**, not to the generic **User** group.

```
dylan:x:500:500:Dylan:/home/dylan:/bin/bash
chris:x:501:501:Chris:/home/chris:/bin/bash
```

NOTE *If you turn off shadow password support, entries in your **passwd** file will display encrypted passwords. Because any user can read the **/etc/passwd** file, intruders can access and possibly crack the encrypted passwords.*

/etc/shadow and /etc/gshadow

The **/etc/passwd** file is a simple text file and is vulnerable to security breaches. Anyone who gains access to the **/etc/password** file might be able to decipher or crack the encrypted passwords through a brute-force attack. The shadow suite of applications implements a greater level of security. These include versions of `useradd`, `groupadd`, and their corresponding update and delete programs. Most other user configuration tools support shadow security measures. With shadow security, passwords are no longer kept in the **/etc/password** file. Instead, passwords are kept in a separate file called **/etc/shadow**. Access is restricted to the root user.

The following example shows the **/etc/passwd** entry for a user:

```
chris:x:501:501:Chris:/home/chris:/bin/bash
```

A corresponding password file, called **/etc/gshadow**, is also maintained for groups that require passwords.

Password Tools

To change any particular field for a user, you use the user management tools provided, such as the `passwd` command, `usermod`, `useradd`, and `chage`, which are discussed in this chapter. The `passwd` command lets you change the password only. Other tools not only add entries to the **/etc/passwd** file, but they create a home directory for the user and install initialization files in the user's home directory.

These tools also let administrators control users' access to their accounts. You can set expiration dates for users or lock them out of their accounts. Users locked out of their accounts will have a their password in the **/etc/shadow** file prefixed by the invalid string, **!!**. Unlocking the account removes this prefix.

Managing User Environments

Each time a user logs in, two profile scripts are executed: a system profile script that is the same for every user, and a user login profile script that can be customized to each user's needs. When the user logs out, a user logout script is run. In addition, each time a shell is generated, including the login shell, a user shell script is run. Different kinds of scripts are used for different shells. The default shell commonly used is the BASH shell. As an alternative, users can use shells such as TCSH or the Z shell.

Profile Scripts

For the BASH shell, each user has his or her own BASH login profile script named **.profile** in the user's home directory. The system profile script is located in the **/etc** directory and named **profile** with no preceding period. The BASH shell user shell script is called **.bashrc**. The **.bashrc** file also runs the **/etc/bashrc** file to implement any global definitions such as the **PS1** and **TERM** variables. The **.profile** file runs the **.bashrc** file, and through it, the **/etc/bashrc** file, which implements global definitions.

As a superuser, you can edit any of these profile or shell scripts and put in any commands you want executed for each user when that user logs in. For example, you may want to define a default path for commands, in case the user has not done so. Or you may want to notify the user of recent system news or account changes.

/etc/login.defs

Systemwide values used by user and group creation utilities such as **useradd** and **usergroup** are kept in the **/etc/login.defs** file. Here you will find the range of possible user and group IDs listed. **UID_MIN** holds the minimum number for user IDs and **UID_MAX** the maximum number. Various password options control password controls, such as **PASS_MAX_DAYS**, which determines the maximum days allowable for a password. Many password options, such as password lengths, are now handled by Pluggable Authentication Modules (PAM). Samples of these entries are shown here:

```
UID_MIN      1000
MAIL_DIR    /var/mail
PASS_MAX_DAYS    99999
```

Controlling User Passwords

Once you have created a user account, you can control the user's access to it. The **passwd** tool lets you lock and unlock a user's account. You use the **passwd** command with the **-l** option to lock an account, invalidating its password, and you use the **-u** option to unlock it.

You can also force a user to change his or her password at given intervals by setting an expiration date for that password. The **chage** command lets you specify an expiration limit for a user's password. A user can be required to change her password every month, every week, or at a given date. Once the password expires, the user is prompted to enter a new one. You can issue a warning beforehand, telling the user how much time is left before the password expires.

If you want to close an account, you can permanently expire a password. You can even shut down accounts that are inactive for too long. The **-M** option with the number of days sets the maximum time that a password can be valid. In the next example, the password for the **chris** account will stay valid for seven days:

```
chage -M 7  chris
```

To set a particular date for the account to expire, use the **-E** option with the date specified *mm/dd/yyyy*:

```
chage -E 07/30/2008  chris
```

To find out the current expiration settings for a given account, use the **-l** option:

```
chage -l chris
```

You can also combine your options into one command, like so:

```
chage -M 7 -E 07/30/2008  chris
```

A list of the **chage** options appears in Table 22-2.

Option	Description
-m	Minimum number of days a user must go before being able to change his or her password
-M	Maximum number of days a user can go without changing his or her password
-d	The last day the password was changed
-E	Specific expiration date for a password, date in format in *yyyy-mm-dd* or in commonly used format like *mm/dd/yyyy*
-I	Allowable account inactivity period (in days), after which password will expire
-W	Warning period, number of days before expiration when the user will be sent a warning message
-l	Current password expiration controls display

TABLE 22-2   Options for the chage Command

Adding and Removing Users and Groups with useradd, usermod, and userdel

Linux also provides the **useradd**, **usermod**, and **userdel** commands to manage user accounts. All these commands take in their information as options on the command line. If an option is not specified, they use predetermined default values. To use these command line operations on your desktop, you first need to open a terminal window (right-click the desktop and choose Open Terminal), and then enter the commands at the shell prompt.

If you are using a desktop interface, you should use GUI tools to manage user accounts. Each Linux distribution usually provides a tool to manage users. In addition. you can use the KUser tool or the GNOME **users-admin** tool. Table 22-3 shows user management tools.

NOTE *On KDE, KUser lets you manage both users and groups. The KDE User Manager window displays two tabs for Users and Groups. The Users tab lists user login, full name, home directory, login shell, and user ID. On the toolbar, Add, Edit, and Delete buttons can be used for both users and groups, and Users and Groups menus offer corresponding entries. Initially, all system users and groups will also be displayed. Choose Settings | Hide System Users/Groups to display normal users and groups.*

useradd

With the **useradd** command, you enter values as options on the command line, such as the name of a user, to create a user account. It then creates a new login and directory for that username using all the default features for a new account.

```
# useradd chris
```

The **useradd** utility first checks the **/etc/login.defs** file for default values for creating a new account. For those defaults not defined in the **/etc/login.defs** file, **useradd** supplies its own. You can display these defaults using the **useradd** command with the **-D** option. The default values include the group name, the user ID, the home directory, the **skel** directory,

Tool	Description
GNOME **users-admin**	Adds, removes, and modifies users and groups; primary Ubuntu desktop user management tool
KDE User Manager (KUser)	Adds, removes, and modifies users and groups
useradd *username options*	Adds a user
userdel *username*	Deletes a user
usermod *username options*	Modifies user properties
groupadd *groupname options*	Adds a group
groupdel *groupname*	Deletes a group
groupmod *groupname options*	Modifies a group name

TABLE 22-3 User and Group Management Tools

and the login shell. Values the user enters on the command line will override corresponding defaults. The group name is the name of the group in which the new account is placed. By default, this is **other**, which means the new account belongs to no group. The user ID is a number identifying the user account. The **skel** directory is the system directory that holds copies of initialization files. These initialization files are copied into the user's new home directory when it is created. The login shell is the pathname for the particular shell the user plans to use.

The `useradd` command has options that correspond to each default value. Table 22-4 shows all the options you can use with the `useradd` command. You can use specific values in place of any of these defaults when creating a particular account. The login is inaccessible until you add these specific values. In the next example, the group name for the **chris** account is set to **intro1** and the user ID is set to **578**:

```
# useradd chris -g intro1 -u 578
```

Once you add a new user login, you need to give the new login a password. Password entries are placed in the **/etc/passwd** and **/etc/shadow** files. Use the `passwd` command to create a new password for the user, as shown next. The password you enter will not appear

Option	Description
-d *dir*	Sets the home directory of the new user.
-D	Displays defaults for all settings. Can also be used to reset default settings for the home directory (**-b**), group (**-g**), shell (**-s**), expiration date (**-e**), and password expirations (**-f**).
-e *mm/dd/yy*	Sets an expiration date for the account (none, by default). Specified as *month/day/year*.
-f *days*	Sets the number of days an account remains active after its password expires.
-g *group*	Sets a group.
-m	Creates user's home directory, if it does not exist.
-m **-k** *skl-dir*	Sets the skeleton directory that holds skeleton files, such as **.profile** files, which are copied to the user's home directory automatically when it is created; the default is **/etc/skel**.
-M	Does not create user's home directory.
-p *password*	Supplies an encrypted password (crypt or MD5). With no argument, the account is immediately disabled.
-s *shell*	Sets the login shell of the new user. This is **/bin/bash** by default, the BASH shell.
-u *userid*	Sets the user ID of the new user. The default is the increment of the highest number used so far.

TABLE 22-4   Options for `useradd` and `usermod`

on your screen. You will be prompted to repeat the password. A message will then tell you that the password was successfully changed.

```
# passwd chris
Changing password for user chris
New UNIX password:
Retype new UNIX password:
passwd: all authentication tokens updated successfully
#
```

usermod

The **usermod** command lets you change the values for any of these features. You can change the home directory or the user ID. You can even change the username for the account. The **usermod** command takes the same options as **useradd**, listed in Table 22-4.

userdel

When you want to remove a user from the system, you can use the **userdel** command to delete the user's login. With the **-r** option, the user's home directory will also be removed. In the next example, the user **chris** is removed from the system:

```
# userdel -r chris
```

Managing Groups

Groups are an effective way to manage user access and permissions. Using groups, you can control settings for several users at a time. You can manage groups using either shell commands or GUI utilities.

/etc/group and /etc/gshadow

The system file that holds group entries is called **/etc/group**. The file consists of group records, with one record per line and its fields separated by colons. A group record has four fields: a group name, password, group ID, and the users who are part of this group:

- **Group name** The name of the group, which must be unique
- **Password** With shadow security implemented, this field is an **x**, with the password indicated in the **/etc/gshadow** file; this field can be blank
- **Group ID** The number assigned by the system to identify this group
- **Users** The list of users that belong to the group, separated by commas

Here is an example of an entry in an **/etc/group** file. The group is called **engines**, the password is managed by shadow security, the group ID is **100**, and the users who are part of this group are **chris**, **robert**, **valerie**, and **aleina**:

```
engines:x:100:chris,robert,valerie,aleina
```

As in the case of the **/etc/passwd** file, it is best to change group entries using a group management utility such as **groupmod** or **groupadd**. All users have read access to the

/etc/**group** file. With shadow security, secure group data such as passwords are kept in the /etc/**gshadow** file, to which only the root user has access.

User Private Groups

A new user can be assigned to a special group set up for just that user and given the user's name. Thus, the new user **dylan** is given a default group also called **dylan**. The group **dylan** will also show up in the listing of groups. This method of assigning default user groups is called the *User Private Group (UPG)* scheme. Supplementary groups are additional groups to which the user may want to belong. Traditionally, users were all assigned to one group named **users** that subjected all users to the group permission controls for the **users** group. With UPG, each user has its own group, with its own group permissions.

Group Directories

As with users, you can create a home directory for a group. To do so, you simply create a directory for the group in the /**home** directory and change its home group to that group and allow access by any member of the group. The following example creates a directory called **engines** and changes its group to the **engines** group:

```
mkdir /home/engines
chgrp engines /home/engines
```

Then the read, write, and execute permissions for the group level should be set with the **chmod** command:

```
chmod g+rwx /home/engines
```

Any member of the **engines** group can now access the /**home/engines** directory and any shared files placed therein. This directory becomes a shared directory for the group. You can, in fact, use the same procedure to make other shared directories at any location on the file system.

Files within the shared directory should also have their permissions set to allow access by other users in the group. When a user places a file in a shared directory, the user needs to set the permissions on that file to allow other members of the group to access it. A read permission will let others display it, write lets them change it, and execute lets them run it (used for scripts and programs).

The following example first changes the group for the **mymodel** file to **engines**. Then it copies the **mymodel** file to the /**home/engines** directory and sets the group read and write permission for the **engines** group:

```
$ chgrp engines mymodel
$ cp mymodel /home/engines
$ chmod g+rw /home/engines/mymodel
```

Managing Groups Using groupadd, groupmod, and groupdel

You can also manage groups with the **groupadd**, **groupmod**, and **groupdel** commands. These command line operations let you quickly manage a group from a terminal window.

With the **groupadd** command, you can add new groups to the system; the system places the group's name in the **/etc/group** file and gives it a group ID number. If shadow security is in place, changes are made to the **/etc/gshadow** file. The **groupadd** command creates only the group category; you need to add users to the group individually. In the following example, the **groupadd** command creates the **engines** group:

```
# groupadd engines
```

You can delete a group with the **groupdel** command. In the next example, the **engines** group is deleted:

```
# groupdel engines
```

You can change the name of a group or its ID using the **groupmod** command. Enter **groupmod -g** with the new ID number and the group name. To change the name of a group, you use the **-n** option. Enter **groupmod -n** with the new name of the group, followed by the current name. In the next example, the **engines** group has its name changed to **trains**:

```
# groupmod -n trains engines
```

Disk Quotas

Disk quotas control how much disk space a particular user can access on your system. On your Linux system, unused disk space is held as a common resource that each user can access as he needs it. As users create more files, they take the space they need from the pool of available disk space. In this sense, all the users are sharing a single resource of unused disk space. However, if one user were to use up all the remaining disk space, none of the other users would be able to create files or even run programs. To counter this problem, you can create disk quotas on particular users, limiting the amount of available disk space they can use.

Quota Tools

Quota checks can be implemented on the file system of a hard disk partition mounted on your system (**quota** package, Ubuntu main repository). The quotas are enabled using the **quotacheck** and **quotaon** programs. They are executed in the **/etc/init.d/quota** script, which can be run whenever you start up your system. Each partition needs to be mounted with the quota options, **usrquota** (for user controls) or **grpquota** (for group controls). These options are usually placed in the mount entry in the **/etc/fstab** file for a particular partition. For example, to mount the **/dev/hda6** hard disk partition to the **/home** directory with support for user and group quotas, you would use a mount entry like the following:

```
/dev/hda6 /home ext2 defaults,usrquota,grpquota 1 1
```

You also need to create **quota.user** and **quota.group** files for each partition for which you enable quotas. These are the quota databases that hold the quota information for each user and group. You can create these files by running the **quotacheck** command with the **-a** option or the device name of the file system where you want to enable quotas.

The quota service script will perform a quota check and turn on the quota service for all file systems. It will also use **quotacheck** to create **quota.user** and **quota.group** files for new file systems. You can run this script manually to start, stop, and restart the service. The following command will start the quota service, running **quotacheck** and **quotaon** with the following command:

```
sudo /etc/init.d/quota start
```

You can also use `quotacheck` directly to check quota files for a particular file system. The following example creates the quota database on the **hda1** hard disk partition:

```
sudo quotacheck /dev/hda1
```

Though the **quota** script can be used to turn the quota service on or off (start, stop, and restart options), you can also manually turn the quota service on directly with the `quotaon` command. Using just `quotaon` lets you turn the service on without having to perform a **quotacheck** operation. You can turn quotas off using the `quotaoff` command.

```
sudo quotaon  -aug
```

When you start up your system, the **quota** script will use `quotacheck` to check the quota databases, and then `quotaon` to turn on quotas.

NOTE *The **quotarpc** service enables remote quota controls.*

edquota

You can set disk quotas using the `edquota` command. This command lets you access the quota record for a particular user and group, which is maintained in the disk quota database. You can also set default quotas that will be applied to any user or group on the file system for which quotas have not been set. `edquota` will open the record in your default editor, and you can use your editor to make any changes. To open the record for a particular user, use the **-u** option and the username as an argument for `edquota` (see Table 22-5). The following example opens the disk quota record for the user **larisa**:

```
sudo edquota -u larisa
```

edquota **Option**	**Description**
-u	Edits the user quota; the default
-g	Edits the group quota
-p	Duplicates the quotas of the typical user specified; the normal mechanism used to initialize quotas for groups of users
-t	Edits the soft time limits for each file system

TABLE 22-5   Options for `edquota`

quota Option	Description
-g	Prints group quotas for the user's group
-u	Prints the user's quota
-v	Displays quotas on file systems where no storage is allocated
-q	Prints information on file systems where usage is over quota

TABLE 22-6 Options for quota

The limit you set for a quota can be *hard* or *soft*. A hard limit will deny a user the ability to exceed his or her quota, whereas a soft limit will just issue a warning. For the soft limit, you can designate a grace period (up to 48 hours) during which time the user can reduce her disk space below the limit. If the disk space still exceeds the limit after the grace period expires, the user can be denied access to her account. For example, a soft limit is typically 75MB, whereas the hard limit could be 100MB.

The quota record begins with the hard disk device name and the blocks of memory and inodes in use. The limits segments have parameters for soft and hard limits. If these entries are 0, no limits are in place. You can set both hard and soft limits, using the hard limit as a firm restriction. Blocks in Linux are currently about 1000 bytes. The inodes are used by files to hold information about the memory blocks making up a file. To set the time limit for a soft limit, use the **edquota** command with the **-t** option. The following example displays the quota record for **larisa**:

```
Quotas for user larisa:
/dev/hda3: blocks in use: 9000, limits (soft = 40000, hard = 60000)
  inodes in use: 321, limits (soft = 0, hard = 0)
```

repquota and quota

As the system administrator, you can use the **repquota** command to generate a summary of disk usage for a specified file system, checking to see what users are approaching or exceeding quota limits. **repquota** takes as its argument the file system to check; the **-a** option checks all file systems. Here's an example:

```
repquota /dev/hda1
```

Individual users can use the **quota** command to check memory use and determine how much disk space is left in their quota. Table 22-6 shows the options for the command.

Lightweight Directory Access Protocol

The Lightweight Directory Access Protocol (LDAP) is designed to implement network-accessible directories of information. In this context, the term *directory* is defined as a database of primarily read-only, simple, small, widely accessible, and quickly distributable information. It is not designed for transactions or updates. It is primarily used to provide information about users on a network, such as their e-mail addresses or phone numbers. Such directories can also be used for authentication purposes, identifying that a certain user belongs to a specified network. You can find out more information on LDAP at **http://ldapman.org**.

You can think of an LDAP directory for users as an Internet-accessible phone book, where anyone can look up your e-mail address or other information. In fact, it may be more accurate to refer to such directories as databases of user information that are accessible over networks such as the Internet. Normally, users on a local network are spread across several different systems, and to obtain information about a particular user, you have to know what system the user is on and then query that system. With LDAP, user information for all users on a network is kept in the LDAP server, so you can query only the network's LDAP server to obtain information about a user. For example, Sendmail can use LDAP to look up user addresses. You can also use Firefox or Netscape to query LDAP.

NOTE *LDAP is a directory access protocol to an X.500 directory service, the OSI Directory Service.*

LDAP directories are implemented as clients and servers; you use an LDAP client to access an LDAP server that manages the LDAP database. Ubuntu uses OpenLDAP, an open-source version of LDAP (see **www.openldap.org**). OpenLDAP provides an LDAP server (**slapd**), an LDAP replication server (**slurpd**), an LDAP client, and LDAP utilities.

On Ubuntu, you install the LDAP packages using the **ldap-auth-config** metapackage. This package will also select and install the **ldap-auth-client**, **libpam-ldap**, and **libnss-ldap** packages. For the LDAP server, you select the **slapd** package. If you are running Postfix mail server, you may want to use **postfix-ldap**.

When installing **ldap-auth-config**, you are prompted to enter in the URI for the LDAP server, the distinguishing name of the search base, and the version to use. You are then prompted to specify whether the administrator on your system has administrative access to the LDAP server and if the LDAP database requires a login. Then specify the LDAP account for the root and the LDAP root account password.

For documentation of the LDAP server on Ubuntu, check the OpenLDAP Server entry for your distribution at **https://help.ubuntu.com**.

LDAP Configuration Files

All LDAP configuration files are kept in the **/etc/ldap** directory. These include **slapd.conf**, the LDAP server configuration file, and **ldap.conf**, the LDAP clients and tools configuration file. To enable the LDAP server, you have to edit the **slapd.conf** file manually and change the domain value (**dc**) for the **suffix** and **rootdn** entries to your own network's domain address. This is the network that will be serviced by the LDAP server.

To enable LDAP clients and their tools, you must specify the correct domain address in the **ldap.conf** file in the BASE option, along with the server's address in the URI option (domain name or IP address). For clients, this is the configuration information you entered when installing the **ldap-auth-config** package. You can also edit the **ldap.conf** file directly. See the **ldap.conf** man entry for detailed descriptions of LDAP options.

If you installed the LDAP server, you can start, stop, and restart the LDAP service using the `slapd` script:

```
sudo /etc/init.d/slapd start
```

You can also have the LDAP servers started when your system starts up by checking the LDAP Server entry in the **services-admin** tool: choose System | Administration | Services.

TIP *Keep in mind that the /etc/ldap.conf and /etc/ldap/ldap.conf files are not the same. /etc/ ldap.conf is used to configure LDAP for the Name Service Switch and PAM support, whereas /etc/ldap/ldap.conf is used for all LDAP clients.*

Configuring the LDAP Server: /etc/ldap/slapd.conf

You configure the LDAP server with the **/etc/ldap/slapd.conf** file, where you will find entries for loading schemas and for specifying access controls, the database directory, and passwords. The file is commented in detail, with default settings for most options, although you will have to enter settings for several. First you need to specify your domain suffix and root domain manager. The default settings are shown here:

```
suffix          "dc=my-domain,dc=com"
rootdn          "cn=Manager,dc=my-domain,dc=com"
```

In the next example, the **suffix** is changed to **mytrek**, for **mytrek.com**. The **rootdn** remains the same.

```
suffix          "dc=mytrek,dc=com"
rootdn          "cn=Manager,dc=mytrek,dc=com"
```

Next you will have to specify a password with **rootpw**. Entries are available for both plain text and encrypted versions, and both are commented. Remove the comment for one. In the following example, the plain text password option, **secret**, is used:

```
rootpw          secret
# rootpw        {crypt}ijFYNcSNctBYg
```

For an encrypted password, you can first create the encrypted version with **slappasswd**, as shown next. This will generate a text encryption string for the password. Then copy the generated encrypted string to the **rootpw** entry. On GNOME, you can simply cut and paste from a terminal window to the **/etc/ldap/slapd.conf** file in Text Editor (Accessories). You can also redirect the encrypted string to a file and read it in later. SSHA encryption is used by default.

```
# slappasswd
New password:
Re-enter new password:
{SSHA}0a+szaAwElK57Y8AoD5uMULSvLfCUfg5
```

The **rootpw** root password entry should then look like this:

```
rootpw          {SSHA}0a+szaAwElK57Y8AoD5uMULSvLfCUfg5
```

Use the password you entered at the **slappasswd** prompt to access your LDAP directory.

The configuration file also lists the schemas to be used. Schemas are included with the **include** directive:

```
include          /etc/ldap/schema/core.schema
include          /etc/ldap/schema/cosine.schema
include          /etc/ldap/schema/inetorgperson.schema
include          /etc/ldap/schema/nis.schema
```

NOTE *LDAP supports the Simple Authentication and Security Layer (SASL) for secure authentication with methods such as MD5 and Kerberos.*

LDAP Directory Database: ldif

A record (also known as entry) in an LDAP database begins with a name, known as a *distinguishing name*, followed by a set of attributes and their values. The distinguishing name uniquely identifies the record. For example, a name could be a username and the attribute would be the user's e-mail address, the address being the attribute's value. Allowable attributes are determined by schemas defined in the **/etc/ldap/schema** directory. This directory will hold various schema definition files, each with a **schema** extension. Some will be dependent on others, enhancing their supported classes and attributes. The basic core set of attributes is defined in the **core.schema** file. Here you will find definitions for attributes such as country name and street address. Other schemas, such as **inetorgperson.schema**, specify **core.schema** as a dependent schema, making its attributes available to the classes. The **inetOrgPerson** schema will also define its own attributes such as **jpegPhoto** for a person's photograph.

Schema Attributes and Classes

Attributes and classes are defined officially by RFC specifications that are listed with each attribute and class entry in the schema files. These are standardized definitions and should not be changed. Attributes are defined by an **attributetype** definition. Each is given a unique identifying number followed by a name by which it can be referenced. Fields include the attribute description (DESC), search features such as EQUALITY and SUBSTR, and the object identifier (SYNTAX). See the OpenLDAP administrative guide for a detailed description.

```
attributetype ( 2.5.4.9 NAME ( 'street' 'streetAddress' )
     DESC 'RFC2256: street address of this object'
     EQUALITY caseIgnoreMatch
     SUBSTR caseIgnoreSubstringsMatch
     SYNTAX 1.3.6.1.4.1.1466.115.121.1.15{123} )
```

A class defines the kind of database (directory) you can create. This will specify the kinds of attributes you can include in your records. Classes can be dependent, where one class becomes and extension of another. The class most often used for LDAP databases is **inetOrgPerson**, defined in the **inetOrgPerson.schema** file, shown next. The term **inetOrgPerson** stands for Internet Organization Person, as many LDAP directories perform Internet tasks. The class is derived from the **organizationalPerson** class defined in **core.schema**, which includes the original attributes for commonly used fields such as street address and name.

```
# inetOrgPerson
# The inetOrgPerson represents people who are associated with an
# organization in some way.  It is a structural class and is derived
# from the organizationalPerson which is defined in X.521 [X521].
objectclass ( 2.16.840.1.113730.3.2.2
    NAME 'inetOrgPerson'
      DESC 'RFC2798: Internet Organizational Person'
    SUP organizationalPerson
    STRUCTURAL
     MAY (
            audio $ businessCategory $ carLicense $ departmentNumber $
            displayName $ employeeNumber $ employeeType $ givenName $
            homePhone $ homePostalAddress $ initials $ jpegPhoto $
            labeledURI $ mail $ manager $ mobile $ o $ pager $
            photo $ roomNumber $ secretary $ uid $ userCertificate $
            x500uniqueIdentifier $ preferredLanguage $
            userSMIMECertificate $ userPKCS12 )
     )
```

You can create your own classes, building on the standard ones already defined. You can also create your own attributes, but each attribute will require a unique object identifier (OID).

Distinguishing Names

Data in an LDAP directory is organized hierarchically, from general categories to specific data. So, for example, an LDAP directory can be organized starting with countries, narrowing to states, then organizations and their subunits, and finally individuals. Commonly, LDAP directories are organized along the lines of Internet domains. In this format, the top category is the domain name extension, such as **.com** or .ca. The directory then breaks down to the network (organization), units, and finally users.

This organization helps define distinguishing names that will identify the LDAP records. In a network-based organization, the top-level organization is defined by a domain component specified by the **dcObject** class, which includes the **domainComponent (dc)** attribute. Usually you define the network and extension as domain components to make up the top-level organization that becomes the distinguishing name for the database itself. Here's an example:

```
dc=mytrek, dc=com
```

Under the organization name is an organizational unit, such as users. These are defined as an **organizationalUnitName (ou)**, which is part of the **organizationalUnit** class. The distinguishing name for the user's organizational unit would be

```
ou=users, dc=mytrek, dc=com
```

Under the organizational unit you can then have individual users. Here the username is defined with the **commonName (cn)** attribute, which is used in various classes, including Person, which is part of **organizationalPerson**, which in turn is part of **inetOrgPerson**. The distinguishing name for the user **dylan** is then

```
cn=dylan,ou=users,dc=mytrek,dc=com
```

LDIF Entries
Database entries are placed in an LDAP Interchange Format (LDIF) file. This format provides a global standard that allows a database to be accessed by any LDAP-compliant client. An LDIF file is a simple text file with an **.ldif** extension placed in the **/etc/ldap** directory. The entries for an LDIF record consist of a distinguishing name or attribute followed by a colon and its list of values. Each record begins with a distinguishing name to uniquely identify the record. Attributes then follow. You can think of the name as a record and the attributes as fields in that record. You end the record with an empty line.

Adding the Records
Once you have created your LDIF file, you can then use the **ldapadd** command to add the records to you LDAP directory. Use the **-D** option to specify the directory in which to add the records and the **-f** option to specify the LDIF file to read from. You could use **ldapadd** to enter fields directly. The **-x** option says to use simple password access, the **-W** will prompt for the password, and the **-D** option specifies the directory manager:

```
ldapadd -x -D "cn=Manager,dc=mytrek,dc=com" -W -f mytrek.ldif
```

Searching LDAP
Once you have added your records, you can use the **ldapsearch** command to search your LDAP directory. The **-x** and **-W** options provide simple password access, and the **-b** option specifies the LDAP database to use. Following the options are the attributes to search for, in this case the **street** attribute:

```
ldapsearch -x -W -D 'cn=Manager,dc=mytrek,dc=com' -b 'dc=mytrek,dc=com' street
```

If you want to see all the records listed in the database, you can use the same search command without any attributes.

LDAP Tools
To make or change entries in the LDAP database, you use the **ldapadd** and **ldapmodify** utilities (**ldap-utils** package, Ubuntu main repository). With **ldapdelete**, you can remove entries. Once you have created an LDAP database, you can then query it, through the LDAP server, with **ldapsearch**. For the LDAP server, you can create a text file of LDAP entries using the LDAP Data Interchange Format (LDIF). Such text files can then be read in all at once to the LDAP database using the **slapadd** tool. The **slapcat** tool extracts entries from the LDAP database and saves them in an LDIF file. To reindex additions and changes, you use the **slapindex** utility. See the LDAP HOWTO at the Linux Documentation Project for details on using and setting up LDAP databases such as address books (**http://tldp.org**).

Pluggable Authentication Modules
Pluggable Authentication Modules (PAM) is an authentication service that lets a system determine the method of authentication to be performed for users. In a Linux system, authentication has traditionally been performed by looking up passwords. When a user logs in, the login process looks up the user's password in the password file. With PAM, users'

requests for authentication are directed to PAM, which in turn uses a specified method to authenticate the user. This could be a simple password lookup or a request to an LDAP server, but it is PAM that provides authentication, not a direct password lookup by the user or application. In this respect, authentication becomes centralized and controlled by a specific service, PAM. The actual authentication procedures can be dynamically configured by the system administrator. Authentication is carried out by modules that can vary according to the kind of authentication needed. An administrator can add or replace modules by simply changing the PAM configuration files. See the PAM Web site at **http://kernel.org/pub/linux/libs/pam** for more information and a listing of PAM modules. PAM modules are located in the **/lib/security** directory.

PAM modules will usually have their own man pages that list options that can be used for particular modules. Some of the more commonly used are **pam_unix** (password check), **pam_deny** (lock out), **pam_env** (PAM environment variables), and **pam_group** (check group membership). The following command in a terminal window will display the man page for **pam_unix**:

```
man pam_unix
```

PAM Configuration Files

PAM uses different configuration files for different services that request authentication. Such configuration files are kept in the **/etc/pam.d** directory. For example, you have a configuration file for logging in to your system (**/etc/pam.d/login**), one for the graphical login (**/etc/pam.d/gdm**), and one for accessing your Samba server (**/etc/pam.d/samba**). A default PAM configuration file, called **/etc/pam.d/other**, is invoked if no services file is present. The **system-auth** file contains standard authentication modules for system services.

PAM Modules

A PAM configuration file contains a list of modules to be used for authentication. They have the following format:

```
module-type  control-flag  module-path  module-args
```

The *module-path* is the module to be run, and *module-args* are the parameters you want passed to that module. Though a few generic arguments can be used, most modules have their own specific ones. The *module-type* refers to different groups of authentication management: account, authentication, session, and password. The account management performs account verification, checking such account aspects as whether the user has access or whether the password has expired. Authentication (**auth**) verifies who the user is, usually through a password confirmation. Password management performs authentication updates such as password changes. Session management refers to tasks performed before a service is accessed and before it is shut down. These include tasks such as initiating a log of a user's activity or mounting and unmounting home directories.

TIP *As an alternative to the **/etc/pam.d** directory, you can create one configuration file called the **/etc/pam.conf** file. Entries in this file have a service field, which refers to the application for which the module is used. If the **/etc/pam.d** directory exists, **/etc/pam.conf** is automatically ignored.*

The *control-flag* field indicates how PAM is to respond if the module fails. The control can be a simple directive or a more complicated response that can specify return codes such as **open_err** with actions to take. The simple directives are **requisite, required, sufficient**, and **optional**. The **requisite** directive ends the authentication process immediately if the module fails to authenticate. The **required** directive ends the authentication only after the remaining modules are run. The **sufficient** directive indicates that success of this module is enough to provide authentication unless a previous required module has failed. The **optional** directive indicates the module's success is not needed unless it is the only authentication module for its service. If you specify return codes, you can refine the conditions for authentication failure or success. Return codes can be given values such as **die** or **ok**. The **open_err** return code could be given the action **die**, which stops all authentication and returns failure.

On Ubuntu, commonly used PAM module entries are placed in the PAM files prefixed with the **common** term. These include **common-account**, **common-auth**, **common-password**, and **common-session**. The **common-account** modules are used to verify that the user has a valid account on the system. The **common-session** modules provide support for login sessions. The **common-auth** modules provide system authentication. The **common-password** modules check passwords. The **common-account** modules include **pam_unix.so** (Unix password authentication), **pam_ldap.so** (LDAP server authentication), and **pam_deny.so** (deny access):

```
account    sufficient    pam_unix.so
account    sufficient    pam_ldap.so
account    required      pam_deny.so
```

The **common-password** modules will also include options for password length, retries, and shadow passwords. Check the man pages for each to see their options, including **pam_cracklib**:

```
password    required     pam_cracklib.so difok=2 minlen=8 dcredit=2
ocredit=2 retry=3
password    sufficient   pam_unix.so nullok md5 shadow use_authtok
password    sufficient   pam_ldap.so use_first_pass
password    required     pam_deny.so
```

A common PAM file is included in a PAM configuration file with the **@include** command:

```
@include   common-account
```

The **/etc/pam.d/vsftpd** configuration file for the FTP server is shown next. The **pam_listfile** module allows a particular file to be used for authentication, in this case, **/etc/ftpusers**. The **deny** setting for the **sense** option will set up **/etc/ftpusers** to deny access to any users listed there. The **pam_shells** module checks for a valid login shell. See the man pages for each for more details and options.

```
auth  required  pam_listfile.so item=user sense=deny file=/etc/ftpusers
        onerr=succeed
@include common-account
@include common-session
@include common-auth
auth  required pam_shells.so
```

File Systems

F iles reside on physical storage devices such as hard drives, CD-ROMs, or floppy disks. The files on each storage device are organized into a *file system,* and the storage devices on your Linux system are presented as a collection of file systems that you can manage. When you want to add a new storage device, you need to format it as a file system and then attach it to your Linux file structure. Hard drives can be divided into separate storage devices called *partitions,* each of which has its own file system. You can perform administrative tasks on your file systems, such as backing them up, attaching or detaching them from your file structure, formatting new devices or erasing old ones, and checking a file system for problems.

To access files on a device, you attach its file system to a specified directory. This is called *mounting* the file system. For example, to access files on a floppy disk, you first mount its file system to a particular directory. With Linux, you can mount a number of different types of file systems. You can even access a Windows hard drive partition or tape drive, as well as file systems on a remote server.

Recently developed file systems for Linux now support *journaling,* which allows your system to recover from a crash or interruption easily. The **ext3**, ReiserFS, XFS, and Journaled File System (JFS) from IBM maintain a record of file and directory changes, called a *journal,* which can be used to recover files and directories in use when a system suddenly crashes due to unforeseen events such as power interruptions. Most distributions currently use the **ext3** file system as their default, though you also have the option of using ReiserFS or JFS, an independently developed journaling system.

Your Linux system is capable of handling any number of storage devices that are connected to it. You can configure your system to access multiple hard drives, partitions on a hard drive, CD-ROM discs, DVDs, floppy disks, and even tapes. You can elect to attach these storage components manually or have them automatically mount when you boot. Automatic mounts are handled by configuring the **/etc/fstab** file. For example, the main partitions holding your Linux system programs are automatically mounted whenever you boot, whereas a floppy disk can be manually mounted when you put one in your floppy drive, though even these can also be automatically mounted. Removable storage devices such as CD-ROMs, as well as removable devices such as USB cameras and printers, are now handled by **udev** and the Hardware Abstraction Layer (HAL), as described in Chapter 25 and partially discussed here.

File Systems and Directory Trees

Although all the files in your Linux system are connected into one overall directory tree, parts of that tree may reside on different storage devices such as hard drives or CD-ROMs. Files on a particular storage device are organized into file systems, formatted devices with their own trees of directories and files. Your Linux directory tree may encompass several file systems, each on different storage devices. On a hard drive with several partitions, a file system exists for each partition. The files themselves are organized into one seamless tree of directories, beginning from the root directory. For example, if you attach a CD-ROM to your system, a pathname will lead directly from the root directory on your hard disk partition's file system to the files in the CD-ROM file system.

TIP *With Linux you can mount file systems of different types, including those created by other operating systems, such as Windows, IBM OS, Unix, and SGI. Within Linux a variety of file systems are supported, including several journaling systems such as ReiserFS and **ext3**.*

A file system has its files organized into its own directory tree. You can think of this as a *subtree* that must be attached to the main directory tree. The tree remains separate from your system's directory tree until you specifically connect it. For example, a floppy disk with Linux files has its own tree of directories. You need to attach this subtree to the main tree on your hard drive partition. Until they are attached, you cannot access the files on your floppy disk.

File System Hierarchy Standard

Linux organizes its files and directories into one overall interconnected tree, beginning from the root directory and extending down to system and user directories. The organization and layout for the system directories are determined by the Filesystem Hierarchy Standard (FHS). The FHS provides a standardized layout that all Linux distributions should follow in setting up their system directories. For example, an **/etc** directory must exist to hold configuration files and a **/dev** directory to hold device files. You can find out more about FHS, including the official documentation, at **http://proton.pathname.com/fhs**. Linux distributions, developers, and administrators all follow the FHS to provide a consistent organization to the Linux file system.

Linux uses a number of specifically named directories for specialized administrative tasks. All these directories are at the very top level of your main Linux file system, the file system root directory, represented by a single slash, **/**. For example, the **/dev** directory holds device files, and the **/home** directory holds the user home directories and all their user files. You have access to these directories and files only as the system administrator (though users normally have read-only access). You need to log in as the root user, placing yourself in a special root user administrative directory called **/root**. From here, you can access any directory on the Linux file system, both administrative and user.

Root Directory: /

The subdirectories held in the root directory, **/**, are listed in Table 23-1 along with other useful subdirectories. Directories that you may commonly access as an administrator are the **/etc** directory, which holds configuration files; the **/dev** directory, which holds dynamically generated device files; and the **/var** directory, which holds server data files for DNS, web, mail, and FTP servers, along with system logs and scheduled tasks. For managing different versions of the kernel, you may need to access the **/boot** and **/lib/modules** directories as well as **/usr/src/linux**. The **/boot** directory holds the kernel image files for any new kernels you install, and the **/lib/modules** directory holds modules for your different kernels.

Directory	Function
/	Begins the file system structure—the root
/bin	Holds the essential user commands and utility programs
/boot	Holds the kernel image files and associated boot information and files
/dev	Holds dynamically generated file interfaces for devices such as the terminal and the printer (see Chapter 25)
/etc	Holds system configuration files and any other system files
/etc/opt	Holds system configuration files for applications in **/opt**
/etc/X11	Holds system configuration files for the X Window System and its applications
/home	Contains users' home directories
/lib	Holds essential shared libraries and kernel modules
/lib/modules	Holds the kernel modules
/media	Holds directories for mounting media-based removable file systems, such as CD-ROMs, floppy disks, USB card readers, and digital cameras, and automatically detected and mounted local partitions, including NTFS partitions
/mnt	Holds directories for additional file systems such as hard disks
/opt	Holds added software applications (for example, KDE on some distributions)
/proc	Process directory, a memory-resident directory that contains files used to provide information about the system
/sbin	Holds administration-level commands and commands used by the root user
/sys	Holds the **sysfs** file system for kernel objects, listing supported kernel devices and modules
/tmp	Holds temporary files
/usr	Holds those files and commands used by the system; this directory breaks down into several subdirectories
/var	Holds files that vary, such as mailbox, web, and FTP files

TABLE 23-1   Linux File System Directories

System Directories

Your Linux directory tree contains certain directories whose files are used for different system functions. For basic system administration, you should be familiar with the system program directories where applications are kept, the system configuration directory (**/etc**) where most configuration files are placed, and the system log directory (**/var/log**) that holds the system logs, recording activity on your system. Both are covered in detail in this chapter. Table 23-2 lists the system directories.

Program Directories

Directories with **bin** in the name are used to hold programs. The **/bin** directory holds basic user programs, such as login, shells (BASH, TCSH, and zsh), and file commands (**cp**, **mv**, **rm**, **ln**, and so on). The **/sbin** directory holds specialized system programs for such tasks as file system management (**fsck**, **fdisk**, **mkfs**) and system operations such as shutdown and startup (**init**). The **/usr/bin** directory holds program files designed for user tasks. The **/usr/sbin**

Directory	Description
/bin	Holds system-related programs
/dev	Holds device files
/etc	Holds configuration files for system and network services and applications
/etc/udev	Holds configuration for device files
/home	Holds user home directories and server data directories, such as Web site and FTP site files
/lib	Holds system libraries
/media	Where removable media file systems such as CD-ROMs, USB drives, and floppy disks are mounted
/sbin	Holds system programs for specialized tasks
/sys	Holds the **sysfs** file system with device information for kernel-supported devices on your system
/tmp	Holds system temporary files
/usr	Holds user-related programs and files; includes several key subdirectories, such as **/usr/bin**, **/usr/X11**, and **/usr/share/doc**
/usr/share/hal	Holds configuration for HAL removable devices
/usr/bin	Holds programs for users
/usr/share	Holds shared files
/usr/share/doc	Holds documentation for applications
/usr/X11	Holds X Window System configuration files
/var	Holds system directories whose files continually change, such as logs, printer spool files, and lock files

TABLE 23-2 System Directories

directory holds user-related system operation, such as **useradd** for adding new users. The **/lib** directory holds all the libraries your system uses, including the main Linux library, **libc**, and subdirectories such as **modules**, which holds all the current kernel modules.

Configuration Directories and Files

When you configure different elements of your system, such as user accounts, applications, servers, or network connections, you make use of configuration files kept in certain system directories. Configuration files are placed in the **/etc** directory.

The /usr Directory

The **/usr** directory contains a multitude of important subdirectories used to support users, providing applications, libraries, and documentation. The **/usr/bin** directory holds numerous user-accessible applications and utilities; **/usr/sbin** holds user-accessible administrative utilities. The **/usr/share** directory holds architecture-independent data that includes an extensive number of subdirectories, including those for documentation, such as **man**, **info**, and **doc** files. Table 23-3 lists the subdirectories of the **/usr** directory.

The /media Directory

The **/media** directory is used for *mountpoints* (the directories in the file structure to which the new file systems are attached) for removable media such as CD-ROM, DVD, floppy, or Zip drives, as well as for other media-based file systems such as USB card readers, cameras, and MP3 players. These are file systems you may be changing frequently, unlike partitions on fixed disks. Most Linux systems use HAL to dynamically manage the creation, mounting, and device assignment of these devices. As instructed by HAL, this tool will create floppy, CD-ROM, storage card, camera, and MP3 player subdirectories in **/media** as needed. The default subdirectory for mounting is **/media/disk**. Additional drives have a number attached to their name.

Directory	Description
/usr/bin	Holds most user commands and utility programs
/usr/sbin	Holds administrative applications
/usr/lib	Holds libraries for applications, programming languages, desktops, and so on
/usr/games	Holds games and educational programs
/usr/include	Holds C programming language header files (**.h**)
/usr/doc	Holds Linux documentation
/usr/local	Holds locally installed software
/usr/share	Holds architecture-independent data such as documentation and configuration files
/usr/src	Holds source code, including the kernel source code
/usr/X11R6	Holds X Window System–based applications and libraries

TABLE 23-3 /usr Directories

The /mnt Directory

The **/mnt** directory is usually used for mountpoints for other mounted file systems such as Windows partitions. You can create directories for any partitions you want to mount, such as **/mnt/windows** for a Windows partition.

The /home Directory

The **/home** directory holds user home directories. When a user account is set up, a home directory is set up here for that account, usually with the same name as the user. As the system administrator, you can access any user's home directory, so you have control over that user's files.

The /var Directory

The **/var** directory holds subdirectories for tasks whose files change frequently, such as lock files, log files, web server files, or printer spool files. For example, the **/var** directory holds server data directories, such as **/var/www** for the Apache web server Web site files or **/var/named** for the DNS server. The **/tmp** directory is simply a directory to hold any temporary files programs that may be needed to perform a particular task.

The **/var** directories are designed to hold data that changes with the normal operation of the Linux system. For example, spool files for documents that you are printing are kept here. A spool file is created as a temporary printing file and is removed after printing. Other files, such as system log files, are changed constantly. Table 23-4 lists the subdirectories of the **/var** directory.

The /proc File System

The **/proc** file system is a special file system that is generated in system memory. It does not exist on any disk. **/proc** contains files that provide important information about the state of your system. For example, **/proc/cpuinfo** holds information about your computer's CPU processor, **/proc/devices** lists those devices currently configured to run with your kernel, **/proc/filesystems** lists the file systems, and **/proc** files are really interfaces to the kernel, obtaining information from the kernel about your system. Table 23-5 lists the **/proc** subdirectories and files.

Like any file system, **/proc** has to be mounted. The **/etc/fstab** file will have a special entry for **/proc** with a file system type of proc and no device specified:

```
none    /proc    proc     defaults   0      0
```

TIP *You can use* **sysctl***, the Kernel Tuning tool, to set* **proc** *file values you are allowed to change, such as the maximum number of files, or to turn on IP forwarding.*

The sysfs File System: /sys

The **sysfs** file system is a virtual file system that provides a hierarchical map of your kernel-supported devices such as PCI devices, buses, and block devices, as well as supporting kernel modules. The **classes** subdirectory will list all your supported devices by category, such as network and sound devices. With **sysfs** your system can easily determine the device file with which a particular device is associated. This is very helpful for managing removable devices

Directory	Description
/var/account	Processes accounting logs
/var/cache	Holds application cache data for man pages, web proxy data, fonts, or application-specific data
/var/crash	Holds system crash dumps
/var/games	Holds varying games data
/var/lib	Holds state information for particular applications
/var/local	Holds data that changes for programs installed in /usr/local
/var/lock	Holds lock files that indicate when a particular program or file is in use
/var/log	Holds log files such as /var/log/messages that contain all kernel and system program messages
/var/mail	Holds user mailbox files
/var/named	Holds DNS server domain configuration files
/var/opt	Holds variable data for applications installed in /opt
/var/run	Holds information about the system's running processes
/var/spool	Holds applications' spool data such as that for mail, news, and printer queues, as well as cron and at jobs
/var/tmp	Holds temporary files that should be preserved between system reboots
/var/www	Holds web server Web site files

TABLE 23-4 /var Subdirectories

as well as dynamically configuring and managing devices as HAL and udev do. The **sysfs** file system is used by udev to generate needed device files dynamically in the **/dev** directory, as well as by HAL to manage removable device files and support as needed (HAL technically provides information only about devices, though it can use tools to change configurations dynamically as needed). The **/sys** file system type is **sysfs**. The **/sys** subdirectories organize your devices into different categories. The file system is used by **systool** to display a listing of your installed devices. The following example will list all your system devices:

```
systool
```

Like **/proc**, the **/sys** directory resides only in memory, but you still need to mount it in the **/etc/fstab** file:

```
none    /sys      sysfs     defaults   0       0
```

Device Files: /dev, udev, and HAL

To mount a file system, you have to specify its device name. The interfaces to the devices that may be attached to your system are provided by special files known as *device files*. The names of these device files are the device names. Device files are located in the **/dev** directories and

File	Description
/**proc**/*num*	Each process is held in a directory that's labeled by its number: /**proc/1** is the directory for process 1, for example
/**proc/cpuinfo**	Contains information about the CPU, such as its type, make, model, and performance
/**proc/devices**	Lists the device drivers configured for the currently running kernel
/**proc/dma**	Displays the Direct Memory Access (DMA) channels currently used
/**proc/filesystems**	Lists file systems configured into the kernel
/**proc/interrupts**	Displays the interrupts in use
/**proc/ioports**	Shows the I/O ports in use
/**proc/kcore**	Holds an image of the physical memory of the system
/**proc/kmsg**	Contains messages generated by the kernel
/**proc/loadavg**	Lists the system load average
/**proc/meminfo**	Displays memory usage
/**proc/modules**	Lists the kernel modules currently loaded
/**proc/net**	Lists status information about network protocols
/**proc/stat**	Contains system operating statistics, such as page fault occurrences
/**proc/uptime**	Displays the time the system has been up
/**proc/version**	Displays the kernel version

TABLE 23-5   /proc Subdirectories and Files

usually have abbreviated names ending with the number of the device. For example, **fd0** may reference the first floppy drive attached to your system. The prefix **sd** references both Serial ATA (SATA) and SCSI hard drives, so **sda2** would reference the second partition on the first SATA or SCSI hard drive. In most cases, you can use the **man** command with a prefix to obtain more detailed information about this kind of device. For example, **man sd** displays the man pages for SCSI devices. A complete listing of all device names can be found in the **devices** file located in the **linux/doc/device-list** directory at the **http://kernel.org** Web site. Table 23-6 lists several commonly used device names.

NOTE *Most newer systems use only Serial ATA (SATA) hard drives and CD/DVD drives. These will have the prefixes **sd** and **scd**. The older IDE drives with the **hd** prefix are rarely used.*

udev and HAL
Device files are no longer handled in a static way; they are now dynamically generated as needed. Previously a device file was created for each possible device, leading to a very large number of device files in the **/etc/dev** directory. Now your system detects only those devices it uses and creates device files for them, resulting in a much smaller listing of device files.

Device Name	Description
hd	IDE hard drives (rarely used on new systems)
fd	Floppy disks
sd	Serial ATA (SATA) and SCSI hard drives, SATA drives are standard on new systems
ht	IDE tape drives
js	Analog joysticks
lp	Printer ports
md	RAID devices
midi	Midi ports
nst	SCSI tape drives, no rewind
pty	Pseudoterminals (used for remote logins)
scd	Serial ATA and SCSI CD-ROM drives
st	SCSI tape drives
tty	Terminals
ttyS	Serial ports
cdrecorder	Links to your CD-R or CD-RW device file, set in **/etc/udev/rules.d**
cdrom	Links to your CD-ROM device file, set in **/etc/udev/rules.d**
floppy	Links to your floppy device file, set in **/etc/udev/rules.d**
modem	Links to your modem device file, set in **/etc/udev/rules.d**
rd/c*n*d*n*	The directory that holds RAID devices is **rd**; **c***n* is the RAID controller and **d***n* is the RAID disk for that controller
scanner	Links to your scanner device file, set in **/etc/udev/rules.d**
tape	Links to your tape device file, set in **/etc/udev/rules.d**

TABLE 23-6   Device Name Prefixes

The tool used to detect and generate device files is **udev**, user devices. Each time your system is booted, **udev** will automatically detect your devices and generate device files for them in the **/etc/dev** directory. This means that the **/etc/dev** directory and its files are re-created each time you boot. It is a dynamic directory, no longer static. To manage these device files, you need to use **udev** configuration files located in the **/etc/udev** directory. This means that **udev** is also able to manage all removable devices dynamically; **udev** will generate and configure device files for removable devices as they are attached and then remove these files when the devices are removed. In this sense, all devices are now considered hotplugged, with fixed devices simply being hotplugged devices that are never removed.

As **/etc/dev** is now dynamic, any changes you would make manually to the **/etc/dev** directory will be lost when you reboot. This includes the creation of any symbolic links such as **/dev/cdrom** that many software applications use. Instead, such symbolic links have to be configured using **udev** rules listed in configuration files located in the **/etc/udev/rules.d** directory. Default rules are already in place for symbolic links, but you can create rules of your own. See Chapter 25 for more details.

In addition to **udev**, information about removable devices such as CD-ROMs and floppy disks, along with cameras and USB printers, used by applications such as the desktop to interface dynamically with them, is managed by HAL, a separate utility. HAL allows a removable device to be recognized no matter what particular connections it may be using. For example, you can attach a USB printer in one USB port at one time and then switch it to another later. The **fstab** file is edited using the **fstab-sync** tool, which is invoked by HAL rules in configuration files in **/usr/share/hal/fdi** directory.

HAL has a key impact on the **/etc/fstab** file used to manage file systems. No longer are entries maintained in the **/etc/fstab** file for removable devices such as a CD-ROM. These devices are managed directly by HAL using its set of storage callouts such as **hal-system-storage-mount** to mount a device or **hal-system-storage-eject** to remove one. In effect, you now have to use the HAL device information files to manage your removable file systems. Should you want to bypass HAL and manually configure a CD-ROM device, you simply place an entry for it in the **/etc/fstab** file.

Floppy and Hard Disk Devices

The device name for your floppy drive is **fd0**; it is located in the directory **/dev. /dev/fd0** references your floppy drive. Notice the numeral **0** after **fd**. If you have more than one floppy drive, additional drives are represented by **fd1**, **fd2**, and so on.

IDE hard drives use the prefix **hd**, whereas SATA and SCSI hard drives use the prefix **sd**. RAID devices, on the other hand, use the prefix **md**. The prefix for a hard disk is followed by a letter that labels the hard drive and a number for the partition. For example, **hda2** references the second partition on the first IDE hard drive, where the first hard drive is referenced with the letter **a**, as in **hda**. The device **sdb3** refers to the third partition on the second SATA hard drive (**sdb**). RAID devices, however, are numbered from 0, like floppy drives. Device **md0** references the first RAID device, and **md1** references the second. On an IDE hard disk device, Linux supports up to four primary IDE hard disk partitions, numbered 1 through 4. You are allowed any number of logical partitions. To find the device name, you can use **df** to display your hard partitions, examine the **/etc/fstab** file, or run the GNOME Partition Manager (GParted).

NOTE *GNOME now manages all removable media directly with HAL, instead of using **fstab** entries.*

CD-ROM Devices

The device name for your CD-ROM drive varies depending on the type of CD-ROM you use. The device name for an IDE CD-ROM has the same prefix as an IDE hard disk partition, **hd**, and is identified by a following letter that distinguishes it from other IDE devices. For example, an IDE CD-ROM connected to your secondary IDE port may have the name **hdc**. An IDE CD-ROM connected as a slave to the secondary port may have the name **hdd**. The actual name is determined when the CD-ROM is installed, as happened when you installed your Linux system. Serial ATA and SCSI CD-ROM drives use a different nomenclature for their device names. They begin with **scd** for SATA or SCSI CD/DVD-ROM and are followed by a distinguishing number. For example, the name of a SATA CD-ROM could be **scd0** or **scd1**. The name of your CD-ROM was determined when you installed your system.

As noted previously, CD-ROM devices are now configured by HAL. HAL does this in a device information file in its policy configuration directory. To configure a CD-ROM device, such as by adding user mount capability, you need to configure its entry in the **storage-methods.fdi** configuration file (see Chapter 25 for details). The GNOME Volume Manager uses HAL and **udev** to access removable media directly and Samba to provide Windows networking support. Media are mounted by **gnome-mount**, a wrapper for accessing HAL and **udev**, which perform the mount (**/etc/fstab** is no longer used).

Mounting File Systems

Attaching a file system on a storage device to your main directory tree is called *mounting* the device. The file system is mounted to an empty directory on the main directory tree. You can then change to that directory and access those files. If the directory does not yet exist, you have to create it. The directory in the file structure to which the new file system is attached is the mountpoint. So, for example, to access files on a CD-ROM, you first have to mount the CD-ROM.

Mounting fixed file systems like internal hard disks can normally be done only as the root user. This is a system administration task and should not usually be performed by a regular user. Removable media, though, such as CD/DVD-ROMs and USB drives, are user mountable, and any user could mount a CD-ROM or USB drive.

Even the file systems on your hard disk partition must be explicitly mounted. When you install your Linux system and create the Linux partition on your hard drive, however, your system is automatically configured to mount your main file system whenever it starts. When your system shuts down, the file systems are automatically unmounted. You have the option of unmounting any file system, removing it from the directory tree, and possibly replacing it with another, as is the case when you replace a CD-ROM.

Once a file system is actually mounted, an entry for it is made by the operating system in the **/etc/mstab** file. Here you will find listed all file systems currently mounted.

File System Information

The file systems on each storage device are formatted to take up a specified amount of space. For example, you may have formatted your hard drive partition to take up 3GB. Files installed or created on that file system take up part of the space, while the remainder is available for new files and directories. To find out how much space you have free on a file system, you can use the **df** command or, on the desktop, either the GNOME System Monitor, the Disk Usage Analyzer, or the KDE KDiskFree utility. KDiskFree displays a list of devices, showing how much space is free on each partition and the percentage used.

For the GNOME System Monitor (System | Administration | System Monitor), click the File Systems tab to display a list of the free space on your file systems (see Figure 23-1). The System Monitor will show the mountpoint (Directory), the file system type (Type), the amount of available space, and the amount of space used (Used) with a percentage graph.

Disk Usage Analyzer

The disk usage analyzer (Baobob) lets you see how much disk space is used and available on all your mounted hard disk partitions (see Figure 23-2). It will also check all mounted Logical Volume Manager (LVM) and RAID arrays. Access it by choosing Applications | Accessories | Disk Usage Analyzer. Usage is shown in simple graph, which shows you how

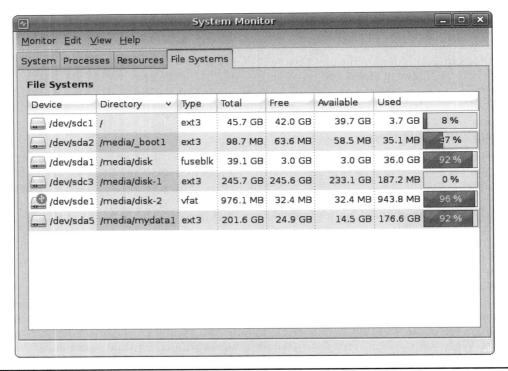

FIGURE 23-1 GNOME System Monitor, File Systems tab

much overall space is available and where it is. When you scan the file system (by clicking the Scan Filesystem button on the toolbar), disk usage for all your directories is analyzed and displayed in the left pane and on a graph in the right pane. Passing your mouse over a section in the graph will display its directory name and disk usage. In the left-hand listing, each files system is first shown with a graph for its usage, as well as its size and number of top-level directories and files. Expanding to the subdirectories, you can select one to show a graph for just its size and contents.

From the Analyzer menu, you can scan just your home folder, a specific folder on your system, or a folder on a remote file system. The remote folders options lets you scan directories on FTP sites, Windows shares (Samba), or WebDAV accessible directories.

df

The **df** command reports file system disk space usage. It lists all your file systems by their device names, how much disk space they take up, and the percentage of the disk space used, as well as where they are mounted. With the **-h** option, it displays information in a more readable format, such as measuring disk space in megabytes instead of memory blocks. The **df** command is also a safe way to obtain a listing of all your partitions, instead

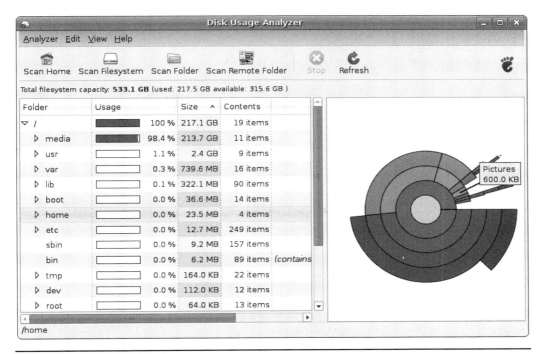

FIGURE 23-2   Disk Usage Analyzer

of using **fdisk** (because with **fdisk** you can erase partitions). **df** shows only mounted partitions, however, whereas **fdisk** shows all partitions. Here's an example:

```
$ df -h
Filesystem Size Used Avail Use% Mounted on
/dev/hda3   9.7G 2.8G 6.4G  31%  /
/dev/hda2   99M  6.3M 88M   7%   /boot
/dev/hda2   22G  36M  21G   1%   /home
/dev/hdc    525M 525M 0     100% /media/disk
```

You can also use **df** to tell you to what file system a given directory belongs. Enter **df** with the directory name or **df .** for the current directory:

```
$ df .
Filesystem 1024-blocks Used Available Capacity Mounted on
/dev/hda3 297635 169499 112764 60% /
```

e2fsck and fsck

To check the consistency of the file system and repair it if it is damaged, you can use file system checking tools. **fsck** checks and repairs a Linux file system. **e2fsck** is designed to support **ext2** and **ext3** file systems, whereas the more generic **fsck** also works on any other file systems. The **ext2** and **ext3** file systems are the file systems normally used for Linux hard disk partitions and floppy disks. Linux file systems are normally **ext3**, which you use

e2fsck to check. **fsck** and **e2fsck** take as their argument the device name of the hard disk partition that the file system uses:

```
fsck    device-name
```

Before you check a file system, be sure that the file system is unmounted. **e2fsck** should not be used on a mounted file system. To use **e2fsck**, enter **e2fsck** and the device name that references the file system. The **-p** option automatically repairs a file system without first requesting approval from the user for each repair task. The following examples check the disk in the floppy drive and the primary hard drive:

```
# e2fsck /dev/fd0
# e2fsck /dev/hda1
```

With **fsck**, the **-t** option lets you specify the type of file system to check, and the **-a** option automatically repairs systems, whereas the **-r** option first asks for confirmation. The **-A** option checks all systems in the **/etc/fstab** file.

Journaling

The **ext3** and ReiserFS file systems introduced journaling capabilities to Linux systems. Journaling provides for fast and effective recovery in case of disk crashes and is used instead of using **e2fsck** or **fsck**. With journaling, a log is kept of all file system actions, which are placed in a journal file. In the event of a crash, Linux needs to read and replay only the journal file to restore the system to its previous (stable) state. Files that were in the process of writing to the disk can be restored to their original state. Journaling also avoids lengthy **fsck** checks on reboots that occur when your system suddenly loses power or freezes and has to be restarted physically. Instead of using **fsck** to check each file and directory manually, your system just reads its journal files to restore the file system.

Keeping a journal entails more work for a file system than any nonjournal method. Though all journaling systems maintain a file system's directory structure (the *metadata*), they offer various levels of file data recovery. Maintaining file data recovery information can be time-consuming, slowing down the file system's response time. At the same time, journaling systems make more efficient use of the file system, providing a faster response time than the nonjournal **ext2** file system.

You can use other kind of journaling file systems on Linux. These include ReiserFS, JFS, and XFS. ReiserFS provides a completely reworked file system structure based on journaling (**namesys.com**). Most distributions also provide support for ReiserFS file systems. JFS is the IBM version of a journaling file system, designed for use on servers providing high throughput such as e-business enterprise servers (**http://jfs.sourceforge.net**). It is freely distributed under the GNU public license. XFS is another high-performance journaling system developed by Silicon Graphics (**http://oss.sgi.com/projects/xfs**). XFS is compatible with RAID and NFS file systems.

ext3 Journaling

Journaling is supported in the Linux kernel with **ext3**. The **ext3** file system is also fully compatible with the earlier **ext2** version it replaces. To create an **ext3** file system, you use the **mkfs.ext3** command. You can even upgrade **ext2** file systems to **ext3** versions automatically, with no loss of data or change in partitions. This upgrade just adds a journal file to an **ext2** file system and enables journaling on it, using the `tune2fs` command. Be sure to change the **ext2** file type to **ext3** in any corresponding **/etc/fstab** entries. The following example converts the **ext2** file system on **/dev/hda3** to an **ext3** file system by adding a journal file (`-j`):

```
tune2fs -j /dev/hda3
```

The **ext3** file system maintains full metadata recovery support (directory tree recovery), but it offers various levels of file data recovery. In effect, you are trading off less file data recovery for more speed. The **ext3** file system supports three options: `writeback`, `ordered`, and `journal`. The default option, `writeback`, provides only metadata recovery, no file data recovery. The `ordered` option supports limited file data recovery, and the `journal` option provides for full file data recovery. Any files in the process of being changed during a crash will be recovered. To specify a **ext3** option, use the `data` option in the `mount` command:

```
mount -t ext3 data=ordered  /dev/sd1a   /mydata
```

ext4 File Systems

The **ext4** file system enhances the **ext3** file system in terms of scalability and access methods. The **ext4** file system type is designed to handle very large files efficiently, supporting a much larger file size. Access methods now use extents instead of direct mapping, making access of large files much more efficient. The **ext3** file system, though, remains a very effective choice for systems managing many smaller files.

ReiserFS

Though journaling is often used to recover from disk crashes, a journal-based file system can do much more. The **ext3**, JFS, and XFS file systems provide only the logging operations used in recovery, whereas ReiserFS uses journaling techniques to rework file system operations completely. In ReiserFS, journaling is used to read and write data, abandoning the block structure used in traditional Unix and Linux systems. This gives it the ability to access a large number of small files very quickly, and they use only the amount of disk space they need. However, efficiency is not that much better with larger files.

Mounting File Systems Automatically: /etc/fstab

File systems are mounted using the `mount` command. Although you can mount a file system directly using a `mount` command, you can simplify the process by placing mount information in the **/etc/fstab** configuration file. Entries in this file can tell Linux to mount certain file systems automatically whenever your system boots. For other file systems, you can specify configuration information, such as mountpoints and access permissions, which can be automatically used whenever you mount the file system. Using the configuration file entries means that you don't need to enter this information as arguments to a `mount` command. For example, if you add a new hard disk partition to your Linux system, you can add mount information in the **/etc/fstab** file to have the partition automatically mounted on startup and then unmounted when you shut down. Otherwise, you must mount and unmount the partition explicitly each time you boot up and shut down your system. Both KDE and GNOME will also automatically mount any unmounted file system using their own file system detection and mount operations. On GNOME, the Gnome virtual file system (GVFS) will detect any unmounted file systems and mount them to the **/media** directory. Should you want a file system mounted to a different directory, you would have to place a mount entry for it in the **/etc/fstab** file, specifying that directory.

HAL and fstab

To have Linux automatically mount a file system on a new hard disk partition, you need to add only its name to the **fstab** file, but this is not the case with removable devices such as CD-ROMs and USB printers. Removable devices are managed by HAL, using the storage policy files located in **/usr/share/hal/fdi** and **/etc/hal/fdi** directories. The devices are automatically detected by the **haldaemon** service and are managed directly by HAL using its set of storage callouts, such as **hal-system-storage-mount** to mount a device or **hal-system-storage-eject** to remove one. In effect, you use the HAL device information files to manage your removable file systems. If you want different options set for the device, you should create your own **storage-methods.fdi** file in the **30user** directory. The configuration is implemented using the XML language. Check the default storage file in **10osvendors/ 20-storage-methods.fdi** as well as samples in **/usr/share/doc/hal**version**/conf** directory. See Chapter 25 for examples of using HAL to set device options.

fstab Fields

An entry in an **fstab** file contains several fields, each separated from the next by a space or tab. These are described as the *device, mountpoint, file system type, options, dump,* and *fsck* fields, arranged in the sequence shown here:

```
<device> <mountpoint> <filesystemtype> <options> <dump> <fsck>
```

The first field is the name of the file system to be mounted. This entry can be either a device name or an **ext2** or **ext3** file system label. A device name usually begins with **/dev**, such as **/dev/hda3** for the third hard disk partition. A label is specified by assigning the label name to the tag **LABEL**, as in **LABEL=/** for an **ext2** root partition. The next field is the mountpoint directory in your file structure where you want the file system on this device to be attached. The third field is the type of file system being mounted. Table 23-7 provides a list of all the different types you can mount. The type for a standard Linux hard disk partition is **ext3**. The next example shows an entry for the main Linux hard disk partition. This entry is mounted at the root directory, /, and has a file type of **ext3**:

```
/dev/hda3   /    ext3    defaults   0   1
```

The following example shows a **LABEL** entry for the hard disk partition, where the label name is /:

```
LABEL=/     /    ext3    defaults   0   1
```

Auto Mounts

The file system type for a floppy disk may differ depending on the disk you are trying to mount. For example, you may want to read a Windows-formatted floppy disk at one time and a Linux-formatted floppy disk at another time. For this reason, the file system type

Type	Description
adfs	Apple DOS file systems
affs	Amiga fast file systems
auto	Attempts to detect the file system type automatically
devpts	Unix 98 Pseudo Terminals (TTYs, kernel interface file system)
ext	Earlier version of Linux file system, no longer in use
ext4	New Linux file system format supporting long filenames and very large file sizes; includes journaling
ext3	Standard Linux file system supporting long filenames and large file sizes; includes journaling
ext2	Older standard Linux file system supporting long filenames and large file sizes; does not have journaling
hpfs	File system for OS/2 high-performance partitions
iso9660	File system for mounting CD-ROM
minux	Minux file systems (filenames are limited to 30 characters)
msdos	File system for MS-DOS partitions (16-bit)
nfs	NFS file system for mounting partitions from remote systems
nfs4	NFSv4 file system for mounting partitions from remote systems
ntfs	Windows NT, XP, Vista, and 2000 file systems (affords read-only access)
ntfs3g	Windows NT, XP Vista, and 2000 file systems with write capability, NTFS-3g project
proc	Used by operating system for processes (kernel support file system)
ramfs	RAM-based file systems
reiserfs	A ReiserFS journaling file system
shmfs and tmpfs	Linux Virtual Memory, POSIX shared memory maintenance access (kernel interface file system)
smbfs	Samba remote file systems, such as NFS
swap	Linux swap partition or swap file
sysfs	Used by operating system for devices (kernel support file system)
sysv	Unix System V file systems
udf	Universal Disk Format used on CD/DVD-ROMs
ufs	Unix File System, found on Unix system (older format)
umsdos	UMS-DOS file system
usbfs	Used by operating system for USB devices (kernel support file system)
vfat	File system for Windows 95, 98, and Millennium partitions (32-bit)
xfs	A Silicon Graphics (SGI) file system
xiaf	Xiaf file system

TABLE 23-7 File System Types

specified for the floppy device is **auto**. With this option, the type of file system formatted on the floppy disk is detected automatically, and the appropriate file system type is used. Here's an example:

```
/dev/fd0  /media/floppy  auto   defaults,noauto   0  0
```

mount Options

The field after the file system type lists the different options for mounting the file system. The default set of options is specified by **defaults**, and specific options are listed next to each other separated by a comma (no spaces). The **defaults** option specifies that a device is read/write (**rw**), it is asynchronous (**async**), it is a block device (**dev**), that it cannot be mounted by ordinary users (**nouser**), and that programs can be executed on it (**exec**).

Removable devices such as CD-ROMs and floppy disks are managed by HAL, which uses its own configuration files to set the options for these devices. You can place your own entries in the **/etc/fstab** file for CD-ROMs to bypass HAL. This will, however, no longer let your CD-ROMs and DVD-ROMs be automatically detected.

In a HAL configuration, a CD-ROM has **ro** (read-only) and **noauto** (not automatically mounted) options. The **noauto** option is used with both CD-ROMs and floppy drives so that they will not automount, because you might not know if anything is stored on a drive when you start up. At the same time, the HAL entries for both the CD-ROM and the floppy drives can specify where they are to be mounted when you decide to mount them. The **user** option allows any user to mount the system, useful for removable devices. The **group** option allows only users belonging to the device's group to mount it. The **fscontext** option is used by SELinux. Table 23-8 lists the options for mounting a file system. An example of a hard drive entry follows:

```
/dev/VolGroup00/LogVol00   /  ext3    defaults      1 1
```

Boot and Disk Check

The last two fields of an **fstab** entry consist of integer values. The first one is used by the **dump** command to determine whether a file system needs to be dumped, backing up the file system. The second value is used by **fsck** to determine whether a file system should be checked at reboot, and in what order with other file systems. If the field has a value of **1**, it indicates a boot partition, and **2** indicates other partitions. The **0** value means **fsck** needn't check the file system.

fstab Sample

A copy of an **/etc/fstab** file is shown next. Notice that the first line is a comment. All comment lines begin with a **#**. The entries for the **/proc** and **/sys** file systems are special entries used by your Linux operating system for managing its processes and devices; they are not actual devices. To create an entry in the **/etc/fstab** file, you can edit the **/etc/fstab** file directly. You can use the example **/etc/fstab** file shown here as a guide to show how your entries should look. The **/proc** and **swap** partition entries are particularly critical. To identify a disk, Ubuntu uses an UUID (Universally Unique Identifier) label. The UUID ensures that the correct disk will be accessed. The **/dev/disk/by-uuid** directory will list the UUIDs for all your disks. In this example, the UUID has been shortened to allow the entry

Option	Description
async	Indicates that all I/O to the file system should be done asynchronously.
auto	Indicates that the file system can be mounted with the -a option. A mount -a command executed when the system boots, in effect, mounts file systems automatically.
defaults	Uses default options: rw, suid, dev, exec, auto, nouser, and async.
dev	Interprets character or block special devices on the file system.
exec	Permits execution of binaries.
fscontext	Provide SELinux security context to those file systems without one.
group	Allows users who belong to the device's group to mount it.
noauto	Indicates that the file system can only be mounted explicitly. The -a option does not cause the file system to be mounted.
owner	Allows a user who is the owner of device to mount the file system.
nodev	Does not interpret character or block special devices on the file system.
noexec	Does not allow execution of binaries on the mounted file systems.
nosuid	Does not allow **set-user-identifier** or **set-group-identifier** bits to take effect.
nouser	Forbids an ordinary (that is, nonroot) user to mount the file system.
remount	Attempts to remount an already-mounted file system. This is commonly used to change the mount flags for a file system, especially to make a read-only file system writable.
ro	Mounts the file system as read-only.
rw	Mounts the file system as read/write.
suid	Allows **set-user-identifier** or **set-group-identifier** bits to take effect.
sync	Indicates that all I/O to the file system should be done synchronously.
user	Enables an ordinary user to mount the file system. Ordinary users always have the following options activated: noexec, nosuid, and nodev.

TABLE 23-8   Mount Options for File Systems

to display on a single line. The actual UUID for the swap and root (/) entries would be lengthy strings such as **UUID=a179d6e6-b90c-4cc4-982d-a4cfcedea7df**.

/etc/fstab
```
# /etc/fstab: static file system information.
#
# <file system>  <mountpoint>    <type>      <options>          <dump>   <pass>
proc               /proc         proc        defaults           0       0
# /dev/sda2      UUID=a179d         /        ext3      defaults,errors=remount-ro 0    1
# /dev/sda1      UUID=48b9      none         swap      sw                 0         0
/dev/hdc         /media/cdrom0  udf,iso9660            user,noauto,exec 0          0
/dev/fd0         /media/floppy0   auto               rw,user,noauto,exec 0          0
/dev/hda1        /mnt/windows     vfat              defaults            0          0
```

Partition Labels: e2label

Linux can use file system labels for **ext2** and **ext3** file systems on hard disk partitions. Thus, in the **/etc/fstab** file just shown, the first entry uses a label for its device name, as shown here. In this case, the label is the slash, **/**, indicating the root partition. You can change this device's label with **e2label**, but be sure to also change the **/etc/fstab** entry for it.

```
LABEL=/     /     ext3    defaults    0   1
```

For **ext2** and **ext3** partitions, you can change or add a label with the **e2label** tool or **tune2fs** with the **-L** option. Specify the device and the label name. If you change a label, be sure to change corresponding entries in the **/etc/fstab** file. Just use **e2label** with the device name to find out what is the current label. In the next example, the user changes the label of the **/dev/hda3** device to **TURTLE**:

```
e2label /dev/hda3   TURTLE
```

Windows Partitions

Windows partitions attached to your system are automatically detected and mounted in the **/media** directory using the NTFS-3G drivers. You can, however, manually mount Windows file systems if you want, and you might have to do this for server systems. You can mount MS-DOS; Windows 95/98/Me onto your Linux file structure, just as you would mount any Linux file system. You have to specify the file type of **vfat** for Windows 95/98/Me and **msdos** for MS-DOS. Windows XP, Vista, NT, and 2000 use the **ntfs** file type. To have your manual mounts performed automatically, you need to add an entry for your Windows partitions in your **/etc/fstab** file and give it the **defaults** option or be sure to include an **auto** option. You make an entry for each Windows partition you want to mount and then specify the device name for that partition, followed by the directory in which you want to mount it. The next example shows a Windows 95/98/ME partition (**vfat**) entry for an **/etc/fstab** file. Notice the last entry in the **/etc/fstab** file example is an entry for mounting a Windows partition.

```
/dev/hda1 /mnt/windows vfat defaults 0 0
```

For Windows XP, NT, Vista, and 2000, you specify the NTFS-3G driver type. The NTFS-3G project's read/write driver (**www.ntfs-3g.org**) are installed by default by the Ubuntu desktop disk. The NTFS-3G driver provides both read and stable write support. In addition, the **ntfs-config** configuration tool lets you manually set up your partitions easily on GNOME or KDE using NTFS-3G, as shown next. The Linux-NTFS Project's kernel module is an older solution that provides only read capability.

```
/dev/hda2 /mnt/windows ntfs-3g defaults 0 0
```

NOTE *The NTFS-3G driver makes use the Filesystem in Userspace (FUSE). FUSE implements virtual file systems in userspace, acting as a connection to the kernel's file system management operations. With NTFS-3G, users set up a virtual file system for an NTFS partition, on which actions are handled by the kernel. FUSE has been implemented on other operating systems such as Mac OS X and Windows XP for different tasks. Of note is the GmailFS file system that treats Gmail storage as if it were a file system. See* ***http://fuse.sourceforge.net*** *for more details.*

noauto

File systems listed in the **/etc/fstab** file are automatically mounted whenever you boot, unless this feature is explicitly turned off with the **noauto** option. Notice that the CD-ROM and floppy disks in the sample **fstab** file earlier in this chapter have a **noauto** option. Also, if you issue a **mount -a** command, all the file systems without a **noauto** option are mounted. If you want to make the CD-ROM user-mountable, add the **user** option:

```
/dev/hdc /media/cdrom iso9660 ro,noauto,user 0 0
```

> **TIP** *The "automatic" mounting of file systems from **/etc/fstab** is actually implemented by executing a **mount -a** command in the **/etc/rc.d/rc.sysinit** file that is run whenever you boot. The **mount -a** command mounts any file system listed in your **/etc/fstab** file that does not have a **noauto** option. The **umount -a** command (which is executed when you shut down your system) unmounts the file systems in **/etc/fstab**.*

Mounting File Systems Manually: mount and umount

You can also mount or unmount any file system using the **mount** and **umount** commands directly (notice that **umount** lacks an *n*). The mount operations discussed in the preceding sections use the **mount** command to mount a file system. Normally, file systems can be mounted on hard disk partitions only by the root user, whereas CD-ROMs and floppy disks can be mounted by any user. Table 23-9 lists the different options for the **mount** command.

The mount Command

The **mount** command takes two arguments: the storage device through which Linux accesses the file system, and the mountpoint directory in the file structure to which the new

Option	Description
-a	Mounts all file systems listed in **/etc/fstab**
-f	Fakes the mounting of a file system; use it to check whether a file system can be mounted
-n	Mounts the file system without placing an entry for it in the **mstab** file
-o option-list	Mounts the file system using a list of options; this comma-separated list of options follows -o (see Table 23-8 for a list of the options)
-r	Mounts the file system with read-only permission
-t type	Specifies the type of file system to be mounted (see Table 23-7 for valid file system types)
-v	Verbose mode in which **mount** displays descriptions of the actions it is taking; use with -f to check for any problems mounting a file system, -fv
-w	Mounts the file system with read/write permission

TABLE 23-9   The mount Command Options

file system is attached. The *device* is a special device file that connects your system to the hardware device. The syntax for the **mount** command is as follows:

```
mount device mountpoint
```

As noted, device files are located in the **/dev** directories and usually have abbreviated names ending with the number of the device. For example, **fd0** may refer to the first floppy drive attached to your system. The following example mounts a hard disk in the first (**hdc2**) to the **/mymedia** directory. The mountpoint directory needs to be empty. If you already have a file system mounted there, you will receive a message that another file system is already mounted there and that the directory is busy. If you mount a file system to a directory that already has files and subdirectories in it, those will be bypassed, giving you access only to the files in the mounted file system. Unmounting the file system, of course, restores access to the original directory files. Mounting internal hard disk partitions requires administrative access; use the **sudo** command:

```
sudo mount /dev/hdc2 /mymedia
```

For any partition with an entry in the **/etc/fstab** file, you can mount the partition using only the mount directory specified in its **fstab** entry; you needn't enter the device filename. The **mount** command looks up the entry for the partition in the **fstab** file, using the directory to identify the entry and, in that way, finding the device name. For example, to mount the **/dev/hda1** Windows partition in the preceding example, the **mount** command needs to know only the directory to which it is mounted—in this case, **/mnt/windows**:

```
sudo mount /mnt/windows
```

If you are unsure about the type of file system that a disk holds, you can mount it specifying the **auto** file system type with the **-t** option. Given the **auto** file system type, **mount** attempts to detect the type of file system on the disk automatically. This is useful if you are manually mounting a floppy disk whose file system type you are unsure of (HAL also automatically detects the file system type of any removable media, including floppies). Here's an example:

```
mount -t auto /dev/fd0 /media/floppy
```

The umount Command

If you want to replace one mounted file system with another, you must first explicitly unmount the one already mounted. Say you have mounted a floppy disk, and now you want to take it out and insert a new one. You must unmount that floppy disk before you insert and mount the new one. You unmount a file system with the **umount** command, which can take as its argument either a device name or the directory where it was mounted. Here is the syntax:

```
umount device-or-mountpoint
```

The following example unmounts the floppy disk wherever it is mounted:

```
umount /dev/fd0
```

Using the example in which the device is mounted on the **/mydir** directory, you can use that directory to unmount the file system:

```
sudo umount /mydir
```

One important constraint applies to the **umount** command: You can never unmount a file system in which you are currently working. If you change to a directory within a file system that you then try to unmount, you receive an error message stating that the file system is busy. For example, suppose a CD-ROM is mounted on the **/media/disk** directory, and then you change to that **/media/disk** directory. If you decide to change CD-ROMs, you first have to unmount the current one with the **umount** command. This will fail because you are currently working in the directory in which it is mounted. You have to leave that directory before you can unmount the CD-ROM. Here's an example:

```
sudo mount /dev/hdc /media/disk
cd /media/disk
umount /media/disk
      umount: /dev/hdc: device is busy
cd /root
umount /media/disk
```

TIP *If other users are using a file system you are trying to unmount, you can use the* **lsof** *or* **fuser** *command to find out who they are.*

Managing CDs/DVDs, USB Drives, and Floppy Disks

When you mount a CD/DVD, USB drive, or floppy disk, you cannot then simply remove the device to insert or install another device. You must first unmount it, detaching the file system from the overall directory tree. In fact, the CD/DVD drive remains locked until you unmount it. Once you unmount a CD/DVD disc, you can then take it out and insert another one, which you then must mount before you can access it. When changing several CD/DVDs or floppy disks, you are continually mounting and unmounting them. For a CD-ROM, instead of using the **umount** command, you can use the **eject** command with the device name or mountpoint, which will unmount and then eject the CD-ROM from the drive.

To mount a CD/DVD disc, USB drive, or floppy disk, you simply insert it into the drive. HAL will detect it and mount it automatically in the **/media/disk** directory.

If, instead, you want to mount the drive manually from the command line with the **mount** command, you will first have to decide on a directory in which to mount it to (you can create it if it does not exist). The **/media/disk** directory is created dynamically when a disk is inserted and deleted when the disk is removed. To mount a disk manually, use the **mount** command, the device name such as **/dev/cdrom**, and the directory to which it is mounted:

```
# mount /dev/cdrom  /media/cdrom1
```

If you want to unmount the drive manually, say from the command line, you can use the **umount** command and the name of the directory on which it is mounted:

```
# umount /media/cdrom1
```

Or if mounted by HAL, you could use this:

```
# umount /media/disk
```

When you burn a CD, you may need to create a CD image file. You can access such an image file from your hard drive, mounting it as if it were another file system (even ripped images can be mounted in this way). For this, you use the **loop** option, specifying an open loop device such as **/dev/loop0**. If no loop device is indicated, **mount** will try to find a open one. The file system type is **iso9660**, a CD-ROM ISO image file type:

```
# mount -t iso9660 -o loop=/dev/loop0 image-file mount-directory
```

To mount the image file **mymusic.cdimage** to the **/mnt/mystuff** directory and make it read-only, you would use this:

```
# mount -t iso9660 -o ro,loop=/dev/loop0 mymusic.cdimage /mnt/mystuff
```

Once the CD image file is mounted, you can access files on the CD-ROM as you would in any directory.

TIP *You use* **mkisofs** *to create a CD-ROM image made up from your files or another CD-ROM.*

Mounting Hard Drive Partitions: Linux and Windows

You can mount either Linux or Windows hard drive partitions with the **mount** command. However, it is much more practical to have them mounted automatically using the **/etc/fstab** file as described. The Linux hard disk partitions you created during installation are already automatically mounted for you. As noted, to mount a Linux hard disk partition, enter the **mount** command with the device name of the partition and the directory to which you want to mount it. IDE hard drives use the prefix **hd**, and SCSI hard drives use the prefix **sd**. The next example mounts the Linux hard disk partition on **/dev/hda4** to the directory **/mnt/mydata**:

```
# mount -t ext3 /dev/hda4 /mnt/mydata
```

Mounting DVD/CD Disc Images

Mounting a DVD/CD disc image is also performed with the **mount** command, but it requires the use of a loop device. Specify the loop device with the **loop** option as shown in the next example. Here the **mydoc.iso** is mounted to the **/media/cdrom** directory as a file system of type **iso9660**. Be sure to unmount it when you finish. The image can be mounted to an empty directory on your system.

```
mount -t iso9660 -o ro,loop=/dev/loop0 mydocuments.iso /media/mycdrom
```

Creating File Systems: mkfs, mke2fs, mkswap, parted, and fdisk

Linux provides a variety of tools for creating and managing file systems, letting you add new hard disk partitions, create CD images, and format floppies. To use a new hard drive, you will first have to partition it and then create a file system on it. You can use either

parted or **fdisk** to partition your hard drive. It may be easier and safer, though, to use the GUI front ends for parted, GParted and QTParted. Both provide clear graphics and an easy-to-use interface for managing, creating, and removing file systems.

To create the file system on the partitions, you can use the **mkfs** command in a terminal window, which is a front end for various file system builders. For swap partitions, you use a special tool, **mkswap**, and to create file systems on a CD-ROM, you use the **mkisofs** tool. Linux partition and file system tools are listed in Table 23-10.

Tool	Description
cfdisk	Screen-based interface for **fdisk**
dumpe2fs	Displays lower-level block information for a file system
fdisk	Menu-driven program that creates and deletes partitions
GParted	GNOME GParted, partitioning and file system creation
hdparm	IDE hard disk tuner that sets IDE hard disk features
mkfs	Creates a file system on a partition or floppy disk using the specified file system type; front end to formatting utilities
mke2fs	Creates an **ext2** file system on a Linux partition; use the **-j** option to create an **ext3** file system
mkfs.ext3	Creates an **ext3** file system on a Linux partition
mkfs.ext2	Creates an **ext2** file system on a Linux partition
mkfs.reiserfs	Creates a ReiserFS journaling file system on a Linux partition (links to **mkreiserfs**)
mkfs.bfs	Creates a SCO bfs file system on a Linux partition
mkfs.msdos	Creates a DOS file system on a given partition
mkfs.vfat	Creates a Windows 16-bit file system on a given partition (Windows 95/98/Me)
mkfs.cramfs	Creates a CRAMFS compressed flash memory file system, read-only (used for embedded devices)
mkswap	Sets up a Linux swap area on a device or in a file
mkdosfs	Creates an MS-DOS file system under Linux
mkisofs	Creates an ISO CD-ROM disk image
parted	Manages GNU partition
QTParted	KDE GUI interface for partitioning and file system creation
resize2fs	Extends the size of a partition, using unused space currently available on a disk
tune2fs	Tunes a file system, setting features such as the label, journaling, and reserved block space

TABLE **23-10**   Linux Partition and File System Creation Tools

Parted and GParted

Most users will use GNU Parted (**www.gnu.org/software/parted/index.shtml**) to manage hard disk partitions, create new ones, and delete old ones. Unlike Fdisk, Parted lets you resize partitions. To use Parted on the partitions in a given hard drive, none of the partitions on that drive can be in use. This means that if you want to use Parted on partitions located on that same hard drive as your kernel, you have to boot your system in rescue mode and choose not to mount your system files. For any other hard drives, you only need to unmount their partitions and turn your swap space off with the **swapoff** command.

NOTE *QTParted works in much the same way as GParted. You will need to have supporting KDE libraries installed. A sidebar shows available disks. It also uses a graphical display and expandable tree for partitions. See **http://qtparted.sourceforge.net** for more information.*

GParted: The GNOME Partition Editor

Parted can be used in its original command line interface from a terminal window or with a desktop interface such as GNOME's GParted or KDE's QTParted. Most users prefer the GNOME GParted (GNOME Partition Editor) interface, which provides an easy-to-use graphical display for all your partitions (see Figure 23-3). GParted is part of the main Ubuntu repository, and accessible by choosing System I Administration I GParted. GParted can create most file system partitions, including Linux **ext3** and ReiserFS, as well as Windows NTFS and **vfat**, and MAC HFS. GParted makes use of supporting software such as

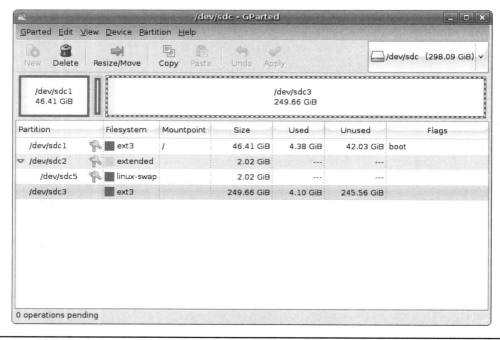

FIGURE 23-3   GParted

e2fsprogs for **ext3** partitions and **ntfsprogs** for NFTS partitions, both installed with the desktop disc. See **http://gparted.sourceforge.net** for more information. Keep in mind that both GParted and QTParted, though proven reliable, are still under development. The command line tools such as Parted and Fdisk remain the primary partition tools.

A graphical display shows the partitions on a selected hard disk, showing you the partition labels and device names as well as the proportional size of each. You use a pop-up menu in the upper-right to select a particular disk on your system. The disk will be identified with its device name, such as **/dev/sda**, and its size. The lower part of the GParted window shows the hard disk partitions for the selected drives in an expandable tree. Each partition's file system, mountpoint, and size are shown. The amount of space used and any flags such as whether the disk is bootable, are also displayed. From the View menu, you can choose to display information about the selected device and list the tasks to be applied.

You can create, resize, format, and delete partitions. Free space will be listed as unallocated space. Mounted partitions show a lock icon on their entries. If you want to perform any action on those partitions, you have to first unmount them. Right-click the partition entry and choose Unmount from the pop-up menu.

To create a partition, click the New button. This will open a Create New Partition window, where you can specify the partitions size, whether it is primary or extended, and its file system type.

To perform any operations on partitions, right-click the partition name to display a pop-up menu where you can choose these tasks. You can also select the entry and then choose a task form the Partition menu. The Format entry expands to another submenu listing all the supported file system types, such as **ntfs** or **ext3**. Deleting a partition (Delete button) will remove it permanently, losing all data. You can resize a partition to a larger size if space is available on either side. A partition can be reduced if unused space resides within the partition. A resize window shows the open space and lets you change sizes.

You can also add disk labels and flags. To change a disk label, choose Device | Set DiskLabel. A disk label names the partition, allowing your system to reference it by its label name instead of using its device name. This is helpful for removable devices whose device names may change, but labels will not. The flags indicate partition use, such as *boot* for bootable partition, *lvm* for one that supports an lvm file system, and *raid* for a member of a RAID array.

Once you have finished making changes, click the Apply button to have those changes take effect. Nothing will change until you click the Apply button.

The parted Command

Alternatively you can use the **parted** command in a terminal window to manage partitions. You can start Parted with the **parted** command and the device name of the hard disk you want to work on. Alternatively, you can use GParted on GNOME or QTParted on KDE. The following example starts **parted** for the hard disk **/dev/hda**:

```
parted /dev/hda
```

Use the **print** command to list all your partitions. The partition number for each partition will be listed in the first column under the Minor heading. The Start and End columns list the beginning and end positions that the partition uses on the hard drive. The numbers are in megabytes, starting from the first megabyte to the total available.

To create a new partition, use the **mkpart** command with either **primary** or **extended**, the file system type, and the beginning and end positions. You can create up to three primary partitions and one extended partition (or four primary partitions if no extended partition exists). The extended partition can, in turn, have several logical partitions. Once you have created the partition, you can later use **mkfs** to format it with a file system.

To remove a partition, use the **rm** command and the partition number. To resize a partition, use the **resize** command with the partition number and the beginning and end positions. You can even move a partition using the **move** command. The **help** command lists all commands.

Fdisk

To start Fdisk, enter **fdisk** on the command line with the device name of the hard disk you are partitioning. This brings up an interactive program you can use to create your Linux partition. The following command invokes **fdisk** for creating partitions on the **hdb** hard drive:

```
fdisk    /dev/hdb
```

CAUTION *Be careful when using Linux Fdisk. It can literally erase entire hard disk partitions and all the data on those partitions if you are not careful.*

The partitions have different types that you need to specify. Linux Fdisk is a line-oriented program. It has a set of one-character commands that you press from the keyboard. You may then be prompted to type in certain information and press ENTER. If you run into trouble during the **fdisk** procedure, you can press Q at any time, and you will return to the previous screen without any changes having been made. No changes are actually made to your hard disk until you press W. This should be your very last command; it makes the actual changes to your hard disk and then quits Fdisk, returning you to the installation program.

Table 23-11 lists the commonly used **fdisk** commands. Perform the following steps to create a Linux partition:

1. Press N to define a new partition; you will be asked if it is a primary partition.

2. Press P to indicate that it is a primary partition. Linux supports up to four primary partitions.

3. Enter the partition number for the partition you are creating and enter the beginning cylinder for the partition (this is the first number in parentheses at the end of the prompt).

4. You are then prompted to enter the last cylinder number. You can enter either the last cylinder you want for this partition or a size. For example, you can enter the size as **+1000M** for 1GB, preceding the amount with a + sign. Bear in mind that the size cannot exceed your free space.

5. You then specify the partition type. The default type for a Linux partition is 83. If you are creating a different type of partition, such as a swap partition, press T to indicate that this is the type you want.

Command	Action
a	Toggle a bootable flag
l	List known partition types
m	List commands
n	Add a new partition
p	Print the partition table
q	Quit without saving changes
t	Change a partition's system ID
w	Write table to disk and exit

TABLE 23-11   Commonly Used fdisk Commands

6. Enter the partition number, such as 82 for a swap partition.

7. When you are finished, press w to write out the changes to the hard disk, and then press ENTER to continue.

mkfs

Once you create your partition, you have to create a file system on it. To do this, use the **mkfs** command to build the Linux file system and pass the name of the hard disk partition as a parameter. You must specify its full pathname with the **mkfs** command. Table 23-12 lists the options for the **mkfs** command. For example, the second partition on the first hard drive has the device name **/dev/hdb1**. You can now mount your new hard disk partition, attaching it to your file structure. The next example formats that partition:

```
# mkfs -t ext3 /dev/hdb1
```

Option	Description
Blocks	Specifies number of blocks for the file system; 1440 blocks for a 1.44MB floppy disk
-c	Checks a partition for bad blocks before formatting it (may take some time)
file-system-options	Options for the type of file system specified; listed before the device name, but after the file system type
-l *filename*	Reads a list of bad blocks
-t *file-system-type*	Specifies the type of file system to format; default is the standard Linux file system type, **ext3**
-V	Verbose mode; displays description of each action **mkfs** takes
-v	Instructs the file system builder program that **mkfs** invokes to show actions it takes

TABLE 23-12   The mkfs Options

The **mkfs** command is just a front end for several different file system builders. A *file system builder* performs the actual task of creating a file system. Linux supports various file system builders, including several journaling file systems and Windows file systems. The name of a file system builder has the prefix **mkfs** and a suffix for the name of the type of file system. For example, the file system builder for the **ext3** file system is **mkfs.ext3**. For ReiserFS file systems, it is **mkfs.reiserfs** (link to **mkreiserfs**, which is part of **reiser-utils** package). For Windows 16-bit file systems (95/98/Me), it is **mkfs.vfat**.

Some of these file builders are simply other names for traditional file system creation tools. For example, the **mkfs.ext2** file builder is just another name for the **mke2fs ext2** file system creation tool, and **mkfs.msdos** is the **mkdosfs** command. As **ext3** is an extension of **ext2**, the command **mkfs.ext3** simply invokes **mke2fs**, the tool for creating **ext2** and **ext3** file systems, and directs it to create an **ext3** file system (using the **-j** option). Any of the file builders can be used directly to create a file system of that type. Options are listed before the device name. The next example is equivalent to the preceding one, creating an **ext3** file system on the **hdb1** device:

```
mkfs.ext3 /dev/hdb1
```

The syntax for the **mkfs** command is as follows. You can add options for a particular file system after the type and before the device. The block size is used for file builders that do not detect the disk size.

```
mkfs options [-t type] file-sysoptions device size
```

TIP *Once you have formatted your disk, you can label it with the **e2label** command.*

The same procedure works for floppy disks. In this case, the **mkfs** command takes as its argument the device name. It uses the **ext2** file system (the default for **mkfs**), because a floppy is too small to support a journaling file system.

```
# mkfs /dev/fd0
```

mkswap

If you want to create a swap partition, you first use Fdisk or Parted to create the partition, if it does not already exist, and then you use the **mkswap** command to format it as a swap partition. **mkswap** formats the entire partition unless otherwise instructed. It takes as its argument the device name for the swap partition:

```
mkswap /dev/hdb2
```

You then need to create an entry for it in the **/etc/fstab** file so that it will be automatically mounted when your system boots.

CD/DVD Disc Recording

Recording data to DVD/CD discs on Linux is now handled directly by the GNOME and KDE desktops. Simple drag-and-drop operations on a blank DVD/CD lets you burn the disc. You can also use GNOME and KDE CD recording applications such as Brasero on

GNOME (see Chapter 3) and KOnCD to create your DVD/CDs easily. All are front ends to the **mkisofs** and **cdrecord** tools. To record DVDs on DVD writers, you can use **cdrecord** for DVD-R/RW drives and the DVD+RW tools for DVD+RW/R drives. If you want to record CD-ROMs on a DVD writer, you can just use the **cdrecord** application with many options.

The **cdrecord** application currently works only on DVD-R/RW drives; it is part of the **dvdrtools** package. If you want to use DVD+RW/R drives, use the DVD+RW tools such as **growisofs** and **dvd+rw-format**. Some DVD+RW tools are included in the **dvd+rw-tools** package. Check the DVD+RW tools Web site for more information: **http://fy.chalmers.se/~appro/linux/DVD+RW**.

With the `mkisofs` command, you can create a CD image file, which you can then write to a CD-R/RW write device. Once you create your CD image file, you can write it to a CD-Write device, using the **cdrecord** application.

Mono and .NET Support

With Mono, Linux now provides .NET support, along with .NET applications such as the Beagle desktop search tool and the F-Spot photo management tool. Mono provides an open source development environment for .NET applications. The Mono project is an open source project supported by Novell that implements the .NET Framework on Unix, Linux, and OS X systems. Currently, Mono 1.2 and 2.0 are offered. Mono 1.2 corresponds generally with .NET 1.1 features, and Mono 2.0 corresponds with .NET 2.0. See **http://mono-project.com** for detailed information.

Mono is implemented on Linux using several components: the basic Mono .NET application includes tools such as the Mono certification manager (**certmgr**), the Global Assemblies Cache Manager tool (**gacutil**) for making assemblies available at runtime, and **mcs**, the Mono C# compiler. Several additional tools are available for distinct features such as Visual Basic support, SQL database queries, and .NET web support. The Mono language testing tool, **NUnit**, is also included.

Configuration is found in the **/etc/mono/config** file, which is an XML-like file that maps dynamic link library (DLL) references to Linux libraries. The **/etc/mono** file also contains configuration files for Mono 1.0 and 2.0. Mono is installed in **/usr/lib/mono**. In the corresponding **1.0** and **2.0** directories you will find the DLL and EXE .NET support assemblies for different Mono applications. Other directories will hold .NET DLLs and configuration for several applications and services, including Evolution, D-Bus, and GTK.

Local configuration information and runtime applications are placed in the user's **.config** directory.

RAID and LVM

W ith onset of cheap, efficient, and very large hard drives, even simple home systems can employ several hard drives. The use of multiple hard drives creates opportunities for ensuring storage reliability and more easily organizing access to your hard disks. Linux provides two methods for managing your hard disks: Logical Volume Manager (LVM) and Redundant Arrays of Independent Disks (RAID). LVM is a method for organizing all your hard disks into logical volumes, letting you pool the storage capabilities of several hard disks into a single logical volume. Your system then sees one large storage device, and you do not have to micromanage each underlying hard disk and its partitions. LVM is perhaps the most effective way to add hard drives to your system and creates a large accessible pool of storage. RAID lets you store the same data in different places on multiple hard drives that are treated as a single hard drive. They include recovery information that allows you to restore your files should one of the drives fail. The two methods can be mixed, implementing LVM volumes on RAID arrays. LVM provides flexibility, and RAID can provide data protection.

With LVM you no longer have to keep track of separate disks and their partitions; nor do you need to remember where files are stored on what partitions located in what drive. Partitions and their drives are combined into logical file systems that you can attach to your system directory tree. Several logical file systems can each have their own drives and/or partitions.

In a system with several hard drives using both LVM and RAID, you can combine the hard drives into one logical file system that accesses the storage as one large pool. Files are stored in a single directory structure, not on directories on a particular partition. Instead of mounting file systems for each individual hard drive, only one file system is used to mount systems for all the hard drives. LVM also lets you implement several logical file systems on different partitions across several hard drives.

RAID is best suited to desktops and servers with multiple hard drives and that require data recovery. The most favored form of RAID, RAID 5, requires a minimum of three hard drives. RAID, with the exception of RAID 0, provides the best protection against hard drive failure and is considered a necessity for storage-intensive tasks such as enterprise, database, and Internet server operations. It can also provide peace of mind for smaller operations, providing recovery from hard disk failure. Keep in mind that different forms of RAID can be used; each has its advantages and weaknesses—for example, RAID 0 provides no recovery capabilities at all. After setting up a RAID array, you can implement LVM volumes on the array.

In comparison to LVM, RAID can provide faster access for applications that work with very large files, such as multimedia, database, or graphics applications. But for normal operations, LVM is just as efficient as RAID. LVM, though, requires running your Linux system and configuring it from your Linux operating system. RAID, which is now supported at the hardware level on most computers, is easier to set up, especially a simple RAID 0 operation that merely combines hard drives into one drive.

Logical Volume Manager

For easier hard disk storage management, you can set up your system to use the LVM, creating partitions that are organized into logical volumes to which free space is automatically allocated. Logical volumes provide a more flexible and powerful way of dealing with disk storage, organizing physical partitions into logical volumes in which you can easily manage disk space. Disk storage for a logical volume is treated as one pool of memory, though the volume can in fact contain several hard disk partitions spread across several hard disks. Adding a new LVM partition merely increases the pool of storage accessible to the entire system. The original LVM package was developed for kernel 2.4. The current LVM2 package is used for kernel 2.6. Check the LVM HOWTO at **http://tldp.org** for detailed examples.

NOTE *On Ubuntu, you can use Red Hat's **system-config-lvm** tool to manage your LVM devices with a simple GUI.*

LVM Structure

In an LVM structure, LVM physical partitions, also known as *extents*, are organized into logical groups, which are in turn used by logical volumes—three different levels of organization. At the lowest level are physical volumes, physical hard disk partitions that you create with partition creation tools such as **parted** or **fdisk**. The partition type will be a Linux LVM partition, code **8e**. These physical volumes are organized into logical groups, known as *volume groups*, that operate much like logical hard disks. You assign collections of physical volumes to different logical groups.

Once you have created logical groups, you can create logical volumes, which function much like hard disk partitions on a standard setup. For example, on the **turtle** group volume, you could create a **/var** logical volume, and on the **rabbit** logical group, you could create **/home** and **/projects** logical volumes. You can have several logical volumes on one logical group, just as you can have several partitions on one hard disk.

You treat the logical volumes as you would any ordinary hard disk partition. You create a file system on one with the **mkfs** command, and then you can mount the file system to use it with the **mount** command. The Linux file system type could be **ext3**.

Storage on logical volumes is managed using extents. A logical group defines a standard size for an extent—say, 4MB—and then divides each physical volume in its group into extents of that size. Logical volumes are, in turn, divided into extents of the same size, which are then mapped to the physical volumes.

Logical volumes can be mirrored, striped, or linear. The mirrored option will create a mirror copy of a logical volume, providing a restore capability. The striped option lets you automatically distribute your logical volume across several partitions as you would a RAID device. This adds better efficiency for very large files but is complicated to implement. As on a RAID device, stripe sizes must be consistent across partitions and, as LVM partitions can be of any size, the stripe sizes must be carefully calculated. The simplest approach is to use a linear implementation, much like a RAID 0 device, which treats the storage as one large ordinary drive, with storage accessed sequentially.

For logical volumes, one restriction and a recommendation apply. The boot partition cannot be part of a logical volume. You must create a separate hard disk partition as your boot partition with the **/boot** mountpoint in which your kernel and all needed boot files are installed. In addition, it is recommended that you not place your root partition on a logical volume. Doing so can complicate any needed data recovery. This is why a default partition configuration for many distributions that are set up during installation will include a separate **/boot** partition of 100MB of type **ext3**, whereas the root and swap partitions will be installed on logical volumes. Two partitions will be set up, one for the logical group (LVM physical volume, **pv**) holding both swap and root volumes, and another for the boot partition (**ext3**). Both logical volumes will be **ext3** file systems.

Creating LVMs During Installation

You can create LVM file systems during installation. LVM may even be the default configuration. First, create physical LVM partitions. Then create the volume groups in which you place these partitions, and then, from the volume groups, create the logical volumes, for which you specify mountpoints and file system types. You can create LVM partitions during the installation process. Create an LVM physical partition on your hard disk, and then create your logical volumes. You need to assign the LVM physical partitions to volume groups, which are essentially logical hard drives. Once the volume groups are created, you are ready to create logical volumes. You can create several logical volumes within each group. The logical volumes function like partitions. You must specify a file system type and mountpoint for each logical volume you create, and you need at least a swap and root volume. The file system type for the swap volume is **swap**, and for the root volume it's a standard Linux file system type such as **ext3**.

system-config-lvm

Ubuntu currently does not provide any configuration tools for LVM. Red Hat and Fedora provide an easy-to-use LVM configuration tool called **system-config-lvm**. This tool provides a GUI for managing your LVM. It lets you obtain information about your logical and physical volumes and perform simple tasks such as deleting and extending logical volumes or migrating and removing physical volumes. It remains, to date, the best GUI tool available for managing LVM and is well worth the effort required to install it on Ubuntu should you use LVM extensively.

Installing system-config-lvm

You can download this tool and install it on your Ubuntu system and it will work similar to the other Fedora tools already included with Ubuntu, such as **system-config-printer**. However, you must use the Fedora package, which then needs to be prepared as an Ubuntu-compliant Debian package.

1. Install the **alien** package from the Synaptic Package Manager. The **alien** package can convert packages from other distributions, including Red Hat and Fedora RPM packages, to Ubuntu-compliant DEB packages.

2. Download the current Fedora version of **system-config-lvm** from a distribution site such as **http://download.fedora.redhat.com/pub/fedora/linux/releases/9/Everything/i386/os/Packages**. You can download directly from your browser.

3. Convert the Fedora RPM package to an Ubuntu DEB package using **alien**. Open a terminal window and enter the **alien** command with the package name:

```
sudo alien system-config-lvm-1.1.4-1.0.fc9.noarch.rpm
```

This will create a DEB version called **system-config-lvm_1.1.4-1_all.deb**. Note the underscores in the name.

4. Create a Python 2 link for the **python2.5** library on Ubuntu. The **system-config-lvm** tool searches for Python as **python2**:

```
sudo ln -s /usr/bin/python2.5  /usr/bin/python2
```

5. Install **system-config-lvm_1.1.1-3_all.deb** with the **dpkg** command:

```
sudo dpkg -i system-config-lvm_1.1.4-1_all.deb
```

An LVM entry will be placed on the System | Administration menu, which you can use to start **system-config-lvm**.

6. Modify the command for this entry to precede the command with the **gksu** command. The **gksu** command provides administrative access that **system-config-lvm** needs to perform its tasks. Choose System | Preferences | Logical Volume Management entry, and right-click and select Properties. This opens a window with an entry for Command. Insert the **gksu** command:

```
gksu  /usr/sbin/system-config-lvm
```

If you add this launcher to the panel or desktop, you should see the **gksu** command in the Launcher panel of its properties window (right-click the launcher icon and choose Properties).

Using system-config-lvm

As mentioned, you can invoke **system-config-lvm** by choosing System | Administration | Logical Volume Management. You can also enter **system-config-lvm** in a terminal window. **system-config-lvm** will display a window showing all your logical and physical volumes, a graphical representation of a selected volume or volume group, and information about the selected volumes. Figure 24-1 shows two volume groups, **VolGroup00** and **mymedia**. In this example, the **mymedia** volume group has one logical volume called **myvideo**, which in turn has two physical volumes, **sdb1** and **sdd1**—these are the **b:** and **d:** SATA drives.

Selecting a physical volume displays buttons with options to extend the volume group or remove physical volumes; selecting a particular partition allows you to migrate a particular volume or remove it from the group. When extending a volume group, you will see a list of possible partitions from which to choose.

Selecting a logical group displays buttons with options to create or remove the volume, and selecting a particular volume in that group lets you remove the logical volume or edit

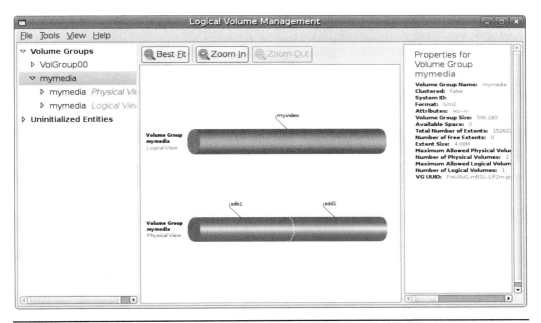

FIGURE 24-1   system-config-lvm on Ubuntu: System | Administration | Logical Volume Management

its properties. You can specify a logical volume's file system type, size, and logical volume name via its properties window. When adding a new logical volume, you can use properties to set the name, size, and file system type, formatting it appropriately. Space permitting, you can even resize current volumes.

Uninitialized Entities are partitions that do not belong to any volume. Recall that the boot partition cannot belong to a volume group, and it cannot be a logical volume. Be sure to leave that partition alone. For other uninitialized partitions, you can select their entries and initialize them to add them to a volume group by choosing Tools | Initialize Block Device.

If you have the free space on a logical group, you can create a new logical volume. Select the logical group entry from the left pane A Create New Logical Volume button will appear which you can click to open a dialog where you can create a new logical volume (Figure 24-2), which includes entries for the LV Name, Size, Filesystem, and location where you want it mounted. You can also specify the size of the extents, though the default normally works well. You can specify whether a logical volume should be linear, mirrored, or striped. These features are similar to the linear, mirrored, or striped implementations used in RAID devices. Normally you would choose the Linear implementation, which is the default.

To extend the size of a volume using free space in the volume group, select the volume group and the Edit Properties button will appear which you can then click. This opens the dialog shown in Figure 24-2. You can then use the Size slider to increase the size of the volume. When you click OK, **system-config-lvm** will unmount your volume group and then resize the volume and check the file system, extending the size while preserving your original data. This capability is a major advantage for LVM devices. Hard disk partitions are fixed, whereas LVM logical disks can easily be expanded. To expand a hard disk partition,

FIGURE 24-2
Creating a new
logical volume

you had to destroy the old one and create a new, larger one that in turn was also fixed. With LVM, you simply add more storage. The logical structure is separated from the physical implementation.

Using the LVM Commands

You can use the collection of LVM tools to manage your LVM volumes, adding new LVM physical partitions and removing current ones from the Ubuntu main repository (see Table 24-1). You can use these tools in a terminal window to manage and create LVM volumes. A GUI LVM tool like **system-config-lvm** is actually a GUI for the LVM tools. You can either use LVM tools directly or use the **lvm** command to generate an interactive shell from which you can run LVM commands. Man pages are available for all the LVM commands. LVM maintains configuration information in the **/etc/lvm/lvm.conf** file, where you can configure LVM options such as the log file, the configuration backup directory, or the directory for LVM devices (see the **lvm.conf** man page for details).

Displaying LVM Information

You can use the **pvdisplay**, **vgdisplay**, and **lvdisplay** commands to show detailed information about a physical partition, volume groups, and logical volumes, respectively. **pvscan**, **vgscan**, and **lvscan** list your physical, group, and logical volumes, respectively.

Managing LVM Physical Volumes with the LVM Commands

A physical volume can be any hard disk partition or RAID device. A RAID device is seen as a single physical volume. You can create physical volumes either from a single hard disk or from partitions on a hard disk. On very large systems with many hard disks, you would more likely use an entire hard disk for each physical volume.

Command	Description
lvm	Open an interactive shell for executing LVM commands
lvmdiskscan	Scan all disks for LVM physical partitions
lvdisplay	Display detailed information about Logical Volumes
lvcreate	Create a logical volume
lvrename	Rename a logical volume
lvchange	Modify a logical volume
lvextend	Extend the size of a logical volume
lvreduce	Reduce the size of a logical volume
lvremove	Remove a logical volume
lvs	List logical volumes with detailed information
lvresize	Change the size of a logical volume
lvscan	Scan system for logical volumes
pvdisplay	Display detailed information about LVM physical partitions
pvchange	Modify an LVM physical partition
pvcreate	Create an LVM physical partition
pvmove	Move content of an LVM physical partition to another partition
pvremove	Delete an LVM physical partition
pvs	List physical partitions with detailed information
pvresize	Resize a physical partition
pvscan	Scan system for physical partitions
vgdisplay	Display detailed information about volume groups
vgexport	Activate a volume group
vgimport	Make an exported volume group known to a new system; useful for moving an activated volume group from one system to another
vgmerge	Combine volume groups
vgreduce	Remove physical partitions from a volume group
vgremove	Delete a volume group
vgs	List volume groups with detailed information
vgslit	Split a volume group
vgscan	Scan system for volume groups
vgck	Check volume groups
vgrename	Rename a volume group
vgcfgbackup	Backup volume group configuration (metadata)
vgcfgrestore	Restore volume group configuration (metadata)

TABLE 24-1 LVM Commands

To initialize a physical volume on an entire hard disk, you use the hard disk device name, as shown here:

```
pvcreate /dev/sdc
```

If you are using a single partition for an entire drive, you create a new physical volume using the partition's device name, as shown here:

```
pvcreate /dev/sdc1
```

This will create one physical partition, **pv**, called **sdc1** on the **sdc** hard drive (the third Serial ATA drive, drive **c:**).

To initialize several drives, just list them. The following creates two physical partitions, **sdc1** and **sdd1**:

```
pvcreate /dev/sdc1 /dev/sdd1
```

You can also use several partitions on different hard drives. This is a situation in which your hard drives each hold several partitions. This condition occurs often when you are using some partitions on your hard drive for different purposes, such as for different operating systems, or if you want to distribute your logical group across several hard drives. To initialize these partitions at once, you simply list them:

```
pvcreate /dev/sda3 /dev/sdb1 /dev/sdb2
```

Once you have initialized your partitions, you must create LVM groups on them.

Managing LVM Groups

Physical LVM partitions are used to make up a volume group. You can manually create a volume group using the **vgcreate** command and the name of the group along with a list of physical partitions you want in the group. If you are then creating a new volume group in which to place these partitions, you can include them in the group when you create the volume group with the **vgcreate** command. The volume group can use one or more physical partitions. The default install configuration used only one physical partition for the **VolGroup00**. In the following example, a volume group called **mymedia** is made up of two physical volumes, **sdb1** and **sdc1**:

```
vgcreate mymedia  /dev/sdb1 /dev/sdc1
```

The example shown in Figure 24-1, sets up a logical group on two serial ATA hard drives, each with its own single partition. Alternatively, you can set up a volume group to span partitions on several hard drives. If you are using partitions for different functions, this approach gives you the flexibility for using all the space available across multiple hard drives. The following example creates a group called **rabbit** consisting of three physical partitions: **/dev/sda3**, **/dev/sdb2**, and **/dev/sdb4**:

```
vgcreate rabbit  /dev/sda3 /dev/sdb2 /dev/sdb4
```

If you later want to add a physical volume to a volume group, you use the **vgextend** command, which adds a new partition to a logical group. In the following example, the partition **/dev/sda3** is added to the volume group **rabbit**. In effect, you are extending the size of the logical group by adding a new physical partition.

```
vgextend  rabbit  /dev/sda3
```

To add an entire new drive to a volume group, you follow a similar procedure. The following example adds a fifth serial ATA hard drive, **sde1**, first creating a physical volume on it and then adding that volume, **sde1**, to the **mymedia** volume group.

```
pvcreate /dev/sde1
vgextend mymedia /dev/sde1
```

To remove a physical partition, first remove it from its logical group. You may have to use the **pmove** command to move any data off the physical partition. Then use the **vgreduce** command to remove it from its logical group.

You can, in turn, remove an entire volume group by first deactivating it with **vgchange -a n** and then using the **vgremove** command.

Activating Volume Groups

In a standard file system structure, you mount and unmount hard disk partitions; however, with an LVM structure, you activate and deactivate entire volume groups. The group volumes are inaccessible until you activate them with the **vgchange** command with the **-a** option. To activate a group, first reboot your system, and then enter the **vgchange** command with the **-a** option and the **y** argument to activate the logical group (an **n** argument will deactivate the group):

```
vgchange -a  y  rabbit
```

Creating LVM Logical Volumes

To create logical volumes, you use the **lvcreate** command and then format your logical volume using the standard formatting command such as **mkfs.ext3**.

With the **-n** option you specify the volume's name, which functions like a hard disk partition's label. You use the **-L** option to specify the size of the volume. Other options can be used to implement features such as a linear, striped, or mirrored volume, or to specify the size of the extents to use. Usually the defaults work well. The following example creates a logical volume named **projects** on the **rabbit** logical group with a size of 20GB.

```
lvcreate -n projects  -L 20GB rabbit
```

The following example sets up a logical volume on the **mymedia** volume group that is 540GB in size. The **mymedia** volume group is made up of two physical volumes, each on 320GB hard drives—the two hard drives are logically seen as one.

```
lvcreate -n myvideos  -L 540GB mymedia
```

Once you have created your logical volume, you can create a file system to use on it. The following creates an **ext3** file system on the **myvideos** logical volume:

```
mkfs.ext3 myvideos
```

You can remove a logical volume with the `lvremove` command. With `lvextend`, you can increase the size of the logical volume, and `lvreduce` will reduce its size.

LVM Device Names: /dev/mapper

The **device-mapper** driver is used by LVM to set up tables for mapping logical devices to a hard disk. The device name for a logical volume is kept in the **/dev/mapper** directory and has the format *logical group–logical volume*. In addition, a corresponding device folder will exist for the logical group, which will contain logical volume names. These device names are links to the **/dev/mapper** names. For example, the **mypics** logical volume in the **mymedia** logical group has the device name **/dev/mapper/mymedia-mypics**. A corresponding folder will be called **/dev/mymedia**. The device name **/dev/mymedia/mypics** is a link to the **/dev/mapper/mymedia-mypics** device name. You can just as easily use the link, as shown in this chapter, as the original device name. The snapshot device described later in this chapter would have the device name **/dev/mapper/mymedia-mypicssnap1** with the link device name being **/dev/mymedia/mypicssnap**.

NOTE *You can back up volume group metadata (configuration) using the **vgcfgbackup** command. This does not back up your logical volumes (no content). Metadata backups are stored in **/etc/ lvm/backup**, and can be restored using **vgcfgrestore**. You may need to restore your volume if you are using the same upgraded system on new computer hardware.*

LVM Example for Multiple Hard Drives

With hard drives becoming cheaper and the demand for storage increasing, many systems now use multiple hard drives. Without RAID, partitions on each hard drive had to be individually managed, and each hard drive had to be managed separately, with files having to fit into remaining storage as the drives filled up. RAID allows you to treat several hard disks as one storage device, but restrictions apply to the sizes and kinds of devices you can combine.

With LVM, these restrictions do not apply. You can combine hard disks into a single storage device. This method is flexible, because it lets you replace disks without losing any data and add new disks to increase your storage automatically (or you can replace smaller disks with larger ones).

For example, suppose you want to add two hard disks to your system, but you want to treat the storage in both disks logically instead of having to manage partitions in each. LVM lets you treat the combined storage of both hard drives as one giant pool. In effect, two 500GB drives can be treated as a single, 1 terabyte storage device.

In the following example, the Linux system makes use of three hard drives. The Linux system and boot partitions are on the first hard drive, **sda**. Added to this system are two hard drives, **sdb** and **sdc**, which will make up an LVM storage device to be added to the system.

The steps involved in creating and accessing logical volumes are described in the following commands. In this example, two hard disk drives will be combined into one LVM drive. The hard drives are Serial ATA drives identified on the systems as **sdb** and **sdc**. Each drive is first partitioned with a single LVM physical partition. Use a partition creation tool such as **fdisk** or **parted** to create the physical partitions on the hard disks **sdb** and **sdc**. We'll create the partitions **sdb1** and **sdc1**.

1. First initialize the physical volumes with the **pvcreate** command. The **sda1** and **sda2** partitions in the **sda** entry are reserved for the boot and root partitions and are never initialized.

   ```
   pvcreate /dev/sda1 /dev/sdb1 /dev/sdc1
   ```

2. Create the logical groups you want using the **vgcreate** command. In this case, one logical group exists. The **mymedia** group uses **sdb1** and **sdc1**. If you create a physical volume later and want to add it to a volume group, you can use the **vgextend** command.

   ```
   vgcreate mymedia  /dev/sdb1 /dev/sdc1
   ```

3. Now create the logical volumes in each volume group, using the **lvcreate** command. In this example, two logical volumes are created: one for **myvideo** and another for **mypics**. The corresponding **lvcreate** commands are shown here:

   ```
   lvcreate  -n myvideo   -l 540GB    mymedia
   lvcreate  -n mypics    -l 60GB    mymedia
   ```

4. Now you can activate the logical volumes. Reboot and use **vgchange** with the **-a y** options to activate the logical volumes:

   ```
   vgchange -a y mymedia
   ```

5. Now make file systems for each logical volume:

   ```
   mkfs.ext3 myvideo
   mkfs.ext3 mypics
   ```

6. Now mount the logical volumes. In this example, they are mounted to subdirectories of the same name in **/mydata**:

   ```
   mount -t ext3 /dev/mymedia/mypics   /mydata/mypics
   mount -t ext3 /dev/mymedia/myvideo /mydata/myvideo
   ```

Using LVM to Replace Drives

LVM can be very useful when you need to replace an old hard drive with a new one. Hard drives are expected to last about six years on average. You might want to replace the older drive with a larger one (available hard drive storage sizes double every year or so). To replace a nonboot hard drive is easy. To replace a boot drive is much more complicated.

To replace a drive, simply incorporate the new drive into your logical volume. The size of your logical volume will increase accordingly. You can use the **pmove** command to move data from the old drive to the new one. Then, issue commands to remove the old drive. From the user and system point of view, no changes are made. Files from your old drive will still be stored in the same directories, though the actual storage will be implemented on the new drive.

Replacement with LVM becomes more complicated if you want to replace your boot drive, from which the hard drive your system starts up and that holds your Linux kernel. The boot drive contains a special boot partition and the master boot record. The boot partition cannot be part of any LVM volume. You first have to create a boot partition on the new drive using a partition tool such as Parted or Fdisk, labeling it as **boot**. The boot drive is usually very small, about 200MB. Then mount the partition on your system and copy the contents of your **/boot** directory to it. Then you add the remainder of the disk to your logical volume and logically remove the old disk, copying the contents of the old disk to the new one. You still have to boot with the Linux rescue DVD (or install a DVD in rescue mode) and issue the **grub-install** command to install the master boot record on your new drive. You can then boot from the new drive.

LVM Snapshots

A *snapshot* records and defines the state of the logical volume at a designated time. It does not create a full copy of data on the volume, just changes since the last snapshot, at a time you define. This allows you to back up the data in a consistent way. In addition, should you need to restore a file to its previous version, you can use its snapshot. Snapshots are treated as logical volumes and can be mounted, copied, or deleted.

To create a snapshot, you use the **lvcreate** command with the -s option. In the following example, the snapshot is named **mypics-snap1** (**-n** option). You need to specify the full device name of the logical group for which you want to create the snapshot. In this example, the snapshot logical volume is created in the **/dev/mymedia** logical group. It could just as easily have been created in any other logical group. Be sure that enough free space is available in the logical group to hold the snapshot. Although a snapshot normally uses very little space, you must guard against overflows. If the snapshot is allocated the same size as the original, it will never overflow. For systems where little of the original data changes, the snapshot can be very small. The following example allocate one third the size of the original (60GB):

```
lvcreate  -s -n mypics-snap1 -l 20GB /dev/mymedia
```

You can then mount the snapshot as you would any other file system:

```
mount /dev/mymedia/mypics-snap1 /mysnaps
```

To delete a snapshot, you use the **lvremove** command, removing it as you would any logical volume:

```
lvremove  -f /dev/mymedia/mypics-snap1
```

Snapshots are useful for making backups while a system is still active. You can use **tar** or **dump** to back up the mounted snapshot to a disk or tape. All the data form the original logical volume will be included, along with the changes noted by the snapshot.

Snapshots also allow you to perform effective undo operations. You can create a snapshot of a logical volume, and then unmount the original and mount the snapshot in its place. Any changes you make will be performed on the snapshot, not the original. Should problems occur, unmount the snapshot and then mount the original. This restores the original state of your data. You could also do this using several snapshots, restoring to a previous snapshot. With this procedure, you could test new software on a snapshot, without endangering your original data, as the software would be operating on the snapshot rather than the original logical volume.

You can also use snapshots as alternative versions of a logical volume. You can read and write to a snapshot. A write will change only the snapshot volume, not the original, creating, in effect, an alternate version.

Configuring RAID Devices

RAID is a method of storing data across several disks to provide greater performance and redundancy. With RAID, several hard disks are treated as a single hard disk by your operating system. RAID efficiently stores and retrieves data across all disks, instead of having the operating system access each disk as a separate file system. Lower level details of storage and retrieval are no longer a concern for the operating system. RAID allows greater flexibility in adding or removing hard disks, as well as implementing redundancy in the storage system to provide greater reliability. With RAID, several hard disks are treated as one virtual disk, where some of the disks are used as real-time mirrors, duplicating data. You can use RAID in several ways, depending on the degree of reliability you need. When you place data on multiple disks, I/O operations can overlap in a balanced way, improving performance. Because having multiple disks increases the mean time between failures (MTBF), storing data redundantly also increases fault tolerance.

RAID can be implemented on a hardware or software level. On a hardware level, you can connect hard disks to a RAID hardware controller, usually a special PC card. Your operating system then accesses storage through the RAID hardware controller. Alternatively, you can implement RAID as a software controller, letting the controller program manage access to hard disks treated as RAID devices. The software version lets you use hard disks as RAID disks. Linux uses the multiple device (MD) driver, supported in the 2.4 kernel, to implement a software RAID controller. Linux software RAID supports several levels (linear, 0, 1, 4, 5, 6, and 10), whereas hardware RAID supports many more. Hardware RAID levels, such as 7–10, provide combinations of greater performance and reliability.

TIP *Before you can use RAID on your system, make sure RAID is supported on your kernel, along with the RAID levels you want to use. If they are not supported, you will have to reconfigure and install a RAID module for the kernel. Check the Multi-Driver Support component in your kernel configuration. You can specify support for any or all of the RAID levels.*

Motherboard RAID Support: dmraid

With kernel 2.6, hardware RAID devices are supported with the Device-Mapper Software RAID support tool (**dmraid**), which currently supports a wide range of motherboard RAID devices. Keep in mind that many "hardware" RAID devices are, in effect, really software RAID (*fakeraid*). Though you configure them in the motherboard BIOS, the drivers operate as software, like any other drivers. In this respect, they could be considered less flexible than a Linux software RAID solution, and they could also depend directly on vendor support for any fixes for updates.

The **dmraid** driver will map your system to hardware RAID devices such as those provided by Intel, Promise, and Silicon Magic and often included on motherboards.

The **dmraid** tool uses the device-mapper driver to set up a virtual file system interface, just as is done for LVM drives. The RAID device names will be located in **/dev/mapper**.

You use the BIOS RAID configuration utility to set up RAID devices as instructed by the hardware documentation. During a Linux installation, the RAID devices are automatically detected and the **dmraid** module is loaded, selecting the appropriate drivers.

Using the **dmraid** command, you can detect and activate RAID devices. The following command displays your RAID devices:

```
dmraid -r
```

To list currently supported devices, use **dmraid** with the **-l** option:

```
dmraid -l
```

NOTE *The **dmraid** tool is improved continually and may not work well with some RAID devices.*

Linux Software RAID Levels

Linux software RAID can be implemented at different levels, depending on whether you want organization, efficiency, redundancy, or reconstruction capability. Each capability corresponds to different RAID levels. For most levels, the size of the hard disk devices should be the same. Linux software RAID supports several levels, as shown in Table 24-2. In addition, a FAULTY raid level is provided for testing purposes.

RAID Level	Capability	Description
Linear	Appending	Treats RAID hard drives as one virtual drive with no striping, mirroring, or parity reconstruction.
0	Striping	Implements disk striping across drives with no redundancy.
1	Mirroring	Implements a high level of redundancy. Each drive is treated as mirror for all data.
4	Parity	Implements data reconstruction capability using parity information, kept on a separate disk.
5	Distributed parity	Implements data reconstruction capability using parity information, which is distributed across all drives, instead of using a separate drive as in RAID 4. Requires at least three hard drives.
6	Distributed parity	Implements data reconstruction capability using dual distributed parity information. Dual sets of parity information are distributed across all drives. Can be considered an enhanced form of RAID 5.
10	Striping and Mirroring	Implements a high level of redundancy with striping. Also know as 1+0.
Multipath	Multiple access to devices	Supports multiple access to the same device.

TABLE 24-2 Linux Software RAID Levels

NOTE *For mirroring for RAID 1, disks of the same size are required, and for RAID 5 they are recommended.*

Linear

The *linear* level lets you organize several hard disks into one logical hard disk, providing a pool of continuous storage. Instead of being forced to set up separate partitions on each hard drive, in effect you have only one hard drive to work with. The storage is managed sequentially. When one hard disk fills up, the next one is used. In effect, you are *appending* one hard disk to the next. So, for example, if you have a hard disk RAID array containing two 80GB disks, after you use up the storage on one, you will automatically start on the next. This level provides no recovery capability.

RAID 0: Striping

For efficiency, RAID stores data using disk *striping*, in which data is organized into standardized stripes that can be stored across the RAID drives for faster access (level 0). RAID 0 also organizes your hard disks into common RAID devices but treats them like single hard disks, storing data randomly across all the disks. For example, if you had a hard disk RAID array containing two 80GB disks, you could access them as one 160GB RAID device.

RAID 1: Mirroring

RAID level 1 implements redundancy through *mirroring*. In mirroring, the same data is written to each RAID drive. Each disk has a complete copy of all the data written, so if one or more disks fail, the others still have your data. Though extremely safe, redundancy can be very inefficient and consumes a great deal of storage. For example, on a RAID array of two 80GB disk drives, one disk is used for standard storage and the other is a real-time backup. This leaves you with only 80GB for use on your system. Write operations also have to be duplicated across as many mirrored hard disks as are used by the RAID array, slowing down operations.

RAID 4: Parity

Though it is not supported in some distributions due to overhead costs, RAID 4, like RAID 5, supports a more compressed form of recovery using parity information instead of mirrored data. With RAID 4, parity information is kept on a separate disk, while the other disks are used for data storage, much like in a linear model.

TIP *Many distributions also allow you to create and format RAID drives during installation. At that time, you can create your RAID partitions and devices.*

RAID 5 and 6: Distributed Parity

As an alternative to mirroring, data can be reconstructed using *parity information* in case of a hard drive crash. Parity information is saved instead of full duplication of the data. Parity information takes up the space equivalent of one drive, leaving most of the space on the RAID drives free for storage. RAID 5 combines both striping and parity (see RAID 4), where parity information is distributed across the hard drives, rather than in one drive dedicated to that purpose. This allows the use of the more efficient access method, striping. With both striping and parity, RAID 5 provides both fast access and recovery capability, making it the most popular RAID level used. For example, a RAID array of four 80GB hard drives would be treated as one 320GB hard drive with part of that storage (80GB) used to hold parity information, leaving 240GB free. RAID 5 requires at least three hard drives.

RAID 6 operates the same as RAID 5, but it uses dual sets of parity information for the data, providing even greater restoration capability.

RAID 10: Striping and Mirroring

RAID 10, also known as RAID 1+0, combines both striping and mirroring (RAID 0 and 1). This provides both redundancies and fast access.

Multipath

Though not actually a RAID level, Multipath allows for multiple access to the same device. Should one controller fail, another can be used to access the device. In effect, it provides controller-level redundancy. Support is implemented using the **mdadmd** daemon. This is started with the **mdadmd** service script:

```
sudo /etc/init.d/mdadmd start
```

RAID Devices and Partitions: md and fd

A RAID device is named an **md** and uses the MD driver. These devices are already defined on your Linux system in the **/etc/dev** directory, starting with **md0**: **/dev/md0** is the first RAID device, and **/dev/md1** is the second, and so on. Each RAID device, in turn, uses hard disk partitions, where each partition contains an entire hard disk. These partitions are usually referred to as *RAID disks*, whereas a RAID device is an array of the RAID disks it uses.

When creating a RAID partition, you should set the partition type to **fd**, instead of the 83 for the standard Linux partition. The **fd** type is used by RAID for automatic detection.

Booting from a RAID Device

Usually, as part of the installation process, you can create RAID devices from which you can also boot your system. Your Linux system will be configured to load RAID kernel support and automatically detect RAID devices. The boot loader will be installed on your RAID device—that is, all the hard disks making up that device.

Most Linux distributions do not support booting from RAID 5, only RAID 1. This means that if you want to use RAID 5 and still boot from RAID disks, you will need to create at least two (or more if you want) RAID devices using corresponding partitions for each device across your hard disks. One device would hold your **/boot** partition and be installed as a RAID 1 device. This RAID 1 device would be the first RAID device, **md0**, consisting of the first partition on each hard disk. The second RAID device, **md1**, could then be a RAID 5 device and would consist of corresponding partitions on the other hard disks. Your system could then boot from the RAID 1 device but use the RAID 5 device.

If you do not create RAID disks during installation but instead create them later and want to boot from them, you must ensure that your system is configured correctly. The RAID devices need to be created with persistent superblocks, and support for the RAID devices has to be enabled in the kernel. On Linux distributions, this support is enabled as a module. Difficulties occur if you are using RAID 5 for your / (root) partition. This partition contains the RAID 5 module, but to access the partition, you must load the RAID 5 module.

To work around this limitation, you can create a RAM disk in the **/boot** partition that contains the RAID 5 module. Use the **mkinitrd** command to create the RAM disk and the **--with** option to specify the module to include:

```
mkinitrd --preload raid5 --with=raid5 raid-ramdisk 2.6.24-10
```

RAID Administration: mdadm

You use the **mdadm** tool to manage and monitor RAID devices. The **mdadm** tool is an all-purpose means of creating, monitoring, administering, and fixing RAID devices. You can run commands directly to create and format RAID disks. It also runs as a daemon to monitor and detect problems with the devices.

The **mdadm** tool has seven different modes of operation, each with its own set of options, including **monitor** with the **-f** option to run it as a daemon, or **create** with the **-l** option to set a RAID level for a disk. Table 24-3 lists the different modes of operation. Check the **mdadm** man page for a detailed listing of the options for each mode.

Creating and Installing RAID Devices

If you created your RAID devices and their partitions during the installation process, you should already have working RAID devices. Your RAID devices will be configured in the **/etc/mdadm.conf** file, and the status of your RAID devices will be listed in the **/proc/mdstat** file. You can manually start or stop your RAID devices with the **raidstart** and **mdadm** commands. The **-a** option operates on all of them, though you can specify particular devices if you want.

To create a new RAID device manually for an already installed system, follow these steps:

1. Make sure that your kernel supports the RAID level you want for the device you are creating.

2. If you have not already done so, create the RAID disks (partitions) you will use for your RAID device.

3. Create your RAID device with **mdadm** command in the build or create mode. The array will also be activated.

Mode	Description
assemble	Assembles RAID array from devices
build	Builds array without per-device superblocks
create	Builds array with per-device superblocks
manage	Manages array devices, adding or removing disks
misc	Performs specific operations on a device, such as making it read only
monitor	Monitors arrays for changes and acts on them (used for RAID 1, 4, 5, 6)
grow	Changes array size, as when replacing smaller devices with larger ones

TABLE 24-3   mdadm Modes

4. Alternatively, you can configure your RAID device (**/dev/md***n*) in the **/etc/mdadm.conf** file, specifying the RAID disks to use, and then use the **mdadm** command specifying the RAID device to create.

5. Create a file system on the RAID device (**mkfs**) and then mount it.

Adding a Separate RAID File System

If you just want to add a RAID file system to a system that already has a standard boot partition, you can dispense with the first RAID 1 partition. Given three hard disks to use for the RAID file system, you just need three partitions, one for each disk: **/dev/sda1**, **/dev/sdc1**, and **/dev/sdb1**.

```
ARRAY /dev/md0   devices=/dev/sda1, /dev/sdc1, /dev/sdb1  level=5 num-devices=2
```

You then create the array with the following command:

```
mdadm -C /dev/md0 -n3 /dev/sda1 /dev/sdc1 /dev/sdb1 -l5
```

You can then format and mount your RAID device.

Creating Hard Disk Partitions: fd

To add new RAID devices or to create them in the first place, you need to create the hard disk partitions they will use manually and then configure RAID devices to use those partitions. To create a hard disk partition for use in a RAID array, use **fdisk** or **parted** and specify **fd** as the file system type. You invoke **fdisk** or **parted** with the device name of the hard disk on which the partition will be created. Be sure to specify **fd** as the partition type. The following example invokes **fdisk** for the hard disk **/dev/sdc** (the first hard disk on the secondary IDE connection):

```
fdisk /dev/sdc
```

Though technically partitions, these hard disk devices are referred to as *disks* in RAID configuration documentation and files.

NOTE *You can also use GParted or QtParted to create your hard disk partitions. These tools provide a GUI for* **parted** *(choose Applications | System Tools).*

Configuring RAID: /etc/mdadm.conf

Once you have created your disks, you need to configure them as RAID devices. RAID devices are configured in the **/etc/mdadm.conf** file, with options shown in Table 24-4. This file will be used by the **mdadm** command in the create mode to create the RAID device. In the **/etc/mdadm.conf** file, you create both **DEVICE** and **ARRAY** entries. The **DEVICE** entries list the RAID devices. The **ARRAY** entries list the RAID arrays and their options. This example implements a simple array on two disks. Serial ATA drives are used:

```
DEVICE  /dev/sda1 /dev/sdb1
```

Directive or Option	Description
DEVICE devices-list	Partitions and drives used for RAID devices.
ARRAY	Array configuration section for a particular RAID device.
level=num	The RAID level for the RAID device, such as 0, 1, 4, 5, and −1 (linear).
devices=disk-device-list	The disk devices (partitions) that make up the RAID array.
num-devices=count	Number of RAID devices in an array. Each RAID device section must have this directive; the maximum is 12.
spare-group=name	Text name for a spare group whose devices can be used for other arrays.
auto=option	Automatically create specified devices if they do not exist. You can create traditional nonpartitioned (**yes** or **md** option) or the newer partitionable arrays (**mdp** or **part** option). For partitionable arrays the default is 4, which you can change.
super-minor	Minor number of the array superblock, same as md device number.
uuid=UUID-number	UUID identifier stored in array superblock, used to identify the RAID array. Can be used to reference an array in commands.
MAILADDR	Monitor mode, mail address where alerts are sent.
PROGRAM	Monitor mode, program to run when events occur.

TABLE 24-4   mdadm.conf Options

You can list more than one device for a **DEVICE** entry, as well as have separate **DEVICE** entries. You can also specify multiple devices using file matching symbols such as *, ?, and []. The following specifies all the partitions on **sda** drive as RAID devices:

```
DEVICE /dev/ sda*  /dev/sdb1
```

For an **ARRAY** entry, you specify the name of the RAID device you are configuring, such as **/dev/md0** for the first RAID device. You then add configuration options such as **devices** to list the partitions that make up the array, **level** for the RAID level, and **num-devices** for the number of devices. The following example configures the RAID array **/dev/md0** as three disks (partitions) using **/dev/sda2**, **/dev/sdc1**, and **/dev/sdb1** and is configured for RAID 5 (**level=5**).

```
ARRAY /dev/md0   devices=/dev/sda2, /dev/sdc1, /dev/sdb1  level=5 num-devices=3
```

Creating a RAID Array

You can create a RAID array by using options specified with the mdadm command or using configurations listed in the **/etc/mdadm.conf** file. Use of the **/etc/mdadm.conf** file is not required, though it does make RAID creation more manageable, especially for large or complex arrays. Once you have created your RAID devices, your RAID device will be automatically activated. The following command creates a RAID array, **/dev/md1**, using three devices, **/dev/sda1**, **/dev/sdc1**, and **/dev/sdb1**, at level 5.

```
mdadm --create /dev/md1 --raid-devices=3 /dev/sda1 /dev/sdc1 /dev/sdb1 --level=5
```

Each option has a corresponding short version, as shown in Table 24-5. The same command is shown here with single-letter options:

```
mdadm -C /dev/md1 -n3 /dev/sda1 /dev/sdc1 /dev/sdb1 -l5
```

If you have configured your RAID devices in the **/etc/mdadm.conf** file, you use the **mdadm** command in the create mode to create your RAID devices. **mdadm** takes as its argument the name of the RAID device, such as **/dev/md0** for the first RAID device. It then locates the entry for that device in the **/etc/mdadm.conf** file and uses that configuration information to create the RAID file system on that device. You can specify an alternative configuration file with the **-c** option, if you wish. **mdadm** operates as a kind of **mkfs** command for RAID devices, initializing the partitions and creating the RAID file systems. Any data on the partitions making up the RAID array will be erased.

```
mdadm  --create /dev/md0
```

Creating Spare Groups

Linux software RAID now allows RAID arrays to share their spare devices. This means that if arrays belong to the same spare group, a device that fails in one array can automatically use the spare in another array. Spare devices from any array can be used in another as needed. You set the spare group to which an array belongs to the **--spare-group** option. The **mdadm** monitoring mode will detect a failed device in an array and automatically replace it with a spare device from arrays in the same spare group. The first command in the next example creates a spare drive called **/dev/sdd1** for the **/dev/md0** array and labels it **mygroup**. In the second command, array **/dev/md1** has no spare drive but belongs to the same spare group as array **/dev/md0**. Should a drive in **/dev/md1** fail, it can automatically

Option	Description
-n --raid-devices	Number of RAID devices
-l --level	RAID level
-C --create	Create mode
-c --chunk	Chunk (stripe) size in powers of 2; default is 64KB
-x --spare-devices	Number of spare devices in the array
-z --size	Size of blocks used in devices, by default set to the smallest device if not the same size
-p --parity	The parity algorithm; left-symmetric is used by default

TABLE 24-5   The mdadm --create Options

use the spare device, **/dev/sdd1**, from **/dev/md0**. The following code lines are really two lines (truncated to fit on this page), each beginning with **mdadm:**

```
mdadm --create /dev/md0 --raid-devices=3 /dev/sda1 /dev/sdc1 -x
      /dev/sdd1 --level=1 --spare-group=mygroup
mdadm --create /dev/md1 --raid-devices=2 /dev/sda2 /dev/sdc2 --level=1
      --spare-group=mygroup
```

Creating a File System

Once the RAID devices are activated, you can create file systems on the RAID devices and mount those file systems. The following example creates a standard Linux file system on the **/dev/md0** device:

```
mkfs -t ext3 /dev/md0
```

In the following example, the user creates a directory called **/myraid** and mounts the RAID device there:

```
mkdir /myraid
mount /dev/md0 /myraid
```

If you plan to use your RAID device for maintaining your user directories and files, you mount the RAID device as your **/home** partition. Such a mounting point might normally be used if you created your RAID devices when installing your system. To transfer your current home directories to a RAID device, first back them up on another partition, and then mount your RAID device, copying your home directories to it.

Managing RAID Arrays

You can manage RAID arrays with the **mdadm** manage mode operations. In this mode you can add or remove devices in arrays, and mark devices as failed. The **--add** option lets you add a device to an active array, essentially a hot swap operation:

```
mdadm /dev/md0 --add /dev/sdd1
```

To remove a device from an active array, you first have to mark it as failed with the **--fail** option and then remove it with **--remove**:

```
mdadm /dev/md0 --fail /dev/sdb1 --remove /dev/sdb1
```

Starting and Stopping RAID Arrays

To start an already existing RAID array, you use **mdadm** command with the assemble mode (newly created arrays are automatically started). To do so directly on the command line requires that you also know what devices make up the array, listing them after the RAID array like so:

```
mdadm -A /dev/md1 /dev/sda2   /dev/sdb1
```

It is easier to configure your RAID arrays in the **/etc/mdadm.conf** file. With the scan option, **-s**, **mdadm** will then read array information from the **/etc/mdadm.conf** file. If you do not specify a RAID array, all arrays will be started.

```
mdadm -s /dev/md0
```

To stop a RAID array, you use the **-S** option:

```
mdadm -S /dev/md0
```

Monitoring RAID Arrays

As a daemon, **mdadm** is started and stopped using the **mdmonitor** service script in **/etc/init.d**. This invokes mdadm in the monitor mode, detecting any problems that arise and logging reports as well as taking appropriate action:

```
service mdadm start
```

You can monitor devices directly by invoking **mdadm** with the monitor mode:

```
mdadm --monitor /dev/md0
```

Monitor-related options can be set in the **/etc/mdadm.conf** file. **MAILADDR** sets the mail address where notification of RAID events are sent. **PROGRAM** sets the program to use if events occur.

If you decide to change your RAID configuration or add new devices, you first have to deactivate your currently active RAID devices. To deactivate a RAID device, you use the **mdadm** command in the misc mode. Be sure to close any open files and unmount any file systems on the device first. Here's an example:

```
umount /dev/md0
mdadm -S /dev/md0
```

Configuring Bootable RAID

Bootable RAID devices use RAID level 0 or 1. In the following example, the first array holds only the boot partition and uses RAID level 1, whereas the second array uses three partitions and is set to RAID level 5:

```
ARRAY /dev/md0    devices=/dev/sda1   level=1 num-devices=1
ARRAY /dev/md1    devices=/dev/sda2, /edev/sdc1, /dev/sdb1   level=5 num-devices=3
```

This example configures the RAID array **/dev/md0** as a RAID 1 (**level=1**) device. Two disks (partitions) make up the second RAID array, **/dev/md1** using **/dev/sda2** and **/dev/sdb1**. It is configured for RAID 5 (**level=5**).

You can create a RAID array either using options specified with the **mdadm** command or using configurations listed in the **/etc/mdadm.conf** file. Use of the **/etc/mdadm.conf** file is not required, though it does make RAID creation more manageable, especially for large or complex arrays. Once you have created your RAID devices, your RAID device will be automatically activated. The following command creates a RAID array, **/dev/md1**, using three devices, **/dev/sda2**, **/edev/sdc1**, and **/dev/sdb1**, at level 5:

```
mdadm --create /dev/md1 --raid-devices=3 /dev/sda2  /edev/sdc1 /dev/sdb1 --level=5
```

Each option has a corresponding short version, as shown earlier in Table 24-4. The same command is shown here using single-letter options:

```
mdadm -C /dev/md1 -n3 /dev/sda2  /edev/sdc1 /dev/sdb1 -l5
```

For the first array in the previous example you use this:

```
mdadm -C /dev/md0 -n1 /dev/sda1 -l1
```

Devices and Modules

All devices, such as printers, terminals, and CD-ROMs, are connected to your Linux operating system through special files called *device files.* Such files contain all the information your operating system needs to control the specified device. This design introduces great flexibility. The operating system is independent of the specific details for managing a particular device because the specifics are all handled by the device file. The operating system simply informs the device what task it is to perform, and the device file tells it how. If you change devices, you have to change only the device file, not the whole system.

To install a device on your Linux system, you need a device file for it, software configuration such as that provided by a configuration tool, and kernel support that is usually supplied by a module or support that is already compiled and built into the kernel. Device files are not handled in a static way. They are dynamically generated as needed by udev and managed by the Hardware Abstraction Layer (HAL). Before udev and HAL were available, a device file was created for each possible device, leading to a large number of device files in the **/etc/dev** directory. Now your system will detect only those devices it uses and create device files for those devices only, for a much smaller listing of device files. Both udev and HAL are hotplug systems, with udev designed for creating devices and HAL designed for providing information about them and managing the configuration for removable devices, such as those with file systems like USB card readers and CD-ROMs.

With udev and HAL, Managing devices in Ubuntu is at the same time easier but much more complex. You now have to use udev and HAL to configure devices, though much of this is now automatic. Device information is maintained in a special device file system called **sysfs** located at **/sys**. This is a virtual file system like **/proc** and is used to keep track of all devices supported by the kernel. Several of the resources you might need to consult and directories you might need to use are listed in Table 25-1.

The sysfs File System: /sys

The system file system is designed to hold detailed information about system devices. This information can be used by hotplug tools such as udev to create device interfaces as they are needed. Instead of having a static and complete manual configuration for a device, the **sysfs** system maintains configuration information about the device, which is then used as needed by the hotplugging system to create device interfaces when a device is attached to the system.

Resource	Description
/sys	The **sysfs** file system listing configuration information for all the devices on your system
/proc	An older process file system listing kernel information, including device information
http://kernel.org/pub/linux/docs/ device-list/devices.txt	Linux device names Web site
http://kernel.org/pub/linux/utils/kernel/ hotplug/udev.html	The udev Web site
/etc/udev	The udev configuration directory
http://freedesktop.org/wiki/Software/hal	The HAL Web site
/etc/hal	The HAL configuration directory
/usr/share/hal/fdi	The HAL device information files, for configuring HAL information support and policies
/etc/hal/fdi	The HAL system administrator's device information files

TABLE 25-1   Device Resources

More and more devices are now removable, and many (cameras, for example) are meant to be attached temporarily. Instead of maintaining separate static and dynamic methods for configuring devices, Linux distributions make all devices structurally hotplugged.

The **sysfs** file system is a virtual file system that provides a hierarchical map of your kernel-supported devices such as PCI devices, buses, and block devices, as well as supporting kernel modules. The **class** subdirectory will list all your supported devices by category, such as net and sound devices. With **sysfs** your system can easily determine the device file with which a particular device is associated. This is very helpful for managing removable devices as well as dynamically managing and configuring devices as HAL and udev do. The **sysfs** file system is used by udev to generate needed device files dynamically in the **/dev** directory, as well as by HAL to manage removable device files as needed. The **/sys** file system type is **sysfs**. The **/sys** subdirectories organize your devices into different categories. The file system is used by **systool** to display a listing of your installed devices. The tool is part of the **sysfsutils** package (universe repository). Use the following command to list all your system devices:

```
systool
```

Like **/proc**, the **/sys** directory resides only in memory, but it is still mounted in the **/etc/fstab** file.

The proc File System: /proc

The **/proc** file system is an older file system that is used to maintain information about kernel processes, including devices. It maintains special information files for your devices, though many of these are now supported by the **sysfs** file system. The **/proc/devices** file

File	Description
/proc/devices	Lists the device drivers configured for the currently running kernel
/proc/dma	Displays the DMA channels currently used
/proc/interrupts	Displays the IRQs (interrupts) in use
/proc/ioports	Shows the I/O ports in use
/proc/pci	Lists PCI devices
/proc/asound	Lists sound devices
/proc/ide	Directory for IDE devices
/proc/net	Directory for network devices

TABLE 25-2   /proc Device Information Files

lists your installed character and block devices along with their major numbers. Interrupt requests (IRQs), direct memory access (DMA) channels, and I/O ports currently used for devices are listed in the **interrupts**, **dma**, and **ioports** files, respectively. Certain files list information covering several devices, such as **pci**, which lists all your PCI devices, and **sound**, which lists all your sound devices. The **sound** file lists detailed information about your sound card. Several subdirectories, such as **net**, **ide**, and **scsi**, contain information files for different devices. Certain files hold configuration information that can be changed dynamically, such as the IP packet–forwarding capability and the maximum number of files. You can change these values with the **sysctl** tool (System | Tools | Kernel Tuning) or by manually editing certain files. Table 25-2 lists several device-related **/proc** files.

udev: Device Files

Devices are *hotpluggable,* meaning they can be easily attached and removed. Their configuration is dynamically detected and does not rely on manual administrative settings. The hotplug tool used to detect device files is udev, user devices. Each time your system is booted, udev automatically detects your devices and generates device files for them in the **/etc/dev** directory. This means that the **/etc/dev** directory and its files are recreated each time you boot. It is a dynamic directory, no longer static. udev uses a set of rules to direct how device files are to be generated, including any corresponding symbolic links. These are located in the **/etc/udev/rules.d** file. You can find out more about udev at **http://kernel.org/pub/linux/utils/kernel/hotplug/udev.html**.

As part of the hotplug system, udev will automatically detect kernel devices that are added or removed from the system. When the device interface is first created, its corresponding **sysfs** file is located and read, determining any additional attributes such as serial numbers and device major and minor numbers that can be used to uniquely identify the device. These can be used as keys in udev rules to create the device interface. Once the device is created, it is listed in the udev database, which keeps track of currently installed devices.

If a device is added, udev is called by hotplug. It checks the **sysfs** file for that device for the major and minor numbers, if provided. It then uses the rules in its rules file to create the device file and any symbolic links to create the device file in **/dev**, with permissions specified for the device in the udev permissions rules.

As **/etc/dev** is now dynamic, any changes you make manually to the **/etc/dev** directory will be lost when you reboot. This includes the creation of any symbolic links you might create manually, such as **/dev/cdrom** that many software applications use. Instead, such symbolic links have to be configured in the udev rules files, located in the **/etc/udev/rules.d** directory. Default rules are already in place for symbolic links, but you can create rules to add your own.

udev Configuration

The configuration file for udev is **/etc/udev/udev.conf**. Here are set global udev options such as the location of the udev database; the defaults for device permissions, owner, and group; and the location of udev rules files. The udev tool uses the udev **rules.d** file to create your device files dynamically.

CAUTION *Be very careful in making any changes, particularly to rules file locations. Support for all devices on your system relies on these rules.*

Device Names and udev Rules: /etc/udev/rules.d

The name of a device file is designed to reflect the device's task. Printer device files begin with **lp** for *line print*. Because you can have more than one printer connected to your system, the particular printer device files are distinguished by two or more numbers or letters following the prefix **lp**, such as **lp0**, **lp1**, **lp2**. The same is true for terminal device files, which begin with the prefix **tty**, for *teletype*; they are further distinguished by numbers or letters such as **tty0**, **tty1**, **ttyS0**, and so on. You can obtain a complete listing of the current device filenames and the devices for which they are used from the **kernel.org** Web site at **http://kernel.org/pub/linux/docs/device-list/devices.txt**.

With udev, device names are determined dynamically by rules listed in the udev rules files at **/etc/udev/rules.d**. The rules files in this directory are generated by your system during installation. *You should never edit them.* If you need to add rules of your own, you should create your own rules file. The rules files are named, beginning with a number to establish priority. They are read sequentially, with the first rules overriding any conflicting later ones. All rules files have a **.rules** extension. Rules can be organized in three general categories: names, permissions/ownership, and symbolic links. In addition various specialized categories are used for certain kinds of devices such as faxes and some mice. On Ubuntu and Debian, the general categories are held in separate file: **20-names.rules**, **40-permissions.rules**, and **60-symlink.rules**. Other rules files are set up for more specialized devices, such as **60-rules-libsane** for scanners, **60-rules-libmtp** for music players, **60-pcmcia .rules** for PCMCIA devices, and **90-alsa.rules** for the sound driver. The **70-persistent-net.rules** sets up your network devices.

The rules files already present in the **rules.d** directory have been provided for your Linux distribution and are designed specifically for it. To customize your setup, create your own separate rules files in **/etc/udev/rules.d.** In your rules file, you normally define only symlinks, using SYMLINK fields alone, as described in the following sections. These set up symbolic links to devices, letting you access them with other device names. NAME fields are used to create the original device interface, a task usually left to udev itself.

CAUTION *You should never modify the rules in the **rules.d** directory.*

Each line maps a device attribute to a device name and specifies any symbolic names (links). Attributes are specified using keys, and more than one key can be used. If all the keys match a device, the associated name is used for it and a device file of that name will be generated. An assignable key, such as NAME for the device name or SYMLINK for a symbolic name, is used to assign the matched value. Instead of listing a device name, a program or script may be specified to generate the name. This is often the case for DVD/CD-ROM devices, where the device name could be a dvdwriter, cdwriter, cdrom, or dvdrom.

The rules consist of a comma-separated list of fields. A field consists of a matching or assignable key. The matching keys use the == and != operators to compare for equality and inequality. The *, ?, and [] operators can match any characters, any single character, or a class of characters, just as in the shell. The assignable keys can use the =, +=, and := operators to assign values. The = operator assigns a single value, the += appends the value to those already assigned, and the := operator makes an assignment final, preventing later changes. The udev keys are listed in Table 25-3. Check the udev man page for detailed descriptions.

Matching Keys	Description
ACTION	Match the event action.
DEVPATH	Match the device path.
ENV{key}	Match an environment variable value.
BUS	Match the bus type of the device. (The sysfs device bus must be able to be determined by a "device" symlink.)
DRIVER	Match the device driver name.
ID	Match the device number on the bus, for instance, the PCI bus ID.
KERNEL	Match the kernel device name.
PROGRAM	Use an external program to determine the device. This key is valid if the program returns successful. The string returned by the program may be additionally matched with the RESULT key.
RESULT	Match the returned string of the last PROGRAM call. This key may be used in any following rule after a PROGRAM call.
SUBSYSTEM	Match the device subsystem.
SYSFS{{filename}}	Match the sysfs device attribute, for instance, a label, vendor, USB serial number, SCSI UUID, or file system label.
Assignable Keys	Description
NAME	The name of the node to be created, or the name the network interface should be renamed to.
OWNER, GROUP, MODE	The permissions for the device.
PLACE	Match the location on the bus, such as the physical port of a USB device.
ENV{key}	Export a variable to an environment.
IMPORT{type}	Import results of a program, contents of a text file, or stored keys in a parent device. The type can be **program**, **file**, or **parent**.
SYMLINK	The name of the symbolic link (symlink) for the device.
RUN	Add program to list of programs to be run by the device.

TABLE 25-3 udev Rule Keys

The key fields such as KERNEL support pattern matching to specify collections of devices. For example, **mouse*** will match all devices beginning with the pattern *mouse*. The following field uses the KERNEL key to match on all mouse devices as listed by the kernel:

```
KERNEL=="mouse*"
```

The next key will match on all printer devices numbered **lp0** through **lp9**. It uses brackets to specify a range of numbers or characters, in this case 0 through 9, **[0-9]**:

```
KERNEL=="lp[0-9]*"
```

The NAME, SYMLINK, and PROGRAM fields support string substitution codes similar to the way printf codes work. Such a code is preceded by a **%** symbol. The code allows several possible devices and names to be referenced in the same rule. Table 25-4 lists the supported codes.

The udev man page provides many examples of udev rules using various fields. The **20-names.rules** files hold rules that primarily use KERNEL keys to designate devices. The KERNEL key is followed by either a NAME key to specify the device filename or a SYMLINK key to set up a symbolic link for a device file. The following rule uses the KERNEL key to match on all mouse devices as listed by the kernel. Corresponding device names are placed in the **/dev/input** directory, and the name used is the kernel name for the device (**%k**):

```
KERNEL=="mouse*",  NAME="input/%k"
```

This rule uses both a SUBSYSTEMS key and a KERNEL key to set up device files for USB printers, whose kernel names will be used to create device files in **/dev/usb**:

```
SUBSYSTEMS=="usb", KERNEL=="lp[0-9]*", NAME="usb/%k"
```

Substitution Code	Description
%n	The kernel number of the device
%k	The kernel name for the device
%M	The kernel major number
%m	The kernel minor number
%p	The device path
%b	The device name matched from the device path
%c	The string returned by a PROGRAM field (can't be used in a PROGRAM field)
%s{*filename*}	Content of **sysfs** attribute
%E{*key*}	Value of environment variable
%N	Name of a temporary device node, to provide access before real node is created
%%	Quotes the % character in case it is needed in the device name

TABLE 25-4   udev Substitution Codes

Symbolic Links

Certain device files are really symbolic links bearing common device names that are often linked to the actual device file used. A *symbolic link* is another name for a file that is used like a shortcut, referencing that file. Common devices such as printers, CD-ROM drives, hard drives, SCSI devices, and sound devices, along with many others, will have corresponding symbolic links. For example, a **/dev/cdrom** symbolic link links to the actual device file used for your CD-ROM. If your CD-ROM is an IDE device, it may use the device file **hdc**. In this case, **/dev/cdrom** is a link to **/dev/hdc**. In effect, **/dev/cdrom** is another name for **/dev/hdc**. Serial ATA DVD/CD drives will be linked to **scd** devices, such as **scd0** for the first Serial ATA CD/DVD drive. If your drive functions both as a CD and DVD writer and reader, several links will exist to the same device. In this case the links **cdrom**, **cdrw**, **cdwriter**, **dvd**, **dvdrw**, and **dvdwriter** will all link to the same CD/DVD RW-ROM device.

A **/dev/modem** link file also exists for your modem. If your modem is connected to the second serial port, its device file will be **/dev/ttyS1**. In this case, **/dev/modem** will be a link to that device file. Applications can then use **/dev/modem** to access your modem instead of having to know the actual device file used. Table 25-5 lists commonly used device links.

Symbolic links are created by udev using the **SYMLINK** field. The symbolic links for a device can be listed either with the same rule creating a device file (**NAME** key) or in a separate rule that will specify only a symbolic link. The inclusion of the **NAME** key does not have to be specific, if the default device name is used. The **+** added to the **=** symbol will automatically create the device with the default name, not requiring an explicit **NAME** key in the rule. The following rule is for parallel printers. It includes both the default name and implied **NAME** key creating the device (**+**) and a symbolic link, **par**. The **%n** will add a number to the symbolic link such as **par1**, **par2**, and so on.

```
KERNEL=="lp[0-9]*",     SYMLINK+="par%n"
```

Link	Description
cdrom	Link to your CD-ROM device file, set in **/etc/udev/rules.d**
dvd	Link to your DVD-ROM device file, set in **/etc/udev/rules.d**
cdwriter	Link to your CD-R or CD-RW device file, set in **/etc/udev/rules.d**
dvdwriter	Link to your DVD-R or DVD-RW device file, set in **/etc/udev/rules.d**
modem	Link to your modem device file, set in **/etc/udev/rules.d**
floppy	Link to your floppy device file, set in **/etc/udev/rules.d**
tape	Link to your tape device file, set in **/etc/udev/rules.d**
scanner	Link to your scanner device file, set in **/etc/udev/rules.d**
mouse	Link to your mouse device file, set in **/etc/udev/rules.d**
tape	Link to your tape device file, set in **/etc/udev/rules.d**

TABLE 25-5 Device Symbolic Links

Should you want to create more than one symbolic link for a device, you can list them in the **SYMLINK** field. The following creates two symbolic links, one named **cdrom** and another named **cdrom-** with the kernel name attached (**%k**):

```
SYMLINK+="cdrom cdrom-%k"
```

In the **70-persistent-cd.rules** files you will find several **SYMLINK** fields for optical devices, one of which is shown here:

```
SYMLINK+="dvd"
```

Symbolic links for CD/DVD aliases are generated for you automatically using a rules generator file, **75-cd-aliases-generator**. You should not have to create any symbolic links for CD/DVD aliases, including removable ones (such as USB/Firewire).

If you decide to set up a separate rule that specifies just a symbolic link, the symbolic link will be kept on a list awaiting the creation of its device. This also allows you to add other symbolic links for a device in other rules files. This situation can be confusing because symbolic links can be created for devices that are not yet generated. The symbolic links will be defined and held until needed, when the device is generated. This is why you can have many more **SYMLINK** rules than **NAME** rules in udev that actually set up device files. In the case of removable devices, they will not have a device name generated until they are connected.

In most cases, you will need symbolic links only for devices, using the official symbolic names. Most of these are already defined for you. Should you need to create just a symbolic link, you can create a **SYMLINK** rule for it. However, a new **SYMLINK** rule needs to be placed before the name rules that name that device. The **SYMLINK** rules for a device are read by udev and kept until a device is named. Then those symbolic names can be used for that device. You can have as many symbolic links for the same device as you want, meaning that you could have several **SYMLINK** rules for the same device. When the **NAME** rule for the device is encountered, the previous **SYMLINK** keys are simply appended.

Persistent Rules

The default name rules will provide names for your devices using the official symbolic names reserved for them, for instance, **lp**n for printer, where n is the number of the printer. For fixed devices, such as fixed printers, this is normally adequate. However, for removable devices, such as USB printers that may be attached in different sequences at different times to USB ports, the names used may not refer to the same printer. For example, if you have two USB printers, an Epson and Canon, and you attach the Epson first and the Canon second, the Epson will be given the name **usb/lp0** and the Canon will have the name **usb/lp1**. If, however, you later detach them and reattach the Canon first and the Epson second, then the Canon will have the name **usb/lp0** and the Epson will have **usb/lp1**. The particular device needs to be correctly identified no matter what connection it is attached to.

To correctly identify a device always, udev uses persistent names. The rules for these names are held in the persistent names files. Currently persistent rule files are used for storage, tape, input, CD, and network devices. The input device persistent rules are held in the **65-input-persistent.rules** file and the storage rules are in the **65-storage-persistent.rules** file. Persistent rules for network devices are in the **70-persistent-net.rules** file and CD/DVD devices are in the **70-persistent-cd.rules** file.

Generated Rules

Devices can have their rules determined using *generator rules* files. These generator rules make use of udev scripts and programs in the **/lib/udev** directory to identify the devices. Network device rules are determined using generator files. Entries for persistent rules files for network devices are created by their generator rules. Any additional rules you want to set up for network devices can also be placed in the network persistent rules file. You must add a generated field, **ENV{GENERATED} = "1"**, at the end of any of your own rules.

The persistent rules file for network interfaces is **75-persistent-net-generator.rules** and the persistent network interface file is **70-persistent-net.rules**. The generator rules file determines the MAC address of the network device and then invokes the **write_net_rules** script in **/lib/udev** to determine the rule. The rule is placed in the **70-persistent-net.rules** file. You will find the entries here for your Ethernet connections, such as **eth0**.

Symbolic links (aliases) for CD/DVD devices are also created by a generator rules file, **75-cd-aliases-generator**. This file is run for devices that have no rule for persistent names. These rules are placed in the **70-persistent-cd.rules** file. For USB- and Firewire-connected CD/DVDs, the generator file invokes the **write_cd_rules** script with the **by-id** option to uniquely identify the CD/DVD device using its device ID, such as a serial number or model. Other CD/DVDs have symbolic names generated using just the **write_cd_rules** program with no option, which defaults to a **by-path** option. This option identifies the device by its pathname on the system and is useful for fixed attached CD/DVD devices.

Creating udev Rules

Default rules for your devices are placed by udev in the **/etc/udev/rules.d/50-udev.rules** or **/etc/udev/rules.d/20-names.rules** file. You should never edit this file, though you can check it to see how device naming is handled. This file will create the device files using the official kernel names. These names are often referenced directly by applications that expect to find devices with these particular names, such as **lp0** for a printer device.

If you want to create rules of your own, you should place them in a separate rules file. The **NAME** rules that name devices are read lexically, where the first **NAME** rule will take precedence over any later ones. Only the first **NAME** rule for a device will be used. Later **NAME** rules for that same device will be ignored. Keep in mind that a **SYMLINK** rule with a += includes a **NAME** rule for the default device, even though the **NAME** field is not explicitly shown.

Since rules are being created that are meant to replace the default rules, they would have to be run first. To do this, you place them in a rules file that begins with a very low number, say 10. Such a rules file would be executed before the **20-names.rules** file, which holds the default rules. Rules files are read in lexical order, with the lower numbers read first. You can create a file called **10-user.rules** in the **/etc/udev/rules.d** directory in which you place your own rules. Conversely, if you want rules that will run only if the defaults fail for some reason, you can use a rules file numbered after 50, such as **96-mydefaults.rules**.

The upcoming section "Manually Creating Persistent Names: udevinfo" describes how to create a **canon-pr** rule to replace the default printer rule for that printer. The new user **canon-pr** rule would be placed in a **10-user.rules** file to be executed before the printer rules in the **20-names.rules** files, thereby taking precedence. The default printer rule in the **20-names.rules** files (shown here) would not be applied to the Canon printer:

```
SUBSYTEM="usb", KERNEL="lp[0-9]*", NAME="usb/%k"
```

SYMLINK Rules

You can also create your own rules that only create symbolic links. However, these need to be placed before the name rules that name the devices. These SYMLINK rules are read by udev and kept until a device is named, then all the symbolic names will be used for that device. You can have as many symbolic links as you want for the same device, meaning that you can have several SYMLINK rules for the same device. When the NAME rule for the device is encountered, the previous **SYMLINK** keys are simply appended.

Most standard symbolic names are already defined. If you always know the name for a device, you can easily add a SYMLINK rule. For example, if you know your DVD-ROM is attached to the first secondary IDE connection (**hdc**), you can create a symbolic name of your own choosing with a **SYMLINK** rule. In the next example a new symbolic link, **mydvdrom**, is created for the DVD-ROM on the **/dev/hdc** device:

```
KERNEL=="hdc",      SYMLINK="mydvdrom"
```

For a **SYMLINK** rule to be used, it must occur before a **NAME** rule that names the device. You should place these rules in a file that will precede the **20-names.rules** or **60-symlink.rules** files, such as **10-user.rules**.

Manually Creating Persistent Names: udevinfo

The key task in creating a persistent name is to use unique information to identify the device. You then create a rule that references the device with the unique information to identify it, and then name it with an official name, and then add a unique symbolic name. You can then use the unique symbolic name, such as **canon-pr**, to reference just that printer always and no other, when it is plugged in. In this example, unique information such as the Canon printer serial number is used to identify the Canon printer. It is next named with the official name, **usb/lp0** or **usb/lp1**, depending on whether another printer was plugged in first, and then it is given a unique symbolic name, **canon-pr**, which will reference that official name, whatever it may be. Keeping the official name, such as **lp0**, preserves standard access to the device as used by many applications.

You use **/sys** file system information about the device to detect the correct device to reference with the symbolic link. Unique **/sys** device information such as the vendor serial number or the vendor name can be used to uniquely reference the device. To obtain this information, you first need to query the **/sys** file system. You do this with the **udevinfo** command.

First you will need to know where the device is located in the **/sys** file system. You plug in your device, which will be automatically configured, and name it, using the official name. For example, plugging in the USB printer will create a **/dev/usb/lp0** device name for it. You can use this device name to find out where the USB printer information is in **/sys**. Use the **udevinfo** command with the **-q path** option to query for the **/sys** pathname, and add the **-n** option with the device's full pathname to identify the device you are searching for. The following command will display the **/sys** path for the printer with the device name **lp0**. In this case, the device is in the **class** subdirectory under **usb**. The path will assume **/sys**.

```
udevinfo -q path -n  /dev/usb/lp0
  /class/usb/lp0
```

Once you have the device's **/sys** path, you can use that path to display information about it. Use the **udevinfo** command again with the **-a** option to display all information about the device and the **-p** option to specify its path in the **/sys** file system. The listing can be extensive, so you should pipe the output to **less** or redirect it to a file:

```
udevinfo -a  -p  /sys/class/usb/lp0 | less
```

Some of the key output to look for is the bus used and information such as the serial number, product name, or manufacturer, as shown next. Look for information that uniquely identifies the device, such as the serial number. Some devices will support different buses, and the information may be different for each. Be sure to use the information for that bus when setting up your keys in the udev rule.

```
BUS="usb"
ATTRS{serial}="300HCR"
ATTRS{manufacturer}="Canon"
ATTRS{idproduct}="1074"
ATTRS{product}="S330"
```

You can use much of this information in an **ATTRS** (attributes) key in an udev rule to identify the device. The **ATTRS** key is used to obtain **/sys** information about a device. You use the **ATTRS** key with the field you want referenced placed in braces. You can then match that field to a value to reference the particular device you want. Use the **=** sign and a valid field value to match against. Once you know the **/sys** serial number of a device, you can use it in **ATTRS** keys in udev rules to reference the device uniquely. The following key checks the serial number of the devices field for the Canon printer's serial number:

```
ATTRS{serial}=="300HCR"
```

A user rule can now be created for the Canon printer.

In another rules file, you can add your own symbolic link using **/sys** information to uniquely identify the printer and name the device with its official kernel name. The first two keys, **BUS** and **ATTRS**, specify the particular printer. In this case the serial number of the printer is used to uniquely identify it. The **NAME** key will name the printer using the official kernel name, always referenced with the **%k** code. Since this is a USB printer, its device file will be placed in the **usb** subdirectory, **usb/%k**. Then the **SYMLINK** key defines the unique symbolic name to use, in this case **canon-pr** in the **/dev/usb** directory:

```
BUS=="usb", ATTRS{serial}=="300HCR", NAME="usb/%k", SYMLINK="usb/canon-pr"
```

The rules are applied dynamically in real time. To run a new rule, simply attach your USB printer (or detach and reattach). You will see the device files automatically generated.

Permission Fields: MODE, GROUP, OWNER

Permissions that will be given to different device files are determined by the permission fields in the udev rules. The permission rules are located in the **40-permissions.rules** file. The **MODE** field is a octal-bit permission setting, the same that is used for file permissions. Usually this is set to 660, owner and group read/write permission. Pattern matching is supported with the *****, **?**, and **[]** operators.

USB printer devices use the **lp** group with mode 660:

```
KERNEL=="usb/lp*",      GROUP="lp", MODE="0660"
```

Tape devices use the disk group:

```
KERNEL=="npt*",     GROUP="disk", MODE="0660"
```

The default settings set the **OWNER** and **GROUP** to root with owner read/write permissions (600):

```
KERNEL=="*",      OWNER="root" GROUP="root", MODE="0600"
```

Hardware Abstraction Layer

The purpose of HAL is to abstract the process of applications accessing devices. Applications should not have to know anything about a device, even its symbolic name. The application should just have to request a device of a certain type, and then a service, such as HAL, should provide what is available. With HAL, device implementation is hidden from applications.

HAL makes devices easily available to desktops and applications using a D-BUS (device bus) structure. Devices are managed as objects that applications can easily access. The D-BUS service is provided by the HAL daemon, **haldaemon**. Interaction with the device object is provided by the **freedesktop.org** HAL service, which is managed by the **/org/freedesktop/ HAL/Manager**.

HAL is an information service for devices. The HAL daemon maintains a dynamic database of connected hardware devices. This information can be used by specialized callout programs to maintain certain device configuration files. This is the case with managing removable storage devices. HAL will invoke the specialized callout programs that will use HAL information to manage devices dynamically. Removable devices such as CD-ROM discs or USB card readers are managed by specialized callouts with HAL information, detecting when such devices are attached. The situation can be confusing: Callout programs perform the actual tasks, but HAL provides the device information. For example, though the callout **hal-system-storage-mount** mounts a device, the options and mountpoints used for CD-ROM entries are specified in HAL device information files that set policies for storage management.

HAL has a key impact on the **/etc/fstab** file used to manage file systems. No longer are entries maintained in the **/etc/fstab** file for removable devices such as CD-ROMs. These devices are managed directly by HAL using its set of storage callouts such as **hal-storage-mount** to mount a device or **hal-storage-eject** to remove one. In effect, you now have to use the HAL device information files to manage your removable file systems.

HAL is a software project of freedesktop.org, which specializes in open source desktop tools. Check the latest HAL specification documentation at **www.freedesktop.org** under the **software/HAL** page for detailed explanations of how HAL works (see the specifications link on the HAL page: Latest HAL Specification). The documentation is very detailed and complete.

The HAL Daemon and hal-device-manager (hal-gnome)

The HAL daemon, **hald**, is run as the **haldaemon** process. Information provided by the HAL daemon for all your devices can be displayed using the HAL device manager, **hal-device-manager**, which is part of the **hal-gnome** package. You can access it, once installed, by choosing System | Administration | Hardware.

When you run the manager, it displays an expandable tree of your devices arranged by category in the left panel. The right panel displays information about the selected device. A Device tab lists the basic device information such as the vendor and the bus type. The Advanced tab lists the HAL device properties defined for this device, as described in later sections, as well as **/sys** file system paths for this device. For device controllers, a USB or PCI tab will appear. For example, a DVD writer could have an entry for the **storage.cdrom.cdr** property that says it can write CD-R discs. You may find an IDE CD/DVD-ROM device under IDE (some third-party IDE controllers may be labeled as SCSI devices). A typical entry would look like the following; the **bool** is the type of entry, namely Boolean:

```
storage.cdrom.cdr       bool      true
```

Numerical values may use an **int** type or a **strlist** type. The following **write_speed** property has a value **7056**:

```
storage.cdrom.write_speed      strlist      7056
```

The **/sys** file system path will also be a string. It will be preceded by a Linux property category. Strings will use a **strlist** type for multiple values and **string** for single values. The following entry locates the **/sys** file system path at **/sys/block/hdc**:

```
linux.sysfs_path    strlist   /sys/block/hdc
```

HAL Configuration: /etc/hal/fdi and /usr/share/hal/fdi

Information about devices and policies to manage devices are held in device information files in the **/etc/hal/fdi** and **/usr/share/hal/fdi** directories. In these directories, you set properties such as options that are to be used for CD-ROMs in **/etc/fstab**.

The implementation of HAL on Linux configures storage management by focusing on storage methods for mountable volumes, instead of particular devices. Volume properties define actions to take and valid options that can be used. Special callouts perform the actions directly, such as **hal-storage-mount** to mount media or **hal-storage-eject** to remove it.

Device Information Files: fdi

HAL properties for these devices are handled by device information files (**fdi**) in the **/usr/share/hal/fdi** and **/etc/hal/fdi** directories. The **/usr/share/hal/fdi** directory is used for configurations provided by the distribution, whereas **/etc/hal/fdi** is used for setting user administrative configurations. In both are listed subdirectories for the different kinds of information that HAL manages, such as **policy**, whose subdirectories have files with policies for how to manage devices. The files, known as *device information files*, have rules for obtaining information about devices, as well rules for detecting and assigning options for removable devices. The device information files use the extension **.fdi**, as in **storage-methods.fdi**. For example, the **policy** directory has two subdirectories: **10osvendor** and **20thirdpary**. The **10osvendor** holds the **fdi** files that have policy rules for managing removable devices on Linux (**10osvendor** replaces **90defaultpolicy** in earlier HAL versions). This directory holds the **20-storage-methods.fdi** policy file used for storage devices. Here you will find the properties that specify options for removable storage devices such as CD-ROMs. The directories begin with numbers, and lower numbers are read first. Unlike with udev, the last property read will override any previous property settings, so priority is given to higher-numbered directories and the **fdi** files they hold. This is why the default policies are in **10osvendor**, whereas the user policies, which override the defaults, are in a higher-numbered directory such as **30user**, as are third-party policies in **20thirdpolicy**.

Three device information file directories are set up in the device information file directories, each for different kinds of information: **information**, **policy**, and **preprobe**:

- **information** Contains information about devices.
- **policy** Contains setting policies such as storage policies. The default policies for a storage device are in a **20-storage-methods.fdi** file in the **policy/10osvendor** directory.
- **preprobe** Handles difficult devices such as unusual drives or drive configurations— for instance, those in **preprobe/10osvendor/10-ide-drives.fdi**. This contains information needed even before the device is probed.

Within these subdirectories are still other subdirectories indicating where the device information files come from, such as **vendor**, **thirdparty**, or **user**, and their priority. Certain critical files are listed here:

- **information/10freedesktop** Information provided by freedesktop.org
- **policy/10osvendor** Default policies (set by system administrator and OS distribution)
- **preprobe/10usevendor** Preprobe policies for difficult devices

Properties

Information for a device is specified with a *property* entry. Such entries consist of a key/value pair, where the key specifies the device and its attribute, and the value is for that attribute. Many kinds of values can be used, such as Boolean true/false, string values such as those used to specify directory mountpoints, or integer values.

Properties are classified according to metadata, physical connection, function, and policies. Metadata provides general information about a device, such as the bus it uses, its driver, or its HAL ID. Metadata properties begin with the key info, as in **info.bus**. Physical properties describe physical connections, namely the buses used. The IDE, PCI, and SCSI bus information is listed in **ide, pci**, and **scsi** keys. The **usb_device** properties are used for the USB bus; an example is **usb_device.number**.

The functional properties apply to specific kinds of devices. Here you will find properties for storage devices, such as the **storage.cdrom** keys that specify whether an optical device has writable capabilities. For example, the **storage.cdrom.cdr** key set to true will specify that an optical drive can write to CD-R discs.

The policies are not properties as such. Policies indicate how devices are to be handled and are, in effect, the directives that callout programs use to carry out tasks. Policies for storage media are handled using Volume properties, specifying methods (callouts) to use and valid options such as mount options. HAL uses scripts in the **/usr/share/hal/scripts** directory to manage media. The following abbreviated entries come from the **20-storage-methods.fdi** policy file. The first specifies the action to take and the second the callout script to execute, **hal-storage-mount**:

```
<append key="Volume.method_names" type="strlist">Mount</append>
<append key="Volume.method_execpaths" type="strlist">hal-storage-mount</append>
```

Mount options are designated using `volume.mount.valid_options` as shown here for `ro` (read only). Options that will be used will be determined when the mount callout is executed.

```
<append key="volume.mount.valid_options"type="strlist">ro</append>
```

Several of the commonly used volume policy properties are listed in Table 25-6.

Device Information File Directives

Properties are defined in directives listed in device information files. As noted, device information files have **.fdi** extensions. A directive is encased in greater-than (>) and less-than (<) symbols. There are three directives:

- **merge**   Merges a new property into a device's information database
- **append**   Appends or modifies a property for that device already in the database
- **match**   Tests device information values

A directive includes a type attribute designating the type of value to be stored, such as `string`, `bool`, `int`, and `double`. The `copy_property` type copies a property. The following discussion of the **storage-methods.fdi** file shows several examples of merge and match directives.

Property	Description
`volume.method.execpath`	Callout script to be run for a device
`volume.policy.desired_mount_point` (*string*)	The preferred mountpoint for the storage device
`volume.mount.valid_options.*` (*bool*)	Mount options to use for specific device, where * can be any mount option, such as **noauto** or **exec**
`volume.method_names`	Action to be taken
`volume.policy.mount_filesystem` (*string*)	File system to use when mounting a volume
`volume.mount.valid.mount_options.*` (*bool*)	Default mount options for volumes, where * can be any mount option, such as **noauto** or **exec**

TABLE 25-6   HAL Storage Policies

storage.fdi

The **20-storage-methods.fdi** file in the **/usr/share/hal/fdi/policy/10osvendor** directory lists the policies for your removable storage devices. This is where your options for storage volumes (for example, CD-ROM) entries are actually specified. The file is organized in sections beginning with particular types of devices to standard defaults. Keys are used to define options, such as **volume.mount.valid_options**, which will specify a mount option for a storage device such as a CD-ROM. Keys are also used to specify exceptions such as hotplugged devices.

The **20-storage-methods.fdi** file begins with default properties and then lists those properties for specific kinds of devices. Unless redefined in a later key, the default will remain in effect. The options you see listed for the default storage volumes will apply to CD-ROMs. For example, the **noexec** option is set as a valid default. The following sets **noexec** as a default mount option for a storage device. There are also entries for **ro** and **quiet**. The **append** operation adds the policy option.

```
<append key="volume.mount.valid_options"type="strlist">noexec</append>
```

The default mountpoint root directory for storage devices is now set by the mount callout script, **hal-storage-mount**. Currently this is **/media**. The default mountpoint is disk. HAL will try to use the Volume property information to generate a mountpoint.

The following example manages blank disks. Instead of being mounted, such disks can only be ejected. To determine possible actions, HAL uses **method_names**, **method_signatures**, and **method_execpaths** for the Volume properties. (The **org.freedesktop.Hal** prefix for the keys has been removed from this example to make it more readable, as in **org.freedesktop.Hal.Volume.method_names**.)

```
<match key="volume.disc.is_blank" bool="true">
<append key="info.interfaces"type="strlist">Volume</append>
<append key="Volume.method_names" type="strlist">Eject</append>
<append key="Volume.method_signatures" type="strlist">as</append>
<append key="Device.Volume.method_execpaths" type="strlist">
hal-storage-eject</append>
</match>
```

After dealing with special cases, the file system devices are matched, as shown here:

```
<match key="volume.fsusage" string="filesystem">
```

Storage devices to ignore, such as recovery partitions, are specified:

```
<merge key="volume.ignore" type="bool">false</merge>
```

Then the actions to take and the callout script to use are specified, such as the action for unmount that uses **hal-storage-mount**:

```
<append key="Device.Volume.method_names" type="strlist">Mount</append>
<append key="Device.Volume.method_signatures" type="strlist">ssas</append>
<append key="Device.Volume.method_execpaths" type="strlist">
hal-storage-mount</append>
```

Options are then specified with **volume.mount.valid_options**, starting with defaults and continuing with special cases, such as **ext3** shown here for access control lists (**acl**) and extended attributes (**xattr**):

```
<!-- allow these mount options for ext3 -->
<match key="volume.fstype" string="ext3">
<append key="volume.mount.valid_options"type="strlist">acl=</append>
<append key="volume.mount.valid_options"type="strlist">user_xattr=</append>
<append key="volume.mount.valid_options"type="strlist">data=</append>
 </match>
```

HAL Callouts

Callouts are programs invoked when the device object list is modified or when a device changes. As such, callouts can be used to maintain systemwide policy (that may be specific to the particular OS) such as changing permissions on device nodes, managing removable devices, or configuring the networking subsystem. Three different kinds of callouts are used for devices, capabilities, and properties. *Device* callouts are run when a device is added or removed. *Capability* callouts add or remove device capabilities, and *property* callouts add or remove a device's property. Callouts are implemented using **info.callout** property rules, such as that which invokes the **hal-storage-mount** callout when CD/DVD-ROMs are inserted or removed, as shown here:

```
<append key="org.freedesktop.Hal.Device.Volume.method_execpaths"
type="strlist">hal-storage-mount</append>
```

Callouts are placed in the **/usr/lib/hal** directory with the HAL callouts prefixed with **hal-**. Here you will find many of storage callouts used by HAL, such as **hal-storage-eject** and **hal-storage-mount**. HAL uses these callouts to manage removable devices such as DVD/CD-ROMs directly instead of editing entries in the **/etc/fstab** file (**fstab-sync** is no longer used). The **gnome-mount** tool used for mounting CD/DVD disk on the GNOME desktop uses the HAL callouts. Other supporting scripts can be found in the **/usr/lib/hal/scripts** directory.

Manual Devices

You can, if you wish, create device file interfaces manually using the **MAKEDEV** or **mknod** command. **MAKEDEV** is a script that can create device files for known fixed devices such as attached hard disks. Check the **MAKEDEV** man page for details. Ubuntu relies on aliases in the **/etc/modprobe.d** directory to manage most fixed devices: **/etc/modprobe.d/aliases**.

Linux implements several types of devices, the most common of which are block and character. A *block device,* such as a hard disk, transmits data a block at a time. A *character device,* such as a printer or modem, transmits data one character at a time, or rather as a continuous stream of data, not as separate blocks. Device driver files for character devices have a *c* as the first character in the permissions segment displayed by the **ls** command. Device driver files for block devices have a *b.* In the next example, **lp0** (the printer) is a character device and **sda1** (the hard disk) is a block device:

```
# ls -l sda1 lp0
brw-rw---- 1 root disk 3, 1 Jan 30 02:04 sda1
crw-rw---- 1 root lp   6, 0 Jan 30 02:04 lp0
```

The device type can be either *b, c, p,* or *u.* The *b* indicates a block device, and *c* is for a character device. The *u* is for an unbuffered character device, and the *p* is for a FIFO (first in, first out) device. Devices of the same type often have the same name; for example, serial interfaces all have the name **ttyS**. Devices of the same type are then uniquely identified by a number attached to the name. This number has two components: the major number and the minor number. Devices may have the same major number, but if so, the minor number is always different. This major and minor number structure is designed to deal with situations in which several devices may be dependent on one larger device, such as several modems connected to the same I/O card. All the modems will have the same major number that references the card, but each modem will have a unique minor number. Both the minor and major numbers are required for block and character devices (*b, c,* and *u*). They are not used for FIFO devices, however.

Valid device names along with their major and minor numbers are listed in the **devices.txt** file located in the **/Documentation** directory for the kernel source code, **/usr/src/linux-*ver*/ Documentation**. When you create a device, you use the major and minor numbers as well as the device name prefix for the particular kind of device you are creating. Most of these devices are already created for you and are listed in the **/etc/dev** directory.

Though the **MAKEDEV** command is preferable for creating device files, it can create only files for which it is configured. For devices not configured for use by **MAKEDEV**, you will have to use the **mknod** command. This is a lower level command that requires manual configuration of all its settings. With the **mknod** command you can create a device file in the traditional manner without any of the configuration support that **MAKEDEV** provides.

The **mknod** command can create either a character or block-type device. The **mknod** command has the following syntax:

```
mknod options device device-type major-num minor-num
```

As a simple example, creating a device file with **mknod** for a printer port is discussed here. Linux systems usually provide device files for printer ports (**lp0–2**). As an example, you can see how an additional port could be created manually with the **mknod** command. Printer devices are character devices and must be owned by the root and daemon. The permissions for printer devices are read and write for the owner and the group, 660. The major device number is set to 6, while the minor device number is set to the port number of the printer, such as 0 for LPT1 and 1 for LPT2. Once the device is created, you use **chown** to change its ownership to the root user, since only the administrator should control it. Change the group to **lp** with the **chgrp** command.

Most devices belong to their own groups, such as **disks** for hard disk partitions, **lp** for printers, **floppy** for floppy disks, and **tty** for terminals. In the next example, a printer device is made on a fourth parallel port, **lp3**. The **-m** option specifies the permissions—in this case, 660. The device is a character device, as indicated by the **c** argument following the device name. The major number is 6, and the minor number is 3. If you were making a device at **lp4**, the major number would still be 6, but the minor number would be 4. Once the device is made, the **chown** command then changes the ownership of the parallel printer device to **root**. For printers, be sure that a spool directory has been created for your device. If not, you need to make one. Spool directories contain files for data that varies according to the device output or input, like that for printers or scanners. As with all manual devices, the device file has to be placed in the **/etc/udev/devices** directory; udev will later put it in **/dev**.

```
# mknod -m 660 /etc/udev/devices/lp3 c 6 3
# chown root /etc/udev/devices/lp3
# chgrp lp /etc/udev/devices/lp3
```

Installing and Managing Terminals and Modems

In Linux, several users may be logged in at the same time. Each user needs his or her own terminal through which to access the Linux system, of course. The monitor on your PC acts as a special terminal, called the *console,* but you can add other terminals through either the serial ports on your PC or a special multiport card installed on your PC. The other terminals can be standalone terminals or PCs using terminal emulation programs. For a detailed explanation of terminal installation, see the **Term-HOWTO** file in **/usr/share/doc/HOWTO** or at the Linux Documentation Project site (**http://tldp.org**). A brief explanation is provided here.

Serial Ports

The serial ports on your PC are referred to as COM1, COM2, COM3, and COM4. These serial ports correspond to the terminal devices **/dev/ttyS0** through **/dev/ttyS3**. Note that several of these serial devices may already be used for other input devices such as your mouse and for communications devices such as your modem. If you have a serial printer, one of these serial devices is already used for that. If you installed a multiport card, you have many more ports from which to choose. For each terminal you add, udev will create the appropriate character device on your Linux system. The permissions for a terminal device are normally 660. *Terminal devices* are character devices with a major number of 4 and minor numbers usually beginning at 64.

> **TIP**   *The **/dev/pts** entry in the **/etc/fstab** file mount a **devpts** file system at **/dev/pts** for Unix98 Pseudo-TTYs. These pseudoterminals are identified by devices named by number.*

mingetty, mgetty, and getty

Terminal devices are managed by your system using the **getty** program and a set of configuration files. When your system starts, it reads the files of connected terminals in the Upstart **/etc/events.d** directory. Terminal files are prefixed with **tty** and have the terminal device number attached, such as **tty2**. The files executes an appropriate `getty` program for each terminal. These **getty** programs set up the communication between your Linux system and a specified terminal. You can install other **getty** applications to use instead, such as **mgetty** and **mingetty**. **mingetty** provides minimal support for virtual consoles. **mgetty** is designed for fax/modem connections, letting you configure dialing, login, and fax parameters. All **getty** programs can read an initial message placed in the **/etc/issue** file, which can contain special codes to provide the system name and current date and time.

Input Devices

Input devices, such as mice and keyboards, are displayed on several levels. Initial detection is performed during installation when you select the mouse and keyboard types. Keyboards and mice will automatically be detected by HAL. You can perform detailed configuration with your desktop configuration tools, such as the GNOME or KDE mouse configuration tools. On GNOME, choose System | Preferences | Mouse to configure your mouse. A Keyboard entry on that same menu is used for keyboards.

Installing Other Cards

To install a new card, your kernel must first be configured to support it. Support for most cards is provided in the form of modules that can be dynamically loaded into the kernel. Installing support for a card is usually a simple matter of loading a module that includes the drivers. For example, drivers for the Sound Blaster sound card are in the module **sb.o**. Loading this module makes your sound card accessible to Linux. Ubuntu automatically detects the cards installed on your system and loads the needed modules. If you change sound cards, the new card is automatically detected. You can also load modules you need manually, removing an older conflicting one. The section "Modules" later in this chapter describes this process.

Sound Devices

Most sound cards are now detected and managed by udev and HAL. A list of various sound devices is provided in Table 25-7. Some sound cards may require more specialized support. You can determine your current sound configuration by listing the contents of the **/proc/asound/oss/sndstat** file. You can test your card by simply redirecting a sound file to it, as shown here:

```
cat sample.au > /dev/audio
```

Older sound devices are supported as part of the Open Sound System (OSS) and are freely distributed as OSS/Free. These are installed as part of Linux distributions. The OSS device drivers are intended to provide a uniform API for all Unix platforms, including Linux. They support Sound Blaster– and Windows Sound System–compatible sound cards (ISA and PCI).

Device	Description
/dev/sndstat	Sound driver status
/dev/audio	Audio output device
/dev/dsp	Sound sampling device
/dev/mixer	Control mixer on sound card
/dev/music	High-level sequencer
/dev/sequencer	Low-level sequencer
/dev/midi	Direct MIDI port

TABLE 25-7 Sound Devices

Device Name	Type of Device
/dev/video	Video capture interface
/dev/vfx	Video effects interface
/dev/codec	Video codec interface
/dev/vout	Video output interface
/dev/radio	AM/FM radio devices
/dev/vtx	Teletext interface chips
/dev/vbi	Data services interface

TABLE 25-8 Video and TV Device Drivers

The Advanced Linux Sound Architecture (ALSA) replaced OSS in the 2.6 Linux kernel; it aims to be a better alternative to OSS, while maintaining compatibility with it. ALSA provides a modular sound driver, an API, and a configuration manager. ALSA is a GNU project and is entirely free; its Web site at **http://alsa-project.org** contains extensive documentation, applications, and drivers. Currently available are the ALSA sound driver, the ALSA Kernel API, the ALSA library to support application development, and the ALSA manager to provide a configuration interface for the driver. ALSA evolved from the Linux Ultra Sound Project. The ALSA project currently supports most Creative sound cards.

Video and TV Devices

Device names used for TV, video, and DVD devices are listed in Table 25-8. Drivers for DVD and TV decoders have been developed, and mga4linux (**http://marvel.sourceforge.net**) is developing video support for the Matrox Multimedia cards. The General ATI TV and Overlay Software (GATOS) (**http://gatos.sourceforge.net**) has developed drivers for the currently unsupported features of ATI video cards, specifically TV features. The BTTV Driver Project has developed drivers for the Booktree video chip. Creative Labs sponsors Linux drivers for the Creative line of DVD DXR2 decoders (**http://opensource.creative.com**).

PCMCIA Devices

PCMCIA devices are card readers commonly found on laptops to connect devices such as modems or wireless cards, though they are becoming standard on many desktop systems as well. The same PCMCIA device can support many different kinds of devices, including network cards, modems, hard disks, and Bluetooth devices.

PCMCIA support and PCMCIA devices are now considered hotplugged devices managed by HAL and udev directly; you can no longer use the cardmgr/pcmcia service. Card information and control is now managed by **pccardctl**. The PCMCIA udev rules are listed in **60-pcmcia.rules**, which automatically probes and installs cards. Check **http://kernel.org/pub/linux/utils/kernel/pcmcia/pcmcia.html** for more information.

You can obtain information about a PCMCIA device by using the **pccardctl** command, or you can manually eject and insert a device. The **status**, **config**, and **ident** options will display the device's socket status, configuration, and identification, respectively. The **insert** and **eject** options will let you add and remove a device. The **cardinfo** command also provides device information.

It is not advisable to hot-swap IDE or SCSI devices. For these, you should first manually shut down the device using the **pccardctl** command:

```
pccardctl eject
pccardctl scheme home
```

Modules

The Linux kernel employs the use of modules to support different operating system features, including support for various devices such as sound and network cards. In many cases, you do have the option of implementing support for a device either as a module or by directly compiling it as a built-in kernel feature, which requires you to rebuild the kernel. A safer and more robust solution is to use modules. *Modules* are components of the Linux kernel that can be loaded as needed. To add support for a new device, you can simply instruct a kernel to load the module for that device. In some cases, you may have to recompile only that module to provide support for your device. The use of modules has the added advantage of reducing the size of the kernel program as well as making your system more stable. The kernel can load modules in memory only as they are needed. Should a module fail, only the module stops running, and it will not affect the entire system.

Kernel Module Tools

The modules needed by your system are determined during installation, according to the kind of configuration information you provided and the automatic detection performed by your Linux distribution. For example, if your system uses an Ethernet card whose type you specified during installation, the system loads the module for that card. You can, however, manually control what modules are to be loaded for your system. In effect, this enables you to customize your kernel whatever way you want. The 2.6 Linux kernel includes the Kernel Module Loader (**Kmod**), which can load modules automatically as they are needed. Kernel module loading support must also be enabled in the kernel, though this is usually considered part of a standard configuration. In addition, several tools enable you to load and unload modules manually. The Kernel Module Loader uses certain kernel commands to perform the task of loading or unloading modules. The **modprobe** command is a general-purpose command that calls **insmod** to load modules and **rmmod** to unload them. These commands are listed in Table 25-9. Options for particular modules, general configuration, and even specific module loading can be specified in the **/etc/modprobe.conf** file. You can use this file to load and configure modules automatically. You can also specify modules to be loaded at the boot prompt or in **grub.conf**.

Module Files and Directories: /lib/modules

The filename for a module has the extension **.o**. Kernel modules reside in the **/lib/modules/** *version* directory, where *version* is the version number for your current kernel with the extension generic. The directory for the 2.6.24-10-generic kernel is **/lib/modules/2.6.24-10-generic**. As you install new kernels on your system, new module directories are generated for them.

Command	Description
`lsmod`	Lists modules currently loaded.
`insmod`	Loads a module into the kernel. Does not check for dependencies.
`rmmod`	Unloads a module currently loaded. Does not check for dependencies.
`modinfo`	Displays information about a module: `-a` (author), `-d` (description), `-p` (module parameters), `-f` (module filename), `-v` (module version).
`depmod`	Creates a dependency file listing all other modules on which the specified module may rely.
`modprobe`	Loads a module with any dependent modules it may also need. Uses the file of dependency listings generated by `depmod`: `-r` (unload a module) and `-l` (list modules).

TABLE 25-9   Kernel Module Commands

One method for accessing the directory for the current kernel is to use the **uname -r** command to generate the kernel version number. This command uses back quotes:

```
cd /lib/modules/`uname -r`
```

In this directory, modules for the kernel reside in the **kernel** directory. Within the **kernel** directory are several subdirectories, including the **drivers** directory that holds subdirectories for modules such as network drivers and video drivers. These subdirectories serve to categorize your modules, making them easier to locate. For example, the **kernel/drivers/net** directory holds modules for your Ethernet cards, and the **kernel/drivers/video** directory contains video card modules. Specialized modules are placed in the **ubuntu** directory instead of the **kernel** directory. These include the sound drivers. The ALSA sound driver are located at **/lib/modules/2.6.24-17/ubuntu/sound/alsa-drivers**.

Managing Modules with modprobe and /etc/modules

As noted, you can use several commands to manage modules. The **lsmod** command lists the modules currently loaded into your kernel, and **modinfo** provides information about particular modules. Though you can use the **insmod** and **rmmod** commands to load or unload modules directly, you should use only **modprobe** for these tasks. Often, however, a given module requires other modules to be loaded.

To have a module loaded automatically at boot, you simply place the module name in the **/etc/modules** file. Here you will also find entries for **fuse** and **lp**. You can use this file to force loading a needed module that may not be detected by udev or HAL. This can be particularly true for specialized vendor kernel modules you may need to download, compile, and install.

The depmod Command

Instead of manually trying to determine module dependencies, you can use the **depmod** command to detect the dependencies for you. The **depmod** command generates a file that lists all the modules on which a given module depends. The **depmod** command generates a hierarchical listing, noting what modules should be loaded first and in what order they will load. Then, to load the module, you use the **modprobe** command using that file. **modprobe** reads the file generated by **depmod** and loads any dependent modules in the correct order, along with the module you want. You need to execute **depmod** with the **-a** option once, before you ever use **modprobe**. Entering **depmod** **-a** creates a complete listing of all module dependencies. This command creates a file called **modules.dep** in the module directory for your current kernel version, **/lib/modules/***version*.

```
depmod -a
```

The modprobe Command

To install a module manually, you use the **modprobe** command and the module name. You can add any parameters the module might require. The following command installs the Intel high-definition sound module. **modprobe** also supports the use of the * character to enable you to use a pattern to select several modules. This example uses several values commonly used for sound cards:

```
modprobe  snd-hda-intel
```

Use the values recommended for your sound card on your system. Most sound card drivers are supported by the ALSA project. Check the driver's Web site to learn what driver module is used for your card.

To discover what parameters a module takes, you can use the **modinfo** command with the **-p** option.

You can use the **-l** option to list modules and the **-t** option to look for modules in a specified subdirectory. Sound modules are located in the **/lib/modules/2.6.version-generic/ ubuntu** directory, where version is the kernel version like 2.6.24-17. Sound modules are arranged in different subdirectories according to the driver and device interface they use, such as **pci**, **isa**, or **usb**. Most internal sound cards use **pci**. Within the interface directory may be further directories such as **emu10k1** used for the Creative Audigy cards and **hda** for high definition drivers. In the next example, the user lists all modules in the **sound/alsa-driver/pci/hda** directory:

```
# modprobe -l -t sound/pci/hda
/lib/modules/2.6.24-17-generic/ubuntu/sound/alsa-driver/sound/pci/hda/
  snd-hda-intel.ko
```

Options for the **modprobe** command are placed in the **/etc/modprobe.d** directory.

The insmod Command

The **insmod** command performs the actual loading of modules. Both **modprobe** and the Kernel Module Loader make use of the **insmod** command to load modules. Though **modprobe** is preferred because it checks for dependencies, you can load or unload particular modules individually with **insmod** and **rmmod** commands. The **insmod** command takes as its argument the name of the module, as does **rmmod**. The name can be the simple base name, such as **snd-ac97-codec** for the **snd-ac97-codec.ko** module. You can specify the complete module filename using the **-o** option. Other helpful options are the **-p** option, which lets you probe your system first to see if the module can be successfully loaded, and the **-n** option, which performs all tasks except actually loading the module (a dummy run). The **-v** option (verbose) lists all actions taken as they occur. In those rare cases where you may have to force a module to load, you can use the **-f** option. In the next example, **insmod** loads the **snd-ac97-codec.ko** sound module:

```
# insmod -v snd-ac97-codec
```

The rmmod Command

The **rmmod** command performs the actual unloading of modules. It is the command used by **modprobe** and the Kernel Module Loader to unload modules. You can use the **rmmod** command to remove a particular module as long as it is not being used or required by other modules. You can remove a module and all its dependent modules by using the **-r** option. The **-a** option removes all unused modules. With the **-e** option, when **rmmod** unloads a module, it saves any persistent data (parameters) in the persistent data directory, usually **/var/lib/modules/persist**.

modprobe Configuration

Module loading can require system renaming as well as specifying options to use when loading specific modules. Even when removing or installing a module, certain additional programs may have to be run or other options specified. These parameters can be set in files located in an **/etc/modprobe.d** directory. Configuration for **modprobe** supports the following actions:

- **alias** *module name*   Provides another name for the module, used for network and sound devices.
- **options** *module options*   Specifies any options a particular module may need.
- **install** *module commands*   Uses the specified commands to install a module, letting you control module loading.
- **remove** *module commands*   Specifies commands to be run when a module is unloaded.
- **include** *config-file*   Includes additional configuration files.
- **blacklist** *module*   Ignores any internal aliases that a given module may define for itself. This allows you to use only aliases defined by **modprobe**. It also avoids conflicting modules where two different modules may have the same alias defined internally. Default blacklist entries are held in one or more blacklist files in the **/etd/modprobe.d** directory. Their names begin with the term **blacklist**. Use the **modinfo** command to list a module's internal aliases.

Among the more common entries are aliases used for network protocols in the **aliases** file. Actual network devices are now managed by udev in the **70-persistent-net.rules** file, not by **modprobe** aliases.

Installing New Modules from Vendors: Driver Packages

You may find that your hardware device is not supported by current Linux modules. In this case, you can download drivers from the hardware vendor or open source development group to create your own driver and install it for use by your kernel. The drivers could be in DEB or compressed archives. The process for installing drivers differs, depending on how a vendor supports the driver. Different kinds of packages are listed here:

- **DEB packages**   Some support sites will provide drivers already packaged in DEB files for direct installation.

- **Drivers compiled in archives**   Some sites will provide drivers already compiled for your distribution but packaged in compressed archives. In this case, a simple install operation will place the supporting module in the **modules** directory and make if available for use by the kernel.

- **Source code**   Other sites provide just the source code, which, when compiled, will detect your system configuration and compile the module accordingly.

- **Scripts with source code**   Some sites will provide customized scripts that may prompt you for basic questions about your system and then both compile and install the module.

For drivers that come in the form of compressed archives (**tar.gz** or **tar.bz2**), the compile and install operations normally make use a makefile script operated by the **make** command. Be sure the kernel headers are installed first. These are normally installed by default with the **linux-headers** package. A simple install usually requires running the following command in the driver's software directory:

```
make install
```

In the case of sites that supply only the source code, you may have to perform both configure and compile operations as you would for any software:

```
./configure
make
make install
```

For packages that have no install option, compiled or source, you will have to move the module manually to the kernel module directory, **/lib/modules**/*version*, and use **depmod** and **modprobe** to load it (see the preceding section).

If a site gives you a customized script, you can run that script. For example, the Marvel gigabit LAN network interfaces found on many motherboards use the SysKonnect Linux drivers held in the **skge.ko** module. The standard kernel configuration will generate and install this module. But if you are using a newer motherboard, you may need to download and install the latest Linux driver. For example, some vendors may provide a script, **install.sh**, that you run to configure, compile, and install the module:

```
./install.sh
```

NOTE *You can create your own kernel using the **linux-source** package from the Ubuntu repository. It is advisable to use the Ubuntu kernel package, as it includes Ubuntu patches. Alternatively, you can use the original Linux kernel from **kernel.org**, but incompatibilities can occur, especially with updates expecting the Ubuntu version. For third party kernel modules, you only need the kernel headers in the **linux-headers** package which is already installed.*

CHAPTER

Backup Management

Backup operations have become an important part of administrative duties. Several backup tools are provided on Linux systems, including Anaconda and the traditional dump/restore tools, as well as the **rsync** command used for making individual copies. Anaconda provides server-based backups, letting different systems on a network back up to a central server. BackupPC provides network and local backup using configured rsync and tar tools. The dump tools let you refine your backup process, detecting data changed since the last backup. Table 26-1 lists Web sites for Linux backup tools.

Individual Backups: archive and rsync

You can back up and restore particular files and directories with archive tools such as tar, restoring the archives later. For backups, tar is usually used with a tape device. To schedule automatic backups, you can schedule appropriate **tar** commands with the **cron** utility. The archives can be also compressed for storage savings. You can then copy the compressed archives to any medium, such as a DVD, floppy disk, or tape. On GNOME, you can use File Roller to create archives easily (Archive Manager under System Tools). The KDAT tool on KDE, a front end to tar, will back up to tapes. See Chapter 12 for a discussion of compressed archives.

If you want to remote-copy a directory or files from one host to another, making a particular backup, you can use rsync, which is designed for network backups of particular directories or files, intelligently copying only those files that have been changed, rather than the contents of an entire directory. In archive mode, it can preserve the original ownership and permissions, providing corresponding users exist on the host system. The following example copies the **/home/george/myproject** directory to the **/backup** directory on the host **rabbit**, creating a corresponding **myproject** subdirectory. The **-t** specifies that this is a transfer. The remote host is referenced with an attached colon, **rabbit:**.

```
rsync -t /home/george/myproject   rabbit:/backup
```

If, instead, you want to preserve the ownership and permissions of the files as well as include all subdirectories, you use the **-a** (archive) option. Adding a **-z** option will compress the file. The **-v** option provides a verbose mode (you can leave this out if you wish):

```
rsync -avz  /home/george/myproject   rabbit:/backup
```

589

Web Site	Tools
http://rsync.samba.org	rsync remote copy backup
http://backuppc.sourceforge.net	BackupPC network or local backup using configured rsync and tar tools
www.amanda.org	Amanda open source network backup and recovery
http://dump.sourceforge.net	Dump and restore tools

TABLE 26-1   Backup Resources

A trailing slash on the source will copy the contents of the directory, rather than generating a subdirectory of that name. Here the contents of the **myproject** directory are copied to the **george-project** directory:

```
rsync -avz  /home/george/myproject/   rabbit:/backup/george-project
```

The **-a** option is the equivalent to the following options: **r** (recursive), **l** (preserve symbolic links), **p** (permissions), **g** (groups), **o** (owner), **t** (times), and **D** (preserve device and special files). The **-a** option does not preserve hard links, as this can be time consuming. If you want hard links preserved, you need to add the **-H** option:

```
rsync -avzH  /home/george/myproject   rabbit:/backup
```

The **rsync** command is configured to use Secure Shell (SSH) remote shell by default. You can specify it or an alternate remote shell to use with the **-e** option. For secure transmission, you can encrypt the copy operation with **ssh**. Either use the **-e ssh** option or set the **RSYNC_RSH** variable to **ssh**:

```
rsync -avz -e ssh  /home/george/myproject   rabbit:/backup/myproject
```

You can also copy from a remote host to the host you are on:

```
rsync -avz  lizard:/home/mark/mypics/  /pic-archive/markpics
```

You can also run rsync as a server daemon. This will allow remote users to sync copies of files on your system with versions on their own, transferring only changed files rather than entire directories. Many mirror and software FTP sites operate as rsync servers, letting you update files without having to download the full versions again. Configuration information for rsync as a server is kept in the **/etc/rsyncd.conf** file. Check the man page documentation for **rsyncd.conf** for details on how to configure the rsync server. You can start, restart, and shut down the rsync server using the **/etc/init.d/rsync** script:

```
sudo /etc/init.d/rsync restart
```

TIP *Though it is designed for copying between hosts, you can also use rsync to make copies within your own system, usually to a directory in another partition or hard drive. In fact, you can use rsync in eight different ways. Check the rsync man page for detailed descriptions of each.*

BackupPC

BackupPC provides an easily managed local or network backup of your system or hosts on a system using configured rsync or tar tools. There is no client application to install, just configuration files. BackupPC can back up hosts on a network, including servers, or just a single system. Data can be backed up to local hard disks or to network storage such as shared partitions or storage servers. BackupPC is included as part of the main Ubuntu repository. You can find out more about BackupPC at **http://backuppc.sourceforge.net**.

You can configure BackupPC using your Web page configuration interface. This is the host name of your computer with the **/backuppc** name attached, like so: **http://rabbit/backuppc**. Detailed documentation is installed at **/usr/share/doc/backuppc**. Configuration files are located at **/etc/backuppc**. The **config.pl** file holds BackupPC configuration options and the hosts file lists hosts to be backed up. You can use **services-admin** to have BackupPC start automatically—check the Remote Backup Server (backuppc) entry. BackupPC has its own service script with which you start, stop, and restart the BackupPC service manually, at **/etc/init.d/backuppc**:

```
sudo /etc/init.d/backuppc
```

When you first install BackupPC, an install screen will display information you will need to access your BackupPC tool (see Figure 26-1). This includes the URL to use, the username, and a password. Be sure to write down the username and password. The URL is simply your computer name with **/backuppc** attached. The username is **backuppc**. You can change the password with the **htpassword** command, as shown next. The password is kept in the **/etc/backuppc/htpasswd** file in an encrypted format.

```
sudo htpassword /etc/backuppc/htpasswd   backuppc
```

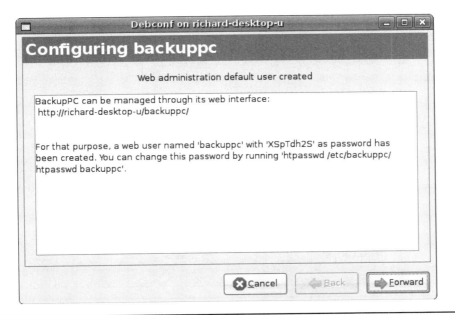

FIGURE 26-1 BackupPC user and password

To access BackupPC, start your browser and enter your URL (computer name with **/backuppc**) and then the **backuppc** username with the password when prompted for authorization. The general status screen is displayed. The left sidebar displays three sections: localhost, Hosts, and Server. The Server section has links for BackupPC server configuration. Host Summary will display host backup status (see Figure 26-2).

BackupPC Server Configuration

To add other hosts, click the Server section's Edit Hosts link on the left sidebar to open a page where you add or modify hosts (Figure 26-3). Here you can add new hosts, change users, and add new users. Host entries are saved to the **/etc/backuppc/hosts** file. Click the Save button to finish.

The Server Edit Config link opens a page with tabbed panels for all your server configuration options. The page opens to the Server tab, but you can also access the Hosts tab to add new users, Xfer to specify the backup method, and the Backup Settings to set backup options. The Server tab will control features such as the hostname of the server and the username to provide access. On the Xfer tab you can configure different backup methods: archive (gzip), rsync, rsyncd, smb (Samba), and tar. The Schedule tab sets the periods for full and incremental backups.

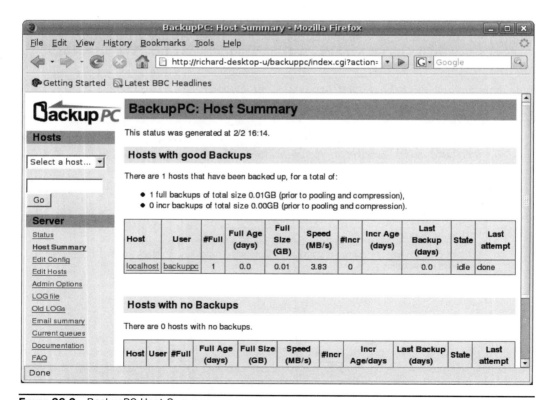

FIGURE 26-2 BackupPC Host Summary screen

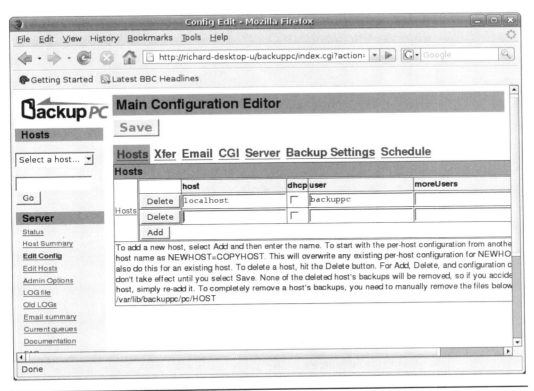

FIGURE 26-3   BackupPC Configuration Editor

BackupPC Host Backup and Configuration

The Hosts pop-up menu is located on the side panel in the Hosts section. Here you choose the host on which to perform backups and restores. The localhost entry will access your own computer. When you select a host, a new section will appear on the side panel above the Hosts section, labeled with that hostname, such as localhost. In this section will be links for the host home page, Browse Backups, Logs, and an Edit Config link to configure the backup for that host.

The host home page will list backups and display buttons for full and incremental backups (see Figure 26-4). Click Start Full Backup to perform a full backup or Start Incre Backup for an incremental backup (changed data only). You will be prompted for confirmation before the backup begins.

To select files to restore, click the Browse Backups link to display a tree of possible files and directories to restore. Select the files or directories you want, or click the Select All check box to choose the entire backup. Then click Restore Backup. A Restore page lets you choose from three kinds of backup: a direct restore, Zip archive, or tar archive. For a direct restore, you can have BackupPC either overwrite your current files with the restored ones or save the files to a specified directory, where you can later choose which ones to use. The Zip and tar restore options create archive files that hold your backup. You can later extract and restore files from the archive.

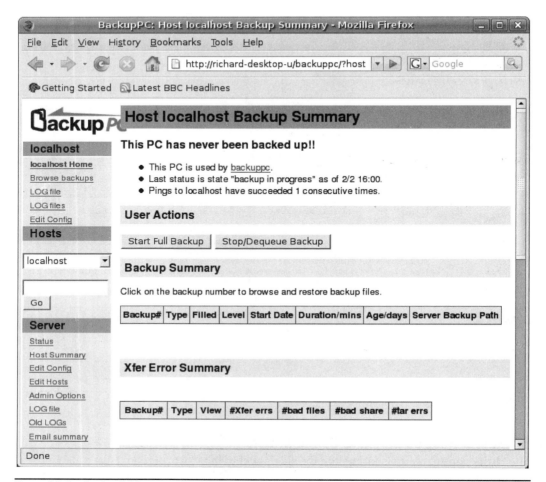

FIGURE 26-4 BackupPC host page

The Edit Config link under Server in the side panel opens a page of tabbed panels for your host backup configuration. On the Xfer tab you can decide on the type of backup you want to perform. You can choose from archive (zip), tar, rsync, rsyncd, and smb (Samba). Here you can set specific settings such as the destination directory for a Zip archive or the Samba share to access for an SMB backup. The Schedule tab is where you specify the backup intervals for full and incremental backups.

BackupPC uses both compression and detection of identical files to reduce the size of the backup, allowing several hosts to be backed up in limited space. Once an initial backup is performed, BackupPC will back up only changed files using incremental backups, reducing the time of the backup significantly.

Amanda

To back up hosts connected to a network to a central backup server, you can use the Advanced Maryland Automatic Network Disk Archiver (Amanda) to archive hosts (universe repository). Amanda uses tar tools to back up all hosts to a single host operating as a backup server. Backup data is sent by each host to the host operating as the Amanda server, where they are written out to a backup medium such as tape. With an Amanda server, the backup operations for all hosts become centralized in one server, instead of each host having to perform its own backup. Any host that needs to restore data simply requests it from the Amanda server, specifying the file system, date, and filenames. Backup data is copied to the server's holding disk and from there to tapes.

Detailed documentation and updates are provided at **www.amanda.org**. For the server, be sure to install the **amanda-server** package, and for clients you use the **amanda-clients** package. Ubuntu also provides an **Amanda-common** package for documentation, shared libraries, and Amanda tools.

Amanda is designed for automatic backups of hosts that may have very different configurations as well as operating systems. You can back up any host that supports GNU tools, including Mac OS X and Windows systems connected through Samba.

Amanda Commands

Amanda has its own commands that correspond to the common backup tasks, beginning with **am**, such as **amdump**, **amrestore**, and **amrecover**, as listed in Table 26-2. The **amdump** command is the primary backup operation.

The **amdump** command performs requested backups; it is not designed for interactive use. For an interactive backup, you use an archive tool such as tar directly. The **amdump** is placed within a **cron** instruction to be run at a specified time. If, for some reason **amdump** cannot save all its data to the backup medium (tape or disk), it will retain the data on the holding disk. The data can then later be directly written with the **amflush** command.

You can restore particular files as well as complete systems with the **amrestore** command. With the **amrecover** command, you can select from a list of backups.

Amanda Configuration

Configuration files are placed in **/etc/amanda**, and log and database files are in **/var/lib/amanda**. These are created automatically when you install Amanda. You will need to create a directory to use as a holding disk where backups are kept before being written to the tape. This should be located on a file system with a large amount of available space, enough to hold the backup of your largest entire host.

/etc/amanda

Within the **/etc/amanda** directory are subdirectories for the different kind of backups you want to perform. Each directory will contain its own **amanda.conf** and **disklist** files. By default a daily backup directory is created called **DailySet1**, with a default **amanda.conf** and a sample **disklist** file. To use them, you will have to edit them to enter your system's own settings. For a different backup configuration, you can create a new directory and copy the **DailySet1 amanda.conf** and **disklist** files to it, editing them as appropriate. When you

Command	Description
`amadmin`	Back up administrative tasks
`amcheck`	Check the backup systems and files as well as the backup tapes before backup operations
`amcleanup`	Clean up if a system failure occurs on the server
`amdump`	Perform automatic backups for the file systems listed in the **disklist** configuration file
`amflush`	Directly back up data from the holding disk to a tape
`amlabel`	Label the backup medium for Amanda
`amrecover`	Select backups to restore using an interactive shell
`amrestore`	Restore backups, either files or complete systems
`amrmtape`	Remove a tape from the Amanda database, used for damaged tapes
`amstatus`	Show the status of the current Amanda backup operation
`amtape`	Manage backup tapes, loading and removing them
`amverify`	Check format of tapes
`amverifyrun`	Check the tapes from the previous run, specifying the configuration directory for the backup

TABLE 26-2   Amanda Commands

issue Amanda commands such as **amdump** to perform backups, you will use the name of the **/etc/amanda** subdirectory to indicate the kind of backup you want performed:

```
amdump DailySet1
```

The **/etc/amanda** directory also contains a sample **cron** file, **crontab.sample**, that shows how a **cron** entry should look.

amanda.conf

The **amanda.conf** file contains basic configuration parameters such as the tape type and logfile as well as holding file locations. In most cases, you can use the defaults as listed in the **DailySet1/amanda.conf** file. The file is commented in detail, telling you what entries you will have to change. You will need to set the Tapedev entries to the tape device you use and the Tape Type entry for your tape drive type. In the Holding Disk segment, you will need to specify the partition and the directory for the holding disk you want to use. See the Amanda man page and documentation for detailed information on various options.

disklist

The **disklist** file is where you specify the file systems and partitions to be backed up. An entry lists the host, the partition, and the dump-type. The possible dump-types are defined in **amanda.conf**. The dump-types set certain parameters such as the priority of the backup and whether or not to use compression. The comp-root type will back up root partitions with compression and low priority, whereas the always-full type will back up an entire partition with no compression and the highest priority. You can define other dump-types in **amanda.conf** and use them for different partitions.

Backups are performed in the order listed; be sure to list the more important ones first. The **disklist** file in **DailySet1** provides detailed examples.

Enabling Amanda on the Network

To use Amanda on the network, you need to run two servers on the Amanda server as well as an Amanda client on each network host. Access must be enabled for both the clients and the server.

Amanda Server

The Amanda server runs through **xinetd**, using **xinetd** service files located in **/etc/xinetd.d**. The two service files are **amidxtape** and **amandaidx**. Restart the **xinetd** daemon to have it take immediate effect.

For clients to be able to recover backups from the server, the clients' hostnames must be placed in the **.amandahosts** file in the server's Amanda user home directory, **/var/lib/amanda**. On the server, **/var/lib/amanda/.amandahosts** will list all the hosts that are backed up by Amanda.

Amanda Hosts

Each host needs to allow access by the Amanda server. To do this, you place the hostname of the Amanda server in each client's **.amandahosts** dot file. This file is located in the client's Amanda user home directory, **/var/lib/amanda**.

Each host needs to run the Amanda client daemon, **amanda**, which also runs under **xinetd**. The **/etc/xinetd.d/amanda** configuration file is used to control enabling Amanda.

TIP *If your server and hosts have firewalls, you will need to allow access through the ports that Amanda uses, usually 10080, 10082, and 10083.*

Using Amanda

Backups are performed by the **amdump** command:

```
amdump DailySet1
```

An **amdump** command for each backup is placed in the Amanda **crontab** file. It is helpful to run an **amcheck** operation to make sure that a tape is ready:

```
0 16 * * 1-5 /usr/sbin/amcheck -m DailySet1
45 0 * * 2-6 /usr/sbin/amdump DailySet1
```

Before you can use a tape, you will have to label it with **amlabel**. Amanda uses the label to determine what tape should be used for a backup. Log in as the Amanda user (not root) and label the tape so that it can be used:

```
amlabel DailySet DailySet1
```

A client can recover a backup using **amrecover**. This needs to be run as the root user, not as the Amanda user. The **amrecover** command works through an interactive shell much like **ftp**, letting you list available files and select them to restore. Within the **amrecover** shell, the **ls** command will list available backups, the **add** command will select one, and the extract operation will restore it. The **lcd** command lets you change the client directory; **amrecover** will use **DailySet1** as the default, but for other configurations you will need to specify their configuration directory with the **-C** option. Should you have more than one Amanda server, you can list the one you want with the **-t** option. Here's an example:

```
amrecover -C DailySet1
```

To restore full system backups, you use the **amrestore** command, specifying the tape device and the hostname:

```
amrestore  /dev/rmt1  rabbit
```

To select certain files, you can pipe the output to a recovery command such as **restore** (discussed in the next section):

```
amrestore -p /dev/rmt1  rabbit mydir  | restore  -ibvf 2 -
```

Backups with Dump and Restore

You can back up and restore your system with the dump and restore utilities (universe repository, **dump** package). Dump can back up your entire system or perform incremental backups, saving only those files that have changed since the last backup. It supports several options for managing the backup operation, such as specifying the size and length of storage media (see Table 26-3).

NOTE *Several disk dump tools are also available. The **diskdumpfmt** command can be used to format tapes for use by dump. **diskdumpctl** registers a dump partition with the system. **savecore** saves a vmcore file from the data in a dump partition. Dumped cores can be read by the **crash** tool. Check the **crash** man page for details.*

The dump Levels

The dump utility uses *dump levels* to determine to what degree you want your system backed up. A dump level of 0 will copy file systems in their entirety. The remaining dump levels perform incremental backups, backing up only files and directories that have been created or modified since the last lower level backup. A dump level of 1 will back up only files that have changed since the last level 0 backup. The dump level 2, in turn, will back up only files that have changed since the last level 1 backup (or 0 if there is no level 1), and so on up to dump level 9. You can run an initial complete backup at dump level 0 to back up your entire system and then run incremental backups at certain later dates, backing up only the changes since the full backup.

Using dump levels, you can devise certain strategies for backing up a file system. It is important to keep in mind that an incremental backup is run on changes from the last lower level backup. For example, if the last backup was 6 and the next backup was 8, then the

Option	Description
-a	Lets dump bypass any tape length calculations and write until an end-of-media indication is detected. Recommended for most modern tape drives and is the default.
-0 through -9	Specifies the dump level. A dump level 0 is a full backup, copying the entire file system (see also the -h option). Dump level numbers above 0 perform incremental backups, copying all new or modified files new in the file system since the last backup at a lower level. The default level is 9.
-B *records*	Lets you specify the number of blocks in a volume, overriding the end-of-media detection or length and density calculations that dump normally uses for multivolume dumps.
-b *blocksize*	Lets you specify the number of kilobytes per dump record. With this option, you can create larger blocks, speeding up backups.
-d *density*	Specifies the density for a tape in bits per inch (default is 1600BPI).
-h *level*	Files that are tagged with a user's **nodump** flag will not be backed up at or above this specified level. The default is 1, which will not back up the tagged files in incremental backups.
-f *file/device*	Backs up the file system to the specified file or device. This can be a file or tape drive. You can specify multiple filenames, separated by commas. A remote device or file can be referenced with a preceding hostname, *hostname:file*.
-k	Uses Kerberos authentication to talk to remote tape servers.
-M *file/device*	Implements a multivolume backup, where the *file* written to is treated as a prefix and the suffix consisting of a numbered sequence from 001 is used for each succeeding file—*file*001, *file*002, and so on. Useful when backup files need to be greater than the Linux **ext3** 2GB file size limit.
-n	Notifies operators if a backup needs operator attention.
-s *feet*	Specifies the length of a tape in feet. Dump will prompt for a new tape when the length is reached.
-S	Estimates the amount of space needed to perform a backup.
-T *date*	Allows you to specify your own date instead of using the **/etc/dumpdates** file.
-u	Writes an entry for a successful update in the **/etc/dumpdates** file.
-W	Detects and displays the file systems that need to be backed up. This information is taken from the **/etc/dumpdates** and **/etc/fstab** files.
-w	Detects and displays the file systems that need to be backed up, drawing only on information in **/etc/fstab**.

TABLE 26-3   Options for dump

level 8 will back up everything from the level 6 backup. The sequence of the backups is important. If, for example, there were three backups with levels 3, then 6, and then 5, the level 5 backup would take everything from the level 3 backup, not stopping at level 6. Level 3 is the next-*lower*-level backup for level 5, in this case. This can make for some complex incremental backup strategies. For example, if you want each succeeding incremental backup to include all the changes from the preceding incremental backups, you can run the backups in descending dump level order. Given a backup sequence of 7, 6, and 5, with 0 as the initial full backup, 6 would include all the changes to 7, because its next lower level is 0. Then 5 would include all the changes for 7 and 6, also because its next lower level is 0, making all the changes since the level 0 full backup. A simpler way to implement this is to make the incremental levels all the same. Given an initial level of 0, and then two backups both with level 1, the last level 1 would include all the changes from the backup with level 0, since level 0 is the next *lower* level—not the previous level 1 backup.

Recording Backups

Backups are recorded in the **/etc/dumpdates** file. This file will list all the previous backups, specifying the file system on which they were performed, the dates on which they were performed, and the dump level used. You can use this information to restore files from a specified backup. Recall that the **/etc/fstab** file records the dump level as well as the recommended backup frequency for each file system. With the **-w** option, dump will analyze both the **/etc/dumpdates** and **/etc/fstab** files to determine which file systems need to be backed up. The **dump** command with the **-w** option uses **/etc/fstab** to report the file systems ready for backup.

Operations with dump

The **dump** command takes as its arguments the dump level, the device on which it is storing the backup, and the device name of the file system that is being backed up. If the storage medium (such as a tape) is too small to accommodate the backup, **dump** will pause and let you insert another. **dump** supports backups on multiple volumes. The **u** option will record the backup in the **/etc/dumpdates** file. In the following example, an entire backup (dump level 0) is performed on the file system on the **/dev/hda3** hard disk partition. The backup is stored on a tape device, **/dev/tape**.

```
dump -0u -f /dev/tape /dev/hda5
```

NOTE *You can use the **mt** command to control your tape device; **mt** has options to rewind, erase, and position the tape. The **rmt** command controls a remote tape device.*

The storage device can be another hard disk partition, but it is usually a tape device. When you installed your system, your system most likely detected the device and set up **/dev/tape** as a link to it (just as it did with your CD-ROMs). If the link was not set up, you have to do it yourself or use the device name directly. Tape devices can have different device names, depending on the model or interface. SCSI tape devices are labeled with the prefix **st**, with a number attached for the particular device: **st0** is the first SCSI tape device. To use the device in the **dump** command, just specify its name:

```
dump -0u -f /dev/st0 /dev/hda5
```

Should you need to back up to a device located on another system on your network, you must specify that hostname for the system and the name of its device. The hostname is entered before the device name and delimited with a colon. In the following example, the user backs up file system **/dev/hda5** to the SCSI tape device with the name **/dev/st0** on the **rabbit.mytrek.com** system:

```
dump -0u -f rabbit.mytrek.com:/dev/st0 /dev/hda5
```

The **dump** command works on one file system at a time. If your system has more than one file system, you will need to issue a separate **dump** command for each.

TIP *You can use the system **cron** utility to schedule backups using **dump** at specified times.*

Recovering Backups

You use the **restore** command either to restore an entire file system or to retrieve particular files. **restore** will extract files or directories from a backup archive and copy them to the current working directory. Make sure you are in the directory to which you want the files restored when you run **restore**. The command will also generate any subdirectories as needed, and it has several options for managing the restore operation.

To recover individual files and directories, you run **restore** in an interactive mode using the **-i** option. This will generate a shell with all the directories and files on the tape, letting you select those you want to restore. When you are finished, **restore** will then retrieve from a backup only those files you selected. This shell has its own set of commands that you can use to select and extract files and directories. The following command will generate an interactive interface listing all the directories and files backed up on the tape in the **/dev/tape** device:

```
restore -ivf /dev/tape
```

This command will generate a shell encompassing the entire directory structure of the backup. You are shown a shell prompt and can use the **cd** command to move to different directories and the **ls** command to list files and subdirectories. You use the **add** command to tag a file or directory for extraction. Should you later decide not to extract it, you can use the **delete** command to remove it from the tagged list. Once you have selected all the items you want, you enter the **extract** command to retrieve them from the backup archive. To quit the restore shell, you enter **quit**. The **help** command will list the restore shell commands.

If you need to restore an entire file system, use **restore** with the **-r** option. You can restore the file system to any blank formatted hard disk partition of adequate size, including the file system's original partition. If may be advisable, if possible, to restore the file system on another partition and check the results.

Restoring an entire file system involves setting up a formatted partition, mounting it to your system, and then changing to its top directory to run the **restore** command. First you should use **mkfs** to format the partition where you are restoring the file system, and then mount it onto your system. Then you use **restore** with the **-r** option and the **-f** option to specify the device holding the file system's backup. In the next example, the user formats and mounts the **/dev/hda5** partition and then restores on that partition the file system backup, currently on a tape in the **/dev/tape** device:

```
mkfs /dev/hda5
mount /dev/hda5 /mystuff
cd /mystuff
restore -rf /dev/tape
```

To restore from a backup device located on another system on your network, you have to specify the hostname for the system and the name of its device. The hostname is entered before the device name and delimited with a colon. In the following example, the user restores a file system from the backup on the tape device with the name **/dev/tape** on the **rabbit.mytrek.com** system:

```
restore -rf rabbit.mytrek.com:/dev/tape
```

CHAPTER 27

Administering TCP/IP Networks

L inux systems are configured to connect with networks that use the TCP/IP protocols. These are the same protocols used by the Internet and many local area networks (LANs). TCP/IP is a robust set of protocols designed to provide communications among systems with different operating systems and hardware. The TCP/IP protocols were developed in the 1970s as a special project of the Defense Advanced Research Projects Agency (DARPA) to enhance communications between universities and research centers. These protocols were originally developed on Unix systems, with much of the research carried out at the University of California, Berkeley.

Linux, as a version of Unix, benefits from much of this original focus on Unix. Currently, the TCP/IP development is managed by the Internet Engineering Task Force (IETF), which, in turn, is supervised by the Internet Society (ISOC). The ISOC oversees several groups responsible for different areas of Internet development, such as the Internet Assigned Numbers Authority (IANA), which is responsible for Internet addressing (see Table 27-1). Over the years, TCP/IP standards and documentation have been issued in the form of Request for Comments (RFC) documents. You can check the most recent RFCs for current developments at the IETF Web site at **www.ietf.org**.

TCP/IP Protocol Suite

The TCP/IP protocol suite consists of several different protocols, each designed for a specific task in a TCP/IP network. The three basic protocols are the Transmission Control Protocol (TCP), which handles receiving and sending out communications; the Internet Protocol (IP), which handles the actual transmissions; and the User Datagram Protocol (UDP), which also handles receiving and sending packets. The Internet Protocol (IP), which is the base protocol that all others use, handles the actual transmissions, the packets of data with sender and receiver information in each.

TCP is designed to work with cohesive messages or data. This protocol checks received packets and sorts them into their designated order, forming the original message. For data sent out, TCP breaks the data into separate packets, designating their order. UDP, meant to work on a much more raw level, also breaks down data into packets but does not check

Web Site	Description
http://isoc.org	Internet Society (ISOC) is a professional membership organization of Internet experts that oversees boards and task forces dealing with network policy issues.
www.ietf.org/iesg.html	The Internet Engineering Steering Group (IESG) is responsible for technical management of IETF activities and the Internet standards process.
http://iana.org	Internet Assigned Numbers Authority (IANA) is responsible for Internet Protocol (IP) addresses.
http://iab.org	Internet Architecture Board (IAB) defines the overall architecture of the Internet, providing guidance and broad direction to the IETF.
www.ietf.org	Internet Engineering Task Force (IETF) is a protocol engineering and development arm of the Internet.

TABLE 27-1   TCP/IP Protocol Development Groups

their order. TCP/IP is designed to provide stable and reliable connections that ensure that all data is received and reorganized into its original order. UDP, on the other hand, is designed simply to send as much data as possible, with no guarantee that packets will all be received or placed in the proper order. UDP is often used for transmitting very large amounts of data of the type that can survive the loss of a few packets—for example, temporary images, video, and banners displayed on the Internet.

Other protocols provide various network and user services. The Domain Name Service (DNS) provides address resolution, the File Transfer Protocol (FTP) provides file transmission, and the Network File System (NFS) provides access to remote file systems. Table 27-2 lists the protocols in the TCP/IP suite. These protocols make use of either TCP or UDP to send and receive packets, which in turn uses IP to transmit the packets.

In a TCP/IP network, messages are broken into small components, called *datagrams,* which are then transmitted through various interlocking routes and delivered to their destination computers. Once received, the datagrams are reassembled into the original message. Datagrams themselves can be broken down into smaller packets. The *packet* is the physical message unit actually transmitted among networks. Sending messages as small components has proven to be far more reliable and faster than sending them as one large, bulky transmission. If one small component is lost or damaged, only that component must be resent, whereas if any part of a large transmission is corrupted or lost, the entire message has to be resent.

The configuration of a TCP/IP network on your Linux system is implemented using a set of network configuration files (see Table 27-5, later in this chapter). Many of these files can be managed using administrative programs provided by your distribution on your root user desktop. You can also use more specialized programs, such as netstat, ifconfig, Wireshark, and route. Some configuration files are easy to modify yourself using a text editor.

TCP/IP networks are configured and managed with a set of utilities called **ifconfig**, **route**, and **netstat**. The ifconfig utility operates from your root user desktop and enables you to configure your network interfaces fully, adding new interfaces and modifying others.

Transport	Description
TCP	Transmission Control Protocol: places systems in direct communication
UDP	User Datagram Protocol
IP	Internet Protocol: transmits data
ICMP	Internet Control Message Protocol: provides status messages for IP
Routing	**Description**
RIP	Routing Information Protocol: determines routing
OSPF	Open Shortest Path First: determines routing
Network Addresses	**Description**
ARP	Address Resolution Protocol: determines unique IP address of systems
DNS	Domain Name Service: translates hostnames into IP addresses
RARP	Reverse Address Resolution Protocol: determines addresses of systems
User Service	**Description**
FTP	File Transfer Protocol: transmits files from one system to another using TCP
TFTP	Trivial File Transfer Protocol: transfers files using UDP
Telnet	Allows remote login to another system on the network
SMTP	Simple Mail Transfer Protocol: transfers e-mail between systems
RPC	Remote Procedure Call: allows programs on remote systems to communicate
Gateway	**Description**
EGP	Exterior Gateway Protocol: provides routing for external networks
GGP	Gateway-to-Gateway Protocol: provides routing between Internet gateways
IGP	Interior Gateway Protocol: provides routing for internal networks
Network Service	**Description**
NFS	Network File System: allows mounting of file systems on remote machines
NIS	Network Information Service: maintains user accounts across a network
BOOTP	Boot Protocol: starts system using boot information on server for network
SNMP	Simple Network Management Protocol: provides status messages on TCP/IP configuration
DHCP	Dynamic Host Configuration Protocol: automatically provides network configuration information to host systems

TABLE 27-2   TCP/IP Protocol Suite

The ifconfig and route utilities are lower level programs that require more specific knowledge of your network to use effectively. The netstat utility provides you with information about the status of your network connections. Wireshark is a network protocol analyzer that lets you capture packets as they are transmitted across your network, selecting those you want to check.

Zero Configuration Networking: Avahi and Link Local Addressing

Zero Configuration Networking (Zeroconf) allows the setup of nonroutable private networks without the need of a DHCP server or static IP addresses. A Zeroconf configuration lets users automatically connect to a network and access all network resources, such as printers, without having to perform any configuration. On Linux, Zeroconf networking is implemented by Avahi (**http://avahi.org**), which includes multicast DNS (mDNS) and DNS service discovery (DNS-SD) support that automatically detects services on a network. IP addresses are determined using either IPv6 or IPv4 Link Local (IPv4LL) addressing. IPv4 Link Local addresses are assigned from the 168.254.0.0 network pool. Derived from Apple's Bonjour Zeroconf implementation, it is a free and open source version currently used by desktop tools such as the GNOME virtual file system. Ubuntu implements full Zeroconf network support with the Avahi daemon that implements multicast DNS discover, and avahi-autoipd that provides dynamic configuration of local IPv4 addresses. Both are installed as part of the desktop configuration. Avahi support tools are located in the **avahi-utilities** package.

The KDE Zeroconf solution is also provided using Avahi (**kdnssd**) located in the **kdnnsd-avahi** packages. Use the KDE control center Service Discovery panel (Internet & Network section) to specify your domain. Then enter **zeorconf:/** in a KDE file manger window.

IPv4 and IPv6

Traditionally, a TCP/IP address is organized into four segments consisting of numbers separated by periods: this is called the *IP address*. The IP address actually represents a 32-bit integer whose binary values identify the network and host. This form of IP addressing adheres to Internet Protocol, version 4, also known as *IPv4*. IPv4, the kind of IP addressing described here, is still in wide use.

Currently, version 6 of IP, IPv6, is gradually replacing the older IPv4 version. IPv6 expands the number of possible IP addresses by using 127 bits. It is fully compatible with systems still using IPv4. IPv6 addresses are represented differently, using a set of eight, 16-bit segments, each separated from the next by a colon. Each segment is represented by a hexadecimal number. Here's a sample address:

```
FEC0:0:0:0:800:BA98:7654:3210
```

Advantages for IPv6 include the following:

- It features simplified headers that allow for faster processing.
- It provides support for encryption and authentication along with virtual private networks (VPNs) using the integrated IPsec protocol.
- It extends the address space to cover 2^{127} possible hosts (billions of billions). This extends far beyond the 4.2 billion supported by IPv4.

- It supports stateless autoconfiguration of addresses for hosts, bypassing the need for DHCP to configure such addresses. Addresses can be generated directly using the Media Access Control (MAC) hardware address of an interface.

- It offers support for Quality of Service (QoS) operations, providing sufficient response times for services such as multimedia and telecom tasks.

- Multicast capabilities are built into the protocol, providing direct support for multimedia tasks. Multicast addressing also provides that same function as IPv4 broadcast addressing.

- More robust transmissions can be ensured with anycast addressing, where packets can be directed to an anycast group of systems, only one of which needs to receive them. Multiple DNS servers supporting a given network can be designated as an anycast group, of which only one DNS server needs to receive the transmission, providing greater likelihood that the transmissions will be successful.

- It provides better access for mobile nodes such as PDAs, notebooks, and cell phones.

TCP/IP Network Addresses

As noted, the traditional IPv4 TCP/IP address is organized into four segments, consisting of numbers separated by periods. This kind of address is still in widespread use and is commonly called the *IP address.* Part of an IP address is used for the network address, and the other part is used to identify a particular interface on a host in that network. You should realize that IP addresses are assigned to interfaces—such as Ethernet cards or modems—and not to the host computer. Usually a computer has only one interface and is accessed using only that interface's IP address. In that regard, an IP address can be thought of as identifying a particular host system on a network, so the IP address is usually referred to as the *host address.*

In fact, though, a host system can have several interfaces, each with its own IP address. This is the case for computers that operate as gateways and firewalls from the local network to the Internet. One interface usually connects to the LAN and another to the Internet, as by two Ethernet cards. Each interface (such as an Ethernet card) has its own IP address. If you use a modem to connect to an ISP, you must set up a Point-to-Point Protocol (PPP) interface that also has its own IP address (usually dynamically assigned by the ISP). Remembering this distinction is important if you plan to use Linux to set up a local or home network, using Linux as your gateway machine to the Internet.

IPv4 Network Addresses

The IP address is divided into two parts: one part identifies the network and the other part identifies a particular host. The network address identifies the network of which a particular interface on a host is a part. Two methods exist for implementing the network and host parts of an IP address: the original class-based IP addressing and the current Classless Interdomain Routing (CIDR) addressing. Class-based IP addressing designates officially predetermined parts of the address for the network and host addresses, whereas CIDR addressing allows the parts to be determined dynamically using a netmask.

Class-Based IP Addressing

Originally, IP addresses were organized according to classes. On the Internet, networks are organized into three classes depending on their size—classes A, B, and C. A class A network uses only the first segment for the network address and the remaining three for the host, allowing a great many computers to be connected to the same network. Most IP addresses reference smaller, class C, networks. For a class C network, the first three segments are used to identify the network, and only the last segment identifies the host. Altogether, this forms a unique address with which to identify any network interface on computers in a TCP/IP network. For example, in the IP address 192.168.1.72, the network part is 192.168.1 and the interface/host part is 72. The interface/host is a part of a network whose own address is 192.168.1.0.

In a class C network, the first three numbers identify the network part of the IP address. This part is divided into three network numbers, each identifying a subnet. Networks on the Internet are organized into subnets, beginning with the largest and narrowing to small subnetworks. The last number is used to identify a particular computer, referred to as a *host*. You can think of the Internet as a series of networks with subnetworks; these subnetworks have their own subnetworks. The rightmost number identifies the host computer, and the number preceding it identifies the subnetwork of which the computer is a part. The number to the left of that identifies the network of which the subnetwork is a part, and so on. The Internet address 192.168.187.4, then, references the fourth computer connected to the network identified by the number 187. Network 187 is a subnet to a larger network identified as 168. This larger network is itself a subnet of the network identified as 192. Here's how it breaks down:

192.168.187.4	IPv4 address
192.168.187	Network identification
4	Host identification

Netmask

Systems derive the network address from the host address using the netmask. You can think of an IP address as a series of 32 binary bits, some of which are used for the network and the remainder for the host. The *netmask* has the network set of bits set to 1s, with the host bits set to 0s (see Figure 27-1). In a standard class-based IP address, all the numbers in the network part of your host address are set to 255, and the host part is set to 0. This has the effect of setting all the binary bits making up the network address to 1s. This, then, is your netmask. So the netmask for the host address 192.168.1.72 is 255.255.255.0. The network part, 192.168.1, has been set to 255.255.255, and the host part, 72, has been set to 0. Systems can then use your netmask to derive your network address from your host address. They can determine what part of your host address makes up your network address and what those numbers are.

For readers familiar with computer programming, a bitwise AND operation on the netmask and the host address results in zeroing the host part, leaving you with the network part of the host address. You can think of the address as being implemented as a 4-byte integer, with each byte corresponding to a segment of the address. In a class C address, the three network segments correspond to the first 3 bytes and the host segment corresponds to

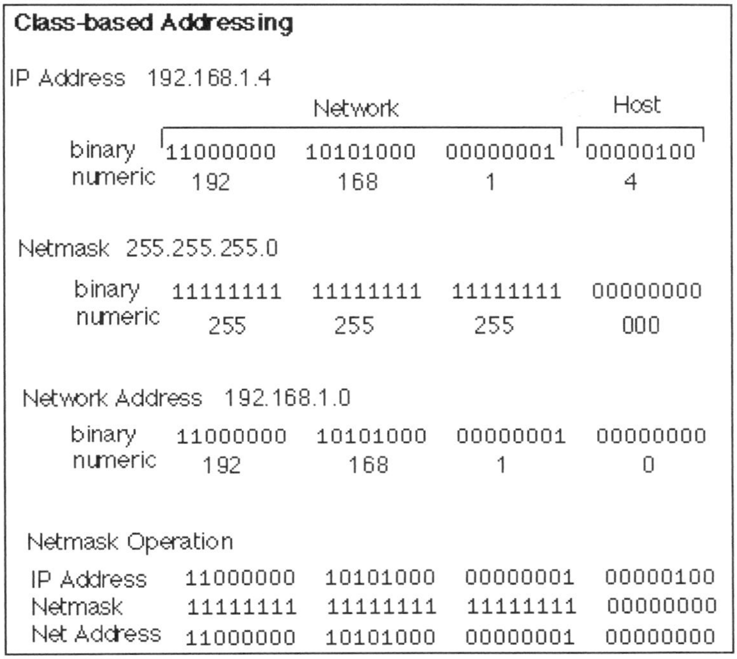

FIGURE 27-1   Class-based netmask operations

the fourth byte. A netmask is designed to mask out the host part of the address, leaving the network segments alone. In the netmask for a standard class C network, the first 3 bytes are all 1s and the last byte consists of 0s. The 0s in the last byte mask out the host part of the address, and the 1s in the first 3 bytes leave the network part of the address alone. Figure 27-1 shows the bitwise operation of the netmask on the address 192.168.1.4. This is a class C address to the mask, which consists of twenty-four 1s making up the first 3 bytes and eight 0s making up the last byte. When it is applied to the address 192.168.1.4, the network address remains (192.168.1) and the host address is masked out (4), giving you 192.168.1.0 as the network address.

Classless Interdomain Routing

Currently, the class-based organization of IP addresses is being replaced by the CIDR format. CIDR was designed for midsized networks, those between a class C and classes with numbers of hosts greater than 256 and smaller than 65,534. A class C network–based IP address using only one segment for hosts, an 8-bit integer, with a maximum value of 256. A class B network–based IP address uses two segments, which make up a 16-bit integer whose maximum value is 65,534. You can think of an address as a 32-bit integer taking up 4 bytes, where each byte is 8 bits. Each segment conforms to 1 of the 4 bytes. A class C network uses three segments, or 24 bits, to make up its network address. A class B network, in turn, uses two segments, or 16 bits, for its address. With this scheme, allowable host and network addresses are changed an entire byte at a time, segment to segment. With CIDR addressing, you can define host and network addresses by bits, instead of whole segments.

Obtaining an IP Address

IP addresses are officially allocated by IANA, which manages all aspects of Internet addressing. IANA oversees Internet Registries (IRs), which, in turn, maintain Internet addresses on regional and local levels. The Internet Registry for the Americas is the American Registry for Internet Numbers (ARIN, at **www.arin.net**). These addresses are provided to users by Internet service providers (ISPs). You can obtain your own Internet address from an ISP, or if you are on a network already connected to the Internet, your network administrator can assign you one. If you are using an ISP, the ISP may temporarily assign one from a pool it has on hand with each use.

IPv4 Reserved Addresses

Certain numbers are reserved—for example, the numbers *127, 0,* and *255* cannot be part of an official IP address. The number *127* is used to designate the network address for the loopback interface on your system, which enables users on your system to communicate with each other within the system without having to route through a network connection. Its network address would be 127.0.0.0, and its IP address is 127.0.0.1. For class-based IP addressing, the number *255* is a special broadcast identifier you can use to broadcast messages to all sites on a network. Using *255* for any part of the IP address references all nodes connected at that level. For example, 192.168.255.255 broadcasts a message to all computers on network 192.168, all its subnetworks, and their hosts. The address 192.168.187.255 broadcasts to every computer on the local network. If you use *0* for the network part of the address, the host number references a computer within your local network. For example, 0.0.0.6 references the sixth computer in your local network. If you want to broadcast to all computers on your local network, you can use the number 0.0.0.255. For CIDR IP addressing, the broadcast address may appear much like a normal IP address. As indicated in the preceding section, CIDR addressing allows the use of any number of bits to make up the IP address for either the network or the host part. For a broadcast address, the host part must have all its bits set to 1.

A special set of numbers is reserved for use on non-Internet LANs (RFC 1918). These are numbers that begin with the special network number *192.168* (for class C networks), as used in these examples. If you are setting up a LAN for a small business or a home network, for example, you are free to use these numbers for your local machines. You can set up an intranet using network cards, such as Ethernet cards and Ethernet hubs, and then configure your machines with IP addresses starting from 192.168.1.1. The host segment can go up to 256. So if you have three machines on your home network, you could give them the addresses 192.168.1.1, 192.168.1.2, and 192.168.1.3.

You can implement Internet services, such as FTP, web, and mail services, on your local machines and use any of the Internet tools to make use of those services. They all use the same TCP/IP protocols used on the Internet. For example, with FTP tools, you can transfer files among the machines on your network. With mail tools, you can send messages from one machine to another, and with a Web browser, you can access local Web sites that may be installed on a machine running its own web servers. If you want to connect one of your machines to the Internet or some other network, you can set it up to be a gateway machine. By convention, the gateway machine is usually given the address 192.168.1.1. With a method called *IP masquerading,* you can have any of the non-Internet machines use a gateway to connect to the Internet.

IPv4 Private Network Addresses	Network Classes
10.0.0.0	Class A network
172.16.0.0–172.31.255.255	Class B network
192.168.0.0	Class C network
127.0.0.0	Loopback network (for system self-communication)

TABLE 27-3   Non-Internet IPv4 Local Network IP Addresses

Numbers are also reserved for class A and class B non-Internet local networks. Table 27-3 lists these addresses. The possible addresses available span from 0 to 255 in the host segment of the address. For example, class B network addresses range from 172.16.0.0 to 172.31.255.255, providing a total of 32,356 possible hosts. The class C network ranges from 192.168.0.0 to 192.168.255.255, providing 256 possible subnetworks, each with 256 possible hosts. The network address 127.0.0.0 is reserved for a system's loopback interface, which allows it to communicate with itself, enabling users on the same system to send messages to each other.

Broadcast Addresses

The broadcast address allows a system to send the same message to all systems on your network at once. With IPv4 class–based IP addressing, you can easily determine the broadcast address using your host address: the broadcast address has the host part of your address set to 255. The network part remains untouched. So the broadcast address for the host address 192.168.1.72 is 192.168.1.255 (you combine the network part of the address with 255 in the host part).

Gateway Addresses

Some networks have a computer designated as the gateway to other networks. Every connection to and from a network to other networks passes through this gateway computer. Most local networks use gateways to establish a connection to the Internet. If you are working on this type of network, you must provide the gateway address. If your network does not have a connection to the Internet or a larger network, you may not need a gateway address. The gateway address is the address of the host system providing the gateway service to the network. On many networks, this host is given a host ID of 1, so the gateway address for a network with the address 192.168.1 would be 192.168.1.1, but this is only a convention. To be sure of your gateway address, ask your network administrator.

Name Server Addresses

Many networks, including the Internet, have computers that provide a DNS that translates the domain names of networks and hosts into IP addresses. These are known as the network's *domain name servers*. The DNS makes your computer identifiable on a network, using your domain name rather than your IP address. You can also use the domain names of other systems to reference them, so you needn't know their IP addresses. You must know the IP addresses of any domain name servers for your network, however. You can obtain the addresses from your system administrator (often more than one address exists). Even if you are using an ISP, you must know the address of the domain name servers your ISP operates for the Internet.

IPv6 Addressing

IPv6 addresses introduce major changes into the format and method of addressing systems under the Internet Protocol (see RFC 3513 at **www.ietf.org/rfc.html** or **www.faqs.org** for more details). Several different kinds of addressing are available with different fields for the network segment. The host segment has been expanded to a 64-bit address, allowing direct addressing for a far larger number of systems. Each address begins with a type field specifying the kind of address, which will then determine how its network segment is organized. These changes are designed not only to expand the address space but also to provide greater control over transmissions at the address level.

> **NOTE** *Most distributions already enable IPv6 support in the kernel. Kernel support for IPv6 is provided by the IPv6 kernel module. Kernel configuration support can be found under Device Drivers | Networking Support | Networking Options | The IPv6 Protocol.*

IPv6 Address Format

An IPv6 address consists of 127 bits, up from the 32 bits used in IPv4 addresses. The first 64 bits are used for network addressing, of which the first few bits are reserved for indicating the address type. The last 64 bits are used for the interface address, known as the *interface identifier field*. The amount of bits used for subnetting can be adjusted with a CIDR mask, much like that in IPv4 CIDR addressing (see the preceding section).

An IPv6 address is written as eight segments representing 16 bits each (127 bits total). To represent 16-bit binary numbers more easily, hexadecimal numbers are used. Hexadecimal numbers use 16 unique numbers, instead of the 8 used in octal numbering. These are 0–9, continuing with the characters A–F.

In the next example, the first four segments represent the network part of the IPv6 address and the following four segments represent the interface (host) address:

```
FEC0:0000:0000:0000:0008:0800:200C:417A
```

You can cut any preceding zeros, but not trailing zeros, in any given segment. Segments with all zeros can be reduced to a single zero, like so:

```
FEC0:0:0:0:8:800:200C:417A
```

The loopback address used for localhost addressing can be written with seven preceding zeros and a one:

```
0:0:0:0:0:0:0:1
```

Many addresses will have sequences of zeros. IPv6 supports a shorthand symbol for representing a sequence of several zeros in adjacent fields. This consists of a double colon (::). Only one :: symbol can be used per address.

```
FEC0::8:800:200C:417A
```

The loopback address 0000000000000001 can be reduced to the following:

```
::1
```

To ease the transition from IPv4 addressing to IPv6, a form of addressing incorporating IPv4 addresses is also supported. In this case, the IPv4 address (32 bits) can be used to represent the last two segments of an IPv6 address and can be written using IPv4 notation:

```
FEC0::192.168.0.3
```

IPv6 Interface Identifiers

The identifier part of the IPv6 address takes up the second 64 bits, consisting of four segments containing four hexadecimal numbers. The interface ID is a 64-bit (four-segment) Extended Unique Identifier (EUI-64) generated from a network device's MAC address.

IPv6 Address Types

Three basic kinds of IPv6 address types exist: unicast, multicast, and anycast. These, in turn, can have their own types of addresses.

- A *unicast* address is used for a packet that is sent to a single destination.
- A *multicast* address is used to broadcast a packet to a range of destinations.
- An *anycast* address is used for a packet that can be sent to more than one destination.

In IPv6, addressing is controlled by the format prefix that operates as a kind of address type. The format prefix is the first field of the IP address. The three major kinds of unicast network addresses are global, link-local, and site-local, which are each indicated by their own format prefix (see Table 27-4).

- Global addresses begin with the address type 3, site local with FEC, and link-local with FE8. Global addresses can be sent across the Internet.
- Link-local addresses are used for physically connected systems on a local network.
- Site-local can be used for any hosts on a local network. Site-local addresses operate like IPv4 private addresses; they are used only for local access and cannot be used to transmit over the Internet.

IPv6 Addresses Format Prefixes and Reserved Addresses	Description
3	Unicast global addresses
FE8	Unicast link-local addresses, used for physically connected hosts on a network
FEC	Unicast site-local addresses, comparable to IPv4 private addresses
0000000000000001	Unicast loopback address (for system self-communication, localhost)
0000000000000000	Unspecified address
FF	Multicast addresses

TABLE 27-4   IPv6 Format Prefixes and Reserved Addresses

In addition, IPv6 has two special reserved addresses. The address 0000000000000001 is reserved for the loopback address used for a system's localhost address, and the address 0000000000000000 is the unspecified address.

IPv6 Unicast Global Addresses

IPv6 global addresses currently use four fields: the format prefix, a global routing prefix, the subnet identifier, and the interface identifier. The format prefix for a unicast global address is 3 (3 bits). The global routing prefix references the network address (45 bits), and the subnet ID references a subnet within the site (16 bits).

IPv6 Unicast Local Use Addresses: Link-Local and Site-Local Addresses

For local use, IPv6 provides both link-local and site-local addresses. Link-local addressing is used for interfaces (hosts) that are physically connected to a network. This is usually a small local network. A link-local address uses only three fields: the format prefix FE8 (10 bits), an empty field (54 bits), and the interface identifier (host address, 64 bits). In effect, the network section is empty.

IPv6 site-local addresses have three fields: the format prefix (10 bits), the subnet identifier (54 bits), and the interface identifier (64 bits). Except for any local subnetting, no network address exists.

IPv6 Multicast Addresses

Multicast addresses have a format prefix of *FF* (8 bits) with flag and scope fields to indicate whether the multicast group is permanent or temporary and whether it is local or global in scope. A group identifier (112 bits) references the multicast group. For the scope, *2* is link-local, *5* is site-local, and *E* is global. In addition to their interface identifiers, hosts will also have a group ID that can be used as a broadcast address. You use this address to broadcast to the hosts. The following example will broadcast only to those hosts on the local network (5) with the group ID 101:

```
FF05:0:0:0:0:0:0:101
```

To broadcast to all the hosts in a link-local scope, you would use this broadcast address:

```
FF02:0:0:0:0:0:0:1
```

For a site-local scope, a local network, you would use this:

```
FF05:0:0:0:0:0:0:2
```

TCP/IP Configuration Files

A set of configuration files in the **/etc** directory, shown in Table 27-5, is used to set up and manage your TCP/IP network. These configuration files specify such network information as host and domain names, IP addresses, and interface options. The IP addresses and domain names of other Internet hosts you want to access are entered in these files. If you configured your network during installation, you can already find that information in these files.

Address	Description
Host address	IP address of your system; includes a network part to identify the network you are on and a host part to identify your own system
Network address	IP address of your network
Broadcast address	IP address for sending messages to all hosts on your network at once
Gateway address	IP address of your gateway system, if you have one (usually the network part of your host IP address with the host part set to 1)
Domain name server addresses	IP addresses of domain name servers your network uses
Netmask	Used to determine the network and host parts of your IP address
File	**Description**
/etc/hosts	Associates hostnames with IP addresses, lists domain names for remote hosts with their IP addresses
/etc/host.conf	Lists resolver options
/etc/nsswitch.conf	Name Switch Service configuration
/etc/resolv.conf	Lists domain name server names, IP addresses (name server), and domain names where remote hosts may be located (search)
/etc/protocols	Lists protocols available on your system
/etc/services	Lists available network services, such as FTP and telnet, and the ports they use
/etc/networking/interfaces	Network interfaces controlled by ip-up and ip-down

TABLE 27-5   TCP/IP Configuration Addresses and Files

Identifying Hostnames: /etc/hosts

Without the unique IP address the TCP/IP network uses to identify computers, a particular computer cannot be located. Because IP addresses are difficult to use or remember, domain names are used instead. For each IP address, a domain name exists. When you use a domain name to reference a computer on the network, your system translates it into its associated IP address, which can then be used by your network to locate that computer.

Originally, every computer on the network was responsible for maintaining a list of the hostnames and their IP addresses. This list is still kept in the **/etc/hosts** file. When you use a domain name, your system looks up its IP address in the **hosts** file. The system administrator is responsible for maintaining this list. Because of the explosive growth of the Internet and the development of more and more large networks, the responsibility for associating domain names and IP addresses has been taken over by domain name servers. The **hosts** file is still used to hold the domain names and IP addresses of frequently accessed hosts, however. Your system normally checks your **hosts** file for the IP address of a domain name before taking the added step of accessing a name server.

The format of a domain name entry in the **hosts** file is the IP address followed by the domain name, separated by a space. You can then add aliases for the hostname. After the entry, on the same line, you can enter a comment. A comment is always preceded by a **#** symbol. You can already find an entry in your **hosts** file for **localhost.localdomain** and **localhost** with the IP address 127.0.0.1; **localhost** is a special identification used by your computer to enable users on your system to communicate locally with each other. The IP address 127.0.0.1 is a special reserved address used by every computer for this purpose. It identifies what is technically referred to as a *loopback device.* The corresponding IPV6 localhost address is **::1** and has the hostname **localhost6**. You should never remove the **localhost** and **localhost6** entries. A sample **/etc/hosts** file is shown here:

```
/etc/hosts
127.0.0.1            localhost.localdomain localhost turtle.mytrek.com
::1                  localhost6.localdomain6   localhost6
192.168.0.1       turtle.mytrek.com
192.168.0.2       rabbit.mytrek.com
192.168.34.56     pango1.mytrain.com
```

/etc/resolv.conf

The **/etc/resolv.conf** file holds the IP addresses for your DNS servers along with domains to search. A DNS entry will begin with the term **nameserver** followed by the name server's IP address. A search entry will list network domain addresses. Check this file to see if your network DNS servers have been correctly listed. If you have a router for a local network, NetworkManager will automatically place an entry for it in this file. The router in turn will reference your ISP's name server.

```
/etc/resolv.conf
nameserver  192.168.0.1
```

/etc/services

The **/etc/services** file lists network services available on your system, such as FTP and telnet, and associates each with a particular port. Here, you can find out what port your web server is checking or what port is used for your FTP server. You can give a service an alias, which you specify after the port number. You can then reference the service using the alias.

/etc/protocols

The **/etc/protocols** file lists the TCP/IP protocols currently supported by your system. Each entry shows the protocol number, its keyword identifier, and a brief description. See **http://iana.org/assignments/protocol-numbers** for a complete listing.

/etc/network

The **/etc/network** directory holds network interface information used by **ifup** and **ifdown** to start up and shut down your networking. Subdirectories hold configuration scripts for certain network-related services such as multicast DNS discover with Avahi or remote file system mounting with NFS. The subdirectories included are **if-down.d**, **if-post-down.d**, **if-pre-up.d**, and **if-up.d**.

/etc/network/interfaces

Interfaces are defined in **/etc/network/interfaces** file, which usually holds only the configuration for the internal loopback interface. NetworkManager will handle all configuration for network interfaces such as your Ethernet card or wireless connection. A standard Ubuntu version defines the loopback interface, the local network interface for your computer. The **auto** command will automatically activate the network interface when you boot up.

```
auto lo
iface lo inet loopback
```

The **/etc/network/interfaces** file holds manual network configuration settings, such as those you set with **network-admin** (System | Administration | Network). Automatic configurations are managed by NetworkManager. NetworkManager, however, will run any if-up and if-down scripts in the **/etc/network** subdirectories.

Should you need to configure your connection manually, you could enter configuration entries directly by editing the **/etc/network/interfaces** file. The **iface** command defines the interface. Its arguments are the interface name, the protocol it uses (**inet** for IPv4 and **inet6** for IPv6), and the connection type: **static**, **dhcp**, **ppp** (dial-up), or **bootp**. Each protocol and connection type can support different options. Check the interface's man page for details.

The following example sets up a static IP address for the first Ethernet device, **eth0,** using the IPv4 protocol. The address entry specifies the IP address, along with netmask and gateway for the IP addresses for those servers:

```
auto eth0
iface lo inet static
address 192.168.0.5
netmask 255.255.255.0
gateway 192.168.0.1
```

Should you be using a DHCP server to set up your address information, you would specify **dhcp**:

```
auto eth0
iface lo inet dhcp
```

You use the **auto** entry to specify whether an interface should be started up with the **ifup -a** command. This command is run by the **/etc/init.d/networking** script, which is run when your system starts up and whenever you restart networking.

If you make changes, you can then restart the network services with the **init** networking script:

```
sudo /etc/init.d/networking restart
```

Network Autoconfiguration with IPv6, DHCPv6, and DHCP

Many networks now provide either IPv6 autoconfiguration or the DHCP service, which automatically provides network configuration for all connected hosts. Autoconfiguration can be either stateless, as in the case of IPv6, or stateful, as with DHCP. Stateless IPv6 autoconfiguration requires no independent server or source to connect to a network. It is a direct plug-and-play operation, where the hardware network interfaces and routers can directly determine the correct addresses. DCHP is an older method that requires a separate server to manage and assign all addresses. Should this server ever fail, hosts cannot connect.

With DHCP, an administrator uses a pool of IP addresses from which the administrator can assign an IP address to a host as needed. The protocol can also be used to provide all necessary network connection information such as the gateway address for the network or the netmask. Instead of having to configure each host separately, network configuration can be handled by a central DHCP server. The length of time that an address can be used can be controlled by means of leases, making effective use of available addresses. If your network is configuring your systems with DHCP, you will not have to configure it.

Two versions of DHCP are currently available—one for the original IPv4 protocol and another, known as DHCPv6, for protocol. IPv6 includes information for dynamic configuration that IPv4 lacks. In this respect, IPv4 is much more dependent on DHCP than is IPv6.

IPv6 Stateless Autoconfiguration

In an IPv6 network, the IPv6 protocol includes information that can directly configure a host. With IPv4 you either had to configure each host manually or rely on a DHCP server to provide configuration information. With IPv6, configuration information is integrated into the Internet protocol directly. IPv6 address autoconfiguration is described in detail in RFC 2462.

IPv6 autoconfiguration capabilities are known as *stateless*, meaning that they can directly configure a host without recourse of an external server. Alternatively, DHCP, including DHCPv6, is *stateful*, where the host relies on an external DHCP server to provide configuration information. Stateless autoconfiguration has the advantage of hosts not having to rely on a DHCP server to maintain connections to a network. Networks can even become mobile, hooking into one subnet or another, automatically generating addresses as needed. Hosts are no longer tied to a particular DHCP server.

Generating the Local Address

To autoconfigure hosts on a local network, IPv6 makes use of the each network device's hardware MAC address. This address is used to generate a temporary address, with which the host can be queried and configured.

The MAC address is used to create a link-local address with a link-local prefix, **FE80::0**, followed by an interface identifier. The link-local prefix is used for physically connected hosts such as those on a small local network.

A uniqueness test is then performed on the generated address. Using the Neighbor Discovery Protocol (NDP), other hosts on the network are checked to determine whether another host is already using the generated link-local address. If no other host is using the address, the address is assigned for that local network. At this point, the host has only a local address valid within the local physical network. Link-local addresses cannot be routed to a larger network.

Generating the Full Address: Router Advertisements

Once the link-local address has been determined, the router for the network is queried for additional configuration information. The information can be stateful, stateless, or both. For stateless configuration, information such as the network address is provided directly, whereas for stateful configuration, the host is referred to a DHCPv6 server where it can obtain configuration information. The two can work together. Often the stateless method is used for addresses, and the stateful DHCPv6 server is used to provide other configuration information such as DNS server addresses.

In the case of stateless addresses, the router provides the larger network address, such as the network's Internet address. This address is then added to the local address, replacing the original link-local prefix, giving either a complete global Internet address or, in the case of private networks, site-local addresses. Routers will routinely advertise this address information, though it can also be specifically requested. The NDP is used to query the information. Before the address is officially assigned, a duplicate address detection procedure checks to see if the address is already in use. The process depends on the router's providing the appropriate addressing information in the form of router advertisements. If no router or route advertisements are provided, then a stateful method such as DHCPv6 or manual configuration must be used to provide the addresses.

Figure 27-2 shows a network that is configured with stateless address autoconfiguration. Each host first determines its interface identifier using its own MAC hardware address to create a temporary link-local address for each host using the **FE80::0** prefix. This allows initial communication with the network's router. The router then uses its network prefix to create full Internet addresses, replacing the link-local prefix.

Router Renumbering

With IPv6, routers can renumber the addresses on their networks by changing the network prefix. Renumbering is carried out through the Router Renumbering (RR) Protocol. (See RFC 2894 for a description of router renumbering.) Renumbering is often used when a network changes ISPs and requires that the net address for all hosts be changed (see Figure 27-3). It can also be used for mobile networks in which a network can be plugged in to different larger networks, renumbering each time.

With renumbering, routers place a time limit on addresses, similar to the lease time in DHCP, by specifying an expiration limit for the network prefix when the address is generated. To ease transition, interfaces still keep their old addresses as deprecated addresses, while the new ones are first being used. The new addresses will be the preferred ones used for any new connections, while deprecated addresses are used for older connections. In effect, a host can have two addresses—one deprecated and one preferred. This regeneration of addresses effectively renumbers the hosts.

IPv6 Stateful Autoconfiguration: DHCPv6

The IPv6 version of DHCP (DHCP IPv6) provides stateful autoconfiguration to those networks that still want a DHCP-like service on IPv6 networks. DHCP IPv6 provides configuration information from a server, just like DHCP, but it is a completely different protocol from the IPv4 version, with different options and capabilities. As a stateful configuration process, information is provided by an independent server. A version of the DHCP IPv6 server and client are available from the WIDE project and located in the Ubuntu universe repository. You can find out more about the WIDE project at **http://sourceforge.net/projects/wide-dhcpv6/**. The server requires its own WIDE DHCPv6 clients.

As with IPv6 autoconfiguration, the host identifier for a local address is first generated automatically. This is a local-link address containing a host identifier address generated from the host interface's MAC address.

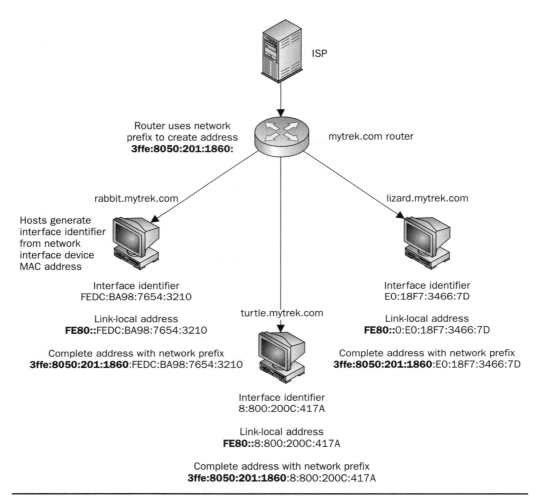

FIGURE 27-2   Stateless IPv6 address autoconfiguration

Once the local-link address is determined, the router is queried for the DHCPv6 server. This information is provided in router advertisements that are broadcast regularly. At this point the two different kinds of stateful information can be provided by the server: addresses and other configuration information. The host is notified which kinds of stateful information are provided. If address information is not given by the DHCPv6 server, addresses will be determined using the stateless autoconfiguration method described in the preceding section. If address information is provided, an address will be obtained from the server instead of being directly generated. Before leasing an address, the server will run a duplicate address detection procedure to make sure the address is unique.

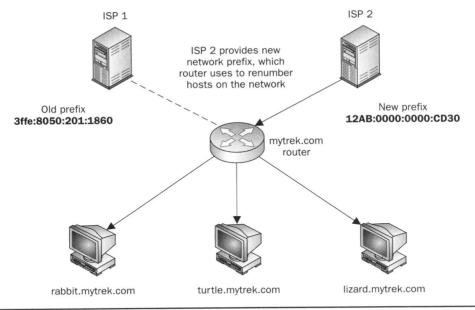

ISP 1

ISP 2

ISP 2 provides new
network prefix, which
router uses to renumber
hosts on the network

Old prefix
3ffe:8050:201:1860

New prefix
12AB:0000:0000:CD30

mytrek.com
router

rabbit.mytrek.com   turtle.mytrek.com   lizard.mytrek.com

FIGURE 27-3   Router renumbering with IPv6 autoconfiguration

Linux as an IPv6 Router: radvd

For a Linux system that operates as a router, you use the **radvd** (Router Advertisement
Daemon) to advertise addresses, specifying a network prefix in the **/etc/radvd.conf** file
(Ubuntu main repository). The **radvd** daemon will detect router network address requests
from hosts, known as *router solicitations,* and provide them with a network address using a
router advertisement. These router advertisements will also be broadcast to provide the
network address to any hosts that do not send in requests. For **radvd** to work, you will have
to turn on IPv6 forwarding. Use **sysctl** and set **net.ipv6.conf.all.forwarding** to **1**.
To start up the **radvd** daemon, you use the **radvd** startup script. To check the router
addresses **radvd** is sending, you can use **radvdump**.

You will have to configure the **radvd** daemon yourself, specifying the network address
to broadcast. Configuration, though, is very simple, as the full address will be automatically
generated using the host's hardware address. A configuration consists of interface entries,
which in turn list interface options, prefix definitions, and options, along with router
definitions if needed. The configuration is placed in the **/etc/radvd.conf** file, which will look
something like this:

```
interface eth0 {
    AdvSendAdvert on;
        prefix fec0:0:0:0::/64
        {
        AdvOnLink on;
        AdvAutonomous on;
        };
};
```

This assumes one interface is used for the local network, **eth0**. This interface configuration lists an interface option (**AdvSendAdvert**) and a prefix definition, along with two prefix options (**AdvOnLink** and **AdvAutonomous**). To specify prefix options for a specific prefix, add them within parentheses following the prefix definition. The prefix definition specifies your IPv6 network address. If a local area network has its own network address, you will need to provide its IPv6 network prefix address. For a private network, such as a home network, you can use the site-local IPv6 prefix, which operates like the IPv4 private network addresses, 192.168.0. The preceding example uses a site-local address that is used for private IPv6 networks, **fec0:0:0:0::**, which has a length of 64 bits.

The **AdvSendAdvert** interface option turns on network address advertising to the hosts. The **AdvAutonomous** network prefix option provides automatic address configuration, and **AdvOnLink** simply means that host requests can be received on the specified network interface.

A second network interface is then used to connect the Linux system to an ISP or larger network. If the ISP supports IPv6, this is simply a matter of sending a router solicitation to the ISP router. This automatically generates your Internet address using the hardware address of the network interface that connects to the Internet and the ISP router's advertised network address. In Figure 27-2, shown earlier, the **eth0** network interface connects to the local network, whereas **eth1** connects to the Internet.

DHCP for IPv4

DHCP provides configuration information to systems connected to an IPv4 TCP/IP network, whether the Internet or an intranet. The machines on the network operate as DHCP clients, obtaining their network configuration information from a DHCP server on their network. A machine on the network runs a DHCP client daemon that automatically receives its network configuration information from its network's DHCP server. The information includes its IP address, along with the network's name server, gateway, and proxy addresses, including the netmask. Nothing has to be configured manually on the local system, except to specify the DHCP server from which it should get its network configuration. This has the added advantage of centralizing control over network configuration for the different systems on the network. A network administrator can manage the network configurations for all the systems on the network from the DHCP server.

A DHCP server also supports several methods for IP address allocation: automatic, dynamic, and manual. Automatic allocation assigns a permanent IP address for a host. Manual allocation assigns an IP address designated by the network administrator. With dynamic allocation, a DHCP server can allocate an IP address to a host on the network only when the host actually needs to use it. Dynamic allocation takes addresses from a pool of IP addresses that hosts can use when needed and releases them when they are finished.

The current version of DHCP supports the DHCP failover protocol, in which two DHCP servers support the same address pool. Should one fail, the other can continue to provide DHCP services for a network. Both servers are in sync and have the same copy of network support information for each host on the network. Primary and secondary servers in this scheme are designated with the primary and secondary statements.

A variety of DHCP servers and clients are available for different operating systems. The Ubuntu main repository provides DHCP version 3 software from the Internet Software Consortium (ISC) at **www.isc.org**. The software available includes a DHCP server, a client, and a relay agent. The DHCP client is called **dhclient**, and the IPv4 server is called **dhcpd**.

Configuring DHCP IPv4 Client Hosts

Configuring hosts to use a DHCP server is a simple matter of setting options for the host's network interface device, such as an Ethernet card. For a Linux host, you can use a distribution network tool to set the host to access a DHCP server automatically for network information. On a network tool's panel for configuring the Internet connection, you will normally find a check box for selecting DHCP. Clicking this box will enable DHCP.

Client support is carried out by the **dhclient** tool. When your network starts up, it uses **dhclient** to set up your DHCP connection. Though defaults are usually adequate, you can further configure the DHCP client using the **/etc/dhclient.conf** file. Consult the **dhclient.conf** man page for a detailed list of configuration options. **dhclient** keeps lease information on the DCHP connection in the **/var/lib/dhcp/dhclient.leases** file. You can also directly run **dhclient** to configure DHCP connections.

```
dhclient
```

Configuring the DHCP IPv4 Server

You can stop and start the DHCP server using the **dhcp3-server** script in the **/etc/rc.d/init.d** directory. Use the **services-admin** tool or the **dhcp3-server** script with the **start**, **restart**, and **stop** options. The following example starts the DHCP server. Use the **stop** option to shut it down and **restart** to restart it.

```
sudo /etc/init.d/dhcp3-server start
```

Dynamically allocated IP addresses, known as *leases,* will be assigned for a given time. When a lease expires, it can be extended or a new one generated. Current leases are listed in the **dhcpd.leases** file located in the **/var/lib/dhcp** directory. A lease entry will specify the IP address and the start and end times of the lease along with the client's hostname.

You can also use the GNOME DHCPD configuration tool (**GDHCPD** package, universe repository) to configure DHCP server graphically. Though still in early development, the GDHCPD tool provides an easy-to-use method for setting up your server. Choose Administration | System Tools to select and start the package. You may need to use **gsku** to start it:

```
gksu gdhcpd
```

On the Scopes tab, you enter the network connection, IP address for that connection, and the netmask. Then click Add. In the Range From boxes, enter a range of addresses to allocate, then click Add.

The Single Hosts tab lets you specify static IP addresses to assign to particular hosts. These are normally used for systems such as servers whose IP addresses do not usually change.

Click the Settings button to see your server configuration settings, such as the configuration and leases files used, and whether to allow DNS updates.

The configuration file for the DHCP server is **/etc/dhcp3/dhcpd.conf**, where you specify parameters and declarations that define how different DHCP clients on your network are accessed by the DHCP server, along with options that define information passed to the clients by the DHCP server. These parameters, declarations, and options can be defined globally for certain subnetworks or for specific hosts. Global parameters, declarations, and options apply to all clients, unless overridden by corresponding declarations and options in subnet or host declarations. Technically, all entries in a **dhcpd.conf** file are statements that can be either declarations or parameters. All statements end with a semicolon. Options are specified in **options** parameter statements. Parameters differ from declarations in that they define if and how to perform tasks, such as how long a lease is allocated. Declarations describe network features such as the range of addresses to allocate or the networks that are accessible.

Domain Name Service

Each computer connected to a TCP/IP network, such as the Internet, is identified by its own IP address. IP addresses are difficult to remember, so a domain name version of each IP address is also used to identify a host. A domain name consists of two parts: the hostname and the domain. The hostname is the computer's specific name, and the domain identifies the network of which the computer is a part. The domains used for the United States usually have extensions that identify the type of host. For example, **.edu** is used for educational institutions and **.com** is used for businesses. International domains usually have extensions that indicate the country in which they are located, such as **.fr** for France or **.au** for Australia. The combination of a hostname, domain, and extension forms a unique name by which a computer can be referenced. The domain can, in turn, be split into further subdomains.

As you know, a computer on a network can still be identified only by its IP address, even if it has a hostname. You can use a hostname to reference a computer on a network, but this involves using the hostname to look up the corresponding IP address in a database. The network then uses the IP address, not the hostname, to access the computer. Before the advent of large TCP/IP networks, such as the Internet, it was feasible for each computer on a network to maintain a file with a list of all the hostnames and IP addresses of the computers connected on its network. Whenever a hostname was used, it was looked up in this file and the corresponding IP address was located. You can still do this on your own system for remote systems you access frequently.

As networks became larger, it became impractical—and, in the case of the Internet, impossible—for each computer to maintain its own list of all the domain names and IP addresses. To provide the service of translating domain addresses to IP addresses, databases of domain names were developed and placed on their own servers. To find the IP address of a domain name, you send a query to a name server, which then looks up the IP address for you and sends it back. In a large network, several name servers can cover different parts of the network. If a name server cannot find a particular IP address, it sends the query on to another name server that is more likely to have it.

If you are administering a network and you need to set up a name server for it, you can configure a Linux system to operate as a name server. To do so, you must start up a name server daemon and then wait for domain name queries. A name server makes use of several configuration files that enable it to answer requests. The name server software used on Linux systems is the Berkeley Internet Name Domain (BIND) server distributed by the ISC.

Name servers are queried by resolvers, which are programs specially designed to obtain addresses from name servers. To use domain names on your system, you must configure your own resolver. Your local resolver is configured with your **/etc/host.conf** and **/etc/resolv.conf** files, but you can use **/etc/nsswitch** in place of **/etc/host.conf**.

host.conf

The **host.conf** file lists resolver options. Each option can have several fields, separated by spaces or tabs. You can add a **#** at the beginning of a line to enter a comment. The options tell the resolver what services to use. The order of the list is important, because the resolver begins with the first option listed and moves on to the next ones in turn. You can find the **host.conf** file in your **/etc** directory, along with other configuration files.

The order entry specifies the sequence of name resolution methods, such as the **hosts** file or the DNS server (**bind**). The **multi** option allows a host to have more then one IP address. In the next example of a **host.conf** file, the **order** option instructs your resolver first to look up names in your local **/etc/hosts** file, and then, if that fails, to query domain name servers.

```
/etc/host.conf
# host.conf file
# Lookup names in host file and then check DNS
order hosts,bind
# There are no multiple addresses
multi on
```

Network Interfaces and Routes: ifconfig and route

Your connection to a network is made by your system through a particular hardware interface, such as an Ethernet card or a modem. Data passing through this interface is then routed to your network. The `ifconfig` command configures your network interfaces, and the `route` command sets up network connections accordingly. If you configure an interface with a network configuration tool provided by your Linux distribution, you needn't use `ifconfig` or `route`. However, you can directly configure interfaces using `ifconfig` and `route`, if you want. Every time you start your system, the network interfaces and their routes must be established. This is done automatically for you by NetworkManager. Also, for manual configurations, interfaces and routes are set up when you star up your system by the `ifup` command run by the **/etc/init.d/networking** initialization file. The `ifup` command uses configuration settings in the **/etc/network/interfaces** file. Alternatively, you can run your own direct configuration with `ifconfig` and `route` commands.

NOTE *As an alternative to* `ifconfig` *and* `route`, *you can use* `ip`. *This is a new tool, included in the **iproute2** package. The syntax is much the same. Route commands use the* `route` *option,* `ip route`. *The* `ifconfig` *operations on addresses would use the* `addr` *option,* `ip addr`.

A packet that is part of a transmission takes a certain *route* to reach its destination. On a large network, packets are transmitted from one computer to another until the destination computer is reached. The route determines where the process starts and to what computer your system needs to send the packet for it to reach its destination. On small networks, routing may be static—that is, the route from one system to another is fixed. One system knows how to reach another, moving through fixed paths. On larger networks and on the Internet, however, routing is dynamic. Your system knows the first computer to send its packet off to, and then that computer takes the packet from there, passing it on to another computer, which then determines where to pass it on. For dynamic routing, your system needs to know little. Static routing, however, can become complex because you have to keep track of all the network connections.

Your routes are listed in your routing table in the **/proc/net/route** file. To display the routing table, enter **route** with no arguments (the **netstat -r** command will also display the routing table). Each entry in the routing table has several fields, providing information such as the route destination and the type of interface used:

```
# route
Kernel routing table
Destination Gateway      Genmask        Flags Metric Ref Use  Iface
192.168.0.0    *         255.255.255.0  U     0      0   0    eth0
127.0.0.0      *         255.0.2055.0   U     0      0   0    lo
default     192.168.0.1  0.0.0.0        UG    0      0   0    eth0
```

Monitoring Your Network: EtherApe, Ping, Ettercap, Wireshark, Tcpdump, and Netstat

Several applications are available on Linux to let you monitor your network activity. Graphical applications such as EtherApe, Ettercap, and Wireshark provide detailed displays and logs to let you analyze and detect network usage patterns. Other tools such as ping offers specific services.

The EtherApe, Ettercap, and Wireshark tools can be accessed by choosing Applications | Internet. Tools such as ping, traceroute, and netstat can be accessed with the GNOME Network Tools application accessible by choosing Applications | System Tools, or they can be called individually from a command line.

EtherApe provides a simple graphical display for your protocol activity. The Preferences dialog lets you set features such as the protocol to check and the kind of traffic to report.

Ping

With the ping program, you can check to see whether you can access another host on your network. The ping program sends a request to the host for a reply. The host then sends a reply back, and it is displayed on your screen. The ping program continually sends such a request until you stop it with a **break** command, by pressing CTRL-C. You see one reply after another scroll by on your screen until you stop the program. If ping cannot access a host, it issues a message saying the host is unreachable. If ping fails, it can indicate that your network connection is not working—only the particular interface, a basic configuration problem, or a bad physical connection. The ping utility uses the ICMP, discussed in Chapter 20. Networks may block these protocols as a security measure, also preventing ping from working. A ping failure may simply indicate a security precaution on the part of the queried network.

To use ping, enter **ping** and the name of the host:

```
$ ping ftp.redhat.com
```

Ettercap

Ettercap is a sniffer program designed to detect Man in the Middle attacks (universe repository). In this kind of attack, packets are detected and modified in transit to let an unauthorized user access a network. You can use either Ettercap's graphical interface or its command line interface. The program can perform unified sniffing on all connections or bridged sniffing on a connection between network interfaces. Ettercap uses plug-ins for specific tasks, such as **dos_attack** to detect Denial of Service attacks and **dns-spoof** for DNS spoofing detection. Check the plug-ins Help panel, or enter `ettercap -P list` for a complete listing. Ettercap can be run in several modes, including a text mode, a command line cursor mode, a script mode using commands in a file, and even as a daemon that logs results automatically.

Wireshark

Wireshark is a network protocol analyzer that lets you capture packets transmitted across your network, selecting and examining those from protocols you want to check (universe repository). You can examine packets from particular transmissions, displaying the data in readable formats. The Wireshark interface displays three panes: a listing of current packets, the protocol tree for the currently selected packet, and a display of the selected packets contents. The first pane categorizes entries by time, source, destination, and protocol, with button headers for each. To sort a set of entries by a particular category, you click its header. For example, to group entries by protocol, you'd click the Protocol button; for destinations, you'd click the Destination button.

Capture Options

To configure Wireshark, choose Capture | Options. This opens an Options window, where you can select the network interface to watch. Here you can also select options such as the file in which to hold your captured information and a size limit for the capture, along with a filter to screen packets. With the Promiscuous mode selected, you can see all network traffic passing through that device; with Promiscuous off, you will see only those packets destined for that device. You can then click the Start button to start Wireshark. To stop and start Wireshark, you select the Stop and Start entries from the Capture menu.

- The Capture Files option lets you select a file in which to save your capture. If no file is selected, data is simply displayed in the Wireshark window. If you want to keep a continuous running snapshot of your network traffic, you can use ring buffers, which are a series of files that are used to save captured data. When they fill up, the capture begins saving again to the first file, and so on. Check Use Multiple Files to enable this option.

- Display options control whether packets are displayed in real time on the Wireshark window.

- Limits let you set a limit for the capture packet size.

- Capture filter lets you choose the type of protocol you want to check.

- Name Resolution enables the display of host and domain names instead of IP addresses, if possible.

Wireshark Filters

A filter lets you select packets that match specified criteria, such as packets from a particular host. Criteria are specified using expressions supported by the Packet Capture Library and implemented by **tcpdump**. Wireshark filters use expressions similar to those used by the **tcpdump** command. Check the **tcpdump** man page for detailed descriptions.

You can set up either a Search filter in the Find panel (accessed via the Edit menu) to search for certain packets, or set up a Capture filter in the Options panel (Capture menu) to select which packets to record. The filter window is the same for both. On the filter window you can select the protocol for which you want to search or capture. The filter name and string will appear in the Properties segment. You can also enter your own string, setting up a new filter of your own. The string must be a filter expression.

To create a new filter, enter the name you want to give it in the Filter Name box. Then in the Filter String box, enter the filter expression, such as **icmp**, and click New. Your new filter will appear in the list. To change a filter, select it and change its expression in the Filter String box, and then click Change.

A filter expression consists of an ID, such as the name or number of the host, and a qualifier. Qualifiers come in three types: type, direction, and protocol. The type can reference the host, network, or port. The type qualifiers are **host**, **net**, and **port**. Direction selects either source or destination packets, or both. The source qualifier is **src**, and the destination qualifier is **dst**. With no destination qualifier, both directions are selected. Protocol lets you specify packets for a certain protocol. Protocols are represented using their lowercase names, such as **icmp** for ICMP. For example, the expression to list all packets coming in from a particular host would be **src host** *hostname*, where *hostname* is the source host. The following example will display all packets from the 192.168.0.3 host:

```
src host 192.168.0.3
```

Using just **host** will check for all packets going out as well as coming in for that host. The **port** qualifier will check for packets passing through a particular port. To check for a particular protocol, you use the protocol name. For example, to check for all ICMP packets you would use this expression:

```
icmp
```

Several special qualifiers let you further control your selection. The **gateway** qualifier lets you detect packets passing through a gateway. The **broadcast** and **multi-cast** qualifiers detect packets broadcast to a network. The **greater** and **less** qualifiers can be applied to numbers such as ports or IP addresses.

You can combine expressions into a single complex Boolean expression using **and**, **or**, or **not**. This lets you create a more refined filter. For example, to capture only the ICMP packets coming in from host 192.168.0.2, you can use this:

```
src host 192.168.0.3 and icmp
```

Tcpdump

Like Wireshark, tcpdump will capture network packets, saving them in a file where you can examine them. Tcpdump operates entirely from the command line. You will have to open a terminal window to run it. Using various options, you can refine your capture, specifying the kinds of packets you want. The **tcpdump** command uses a set of options to specify actions you want to take, which include limiting the size of the capture, deciding to which file to save it, and choosing any filter you want to apply to it. Check the **tcpdump** man page for a complete listing of options; here are a few:

- The **-i** option lets you specify an interface to which you can listen.
- With the **-c** option, you can limit the number of packets to capture.
- Packets will be output to the standard output by default. To save them to a file, you can use the **-w** option.
- You can later read a packet file using the **-r** option and apply a filter expression to it.

The **tcpdump** command takes as its argument a filter expression that you can use to refine your capture. Wireshark uses the same filter expressions as **tcpdump**.

Netstat

The netstat program provides real-time information on the status of your network connections, as well as network statistics and the routing table. The **netstat** command has several options you can use to bring up different sorts of information about your network. Here's an example:

```
# netstat
Active Internet connections
Proto Recv-Q Send-Q Local Address Foreign Address (State) User
tcp 0 0 turtle.mytrek.com:01 pango1.mytrain.com.:ftp ESTABLISHED dylan
Active UNIX domain sockets
Proto RefCnt Flags Type State Path
unix 1 [ ACC ] SOCK_STREAM LISTENING /dev/printer
unix 2 [ ] SOCK_STREAM CONNECTED /dev/log
unix 1 [ ACC ] SOCK_STREAM LISTENING /dev/nwapi
unix 2 [ ] SOCK_STREAM CONNECTED /dev/log
unix 2 [ ] SOCK_STREAM CONNECTED
unix 1 [ ACC ] SOCK_STREAM LISTENING /dev/log
```

The **netstat** command with no options lists the network connections on your system. First, active TCP connections are listed, and then the active domain sockets are listed. The domain sockets contain processes used to set up communications among your system and other systems. You can use **netstat** with the **-r** option to display the routing table, and **netstat** with the **-i** option displays the uses of the different network interfaces.

TIP   *Linux, since the 2.6.10 kernel, includes InfiniBand support. This is a new I/O architecture that is used to replace the older bus architectures used in current systems. InfiniBand is often used as a replacement for local network connections. It is currently implemented in supercomputer and network server clusters. You can find more about InfiniBand at the Linux InfiniBand Project at **http://sourceforge.net/projects/infiniband**. Support for InfiniBand is being carried out as an open source project by OpenFabrics Alliance, at **http://openib.org**.*

Local Services

CHAPTER 28

Managing Services

A single Linux system can provide several different kinds of services, ranging from security to administration and including more obvious Internet services such as Web and FTP sites, e-mail, and printing. Security tools such as Secure Shell (SSH) and Kerberos run as services, along with administrative network tools such as Dynamic Host Control Protocol (DHCP) and Lightweight Directory Access Protocol (LDAP). The network connection interface is itself a service that you can restart at will. Each service operates as a continually running daemon looking for requests for its particular services. In the case of a web service, the requests will come from remote users. You can turn services on or off by starting or shutting down their daemons.

The process of starting up or shutting down a service is handled by service scripts, described in detail in this chapter. This applies to all services and they are covered at this point since you will most likely use service scripts to start and stop Internet services such as web and mail servers. The service scripts are managed by a new startup and shutdown service, Upstart.

Upstart

Linux systems traditionally used the Unix System V init daemon to manage services by setting up runlevels at which systems could be started or shutdown. Ubuntu has since replaced the SystemV init daemon with the Upstart init daemon, while maintaining the System V init runlevel structure for compatibility purposes. Whereas the System V init daemon would start certain services when the entire system started up or shut down, Upstart is entirely event driven. When an event occurs invoking the need for a service, the service is started. This even-oriented approach is designed to work well with removable devices. When a device is added or removed, this change becomes an event that the Upstart daemon detects and then runs any appropriate associated scripts. System V init daemon only ran scripts when its runlevels changed. It saw only runlevels, not events.

Structurally, Upstart can detect and respond to any event. Eventually it may implement scheduled events, replacing cron, atd, an anacron schedulers, as well as support for on-demand service now managed by xinetd and inetd. You can find out more about Upstart at **http://upstart.ubuntu.com**.

Upstart will detect events and run scripts in the **/etc/event.d** directory for those events. These scripts define jobs that Upstart can then run. Jobs that can be performed by Upstart are defined in scripts in Upstart event directory, **/etc/event.d**. Here you will finds Upstart job scripts for emulating runlevels such as the **rc2** script, as well as system services such as TTY terminal connections. In effect, Upstart jobs replace the entries that used to be in the System V init's **/etc/inittab** file.

Upstart operates by running jobs that are defined in job definition files located in the **/etc/event.d** directory. Jobs are already defined for System V init runlevel emulation, TTY system services, and for certain tasks such as a CTRL-ALT-DELETE event to restart your system. A job script will specify an event, the action to take for that event, and any commands to run for that event. The commands can be either a single command run by an **exec** operation, or a set of commands encased in a **script** and **end script** stanza.

To have a job started automatically when a certain event occurs, you place a **start on** directive in its job file, specifying the event. You can use a **stop on** directive to stop the event automatically. You can use several **start on** directives, each for different events. The **start on** directive for the **control-alt-delete** job is shown here:

```
start on control-alt-delete
```

In the **control-alt-delete** job, a CTRL-ALT-DELETE event that runs the **shutdown** command with the **-r** option to restart. The **exec** command is used to run a shell command directly:

```
start on control-alt-delete
   exec/sbin/shutdown -r -now
```

Many jobs define both **start on** and **stop on** directives, for starting and stopping the job. The event can also take an argument. The **rc2** job definition that controls runlevel 2 emulation has **start** and **stop** events, as shown here:

```
start on runlevel 2
stop on runlevel [!2]
```

The **rc2** job will start when a runlevel event occurs with the argument **2**. It will stop when any runlevel even occurs that has an number other than 2, **[!2]**.

NOTE *An Upstart job definition script does not need to have a **start on** directive. It could be started manually with the **start** command.*

A stopped or started event indicates when some other job has been stopped or started. The following **start on** directive would start its job whenever the **myjob** job started:

```
start on started myjob
```

The **startup** event indicates system startup. The **rcS** job (single-user mode) will be started up initially whenever your system starts up. In its **/etc/event.d/rcS** job definition file you will find the following:

```
start on startup
```

The **rc-default** job is started when the **rcS** job stops:

```
start on stopped rcS
```

The TTY1 job used for terminal services will have several start and stop directives, automatically starting at runlevel 2, 3, 4, and 5 events, and stopping on runlevel 0, 1, and 6 events:

```
start on runlevel 2
start on runlevel 3
start on runlevel 4
start on runlevel 5

stop on runlevel 0
stop on runlevel 1
stop on runlevel 6


respawn
exec /sbin/getty 38400 tty1
```

To run several commands, you encase the command in a **script** stanza. A **script** stanza begins with the **script** keyword and ends with **end script**. Most complex jobs use the **script** stanza. The **rc2** job script shown here will start on a runlevel event with the **2** argument. Then the commands in the script structure are run, setting the runlevel to 2 with the **runlevel** command. Then the **/etc/init.d/rc** script is run with the **2** argument to start up any **/etc/init.d** service scripts for runlevel 2, emulating a runlevel change to 2. The **rc2** job is started when **telinit** triggers a runlevel event with a **2** argument. For any runlevel events that are not 2, the **rc2** job will be stopped. The **console** directive specifies where the job output goes, usually to the console (**output**):

```
start on runlevel 2
stop on runlevel [!2]

console output
script
      set $(runlevel --set 2 || true)
      if [ "$1" != "unknown" ]; then
          PREVLEVEL=$1
          RUNLEVEL=$2
          export PREVLEVEL RUNLEVEL
      fi

      exec /etc/init.d/rc 2
end script
```

You can think of the Upstart daemon managing a set of jobs as similar to how the shell manages background jobs. With the **start** and **stop** commands you can start and stop any job. Use **status** to find out the status of a job:

```
$ sudo stop tty1
tty1 (stop) running, process 5109
tty1 (stop) pre-stop, (main) process 5109
tty1 (stop) stopping, process 5109
tty1 (stop) killed, process 5109
tty1 (stop) post-stop
```

```
tty1 (stop) waiting
$ sudo start tty1
tty1 (start) waiting
tty1 (start) starting
tty1 (start) pre-start
tty1 (start) spawned, process 8457
tty1 (start) post-start, (main) process 8457
tty1 (start) running, process 8457
$ sudo status tty1
tty1 (start) running, process 8457
```

The **initctl** command with the **list** option, shown next, will display a complete list of current Upstart jobs. You can add a pattern to search or a particular job. The **initctl** command also has **start**, **stop**, and **status** options form managing jobs.

```
sudo initctl list
```

You can also use the **emit** command to trigger an event manually that would run a certain job.

Upstart and Runlevels: event.d and init.d

Ubuntu still maintain System V init startup and shutdown scripts in the **/etc/init.d** directory that Upstart uses to start and stop services. You can run these scripts directly to start and stop a service. Upstart will also use the System V init links in runlevel directories (**/etc/rc***n***.d**) to start and stop services. In effect, the supporting structure for runlevels remains the same, though in fact services are now handled by Upstart. System V init compatibility scripts, directory structure, and tools, such as **telinit** and **runlevel** equivalents, are held in the **upstart-compat-sysv** package.

You can start up your system at different levels with certain capabilities. For example, you can run your system at an administrative level, locking out user access. Normal full operations are activated by running your system at a certain level of operational capability, such as supporting multiuser access or graphical interfaces. These levels (also known as *states* or *modes*) are referred to as *runlevels,* the level of support at which you are running your system.

> **NOTE** *You can select certain services to run and the runlevel at which to run them. Most services are servers, such as a web server or proxy server. Other services provide security, such as SSH or Kerberos. On Ubuntu, you can use **services-admin** to turn on and off services, specifying the runlevel. The default is runlevel 2.*

Runlevels

Traditionally, a Linux system has several runlevels, numbered from 0 to 6. Support for these are now emulated by Upstart. When you power up your system, you enter the default runlevel. Runlevels 0, 1, and 6 are special runlevels that perform specific functions. Runlevel 0 is the power-down state and is invoked by the **halt** command to shut down the system. Runlevel 6 is the reboot state—it shuts down the system and reboots. Runlevel 1 is the single-user state, which allows access only to the superuser and does not run any network services. This enables you, as the administrator, to perform administrative actions without interference from others.

Other runlevels reflect how you want the system to be used. Ubuntu uses runlevel 2 for graphical logins and the remainder as user defined, also using graphical logins.

TIP *You can use the single-user runlevel (1) as a recovery mode state; this allows you to start up your system without running startup scripts for services such as DNS. This is helpful if your system hangs when you try to start such services. Networking is disabled, as well as any multiuser access. You can also use* `linux –s` *at the boot prompt to enter runlevel 1. If you want to enter the single-user state and also run the startup scripts, you can use the special* `s` *or* `S` *runlevel.*

Runlevels in event.d directory

As noted, runlevel emulation is managed by the Upstart service. But the Upstart service does not actually have runlevels, like System V init does. To maintain compatibility with System V–compliant Linux and Unix applications, Upstart provides runlevel compatibility scripts in the **/etc/event.d** directory that emulate System V init. To start up a runlevel, Upstart uses **telinit** with the runlevel number 2. When your system starts up, it uses the default runlevel as specified by the **rc-default** script in the **/etc/event.d** directory. Runlevel scripts are available for each runlevel in the **/etc/event.d** directory. The default runlevel is 2, which will run the **/etc/event.d/rc2** script, which in turn invokes **telinit** with the argument **2**.

Using telinit

To change to another runlevel, you can use **telinit** with the runlevel number. You can choose from runlevels 2 ,3, 4, and 5. These are all set up as standard multiuser graphical runlevels. The single runlevel (**S**) is reserved for recovery use. The **telinit** command just triggers a runlevel event for Upstart, which then uses the **/etc/init.d/rc** script to emulate a runlevel change. The **telinit** command is then just a wrapper for an Upstart runlevel event, not the **telinit** command used in previous releases with System V init.

The multiuser runlevels are initially all configured the same, though you could make changes in each, such as running different services at different runlevels (use **services-admin**, **update-rc.d**, or **sysv-rc-conf** to make these changes). You could then use **telinit** to start up at that runlevel, like so:

```
sudo telinit 4
```

Formerly, you could also boot to a certain runlevel from the Grub boot menu by specifying the runlevel on the kernel line. With the Upstart emulation, you can now boot directly only to the single-user runlevel from Grub menu. A recovery mode Grub boot entry is set up to do just that. For all other runlevels, you must first lob in as runlevel 2, the default, or **S** (single) and then use the **telinit** command to enter a new runlevel. Alternatively, you could carefully edit the **rc-default** file to detect runlevel numbers other than single on the GRUB command line and invoke the corresponding runlevel with **telinit**. You could then make Grub entries for these runlevels or just edit the Grub kernel line to add the runlevel number. Editing **rc-default** is risky (back it up first) and requires competency in shell programming.

Default Runlevel

As mentioned, the default runlevel is 2, but you can change this default runlevel to 3, 4, or 5 if you want. To change the default runlevel safely, you can create an **/etc/inittab** file and place and **initdefault** entry in it (use vi or Emacs if you're editing from a command line interface). The following command allows you to use gedit to edit the **/etc/inittab** file:

```
gksu gedit /etc/inittab
```

This file would be just a dummy file used only by **rc-default** to read the default entry. A sample default entry is shown next, changing the default to runlevel 3. Your **/etc/inittab** file would have only this line:

```
id:3:initdefault:
```

Command Line Runlevel

On other distributions, such as Fedora, some runlevels are designed for special behavior. On Fedora, runlevel 3 will run just the command line, without the graphical interface. This is not the case with Ubuntu. On Debian, Ubuntu, and similar distributions, the desktop version invokes the X server at all primary runlevels. To run the command line interface as the primary interface for a runlevel, you need to shut down the display managers (your login screen). To set up a particular runlevel to use just the command line, you would have to instruct its startup service for the X server (**/etc/init.d/gdm**) to stop. To set up runlevel 3 to run just the command line interface when you start up your system, you would use the **sysv-rc-conf**, **update-rc.d**, or **admin-users** tool to have the GDM service to stop at runlevel 3, instead of start. This will put a **stop** link in the **/etc/rc3.d** directory for the GDM service, such as **K01gdm**, replacing the **start** link, **S30gdm**. The **K01gdm** link would invoke the **gdm init.d** script with the **stop** option, shutting down the X server. You can then change to runlevel 3 with the **telnet** command and the argument **3**. The screen will blank and start up the command line interface.

```
sudo telinit 3
```

Upon startup in runlevel 3, press ENTER to display the login prompt (also, if you enter runlevel 3 from GRUB, remove the splash option for kernel).

TIP *If you used **/etc/inittab** to change the default runlevel, and you quickly want to change back to using runlevel 2 as the default without having to edit the **/etc/inittab** file, you can just remove the **/etc/inittab** file. The **rc-start** script will start runlevel 2 if there is no **/etc/inittab** file:* **sudo rm /etc/inittab***.*

The runlevel Command

Use the **runlevel** command to see what state you are currently running in. It lists the previous state followed by the current one. If you have not changed states, the previous state will be listed as **N**, indicating no previous state. This is the case for the state in which you boot up. In the next example, the system is running in state 2, with no previous state change:

```
runlevel
N 2
```

System Startup Files and Scripts

Each time you start your system, the Upstart init daemon starts up services defined in startup scripts. Currently, most services still use the older System V init method for starting up services using runlevels. Upstart will use its event-based init daemon to emulate the System V init structure, allowing many services to run as if they were using a System V init daemon. Eventually, service applications will be rewritten to use Upstart directly, without the need for a System V init emulation.

Upstart emulates the System V startup procedure by running a series of startup scripts from system service scripts located in your **/etc/init.d** directory. It uses links in directories with the name **rc***n***.d** to determine what service scripts to run. (The *n* in the name is a number from 1 to 6 indicating a runlevel, such as **rc2.d** for runlevel 2.) These initialization files are organized according to different tasks. You should not have to change any of these files. Table 28-1 shows system startup files and directories.

rc.local

The **/etc/rc.local** file is the last initialization file executed. You can place commands of your own here. When you shut down your system, the system calls the **halt** file, which contains shutdown commands. The files in **init.d** are then called to shut down daemons, and the file systems are unmounted. The **halt** file is located in the **init.d** directory.

/etc/init.d

The **/etc/init.d** directory is designed primarily to hold scripts that start up and shut down different specialized daemons, such as network and printer daemons and those for font and web servers. These files perform double duty, starting a daemon when the system starts up and shutting down the daemon when the system shuts down. The files in **init.d** are designed in a way that makes it easy for you to write scripts for starting up and shutting down specialized applications. Many of these files are set up for you automatically. You shouldn't need to change them, but if you do need to change them, first be sure you know how these files work.

File	Description
/etc/event.d	Upstart job files that actually start services and processes.
/etc/rc*n*.d	Directories that hold system startup and shutdown files, where *n* is the runlevel. The directories hold links to scripts in the **/etc/init.d** directory.
/etc/rc.local	Initialization file for your own commands. You can freely edit this file to add your own startup commands. This is the last startup file executed.
/etc/init.d	Directory that holds system service scripts (see Table 28-2 later in this chapter).
/etc/init.d/rc	Runlevel emulation by Upstart. Upstart runs this script to emulate runlevel changes.

TABLE 28-1   System Startup Files and Directories

When your system starts up, several programs are automatically started and run continuously to provide services such as a Web site or print server. Depending on the kinds of services you want your system to provide, you can add or remove items in a list of services to be started automatically. For example, the web server is run automatically when your system starts up. If you are not hosting a Web site, you have no need for the web server. You can prevent the service from starting, removing an extra task the system does not need to perform, freeing up resources and possibly reducing potential security holes. Several of the servers and daemons perform necessary tasks. The **sendmail** server enables you to send messages across networks, and the **cupsd** server performs printing operations.

/etc/init.d/rc

The **/etc/init.d/rc** script is used by Upstart to emulate System V runlevel changes. The script takes a runlevel as its argument. It then checks the **/etc/rc*n*.d** links for the runlevel to determine what services to start or stop.

/etc/event.d

In the **/etc/event.d** directory, Upstart maintains event scripts for different runlevels, **rc*n***. An **rc2** script exists for runlevel 2. This script simply runs the **/etc/init.d/rc** script with a **2** as its argument. The **/etc/init.d/rc** script will then search the **/etc/rc2.d** directory for links specifying which service script to start and which to stop.

When your system starts, the **/etc/event.d/rc.default** script is run, which will start up with runlevel 2 or the runlevel specified in an **/etc/inittab** dummy file. For runlevel 2, it will invoke the **/etc/init.d/rc** script with the argument **2**.

NOTE *Keep in mind that the System V runlevel system does not exist on Ubuntu, though its service management structure does. Instead, Upstart emulates System V runlevels using the /etc/init.d/rc script and the same service links and startup scripts in the /etc/init.d and /etc/rcn.d directories.*

Service Scripts: /etc/init.d

You can manage server daemon startup and shutdown with special service scripts located in the **/etc/init.d** directory. These scripts often have the same name as the service's program. For example, for the **/usr/sbin/apache2** web server program, the corresponding script is called **/etc/init.d/apache2**. This script starts and stops the web server. This method of using **init.d** service scripts to start servers is called *System V Init*, after the method used in Unix System V. Some of the more commonly used service scripts are listed in Table 28-2.

The service scripts in the **/etc/init.d** directory can be executed automatically whenever you boot your system. Be careful when accessing these scripts, however. They start essential programs, such as your network interface and your printer daemon. These init scripts are accessed from links in subdirectories set up in the **/etc** directory for each possible runlevel. These directories have names in the format **rc*n*.d**, where *n* is a number referring to a runlevel (see Table 28-3).

Service Script	Description
networking	Operations to start up or shut down your network connections
xinetd	Operations to start up or shut down the **xinetd** daemon
cupsys	The CUPS printer daemon
apache2	Apache web server
innd	Internet News service
krb5kdc	Kerberos KDC server
ldap	LDAP service
nfs	Network file system
powernowd	CPU speed control
policykit	Policy authentication tool
postfix	Postfix mail server
pulseaudio	PulseAudio sound server
sendmail	The Sendmail MTA daemon
samba	Samba for Windows hosts
squid	Squid proxy-cache server
sshd	Secure Shell daemon
syslog	System logging daemon
vsftpd	Very Secure FTP server

TABLE 28-2 Selection of Service Scripts in /etc/init.d

Runlevel	Directory	Description
0	rc0.d	Halts (shuts down) the system
1	rc1.d	Single-user mode (limited capabilities)
2	rc2.d	Multiuser mode with graphical login (full operation mode, X server started automatically)
3	rc3.d	User-defined
4	rc4.d	User-defined
5	rc5.d	User-defined
6	rc6.d	Reboots system
S	rcS.d	Single-user mode

TABLE 28-3 Emulated System Runlevels for Ubuntu Distributions

The **rc** script detects the runlevel in which the system was started and then executes only the service scripts specified in the subdirectory for that runlevel. When you start your system, the **rc** script executes the service scripts designated in the default startup directory, such as **rc1.d** (graphical login for Debian and Ubuntu). The **rc*n*.d** directories hold symbolic links to certain service scripts in the **/etc/init.d** directory. Thus, the **apache2** script in the **/etc/init.d** directory is actually called through a symbolic link in an **rc*n*.d** directory. The symbolic link for the **/etc/init.d/apache2** script in the **rc3.d** directory is **S91apache2**. The *S* prefixing the link stands for *startup*; thus, the link calls the corresponding **init.d** script with the **start** option. The number indicates the order in which service scripts are run; lower numbers run first. **S91apache2** invokes **/etc/init.d/apache2** with the option **start**. If you change the name of the link to start with a *K*, the script is invoked with the **stop** option, stopping it. Such links are used in the runlevels 0 and 6 and in directories **rc6.d** and **rc0.d**. Runlevel 0 halts the system, and runlevel 6 reboots it. You can use the **runlevel** command to determine at what runlevel you are currently operating. A listing of runlevels is shown in Table 28-3.

Managing Services

A *service* is a daemon that runs concurrently with your other programs, continually looking for a request for its services either from other users on your system or from remote users connecting to your system through a network. When a server receives a request from a user, it starts up a *session* to provide its services. For example, if users want to download a file from your system, they can use their own FTP client to connect to your FTP server and start up a session. In the session, they can access and download files from your system. Your server needs to be running for a user to access its services. For example, if you set up a Web site on your system with HTML files, you must have the **apache2** web server program running before users can access your site and display those files.

Managing Services Directly

You can use service scripts to start and stop your server manually. These scripts are located in the **/etc/init.d** directory and have the same names as the server programs. For example, the **/etc/init.d/apache2** script with the **start** option starts the web server. Using this script with the **stop** option stops it, and the **restart** option restarts it. Any of the service management tools such as **services-admin** and **rrconf**, can also start, stop, and set runlevels for servers. The **services-admin** tool is installed initially and is accessible by choosing System | Administration | Services. The following commands are equivalent:

```
sudo /etc/init.d/apache2 stop
```

To determine whether your server is running, you can use the **status** option:

```
sudo /etc/init.d/apache2 status
```

Alternatively, you can use the **ps** command with the **-aux** option to list all currently running processes. You should see a process for the server program you started. To refine the list, you can add a **grep** operation with a pattern for the server name you want. The second command lists the process for the web server:

```
ps -aux
ps -aux | grep 'apache2'
```

*TIP   You can just as easily check for the **apache2** process on the GNOME System Monitor.*

Service Management: services-admin, rrconf, sysv-rc-conf, and update-rc.d

Instead of manually executing all the server programs each time you boot your system, you can have your system automatically start the servers for you. You can do this in two ways, depending on how you want to use a server. You can have a server running continuously from the time you start your system until you shut it down, or you can have the server start only when it receives a request from a user for its services. If a server is being used frequently, you may want to have it running all the time. If it is used rarely, you may want the server to start only when it receives a request. For example, if you are hosting a Web site, your web server is receiving requests all the time from remote users on the Internet. For an FTP site, however, you may receive requests infrequently, in which case you may want to have the FTP server start only when it receives a request. Of course, certain FTP sites receive frequent requests, which would warrant a continuously running FTP server.

A server that starts automatically and runs continuously is referred to as a *standalone* server. The System V init procedure can be used to start servers automatically whenever your system boots. This procedure uses service scripts for the servers located in the **/etc/init.d** directory. Most Linux systems configure the web server to start automatically and to run continuously by default. A script for this called **apache2** is in the **/etc/init.d** directory.

Though no distribution-independent tool is available for managing servers, Ubuntu uses the **services-admin** (GNOME), **rcconf** (Debian), **sysv-rc-conf**, or **update-rc.d** tools. The **rcconf** and **update-rc.d** tools were developed by Debian and are used on Debian, Ubuntu, and similar distributions. The **sysv-rc-conf** tool is a generic tool that can be used on all distributions. The **services-admin** tool is part of the GNOME system tools and is installed with Ubuntu.

The tools provide simple interfaces you can use to choose the servers you want started up and how you want them to run. You use these tools to control any daemon you want started up, including system services such as **cron**, the print server, remote file servers for Samba and NFS, authentication servers for Kerberos, and, of course, Internet servers for FTP or HTTP. Such daemons are referred to as *services*, and you should think of these tools as managing these services. Any of these services can be set up to start or stop at different runlevels.

If you add a new service, **services-admin**, **rcconf**, or **sysv-rc-conf** can manage it. As described in the following section, services are started up at specific runlevels using service links in various runlevel directories. These links are connected to the service scripts in the **init.d** directory. Runlevel directories are numbered from 0 to 6 in the **/etc/** directory, such as **/etc/rc2.d** for runlevel 2 and **/etc/rc5.d** for runlevel 5. Removing a service from a runlevel only changes its link in the corresponding runlevel directory. It does not touch the service script in the **init.d** directory.

services-admin

GNOME's **services-admin** tool lets you turn services on or off as well as specify runlevels and the actions to take. It provides a GUI on GNOME, usually accessible by choosing System | Administration | Services. In the Services Settings window (Figure 28-1), every service displays a check box that, when checked, will cause the service to start at boot time; those unchecked will not run. To turn on a service, scroll to its entry and click the check box next to it to add a check mark. To turn off a service, click its check box to remove the check mark.

NOTE *The Boot Up Manager (**bum**) provides a simple desktop interface for turning services on and off. Its features are similar to **rrconf**.*

To turn a service on or off for a specific runlevel, right-click the service to display a pop-up menu and choose Properties. This displays a window that lists the runlevels, where you can indicate whether the service will be started or stopped. To change or set a stop or start action for a runlevel, click and hold down the mouse button on a specific runlevel. This displays a pop-up menu with start and stop options: Select the one you want.

rcconf and sysv-rc-conf

On Ubuntu, you can also use **rcconf** or **sysv-rc-conf** to turn services on or off for different runlevels. Both tools are run from a terminal window on the command line. Both provide an easy cursor-based interface for using arrow keys and the SPACEBAR to turn services on or off. The **rcconf** tool is a more limited Debian tool that turns services on or all for the default runlevels, whereas **sysv-rc-conf** is more refined, allowing you to select specific runlevels.

The **sysv-rc-conf** tool displays a cursor-based screen (Figure 28-2), where you can check which services to start or stop, and at which runlevel. The runlevels will be listed from

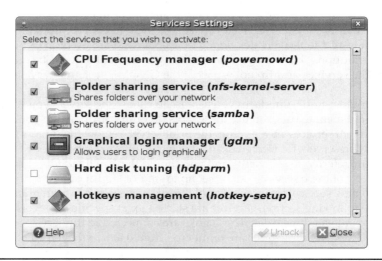

FIGURE 28-1   services-admin tool, System | Administration | Services

```
                   richard@richard-desktop-u: ~
File  Edit  View  Terminal  Tabs  Help

SysV Runlevel Config  -: stop service  =/+: start service  h: help  q: quit

service      1     2     3     4     5     0     6     S
-----------------------------------------------------------------
acpi-supp$  [ ]   [X]   [X]   [X]   [X]   [ ]   [ ]   [ ]
acpid       [ ]   [X]   [X]   [X]   [X]   [ ]   [ ]   [ ]
alsa-utils  [ ]   [ ]   [ ]   [ ]   [ ]   [ ]   [ ]   [ ]
anacron     [ ]   [X]   [X]   [X]   [X]   [ ]   [ ]   [ ]
apache2     [ ]   [X]   [X]   [X]   [X]   [ ]   [ ]   [ ]
apparmor    [ ]   [ ]   [ ]   [ ]   [ ]   [ ]   [ ]   [X]
apport      [ ]   [X]   [X]   [X]   [X]   [ ]   [ ]   [ ]
atd         [ ]   [X]   [X]   [X]   [X]   [ ]   [ ]   [ ]
avahi-dae$  [ ]   [X]   [X]   [X]   [X]   [ ]   [ ]   [ ]
backuppc    [ ]   [X]   [X]   [X]   [X]   [ ]   [ ]   [ ]
bluetooth   [ ]   [X]   [X]   [X]   [X]   [ ]   [ ]   [ ]
bootclean   [ ]   [ ]   [ ]   [ ]   [ ]   [ ]   [ ]   [ ]
bootlogd    [ ]   [ ]   [ ]   [ ]   [ ]   [ ]   [ ]   [ ]


Use the arrow keys or mouse to move around.    ^n: next pg    ^p: prev pg
                   space: toggle service on / off
```

FIGURE 28-2   The sysv-rc-conf service management with runlevels

0 to 6 and S. Use the arrow keys to position to the cell for your service and runlevel. Then press the SPACEBAR to turn a service on or off. You can set the particular runlevel at which to start and stop services.

The **sysv-rc-conf** tool is part of the Ubuntu universe repository. Once installed, you can start it up by entering the following command in a terminal window. **sysv-rc-conf** is a cursor-based keyboard application that runs entirely within the terminal window.

```
sudo sysv-rc-conf
```

update-rc.d

The **update-rc.d** tool is a lower level tool that can install or remove runlevel links. It is usually used when installing service packages to create default runlevel links. You can use it to configure your own runlevels for a service, but this requires that you have a detailed understanding of how runlevel links for services are configured.

The **update-rc.d** tool does not affect links that are already installed. It works only on links that are not already present in the runlevel directories. In this respect, it cannot turn a service on or off directly as can **sysv-rc-conf**. To turn off a service, you would first have to remove all runlevel links in all the **rc*n*.d** directories using the **remove** option and then add in the services you want with the **start** or **stop** options. This makes turning services on and off using the **update-rc.d** tool much more complicated.

You use **start** and **stop** options along with the runlevel to set the runlevels at which to start or stop a service. You will need to provide a link number for ordering the sequence in which it will be run. Enter the runlevel followed by a period. You can specify more than one runlevel. The following line will start the web server on runlevel 5. The order number used for the link name is **91**. The link name will be **S91apache**. Be sure to include the **sudo** command.

```
sudo update-rc.d apache start 91 5 .
```

The stop number is always 100 minus the start number. So the stop number for a service with a start number of 91 would be 09:

```
sudo update-rc.d apache stop 09 6 .
```

The **start** and **stop** options can be combined, like so:

```
update-rc.d apache 99 start 5 . stop 09 6 .
```

A **defaults** option will start and stop the service at a predetermined runlevel. This option can be used to set standard start and stop links for all runlevels. Startup links will be set in runlevels 2, 3, 4, and 5. Stop entries are set in runlevels 0, 1, and 6.

```
update-rc.d apache defaults
```

The following command performs the same operation using the **stop** and **start** options:

```
update-rc.d apache 99 start 2 3 4 5 . stop 09 0 1 6 .
```

The **multiuser** options will start entries at 2, 3, 4 ,5 and stop them at 1:

```
update-rc.d apache multiuser
```

To remove a service you use the **remove** option. The links will not be removed if the service script is still present in the **init.d** directory. Use the **-f** option to force removal of the links without having to remove the service script. The following removes all web service startup and shutdown entries from all runlevels:

```
update-rc.d -f apache  remove
```

To turn off a service at a given runlevel that is already turned on, you would first have to remove all its runlevel links and the add in the links you want. So, to turn off the Apache server at runlevel 3, but still have it turned on at runlevels 2, 4, and 5, you would use the following commands:

```
update-rc.d -f apache remove
update-rc.d apache 99 start 2 4 5 . stop 09 0 1 3 6 .
```

Keep in mind that the **remove** option removes all stop links as well as start ones. So you have to restore the stop links for 0, 1, and 6.

TIP *On Debian and Ubuntu you can use **file-rc** instead of **sysv-rc**. The **file-rc** tool uses a single configuration file instead of links in separate runlevel directories.*

Extended Internet Services Daemon (xinetd)

If your system averages only a few requests for a specific service, you don't need the server for that service to run all the time. You need it only when a remote user is accessing its service. The extended Internet services daemon (**xinetd**) manages Internet servers, invoking them only when your system receives a request for their services. **xinetd** checks continuously for any requests by remote users for a particular Internet service; when it receives a request, it then starts the appropriate server daemon.

The **xinetd** program is designed to be a replacement for **inetd**, providing security enhancements, logging support, and even user notifications. For example, with **xinetd** you can send banner notices to users when they are not able to access a service, telling them why. **xinetd** security capabilities can be used to prevent denial-of-service attacks, limiting remote hosts' simultaneous connections or restricting the rate of incoming connections. **xinetd** also incorporates TCP, providing TCP security without the need to invoke the **tcpd** daemon. Furthermore, you do not have to have a service listed in the **/etc/services** file. **xinetd** can be set up to start any kind of special-purpose server.

Some services on Ubuntu are still configured to use **inetd**, such as the SWAT configuration tool for CUPS print servers. These will use the **openbsd-inetd** package. The **xinetd** and **openbsd-inetd** packages are incompatible, so you must use one or the other. The **inetd** daemon will use an **/etc/inetd.conf** configuration file. Its init script will be **/etc/init.d/openbsd-inetd**.

xinetd and inetd Servers

To start the server only when a request for its services is received, you configure it using the **xinetd** or the older **inetd** daemons. If you add, change, or delete server entries in the **/etc/xinetd** files, you will have to restart the **xinetd** daemon before these changes can take effect. On distributions that support System V init scripts, you can restart the **xinetd** daemon using the **/etc/init.d/xinetd** script with the **restart** argument, as shown here:

```
sudo /etc/init.d/xinetd restart
```

You can also use the **xinetd** script to start and stop the **xinetd** daemon. Stopping effectively shuts down all the servers that the **xinetd** daemon manages (those listed in the **/etc/xinetd.conf** file or the **xinetd.d** directory):

```
sudo /etc/init.d/xinetd stop
sudo /etc/init.d/xinetd start
```

For **inetd**, you would use the **openbsd-inetd** script:

```
sudo /etc/init.d/openbsd-inetd restart
```

You can also directly restart **xinetd** by stopping its process directly. To do this, you use the **killall** command with the **-HUP** signal and the name **xinetd**:

```
killall -HUP xinetd
```

xinetd Configuration: xinetd.conf

The **xinetd.conf** file contains settings for your xinetd server, such as logging and security attributes (see Table 28-4 later in this chapter for a listing of attributes). This file can also contain server configuration entries, or they may be placed into separate configuration files located in the **/etc/xinetd.d** directory. The **includedir** attribute specifies this directory:

```
includedir /etc/xinetd.d
```

Logging xinetd Services

You can add a variety of other attributes such as logging information about connections and server priority (**nice**). In the following example, the **log_on_success** attribute logs the duration (**DURATION**) and the user ID (**USERID**) for connections to a service. **log_on_failure** logs the users that failed to connect, and **nice** sets the priority of the service to 10:

```
log_on_success += DURATION USERID
log_on_failure += USERID
nice = 10
```

The default attributes defined in the defaults block often set global attributes such as default logging activity and security restrictions: **log_type** specifies where logging information is to be sent, such as to a specific file (**FILE**) or to the system logger (**SYSLOG**); **log_on_failure** specifies information to be logged when they fail; and **log_on_success** specifies information to be logged when connections are made:

```
log_type = SYSLOG daemon info
log_on_failure = HOST
log_on_success = PID HOST EXIT
```

xinetd Network Security

For security restrictions, you can use **only_from** to restrict access by certain remote hosts. The **no_access** attribute denies access from the listed hosts, but no others. These controls take IP addresses as their values. You can list individual IP addresses, a range of IP addresses, or a network, using the network address. The **instances** attribute limits the number of server processes that can be active at once for a particular service. The following examples restrict access to a local network 192.168.1.0 and the localhost, deny access from 192.168.1.15, and use the **instances** attribute to limit the number of server processes at one time to 60:

```
only_from = 192.168.1.0
only_from = localhost
no_access = 192.168.1.15
instances = 60
```

The **xinetd** program also provides several internal services, including **services**, **servers**, and **xadmin**. **services** provides a list of currently active services, and **servers** provides information about servers; **xadmin** provides **xinetd** administrative support.

xinetd Service Configuration Files: /etc/xinetd.d Directory

Instead of having one large **xinetd.conf** file for all services, the service configurations are split into several configuration files, one for each service. The directory is specified in the

xinetd.conf file with an **includedir** option. The **xinetd.d** directory holds **xinetd** configuration files for services such as SWAT. This approach has the advantage of letting you add services by creating a new configuration file for them. Modifying a service involves editing only its configuration file, not an entire **xinetd.conf** file.

Configuring Services: xinetd Attributes

Entries in an **xinetd** service file define the server to be activated when requested along with any options and security precautions. An entry consists of a block of attributes defined for different features, such as the name of the server program, the protocol used, and security restrictions. Each block for an Internet service such as a server is preceded by the keyword **service** and the name by which you want to identify the service. A pair of braces encloses the block of attributes. Each attribute entry begins with the attribute name, followed by an assignment operator, such as =, and then the value or values assigned. A special block specified by the keyword **default** contains default attributes for services. The syntax is shown here:

```
service <service_name>
{
<attribute> <assign_op> <value> <value> ...
 ...
}
```

Most attributes take a single value for which you use the standard assignment operator, =. Some attributes can take a list of values. You can assign values with the = operator, but you can also add or remove items from these lists with the =+ and =- operators. Use =+ to add values and =- to remove values. You often use the =+ and =- operators to add values to attributes that may have an initial value assigned in the default block.

Certain attributes are required for a service. These include **socket_type** and **wait**. For a standard Internet service, you also need to provide the **user** (user ID for the service), the **server** (name of the server program), and the **protocol** (protocol used by the server). With **server_args**, you can also list any arguments you want passed to the server program (this does not include the server name). If **protocol** is not defined, the default protocol for the service is used. Attributes are listed in Table 28-4.

Disabling and Enabling xinetd Services

You can turn services on or off manually by editing their **xinetd** configuration file. Services are turned on and off with the **disable** attribute in their configuration file. To enable a service, you set the disable attribute to **no**, as shown here:

```
disable = no
```

You then have to restart **xinetd** to start the service:

```
# /etc/init.d/xinetd restart
```

Attribute	Description
`ids`	Identifies a service. By default, the service ID is the same as the service name.
`type`	Type of service: `RPC`, `INTERNAL` (provided by **xinetd**), or `UNLISTED` (not listed in a standard system file).
`flags`	Possible flags include `REUSE`, `INTERCEPT`, `NORETRY`, `IDONLY`, `NAMEINARGS` (allows use of `tcpd`), `NODELAY`, and `DISABLE` (disables the service). See the **xinetd.conf** man page for more details.
`disable`	Specify **yes** to disable the service.
`socket_type`	Specify `stream` for a stream-based service, `dgram` for a datagram-based service, `raw` for a service that requires direct access to IP, and `seqpacket` for reliable sequential datagram transmission.
`protocol`	Specifies a protocol for the service. The protocol must exist in **/etc/protocols**. If this attribute is not defined, the default protocol employed by the service will be used.
`wait`	Specifies whether the service is single-threaded or multithreaded (**yes** or **no**). If **yes**, the service is single-threaded, which means that **xinetd** will start the server and then stop handling requests for the service until the server stops. If **no**, the service is multithreaded and **xinetd** will continue to handle new requests for it.
`user`	Specifies the user ID (UID) for the server process. The username must exist in **/etc/passwd**.
`group`	Specifies the group ID (GID) for the server process. The group name must exist in **/etc/group**.
`instances`	Specifies the number of server processes that can be simultaneously active for a service.
`nice`	Specifies the server priority.
`server`	Specifies the program to execute for this service.
`server_args`	Lists the arguments passed to the server. This does not include the server name.
`only_from`	Controls the remote hosts to which the particular service is available. Its value is a list of IP addresses. With no value, service is denied to all remote hosts.
`no_access`	Controls the remote hosts to which the particular service is unavailable.
`access_times`	Specifies the time intervals when the service is available. An interval has the form *hour:min-hour:min*.
`log_type`	Specifies where the output of the service log is sent, either the syslog facility (`SYSLOG`) or a file (`FILE`).
`log_on_success`	Specifies the information that is logged when a server starts and stops. Information you can specify includes `PID` (server process ID), `HOST` (the remote host address), `USERID` (the remote user), `EXIT` (exit status and termination signal), and `DURATION` (duration of a service session).
`log_on_failure`	Specifies the information that is logged when a server cannot be started. Information you can specify includes `HOST` (the remote host address), `USERID` (user ID of the remote user), `ATTEMPT` (logs a failed attempt), and `RECORD` (records information from the remote host to allow monitoring of attempts to access the server).

TABLE 28-4   Attributes for xinetd

Attribute	Description
rpc_version	Specifies the RPC version for an RPC service.
rpc_number	Specifies the number for an UNLISTED RPC service.
env	Defines environment variables for a service.
passenv	The list of environment variables from **xinetd**'s environment that will be passed to the server.
port	Specifies the service port.
redirect	Allows a TCP service to be redirected to another host.
bind	Allows a service to be bound to a specific interface on the machine.
interface	Synonym for **bind**.
banner	The name of a file to be displayed for a remote host when a connection to that service is established.
banner_success	The name of a file to be displayed at the remote host when a connection to that service is granted.
banner_fail	The name of a file to be displayed at the remote host when a connection to that service is denied.
groups	Allows access to groups the service has access to (**yes** or **no**).
enabled	Specifies the list of service names to enable.
include	Inserts the contents of a specified file as part of the configuration file.
includedir	Takes a directory name in the form of `includedir /etc/xinetd.d`. Every file inside that directory will be read sequentially as an **xinetd** configuration file, combining to form the **xinetd** configuration.

TABLE 28-4 Attributes for xinetd

If you want to turn on a service that is off by default, you can set its `disable` attribute to **no** and restart **xinetd**. The entry for the TFTP FTP server, **tftpd**, is shown here. An initial comment tells you that it is off by default, but then the `disable` attribute turns it on:

```
service tftp
{
        socket_type     = dgram
        protocol        = udp
        wait            = yes
        user            = root
        server          = /usr/sbin/in.tftpd
        server_args     = -s /tftpboot
        disable         = yes
        per_source      = 11
        cps             = 100 2
        flags           = IPv4
}
```

NOTE *You can also use* **xinetd** *to implement SSH port forwarding, should your system be used to tunnel connections between hosts or services.*

TCP Wrappers

TCP wrappers add another level of security to **xinetd**-managed servers. In effect, the server is wrapped with an intervening level of security, monitoring connections and controlling access. A server connection made through **xinetd** is monitored, verifying remote user identities and checking to make sure they are making valid requests. Connections are logged with the **syslogd** daemon (see Chapter 21) and may be found in **syslogd** files such as **/var/log/secure**. With TCP wrappers, you can also restrict access to your system by remote hosts. Lists of hosts are kept in the **hosts.allow** and **hosts.deny** files. Entries in these files have the format *service:hostname:domain*. The domain is optional. For the service, you can specify a particular service, such as FTP, or you can enter **ALL** for all services. For the hostname, you can specify a particular host or use a wildcard to match several hosts. For example, **ALL** will match on all hosts.

Table 28-5 lists the available wildcards. In the following example, the first entry allows access by all hosts to the web service **http**. The second entry allows access to all services by the **pango1.train.com** host. The third and fourth entries allow FTP access to **rabbit.trek.com** and **sparrow.com**:

```
http:ALL
ALL:pango1.train.com
ftp:rabbit.trek.com
ftp:sparrow.com
```

The **hosts.allow** file holds hosts to which you allow access. If you want to allow access to all but a few specific hosts, you can specify **ALL** for a service in the **hosts.allow** file but list the hosts to which you are denying access in the **hosts.deny** file. Using IP addresses instead of hostnames is more secure because hostnames can be compromised through the DNS records by spoofing attacks, where an attacker pretends to be another host.

Wildcard	Description
ALL	Matches all hosts or services.
LOCAL	Matches any host specified with just a hostname without a domain name. Used to match on hosts in the local domain.
UNKNOWN	Matches any user or host whose name or address is unknown.
KNOWN	Matches any user or host whose name or address is known.
PARANOID	Matches any host whose hostname does not match its IP address.
EXCEPT	An operator that lets you provide exceptions to matches. It takes the form of *list1* **EXCEPT** *list2* where those hosts matched in *list1* that are also matched in *list2* are excluded.

TABLE 28-5   TCP Wrapper Wildcards

When **xinetd** receives a request for an FTP service, a TCP wrapper monitors the connection and starts up the **in.ftpd** server program. By default, all requests are allowed. To allow all requests specifically for the FTP service, you enter the following in your **/etc/hosts.allow** file:

```
ftp:ALL
```

The entry **ALL:ALL** opens your system to all hosts for all services.

TIP *Originally, TCP wrappers were managed by the **tcpd** daemon. However, **xinetd** has since integrated support for TCP wrappers into its own program. You can explicitly invoke the **tcpd** daemon to handle services if you wish. The **tcpd** man pages (**man tcpd**) provide more detailed information about **tcpd**.*

Print, News, and Database Services

Print services are now integrated into every Linux system and allow you to use any printer on your system or network. Newsgroup severs are more rare and are used for setting up newsgroups for local networks or for supporting the Internet's Usenet News Service. Database servers are becoming more common for managing large collections of data on local networks as well as for Internet services.

Printer Services: CUPS

Once treated as devices attached to a system directly, printers are now treated as network resources managed by print servers. In the case of a single printer attached directly to a system, the networking features become transparent and the printer appears as just one more device. On the other hand, you could easily use a print server's networking capability to let several systems access the same printer. Although printer installation is almost automatic on most Linux distributions, your understanding the underlying process can be helpful. Printing sites and resources are listed in Table 29-1.

The Common Unix Printing System (CUPS) provides printing services and is freely available under the GNU Public License. Although CUPS is now included with most distributions, you can also download the most recent source-code version from **http://cups.org**, which provides detailed documentation on installing and managing printers. CUPS is based on the Internet Printing Protocol (IPP), which was designed to establish a printing standard for the Internet. Whereas the older line printer (LPD)–based printing systems focused primarily on line printers, an IPP-based system provides networking, PostScript, and web support. CUPS works like an Internet server and employs a configuration setup much like that of the Apache web server. Its network support lets clients directly access printers on remote servers, without having to configure the printers themselves. Configuration needs to be maintained only on the print servers.

CUPS is the primary print server for most Linux distributions. With **libgnomecups**, GNOME now provides integrated support for CUPS, allowing GNOME-based applications to directly access CUPS printers.

Resource	Description
http://cups.org	Common Unix Printing System
http://pwg.org/ipp	PWG site with Internet Printing Protocol
http://sourceforge.net/projects/lprng	LPRng print server (Universe repository)

TABLE 29-1 Print Resources

Once you have installed your printers and configured your print server, you can print and manage your print queue using print clients. A variety of print clients are available for the CUPS server, GNOME print manager, the CUPS configuration tool, and various line printing tools such as **lpq** and **lpc**, described in detail later in this chapter. The CUPS configuration tool is a Web-based tool that can also manage printers and print jobs (open your browser and enter the URL **http://localhost:631**). A Web page is displayed with entries for managing jobs, managing printers, and performing administrative tasks. Select the Manage Jobs entry to remove or reorder jobs you have submitted.

NOTE *Line Printer, Next Generation (LPRng) was the traditional print server for Linux and Unix systems, but it has since been dropped from many Linux distributions. You can find out more about LPRng at **http://sourceforge.net/projects/lprng**.*

Printer Devices and Configuration

Before you can use any printer, you must install it on a Linux system on your network. A local printer is installed directly on your own system. This involves creating an entry for the printer in a printer configuration file that defines printer type, along with other features such as the device file and spool directory it uses. On CUPS, the printer configuration file is at **/etc/cups/printers.conf**. Installing a printer is fairly simple: You determine which device file to use for the printer and the configuration entries for it.

TIP *If you cannot find the drivers for your printer, you may be able to download them from OpenPrinting database at **www.linux-foundation.org/en/OpenPrinting**. The site maintains an extensive listing of drivers.*

Printer Device Files

Linux dynamically creates the device names for printers that are installed. For parallel printers, the device names will be **lp0**, **lp1**, **lp2**, and so on, depending on how many parallel printers are connected. The number used in these names corresponds to a parallel port on your PC; **lp0** references the LPT1 parallel port, **lp1** references the LPT2 parallel port, and so on. Serial printers will use serial ports, referenced by the device files like **ttyS0**, **ttyS1**, **ttyS2**, and so on. USB-connected printers will have a Hardware Abstract Layer (HAL) device connection. HAL is designed for removable devices that can easily be attached to other connections and still be recognized.

Spool Directories

When your system prints a file, it makes use of special directories called *spool directories*. When you send a file to a printer, a copy of it is made and placed in a spool directory set up for that printer. The location of the spool directory is obtained from the printer's entry in its configuration file. On Linux, the spool directory is located at **/var/spool/cups** under a directory with the name of the printer. For example, the spool directory for the **myepson** printer would be located at **/var/spool/cups/myepson**. The spool directory contains several files for managing print jobs. Some files use the name of the printer as their extension. For example, the **myepson** printer has the files **control.myepson**, which provides printer queue control, and **active.myepson** for the active print job, as well as **log.myepson**, which is the log file.

Installing Printers

Several tools are available for installing CUPS printers. The easiest method is to use the Ubuntu **system-config-printer** tool. You can also use the CUPS Web browser–based configuration tools, included with the CUPS software. Or you can just edit the CUPS printer configuration files directly.

Configuring Printers on Ubuntu with system-config-printer

As noted in Chapter 3, any printer is automatically detected by Ubuntu when you first attach it. You are prompted to confirm automatically selected model and drivers. The tool used to configure printers is **system-config-printers**, accessible by choosing System | Administration | Printing. You can also modify your configuration as well as add access to remote printers on your network.

When you start up **system-config-printer**, you see a window that displays two panes: one that lists your servers and their printers and the other for configuration panels for those printers (see Figure 29-1). To display the configuration details for a particular printer, click the printer's entry in the Server Settings pane; printers are listed in an expandable tree under the servers to which the printers are connected. Printers connected directly to your computer will be listed under Local Printers. Clicking the Server Settings entry will display a pane for setting global printing options such as allowing users to cancel their own print jobs or sharing your printers on your network.

To add a new printer, click New Printer. To edit an installed printer, click its entry in the Server Settings pane to display its configuration panels with tabs for Settings, Policies, Access Control, Printer Options, and Job Control. Once you have made your changes, click Apply to save your changes and restart the printer daemon. If you have more than one printer on your system, you can make one printer the default by clicking Make Default Printer button in its Settings tab. Click the Delete button to remove a printer configuration. You can test your printer with a PostScript, A4, or ASCII test sheet selected from the Test menu.

You can connect to other CUPS print servers by clicking the Go To Server button on the main window. This opens a Connect to CUPS Server window, where you can enter the location of the server and your username.

The New Class button on the main window lets you create a print *class*: you can select a group of printers to print a job instead of selecting just one. That way, if one printer is busy or down, another printer can be automatically selected to perform the job. Installed printers

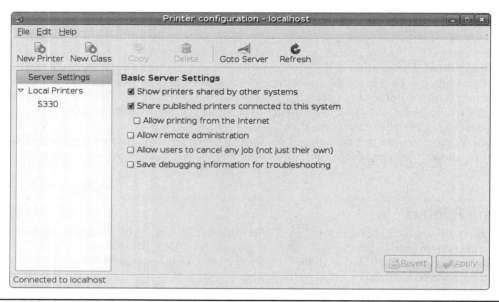

FIGURE 29-1   The Ubuntu system-config-printer tool

can be assigned to different classes. To create a class, click the New Class button to open the New Class window, where you can enter the name for the class, any comments, and the location (your hostname is entered by default). The next screen lists available printers and the printers you assigned to the class. Use the arrow button to add or remove printers to the class. Click Apply when finished. The class will appear under the Local Classes heading on the main **system-config-printer** window. Panels for a selected class are much the same as those for a printer, with a Members panel instead of a Print Control panel. In the Members panel, you can change which printers belong to the class.

Adding a New Printer Manually

When you click New Printer, a series of dialog boxes are displayed, where you can enter the printer name, its type, and its model. In the Printer Name dialog box, type the printer name along with any particular description.

On the following Select Connection screen (Figure 29-2), you select the appropriate printer connection information. Connected local printer brands will be listed by name, such as Canon, whereas for remote printers you specify the type of network connection, such as Windows printers via Samba for printers connected to a Windows system, Internet Printing Protocol (IPP) for printers connected to other Linux systems, or AppSocket/HP JetDirect for HP printers connected directly to your network.

For most connected printers, the connection is usually determined by the device hotplug services udev and HAL, which now manage all devices. This will be the first entry in the list, and the description will show that it was detected by HAL It is always preferable to use the HAL connection; with it, you can plug the printer into any USB port and HAL will automatically detect it. If, instead, you always want the USB printer to use a specific USB port, you can choose the USB-specific connection, such as Canon S330 USB #1. If for some reason your device is not detected, you can use the Other entry to enter the device name.

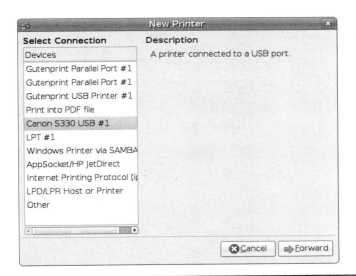

FIGURE 29-2   Printer type for new printers

For an older local printer, you will need to specify the port to which the printer is connected, such as LPT1 for the first parallel port used for older parallel printers, or Serial Port #1 for a printer connected to the first serial port.

On the next screen, you select your printer manufacturer, choosing it from a printer database. Then, on the next screen, you select that manufacturer's model along with its driver (Figure 29-3). The selected drivers for your printer will be listed (on future versions of **system-config-printer**, you can find out more about the printer and driver by clicking the Printer and Driver buttons at the bottom of the screen). Then click the Forward button.

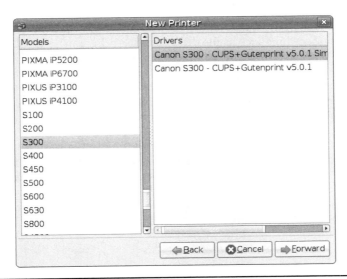

FIGURE 29-3   Printer models and drivers for new printers

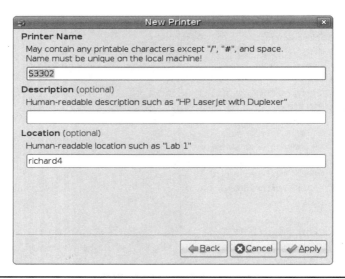

FIGURE 29-4 Printer name and location for new printers

On the next screen, you can enter the printer name, description, and location (Figure 29-4). A printer name and location will already be entered for you. You can change them if you wish—they are only labels to help you identify the printer. When you are finished, click the Apply button. You then see your printer listed in the **system-config-printer** window, with its configuration panel displayed. You are now ready to print.

Modifying Printer Properties

You can also change a printer configuration by selecting its entry in the Printer Configuration window. Once selected, a set of five tabs are displayed for that printer: Settings, Policies, Access Control, Printer Options, and Job Options (Figure 29-5). On the Settings tab, you can change configuration settings such as the driver and the printer name, enable or disable the printer, or specify whether to share it or not. You can also make it the default printer.

The Policies tab lets you specify a start and end banner and an error policy that specifies whether to retry or abort the print job or stop the printer should an error occur. The Access Control tab allows you to deny access to certain users. The Printer Options tab is where you set particular printing features such as paper size and type, print quality, and the input tray to use (Figure 29-6).

On the Job Options tab, you can select default printing features. A pop-up menu provides a list of printing feature categories from which to choose. Click the Add button to add the category, selecting a particular feature from a pop-up menu. You can set such features as the number of copies (Copies); letter, glossy, or A4-sized paper (Media); the kind of document, for instance, text, PDF, PostScript, or image (Document Format); and single- or double-sided printing (Sides).

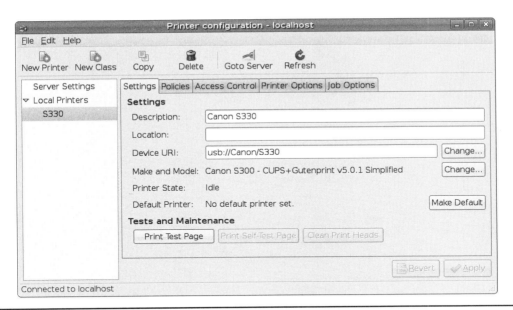

FIGURE 29-5   Modify installed printers

Configuring Printers with KDE

K Desktop Environment (KDE) provides support for adding and configuring CUPS printers through the KDE Control Center or System Settings. On the Control Panel, under Peripherals, select the Printers entry. On System Settings, in the Computer Administration section, click Printers. The KDE Printer tool is the displayed. It can perform many different kinds of printing, such as sending faxes or saving to PDF files. USB printers that are automatically detected are listed in the KDE Printer window. When you click the printer entry, the Information, Jobs, Properties, and Instances tabs let you manage your printer and its print jobs. The Properties tab has options for controlling user access, setting quotas, selecting a banner, and even changing your driver.

To change printer options such as page size and resolution, you choose Configure from the Printer menu. The Printer menu also lets you disable or test the printer, and the printer toolbar provides buttons for these commonly performed tasks. The printer manager lets you configure general features such as the fonts available, the previewer to use, or the printers to display. A pop-up menu, located on the lower right side of the window, displays available printer systems you can use. CUPS is selected by default. You could switch to LPRng if needed. Check the KDEPrint Handbook, accessible from the Documentation menu, for detailed information.

CUPS Web Browser–based Configuration Tool

One of the easiest way to configure and install printers with CUPS is to use the CUPS configuration tool, a Web browser–based tool. To start the Web interface, enter the following URL into your Web browser: **http://localhost:631**. This opens an administration screen,

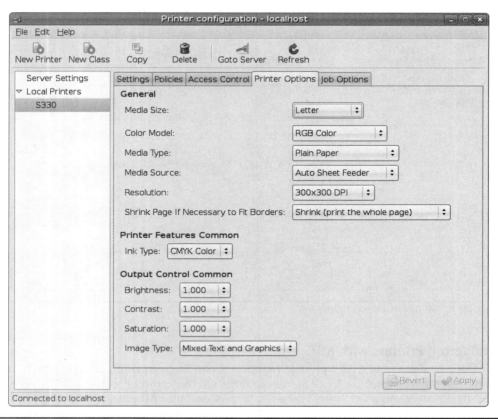

FIGURE 29-6   Printer Options tab

where you can manage and add printers. Users with administrative access will be given full access. Any printers that you set up with **system-config-printer** will already be configured.

With the CUPS configuration tool, you install a printer on CUPS through a series of Web pages, each of which requests different information. To install a printer, click the Add Printer button to display a page where you enter the printer name and location. The location is the host to which the printer is connected.

Subsequent pages will prompt you to enter the model of the printer and driver, which you select from available listings. Once you have added the printer, you can configure it. Clicking the Manage Printers entry in the Administration page lists your installed printers. You can then click a printer to display a page that lets you control the printer. You can stop the printer, configure its printing, modify its installation, and even delete the printer. Clicking the Configure Printer button displays a page where you can configure how your printer prints, by specifying the resolution or paper size.

Configured information for a printer will be stored in the **/etc/cups/printers.conf** file. You can examine this file directly, even making changes. Here is an example of a printer configuration entry. The **DeviceURI** entry specifies the device used, in this case a USB printer managed by HAL. It is currently idle, with no jobs:

```
# Printer configuration file for CUPS
# Written by cupsd
<Printer mycannon>
Info Cannon s330
Location
DeviceURI hal:///org/freedesktop/Hal/devices/usb_device_4a9_1074_300HCR_
  if0_printer_noserial
State Idle
StateTime 1166554036
Accepting Yes
Shared Yes
JobSheets none none
QuotaPeriod 0
PageLimit 0
KLimit 0
OpPolicy default
ErrorPolicy stop-printer
</Printer>
```

NOTE *You can perform all administrative tasks from the command line using the* **lpadmin** *command. See the CUPS documentation for more details.*

Configuring Remote Printers on CUPS

To install a remote printer that is attached to a Windows system or another Linux system running CUPS, you specify its location using special URL protocols. For another CUPS printer on a remote host, the protocol used is **ipp**, for Internet Printing Protocol, whereas for a Windows printer, it would be **smb**. Older Unix or Linux systems using LPRng would use the **lpd** protocol.

Configuring Remote Printers with system-config-printers

You can also use **system-config-printer** to set up a remote printer on Linux, Unix, or Windows networks. Access **system-config-printers** by choosing System | Administration | Printing. When you add a new printer or edit a printer settings, the New Printer/Select Connection dialog will list possible remote connection types (Figure 29-7). When you select a remote connection entry, a panel will be displayed, where you can enter configuration information. For a remote Linux or UNIX printer, select either Internet Printing Protocol (IPP), which is used for newer systems, or LPD/LPR Host or Printer, which is used for older systems. Both panels display entries for the Host Name and the Printer Name. For the Host Name, enter the hostname for the system that controls the printer. For the Printer Name, enter the device name on that host for the printer. The LPD/LPR dialog also has a Probe button for detecting the printer.

A Windows Printer Via Samba is a printer located on a Windows network. You need to specify the Windows server (hostname or IP address), the name of the share, the name of the printer's workgroup, and the username and password if required. The format of the printer SMB URL is shown on the SMP Printer panel. The SMB URL is the hostname and

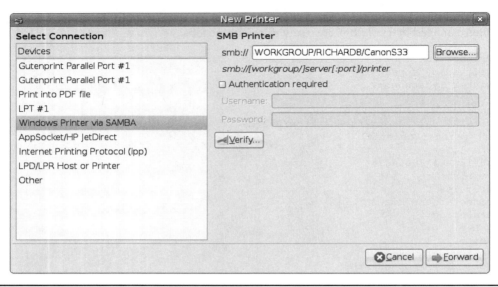

FIGURE 29-7 Windows printer connection configuration

printer name in the SMB URL format, *//workgroup/server/printername*. The Workgroup is the workgroup name for the Windows network. The Server is the computer where the printer is located. The Username and Password can be for the printer resource itself or for access by a particular user. The panel will display a field at the top where you can enter the share host and printer name as an SMB URL.

Instead of typing in the URL, you can click the Browse button to open an SMB Browser window, where you can select the printer from a list of Windows hosts on your network (see Figure 29-8). For example, if your Windows network is WORKGROUP, the entry WORKGROUP will be shown, which you can then expand to list all the Windows hosts on that network (if your network is MSHOME, then that will be listed). When you make your selection, the corresponding URL will show up in the **smb://** box on the New Printer window.

FIGURE 29-8
Selecting a
remote printer

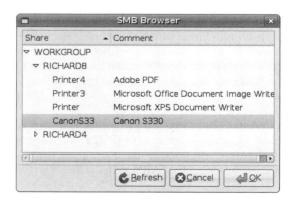

If you are using the Firestarter firewall, be sure to turn it off before browsing a Windows workgroup for a printer, unless it's already configured to allow Samba access.

Also on the panel, you can enter any needed Samba authentication, if required, such as username or password. Check Authentication Required to allow you to enter the Samba username and password.

You will still need the Linux drivers for that Windows printer. Click the Forward button to start the New Printer wizard, first selecting the manufacturer and then the model on the following screen. Then enter a name and location for the printer. Once you finish the wizard, the new printer will appear as an installed printer in **system-config-printers**.

To access an SMB-shared remote printer, you need to install Samba and have the Server Message Block services enabled using the **smb** and **nmb** daemons. The Samba service will be enabled by default. The service is enabled by checking the Windows Folders entry in the Gnome Services tool (System | Administration | Services). Printer sharing must, in turn, be enabled on the Windows network.

Configuring Remote Printers Manually

In the **cupsd.conf** file for a remote printer, the `DeviceURI` entry will have an Internet address along with its protocol instead of listing the device name. For example, a remote printer on a CUPS server (**ipp**) would be indicated as shown here (a Windows printer would use an **smb** protocol):

```
DeviceURI ipp://mytsuff.com/printers/queue1
```

For a Windows printer, you first need to install, configure, and run Samba. (CUPS uses Samba to access Windows printers.) When you install the Windows printer on CUPS, you specify its location using the URL protocol **smb**. The username of the user allowed to log in to the printer is entered before the hostname and separated from the hostname by an **@** sign. On most configurations, this is the **guest** user. The location entry for a Windows printer called **myhp** attached to a Windows host named **lizard** is shown next; its Samba share reference would be **//lizard/myhp**:

```
DeviceURI smb://guest@lizard/myhp
```

To enable CUPS on Samba, you also have to set the printing option in the **/etc/samba/smb.conf** file to **cups**, as shown here:

```
printing = cups
printcap name = cups
```

To enable CUPS to work with Samba, a link named **/usr/lib/cups/backent/smb** is set up to connect to Samba's **/ust/bin/smbpool**. Ubuntu should set up this link for you.

NOTE *To configure a shared Linux printer for access by Windows hosts, you need to configure it as an SMB-shared printer. You do this with Samba.*

CUPS Printer Classes

CUPS lets you select a group of printers for print a job instead of selecting just one. That way, if one printer is busy or down, another printer can be automatically selected to print the job. Such groupings of printers are called *classes*. Once you have installed your printers, you can group them into different classes. For example, you may want to group all inkjet printers into one class and laser printers into another, or you may want to group printers connected to one specific printer server in their own class. To create a class, select Classes on the Administration page and enter the name of the class. You can then add printers to it.

CUPS Configuration Files

CUPS configuration files are placed in the **/etc/cups** directory (see Table 29-2). The **classes.conf**, **printers.conf**, and **client.conf** files can be managed by the web interface. The **printers.conf** file contains the configuration information for the different printers you have installed. Any of these files can be edited manually, if you want.

cupsd.conf

The CUPS server is configured with the **cupsd.conf** file located in **/etc/cups**. You must edit configuration options manually; the server is not configured with the web interface. Your installation of CUPS installs a commented version of the **cupsd.conf** file with each option listed, though most options will be commented out. Commented lines are preceded with a **#** symbol. Each option is documented in detail. The server configuration uses an Apache web server syntax consisting of a set of directives. As with Apache, several of these directives can group other directives into blocks.

CUPS Directives

Certain directives allow you to place access controls on specific locations. These can be printers or resources, such as the administrative tool or the spool directories. Location controls are implemented with the **Location** directive. **Allow From** and **Deny From** directives can permit or deny access from specific hosts. CUPS supports both Basic and Digest forms of authentication, specified in the **AuthType** directive. Basic authentication uses a user and password. For example, to use the Web interface, you are prompted to enter the root user and the root user password. Digest authentication makes use of user and password information kept in the CUPS **/etc/cups/passwd.md5** file, using MD5 versions of a user and password for authentication. The **AuthClass** directive specifies the class

Filename	Description
classes.conf	Contains configurations for different local printer classes
client.conf	Lists specific options for specified clients
cupsd.conf	Configures the CUPS server, **cupsd**
printers.conf	Contains printer configurations for available local printers

TABLE 29-2   CUPS Configuration Files

allowed access. The **System** class includes the root, sys, and system users. The following example shows the **Location** directive for the **/admin** resource, the administrative tool:

```
<Location /admin>

AuthType Basic
AuthClass System

## Restrict access to local domain
Order Deny,Allow
Deny From All
Allow From 127.0.0.1

</Location>
```

CUPS Command Line Print Clients

Once a print job is placed on a print queue, you can use any of several print clients to manage the jobs on your printer or printers, such as **klpq**, the GNOME Print Manager, and the CUPS Printer Configuration tool for CUPS. You can also use several command line print CUPS clients, which include the **lpr**, **lpc**, **lpq**, and **lprm** commands. The Printer System Switcher moves you from one set to the other. With these clients, you can print documents, list a print queue, reorder it, and remove print jobs, effectively canceling them. For network connections, CUPS features an encryption option for its commands, **-E**, to encrypt print jobs and print information sent from a network. Table 29-3 shows various printer commands.

NOTE   *The command line clients have the same name, and much the same syntax, as the older LPR and LPRng command line clients used in Unix and older Linux systems.*

Printer Management	Description
GNOME Print Manager	GNOME print queue management tool (CUPS).
CUPS Configuration Tool	Prints, manages, and configures CUPS.
lpr *options file-list*	Prints a file, copies the file to the printer's spool directory, and places it on the print queue to be printed in turn. **-P** *printer* prints the file on the specified printer.
lpq *options*	Displays the print jobs in the print queue. **-P** *printer* prints the queue for the specified printer. **-l** prints a detailed listing.
lpstat *options*	Displays printer status.
lprm *options printjob-id* **or** *printer*	Removes a print job from the print queue. You identify a particular print job by its number as listed by **lpq**. The **-P** *printer* option removes all print jobs for the specified printer.
lpc	Manages your printers. At the **lpc>** prompt, you can enter commands to check the status of your printers and take other actions.

TABLE 29-3   CUPS Print Clients

lpr

The **lpr** client submits a job, and **lpd** then takes it in turn and places it on the appropriate print queue; **lpr** takes as its argument the name of a file. If no printer is specified, the default printer is used. The **-P** option lets you specify a particular printer. In the next example, the user first prints the file **preface** and then prints the file **report** to the printer with the name **myepson**:

```
$ lpr preface
$ lpr -P myepson report
```

lpc

You can use **lpc** to enable or disable printers, reorder their print queues, and re-execute configuration files. To use **lpc**, enter the command **lpc** at the shell prompt. You will see an **lpc>** prompt, where you can enter **lpc** commands to manage your printers and reorder their jobs. The **status** command with the name of the printer displays whether the printer is ready, how many print jobs it has, and so on. The **stop** and **start** commands can stop a printer and start it back up. The printers shown depend on the printers configured for a particular print servers. A printer configured on CUPS will appear only if you have switched to CUPS.

```
# lpc
lpc> status myepson
myepson:
 printer is on device 'hal' speed -1
 queuing is enabled
 printing is enabled
 1 entry in spool area
```

lpq and lpstat

You can manage the print queue using the **lpq** and **lprm** commands. The **lpq** command lists the print jobs currently on the print queue:

```
# lpq
myepson is ready and printing
Rank    Owner   Jobs   File(s)        Total Size
active   chris    1     report         1024
```

With the **-P** option and the printer name, you can list the jobs for a particular printer. If you specify a username, you can list the print jobs for that user. With the **-l** option, **lpq** displays detailed information about each job. If you want information on a specific job, simply use that job's ID number with **lpq**. To check the status of a printer, use **lpstat**.

lprm

The **lprm** command lets you remove a print job from the queue, erasing the job before it can be printed. The **lprm** command takes many of the same options as **lpq**. To remove a specific job, use **lprm** with the job number. To remove all printing jobs for a particular printer, use the **-P** option with the printer name. **lprm** with no options removes the job printing currently. The following command removes the first print job in the queue (use **lpq** to obtain the job number):

```
# lprm 1
```

CUPS Command Line Administrative Tools

CUPS provides command line administrative tools such as **lpadmin**, **lpoptions**, **lpinfo**, **enable**, **disable**, **accept**, and **reject**. The **enable** and **disable** commands start and stop print queues directly, whereas the **accept** and **reject** commands start and stop particular jobs. The **lpinfo** command provides information about printers, and **lpoptions** lets you set printing options. The **lpadmin** command lets you perform administrative tasks such as adding printers and changing configurations. CUPS administrative tools are listed in Table 29-4.

lpadmin

You can use the **lpadmin** command either to set the default printer or configure various options for a printer. You can use the **-d** option to specify a particular printer as the default destination. Here **myepson** is made the default printer:

```
lpadmin -d myepson
```

The **-p** option lets you designate a printer for which to set various options. The following example sets printer description information:

```
lpadmin -p myepson  -D  Epson550
```

Certain options let you control per-user quotas for print jobs. The **job-k-limit** option sets the size of a job allowed per user, **job-page-limit** sets the page limit for a job, and **job-quota-period** limits the number of jobs with a specified timeframe. The following command sets a page limit of 100 for each user:

```
lpadmin -p myepson  -o job-page-limit=100
```

Administration Tool	Description
lpadmin	CUPS printer configuration
lpoptions	Sets printing options
enable	Activates a printer
disable	Stops a printer
accept	Allows a printer to accept new jobs
reject	Prevents a printer from accepting print jobs
lpinfo	Lists CUPS devices available

TABLE 29-4 CUPS Administrative Tools

User access control is determined with the **-u** option with an **allow** or **deny** list. Users allowed access are listed following the **allow**: entry, and those denied access are listed with a **deny:** entry. Here access is granted to **chris** but denied to **aleina** and **larisa**:

```
lpadmin -p myepson -u allow:chris  deny:aleina,larisa
```

Use **all** or **none** to permit or deny access to all or no users. You can create exceptions by using **all** or **none** in combination with user-specific access. The following example allows access to all users except **justin**:

```
lpadmin -p myepson  -u allow:all   deny:justin
```

lpoptions

The **lpoptions** command lets you set printing options and defaults that mostly govern how your print jobs will be printed. For example, you can set the color or page format to be used with a particular printer. Default settings for all users are maintained by the root user in the **/etc/cups/lpoptions** file, and each user can create her own configurations, which are saved in her **.lpoptions** files. The **-l** option lists current options for a printer, and the **-p** option designates a printer (you can also set the default printer to use with the **-d** option). The following command lists the current options for the myepson printer:

```
lpoptions -p myepson -l
```

Printer options are set using the **-o** option along with the option name and value, **-o** *option=value*. You can remove a printer option with the **-r** option. For example, to print on both sides of your sheets, you can set the **sides** option to **two-sided**:

```
lpoptions -p myepson -o sides=two-sided
```

To remove the option, use **-r**:

```
lpoptions -p myepson -r sides
```

To display a listing of available options, check the standard printing options in the CUPS Software Manual at **http://cups.org**.

enable and disable

The **enable** command starts a printer, and the **disable** command stops it. With the **-c** option, you can cancel all jobs on the printer's queue, and the **-r** option broadcasts a message explaining the shutdown. This command disables the printer named **myepson**:

```
disable myepson
```

accept and reject

The **accept** and **reject** commands let you control access to the printer queues for specific printers. The **reject** command prevents a printer from accepting jobs, whereas **accept** allows new print jobs. The following command prevents the **myepson** printer from accepting print jobs:

```
reject myepson
```

lpinfo
The **lpinfo** command is a handy tool for letting you know what CUPS devices and drivers are available on your system. Use the **-v** option for devices and the **-m** option for drivers:

```
lpinfo -m
```

News Servers

News servers provide Internet users with Usenet news services. They have their own TCP/IP protocol, the Network News Transfer Protocol (NNTP). On most Linux systems, the InterNetNews (INN) news server provides news services (**www.isc.org**). In addition, servers are available that provide better access to Internet resources.

INN news servers access Usenet newsfeeds, providing news clients on your network with the full range of newsgroups and articles. Newsgroup articles are transferred using NNTP, and servers that support this protocol are known as *NNTP servers*. INN was written by Rich Salz and is currently maintained and supported by the Internet Software Consortium (ISC). You can download current versions from its Web site at **www.isc.org**. INN is also included with most Linux distributions. The documentation directory for INN in **/usr/share/doc** contains extensive samples. The primary program for INN is the **innd** daemon.

Two versions of INN area available: a smaller INN used for local networks, and a much more complex INN2 used for large networks. Normally Ubuntu uses INN.

INN also includes several support programs to provide maintenance and crash recovery and to perform statistical analysis on server performance and usage. Cleanfeed implements spam protection, and innreport generates INN reports based on logs. INN also features a strong filter system for screening unwanted articles.

NOTE *Leafnode is an NNTP news server designed for small networks that may have slow connections to the Internet. You can obtain the Leafnode software package along with documentation from its Web site at **http://leafnode.org**. Along with the Leafnode NNTP server, the software package includes several utilities such as Fetchnews, Texpire, and NewsQ that send, delete, and display news articles. Slrnpull is a simple single-user version of Leafnode that can be used only with the slrn newsreader.*

Database Servers: MySQL and PostgreSQL

Two fully functional database servers are included with most Linux distributions, MySQL and PostgreSQL. MySQL is by far the more popular of the two, though PostgreSQL is noted for providing more features. Recently, the MySQL AB project added MaxDB, formerly SAP DB, which provides capabilities comparable to many professional-level database management systems. You can learn more about these products through the sites listed in Table 29-5.

Database	Resource
MySQL	**http://mysql.com**
PostgreSQL	**www.postgresql.org**
MaxDB	**http://mysql.com**

TABLE 29-5 Database Resources

Relational Database Structure

MySQL and PostgreSQL both use a relational database structure, in which data is placed in tables, with identifier fields used to relate the data to entries in other tables. Each row in the table is a record, and each has a unique identifier, like a record number. The connections between records in different tables are implemented by special tables that associate the unique identifiers from records in one table with those of another. Relational database theory and implementation are subjects beyond the scope of this chapter.

A simple, single-table database has no need for a unique identifier. A simple address book listing names and addresses is an example of a single-table database. However, most databases access complex information of different types, related in various ways. Instead of having large records with repeated information, you divide the data in different tables, each holding the unique instance of the data. This way, data is not repeated; only one table holds a single record for a person's name, rather than repeating that person's name each time the data references him or her. The relational organization then takes on the task of relating one piece of data to another. This way, you can store a great deal of information using relatively small database files.

Though you can implement a relational database in many ways, a simple rule of thumb is to organize data into tables where you have a unique instance of each item of data. Each record is given a unique identifier, usually a number. To associate the records in one table with another, you create tables that associate their identifiers.

The Structured Query Language (SQL) is used by most relational database management systems (RDBMSs), including both MySQL and PostgreSQL. Though many RDBMSs use administrative tools to manage databases, on Linux MySQL and PostgreSQL, you still have to use SQL commands directly. The following command will create the database:

```
CREATE DATABASE myphotos
```

Before performing any operations on a database, you first access it with the **USE** command.

```
USE myphotos
```

The tables are created using the **CREATE TABLE** command; the fields for each table are listed within parentheses following the table name. For each field, you need to specify a name, data type, and other options, such as whether it can have a null value or not:

```
CREATE TABLE names (
    personid INT(5) UNSIGNED NOT NULL,
    name VARCHAR(20) NOT NULL,
    street VARCHAR(30) NOT NULL,
    phone CHAR(8)
    );
```

MySQL

MySQL is structured on a client/server model with a server daemon (**mysqld**) filling requests from client programs. MySQL is designed for speed, reliability, and ease of use. It is meant to be a fast database management system for large databases and, at the same time, a reliable system that's suitable for intensive use. To create databases, you use standard SQL. User access can be controlled by assigning privileges.

On Ubuntu, you can install MySQL server and client packages, along with numerous MySQL configuration packages for certain services such as Postfix, Exim, and Apache. Packages to install are **mysql-client**, **mysql-common**, and **mysql-server**. Documentation is held in the **mysql-doc** package and installed at **/usr/share/doc/mysql-doc**.

MySQL Configuration

The MySQL supports three different configuration files—one for global settings, another for server-specific settings, and an optional one for user-customized settings:

- The **/etc/mysql/my.cnf** configuration file is used for global settings applied to both clients and servers. The **/etc/mysql/my.cnf** file provides information such as the data directory (**/var/lib/mysql**) and log files (**/var/log/mysql**) locations, as well as the server base directory (**/var/lib**).

- The **/var/lib/mysql/my.cnf** file is used for server settings only.

- The **.my.cnf** file allows users to customize their access to MySQL. It is located in a user's home directory. Note that this is a dot file.

Sample configuration files can be found in the **mysql-server** directory at **/usr/share/doc**. The **mysql-server** directory lists configurations for small, medium, large, and huge implementations, such as **my-small.cnf**. The administrative manual is located in the **mysql** directory for **/usr/share/doc**. It is in the info format. Use `info mysql` to start it and the arrow and ENTER keys to move through the menus. Here you can find more information about different options.

Global Configuration: /etc/mysql/my.cnf

MySQL specifies options according to different groups, usually the names of server tools. The options are arranged in group segments. The group name is placed within brackets, and options applied to it follow. The default **/etc/mysql/my.cnf** file is shown here:

```
[mysqld]
user=mysql
datadir=/var/lib/mysql
pid-file = /var/run/mysqld/mysqld.pid
socket = /var/run/mysqld/mysqld.sock
port = 3306
basedir = /usr
datadir = /var/lib/mysql
tmpdir = /tmp
language = /usr/share/mysql/English
```

MySQL global options are listed in the **/etc/mysql/my.cnf** file. Options are set up according to groups that control different behaviors of the MySQL server: `mysqld` for the daemon and **safe_mysqld** for the MySQL startup script. The **datadir** directory, **/var/lib/mysql**, is where your database files will be placed. Server tools and daemons are located in the **basedir** directory, **/usr**, and the user that MySQL will run as has the name **mysql**, as specified in the **user** option.

A client group will set up options to be sent to clients, such as the port and socket to use to access the MySQL database:

```
[client]
port=3306
socket=/var/lib/mysqld/mysqld.sock
```

To see what options are currently set for both client and server, you run **mysqld** directly with the **--help** option:

```
/usr/libexec/mysqld --help
```

User Configuration: .my.cnf

Users who access the database server will have their own configuration file in their home directory: **.my.cnf**. Here the user can specify connection options such as the password used to access the database and the connection timeouts:

```
[client]
password=mypassword

[mysql]
no-auto-rehash
set-variable = connect_timeout=2

[mysql-hotcopy]
interactive-timeout
```

MySQL Tools

MySQL provides a variety of tools (as shown in Table 29-6), including server, client, and administrative tools. Backups can be handled with the **mysqldump** command. The **mysqlshow** command will display a database, just as issuing the SQL command **SELECT** ***.*** does, and **mysqlimport** can import text files, just like **LOAD INFILE**.

Command	Description
mysqld	MySQL server
mysql	MySQL client
mysqladmin	Creates and administers databases
mysqldump	Database backup
mysqlimport	Imports text files
mysqlshow	Displays databases

TABLE 29-6   MySQL Commands

MySQL Management with mysql and mysqladmin

To manage your MySQL database, you use **mysql** as the root user. The **mysql** client starts up the MySQL monitor. As the root user, you can enter administrative commands to create databases and database tables, add or remove entries, and carry out standard client tasks such as displaying data.

Log in as the root user and open a terminal window. Then enter the **mysql** command. This will start a MySQL monitor shell with a **mysql>** prompt, as shown. Be sure to end your commands with a semicolon; otherwise, the monitor will provide an indented arrow prompt waiting for added arguments. In the monitor, the semicolon, not the ENTER key, ends commands.

```
 # mysql -u root -p
mysql>
```

If you have set up a MySQL root user, you can use the **-u root** with the **-p** option, as shown next. You will be prompted for a password.

```
# mysql -u root -p
```

Once the **mysql** client has started, you can use the **status** command to check the status of your server and **show databases** to list current databases:

```
mysql> status;
mysql> show databases;
```

Initially two databases set up by MySQL for its own management are displayed: **mysql** and **test**. The **mysql** database holds MySQL user information, and the **test** database is used to test the server.

PostgreSQL

PostgreSQL is based on the POSTGRES database management system, though it uses SQL as its query language. POSTGRES is a next-generation research prototype developed at the University of California, Berkeley. You can learn more about it from the PostgreSQL Web site at **www.postgresql.org**. PostgreSQL is an open source project, developed under the GPL license.

PostgreSQL is often used to provide database support for Internet servers with heavy demands, such as Web servers. With a few simple commands, you can create relational database tables. Use the **createuser** command to create a PostgreSQL user with which you can then log in to the server. You can then create a database with the **createdb** command and construct relational tables using the **create table** directive. With an **insert** command, you can add records and then view them with the **select** command. Access to the server by remote users is controlled by entries in the **pg_hba.conf** file located in PostgreSQL directory, usually at **/var/lib/pgsql**.

NOTE *The search and indexing server **ht://Dig** enables document searches of Web and FTP sites (**http://htdig.org**). With it, you can index documents and carry out complex search requests.*

CHAPTER

Shared Resources: Samba and NFS

L inux provides several tools for accessing files on remote systems connected to a network. The Network File System (NFS) lets you connect to and directly access resources such as files or devices (such as CD-ROMs) that reside on another machine. The newest version, NFS4, provides greater security, with access allowed by your firewall. The Network Information Service (NIS) maintains configuration files for all systems on a network.

With Samba, you can connect your Windows clients on a Microsoft Windows network to services such as shared files, systems, and printers controlled by the Linux Samba server and, at the same time, allow Linux systems to access shared files and printers on Windows systems.

Samba

Samba is a collection of Linux tools that allow you to communicate with Windows systems over a Windows network. In effect, Samba allows a Linux system or network to act as if it were a Windows server, using the same protocols used in a Windows network. Whereas most Unix and Linux systems use TCP/IP for networking, Microsoft networking with Windows uses a protocol called *Server Message Block (SMB)* that implements a local area network (LAN) of PCs running Windows. SMB makes use of a network interface called *Network Basic Input Output System (NetBIOS)* that allows Windows PCs to share resources, such as printers and disk space. One Windows PC on such a network can access part of another Windows PC's disk drive as if the drive were its own.

SMB was originally designed for small LANs. To connect it to larger networks, including those with Unix systems, Microsoft developed the Common Internet File System (CIFS), which still uses SMB and NetBIOS for Windows networking. Wanting to connect his Linux system to a Windows PC, programmer Andrew Tridgell wrote an SMB client and server that he called Samba. Samba allows Unix and Linux systems to connect to such a Windows network, as if they were Windows PCs. Unix systems can share resources on Windows systems as they would if they were just another Windows PC. Windows PCs can also access resources on Unix systems as if they were Windows systems. Samba, in effect, has become a professional-level, open source, and free version of CIFS. It also runs much faster than CIFS. Samba lets you use a Linux or Unix server as a network server for a group of Windows machines operating on a Windows network. You can also use it to share files on your Linux system with other Windows PCs, or to access files on a Windows PC from your Linux system, as well as between Windows PCs. On Linux systems, a **cifs** file system enables you to mount a remote SMB-shared directory on your own file system. You can then access it as you would a directory on your local system.

You can obtain extensive documentation and current releases from the Samba Web and FTP sites at **www.samba.org** and **ftp.samba.org**. Samba HOWTO documentation is also available at **www.tldp.org**. Packages can be obtained from your distribution software repositories.

Extensive documentation is provided with the software package and installed on your system in the **/usr/share/doc/samba-doc** directory. Be sure to install the **samba-doc** package. The **htmldocs** subdirectory holds a variety of documentation. All are in Web page format. Documentation includes the HOWTO, *By Example*, *Using Samba*, and *Developers Guide*. The examples include sample **smb.conf** files for different kinds of configuration. For PDF versions, install the **samba-doc-pdf** package, at **/usr/share/doc/samba-doc-pdf**.

On Ubuntu, Samba software is incorporated into several packages, with configuration tools such as SWAT and **system-config-samba** (see Table 30-1). By selecting the **samba** server package, necessary supporting packages such as **smbclient** and **samba-common** will be automatically selected. Documentation and configuration tools have to be selected manually.

Samba Applications

The Samba software package consists of two server daemons and several utility programs (see Table 30-2). The **smbd** daemon provides file and printer services to SMB clients and other systems, such as Windows, that support SMB. The **nmbd** daemon provides NetBIOS name resolution and service browser support. The **smbclient** tool provides FTP-like access

Package name	Description
samba	The Samba server
samba-common	Samba Ubuntu configuration files and support tools
samba-doc	Documentation for Samba, including examples
system-config-samba	Samba GUI configuration tool from Red Hat
samba-doc-pdf	PDF versions for Samba documentation
swat	SWAT Samba Web interface for Samba configuration
smbclient	Samba clients for accessing Windows shares
smbfs	Mounts and unmounts tools for Samba shares
kdenetwork-filesharing	Implements Samba file sharing by KDE
shares-admin	GNOME Samba file sharing support, installed with GNOME Desktop
nautilus-share	GNOME Nautilus file manager Samba and NFS basic file and folder sharing

TABLE 30-1 Samba Packages on Ubuntu

Application	Description
system-config-samba	Ubuntu Samba administration tool for configuring **smb.conf** with a GNOME GUI
SWAT	Samba Web administration tool for configuring **smb.conf** with a Web browser
smbd	Samba server daemon that provides file and printer services to SMB clients
nmbd	Samba daemon that provides NetBIOS name resolution and service browser support
winbindd	Uses authentication services provided by Windows domain
smbclient	Provides FTP-like access by Linux clients to Samba services
mount.cifs	Mounts Samba share directories on Linux clients (used by the **mount** command with the **-t cifs** option)
smbpasswd	Changes SMB-encrypted passwords on Samba servers
smbstatus	Displays the current status of the SMB network connections
smbrun	Interface program between **smbd** and external programs
testparm	Tests the Samba configuration file, **smb.conf**
smbtar	Backs up SMB/CIFS-shared resources directly to a Unix tape drive
nmblookup	Maps the NetBIOS name of a Windows PC to its IP address
/etc/init.d/samba	Samba init script to start, stop, and restart the Samba server

TABLE 30-2   Samba Applications

by Linux clients to Samba services. **mount.cifs** and **umount.cifs** enable Linux clients to mount and unmount Samba-shared directories (used by the **mount** command with the **-t samba** option). The **smbstatus** utility displays the current status of the SMB server and who is using it. You use **testparm** to test your Samba configuration. **smbtar** is a shell script that backs up SMB/CIFS-shared resources directly to a Unix tape drive. You use **nmblookup** to map the NetBIOS name of a Windows PC to its IP address. The primary Samba configuration tool for Ubuntu is **system-config-samba**, which enables you to use a GUI to create and maintain your Samba configuration file, **/etc/samba/smb.conf**. Alternatively, use the Samba Web administration tool (SWAT) to configure Samba. Configuration files are kept in the **/etc/samba** directory.

Samba provides four main services: file and printer services, authentication and authorization, name resolution, and service announcement. The SMB daemon **smbd** provides the file and printer services, as well as authentication and authorization for those services. This means users on the network can share files and printers. You can control access to these services by requiring that users provide a password. When users try to access a shared directory, they are prompted for the password. Control can be implemented in share mode or user mode. The *share* mode sets up one password for the shared resource and then enables any user who has that password to access it. The *user* mode provides a different password for each user. Samba maintains its own password file for this purpose: **/etc/samba/smbpasswd**.

Name resolution and service announcements are handled by the **nmbd** server. Name resolution essentially resolves NetBIOS names with IP addresses. Service announcements, also known as *browsing,* are the way a list of services available on the network is made known to the connected Windows PCs (and Linux PCs connected through Samba).

Samba also includes the **winbindd** daemon, which allows Samba servers to use authentication services provided by a Windows domain. Instead of a Samba server maintaining its own set of users to allow access, it can make use of a Windows domain authentication service to authenticate users.

Starting Samba

To allow Windows to access a Linux system, and vice versa, you use the Samba server. First be sure that Samba is installed along with the **system-config-samba** or SWAT tool. Open the Synaptic Package Manager and do a search on *samba*. Be sure to install both the **samba** and **system-config-samba** packages.

NOTE   *It is possible to set up Samba-shared directories with the GNOME's **nautilus-share** or **shares-admin** (see Chapter 4). However, this tool does not provide for user-level security, which is now deprecated. It provides very open share-level access to any user.*

Once installed, Samba is normally configured to start up automatically. You can turn this option on or off using the GNOME Services Manager (System | Administration | Services). Make sure the Windows File Sharing entry with the Samba name is checked to start up Samba.

For a simple Samba setup, you can use Ubuntu version of **system-config-samba** or SWAT to configure your **/etc/samba/smb.conf** file. If you make changes, you must restart the Samba server to have the changes take effect. To restart Samba with your new configuration, use the **samba** init script with the `restart` option, **/etc/init.d/samba**. The `start`, `stop`, and `restart` options will start, stop, and restart the server. Run the following command from a terminal window to restart Samba:

```
sudo /etc/init.d/samba restart
```

TIP   *The Samba server needs to run both the **nmb** and the **smbd** servers. Without the **nmbd** server, Windows cannot detect your Samba server. These are both started by the **samba** init script, /etc/init.d/samba.*

Firewall Access

The iptables firewall prevents browsing Samba and Windows shares from your Linux desktop. To work around this restriction, you need to make sure your firewall treats Samba as a trusted service. To allow firewall access to the Samba ports, usually ports 137–139 and 445, you should enable access using a firewall configuration tool like Firestarter or ufw.

For Firestarter, on the Policy panel, select the Inbound menu item and then right-click the Services pane to add a rule. On Add new inbound rule window, select Samba (SMB) from the Name pop-up menu, and the 137–139 and 445 ports will be selected for you.

The Samba rule will show up in the Allow Service section of the Policy Inbound panel. Firestarter maintains its own set of iptables files in **/etc/Firestarter**. Firestarter should show your Samba connection (**Microsoft-ds**).

For the ufw default firewall, you would use the following command. The ufw firewall maintains its iptables files in **/etc/ufw**:

```
ufw allow 137/tcp
```

If you are managing your iptables firewall directly, you could manage access directly by adding the following iptables rule. This accepts input on port 21 for TCP/IP packages.

```
iptables -A INPUT -p tcp --dport 137-139 -j ACCEPT
```

Setting Up Samba with Configuration Tools

To set up simple file sharing on a Linux system, you first need to configure your Samba server. You can do this by directly editing the **/etc/samba/samba.conf** file or by using the configuration tools (see Figure 30-1). On Ubuntu you can use **nautilus-share** (GNOME file manager sharing feature), **shares-admin**, **gsambad**, **system-config-samba**, and **swat** utilities for configuring Samba from your desktop. You will have to first install these packages with Synaptic.

TIP *You can also use the **gsambad** utility for GNOME to graphically configure your Samba service. Be sure to start it with **gksu** for administrative access.*

systemc-config-samba

You will first have to configure the Samba server, designating users that can have access to shared resources such as directories and printers. Due to a compatibility issue with Ubuntu, you may have to issue the following command in order to have the **system-config-samba** tool install correctly.

```
sudo touch /etc/libuser.conf
```

FIGURE 30-1
Samba Server
Configuration with
system-config-
samba

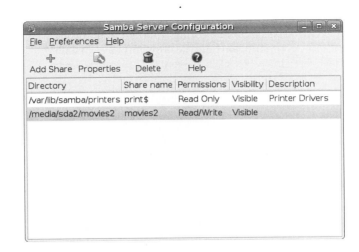

Then you can use **system-config-samba** on Ubuntu.

1. Open the **system-config-samba** tool by choosing System | Administration | Samba.

2. Then, choose Preferences | Server Settings.

3. On the Basic tab, enter the name of your Windows network workgroup (see Figure 30-2). The default names given by Windows are MSHOME or WORKGROUP. Use the name already given to your Windows network. For home networks, you can decide on your own. Just make sure all your computers use the same network name. Check your Windows Control Panel's System applet to make sure.

4. On the Security tab, you can select the kind of authentication you want to use. By default, User security is selected. You could also use share or server security; these are more open, but both have been deprecated and may be dropped in later versions.

Samba Users   For user authentication, you will have to associate a Windows user with a particular Linux account. Select Samba Users in the Preferences window. Then select a Linux user to use. If you want to add a new Samba user, select Add User.

You should then edit the selected user, to enter the corresponding Windows user and then a password that user can type to access Linux. This is the Samba password for that user. Samba maintains its own set of passwords that users will need to access a Samba share. When a Windows user wants to access a Samba share, he or she will need to enter his or her Samba password.

Samba Shares   To set up a simple share, click Add Share in the Preferences window, which opens a Create Samba Share window (see Figure 30-3). On the Basic tab, select the Linux directory to share (click Browse to find it), and then specify whether it will be writable and visible.

On the Access tab, you can choose to open the share to everyone or just for specific users. Your new share will then be displayed in the Samba Server Configuration window.

SWAT

SWAT is a network-based Samba configuration tool that uses a Web page interface to enable you to configure your **smb.conf** file. Be sure you have installed the **swat** package from the Ubuntu main repository. SWAT is an easy way to configure your Samba server, providing the

---

Figure 30-2
Samba Server
Settings, Basic tab

FIGURE **30-3**
New Samba Share,
Basic tab

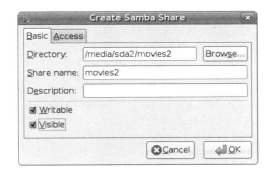

full range of configuration options. SWAT provides a simple-to-use Web page interface with buttons, menus, and text boxes for entering values. A simple button bar across the top lets you select the sections you want to configure. A button bar is included to add passwords. To see the contents of the **smb.conf** file as SWAT changes it, click View. The initial screen (HOME) displays the index for Samba documentation. One of SWAT's more helpful features is its context-sensitive help. For each parameter and option SWAT displays, you can click a Help button to display a detailed explanation of the option and examples of its use.

Activating SWAT SWAT is installed as a separate package on Ubuntu as an **inetd** service, not an **xinetd** service. You will also have to install the **inetd** package to run SWAT. If you have installed **xinetd** (the enhanced version of **xinetd**), then **xinetd** will be removed to allow **inetd** to operate. As an **inetd** service, it will be listed in the **/etc/services** and **/etc/inetd.conf** files. The SWAT program uses port 901, as designated in the **/etc/services** file and shown here:

```
swat 901/tcp # Samba Web Administration Tool
```

Before you use SWAT, back up your current **smb.conf** file. SWAT overwrites the original, replacing it with a shorter and more concise version of its own. The **smb.conf** file originally installed lists an extensive number of options with detailed explanations. This is a good learning tool, with excellent examples for creating various kinds of printer and directory sections. Simply make a backup copy:

```
cp /etc/samba/smb.conf /etc/samba/smb.bk
```

Accessing SWAT You can start SWAT by opening your browser and entering the IP address 127.0.0.1 with port 901 to access SWAT:

http://127.0.0.1:901

Instead of 127.0.0.1, you can use **localhost**:

http://localhost.localhost:901

You can start SWAT from a remote location by entering the address of the Samba server on which it is running, along with its port (901), into a Web browser.

You are first asked to enter a username and a password. To configure Samba, you need to enter your user name and password. Access is given only to those users provided administrative access.

The main SWAT page is displayed with a button bar, with buttons for links for HOME, GLOBALS, SHARES, PRINTERS, WIZARD, STATUS, VIEW, and PASSWORD pages (see Table 30-3). You can use the STATUS page to list your active SMB network connections.

For the various sections, SWAT can display either a basic or advanced version. When you finish working on a section, click the Commit Changes button on its page to save your changes. Do this for each separate page you work on, including the GLOBALS page. Clicking Commit Changes generates a new version of the **smb.conf** file. To have the Samba server read these changes, you have to restart it. You can do this by clicking the Restart SMB button on the Status page.

Configuring Samba Access from Windows

To set up a connection for a Windows client, you need to specify the Windows workgroup name and configure the password. The workgroup name appears in My Network Places on Windows 2000, NT, and XP (or in the Entire Network window in the Network Neighborhood on earlier Windows versions). On Vista, this is simply called *Network*. To set the workgroup name on Windows XP, open the Control Panel and click System, and on the Computer Name tab, click the Change button. This opens a dialog with a setting for the Workgroup, where you can enter the workgroup name. The default may be WORKGROUP or MSHOME. You can set up your own workgroup name, but all your computers would have to be configured to use that name.

On your Ubuntu Samba server, you specify the network name in the Sever Settings window on **system-config-samba**. Alternatively, you can manually enter the network name in the **smb.conf** file, specifying the workgroup name in the **workgroup=** entry in the **global** section. The workgroup name should be uppercase and contain no spaces. The default name used on Windows XP systems is a simple WORKGROUP. The **smb.conf** **workgroup** entry would then look like this:

```
workgroup = WORKGROUP
```

Page	Description
HOME	SWAT home page that lists documentation resources.
GLOBALS	Configures the global section for Samba.
SHARES	Selects and configures directories to be shared (shares).
PRINTERS	Sets up access to printers.
WIZARD	Sets up server, rewrites original **smb.conf** file to remove all comments and default values.
STATUS	Checks the status of the Samba server, both **smbd** and **nmbd**; lists clients currently active and the actions they are performing. You can restart, stop, or start the Samba server from this page.
VIEW	Displays the **smb.conf** configuration file.
PASSWORD	Sets up password access for the server and users that have access.

TABLE 30-3 SWAT Configuration Pages

Accessing Samba Shares from Windows

On a Windows-client, you'll see the Samba server listed when you select View Workgroups Computers from My Network Places (Network on Vista). On older Windows versions, use the Entire Network folder in your Network Neighborhood. The Samba server will have as a name the description you gave it in your Samba configuration. Clicking the icon will display a window with all the configured shares and printers on that Samba server.

If you're a Windows user and you want to access a new share on the Linux system, you can open your My Network Places (Network on Vista) and then click Add A Network Place to add a network place entry for the share or View Workgroup Computers to see computers on your Windows network. Selecting the Linux Samba server will display Samba shares. To access the share, you will need to enter in your username and the Samba password, with the option of having your username and password remembered for automatic access.

You need to make sure that your Windows system has enabled TCP/IP networking. This may already be the case if your Windows client is connected to a Microsoft network. If you need to connect a Windows system directly to a TCP/IP network on which your Linux Samba server is running, you should check to see if TCP/IP networking is enabled on that Windows system. This involves making sure that the Microsoft Network client and TCP/IP are installed, and that your network interface card (NIC adapter) is configured to use TCP/IP. The procedures differ slightly on Windows 2000 and XP, and Windows 95, 98, and ME.

Sharing Windows Directories and Printers with Samba Clients

To manage directory shares, open the Computer Management tool in the Administrative window in the Control Panel. Click Shared Folders and there you'll see the Shares, Sessions, and Open folders. To add a new share, click the Shares folder and then choose Action | New File Share. The Sessions and Open folders' Action menus let you disconnect active sessions and folders.

To share a directory, right-click the directory and choose Sharing from the pop-up menu (Sharing And Security on Windows XP). Click Share This Folder and then enter the share name, the name by which the directory will be known by Samba. You can specify whether you want to allow others to change files on the share. You can also specify a user limit (maximum allowed is the default). You can further click the Permissions button to control access by users. Here, you can specify which users will have access, as well as the type of access. For example, you could allow only read access to the directory.

To share a printer, locate the printer in the Printers window and right-click it, selecting the Sharing option. This opens the Sharing tab of a Properties window, where you can click the Shared As button and enter the name under which the printer will be known by other hosts. For example, on a Windows client named **lizard**, to have a printer called **Epson Stylus Color** shared as **myepson**, the Sharing tab for this printer would have the Shared As button selected and the name **myepson** entered. Then when the user double-clicks the **lizard** icon in the Computers Near Me window, the printer icon labeled **myepson** will appear.

For a Linux system to use this printer, it must first be configured as a remote Windows printer on that Linux system. You can do this easily with the **system-config-printer** tool.

User-Level Security

Samba provides primarily user-level security, requiring users on remote systems to log in using Samba-registered passwords. Samba still provides share- and server-level access, but these methods have been deprecated and are not recommended. User-level security requires

the use of Windows-encrypted passwords. Windows uses its own methods of encryption.
For Samba to handle such passwords, it has to maintain its own Windows-compatible
password database. It cannot use the Linux password databases. Windows also uses
additional information for the login process, such as where the user logged in.

User-level security requires that each user who wants to log in to a Samba share from a
Windows system have a corresponding user account on the Samba server. These are the
users listed in the **system-config-samba** Samba Users window. In addition, this account has
to have a separate Samba password with which to log in to the Samba share. In effect, the
user becomes a Samba user.

The account on the Samba server does not need to use the same username as that used
on the Windows system. A Windows username can be specified for a Samba user. On
system-config-samba, the Create New Samba User window lets you enter a Windows
username in the Windows Username entry. This mapping of windows users to Samba
(Linux) users is listed in the **/etc/smbusers file**. The following maps the Windows user
rpetersen to the Samba (Linux) user **richard**:

```
richard = rpetersen
```

When the Windows user in Windows tries to access the Samba share, the user will be
prompt to log in. The Windows user would then enter **rpetersen** as the username and the
Samba password that was set up for **richard**. On **system-config-samba**, this is the Samba
password entered in the Samba Password entries in the Create New Samba Users window.

User-level security is managed by password back-end databases. By default, the **tdbsam**
back-end database is used. This is a **tdb** database file (trivial data base) that stores Samba
passwords along with Windows extended information. The **tdbsam** database is designed for
small networks. For systems using LDAP to manage users, you can use the LDAP-enabled
back end, **ldbsam**. The **ldbsam** database is designed for larger networks. The **smbpasswd**
file previously used is still available, but it is included only for backward compatibility. The
default configuration entries for user access in the **smb.conf** file are shown here:

```
security = user
passdb backend = tdbsam
```

The **username map** option specifies the file used to associate Windows and Linux
users. Windows users can use the Windows username to log in as the associated user. The
username map file is usually **/etc/samba/smbusers**.

```
username map = /etc/samba/smbusers
```

If you are using an LDAP-enabled Samba database, **ldbsam**, you would use special
LDAP Samba tools to manage users. These are provided in the **smbldap-tools** package. They
are prefixed with the term **smbldap**. You'll find tools for adding, modifying, and deleting
users and groups such as **smbldap-useradd**, **smbldap-userdelete**, and **smbldap-groupmod**.
You use the **smbldap-passwd** command to manage Samba passwords with LDAP. The
smdbldap-userinfo command is used to obtain information about a user. You configure
your LDAP Samba tools' support using the **/etc/smbldap-tools/smbldap.conf** file.

Samba also provides its own Samba password Pluggable Authentication Module (PAM)
module, **pam_smbpass.so**. With this module, you provide PAM authentication support for

Samba passwords, enabling the use of Windows hosts on a PAM-controlled network. The module could be used for authentication and password management in your PAM **samba** file. The following entries in the PAM **samba** file would implement PAM authentication and passwords using the Samba password database:

```
auth required pam_smbpass.so nodelay
password required pam_smbpass.so nodelay
```

Be sure to enable PAM in the **smb.conf** file:

```
obey pam restrictions = yes
```

Samba Passwords: smbpasswd

With user-level security, access to Samba server resources by a Windows client is allowed only to users on that client. The username and Samba password used to access the Samba server must be registered in the Samba password database.

NOTE *If you are using the older **smbpasswd** file, you can use the **mksmbpasswd.sh** script to generate an **smbpasswd** file made up of all the users listed in your /etc/passwd file. You pipe the contents of the passwd file to **mksmbpasswd.sh** and then use redirection (>) to create the file.*

You can use either **system-config-samba** or the **smbpasswd** tool to manage Samba passwords. On **system-config-samba** you use the Samba Users window (Preferences | Samba Users) to add or edit passwords. Alternatively, you can use the **smbpasswd** command in a terminal window to add, or later change, passwords. To add or change a password for a particular user, you use the **smbpasswd** command with the username:

```
# smbpasswd dylan
New SMB Password: new-password
Repeat New SMB Password: new-password
```

Users can use **smbpasswd** to change their own passwords. The following example shows how you would use **smbpasswd** to change your Samba password. If you have no Samba password, you can press the ENTER key to move to the next line.

```
$ smbpasswd
Old SMB password: old-password
New SMB Password: new-password
Repeat New SMB Password: new-password
```

Should you want to use no passwords, you can use **smbpasswd** with the **-n** option. The **smb.conf** file will need to have the **null passwords** option set to **yes**.

NOTE *If you are using the older smbpasswords file, be sure that Samba is configured to use encrypted passwords. Set the **encrypt passwords** option to **yes** and specify the SMB password file.*

Managing Samba Users: smbasswd and pdbedit

To manage users, you can use either the **smbpasswd** command or the **pdbedit** tool, as well as **system-config-samba**. The **smbpasswd** command with the **-a** option will add a user, as shown next, and with the **-x** option will remove one. To enable or disable users you would use the **-e** and **-d** options.

```
smbpasswd -a aleina
```

The **smbpasswd** command will operate on either the older **smbasswd** file or the newer **tdbsam** back-end database files. For the **tdbsam** back-end database files you can use **pdbedit** instead. To add a user, you would use the **-a** option, as shown, and to remove a user, you use the **-x** option:

```
pdbedit -a larisa
```

pdbedit is a command line tool with options for adding and removing users, as well as features such as changing passwords and setting the home directory. You can also import or export the user entries to or from other back-end databases.

The **pdbedit** command lets you display more information about users. To display users from the back-end database you could use the **-L** option. Add the **-v** option for detailed information. For a particular user, add the username:

```
pdbedit -Lv richard
```

For domain policies such as minimum password lengths or retries, you use the **-P** option:

```
pdbedit -P
```

You use the **-i** and **-e** options to import and export database entries. The following will import entries from the old **smbpasswd** file to the new **tdbsam** back-end database:

```
pdbedit -i smbpasswd -e tdbsam
```

If your system is using an LDAP-enabled Samba database, use the **smbldap** tools to manage users and groups.

The Samba smb.conf Configuration File

Samba configuration is held in the **smb.conf** file located in the **/etc/samba** directory. Samba configuration tools such as **system-config-samba** and SWAT will maintain this file for you. Alternatively, you can manually edit the file directly, creating your own Samba configuration. You may have to do this if your Samba configuration proves to be very complex. Direct editing can provide more refined control over your shares.

You use the **testparm** command in a terminal window to check the syntax of any changes you have made to the **/etc/samba/smb.conf** file:

```
testparm
```

The file is separated into two basic parts: one for global options and the other for shared services. Shared services, also known as *shares,* can either be file space services (used by clients as an extension of their native file systems) or printable services (used by clients to access print services on the host running the server). The file space service is a directory to which clients are given access; they can use the space in it as an extension of their local file system. A printable service provides access by clients to print services, such as printers managed by the Samba server.

The **/etc/samba/smb.conf** file holds the configuration for the various shared resources as well as global options that apply to all resources. Linux installs an **smb.conf** file in your **/etc/samba** directory. The file contains default settings used for your distribution. You can edit the file to customize your configuration to suit your needs. Many entries are commented with either a semicolon or a **#** sign, and you can remove the initial comment symbol to make them effective. For a complete listing of the Samba configuration parameters, check the man page for **smb.conf**. An extensive set of sample **smb.conf** files is located in the **/usr/share/doc/ samba*** directory in the **examples** subdirectory.

In the **smb.conf** file, global options are set first, followed by each shared resource's configuration. The basic organizing component of the **smb.conf** file is called a *section*. Each resource has its own section that holds its service name and definitions of its attributes. Even global options are placed in a section of their own, labeled **global**. For example, each section for a filespace share consists of the directory and the access rights allowed to users of the filespace. The section of each share is labeled with the name of the shared resource. Special sections, called **printers** and **homes**, provide default descriptions for user directories and printers accessible on the Samba server. Following the special sections, other sections are entered for specific services, namely access to specific directories or printers.

A section begins with a section label, consisting of the name of the shared resource encased in brackets. Other than the special sections, the section label can be any name you choose. Following the section label, on separate lines, different parameters for this service are entered. The parameters define the access rights to be granted to the user of the service. For example, for a directory, you may want it to be browseable, but read-only, and use a certain printer. Parameters are entered in the format *parameter name = value*. You can enter a comment by placing a semicolon at the beginning of the comment line.

A simple example of a section configuration follows. The section label is encased in brackets and followed by two parameter entries. The **path** parameter specifies the directory to which access is allowed. The **writeable** parameter specifies whether the user has write access to this directory and its filespace.

```
[mysection]
 path = /home/chris
 writeable = true
```

A printer service has the same format but requires certain other parameters. The **path** parameter specifies the location of the printer spool directory. The **read-only** and **printable** parameters are set to **true**, indicating the service is read-only and printable. **public** indicates anyone can access the service.

```
[myprinter]
 path = /var/spool/samba
 read only = true
 printable = true
 public = true
```

Parameter entries can be synonymous yet use different entries with the same meaning. For example, **read only = no**, **writeable = yes**, and **write ok = yes** all mean the same thing, providing write access to the user.

---

*TIP The **writeable** option is an alias for the inverse of the **read only** option. The **writeable = yes** entry is the same as **read only = no** entry.*

Global Section

The **global** section determines configuration for the entire server, as well as specifying default entries to be used in the home and directory segments. In this section, you find entries for the workgroup name, password configuration, and directory settings. Several of the more important entries are discussed here.

The workgroup entry specifies the workgroup name you want to give your network. This is the workgroup name that appears on the Windows client's Network window. The default workgroup entry in the **smb.conf** file is shown here:

```
[global]

# workgroup = NT-Domain-Name or Workgroup-Name
 workgroup = WORKGROUP
```

The workgroup name has to be the same for each Windows client that the Samba server supports. On a Windows client, the workgroup name is usually found on the Network Identification or General tab in the System tool located in the Control Panel. On many clients, this is defaulted to **WORKGROUP**. If you want to keep this name, you have to change the workgroup entry in the **smb.conf** file accordingly. The workgroup entry and the workgroup name on each Windows client have to be the same. In this example the workgroup name is **mygroup**:

```
workgroup = mygroup
```

The server string entry (shown here) holds the descriptive name you want displayed for the server on the client systems. On Windows systems, this is the name displayed on the Samba server icon. The default is **Samba Server**, but you can change this to any name you want.

```
# server string is the equivalent of the NT Description field
    server string = %h server (Samba, Ubuntu)
```

NOTE You can also configure Samba to be a Primary Domain Controller (PDC) for Windows NT networks. As a PDC, Samba sets up the Windows domain that other systems will use, instead of participating in an already established workgroup.

Name service resolution is normally provided by the WINS server (Windows NetBIOS Name Service, **nmbd**), which is started by the **samba** init script. If your local network already has a WINS server, you can specify that instead. The commented default entry is shown here. Replace *w.x.y.z* with your network's WINS server name:

```
;    wins server = w.x.y.z
```

WINS server support by your Samba **nmbd** server would have to be turned off to avoid conflicts, turning your Samba name resolution server into just a client. The commented entry to turn off WINS support is shown here:

```
;   wins support = no
```

If your network also has its own Domain Name Service (DNS) server that it wants to use for name resolution, you can enable that instead. By default, this is turned off, as shown next. Change the **no** to **yes** to allow use of your network's DNS server for Windows name resolution. Also, WINS server support would have to be turned off to make this change.

```
dns proxy = no
```

Name resolution can also be instructed to check the **lmhosts** and **/etc/hosts** files first. The commented default entry is shown here:

```
;   name resolve order = lmhosts host wins bcast
```

Samba resources are normally accessed with either share- or user-level security. On a share level, any user can access the resource without having to log in to the server. On a user level, each user has to log in, using a password. Furthermore, Windows 98, ME, NT, and XP clients use encrypted passwords for the login process. Passwords are encrypted by default and managed by the password database, as noted previously. In the following entries, the security is set to the user level, and the password database file uses tdbsam.

```
security = user
passdb backend = tdbsam
```

If you want share-level security, specify **share** as the security option. This option is deprecated, however. User-level security is considered the standard:

```
security = share
```

As a security measure, you can restrict access to SMB services to certain specified local networks. On the host's network, type the network addresses of the local networks for which you want to permit access. To deny access to everyone in a network except a few particular hosts, you can use the **EXCEPT** option after the network address with the IP addresses of those hosts. The localhost (127) is always automatically included. The next example allows access to two local networks:

```
hosts allow = 192.168.1. 192.168.2.
```

To enable printing, specify the **load printers** configuration:

```
load printers = yes
```

Other options such as **printing** let you specify a different printing server (CUPS is the default):

```
printing = cups
```

PART VIII

You can use a guest user login to make resources available to anyone without requiring a password. A guest user login would handle any users who log in without a specific account. On Linux systems, by default Samba will use the **nobody** user as the guest user. Alternatively, you can set up and designate a specific user to use as the guest user. You designate the guest user with the **guest account** entry in the **smb.conf** file. The commented **smb.conf** file provided with Samba currently lists a commented entry for setting up a guest user called **nobody**. You can make this the user you want to be used as the guest user. Be sure to add the guest user to the password file:

```
guest account = nobody
```

Homes Section
The **homes** section specifies default controls for accessing a user home directory through the SMB protocol by remote users. Setting the **browseable** entry to **no** prevents the client from listing the files in a file browser. The **writeable** entry specifies whether users have read and write control over files in their home directories. The **create mode** and **directory mode** entries set default permissions for new files and directories. The **valid users** entry uses the %S macro to map to the current service.

```
[homes]
 comment = Home Directories
 browseable = no
 read only = no
 valid users = %S
 create mode = yes
 directory mask = 775
```

The printers and print$ Sections
The **printers** section specifies the default controls for accessing printers. These are used for printers for which no specific sections exist. Setting **browseable** to **no** simply hides the **printers** section from the client, not the printers. The **path** entry specifies the location of the spool directory Samba will use for printer files. To enable printing at all, the **printable** entry must be set to **yes**. To allow guest users to print, set the **guest ok** entry to **yes**. The standard implementation of the **printers** section is shown here:

```
 [printers]
 comment = All Printers
 path = /var/spool/samba
 browseable = no
 guest ok = yes
 writable = no
 printable = yes
 read only = yes
 create mask = 0700
```

The **print$** section, shown next, specifies where a Windows client can find a printer driver on your Samba server. The printer drivers are located in the **/var/lib/samba/printers** directory and are read-only.

```
# Windows clients look for this share name as a source of downloadable
# printer drivers
[print$]
   comment = Printer Drivers
   path = /var/lib/samba/printers
   browseable = yes
   read only = yes
   guest ok = no
```

Shares

Sections for specific shared resources, such as directories on your system, are usually placed after the **homes** and **printers** sections. For a section defining a shared directory, enter a label for the system. Then, on separate lines, enter options for its pathname and the different permissions you want to set. In the **path** = *option*, specify the full pathname for the directory. The **comment** = *option* holds the label to be given the share. You can make a directory writeable, public, or read-only. You can control access to the directory with the **valid users** entry, which you can use to list those users permitted access. For those options not set, the defaults entered in the **global**, **homes**, and **printers** segments are used.

The following example is the **myprojects** share. Here the **/myprojects** directory is defined as a *share resource* that is open to any user with guest access:

```
[myprojects]
    comment = Great Project Ideas
    path = /myprojects
    read only = no
    guest ok = yes
```

To limit access to certain users, you can list a set of valid users. Setting the **guest ok** option to **no** closes it off from access by others:

```
[mynewmusic]
 comment =  New Music
 path = /home/specialprojects
 valid users = mark
 guest ok = no
 read only = no
```

To allow complete public access, set the **guest ok** entry to **yes**, with no valid user's entry:

```
[newdocs]
 comment =  New Documents
 path = /home/newdocs
 guest ok = yes
 read only = no
```

Printers

Access to specific printers is defined in the **printers** section of the **smb.conf** file. For a printer, you need to include the **printer** and **printable** entries, as well as specify the type of printing server used. With the **printer** entry, you name the printer, and by setting the **printable** entry to **yes**, you allow it to print. You can control access to specific users with the valid users entry and by setting the **public** entry to **no**. For public access, set the **public** entry to **yes**. For the CUPS server, set the **printing** option to **cups**.

The following example sets up a printer accessible to guest users. This opens the printer to use by any user on the network. Users need to have write access to the printer's spool directory, located in **/var/spool/samba**. Keep in mind that any printer must first be installed on your system. The following printer was already installed as **myhp** and has an **/etc/printcap** entry with that name. You use the CUPS administrative tool to set up printers for the CUPS server. The **printing** option can be inherited from general **printers** share.

```
[myhp]
      path = /var/spool/samba
      read only = no
      guest ok = yes
      printable = yes
      printer = myhp
      oplocks = no
      share modes = no
      printing = cups
```

As with shares, you can restrict printer use to certain users, denying it public access.

Testing the Samba Configuration

After you make your changes to the **smb.conf** file, you can then use the **testparm** program to see if the entries are correctly entered. **testparm** checks the syntax and validity of Samba entries. By default, **testparm** checks the **/etc/samba/smb.conf** file. If you are using a different file as your configuration file, you can specify it as an argument to **testparm**. You can also have **testparm** check to see if a particular host has access to the service set up by the configuration file.

With SWAT, the Status page will list your connections and shares. From the command line, you can use the **smbstatus** command to check on current Samba connections on your network.

To check the real-time operation of your Samba server, you can log in to a user account on the Linux system running the Samba server and connect to the server.

Accessing Samba Services with Clients

Client systems connected to the SMB network can access the shared services provided by the Samba server. Windows clients should be able to access shared directories and services automatically through the Network Neighborhood and the Entire Network icons on a Windows desktop. For Linux systems connected to the same network, Samba services can be accessed using the GNOME Nautilus file manager and KDE file manager, as well as special Samba client programs.

With the Samba **smbclient**, a command line client, a local Linux system can connect to a shared directory on the Samba server and transfer files and run shell programs. Using the **mount** command with the **-t cifs** option, directories on the Samba server can be mounted to local directories on the Linux client. The **cifs** option invokes **mount.cifs** to mount the directory.

Accessing Windows Samba Shares from GNOME

You can use Nautilus (the GNOME file manager) to access your Samba shares. You can open the My Computer icon and then the Network icon. This will display the icons for your network. The Windows Network icon will hold the Windows workgroups of which your Windows hosts are a part. Opening up the Windows Network icon will list your Windows network groups, such as **WORKGROUP**. Opening up the Windows group icon will list the hosts in that group. These will show host icon for your shared Windows hosts. Clicking a host icon will list all the shared resources on it.

Alternatively, you can start Nautilus in browser mode and enter the **smb:** protocol to display all the Samba and Windows networks, from which you can access the Samba and Windows shares.

smbclient

The **smbclient** utility operates like FTP to access systems using the SMB protocols. Whereas with an FTP client you can access other FTP servers or Unix systems, with **smbclient** you can access SMB-shared services, either on the Samba server or on Windows systems. Many **smbclient** commands are similar to those of FTP, such as **mget** to transfer a file or **del** to delete a file. The **smbclient** program has several options for querying a remote system, as well as connecting to it. See the **smbclient** man page for a complete list of options and commands. The **smbclient** program takes as its argument a server name and the service you want to access on that server. A double slash precedes the server name, and a single slash separates it from the service. The service can be any shared resource, such as a directory or a printer. The server name is its NetBIOS name, which may or may not be the same as its IP name. For example, to specify the **myreports** shared directory on the server named **turtle.mytrek.com**, use **//turtle.mytrek.com/myreports**. If you must specify a pathname, use backslashes for Windows files and forward slashes for Unix/Linux files:

```
//server-name/service
```

You can also supply the password for accessing the service. Enter it as an argument following the service name. If you do not supply the password, you are prompted to enter it.

You can then add several options to access shares, such as the remote username or the list of services available. With the **-I** option, you can specify the system using its IP address. You use the **-U** option and a login name for the remote login name you want to use on the remote system. Attach **%** with the password if a password is required. With the **-L** option, you can obtain a list of the services provided on a server, such as shared directories or printers. The following command will list the shares available on the host **turtle.mytrek.com**:

```
smbclient -L turtle.mytrek.com
```

To access a particular directory on a remote system, enter the directory as an argument to the **smbclient** command, followed by any options. For Windows files, you use backslashes for the pathnames, and for Unix/Linux files, you use forward slashes. Once connected, an SMB prompt is displayed and you can use **smbclient** commands such as **get** and **put** to transfer files. The **quit** and **exit** commands quit the **smbclient** program. In the following example, **smbclient** accesses the directory **myreports** on the **turtle.mytrek.com** system, using the **dylan** login name:

```
smbclient //turtle.mytrek.com/myreports -I 192.168.0.1 -U dylan
```

In most cases, you can simply use the server name to reference the server, as shown here:

```
smbclient //turtle.mytrek.com/myreports -U dylan
```

If you are accessing the home directory of a particular account on the Samba server, you can simply specify the **homes** service. In the next example, the user accesses the home directory of the **aleina** account on the Samba server, after being prompted to enter that account's password:

```
smbclient //turtle.mytrek.com/homes -U aleina
```

You can also use **smbclient** to access shared resources located on Windows clients. Specify the computer name of the Windows client along with its shared folder. In the next example, the user accesses the **windata** folder on the Windows client named **lizard**. The folder is configured to allow access by anyone, so the user just presses the ENTER key at the password prompt.

```
$ smbclient //lizard/windata
```

Once logged in, you can execute **smbclient** commands to manage files and change directories. Shell commands can be executed with the ! operator. To transfer files, you can use the **mget** and **mput** commands, much as they are used in the FTP program. The **recurse** command enables you to turn on recursion to copy whole subdirectories at a time. You can use file-matching operators, referred to here as *masks*, to select a certain collection of files. The file-matching (mask) operators are *****, **[]**, and **?** (see Chapter 10). The default mask is *****, which matches everything. The following example uses **mget** to copy all files with a .c suffix, as in **myprog.c**:

```
smb> mget *.c
```

mount.cifs: mount -t cifs

Using the **mount** command with the `-t cifs` option, a Linux or Unix client can mount a shared directory onto its local system. The **cifs** option invokes the **mount.cifs** command to perform the mount operation. The syntax for the **mount.cifs** command is similar to that for the **smbclient** command, with many corresponding options. The **mount.cifs** command takes as its arguments the Samba server and shared directory, followed by the local directory where you want to mount the directory. The following example mounts the **myreports** directory onto the **/mnt/myreps** directory on the local system.

Instead of using **mount.cifs** explicitly, you use the **mount** command with the file system type **cifs**. **mount** will then run the **/sbin/mount.cifs** command, which will invoke **smbclient** to mount the file system:

```
mount -t cifs //turtle.mytrek.com/myreports /mnt/myreps -U dylan
```

To unmount the directory, use the **cifs.umount** command with the local directory name, as shown here:

```
umount /mnt/myreps
```

To mount the home directory of a particular user on the server, specify the **homes** service and the user's login name. The following example mounts the home directory of the user **larisa** to the **/home/chris/larisastuff** directory on the local system:

```
mount -t cifs //turtle.mytrek.com/homes /home/chris/larisastuff -U larisa
```

You can also mount shared folders on Windows clients. Just specify the computer name of the Windows client along with its folder. If the folder name contains spaces, enclose it in single quotes. In the following example, the user mounts the **windata** folder on **lizard** as the **/mylinux** directory. For a folder with access to anyone, just press ENTER at the password prompt:

```
$ mount -t cifs //lizard/windata  /mylinux
Password:
$ ls /mylinux
_hi_mynewdoc.doc_myreport.txt
```

To unmount the shared folder when you are finished with it, use the `cifs.umount` command:

```
cifs.umount /mylinux
```

You could also specify a username and password as options, if user-level access is required:

```
mount -t cifs -o username=chris passwd=mypass //lizard/windata /mylinux
```

You can also use the `cifs` type in an **/etc/fstab** entry to have a Samba file system mounted automatically:

```
//lizard/windata /mylinux cifs defaults 0 0
```

Network File Systems: NFS and /etc/exports

NFS enables you to mount a file system on a remote computer as if it were local to your own system. You can then directly access any of the files on that remote file system. This has the advantage of allowing different systems on a network to access the same files directly, without each having to keep its own copy. Only one copy will be on a remote file system, which each computer can then access. You can find out more about NFS at its Web site at **http://nfs.sourceforge.net**.

NFS operates over a TCP/IP network. The remote computer that holds the file system makes it available to other computers on the network. It does so by exporting the file system, which entails making entries in an NFS configuration file called **/etc/exports**, as well as by running several daemons to support access by other systems. These include **rpc.mountd**, **rpc.nfsd**, and **rpc.portmapper**.

The `nfs-kernel-server` service script will start up the **portmapper**, **nfsd**, **mountd**, and **rquotad** daemons. NFS locking provides for better recovery from interrupted operations that can occur from system crashes on remote hosts. You can use **services-admin** or **sysv-rc-conf** to have NFS start up automatically. On s**ervices-admin** (System | Administration | Services), select the Folder Sharing Service (**nfs-kernel-server**) entry.

To see if NFS is actually running, you can use the **rpcinfo** command with the **-p** option. You should see entries for **mountd** and **nfs**. If not, NFS is not running.

Setting Up NFS Directories with shares-admin: Shared Folders

You can still set up an NFS-shared folder easily using the **shares-admin** tool on the Ubuntu desktop. No longer listed in the Administrative menu, you would have to enter the **shares-admin** command in a terminal window. This opens the Shared folders tool (see Figure 30-4). You will first have to click Unlock button to gain administrative access. The GNOME **shares-admin** tool provides more refined access than **nautilus-share**, the GNOME Nautilus file manager folder and file sharing feature (see Chapter 4). The Shared Folders window has three tabs: Shared Folders, General Properties, and Users.

To add a new shared folder, click the Add button to open a Share Folder window (Figure 30-5). On the Path pop-up menu, select the folder you want to share. If the one you want is not listed, select Other to open a file browser for the entire system. You then select the server to share through. For NFS, select Unix networks (NFS).

You then select the host or network to allow access to this folder. Click Add to open the Add Allowed Hosts window (Figure 30-6). Here you can select the a hostname, IP address, or network address, and then enter the name or address. You can also specify Read Only; otherwise access is writeable.

The allowed host will then appear in the Share Folder window (see Figure 30-7). You can add more hosts or delete others to deny access. When finished, click the Share button.

The shared folder will then appear in the Share Folder window.

NFS Configuration: /etc/exports

An entry in the **/etc/exports** file specifies the file system to be exported and the hosts on the network that can access it. For the file system, enter its *mountpoint,* the directory to which it was mounted on the host system. This is followed by a list of hosts that can access this file

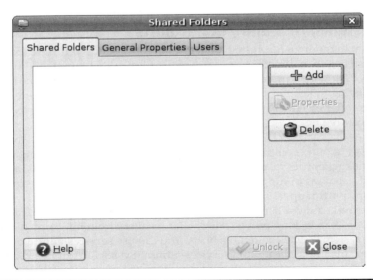

Figure 30-4 Shared Folders tool

FIGURE 30-5
Adding a new
shared folder

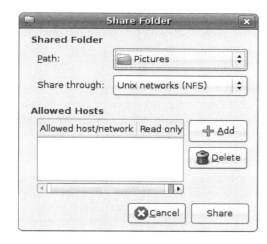

FIGURE 30-6
Specifying allowed
hosts or networks

FIGURE 30-7
Share Folder
window with host
access

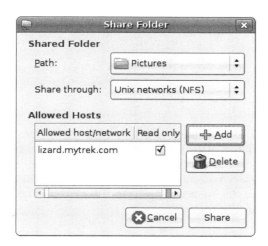

system along with options to control that access. A comma-separated list of export options placed within a set of parentheses may follow each host. For example, you might want to give one host read-only access and another read and write access. If the options are preceded by an * symbol, they are applied to any host.

NFS User-Level Access

Along with general options are options that apply to user-level access. As a security measure, the client's root user is treated as an anonymous user by the NFS server. This is known as *squashing* the user. In the case of the client root user, squashing prevents the client from attempting to appear as the NFS server's root user. Should you want a particular client's root user to have root-level control over the NFS server, you can specify the **no_root_squash** option. To prevent any client user from attempting to appear as a user on the NFS server, you can classify them as anonymous users (the **all_squash** option). Such anonymous users can access only directories and files that are part of the anonymous group.

Normally, if a user on a client system has a user account on the NFS server, that user can mount and access her files on the NFS server. However, NFS requires the user ID for the user be the same on both systems. If this is not the case, the user is considered to be two different users.

Each time your system starts up the NFS server (usually when the system starts up), the **/etc/exports** file will be read and any directories specified will be exported. When a directory is exported, an entry for it is made in the **/var/lib/nfs/xtab** file. It is this file that NFS reads and uses to perform the actual exports. Entries are read from **/etc/exports** and corresponding entries made in **/var/lib/nfs/xtab**. The **xtab** file maintains the list of actual exports.

If you want to export added entries in the **/etc/exports** file immediately, without rebooting, you can use the **exportfs** command with the **-a** option. It is helpful to add the **-v** option to display the actions that NFS is taking. Use the same options to effect any changes you make to the **/etc/exports** file:

```
exportfs -a -v
```

If you later make changes to the **/etc/exports** file, you can use the **-r** option to re-export its entries. The **-r** option will resync the **/var/lib/nfs/xtab** file with the **/etc/exports** entries, removing any other exports or any with different options:

```
exportfs -r -v
```

To export added entries and re-export changed ones, you can combine the **-r** and **-a** options:

```
exportfs -r -a -v
```

You can also use the **exportfs** command to export file systems manually instead of using entries for them in the **/etc/exports** file. Export entries will be added to the **/var/lib/nfs/xtab** file directly. With the **-o** option, you can list various permissions and then follow them with the host and file system to export. The host and file system are separated by a colon. For example, to export the **/home/myprojects** directory manually to **golf.mytrek.com** with the permissions **ro** and **insecure**.

NFSv4

NFS version 4 is a latest version of the NFS protocol (as of this writing) with enhanced features such as greater security, reliability, and speed. Most of the commands are the same as the earlier version, with a few changes. For example, when you mount an NFSv4 file system, you need to specify the **nfs4** file type:

```
# mount -t nfs4  rabbit.mytrek.com:/  /home/dylan/projects
```

In addition, for NFSv4, in the **/etc/exports** file, you can use the **fsid=0** option to specify the root export location. The following entry lets you mount the file system to the **/home/ richlp** directory without having to specify it in the **mount** operation:

```
/home/richlp          *(fsid=0,ro,sync)
```

NFSv4 also supports the RPCSEC_GSS (Remote Procedure Call Security, Generic Security Services) security mechanism, which provides for private/public keys, encryption, and authentication with support for Kerberos.

Mounting NFS File Systems: NFS Clients

Once NFS makes directories available to different hosts, those hosts can then mount those directories on their own systems and access them. The host needs to be able to operate as an NFS client. Current Linux kernels all have NFS client capability built in. This means that any NFS client can mount a remote NFS directory that it has access to by performing a simple **mount** operation.

You can mount an NFS directory either by an entry in the **/etc/fstab** file or by an explicit **mount** command. You have your NFS file systems mounted automatically by placing entries for them in the **/etc/fstab** file. An NFS entry in the **/etc/fstab** file has a mount type of **NFS**. An NFS file system name consists of the hostname of the computer on which it is located, followed by the pathname of the directory where it is mounted. The two are separated by a colon. For example, **rabbit.trek.com:/home/project** specifies a file system mounted at **/home/project** on the **rabbit.trek.com** computer. The format for an NFS entry in the **/etc/fstab** file follows; the file type for NFS versions 1 through 3 is **nfs**, whereas for NFS version 4 it is **nfs4**:

```
host:remote-directory    local-directory      nfs    options    0   0
```

You can also include several NFS-specific **mount** options with your NFS entry. You can specify the size of datagrams sent back and forth and the amount of time your computer waits for a response from the host system. You can also specify whether a file system is to be hard-mounted or soft-mounted. For a *hard-mounted* file system, your computer continually tries to make contact if for some reason the remote system fails to respond. A *soft-mounted* file system, after a specified interval, gives up trying to make contact and issues an error message. A hard mount is the default. A system making a hard-mount attempt that continues to fail will stop responding to user input as it tries continually to achieve the mount. For this reason, soft mounts may be preferable, as they will simply stop attempting a mount that continually fails. The man pages for **mount** contain a listing of these NFS client options. They differ from the NFS server options.

You can also use the **mount** command with the **-t nfs** option to mount an NFS file system explicitly. For an NFSv4 file system, you use **-t nfs4**. To mount the previous entry explicitly, use the following command:

```
# mount -t nfs -o soft,intr,timeo=20   \
        rabbit.mytrek.com:/home/projects   /home/dylan/projects
```

You can, of course, unmount an NFS directory with the **umount** command. You can specify either the local mountpoint or the remote host and directory, as shown here:

```
umount /home/dylan/projects
umount  rabbit.mytrek.com:/home/projects
```

Distributed Network File Systems

For very large distributed systems such as Linux clusters, Linux also supports distributed network file systems, such as Oracle Cluster File System for Linux (OCFS2), InterMezzo, and Red Hat Global File System (GFS and GFS 2). These systems build on the basic concept of NFS as well as RAID techniques to create a file system implemented on multiple hosts across a large network—in effect, distributing the same file system among different hosts at a very low level (see Table 30-4). You can think of it as a kind of RAID array implemented across network hosts instead of just a single system. Instead of each host relying on its own file systems on its own hard drive, they all share the same distributed file system that uses hard drives collected on different distributed servers. This provides far more efficient use of storage available to the hosts, and provides for more centralized management of file system use.

Web Site	Name
http://fedoraproject.org/wiki/Tools/GFS	Fedora GFS resources and links
http://oss.oracle.com/projects/ocfs2/	OCFS2, Oracle Cluster File System for Linux
http://sources.redhat.com/cluster/gfs/	Global File System
www.sun.com/software/products/lustre/	Lustre

TABLE 30-4   Distributed File Systems

Obtaining the Distribution

The Ubuntu distribution installs a professional-level and very stable Linux system along with the KDE and GNOME GUIs, flexible and easy-to-use system configuration tools, an extensive set of Internet servers, a variety of different multimedia applications, and thousands of Linux applications of all kinds. You can find recent information about Ubuntu at **www.ubuntu.com**.

Most Ubuntu software is available for download from the Ubuntu repository. Install disks are also available, either as smaller desktop only installs or larger server installs. You normally use the Ubuntu Desktop Live CD to install Ubuntu. Ubuntu distribution strategy relies on install disks with a selected collection of software that can be later updated and enhanced from the large collection of software on the Ubuntu repository. This means that the collection of software in an initial installation can be relatively small. Software on the Ubuntu repository is also continually updated, so any installation will likely have to undergo extensive updates from the repository.

With smaller install disks, you can quickly download and burn a Ubuntu install image. The Desktop Live CD is available from the GetUbuntu page on the Ubuntu Web site. Both 32-bit and 64-bit versions are available for all current releases. The release covered in this book is the 8.04 LTR release, Hardy Heron.

www.ubuntu.com/getubuntu

In addition, there are Server and Alternate versions as well as an Install DVD are also available. These you can download as ISO images for all versions directly from the following site:

http://releases.ubuntu.com/hardy

This site also includes the torrents for the versions, letting you use a BitTorrent client to download the CD or DVD image. Torrents are also listed at:

http://torrent.ubuntu.com

In addition, you can download several editions of Ubuntu from the respective edition's Web site. Edubuntu and Kubuntu are available at **http://releases.ubuntu.com**. The others can be downloaded from **http://cdimage.ubuntu.com**.

- **www.edubuntu.com**   Educational version
- **www.xubuntu.com**   Xfce desktop version

- **www.kubuntu.com**   KDE desktop version
- **https://wiki.ubuntu.com/Gobuntu**   Open Source–only version

Additional community-supported editions are also available, such as Kubuntu-4 with KDE release 4, Mythbuntu for MythTV, and Ubuntu Studio with image development software. You can download these, along with the other editions from **http://cdimage.ubuntu.com**.

Once you have the install image, you will need to burn it to a DVD or CD disc, which you can then use to install your system.

If you are a first-time user, you may want to run the LiveCD first to see how Ubuntu operates, before you decide to install. The LiveCD can run from system memory.

Check the Ubuntu install guide before installing at the following site; Chapter 2 in this book also offers information.

help.ubuntu.com

Index